'The best history of Pakistan cricket to da[...] thoroughness of a historical reference book [...] A remarkable feat of journalism and enthusiasm,' *Cricketer*

'Peter Oborne's affectionate and immensely authoritative book fizzes along,' *Times Literary Supplement*

'A compelling, superbly researched history of cricket in Pakistan,' David Kynaston, *New Statesman*

'This great book,' Imran Khan

'Masterly,' Neil Clark, *Spectator Australia*

'The most complete, best researched, roses-and-thorns history of cricket in Pakistan,' Suresh Menon, *Independent*

'Intelligent, detailed and highly affectionate history of the Pakistani game ... An encyclopaedic but often thrilling portrait of a beautiful country,' Alex Preston, *Observer*

'*Wounded Tiger* celebrates the triumphs and castigates the offences fairly ... This is a monumental telling of one of sport's great stories, based on thorough, sometimes groundbreaking research,' *The Economist*

'It has drama, intrigue, politics, heroism, villainy, and quite a bit of violence. For anyone wanting to understand the complexities of Pakistan cricket ... this is as good as it's likely to get,' Peter Wilby, *Guardian*

'*Wounded Tiger* ... juxtaposes the building of Pakistan as a nation, an improbable, heroic and, at times, paradoxical task, with the history of its most cherished sport: cricket ... The book is, above all, an ode to a sport and a nation for which the author has obvious affection,' Matthew Syed, *The Times*

'A rich, fascinating and sometimes surprising read ... carefully researched and metic[...]

PETER OBORNE is a regular commentator on politics for television and radio, and recently resigned as the chief political commentator of the *Daily Telegraph*. He is the author of several previous books, including the acclaimed *Alastair Campbell: New Labour and the Rise of the Media Class*, *The Rise of Political Lying*, *The Triumph of the Political Class* and *Basil D'Oliveira, Cricket and Conspiracy: The Untold Story*, which won the William Hill Sports Book of the Year Award in 2004.

WOUNDED TIGER

A History of Cricket in Pakistan

PETER OBORNE

SIMON &
SCHUSTER

London · New York · Sydney · Toronto · New Delhi

A CBS COMPANY

First published in Great Britain by Simon & Schuster UK Ltd, 2014
This paperback edition published by Simon & Schuster UK Ltd, 2015
A CBS COMPANY

1 3 5 7 9 10 8 6 4 2

Simon and Schuster UK Ltd
1st Floor
222 Gray's Inn Road
London WC1X 8HB

www.simonandschuster.co.uk

Simon & Schuster Australia, Sydney
Simon & Schuster India, New Delhi

A CIP catalogue record for this book
is available from the British Library

ISBN 978-1-84983-248-9
eBook ISBN 978-0-85720-075-4

Maps designed by Liane Payne

Typeset in UK by M Rules
Printed and bound by CPI Group (UK) Ltd, Croydon, CR0 4YY

To Saad and Ramma

Contents

Acknowledgements

I have acquired more debts than I can easily repay while researching and writing this book. Najum Latif, curator of the Lahore Gymkhana Cricket Club museum, has been a constant source of advice, insight, information, anecdote and encouragement. His logistical support was also invaluable, especially in Lahore.

In Karachi, Afzal Ahmed and Qamar Ahmed have helped me understand the well-springs of Pakistan cricket. Qamar has saved me from countless misunderstandings and mistakes, while Afzal placed at my disposal his astonishing bibliographical expertise and statistical knowledge and understanding. I am especially grateful for Afzal's patient and detailed readings of successive drafts amid the demands of his business and family life.

Back in England, I originally asked my old friend and cricket novelist Richard Heller to be my researcher. As this project grew ever larger and more ambitious, he became more like a collaborator. Richard bears the main responsibility for some of the most striking sections of this work, including the chapters on women's cricket and reverse swing, and the narratives of Pakistan domestic cricket and many of the accounts of Test cricket. He has also been an inexhaustible source of wisdom and humour and has a wonderful gift for illuminating phrases. The book would not have been finished without him and I would not have enjoyed writing it half as much.

Charles Alexander, formerly President of GE Capital Europe, carried out the research, did the analysis, and wrote the first draft of the chapter on the finances of Pakistan cricket. He also provided cheerful companionship around Pakistan, and our discussions have guided the shape of this book. Stuart Jackson also carried out superb archival research on cricket under the British Empire, the early Indian tours (the subject of his undergraduate dissertation at Cambridge University) and DB Carr's controversial 1956 MCC tour of Pakistan.

Without access to the collections held by the British Library in St Pancras and Colindale, the National Army Museum in Chelsea and the Imperial War Museum in Lambeth, this book would have been impossible. Special mention must be made of Lord's Cricket Ground and the team working in their library and archives. Led by Neil Robinson, the Lord's Library has been spectacularly renovated, revealing a treasure trove of information for any cricket enthusiast. Neil and his assistant Andrew Trigg helped me mine it, and dealt patiently with any request, whether arcane or banal. I am grateful to Robert Athol, archivist at Selwyn College, Cambridge for his help in tracing AR Cornelius during his time at the university. I would also like to thank Government College University, Lahore; Islamia College, Lahore; and of course the Lahore Gymkhana. I would also like to thank Mr Habib A Khan, Director General of the National Archives of Pakistan, and his especially helpful staff

Abdul Waheed, Chief Librarian at Government College University in Lahore, made available over a century's worth of college magazines and history. Librarians Khurram Shahzad and Muhammad Tufail Khan not only helped organise and study the mass of information made available, but also organised access to the Punjab Public Library and various image databases of GCU. At Islamia College, Lahore, I was fortunate to sit down for half a day with Principal of the College, Professor Amjad Ali Shakir, who recounted the history and ideology of this revolutionary institution, and who kindly granted me access to the college archives. Fayaz Ali Shah (President of the Peshawar District Cricket Association) and the staff at the Archives of Islamia College Peshawar, were essential contributors to the history of cricket in the northwest. Mohammed Yaseen of the Lahore Gymkhana library spent many hours helping to scan illustrations for the book.

Nazia Hassan Shah, Sehar Mushtaq and Syed Mohammad Saqib worked in libraries across Lahore, sourcing and translating numerous materials from the last sixty years of Urdu press publications. This alone went some way in providing a counterpoint to the official, and often less descriptive, English-language press of the period.

Max Grodecki, Livvy Moore, James Bowker, Fabia Martin (in the archives of Aligarh Muslim University), Alice Audley, Lorna Studholme and Jess Stafford have done invaluable research and a great deal of essential administration over the course of this project. Gail Marriner transcribed long interviews on women's cricket. Lancing College assisted me with details of Claude Rubie's career.

Sabin Agha guided me around Karachi, and Abdur Rauf and Irfan Ashraf around Peshawar, where Humayun Khan and Munawwar Khan were wonderful hosts. Saad Bari Cheema and Ramma S Cheema were always hospitable company in Lahore, while Professor Omer Tarin generously shared his deep understanding of the North-West Frontier. Murtaza Shibli provided expertise on Pakistani names, Kashmir, and much else. In Islamabad, Muna Habib carried out important research in the National Archive. The book was read in draft form by Joe and Rachel Studholme, Charles Lysacht, James Oborne, Najum Latif, Qamar Ahmed, Afzal Ahmed, Richard Heller, Max Grodecki, and that extraordinary cricketing statistical maestro Steven Lynch. They all saved me from error, although I am responsible for all surviving mistakes of fact and judgement.

Sultan Mahmud, Majid Khan, Giles Clarke, Aftab Gul, Wasim Bari, Shahid Hafiz Kardar, Jamil (Jimmy) Rana and Arif Abbasi were extraordinarily generous with their time and understanding. So were the following, so numerous and so eclectic in their contributions of information and courtesy that I could not sort them into any kind of order. No priority should be read into the following list: Professor Sarah Ansari, Professor Humayun Ansari, Khalid Aziz, Imtiaz Ahmed, Saeed Ahmed, Mushtaq Mohammad, Moin Khan, Mukhtar Bhatti, Khalid Butt, Khalid Qureshi, Nasim-ul-Ghani, Ghulam Mustafa Khan, Colonel (rtd) Rafi Nasim, Aamer Sohail, Asif Iqbal, Mohammad Ilyas, Mohammed Aamer, Hanif Mohammad, Misbah-ul-Haq, the Earl of Home, Mohammad Amir, Sajida Malik, Gareth Pierce, Shandana Khan, Ehsanullah Khan, Imran Khan, Faizan Lakhani, Abad ul-Haq, Syed Iftikhar Ali Bokhari, Khalid Ibadulla, Mohammad Hanif Shahid, Ivo Tennant, Scyld Berry, Syed Zulfiqar Ali Bukhari, Dr Khadim Hussain Baloch, Mohammad Salim Parvez, Shehzar Mohammad (grandson of Hanif), Jalil Kardar (nephew of AH Kardar), Rashid Latif, Mustafa Kamal, Brooks Newmark, Derek Pringle, Henry Blofeld, Mike Brearley, Jonathan Agnew, Mike Atherton, Saleem Altaf, Pervez Sajjad, Shafqat Rana, Dr Zafar Altaf, Ikram Bari Cheema, Shahid Maqbool Cheema, Saad Bari, Sarfraz Nawaz, Javed Burki, Mian Mohammad,

Waqar Hasan, Yawar Saeed, Javed Zaman Khan, Masood Hasan, Irfan Hyder, Anis Hyder, Professor Shaista Sirajuddin, Majid Sheikh, Naghma Raheela, Dr Ambereen Latif September, Abdul Rauf Malik, Professor Francis Robinson, Sohail Khan, Syed Irfan Ashraf, Shamsa Hashmi, IA Rehman, Dr Mubashar Hassan, Mahmud-ul-Hassan, Dr David Washbrook, Dr Prashant Kidambi, Mueen Afzal, Abdul Qadir, Aftab Baloch, Intikhab Alam, Inzamam-ul-Haq, Kiran Baloch Yusuf Garda, George Oborne, Rajinder Amarnath, MJ Akbar, Ramachandra Guha, William Dalrymple, Shameen Khan, Shaiza Khan, Sadiq Mohammad, Wazir Mohammad, Mrs Bushra Aitzaz (chair, PCB women's wing), Ayesha Ashhar (manager PCB women's wing and of Pakistan women's team), Iram Javed (women's team member), Nahida Bibi (women's team member), Ijaz Chaudhry, Gen. Tauqir Zia, Hafsa Adil (Sports Producer; *Dawn* newspaper), Sabahat Kalim (Head of Library: *Dawn*), David Page (editor of the *Kipling Journal*), Professor Dr Farrakh Khan (who sadly died shortly before this book was published), Jamsheed Marker, Dr Saad Shafqat, Gen. Pervez Musharraf, Khalid Mahmood, Abdul Hafeez Pirzada, Nawabzada Mohammad Idrees Khan (brother of Prince Aslam), Nawabzada Abdul Khalik Nasiruddin (cousin of Prince Aslam), Faisal Choudry, Shehzad Mahmood (son of the great Fazal, National Cricket Academy Librarian), Faiysal Ali Khan, Ali Amin Gandapur (Revenue Minister, Khyber-Pakhtunkhwa government), SF Rehman, Carey Schofield, Shaharyar M Khan, Asif Sohail, Badar M Khan (Chief Financial Officer PCB), Subhan Ahmed (Chief Operating Officer PCB), Mubashir Manan (Finance Manager PCB), Muhammad Ali (Geo TV), Ehsan Mani, Faisal Hasnain (CFO ICC), Zahid Noorani (Director Ten Sports), Najam Sethi (a hard-pressed Chairman of the PCB when I spoke to him), Khan Shehram Eusufzye, Brigadier Taimur Dotani and Shahid Javaid Khan (both former members of the Dera Ismail Khan cricket XI in 1964–65).

I would like to thank my wife Martine for tolerating frequent absences in Pakistan. So did Tony Gallagher, then Editor, and Chris Deerin, Comment Editor, of the *Daily Telegraph*. Con Coughlin proved an exhilarating travelling companion. Mike Jones, of publishers Simon & Schuster, has been very tolerant, as this book took much more time to write than originally envisaged and became twice as long. Jo Whitford from the publishers showed notable patience and efficiency, as did Liane Payne, despite being asked repeatedly to redraw the elegant maps. My thanks to Marie Lorimer for coping with the demands of the index. Tom Whiting has done a splendid job as editor, and as always I am grateful to my agent Andrew Gordon.

Finally, I would like to express my appreciation to: Wajid Shamsul Hasan, Shabbir Anwar and Muneer Ahmad (High Commissioner, Press Minister and Press Attaché at the Pakistan High Commission in London); Major Ahmed of Galaxy Travel; the helpful staff of the Lahore Gymkhana; Mr Shuja Baig; the amiable secretary of the Sind Club in Karachi, and all of its courteous staff, notably Umar, the squash professional who demonstrated the depth of talent in Pakistan cricket by bowling unplayable leg-breaks in the club nets. Richard Heller and I hope that our acquaintance with Pakistan is far from finished, because we are already at work on our forthcoming *Companion Volume to Pakistan Cricket*.

Peter Oborne
London, March 2014

Author Note

One encounters many different English transliterations of Pakistani or Indian proper names, places and expressions. With cricketers' proper names, I have followed the form used in *Wisden*. In other cases, I have followed that recommended to me by Pakistani or Indian authorities. When shortening names, I have tried to use the version in which cricketers became known in Pakistan, hence Imran (Khan), Javed (Miandad), Hanif (Mohammad) and likewise for his four brothers, but (Abdul Hafeez) Kardar, (Javed) Burki, (Abdul) Qadir. However, cricketers' names are indexed as in *Wisden*: hence Abdul Qadir among the As and Javed Burki among the Js, but Kardar, AH among the Ks. Other names are indexed in the place where I thought English readers most likely to find them.

Several places have changed names or spellings during the period of this book (for example, Lyallpur became Faisalabad). I have used the form and English spelling which prevailed at the time of the events described in the narrative. However, in direct quotation I have adopted the form used originally by the speaker or writer.

Wisden Cricketers' Almanack has been shortened to the familiar *Wisden* throughout.

To save endless citations, unless otherwise sourced all cricket scores and statistics are taken from www.cricketarchive.com.

Preface

Cricket writing about Pakistan has sometimes fallen into the wrong hands. It has been carried out by people who do not like Pakistan, are suspicious of Pakistanis, and have their own preconceptions. Autobiographies by England cricketers, with some exceptions, are blind to the beauty of Pakistan and the warmth and generosity of its people.

English journalists have tended to follow suit, with the result that Pakistan cricketers emerge as caricatures: Javed Miandad as a hooligan; Imran Khan as a princely scion in the tradition of Ranji; AH Kardar as a fanatic. None of these crude images bear much connection with reality. Pakistan cricket was at first the object of indifference, then avuncular contempt, and in recent decades of vilification and fear.

Another problem is that India has shaped perceptions of the game on the subcontinent. India has been such a wonderful and creative force in world cricket, yet her attitudes to Pakistan cricket are inevitably coloured by nearly seven decades of on-off conflict since Partition.

Ramachandra Guha's masterpiece *A Corner of a Foreign Field* is one of the best cricket books ever written. But AH Kardar was a great deal more interesting than the Muslim nationalist – 'perhaps the greatest cricketer-ideologue born outside the west' – exhumed in Guha's dazzling prose.

Let us consider how Guha compares the Indian and Pakistani commemorative brochures issued ahead of Fazal's 1960 tour. Guha notes that in the Pakistan brochure the 'preliminary pages printed the Pakistani national anthem' and contained pictures of Jinnah and Ayub Khan. He then observes that 'in the Indian brochure there was no national anthem printed, nor a photo of Gandhi. At this time the Pakistan elite had more reason to associate sport with nationalism.'

I tracked down both brochures. The Indian version contained a full page dedicated to a message from Prime Minister Nehru. Another page is dedicated to photographs of the president and vice-president of India, Dr Rajendra Prasad and Dr DS Radhakrishnan; yet another to a full-page message from the Indian Transport and Communications minister; a further page to a bulletin from the chief minister of Maharashtra, shortly followed by a large recruitment advertisement for the Indian Air Force, which was to bomb Pakistan five years later.

The cover illustration of Anthony de Mello's *Portrait of Indian Sport*, published the previous year, portrayed Nehru going out to bat. So although Guha is surely right to assert that Pakistan cricket was nationalistic, the contrast with India is less marked than he claims.

Far less scrupulous than Guha is the Indian novelist and United Nations official Shashi Tharoor. *Shadows Across the Playing Field*, Tharoor's long essay on Pakistan cricket, is littered with errors of fact and interpretation. Tharoor lazily claims that Pakistan lost the 1954 tour of England; gets Hanif's score wrong on the opening day of the first Test in India in 1961 (it was 128 not out, not 90); falsely asserts that Kardar was an aristocrat; omits Ramiz Raja from an account of centuries scored in the 1986 series.

These errors may just be carelessness. Much more serious is the way that Tharoor skews facts in order to prove his thesis. He states that 'whereas a non-Muslim playing for Pakistan remains a rarity in a country where passports are stamped "non-Muslim" to denote their bearer's inferior status, thirty of secular India's 258 Test caps have been awarded to Muslim cricketers.' The implication here could not be more damning: Pakistan Test selectors discriminate against non-Muslims.

As Tharoor, who worked thirty years for the United Nations, must have known, he was making a misleading comparison. Approximately 150 million Muslims are thought to live in India, more than 15% of the population. On that basis, it should come as little surprise that approximately 12% of Indian Test players have been Muslims.

It is true that non-Muslims are a rarity in the Pakistan team, but that may be because non-Muslims are a rarity in Pakistan itself. The figures are disputed but Hindus and Christians between them are generally estimated to total no more than 3% of Pakistanis. As I have shown in this book, they have provided six of the country's approximately 230 Test players – just under 3%. Unfortunately for Tharoor, the statistics suggest that a non-Muslim in Pakistan has roughly the same percentage chance of representing his country as a Muslim in India.

Tharoor states that Pakistan never had a non-Muslim cricket captain. In fact, Yousuf Youhana (both before and after his conversion to Islam) did indeed captain his country.* Tharoor omits the essential fact that when the Board of Control for Cricket in Pakistan (BCCP) was founded in 1948, its senior vice-president (AR Cornelius) was a Christian, and its secretary (KR Collector) was a Parsi.

Even his accounts of action on the field are twisted to prove his point. For instance, here is Tharoor's description of the 1978 Pakistan-India series: 'The Indians' frustration with the Pakistani umpiring frequently bubbled up to the surface and in one episode an altercation between the egregiously biased umpire Shakoor Rana and the Indian opener Sunil Gavaskar actually delayed the start of the final day's play in the first Test by eleven minutes.' Yet *Wisden 1980* tells a different story: 'Gavaskar, the Indian vice captain, used insulting language against the umpire concerned. Mr Rana and his colleague refused to go out the next morning until action was taken ...'

There have been three major histories of Pakistan cricket. In 1998, Omar Noman published *Pride and Passion: An Exhilarating Half Century of Cricket in Pakistan*. This is a serious, scrupulous, sympathetic and well-written work which handles complex material with great skill. This was followed by Shuja-ud-Din and Salim Parvez's *Chequered History of Pakistan Cricket*, published in 2005. Shuja is one of the original band of cricketers who formed Kardar's national team, and Parvez is a famous scholar of the game. Their book is a rare combination of authority with the insight that comes from inside knowledge. I have returned to both books again and again while compiling this volume.

Dr Nauman Niaz has written an extraordinary work – five large, heavy volumes and, in total, I would guess more than one million words. It is a monument to his energy and passion. Niaz synthesises several earlier books

*On three occasions before his 2005 conversion, six times thereafter.

and the work contains numerous character studies of individual players, though at times he is not reliable. This is a work of verve, brio, vaulting ambition and very strong opinions.

There has been one academic study of Pakistan cricket, by Chris Valiotis, which interprets the game as an emanation of post-colonial society. He is acute about its social and cultural impact, but reluctant to cover events and leading personalities. None of these four studies deal with women's cricket. However, this is discussed by the former PCB chairman, Shaharyar Khan, in his thoughtful and absorbing *Cricket Cauldron*. Although primarily an account of his chairmanship from 2003 to 2006, it has many social and historical insights.

There were few cricket writers in the early days, and the most dogged and persistent was Qamaruddin Butt. He was a former first-class cricketer turned umpire who liked to cycle between matches. A noble and indispensable figure, he was the Hansard reporter of the early Test series, describing proceedings with a thoroughness and solemnity which never concealed his deep love and understanding of the game. Occasionally, he would unveil a brilliant phrase, like Hanif Mohammad suddenly producing a beautiful cover drive. Qamaruddin Butt died of a heart attack in 1974 while cycling home from a cricket match at Rawalpindi. MH Maqsood produced an admirable record of the first twenty years of Pakistan cricket. Abid Ali Kazi's compilations of Pakistan cricket statistics are especially important in the early years.

A radio commentator and writer, Omar Kureishi, is Pakistan's answer to England's great John Arlott. Sultan Mahmud has written an essential study of Pakistan cricket during the first fifty years after Partition, *Cricket after Midnight*. The most important source for early Pakistan cricket, however, remains AH Kardar. The author of numerous works, Oxford-educated Kardar was a chronicler as well as a player of the game. *Memoirs of an All-Rounder* is the nearest he got to autobiography, and contains invaluable recollections of pre-Partition cricket.

Few Pakistan cricketers have written autobiographies, and such early memoirs that exist tend to be emotionally reticent. Many great players, including Saeed Ahmed, Waqar Younis, Inzamam-ul-Haq, Intikhab Alam, Asif Iqbal and Abdul Qadir, have never published one at all.

Pioneering work by Qamar Ahmed has ensured that Hanif Mohammad and Waqar Hasan have ghost-written memoirs. Both works are indispensable.

In recent years, two autobiographies have been outstanding. *Cutting Edge*, by Javed Miandad, was ghost-written by Saad Shafqat, a Karachi novelist and neurosurgeon. Shoaib Akhtar was also extremely well served in *Controversially Yours* by his ghost-writer Anshu Dogra, a social anthropologist.

Pakistan newspaper and media reporting is a rich source of material but often highly partisan, reflecting regional and personal rivalries, of which the most enduring has been the divide between Lahore and Karachi. More reliable is the *Encyclopaedia of Pakistan Cricket*, by Baloch and Parvez. It is hard to praise this volume too highly. It is an essential work of reference, lovingly compiled.

Pakistan cricket is a relatively unexplored subject. The library at Lord's is rich in volumes from every major cricketing nation. Pakistan occupies barely half a shelf. If this book does nothing else, I hope it will stimulate an interest in Pakistan cricket.

'Sport has the power to change the world. It has the power to unite in a way that little else does. It speaks to youth in a language they understand. Sport can create hope where once there was only despair. It is more powerful than government in breaking down racial barriers. It laughs in the face of all types of discrimination.'

– NELSON MANDELA[1]

'If all its human resources were developed, Pakistan would be one of the greatest nations in the world. Cricket unites Pakistan and makes its talents bloom. It has no barriers between rich and poor. Cricket teaches people how to live their lives in this world. It makes you a better human being.'

– WASIM BARI, FORMER TEST WICKETKEEPER AND CAPTAIN OF PAKISTAN, IN CONVERSATION WITH THE AUTHOR

The Greatest Game

A mong the crowd at The Oval cricket ground when England regained the Ashes on 19 August 1953 was an off-duty policeman. Tall, muscular and strikingly good-looking, with pale skin and blue eyes, he might have been mistaken for an Englishman by casual observers. But Fazal Mahmood came from the freshly minted state of Pakistan.

Fazal had attended every single day of that decisive Oval Test match. He had witnessed fast-bowling prodigy Fred Trueman rip the guts out of the Australian batting order in a terrifying spell. He had seen the top England batsmen destroyed in turn by the great Ray Lindwall, with only Len Hutton and Trevor Bailey holding the innings together. After that Lindwall spell, Australia held the initiative, but in the second innings their own batting was wrecked by the English spinners Tony Lock and Jim Laker.

On the final day, Fazal – who, like many Pakistanis, felt a loyalty towards England – cheered on Peter May, Bill Edrich and Denis Compton as they painstakingly steered England towards victory. That year, 1953, had produced the most memorable of summers. Two months earlier, Elizabeth II had been crowned Queen at Westminster Abbey just days after news came through that, as part of a British expedition, Sir Edmund Hillary had conquered Everest. That same week, in a moment of national elation, the jockey Sir Gordon Richards won the Derby after twenty-eight years of failure. Now the national cricket team had regained the Ashes which they had lost in 1934.

Fazal ran to join the spectators as they burst forth from the stands and gathered in front of the pavilion to watch the winning team appear on the balcony. In the eyes of Fazal, these England and Australia cricketers seemed incredibly remote, almost godlike figures. In particular, the England captain Len Hutton impressed the young Pakistani. 'Watching him, it felt as if he was the victor of the whole world and that a whole sea of humanity had knelt in front of him,' Fazal said later.[1] 'Even I was shouting, "Hip hip hurrah!" I was also overwhelmed by the persona of Hutton and looked towards him with awe.'

But at that moment, Fazal forgot the noise and the gaiety all around him. Looking upwards, he experienced a vision. He saw Hutton not as a victor but the loser. He saw himself, not Hutton, waving to the crowd – in the aftermath of a famous Pakistan victory over England. It is said that men and women carry their destiny within them. Fazal Mahmood, as he walked away from The Oval on that sunlit afternoon after his near-mystical experience, had acquired a sense of overwhelming purpose. From now on, he was eerily certain that the Pakistan cricket team would defeat their former colonial masters when they arrived in England for their first tour, scheduled for the following year. It was an improbable notion. England were then the greatest team in world cricket, while Pakistan had been a Test nation for scarcely a year, and had won only a single match, and that against lowly regarded India. No country had ever beaten England on home soil at their first attempt. Pakistan's players were almost all amateurs, with limited experience, if any, of English conditions, which were dramatically different from those that prevailed on the subcontinent. By any objective measure, expecting Pakistan to defeat England any time in the near future was lunacy.

Yet Fazal Mahmood did not just hope that Pakistan could pull off this feat. In his soul, he knew he was as great a bowler as Lindwall or Trueman, and equally capable of inflicting devastation on top-class batsmen. Like his fellow countrymen, all he needed was the chance to show his extraordinary talent for the greatest of games.

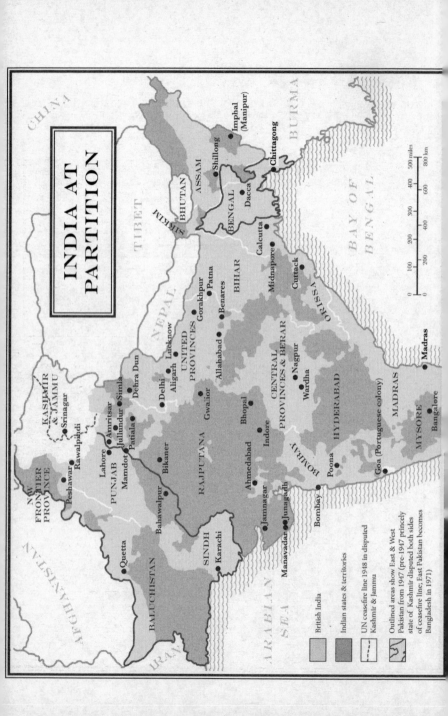

PAKISTAN FIRST-CLASS CRICKET CENTRES SINCE 1947

1947 Date when first-class cricket was first played

This map is about cricket administration only and has no political significance. Dark grey areas were under administration of Pakistan Cricket Board at time of publication. Northern Areas, Azad Kashmir, Jammu and Kashmir disputed between India and Pakistan.

Line of control after 1972

CHINA

NEPAL

INDIA

EAST PAKISTAN (BANGLADESH SINCE 1971)

Dacca 1955

Chittagong 1955

CHINA

NEPAL

INDIA

JAMMU AND KASHMIR

NORTHERN AREAS

AZAD KASHMIR

KHYBER PAKHTUNKHWA

Swabi 2010
Abbottabad 2004
Islamabad 1993
Rawalpindi 1926
Mirpur 2005
Sialkot 1951
Gujrat 2012
Gujranwala 1983
Sheikhupura 1976
Lahore 1923
Okara 2002
Mardan 2010
Peshawar 1938
Wah Cantonment 1984
Muridke 2002
Sargodha 1956
Faisalabad 1955
Sahiwal 1955
Multan 1956
Bahawalpur 1951
Rahimyar Khan 1995

FATA

AFGHANISTAN

PUNJAB

SIND

Sukkur 1957
Nawabshah 2009
Mirpur Khas 1974
Hyderabad 1955
Thatta 1995

Quetta 1954

BALUCHISTAN

Karachi 1926

IRAN

ARABIAN SEA

AFGHANISTAN

200 miles

100   200 km

0   50   100

0   50   100   200

PART ONE

THE AGE OF KARDAR

1947–75

FOUNDING FATHERS

'If I had shown any sign of faltering then, it may have been that defeat would have buried me into oblivion for all time.'

– FAZAL MAHMOOD

The audacity of Fazal Mahmood's ambition can only be understood if it is placed in a historical, personal and religious context. There was no such country as Pakistan when he was born twenty-six years earlier in the north Indian town of Lahore. Even the name had yet to be invented. The British Empire had recently reached its fullest extent as it absorbed new territories in the Middle East following the collapse of the Ottoman Empire, and most observers believed that the British would remain in charge of India for the foreseeable future.

Certainly a small number of agitators struggled against British rule. One of the bravest was Fazal Mahmood's father, Professor Ghulam Hussain. Ghulam had been brilliant and hard-working enough to pass the hugely competitive Indian Civil Service exams, offering the prospect of status and security for the rest of his life.[1] But Ghulam turned instead to revolution, enduring jail and making other sacrifices in the battle to drive the British out of India. Fazal's father was never a member of Mahatma Gandhi's Congress Party, which led the struggle for independence. He was more fearless, and more radical. When Britain declared war on Germany in 1914,

Gandhi played a long game, throwing the weight of Congress behind the allied war effort, with the intention of extracting concessions in return. Ghulam Hussain saw a more immediate opportunity. He believed that the war, by tying down British forces in Europe, offered the opportunity to drive the British occupiers out of India. This appraisal was given overwhelming emotional strength by the Allied declaration of war against the Turks. To British eyes, Turkey looked backward, worthless, decadent, corrupt and a friend of Germany. But Ghulam Hussain and his friends saw something else. The Ottoman Sultan, Mehmet V, carried the title of the Caliph. He was therefore the temporal ruler of Islam and protector of the three holiest Islamic sites, Mecca, Medina and Jerusalem. For Muslims, he was the nearest equivalent to the Pope for Roman Catholics. Many believed that Britain's war against the Sultan and the Caliph was a war on Islam itself, and Muslims had an overriding duty to fight back.

So Ghulam Hussain (like many Muslims before and since) concluded that Afghanistan would represent an ideal base from which to mount an insurrection against Western colonial occupiers. He became a disciple of the famous Islamic scholar Ubaidullah Sindhi,* who envisaged a global Islamic uprising to wash away British rule. To further this end, Ubaidullah travelled to Afghanistan, encouraging Ghulam Hussain (and a number of other followers) to come with him. They hoped that an Islamic army in Saudi Arabia would join with Indian forces based in Kabul. Two German officers, Werner Otto von Hentig and Oskar von Niedermayer, encouraged the scheme, and by December 1915 a Provisional Government of India was operational in Kabul, with a mission to wage Jihad against the British.

In due course, the plan collapsed. Habibullah, Emir of Aghanistan, was urged to lend his blessing to the scheme. But the Emir proved too canny to commit himself either way, and was then assassinated and replaced by a ruler more acceptable to the British. Undismayed, Ubaidullah travelled on to Soviet Russia (where he unsuccessfully sought to meet Lenin), and later Turkey and Saudi Arabia. But his disciple Ghulam Hussain went back to India, settling in Lahore, where the British authorities threw him into jail.

*Ubaidullah Sindhi was a Sikh convert to Islam. After his education at Deoband, he settled in Sindh to avoid family bickering over his conversion. He is best known for organising the Reshmi Roomal Tehrik (Silk Letter Conspiracy) in 1914–15, an Indian movement aiming to oust the British from the subcontinent. Members communicated secretly through letters embroidered in silk handkerchiefs. See *The Oxford Companion to Pakistani History*, ed. Ayesha Jalal (OUP, 2012).

Upon release, he brought out his own newspaper, *Inquilab* (*Revolution*). Inevitably the British seized the presses, and reincarcerated Ghulam. In jail on 18 February 1927, he received news of one of the most significant events in the history of Pakistan cricket: the birth of his son Fazal.

From that moment, Ghulam took a back seat in the revolutionary struggle and devoted his energies to fatherhood and academic life. By the time Fazal was growing up, his father enjoyed respectability as vice-principal of Islamia College. Located just outside the old city of Lahore, this establishment – half high school and half university – was regarded with justifiable suspicion by the British, who disliked its subversive tendencies. Islamia was to provide no fewer than six members of the Pakistan cricket team which played England at The Oval in August 1954.

Fazal would always acknowledge two great inheritances from his father. The first of these was dedication to the faith of Islam. Much later in life, Fazal Mahmood was to publish a book, *Urge to Faith*, a meditation on the wisdom of the Prophet Muhammad, in which he acknowledged the 'constant instruction and guidance of my respected father Professor Ghulam Hussain', adding that he 'urged me to collect and state to the best of my understanding the teachings of the Holy Quran – the light celestial.'[2]

The second inheritance was cricket. Fazal's father, a lover of this most English of sports, was teaching his son how to play by the age of six. Ghulam instructed Fazal on the leg-cutter, twenty years later to be deployed with devastating effect upon the English top order. Fazal would go on to recall how his father told him: 'Mahmood, keep this well in mind. Playing the leg-break is a very vulnerable moment for a batsman and very few players are able to master it. Therefore, focus all your attention on this ball.'[3] Young Fazal spent his childhood mastering the art of bowling in the alleyways of old Lahore, or in Minto Park, a vast open space outside the city walls.

At Kinnaird High School, hard by Lahore Railway Station, Fazal and his classmates would play cricket in the playground, using a small garden shrub instead of stumps. Before the age of twelve, he was attending nets with the Punjab Cricket Club, one of Lahore's better teams, whose practice facilities, Fazal would later recall, were close to Bibian Pak Daman (Ladies of Purity), a shrine to six women from the household of the Prophet who are still celebrated because they brought Islam to South Asia. 'I would go an hour before the net schedule,' Fazal remembered, 'help the groundsman fix the matting, and then bowl in the nets alone till the other players arrived.'

Fazal was fanatical about fitness. He would go for a ten-mile jog every day, and perform five hundred jumps with a skipping rope each morning. In summer, he would swim seventy or eighty lengths at a stretch in the swimming pool of the King Edward Medical College. 'The swimming exercise was a great boon to my health,' Fazal would later remember, 'as throughout my cricketing career, I never felt the slightest pain in my groin, the tenderest muscle in the body.'⁴ His admission at the age of thirteen into Islamia College, where his father taught, was an important step. This was 1940, a momentous year in the formation of Pakistan. Whatever warmth might once have existed between Mahatma Gandhi and Mohammad Ali Jinnah, the leader of the Muslim League, had dissipated. Long ago these two great nation-builders had engaged in a common struggle against British rule. Now events were propelling Jinnah, with trepidation and reluctance, towards the concept of a separate homeland for the Muslims of British India. In March 1940, Jinnah took a vital step away from the dream of Muslim-Hindu unity when he called a special session of the Muslim League at Minto Park (probably disrupting young Fazal's cricket), where the Lahore Resolution, calling for the creation of 'independent states' for Muslims in India, was announced.

As a student at Islamia, young Fazal was naturally caught up in the political agitation. 'I took part in rallies and processions along with my college fellows,' he later remembered. 'Often we were baton-charged and tear-gassed.'⁵ But for Fazal personally, cricket mattered even more. By 1941, aged just fourteen and in his second year, he was selected for the Islamia College First XI. World war raged and the British rule in India was under mortal threat, but Fazal mainly thought about cricket. Soon his leg-cutters were the talk of all India. In early 1944, young Fazal received notification that he had been selected to play for the Northern India Cricket Association in the Ranji Trophy, India's domestic first-class cricket championship. He was just a few days past his seventeenth birthday.⁶

This Northern India cricket team is of exceptional importance for the student of cricket in Pakistan, because it was a prototype for the national side that was to emerge ten years later. The captain was Jahangir Khan, one of the most memorable players from the princely epoch of Indian cricket which was coming to an extremely rapid end. As a young man, Jahangir had played in India's first-ever Test match, against England at Lord's in June 1932. Four years later, while representing Cambridge University at Lord's, he bowled a historic lethal delivery. Directed towards the MCC batsman Tom Pearce, Jahangir Khan's fast-medium ball struck a sparrow on its way to the stumps. The bird collapsed dead on the wicket, and its stuffed body has been preserved at the Lord's museum ever since.

Jahangir's influence on Pakistan cricket was to be immense. His son, Majid Jahangir Khan and grandson Bazid Khan were both to represent Pakistan.* Jahangir's home at Zaman Park in central Lahore would become one of the great seminaries of Pakistan cricket. Imran Khan, Jahangir's nephew, was much later to emerge as Pakistan's greatest ever cricketer. Another nephew, Javed Burki, would captain Pakistan.

Fazal was not the only novice in Jahangir Khan's team. Just as significant, this match between Northern India and the Southern Punjab marked the debut of Abdul Hafeez Kardar, later to become Pakistan's first official Test captain. It is appropriate that Jahangir Khan, the old master, was skipper of the auspicious side in which both men made their first-class debut; a hinge between the old and the new. Both debutants did well. Kardar, opening the batting, was unlucky to be dismissed for 94, whereupon Fazal, who propped up the batting order at number 11, came in to strike a fluent 38. By the time Fazal's turn came to bowl, the great Lala Amarnath was at the wicket, well set and dangerous. 'My hands were shivering as I held fast my grip to the ball,' Fazal would tell the journalist Sheikh Inam Ashraf ten years later when he was at the height of his fame and power. Translated from the Urdu, the passage that follows is a beautiful account of the emotions felt by a seventeen-year-old boy as he prepared to bowl against one of the great batsmen of the age, in his debut first-class match:

My legs were wobbling, my heart was full of apprehensions and my mind was germinating with discouraging thoughts. In front of me was the world famous batsman who was continually prodding the ground with

*Only one other cricketing family, the Headleys, can boast three generations of Test cricketers. George Headley, one of the greatest cricketers of all time, represented West Indies in 22 Tests. His son Ron Headley played two Tests for the West Indies. Ron's son Dean Headley played 15 Test matches for England. Note that neither family represented just one country.

his bat in a strange but victorious disposition. He was waiting for my ball to hit it without wasting any time. I have no qualms in admitting that I was feeling scared, but I braved my heart and with full confidence I threw my first ball. He hit it very hard but the famous Indian cricketer, Gul Mohammad, stopped it with great quickness. I bowled four similar deliveries and Amarnath treated them ruthlessly. If I had shown any sign of faltering then it may have been that sense of defeat would have buried me into oblivion for all time. Before my fifth throw I strengthened my resolve and went ahead with an unshakeable faith. The ball touched Amarnath's bat and went straight into the hands of Dr Jahangir Khan. The ground broke into an applause.[7]

Shortly afterwards Jahangir Khan, muttering, 'Fazal you have done your job', gave the youngster a rest. Two years later, in the summer of 1946, Fazal Mahmood narrowly missed selection for the All-India tour of England led by the Nawab of Pataudi.* This was the last tour India would make under British rule, and before the creation of Pakistan at Partition.

Young Fazal would have felt mixed emotions as he studied the Indian performance from afar. Upon its return to the subcontinent, Pataudi's vanquished All-India team was invited to Delhi for a challenge match against the Rest of India. Fazal had a point to prove, and he made it by scything through the All-India batting order with seven wickets. This match-winning performance was witnessed by two legendary figures in the Indian cricket firmament, Pataudi and the former England Test batsman Prince Duleepsinhji. According to the sports journalist Sultan F Hussain, this pair observed Fazal Mahmood in action for a few overs and then Pataudi asked Duleep: 'Well, prince, what do you think of this young bowler?' Duleep paused to contemplate, and then came the verdict: 'He is good. He should romp home. I wish I could be in Sydney to watch him bowl on that track. He could be lethal.'[8]

This endorsement from such a famous and elegant cricketer, nephew of the great Prince Ranjitsinhji himself, lifted Fazal into a fresh dimension.

---

*Mohammad Iftikhar Ali Khan, Nawab of Pataudi (1910–52). Born in the small princely state of Pataudi, educated at Aitchison College, Lahore. Could have led India against England on either of its inaugural tours of 1932 or 1936, but chose not to do so. Played for England instead, making his Test debut at Sydney in December 1932, a match in which he scored a century. Eventually captained India in 1946. Died tragically young in 1952 after suffering a heart attack while playing polo.

From that moment, Fazal's life was to be directed at one purpose: selection for India's tour of Australia. This contest, the first undertaken by India as an independent nation, was to demonstrate the ease with which ordinary life coexists with horror.

In the final weeks of the British Empire, there was no military force or civil authority capable of keeping order. 'Before the orgy of slaughter had run its course, an estimated twenty million people would become refugees, while perhaps as many as three million would perish in the arbitrary butchering of the innocent,' wrote the historian Lawrence Ziring.[9] Amid all of this, cricket carried on uninterrupted.

The first serious indication of calamity had come the previous year, on the eve of India's Oval Test match against England on 17 August 1946. Jinnah, who believed that the Congress Party and the British were conspiring together to deny rights to India's Muslim minority, ordered a day of action. Riots broke out in many Indian cities, in particular those where Muslim and Hindus lived close together. The situation was worst in Calcutta, the capital of Bengal, where it is estimated that 5,000 people were massacred by rampaging mobs. The 'Great Calcutta Killing' convinced the British Viceroy, Lord Wavell, that Britain's presence on the subcontinent must end at once. Wavell judged that it was useless to use British troops to interpose between rival mobs, since they would themselves become the target.

The cricket team in London was divided between Hindus and Muslims, while one of the touring party, pace bowler Shute Banerjee, came from Calcutta and must have been beside himself with anxiety. *The Times* of 20 August ran a detailed account of the four days of riots, the bodies lying on the streets, the ransacked shops, the stench of death, the fear of epidemic, and desperate attempts by politicians to bring the slaughter to a close. Elsewhere in the paper, the sports pages celebrated a skilful century from Vijay Merchant, the greatest Indian batsman of the era.

In his review of the tour in the following year's *Wisden Cricketers' Almanack* (hereinafter *Wisden*), the journalist Reg Hayter noted that 'while the politicians at home argued the rights of independence, the cricketers abroad showed to the world they could put aside differences of race and creed and join together on and off the field as a single unit, working as one for the same cause.'[10] Whatever their private emotions, the Nawab of

Pataudi's cricketers carried on with stoicism. Perhaps it was the only way they could cope.

Young Fazal Mahmood's obsession with cricket was, in many ways, admirable. As many of his countrymen slaughtered each other, he dealt out non-lethal destruction on the cricket pitch, choosing his victims irrespective of faith and denomination. Growing in confidence and ability all the time, he could do little wrong. In February 1947, nineteen-year-old Fazal made the uneasy journey from Lahore to Bombay to play in a tournament for North Zone under the captaincy of his hero, Lala Amarnath. Fazal, a generally defensive batsman, scored his maiden first-class century and picked up another hatful of wickets.[11]

As Fazal relaxed from his cricketing exploits, the British at last bowed to the inevitable. On 20 February, the Attlee government announced that Britain was quitting India for good, setting June 1948 as the exit date. But this news only added to the uncertainty. The British might have given a date, but the future shape of India was, even at this late stage, completely uncertain. Attlee instructed the new Viceroy, Lord Louis Mountbatten, 'to obtain a unitary government for British India and the India [princely] states.'[12] This prospect was becoming less likely by the day.

In Lahore on 4 March, Hindus and Sikhs joined together to march in favour of a united India. They were fired on by local Punjabi police. The following day, religious minority leaders stubbornly resolved on holding an 'anti-Pakistan day', but this only made things much worse, helping to spark a wave of attacks on Sikhs, Muslims and Hindus across the Punjab. A particularly vicious tactic was beginning to emerge: mass rape as a method of dishonouring entire communities.

Fazal Mahmood, apparently oblivious to the mayhem, was making his way from Bombay to Delhi for the final trial match ahead of the forthcoming tour of Australia. Fazal was especially keen to do well in the fixture, because the selectors would make their choice when it ended. Bathed in the light of hindsight, this otherwise not especially memorable game becomes pregnant with meaning.[13] Many of the great or future great players were there: Vijay Merchant, Vinoo Mankad, Rusi Modi, Imtiaz Ahmed, Fazal Mahmood, Lala Amarnath. Strikingly, in view of the carnage brewing elsewhere, the match was an advertisement for warm inter-communal relations. There were Muslims, such as Ghulam Ahmed from Hyderabad, uncle of the future Pakistan Test cricketer Asif Iqbal, who lived in what would soon become India. There was a Hindu – the great Lala Amarnath, who had been raised in Lahore, the most important city in what would soon become Pakistan. The finest innings of the match was a fighting 158 in a losing cause played by K Rai Singh, a Sikh from the Punjab. Most of these men knew each other well, and were part of a cricketing culture that had steadily spread across much of India over the course of two centuries of British rule. All of the cricketers – Muslim, Sikh and Hindu alike – wanted to represent India against Sir Donald Bradman's Australians that autumn. A degree of naivety was involved. Even at this late stage, the players seem to have assumed that their peaceful world would continue.

Fazal Mahmood was the destroyer, his leg-cutters capturing five opposition wickets for a meagre 45 runs and setting up victory. Afterwards, the touring party was disclosed. 'As I heard my name being called out,' Fazal would later recall, 'I rushed to the telegraph office to send a telegram to my parents in Lahore.'[14] Fazal was requested to report to a pre-tour training camp at Poona on 15 August 1947. Professional fulfillment, fame, recognition and the rewarding life of an international cricketer all seemed to lie ahead for twenty-year-old Fazal Mahmood.

Secure in his place, Fazal now returned to his native Punjab, where the communal violence had been suppressed, though only after several thousand had died. The British panicked. In June 1947, Jinnah, Nehru and representatives of the Dalit (untouchable) community and the Sikhs, agreed in principle to partition along religious lines, against the wish of the absent Gandhi. Mountbatten then abandoned Attlee's intended timetable for British departure in June 1948. He announced that Britain would leave on 15 August, just ten weeks away. Only then did the British think of drawing the partition frontiers. On 9 July 1947, the barrister Sir Cyril Radcliffe was appointed to chair the two boundary commissions which would assess areas of Hindu and Muslim predominance and thus determine the division of the Punjab in the West and Bengal in the East. Less than six weeks remained before independence.[15] Lawrence Ziring notes that Radcliffe 'had never visited India, let alone served there, and did not possess even the most basic understanding of India demography or cultures.' According to Majid Khan, his father Jahangir Khan served on

Radcliffe's commission. He never spoke about this episode for the rest of his life.[16]

Fazal Mahmood's Lahore, just a few miles from Radcliffe's new border, was at the heart of the resulting chaos. For the first half of the twentieth century, it had been an eclectic, tolerant and open city, famed for its restaurants and cafes, artists and poets, and an easy-going outdoor life. Now the religious groups which had lived together relatively amicably for years formed armed bands. The Hindus sealed themselves off against the outside world. Barriers were erected at the end of every street, protected by heavily armed guards. To venture out was dangerous. 'When I arrived in Lahore, the mayhem was at its peak and the curfew was a daily routine,' Fazal noted in his 1954 autobiography. 'Therefore, it was not possible to practise any cricket.'

Fazal was still in Lahore on 14 August 1947, the day that Pakistan came into being. In the West, it comprised the provinces of Baluchistan, North-West Frontier, Sindh and West Punjab (with Kashmir still unresolved). In the East, separated from the West by over a thousand miles of hostile territory and deep-seated linguistic, social and economic differences, East Bengal joined the new state. It remained a monarchy (as briefly did India): Jinnah, its first head of state, was inaugurated governor-general. Though a moment of enormous consequence, it was scarcely a time for celebration. Lahore erupted and the last British officers left the corpse-strewn streets for the final time. The whole of the Punjab was aflame amid the complete collapse of civilisation.

Fazal's overriding concern, however, was to report to the All-India training camp in Poona. Leaving Lahore, he witnessed the smoke rising from burnt and destroyed villages. He made the 650-mile journey through Punjab and Sindh to the port of Karachi on the Arabian Sea.[17] From there he proceeded to Bombay by air. Millions of Muslims were making the same journey, by whatever means they could find – but in the opposite direction. Fazal was travelling directly into the headwinds of the greatest mass migration in history. It was an insanely dangerous journey for a twenty-year-old Muslim male.

From Bombay, Fazal proceeded to Poona, where he joined his new team-mates for training. These training camps, which were also a feature of Pakistan Test cricket in its early years, reflected the deep seriousness with which the emergent nations of India and Pakistan took their sport. At Poona, however, there was very little training to be had. The Indian team was thrown into chronic disarray. When the squad had been chosen five months earlier, the selectors were working to the original timetable, which assumed independence in the summer of 1948. They had optimistically assumed that an All-Indian team would travel to Australia.[18]

Vice-captain Mushtaq Ali, one of the finest Muslim cricketers of the era, had pulled out, citing a family bereavement.* Further confusion was caused by the last-minute withdrawal of Vijay Merchant, the designated captain. Lala Amarnath was appointed in his place. As he absorbed the news that he was to be the first captain of independent India, chilling accounts of bloodshed emerged from his home town of Lahore, including the destruction of the Hindu quarter where he had been raised.

Practice was impossible because of torrential monsoon rains. The team was staying in a bungalow belonging to Shanta Apte, an Indian actress. She filled in the empty hours by singing to the players. Finally the camp was abandoned, and the cricketers were told to return to their homes to gather up their belongings and say farewell to their families ahead of the Australian ordeal which lay ahead. Fazal now faced the task of making his way back to what was now a foreign country. 'This was difficult,' he was to remark later, 'amid the bloodshed in some parts of the subcontinent.' He very nearly met a bloody end on the train back from Poona to Bombay. Hindu fanatics would have lynched him but for the intervention of his travelling companion, the India cricket legend CK Nayudu, who defended Fazal against assailants with a cricket bat.[19]

Arriving in Bombay on 9 September, Fazal at first sought to go onto Lahore via Delhi. But he was warned that he would probably be killed if he took this route. Instead, he managed to fix a flight to Karachi and by 13 September he arrived back home in Lahore. There he found his parents frantic with worry. They had heard nothing from him for a month because none of his letters or telegrams had arrived. They urged him not to risk making a further journey to India. With immense reluctance, Fazal cabled Lala Amarnath saying that he would not be able to join the tour.[20] This

---

* There is no evidence that his decision had anything to do with the creation of Pakistan. Indeed Mushtaq Ali would later try to clamber back on board, only to discover the Indian selectors no longer wanted him.

decision, the most important of Fazal's life, had the most profound consequences for cricket in Pakistan. Half a century later, when Fazal had become one of the grand old men of Pakistan cricket, he would present his refusal to play for India as a principled action, born out of patriotism. Circumstances suggest the story was more complicated.

It should be noted that Partition was not agreed or given a timetable until June 1947. Only from that point was the creation of Pakistan a stone-cold certainty. Had national loyalty been his overriding concern, Fazal would have withdrawn at that moment, and there would have been no need for any of his perilous journeys round northern India.

So what was driving Fazal? It is hard to say for certain, because he has given two conflicting accounts. This is what he wrote in his 2003 autobiography: 'I had grown up in pre-Partition India and had seen communal clashes. But the ferocity, savagery and bloodshed that was committed during Partition jolted me. I did not have the faintest idea that there existed such deep-rooted hatred among the people who had been living together for decades. I decided not to go on the India tour.'

Fazal is suggesting in this account that his loyalty to Muslim Pakistan was stimulated by his experience of the August 1947 carnage. But even as late as 9 September, when the scale of the killing was obvious to all, Fazal left the Poona training camp committed to India. Fazal's earlier autobiography, published in 1955, gives a different version. He states that 'while I was torn between these uncertainties I got a job offer as a police inspector. As the situation was deteriorating and my parents were not willing to let me travel and now that I had a job, all these things cooled down my passion to travel to Australia.' This sounds more accurate. In truth, all kinds of factors must have been at work in Fazal's mind at a time of tumult, tragedy and very rapidly changing events. On the one hand, he had a natural desire to realise his potential as a sportsman. On the other hand, he risked being killed if he made the journey back to India. Furthermore, he can hardly have been unaffected by the massacres of his fellow Muslims. Some voices would have whispered in his ear that he would be mad not to tour, others that he would be betraying his new country if he did so. Most probably Fazal changed his mind from day to day, if not hour to hour, before sending the telegram to Lala Amarnath.

There is one further crucial factor that must have shaped Fazal's thinking. He had just become engaged to be married. His fiancee was fair-complexioned, green-eyed Naaz Parwar, the daughter of Mian Mohammad Saeed, one of the most influential cricketers in the new Pakistan. It was Saeed who had fixed up the job offer from the police, and it is tempting to speculate that he arranged the job deliberately to detain his future son-in-law in Lahore and thus deter him from his Australian mission. On 21 September, two weeks before India set off to Australia, Fazal Mahmood attended Birdwood Barracks in Lahore for his first day of police training.

To Fazal, it may have seemed that he had turned his back on cricket for good. From Lahore, he was dispatched to the police training school in Hangu, a remote rural outpost not far from Peshawar and close to the Afghan border. 'Cricket was unknown in that part of the world,' Fazal recorded in his 2003 autobiography. 'It disappointed me and lowered my morale. However, I developed a plan to carry on my bowling practice. I selected the lawn in my residence and measured the length of the wicket from its back wall. I would bowl almost thirty-five overs a day against the wall. The drill instructor of the school was amazed with my daily routine and asked me about the game. After listening to a one-hour lecture he remarked, "I know the game well – ha'ki" by which he meant hockey.'[21]

As Fazal pounded away at his cricket in the rural oblivion of Hangu – today the scene of deadly skirmishes between the Taliban and Pakistan security forces[22] – he was badly missed by Amarnath's team. Without Fazal the Indian attack was toothless, and the Australians piled up giant scores, Donald Bradman alone amassing 715 runs at an average of 178.75. Fazal suffered agonies of regret, and constantly wondered whether he had made a terrible and irrevocable error.[23] In search of competitive sport, he resorted to the desperate step of taking up hockey and badminton. 'At times,' Fazal was later to reveal, 'I was so disheartened that I wanted to leave the game altogether, because at that time the future of the game in Pakistan looked to be totally dark.'[24]

There for the time being we must leave Fazal Mahmood to his constabulary duties on the North-West frontier. There is surely no question that he would have established himself as an important member of the Indian national team, with the prestige and material rewards that implied. Would he have reverted to Pakistan when it finally became a Test-playing nation? Or would Fazal have spearheaded the Indian attack in the inaugural contest between the two South Asian giants at the Feroz Shah Kotla ground in Delhi five years later?

Such questions, though no more than speculation, illustrate how much was at stake, not just for Fazal Mahmood but also Pakistan, as he made his journeys across northern India in the summer of 1947. The history of cricket on the subcontinent would have been very different had Fazal plumped for India or – as could so very easily have happened – been hacked to death by a Hindu mob.

THE STRUCTURE OF CRICKET IN PAKISTAN AT INDEPENDENCE

Today, we think of cricket as Pakistan's national sport, but this was by no means the case in 1947. Even in the urban centres of Lahore and Karachi, cricket was played mainly by the middle classes, and otherwise thinly spread. It was unknown throughout much of Pakistan's rural hinterland.[25]

Across the Pashtun belt in northern Pakistan, the game was rejected by the tribes, because of its association with British rule – hence Fazal Mahmood's sense of isolation in Hangu. Hockey, cheaper and less time-consuming, was probably more popular than cricket in 1947.

National organisation of the game was pitiful. After independence, the Board of Control of Cricket in India (BCCI) continued to operate out of Bombay,[26] meaning that Pakistan cricket was left without a central structure. There were no Pakistan Test match grounds and no first-class cricket competition. Indeed, there were scarcely any turf wickets – just two in Lahore and none in Karachi.[27] India retained membership of the Imperial Cricket Conference, which conferred Test match status, while Pakistan was cast into the cold. After Partition, Pakistani cricketers found themselves members of a third-class cricketing nation.

There is a comparison here with Irish cricket – a flourishing concern at the start of the twentieth century which was marginalised and suppressed following Partition in 1922. As a result, the most talented Irish players have recently been forced to travel to England to pursue their careers. This nearly happened in Pakistan. We have already noted the temptation felt by Fazal Mahmood to play for the India Test side. Other Pakistani cricketers did take this route after

Partition. For example Jamshed Irani, the Karachi-born wicketkeeper, joined the 1947–48 tour of Australia, playing in the first two Tests.*

So it is possible to imagine Pakistan becoming a kind of satellite cricketing nation, perhaps providing the occasional player for its Test-playing neighbour. Had this happened, Pakistan might well have followed the pattern of the South Asian nation of Ceylon (now Sri Lanka), which became independent in 1948, but did not become a Test-playing nation until 1981.

This was averted. Pakistan cricket acquired an identity of its own, but only after powerful resistance. India was not minded to allow Pakistan its cricketing sovereignty without a fight. Anthony de Mello, president of the BCCI, greeted the prospect of a Pakistani breakaway with horror. 'I call upon sportsmen in all parts of the land to rally round the idea of unity in Indian sport,' declared De Mello on 11 August 1947, four days before independence.[28] 'The other nations will always refer to us as Indians, irrespective of whether some of us belong to new India or to Pakistan.'

When the BCCI held its annual meeting a week later, De Mello 'removed that question [a Pakistan breakaway] from the agenda and the matter was simply left as it was.'[29] De Mello received heavyweight support from Prince Duleepsinhji, who melodramatically warned that if the BCCI was split 'the harm that may result could either give the game a severe setback or even put an end to cricket, as we know it, in this country.'[30]

The BCCI was holding Pakistan to ransom. Either it could have first-class and Test cricket as part of India – or not have first-class cricket at all. *The Times of India*, the country's largest English-language newspaper, spelt this out when it warned that Pakistan 'would have either to accept unity of control or, in the alternative, to negotiate with the Imperial Cricket Conference for recognition as a first-class cricket-playing country so as to avail itself of the opportunity to invite foreign touring teams, coming to India, to extend their programmes to include a match or two in Pakistan. This is also likely to be a

---

*Jamshed Khudadad Irani, born in Karachi 18 August 1923, is the only Pakistani to have played for India without playing for Pakistan. Irani, a Parsi, was keeping wicket when Sir Donald Bradman completed his 100th first-class century at Sydney for an Australian XI against the Indians. After the tour, Irani returned to his native Karachi. In 1949–50 he also stood as umpire in a match between Pakistan & Commonwealth XI at Lahore. Four days later he played for Karachi against the same Commonwealth XI, thus making his first-class debut in Pakistan cricket. Christopher Martin-Jenkins's *Complete Who's Who of Test Cricketers* gives the full name of JK Irani as Jahangir Khan Irani, which is not correct. Irani, a lower order bat (sometimes an opener) and wicketkeeper, made his first-class debut for Sindh against Lord Tennyson's MCC touring party at Karachi in 1937–38, aged only fourteen.

big hurdle for Pakistan and, therefore, the Indian Control Board can afford to watch and wait for moves from the seceding party.'[31]

De Mello had powerful supporters outside India. MCC sent out signals that it would prefer India to remain, for cricketing purposes, a single country.[32] Indian press reports suggested that the Sindh Cricket Association, disturbingly from within Pakistan itself, was nervous about breaking with the BCCI.* India had the money, infrastructure, assets, organisation and best pitches. For Pakistan, to go it alone meant a giant leap in the dark.

But go it alone it was determined to do.[33] The Board of Control of Cricket in Pakistan was first mooted in the summer of 1947, shortly after Lord Mountbatten brought forward independence.† After preliminary work over the winter, the BCCP was formally founded on 1 May 1948 at a meeting in the pavilion of Lahore Gymkhana cricket ground. In cricketing terms, this was as important an event as the swearing in of Jinnah as governor-general the previous 14 August. Pakistan, so long subject to the British, was at last asserting her cricketing sovereignty. But by doing so, she was estranging herself from world cricket.

Three vice-presidents were nominated: Justice AR Cornelius, from the Punjab;‡ Lt Col. Baker from the North-West Frontier Province (NWFP);

---

* *The Times of India*, 24 August 1947. 'But when the Sindh authorities came to brass tacks they were confronted by the many varied difficulties of immense magnitude in forming a Pakistan Board and they found that Pakistan territory would be very weak financially as well as from the point of view of first-class players as it would have to depend on only three provinces – NWFP, Punjab and Sindh – for their cricket talent and money.'

†In its very early days it was sometimes known as the Pakistan Cricket Control Board. For simplicity's sake, however, I refer throughout to the BCCP, until its change of name to the Pakistan Cricket Board (PCB) in the mid-1990s. *The Times of India* reported on 14 August 1947, the eve of independence, that 'certain interested persons in Lahore' had taken steps towards forming 'a Pakistan Board of Control for Cricket'. The report added that the 'Sindh Cricket Association consider that there should not be a division in Indian cricket.' What were *The Times of India* sources? Was the newspaper being mischievous? Or was there a genuine breakaway movement in Sindh? It is impossible to say.

‡Alvin Robert Cornelius was the first of only two non-Muslims to stand at the pinnacle of the judicial system of any of the 55 Islamic states. He was responsible for a series of brilliant court judgements which protected minorities, upheld human rights, and arrested the march of dictatorship. During these formative years, Cornelius also found the time to rescue cricket in Pakistan from oblivion. Born in Agra in 1903, Cornelius was sent to Selwyn College Cambridge in 1924 after winning a government scholarship to study abroad. The college archive contains no record at all of Cornelius as a cricketer. He played tennis and was an active member of the college debating society. Upon his return to India, he passed the Indian Civil Service examinations and was sent to the Punjab. Soon he moved into the judicial branch of the ICS.

One of his earliest postings was at Jullundur, home of the Burki clan, where he played cricket for the Jullundur Club. The only other non-European player was Ahmed Raza Khan, better known today as uncle of three national captains, Javed Burki, Majid Khan and Imran Khan. Ahmed Raza Khan regarded Cornelius as a 'very conscientious, honest and dignified man and a thorough gentleman.' Some 1,000 ICS officers chose to remain in India, but Cornelius was one of the 157 officers who left to join Pakistan.

and Mr Britto from Sindh.* KR Collector, secretary of the Sindh Cricket
Association, was made Board secretary and Professor Mohammad Aslam
of Islamia College Lahore honorary treasurer.† The first president of the
BCCP was Khan Iftikhar Hussain Nawab of Mamdot.

The three key figures were Mamdot, Collector, and Justice Cornelius, a
brilliant man who would later become Chief Justice of Pakistan.‡ Cornelius
provided the intellect and drive and has been credited with organising a
BCCP constitution, a document which I have been unable to find and perhaps does not exist.§ Mamdot delivered social and political muscle. One of
the great feudal magnates in Pakistan, he had thrown his weight behind
Jinnah and the Muslim League in the run-up to independence, and was
rewarded with the post of chief minister of West Punjab after Partition. His
family had patronised the Mamdot Cricket Club since its foundation. KR
Collector, a Parsi, had already established an excellent reputation as secretary
of the Sindh Cricket Association. He did the paperwork, and would carry
his documents around with him in a trunk. For a number of years following Partition, Collector's trunk was effectively the head office of the BCCP.

So one Parsi, one Christian and one Muslim were at the helm, a con-
fessional eclecticism which mirrored Jinnah's vision for Pakistan. In other
ways, the early composition of the BCCP was a less exact reflection. Punjab,

*Diego Britto, originally from Goa, was a leading sports organiser in Sindh and President of the Sindh
Cricket Association in 1947–48. Not to be confused with Jack Britto, who represented Pakistan at
hockey in the 1952 Helsinki Olympics.
†KR Collector, the first secretary of the BCCP, asserted that the organisation was founded on 1 May
1949 (Maqsood, op. cit. pp.26–7). Collector was in a position to know, but other accounts locate it earlier. *The Times of India*, the best newspaper source, refers to a 'special meeting of the organizing Board
of Control for Cricket in Pakistan' in late 1947 (*The Times of India*, 2 December 1947). By March 1948
a constitution was being discussed at a meeting in Lahore. (*The Times of India*, 10 March 1948). The
Souvenir Programme for the Pakistan-West Indies unofficial Test match at Lahore in November 1948,
declared that the Board of Control was founded on 1 May 1948 (p.5). Unfortunately it is dangerous
to make any kind of definitive statement about the BCCP, because no hard documentary evidence exists.
I have been able to find no BCCP archives of any kind for this, or any other period. As a result the historian of Pakistan cricket is forced to resort to oral testimony, or rely on earlier accounts whose accuracy
can by no means be guaranteed. For example, Lt Col (Ret'd) Shuja-ud-Din Butt's normally reliable history asserts that Cornelius was the first President of the BCCP. I have found no evidence that Cornelius
was the first President. See Shuja-ud-Din, p.3. Also see 'Eight Years of Pakistan Cricket' from the official souvenir of the first match between MCC A versus Pakistan in Lahore, 20–26 January 1956.
‡Lt Col. Shuja-ud-Din Butt, who pursued an army career while representing early Pakistan teams in Test
matches, called him the 'Father of Pakistan Cricket' on account of his 'strong organisational skills and
dedication in various administrative roles in the formative years.' Shuja-ud-Din, p.3.
§The BCCP Constitution still had not been completed two years later. See Stephen Menzes, 'Future of
Cricket in Pakistan', published in *Cricket in Pakistan 1948–49 Edition*, p.61. 'The Pakistan Cricket
Control Board will hold the key to the future of the game in this country. The controlling authority is
still in a nascent state with its work in framing a constitution yet unfinished.'

Sindh and NWFP were well represented on the board. Baluchistan and East Pakistan – the other two provinces which came together at the creation of Pakistan – had no representatives at all.

The omission of the thinly populated Western province of Baluchistan was merely insensitive. The omission of East Pakistan was an insult. Right from the beginning, it was excluded from national Pakistan cricket, an estrangement that would have long-term consequences.

One further important decision was made at this meeting. It was resolved to ask Governor-general Jinnah to become BCCP patron, thus linking the interests of cricket to the Pakistan state. In practice, it is unlikely that the founder of the Pakistan nation, by now in the last months of his life and struggling with a multitude of crises, ever accepted this symbolic role.* Jinnah, unlike most of his successors, had little interest in cricket, though he probably played it while at school in the Sindh Madrassah in Karachi.†

While the decision to place cricket under the patronage of the head of state was understandable – perhaps even necessary – there was a heavy price to pay. Jinnah's less fastidious successors were to treat the presidency of the BCCP, and its successor organisation, the Pakistan Cricket Board, as a bauble to be handed out to cronies, with lamentable consequences.

But at least Pakistan cricket now had an address, though not a grand one: Collector's home at 72 Garden Road, Karachi. It scarcely bears comparison to the lavish headquarters and countless employees that Pakistan cricket enjoys today.[34] It was all very precarious: 'There was no infrastructure available in the

---

*Fazal Mahmood, p.20. 'Mohammad Ali Jinnah, the governor-general of Pakistan, very graciously became its first patron.' But did he? I have found no contemporary mentions of Jinnah taking up this important symbolic role. The head of the state nevertheless continued to be patron of cricket, till Nawaz Sharif recently took that position himself as Prime Minister.

†There is no record of Jinnah showing interest in the game after his departure to study law in London in 1892, aged just sixteen. However, Hector Bolitho, Jinnah's first biographer, tells the following story: 'One morning, when Nanji Jafar was playing in the street, Jinnah, then aged about fourteen, came up to him and said, "Don't play marbles in the dust; it spoils your clothes and dirties your hands. We must stand up and play cricket." The boys in Newnham Road were obedient: they gave up playing marbles and allowed Jinnah to lead them from the dusty street to a bright field where he brought his bat and stump for them to use. When he sailed for England at the age of sixteen, he gave Nanji Jafar his bat and said: "You will go on teaching the boys to play cricket while I am away."' Hector Bolitho met Nanji Jafar, 'a smiling old Muslim with tousled, snow-white hair', by chance while interviewing Fatima Bai, who was related to Jinnah by marriage. Jinnah could scarcely have avoided playing cricket while studying at the Sindh Madrassah High School, even though there is no reference to Jinnah the cricketer in the school museum set aside for Jinnah. Fazal Mahmood, however, claimed that Jinnah was a 'follower of cricket', and that Jinnah encouraged him to play on one of his regular visits to Islamia College. See Fazal Mahmood, p.13.

new country. The financial position of the BCCP was zero,'[35] remembered
Fazal Mahmood.

The BCCP's most urgent task was to build up the first-class game. Before
Partition, cricketers from what had suddenly become Pakistan enjoyed
access to first-class cricket because the Northern India Cricket Association's
membership of BCCI entitled it to play in the Ranji Trophy. This halted,
leaving Pakistan almost completely bereft.*

Indeed the situation was so dire that throughout the 1947–48 season
(in the subcontinent cricket is played in the winter months in order to
avoid the scorching summers) only one first-class game was played in
Pakistan. This was the traditional fixture between Punjab University and
the Governor of West Punjab's XI, and ended up in a draw.† The location
was the glorious Lawrence Gardens, the Lahore Gymkhana ground, one
of the most beautiful cricket venues in the world. Flanked by century-old
shisham and peepal trees, which gave it the faint air of The Parks at
Oxford, it had been built by the British in 1880. Without permission no
native – as the locals were often called during British rule – could enter the
pavilion, a masterpiece in the oriental style. Later in life, Fazal Mahmood
would recall that the Lahore Gymkhana was 'the most prestigious in the
province. Every cricketer dreamt of playing there.' But they had to swallow their pride to do so. As a young man before 1947 wanting a game,
Fazal had been forced to stand at the gate of the club, kept at arm's length
by a doorman, while he shouted out that he was available to play in case
either side was short.[36] At last this famous cricket ground, re-named Bagh-
e-Jinnah, belonged to Pakistanis.

However, the match itself was hosted by a Briton, Sir Francis Mudie, governor of West Punjab. Sir Francis was one of a handful of officials and
military officers who had been personally requested by Jinnah to stay behind

---

*Northern India's final Ranji Trophy game before Partition was played in Patiala against the Southern
Punjab at the beginning of February 1947. The Northern India side was an important seedbed for future
Pakistani cricketers.

†Fifty years later cricket statisticians concluded that an earlier fixture, played between Sindh and West
Punjab on 27, 28 and 29 December 1947, met the criteria to be regarded as first-class. The game, in
aid of the Quaid-e-Azam's fund for refugees, was played at Bagh-e-Jinnah and won decisively by the West
Punjab, with the inevitable Fazal taking 6–45 for the winning team. However, this retrospective judgement meant nothing to Pakistani cricketers playing the game at the time. As far as they were concerned
it was not first-class – and on that basis I have chosen to concentrate on Punjab University v Governor
of West Punjab's XI. For more details of both matches, including scorecards, see Abid Ali Kazi's *First-
Class Cricket in Pakistan, Vol 1*, pp.7–8.

after independence. A strong supporter of the Pakistan movement,* Sir Francis had collected many of the country's greatest cricketers into his team, including Jahangir Khan and Fazal Mahmood.

Sir Francis asked for Mian Saeed rather than Jahangir to be captain, an indication that Saeed was being groomed as the leader of the Pakistan national team. His son-in-law Fazal, instead of languishing as he normally did towards the bottom end of the batting order, was promoted to the number 6 slot in the first innings, from which he scored 78. In the second innings he was promoted to number 4, and scored an almost identical 77, highlighting his credentials as an all-rounder.

Mian Mohammad Saeed, who had played Ranji Trophy cricket for Northern India in pre-Partition days, is one of the most attractive figures in the history of Pakistan cricket. Photographs from this period show a bear-like man, looking cheerful and at ease with himself and the world. He worked as a magistrate in post-Partition Lahore.[37] Saeed's role in the creation of the national team has been obscured by the subsequent emergence of AH Kardar.

Almost all of the greatest cricketers of the time played in Sir Francis Mudie's fixture. No wonder – they were starved of first-class cricket. There were just four domestic first-class fixtures in the five years after independence (or five, if we include the match included by statisticians years later).† By contrast, India hosted 88 Ranji Trophy fixtures during this period, with plenty of other first-class cricket besides. Cricket in Pakistan was confined to club games, mainly played over the course of a single day, and certain school

---

*He warned in 1948 that Pakistan 'has a powerful, truculent and unscrupulous neighbour [i.e. India]. She is a member of the Commonwealth and expects help and support from that neighbour. Instead she sees Britain giving way to India on every point – why should she remain with the Commonwealth? Pakistan will seek her friends elsewhere with disastrous consequence to the whole of Asia and the Middle East.' MSS Eur F164/48. India Office Records. British Library, London.

†First-class cricket is the senior level of the game, often played between counties or provinces, subject to special rules and entering the official record. On 19 May 1947, at a meeting of the Imperial Cricket Conference, the following definition of first-class cricket was agreed: 'A match of three or more days duration between two sides of eleven players officially adjudged first-class, shall be regarded as a first-class fixture. Matches in which either team shall have more than eleven players or which are scheduled for less than three days shall not be regarded as first-class. The Governing body in each country shall decide the status of teams.' There is an unsatisfactory circularity about this definition, with its assertion that first-class games are those which are 'officially adjudged' first-class. In addition the first-class game must adhere to the Laws of Cricket, still controlled by the MCC, and the game must be played over two innings. Test matches are always first-class matches. They are played between two countries acknowledged as Test match standard by the International Cricket Conference, and modern Tests are almost always scheduled to be contested over five days.

and inter-university fixtures. These types of cricket played an essential role in maintaining a cricket culture after Partition, but they were not enough.

BCCP vice-president Cornelius needed to take urgent measures to prevent the nation's best players drifting away from the game. In the absence of serious domestic cricket, the only way to do this was to attract international teams to Pakistan, but here again he faced difficulties. Stranded outside the Imperial Cricket Conference, Pakistan was reduced to supplicant status. Its best hope of attracting Test match teams was to entice them northwards during tours of India, or attempt to convince Australia or New Zealand to pause at Lahore or Karachi when they flew to England and back. AH Kardar later referred to this period as the 'nebulous years', a phrase which conjures up uncertainty and isolation. But it does not do justice to the sense of humiliation the country's cricketers must have felt, made worse by the painful fact that India, Pakistan's local rival, was already a member of the cricketing elite.

West Indies holds the honour of producing the first international team which toured Pakistan. For Pakistan's cricketers, the arrival of a Test-playing nation in November 1948 was a momentous event.* But it probably meant little to the West Indies, who had broken their five-Test tour of India after the first Test at Delhi. They were expecting a relaxing intermission. Back in India, Lala Amarnath had encouraged them in this view. When the West Indies captain John Goddard enquired just before the tour of the likely standard in Pakistan, Amarnath reportedly told him, 'It is just a schoolboys' team.' This remark got back to the Pakistan players, who were furious.[38]

The West Indies started with a gentle, drawn game against Sindh Province in Karachi, a city that was soon to emerge as a force in cricket but at the time was essentially a gigantic refugee camp. From Karachi, the West Indians travelled to the garrison town of Rawalpindi, where they played against an XI raised by the cricket-mad commander-in-chief, General Sir Douglas Gracey. The British had been playing cricket at Rawalpindi, strategically close to the North-West frontier, for around a century. An enormous

---

*Fazal Mahmood (2003) claimed that this tour came at his personal instigation, stating that, 'We went to Mamdot Villa, the residence of the chief minister of West Punjab, Nawab Iftikar Hussain Mamdot, who was also the president of the BCCP, and requested him to invite the West Indies team for a Test match at Lahore. The invitation was conveyed through the Board of Control for Cricket in India.' He dates the meeting with the Nawab of Mamdot to September, just a few weeks before the tour began, very late indeed for such a radical change to the West Indies itinerary.

statue of Queen Victoria stood to the right of the sightscreen.* Pakistan's cricketers succumbed ignominiously, dismissed for 96 in their first innings, and lost the match by nine wickets.†

Now came the major event of the short, two-week tour. The West Indies made the journey south from Rawalpindi to the Bagh-e-Jinnah cricket ground in Lahore. Treated as a routine fixture by the international cricket authorities – *Wisden* humiliatingly gives it the same billing as West Indies' match against West Zone at Poona – for Pakistanis it counted for much more. They called it a Test match, even though its official status was nothing of the sort.[39] The pride of the nation was at stake, and here at last the shape of Pakistan's international team was beginning to emerge. Mian Mohammad Saeed was confirmed as captain. The opening pair, Imtiaz Ahmed‡ and Nazar Mohammad,§ put on 148 for the first wicket, but thereafter the team subsided to a disappointing 241.

The Pakistan opening bowler, Munawwar Ali Khan,¶ got his team off to a spellbinding start in the field. The fastest bowler in Pakistan, he bowled George Carew, the West Indies opening batsman, first ball. His second delivery blew away the West Indies captain John Goddard. 'It broke his stump in two,' recollects Sultan Mahmud, a witness. 'I can still visualise one part of the stump flying through the air. Goddard was very much annoyed that he had been misled by the Indians.'[40] Amarnath's contemptuous remark was being disproved.

Clyde Walcott came next to the wicket. He edged his first ball to Nazar in the gully who dropped the catch, depriving Munawwar of a hat-trick. West Indies recovered to the respectability of 308 thanks in part to a fine innings of 57 not out from the injured George Headley, a great batsman now in the veteran stage. In the second innings, Imtiaz Ahmed and Mian

*Later she was to be thrown away by the Pakistanis, only to be reclaimed by the British High Commission in whose grounds in the Islamabad diplomatic enclave it now stands.
†The West Indies, meanwhile, had not thrown off their colonial status either. Despite the presence in their team of the great and experienced George Headley, they were captained by John Goddard, one of the white elite.
‡Wicketkeeper-batsman who played in all but one of Pakistan's first 42 Tests.
§Brilliant opening batsman who scored Pakistan's first century in Test cricket, at Lucknow in 1952. His retirement from cricket as a result of an arm injury in 1953 was a disaster for Pakistan cricket. Nazar broke his arm jumping out of an upstairs window, damaging himself so badly that he was never able to play cricket again. He was widely believed to be fleeing from a jealous husband. Nazar's son Mudassar Nazar also played Test cricket for Pakistan.
¶Fast bowler, played for Mamdot Cricket Club, made debut for Northern India against Bombay 1944–45. He was selected for the 1952–53 Test tour of India, but was refused leave of absence by an unsympathetic employer.

Saeed scored centuries as they put on 205 for the second wicket. 'They gave a wonderful thrashing to the West Indies fast-bowlers,' recollects Mahmood.

Eventually the game petered out as a draw. In Pakistan this was felt as a victory, commented the historian Shuja-ud-Din. By holding at bay such a strong side in an important fixture, Pakistan cricketers had made a perfect start in their pursuit of ICC recognition as a Test-playing country.[41]

Shuja-ud-Din himself played in this match, and was to be a useful player for Pakistan as a left-arm spinner and dogged lower middle-order batsman. He retired from the Pakistan army as a Lieutenant-Colonel in 1978 after twenty-six years' service, including eighteen months in an Indian prisoner-of-war camp after being captured during the 1971 Bangladesh War.

Pakistan gained yet more confidence the following April when Mian Saeed, now established as the first national captain, led his team to Ceylon. Saeed, who had served with British Army intelligence in Cairo during World War Two, had a natural authority and command. Ceylon enjoyed similar status to Pakistan – outside the Imperial Cricket Conference. So any cricketing encounter between the two countries had the air of a knockout contest. Pakistan beat the Ceylonese by an innings in the first 'unofficial Test' and by ten wickets in the second.

The Pakistan team was beginning to acquire a settled look. Nazar Mohammad and Imtiaz Ahmed made a strong opening pair, confident and aggressive, capable of destructive batting even against the very best attacks. In the middle order, Mian Saeed was a solid presence, as was the up and coming Alimuddin, who had officially been just twelve years old when he had first played in the Ranji Trophy.* This series also saw the emergence of Murawwat Hussain as a short-lived force in Pakistan cricket.

The bowling attack was spearheaded by Khan Mohammad, who had formed a strong partnership with Fazal Mahmood. For Fazal this series represented an essential boost to morale. Deprived of access to cricket thanks to his police commitments, he had feared that he was losing his touch.

*Born in Ajmer, reportedly on 15 December 1930, Alimuddin would have been just 12 years and 73 days old when he first played first-class cricket for Rajputana. He spent the 1947–48 season playing for Gujrat in the Ranji Trophy but moved to Pakistan the following year, settling in Karachi and playing first-class cricket for Sindh. Not initially selected for Pakistan on the inaugural tour of India in 1952–53, Alimuddin got his chance as opening batsman alongside Hanif Mohammad on the 1954 tour of England through the freak injury to Nazar Mohammad. Qamar Ahmed, who knew Alimuddin well, refuses to believe that he made his debut aged twelve. (Qamar Ahmed: personal interview).

Fazal's failure against the West Indies the previous year had made him nerv-ous he would be written off. In addition, Fazal was establishing himself as a dangerous lower middle-order batsman. But it was at exactly this moment of maximum national confidence that disaster struck.

To the modern eye there was nothing very menacing about the Commonwealth XI which visited Pakistan in November 1949. It was mainly composed of players, like the Australians George Tribe and Bill Alley, and the Lancashire opening batsman Buddy Oldfield, whose Test careers were over or never began. But the result was humiliation for Pakistan. The Commonwealth XI played five matches against India* and one against Pakistan. In this game, played at the Bagh-e-Jinnah, the Pakistan batting failed twice against the left-arm wrist spin of Tribe in partnership with his fellow Australian Cec Pepper. In the second innings, Mian Saeed's team were bowled out for 66.

At the end of the game, the furious crowd threw stones and verbal abuse at the Pakistan cricketers, who had to shelter in the pavilion before being smuggled out of the back-door in an ambulance. Five years later, Fazal Mahmood (who had taken just one wicket in the match) recalled how the defeat 'destroyed whatever little reputation cricket had in Pakistan. People were disheartened and started calling for the game in Pakistan to be aban-doned.' Fazal recorded that 'cricket in Pakistan was breathing its last.'† It was time for a change of plan.

---

*These games were all titled 'unofficial Tests' by *Wisden*, which awarded no such recognition to poor Pakistan's lonely effort against the Commonwealth XI.
† *Fazal Mahmood aur Cricket*, p.64, sums up the sense of malaise. 'Soon after the Commonwealth team left, the team from Ceylon visited Pakistan. During both the Test matches at Karachi and Lahore, the number of players on the ground was more than that of the spectators. Although we won both the Tests and I alone got 18 wickets, the press and public both ignored it.'

A FAMOUS VICTORY AT KARACHI

'The lithe grace and elegance of Kardar leading his team onto the field; the unending flow of linear rhythm by which Evans accommodated himself to returns from the field; the dignity which radiates from every motion of Frank Worrell; the magnificence and magnanimity of Keith Miller.'

– CLR JAMES[1]

Mian Saeed had got Pakistan off to a flying start. Surely he deserved to be forgiven for the debacle at the Bagh-e-Jinnah against the Commonwealth XI?

He probably would have been but for the fact that Abdul Hafeez Kardar had returned to Pakistan after an absence of almost five years. We last met Kardar making his debut for the Northern Indian Cricket Association in March 1944. Then a debonair cricketer, known for his lavish strokeplay and medium-fast bowling, both left-handed, he was now a very different proposition. Even his name had changed. Known to his friends as Abdul Hafeez before he left for England, now he was AH Kardar, remote and distant, and a purveyor of slow, left-arm orthodox spin.

He had played three Test matches for the Nawab of Pataudi's India team which toured England in 1946, gained a Blue in three successive years for Oxford University and played two seasons as an all-rounder for

Warwickshire in the county championship. Sultan Mahmud, then a prom-ising teenage cricketer, recalls the first time he met Kardar, in Pakistan. It was in the winter of 1949–50, not long after Kardar had come over from Oxford: 'One day we were at the nets with the famous leg-spin bowler Amir Elahi,* when we saw someone in the far distance walking towards us in a white sharkskin suit. A three-piece suit and a tie, on a very hot summer's day. Who on earth could it be? As he came closer Amir Elahi turned to us and said: "Don't you recognise him? The man with the stiff neck. Kardar."

'Everybody welcomed him as he reached the nets. As a kid I was very excited to see Kardar, about whom I had been reading so many stories in the newspapers. He seemed very smart and handsome.

'Amir Elahi asked Kardar: "What brings you to Pakistan?"

'Kardar replied that he was not there long and would soon be travelling to Bombay to meet his cousin AR Kardar, the film director.'[2] Kardar did not at once make himself available for Pakistan. When a Commonwealth team visited in the winter of 1949, he was asked to play. He turned down the opportunity, claiming that his left shoulder was damaged. This claim has been widely disbelieved.[†]

Most of Kardar's fellow cricketers agree that he was set upon dislodging Mian Saeed, and undermined his standing by refusing to play under his cap-taincy. Some even assert that Kardar – who watched the Commonwealth debacle as a spectator – was responsible for the riot that followed the match. Sultan Mahmud, who was there at the time, states today that 'the boys from Bhati Gate and Sanda orchestrated the demonstrations against Mian Saeed.' Bhati Gate and Sanda were the areas where the Kardar family influence was strongest. (No hard evidence has ever been provided for this claim.)

Then Kardar was invited to play against the visiting Ceylonese, who arrived in March 1950. This time he did make himself available, and was named as Mian Saeed's vice-captain. The next day, Kardar suddenly announced he had an injury and needed to return to England.[‡] The real

---

*Amir Elahi, one of the select band of eleven cricketers who have played for two countries. He played for India against Australia in Sydney in 1947 and for Pakistan against India in 1952–53.

†Kardar substantiates the story of the shoulder injury in his *Memoirs of an All-rounder*, p.113. 'However, due to long spells of bowling I ended up with a bad left shoulder and the stage came where I could hardly lift my arm to bowl.'

‡*Dawn*, 21 March 1950, p.8. Kardar cited calcium in his left arm, adding that he would need to return to the UK for treatment. He departed by BOAC to London three days later.

reason, asserts Sultan Mahmud, is that 'Kardar wanted to play as captain. I was part of that team. It was no secret.'[3] More than a year would pass before Kardar finally supplanted Mian Saeed.

It would have been more natural if Kardar could have served first of all as understudy to Saeed. But Kardar would not allow this. For him, it was the captaincy that he wanted, and on his own terms. He was merciless. Mian Saeed had served Pakistan cricket with loyalty and understanding. Along with Jahangir Khan and Syed Fida Hassan* he had been part of the inner core who had brought national cricket into being. Many of the meetings where the BCCP had been conceived had taken place in his home in White House Lane, just behind Aitchison College, across the table with his close friends Jahangir Khan and Justice Cornelius.

Mian Saeed never protested, either in public or even to family or close friends, about the way he had been treated. His son, Yawar Saeed, recalls: 'My father learnt about it through the media. He didn't say a word for forty-eight hours. He went to bed, not even coming down for meals. He said absolutely nothing.'[4] The switch from Mian Saeed to Kardar was to define Pakistan cricket for the next quarter-century. It could have been handled with much more generosity and grace.

THE KARDAR–CORNELIUS CORRESPONDENCE

Justice Cornelius, as chairman of the selectors, cannot have enjoyed making the decision to sack Mian Saeed and install Kardar. Indeed this episode is

---

*Syed Fida Hassan (sometimes wrongly called Fida Hussain) is one of the formative figures in early Pakistan cricket. Educated at Government College, he led a Punjab University team in the 1920s which included Jahangir Khan and Mohammad Nissar. A right-handed batsman of high talent he might have been selected for India's 1932 inaugural tour of England but for competing in the India Civil Service exams. After passing the exams he was sent to Oxford University where he played for the Authentics. In the 1930s he played for Northern India in the Ranji Trophy. In the first Ranji Trophy semi-final at Amritsar he added 125 in a famous partnership with George Abell as Northern India beat Central India by four wickets, the two batsmen coming together with their team a precarious 47–4 chasing 243 to win. After Partition he became a senior civil servant, serving as Chief Secretary for the Punjab and as Adviser to President Ayub Khan. Managed Pakistan on its 1954 tour of England while serving as Chief Secretary for the Punjab, having been a key agitator in the attempt to strip Kardar of the captaincy ahead of the tour. He retained a strong connection with cricket and became President of the BCCP. Fida Hassan, Jahangir Khan, Mian Saeed and Dilawar Hussain formed the selection committee that chose the team for the Lahore 'Test' against Ceylon from which Kardar dropped out, citing injury (see *Dawn*, 21 March 1950, p.8).

mysterious, for Cornelius behaved entirely out of character. He must have
come under intolerable political pressure, and from a very high level, to
decide in favour of Kardar, though there are no records to show how this was
applied, or by whom.

Part of the letter sent by Cornelius to Kardar, offering him the post of
national cricket captain, along with sections of Kardar's reply, survive. The
original correspondence has vanished, as is invariably the case when it comes
to Pakistani cricket records. However, Kardar published sections in his
Memoirs of an All-rounder.[5] 'Your qualifications for the position were fully
recognised by all those who participated in making the choice,' wrote
Cornelius. He went on to spell out the qualities that had recommended
Kardar to the selectors:

> Having participated in county cricket for two full seasons, besides play-
> ing several full seasons for Oxford, you have a wider experience of English
> county players and their tactics than perhaps any cricketer from the sub-
> continent since Pataudi, and what is more, all your experience is very
> recent. Your ability to lead young sides successfully, and to inspire them
> by your own outstanding ability in every department of the game, is fully
> recognised, as also your knack of taking up your vigilance and concen-
> tration for a moment. With all this you will need, besides every ounce of
> support from your side, the good wishes of all Pakistanis, and something
> of supernatural aid as well, to carry your side to victory. All will be forth-
> coming, I feel assured.*

Kardar wrote back:

> There are times when it is absolutely difficult to find words for the proper
> expression of one's sentiments. This is such an occasion. To be a captain
> of one's country is a great honour, for in electing me to this station you
> and your colleagues have bestowed upon me their greatest gift, and have
> shown me the confidence in which I may be held. I accept the trust will-
> ingly and hope to execute it faithfully ... My chief feeling is one of relief

*Cornelius did not mention that Kardar was fifteen years younger than Mian Saeed and much fitter,
important factors on a long, demanding tour.

that I have been asked to assist Pakistan and my chief concern in the next few months will be to perform my duties with efficiency, thoughtfulness and conscientiousness.

Cornelius was exaggerating Kardar's captaincy experience. He never skippered either Oxford or Warwickshire, and his only experience of captaincy was leadership of the Punjab University team in the 1944–45 cricket season. If anyone had shown a proven ability to motivate young sides, it was Mian Saeed.

Some stretching of the truth was forgiveable. Both men were aware of the magnitude of the task that lay ahead: the establishment of Pakistan as a Test-playing nation. Kardar emerged at a unique moment in Pakistan's development. He became captain of a marginalised cricket team representing a traumatised nation neurotic about its status and desperate for recognition. Kardar was a personal manifestation of this neurosis in a way that Mian Saeed – easy in himself, relaxed, a man of the world – was not. This is why cricket under Kardar came to stand for a common national consciousness.

The Indian historian Ramachandra Guha has noted that Kardar was 'a cricketer who was also an ideologue, and through whose life one can read the coming into being of the nation of Pakistan.'[6] This observation captures the most important element of Kardar's sporting personality. Most cricketers are motivated by a mixture of motives: joy in playing the game, personal ambition, financial gain, pride in playing for one's country. But Kardar was ultimately driven by passionate belief in the honour of Pakistan. This overwhelming mission at times made him blind to the humanity of his fellow cricketers. He could often, as we shall see, be cruel and intolerant. But there was more to Kardar than just an ideologue. He relished parties, revelled in the company of fashionable women, and saw no contradiction between his Muslim faith and enjoyment of alcohol. When later in life he entered politics it was as a defender of the humane and egalitarian values he had discovered through his reading of the Holy Quran. The cricket team he sculpted was the near-exact expression of the vision of Pakistan's founder, Mohammad Ali Jinnah.

It is sometimes assumed that Kardar came from a grand background – an impression which his aloof demeanour did nothing to discourage. There were no great ancestral lands, however, and he did not attend Lahore's Aitchison College, the Eton of Pakistan, which educated much of the Indian feudal elite in the first half of the twentieth century. The son of a bank director, Sain Jalaluddin, he was raised in the orthodox Muslim tradition, hard by Bhati Gate inside the walled city of Old Lahore.

Abdul Hafeez's mother was his father's second wife. The senior wife, Umme Kalsoom, was intensely devout and, according to close family, disliked the physical side of married life. So she encouraged her husband to marry again. He chose a fair-skinned Farsi-speaker from Herat in Afghanistan, Zubeida, who is remembered today as 'the most good-looking woman in the Kardar family.' The two wives lived together, one family member recalls, 'like sisters. They were no trouble to each other.' They are said to have been equally devoted to the young Abdul Hafeez.

Kardar's childhood home was a three-storey merchant's house, built in Moghal times with the *choti eent* (small brick) characteristic of the era, abutting an alleyway leading up to one of the little courtyards where so much of the social life of Lahore takes place – weddings, festivals and, of course, street cricket. Except that street lighting had now been introduced, the Lahore of Kardar's childhood had scarcely moved on from the city of courtesans, intrigue and opium dens Rudyard Kipling would explore as a young reporter on his walks after dark, after the final edition of the *Civil and Military Gazette* had gone to bed, and which he would immortalise in his masterpiece *Kim*. Like Kim, Kardar would have been familiar with the 'stealthy prowl through the dark gullies and lanes, the crawl up a water-pipe, the sights and sounds of the women's world on the flat roofs and the headlong flight from housetop to housetop under cover of the hot dark.'

Like Kim, Kardar would have seen the 'ash-smeared fakirs by their brick shrines under the trees at the riverside'. It was one such holy man who came into his parents' house when Kardar was a small boy and informed them that 'this boy of yours is going to make a name for himself.'[7] But while Kim found himself drawn towards the great game of espionage, Kardar stayed aloof from the perfervid political plotting of the time, devoting his time to what he regarded as the greater game of cricket.

Kardar began his early schooling at a madrassah near his home. He learnt the Quran from the prominent scholar Maulana Ghulam Murshid Arain, who led the prayers at the Oonchi Masjid mosque, at the bottom of the little alleyway leading up to his family home. Kardar's membership of the high-ranking Arain caste – defined by Lt Col. JM Wikeley in 1913 as 'a fighting race which has produced many Civil and Military officers who have rendered good services to the nation . . . '8 – was always to be a source of great pride, Arains being admired for their self-discipline and hard work.

Kardar attended the Islamia High School at Bhati Gate,* moving onto the Dayal Singh College. The Dayal Singh College then ranked low down the academic pecking order, a reflection perhaps of the fact that Kardar lived only for cricket and not schoolwork. He would later recall:

> Like all young fans of the game at school I was fascinated by the per-
> sonalities of English county cricket and of the Test matches. My heroes
> were Don Bradman, Wally Hammond, Woodfull, Ponsford, Ranji,
> Pataudi, Duleep, Nissar, Amar Singh, Amarnath, Wazir Ali, Larwood,
> Jardine, Grimmett, Leyland, Mushtaq. My favourite writer-cricketers
> were Ranji, Grimmett and Jardine. It was my good fortune in later years
> to play against some and meet some of them. It was a thrilling experience
> to meet them and learn from their vast knowledge of the game. Whether
> reading the score-card or books by my favourite authors I was all the time
> wanting to reach international standards and to play Test cricket. This
> urge to play Test cricket became a burning passion with me.9

So Kardar's heroes were a mixture of Englishmen, Australians, Muslims like the great Wazir Ali, Hindus like Amarnath, and princely potentates like Ranji and Pataudi. But they were all cricketers – and they formed his moral universe. As a small boy, he would have played cricket in the courtyard outside his home. Later on, he and his schoolfriends would stroll down together to practise or play at Minto Park. The most direct route took them through Lahore's red-light district, a journey which was forbidden by their respectable families. Kardar's father discouraged cricket altogether, fruitlessly urging his son to concentrate on academic studies.

Yet it was Kardar's passion for cricket which rescued him from a career of intellectual mediocrity. In his second year at Dayal Singh College, aged around thirteen, he was talent-spotted by one of the most influential cricket coaches of the era, Khawaja Saeed Ahmed, and prevailed upon to migrate

*The school has since been demolished on the orders of Nawaz Sharif, in his second term as Prime Minister of Pakistan, in order to make way for the extension of the Shrine of Ali Hajveri, the patron saint of Lahore.

to Islamia College. With this move Kardar entered Lahore's cricketing elite.*
By 1941, at the age of sixteen, he was playing for Punjab University and
starting to travel further afield. On one of these journeys in 1942, playing
in a cricket tournament in Bombay, he realised that his fielding skills were
nowhere near those of his potential rivals for Test selection. Kardar's response
indicated his seriousness of purpose:

> On my return to Lahore I set myself the target of gaining maximum
> speed in rushing up to the ball, neat collection and immaculate return to
> the wicketkeeper. To build up my stamina I would go the field at 3 in the
> morning for a gruelling programme. This would begin with a 3- to 4-mile
> run. The road work was followed by short spurts of 40 to 50 yards as are
> required in chasing a ball to the boundary. The morning session would
> conclude with fielding full-blooded drives and high catching. The
> evenings were devoted to net practice. In winding up the day's pro-
> gramme I would run another mile or so. My word, I was tired after the
> full day's programme.[10]

With fierce intelligence, total commitment and plenty of talent, Kardar was
turning himself into an outstanding cricketer. As we have seen, he scored 94
on first-class debut in the spring of 1944. A series of even higher scores followed. Whereas Fazal Mahmood narrowly missed selection for the Nawab
of Pataudi's 1946 India tour of England, Kardar had made himself an automatic choice.

That summer marked the turning point in Kardar's life, even though his
performances on the pitch (he averaged just 16 with the bat in Tests) were
a disappointment. He developed a friendship with Pataudi that would last
until the Nawab's premature death some five years later. There is a photograph of the two together on that 1946 tour, in which Kardar appears to be
helping Pataudi put on his batting gloves. It is a picture of emperor and
retainer, client and patron.

*Nevertheless, in later life Kardar would insist that his time at Dayal Singh had done him good. 'Had I
gone to any of the two premier institutions I would have been overshadowed by other equally good if not
better players. It so transpired that I became the backbone of my college team ... I seemed to revel in
adverse circumstances and nothing ever deterred me from fighting it out from down under.' *Memoirs of
an All-Rounder* [MOAR], p.18.

The Nawab of Pataudi asked his friend CB Fry, the famous English amateur cricketer and sportsman, to help Kardar find a place at Oxford University.[11] At the end of the 1946 tour, Kardar stayed behind in Britain, going up to University College in the autumn, a move which meant that he escaped the horror of Partition and its aftermath.* He was also unavailable for India's 1947–48 tour of Australia, meaning that he was spared the agonising decision which confronted Fazal Mahmood.

Above all, Kardar emerged from Oxford marked out as a future leader of Pakistan. The Dean of University College, Giles Alington, took the young Pakistani under his wing. Alington, who died tragically young, was connected through marriage to the Douglas-Home family in Berwickshire. In his holidays Kardar would go to stay at the family home in the Borders. Alec Douglas-Home, the heir to the Earldom, had played first-class cricket for Oxford University and Middlesex in the 1920s.† He was now a rising politician who would in due course go on to become British prime minister and foreign secretary. Kardar family records show that he would dispatch regular crates of mangoes to the Foreign Office twenty-five years later. Letters of thanks from Sir Alec assert that Kardar's mangoes were eagerly consumed. The strongest influence on the young Pakistani cricketer, however, was Giles Alington. At the end of Kardar's Oxford career, he was offered the post of assistant secretary at Warwickshire Cricket Club.‡ Alington told Kardar that he must turn the job down because the new state of Pakistan was in urgent need of talented young men. Such was the intense, solemn and very proud Oxford graduate who, in late September 1951, took on the task of leading the Pakistan cricket team against the MCC.

---

*I have been unable to track down all of Kardar's movements during the long vacation of 1947. He was certainly in England for the Oxford v Cambridge match at Lord's which finished on 8 July 1947, and presumably back in Oxford for the start of Michaelmas term in October. So he could have gone back home for the summer. But Kardar never subsequently referred to being in Lahore for the unforgettable events of August and September 1947, and surely would have done had he been present. Probably he was in the Deeside village of Hawarden: 'As a result of having to keep pace with academic life, especially after the cricket season in summer, I used to take refuge in a residential library donated to the nation by the great English politician and statesman, Mr Gladstone . . . I used to take rooms plus a private study and in seclusion tried to catch up with what I had missed during the cricket season.' *MOAR*, p.104.

†According to Shahid Kardar. The present Earl of Home (who would have been four or five at the time) has no memories of a visiting Pakistan cricketer, adding there is no record in the visitors' book at the Hirsel.

‡This was a job, much used by county teams at the time, which allowed 'gentlemen' cricketers to retain their 'amateur' status while still getting paid.

PAKISTAN v MCC, SEPTEMBER 1951

Kardar had six weeks to prepare. This was not easy. Upon his return to Pakistan he had taken a job in an oil company in Chittagong, East Pakistan. So first he faced the task of detaching himself from his employer, who was not sympathetic. Kardar found an outlet for his frustration by embarking on another of his ferocious training regimes, while dispatching a letter to Cornelius setting out the qualities he sought in a cricketer: 'I want aggressive players who can set their guts and heart on a purpose.'[12]

Arriving in Lahore at the start of November, the new Pakistan captain immediately produced a display of the kind of imperious judgement that always made him hard to deal with. The problem concerned the number 3 slot in the team's batting order. By general consent the best candidate was Murawwat Hussain, who played a sparkling 36 in a trial match.* Kardar disliked the way he got out to a loose shot, and rebuked him. Murawwat's flippant response infuriated Kardar. Murawwat was dropped, and never played cricket for Pakistan again.†

But this left a bigger hole than ever at number 3, a vacancy which was discussed at the final meeting of selectors. Cornelius put forward Jahangir Khan, who had been enjoying a run of good scores for his club side, the Lahore Gymkhana. Most cricket lovers would forgive Cornelius the moment of romanticism which led him to agitate for his old friend, who was not necessarily past it at forty-one. At worst, Cornelius's idea was a harmless enough conceit, which was swiftly shot down by the other selectors. But for Kardar this 'basic ignorance on the part of the chairman of the difference between club cricket and Test cricket' was unforgiveable. He held it against Cornelius forever after.[13]

MCC – the name under which England teams toured overseas until 1977 – were playing a five-month tour in India, lured north for three weeks in Pakistan. Once again, Pakistan was forced to play a subordinate role. Once

---

*Murawwat Hussain, born in Sialkot 1918, made his first-class debut in the Ranji Trophy for Southern Punjab against Northern India in 1934–35. Hurt by his non-selection for Kardar's 1952 tour of India, later he took to umpiring and besides several first-class matches he stood in one Test match, between the West Indies and Pakistan at Karachi in 1959.

†From retirement years later, Kardar was still glowering about the Murawwat dismissal. 'Here a word of advice to young players would not be out of place. Remember that you are playing for the team and you must play for the team to the end. When you are well set you must not get out before you have put your team on top and have fully discouraged all the bowlers.' *MOAR*, p.129.

again, the tour was of overwhelming importance to the Pakistanis, while it was probably regarded as an upcountry diversion by their opponents.

The Pakistanis' first contest against MCC was at the Bagh-e-Jinnah, Lahore, over four days at the end of November 1951. MCC batted first when the pitch had some life, and struggled against the pace of Khan Mohammad, who took five wickets, and the leg-spin of Amir Elahi, who took four. In reply, a sixteen-year-old opening batsman impressed with his calm and application against an attack of Test quality, spearheaded by Brian Statham. He batted for 165 minutes in scoring 26 and shared an opening stand of 96 with the more fluent Nazar Mohammad, who made 66. More would be heard of Hanif Mohammad. The aggressive Maqsood Ahmed, known always as Merry Max, scored a sparkling hundred, MEZ Ghazali* made 86, and Kardar contributed 48. He eventually declared on 428 for 8, with a lead of 174. By now the pitch was sedated, and MCC lost only one wicket in scoring 368 to save the game. *Wisden*'s comment on this match is significant: 'Expecting a reasonably quiet time in Pakistan, MCC found the standard of cricket higher than expected.'[14]

The match coincided with Kardar's marriage to Shahzadi, sister to his team-mate Zulfiqar Ahmed. The wedding procession set out from the Kardar family home in Old Lahore and travelled to Sanda Kalan, the village on the outskirts of town where the land holdings of Zulfiqar Ahmed's family were concentrated. The MCC travelled to the wedding on special *tongas* (horse-drawn carriages) from Faletti's Hotel, where they were staying.[15]

The next contest against the MCC, played at Karachi at the end of November, may not have been a Test match, as the local cricketers and press insisted on calling it, but it was the most important game of cricket in the nation's history, with only the World Cup final victory of 1992 to rival it. It was also a superb game of cricket, with fortunes changing hour by hour and the result uncertain until the very end.

Kardar was lucky to lose the toss to the MCC captain Nigel Howard.

*Mohammad Ebrahim Zain-ud-din Ghazali, often known as 'Ebbu'. Born in 1924 in Bombay, where he represented Muslims in the Bombay Pentangular, as well as playing for Mahrashtra in the Ranji Trophy. Migrated at Partition, and played for Sindh against the West Punjab on the inaugural first-class match on the soil of the newly created Islamic Republic of Pakistan. Sindh, led by legendary Syed Wazir Ali, were defeated by an innings notwithstanding Ghazali's fighting unbeaten century in the second innings. Ghazali scored only 32 runs in four Test innings on the 1954 tour of England, including the fastest pair in Test cricket. On the third day of the third Test at Old Trafford, Ghazali was dismissed for nought twice within two hours.

Wisden describes the ground as 'remarkable, being partly grass, but most of the outfield was baked mud, with the pitch coir matting stretching the length of the bowler's run instead of ending at the stumps as in previous matches. From the table to the boundary there was a drop of over two feet. The ball flew nastily for two days.' MCC were all out for 123, unable to cope with Khan Mohammad and in particular Fazal Mahmood, who conceded 40 runs while taking six wickets.* However, Pakistan then fell apart in their turn, dismissed for 130, a score which would have been even less impressive but for a vital 29 by Fazal. The MCC managed much better in the second innings, mainly thanks to a century by a young Tom Graveney. Eventually the English were all out for 291, setting Pakistan 285 to win, a task that looked beyond them. It became more distant then ever when Kardar's star opening bat, Nazar Mohammad, succumbed early on to Shackleton. This critical point was the moment when Hanif Mohammad announced himself in international cricket.

At 5ft 3in tall and weighing barely nine stone (probably much less when he embarked on his career), Hanif is one of the smallest players ever to have played Test match cricket. With his crouching stance, ultra-defensive technique, and lack of inches, he was rarely an attractive player to watch. He lacked a sense of cricket as a sport, let alone entertainment. For Hanif it was a solemn duty, indeed a vocation, whose fundamental purpose was to ensure that his country was not defeated. For nearly two decades, he was to be the foundation stone upon which Pakistan teams were built, showing prodigious concentration and on many occasions great courage and physical endurance; first the mascot and as time passed, the emblem of cricket in Pakistan.

Hanif was just sixteen years old and playing only his third first-class match. For over four hours he again defied the MCC Test-class attack of Statham, Shackleton and Tattersall. Once Hanif was dismissed for 64, Pakistan were at once in trouble – five wickets down with only 178 runs on the board. At this point Kardar took on Hanif's mantle, wrestling his way to

---

*Fazal claims that his selection was in doubt right up to the last moment, that he was originally left out by the selectors, and only brought back in thanks to a rearguard action by one of them, Dr Dilawar Hussein. See Fazal Mahmood, p.22. However, Kardar provides a rival account of this incident, saying that a twelfth man was picked as a precaution because of doubts concerning Fazal's fitness. 'I was relieved to hear him announce himself fit,' claims Kardar. *MOAR*, p.146. At this distance in time, it is impossible to separate truth from fiction. However, these conflicting accounts point to underlying tensions which haunted the relationship between Kardar and Fazal Mahmood throughout their careers.

an unbeaten half-century as he steered his side home. Kardar was later to claim that 'I did not play a single aggressive shot in a stay of 165 minutes at the wicket.'[16] Kardar's innings was the most important of his career. He and Fazal were together at the end, and it was Fazal who struck the winning runs.

Everybody recognised the significance of the result. After the game many of the 20,000 spectators stayed behind to celebrate.[17] Among them was Prime Minister Khawaja Nazimuddin. Seizing Fazal and Kardar by the arms, he led the crowd in cries of 'Pakistan Zindabad!' ('Long Live Pakistan!'). The bulbous Nazimuddin, one of Pakistan's most obscure political leaders, had taken over the premiership only six weeks earlier following the (still mysterious) assassination of Liaquat Ali Khan. Only Jinnah had played a greater role in the creation of the state of Pakistan than Liaquat, a powerful and energetic prime minister from 1947 to 1951, and the country never recovered from the death of these two great men. Certainly, Nazimuddin was not capable of realising the vision of his two predecessors.

Politically, Pakistan had reached a turning point. The attempt to create a strong central power had failed. From now on, politicians would interpret their task as navigating between a weak centre and strong but diverse local interests.[18] This moment of acute political crisis provides part of the context for the ecstatic response to the success of the national cricket team that day in Karachi. As the rest of the country fell apart, cricket was one of the few elements of Pakistan life that seemed to guarantee unity and offer triumph. Even Nazimuddin was smart enough to realise this. When that day's celebrations were over, Fazal Mahmood caught the Frontier Mail to Rawalpindi so that he could resume his constabulary duties. On arrival, he asked his superintendent for permission to attend the dinner the prime minister had announced to celebrate the victory, scheduled to take place in Karachi the following week. 'It is a mere dinner,' he was told. 'Forget about that and take care of your duty.'

When Nazimuddin got to hear of this, he ordered Fazal to attend Karachi, and announced during his after-dinner speech that 'players who serve Pakistan would be considered on duty during all national and international competitions.'[19] Overnight, cricket had become a form of service to the state. This national expectation was in due course to become a heavy burden, and bring with it undesirable consequences. But it was one that for the time being Abdul Hafeez Kardar and his team were capable of bearing with equanimity, fortitude and grace.

CRICKET BEFORE PARTITION

'The simpler native games are gradually giving place to the superior attractions of cricket and football, and the tournaments which of recent years have been organised between the various native regiments and between the different tribes inhabiting each district and between the schools of the provinces are doing much to create a spirit of friendly rivalry, and to develop among these frontier people a fascination for those sports which have done so much to make England what she is.'

– TL PENNELL, FRONTIER MISSIONARY, IN HIS 1909 MEMOIRS,
*AMONG THE WILD TRIBES OF THE AFGHAN FRONTIER:
A RECORD OF SIXTEEN YEARS' CLOSE INTERCOURSE
WITH THE NATIVES OF THE INDIAN MARCHES*

Why did this victory over MCC matter so much? This question cannot be addressed without travelling back into the deep history of cricket in (pre-Partition) Pakistan and India. The two countries have evolved radically contrasting cricketing traditions, but they also enjoy a common inheritance.[1]

Indian cricket is a story which starts with the East India Company trading stations dotted around the Indian coastline of the eighteenth and early nineteenth centuries. The Calcutta Cricket Club was founded in 1792, but there is evidence of cricket in Calcutta even before then. Cricket started in

Madras, on India's south-east coast, around the same date, with Bombay following suit soon after.

Cricket began in all these places as an English sport, but over time it was copied by the locals. First to take to cricket were the Parsis of Bombay. Culturally and racially distinct from the Hindus, the Parsis were fire-worshippers (Zoroastrians) who had fled Persia more than a thousand years earlier. They were the first group to adapt themselves to the British, taking jobs others did not want, the reason so many Parsis today carry names that distinguish their occupations. For example, the Indian Test cricketers Nari Contractor and Farokh Engineer were Parsis, as was the first secretary of the Pakistan cricket board, KR Collector.

The Parsis were quicker to wear western dress, and to adopt western customs. By 1848, the year of European revolutions, the Parsis had founded their first club, the Oriental Cricket Club, soon to be replaced by the Young Zoroastrian cricket club, which still flourishes today. According to Ramachandra Guha, 'at least thirty Parsi clubs were formed in the 1850s and 1860s, named after Roman gods or British statesmen: Jupiter, Mars, Gladstone and Ripon for example.'[2] The first two informal cricket tours of England by Indian cricket teams, in 1886 and 1888, were carried out by pioneering Parsi teams.[3]

A few years after the Parsis, the Hindus took to the game. Finally the Muslims (of special interest to the historian of Pakistan cricket) also came to accept that the sport had its merits. The easiest way to illustrate the pace at which the various religious groups came to terms with cricket is through the development of communal sport in Bombay, which soon established itself as the largest centre for cricket on the subcontinent. Communal cricket, however, started with the Parsis. For example, in the winter of 1889–90 the Middlesex cricketer GF Vernon brought a touring side to India, playing almost entirely against local English teams. The only Indian side Vernon played was the Parsis in Bombay which defeated Vernon after an enthralling two-innings contest by four wickets.[4]

By 1907 the Bombay Triangular came into being, an annual competition fought out between the Hindus, the Europeans and the Parsis. In 1912 the Muslims joined in, creating the Quadrangular (which in turn developed in 1937 into the Pentangular, the fifth team incorporating a miscellany known as 'the Rest'). This contest became the dominant event in the Bombay social and sporting calendar, was copied across India, and was followed with what some considered an unhealthy fanaticism. The Congress Party in particular hated the Pentangular, because it claimed it played into the British policy of 'divide and rule'. Mahatma Gandhi believed that the Pentangular encouraged Indians to create a sectarian identity, and made attempts to stop it.[5]

Meanwhile, by the start of the twentieth century princely patronage of cricket was under way. Indian maharajahs, many of whom possessed prodigious wealth, started to lavish their resources on the game. They formed their own teams, lured star players and for a time came to exercise great influence on the development of the sport. Many of them, such as the Maharajah of Patiala or the Maharajkumar of Vizianagram, used cricket as a way of engaging more deeply in the politics of British India. Vizianagram (Vizzy) notoriously courted favour with the Viceroy, and this was the major reason for his appointment as captain of India in their England tour of 1936, a task for which he was totally unsuited.[6] This cult of the exotic Indian prince (which spread into English schoolboy literature in the shape of Hurree Singh, Nawab of Bhanipur, Harry Wharton's and Billy Bunter's boyhood chum at Greyfriars School) was greatly encouraged by the authorities and exerted a malign influence on the Indian game right up to independence, and even beyond.

Thus, through princely patronage and sectarian division, cricket in India tended to reinforce existing structures, encourage political quiescence, and to divert energy and attention from the anti-colonial struggle. Indian cricket before Partition repudiated everything that the Congress Party and Indian independence movement was about. It was collaborationist, divisive, celebrated the British Empire, and used cricket as a method of ingratiation with the ruling elite.

The greatest princely cricketers had at best a lukewarm relationship with Indian cricket. Ranjitsinhji, who never had the opportunity to play Test cricket for India, rejected the chance to serve Indian cricket as an administrator or even figurehead when India joined the Imperial Cricket Conference in 1929. Under Ranji's influence, his nephew Duleepsinhji opted to play for England rather than make himself available as India's first captain.[7] Iftikhar Ali Khan, the Nawab of Pataudi, also chose England over his native country at first. He showed interest in leading India on its tours of

England in 1932 and 1936 but then absented himself at crucial times, was outmanoeuvred in selection politics, and allowed the post to go to inferior talents.[8] When he finally led the Indian touring party to England in 1946, Test cricket was beyond his powers.

Duleepsinhji played only two first-class cricket matches in India, out of a career total of 205. Pataudi played six in India, out of 127 and Ranji none at all. Ranji's *Jubilee Book of Cricket*, written in 1897, celebrated Queen Victoria's Diamond Jubilee and thereby treated cricket as a manifestation of British imperial dominance.

Cricket in what is now Pakistan could offer nothing comparable. Feudal potentates such as the Nawab of Bahawalpur never came close to rivalling either Patiala in influence or Vizianagram in servility. Cricket represented a separate national identity, doubly so because it defined itself in opposition not just to England but also to neighbouring India. In its formative years, it was almost exclusively a middle-class sport. Its roots neither spread down into the rural peasantry or the urban poor, nor (with a handful of evocative exceptions) upwards into the ranks of the aristocracy and land-owning class. Whereas Indian cricket in its early stages was a denial of everything Gandhi's Congress Party stood for, Pakistan cricket can be understood as a sporting manifestation of Jinnah's Pakistan movement.

CRICKET AND CONQUEST

The early history of British involvement with the Indian subcontinent coincided with the earliest years of the Empire's overseas expansion. During this period, which stretches from the formation of the East India Company in 1600 to the early nineteenth century, the main British interest was trade.[9] There was a haphazard military presence; however, its purpose was the protection of commercial ambitions either against rival European powers or hostile local interests, normally a combination of the two.

By contrast, the British arrived in Pakistan through conquest. With the important exception of Bengal in the East, the territories which came to comprise Pakistan (the Punjab, Baluchistan, Sindh Province and North-West Frontier Province, now Khyber Pakhtunkhwa) were governed by independent rulers. These powers and the British eyed each other warily.

Sometimes relations were friendly, sometimes cool. Right up until the 1840s, the area which now comprises modern Pakistan was mostly immune from British, and indeed western, influence. Certainly there is no evidence of cricket.

So while cultures intermingled in the southern centres of Bombay and Madras, the same could not be said of Peshawar or Lahore. British traders might sometimes travel as far north as Karachi. But at this stage the future metropolis, and bastion of global cricket, was little more than a fishing village. To sum up: British merchants brought cricket to India while it was British soldiers who first took cricket to Pakistan where it was at first rejected by the locals, who associated the game with barbarian invasion.

As they marched forward on their campaigns into Sindh (conquered in 1842 and made part of the Bombay presidency), the Punjab and Afghanistan, the British troops certainly took cricket with them, as a study of regimental records and contemporary newspapers shows. But the records also suggest that in these early days they only played among themselves, and the subject population made no serious attempt to emulate them.

In the Punjabi town of Ferozepore (Firozpur) in October 1842, camp reporters passed on to *The Bombay Times and Journal of Commerce* (predecessor to *The Times of India*) news that 'Parades and Cricket seem to be the order of the day.'[10] The same paper carried reports in August 1843, from their enthusiastic correspondent 'Stumps', of the foundation of a Cricket Club in Karachi, 'the first meeting of which took place on last Saturday the 5th instant, when the officers and men of the 2nd European Light Infantry played against the station.'[11]

By 1844 there were cricket matches in Karachi 'once or twice a week, but the ground [was] very bad.'[12] In Lucknow, reports of cricket date back to January 1844, while in Lahore there were reports of the artillery playing 'the rest of the force' during November 1846.[13] Reports travelled back to Bombay of matches in Allahabad and Peshawar before 1850.

The frontier was established at the Khyber Pass following the Second Anglo-Sikh War in 1849,[14] and *The Bombay Times and Journal of Commerce* places the origin of cricket among the garrisoned forces in that very year. It noted that 'A cricket match occasionally comes off among the officers and men of the artillery and other corps. This in itself is an excellent amusement for the men; the games are well played and becoming more frequent.'[15]

The British forces also took cricket with them on their ill-fated excursion to Kabul during the First Afghan War between 1839 and 1842. The Revd GR Gleig, writing four years later, recounts that 'horse-racing and cricket were both got up in the vicinity of Kabul; and in both the chiefs and people soon learned to take a lively interest.' Gleig records that the 'native gentry' entered their horses in British races. 'The game of cricket was not, however, so congenial to the taste of the Afghans,' recorded Gleig. 'They looked on with astonishment at the bowling, batting and fagging out of the English players; but it does not appear that they were ever tempted to lay aside their flowing robes and huge turbans and enter the field as competitors.'[16] But all traces of cricket vanished when the British were driven out in 1842, and the game was not to return to Kabul in a meaningful way until NATO forces entered the city in 2001.

Infantry Cadet Gordon Davidson, stationed at Sabathu, Himachal Pradesh (a hill station about 100 miles east of Lahore and now in India) wrote home to his parents in November 1844 that 'the weather up here is very agreeable and we very often play at cricket. We have no good ground, the parade is the only place that we can play upon and that is far from level, but we manage to get up a capital game.'[17] Again, in January 1845, he wrote home, 'we have two fixed days every week for playing and on those days we have very good games; it is a most difficult thing to get good bats out here, they always send the worst out.'[18] Davidson remained in the Subathu garrison for a further year, playing cricket regularly before being killed during the assault against Ferozeshah in the Sikh War on 21–22 December 1845.

In 1852 stringent regulations were imposed on those officers stationed in the Lahore Fort, preventing them from leaving their post, and one of the problems raised by *The Bombay Times*' correspondent was that such limitations prevented the young officers from enjoying games of cricket.[19]

The annexation of the north continued beyond the victory in Lahore, and in January 1853 a small town was founded which was later named Abbottabad, after Major James Abbott, the first British Deputy Commissioner of the Hazara District.[20] As Professor Omer Tarin, an historian of the North-West frontier has highlighted, cricket soon emerged in the town, following the arrival of the famed Punjab Irregular Frontier Force.

By contrast, Professor Tarin places the development of cricket in Rawalpindi from the 1870s when he says a proper cricket pitch was first created. However, he adds that sports generally, including cricket, were played occasionally on the cavalry exercise ground before that. Today the old 'Pindi' ground is still very much in use. A board at the entrance (which is guarded by soldiers) claims that it was established in 1849 by the Royal Artillery Company, adding that Lord Vansittart, 'a royal progeny', struck a six there in 1852. This would have been an enormous blow since sixes at this stage of the evolution of the game required the ball to be hit out of the ground altogether, not merely over the boundary as is the case today.* The board also recalls that Prince Christian Victor, Queen Victoria's grandson, struck 205 for the King's Royal Rifles against the Devonshire Regiment, an innings which some claim to be the first double-century struck in what is now Pakistan. He remains the only member of the royal family to have played first-class cricket, for I Zingari against the Gentlemen of England in August 1887.[21]

References to cricket emerge rather earlier in the hill station of Murree, a sports ground established for Europeans in the 1850s. By 1860 the Lawrence Asylum and associated schools were established for the sons and daughters of poor Europeans, the grounds of which included one cricket pitch that was good, even if the boundaries fell away into mountain *khuds*[22] – clefts in the hills which must have made the ball very hard to retrieve.

It is important to bear in mind that the earliest frontier cricketers were playing a very different game from the cricket with which we are familiar today. Over-arm bowling (defined as the hand being raised higher than the shoulder) remained illegal until 1864, and may only have been introduced gradually thereafter in northern India. There were four balls to the over. Creases were still dug into the pitch, not marked with whitewash as today. The lbw rule was at a rudimentary stage: decisions were rare, partly because

---

*It is hard to pin down which Vansittart, if any, scored the six. As far back as 1804 Robert Vansittart scored the first century on Indian soil, in Calcutta, for Old Etonians against the Rest of Calcutta (see Rowland Bowen in *Wisden 1967*, p.148, and Berry Sarbadhikary, *My World Of Cricket (A Century Of Tests) 1964*, pp.308–9). The Vansittarts were a well-connected family and some served in India during the nineteenth century but none had royal blood and none became a peer until the first Lord Vansittart was raised to the peerage in 1941. The most likely Vansittart to have visited 'Pindi' in 1852 was Frederick Vansittart, an officer in the 14th (King's) Hussars. His regiment was in Meerut throughout 1852. (See Col. Henry Blackburne Hamilton, *Historical Record of the 14th (King's) Hussars from 1715 to 1900*, (London, Greene & Co, 1901)). Perhaps it was this Frederick Vansittart who struck the great blow at Rawalpindi.

the rules demanded that the ball must pitch on a line between wicket and wicket. Equipment was at a relatively early stage of evolution. Cricket balls could be larger than today. Wicketkeeping gloves, not introduced until 1850, did not come into general use for some time later and would have surely been a rare sight in early frontier cricket. Batting gloves were in use, but far from universal (the then new I Zingari cricket club obliged candidates to face a net without them). Pads, if used, were fastened with string (the sadistic I Zingari examiners forced candidates to do without them as well). The first modern cricket bats, with willow blades and cane handles, were gradually being introduced in England in the 1850s, and, as Infantry Cadet Davidson noted, were slow to spread to the remoter parts of India.

Clothing was hit and miss: coloured trousers, shirts, ties and all kinds of headgear were normal. Photographs held at the National Army Museum, immortalising a number of regimental cricket teams from this period, display not just the prodigious extent to which cricket was played, but also the appearance of the teams. Most glorious of all is an action shot of the 1st Punjab Infantry playing cricket in their cantonment in Kohat close to Peshawar on the North-West Frontier (see plate no. 2).[23] Before the arrival of the British, Kohat had been a small hamlet with a small mud-walled fort and a scruffy bazaar. It had been part of the Afghan kingdom, and ruled from Kabul, then fell into the hands of the Sikhs in 1836, before being captured by the British thirteen years later.

Cricket is mentioned in one of the histories of the Queen's Own Corps of Guides, the famous elite regiment of the Punjab Frontier Force. Alongside the parade ground, which doubled up as a polo ground, on the dusty plain in Mardan, 'there was a cricket ground, dependent on well water, in the centre of the cantonment', which became more permanent with irrigation from the lower Swat canal from 1876.[24] Indian ranks played in matches at Nowshera as there were not enough European officers to make up two teams. For practice at the nets, men from the Afridi Company were employed; they could throw hard and straight and were an excellent substitute for fast bowlers.[25]

One of the most interesting characters in the cricketing story of the Guides is Major Wigram Battye, the man who introduced the game to the regiment;[26] he was killed in the Battle of Futtehabad in 1879, during the Second Anglo-Afghan War. His soldiers, mostly Pashtun and Sikh cavalry rankers, refused to let the stretcher bearers carry him from the battlefield, instead paying him the greatest respect: 'reverently they lifted the body of their dead comrade, and through the hot spring night carried it themselves' on the first leg of his journey to the regimental cemetery at Mardan.[27]

Episodes like these show warmth and respect between British officers and Indian soldiers. But when the military played matches against civilians, it tended to be in the context of the gymkhanas, private clubs controlled by the British. For example on 27 December 1906, Lahore's *Civil and Military Gazette* reported a cricket match between the British Army and the World. Both teams in this cosmopolitan-sounding match were composed fully of players with British names. Anecdotal reports suggest that when the British did play against local teams, they could be aloof and distant. British officers would enjoy lunch in the pavilion during contests against the local teams in Lyallpur (now Faisalabad) at the start of the twentieth century. But their opponents would sit outside while the British sent out a bucket of tea.[28]

Local Indian troops and citizens began playing long after their European counterparts. Thus Professor Tarin has shown how cricket spread into the local population of Abbottabad following the establishment of two schools, the Prince Albert Victor Memorial Anglo-Vernacular High School in the 1870s and the Municipal Vernacular Higher Secondary School by the 1890s.[29]

In Rawalpindi, the game remained the preserve of the Europeans stationed in the town until almost the turn of the century. While some schools had a sporting curriculum by the 1870s, a District Schools Report revealed that by 1882 there were 'no proper grounds or equipment for sports such as cricket and hockey, although on occasion impromptu arrangements are sometimes possible.'[30] In fact, it was not until 1893, as noted by the *Rawalpindi District Gazetteer*, that local students received their first proper sports instruction. Even then, this instruction consisted of one 'itinerant instructor' who was 'shared between several institutions' in the area.[31] Unfortunately the identity of this pioneer remains unknown.

An early indication of the important role schools were to play in the growth of north Indian cricket comes from TL Pennell's record of his time as a missionary in Bannu, another frontier town with a significant military presence. The launch of this Mission school was at first greeted with a fatwa declared by local Mullahs, they later limited their criticisms to the teaching of English and the subversive impact of Christianity on the minds of its young pupils. However, the school went from strength to strength and local opposition quietened with Indian families recognising the necessity of English in consideration for any Government position in the future.[32]

Cricket in the school flourished and regular games took place between garrison officers and the Mission High School students despite the constant dangers of living on the frontier. 'The old order changes and gives place to the new. Tent-pegging will always retain its charm, with its brave show and splendid opportunities for the display of manly courage,' recorded Pennell, adding that 'the simpler native games are gradually giving place to the superior attractions of cricket and football, and the tournaments which of recent years have been organised between the various native regiments and between the different tribes inhabiting each district and between the schools of the provinces are doing much to create a spirit of friendly rivalry, and to develop among these frontier people a fascination for those sports which have done so much to make England what she is.'[33]

Pennell recalls one game in which a garrison officer allowed his son to score the winning run for the school off his bowling. The following week he was killed in action and buried in the small military cemetery opposite the entrance to the cricket ground.[34]

ENGLISH VISITORS

Towards the end of the nineteenth century, English touring teams started to visit. The first to venture towards the territory of what is today Pakistan was GF Vernon's tour of amateurs in 1889–90, which played a three-day fixture in Lahore. They won by an innings. Lord Hawke of Yorkshire and England was one of Vernon's party. He brought a team of his own over in 1892–93, playing twice in Lahore and finishing the tour in Peshawar. They had three comfortable victories against opponents who were exclusively English apart from one Parsi, C Contractor, who contributed 0 and 1 to the Sindh XI in Lahore. Neither of these tours attracted much attention at home.[35]

However, exactly ten years later the Oxford Authentics (the University second XI) made the journey. The Authentic wicketkeeper, Cecil Headlam, wrote a book about this tour which provides the first literary account of the state of cricket in the Punjab, the North-West Frontier and Sindh, as seen through British eyes. The Authentics travelled north immediately after beating the Gentlemen of India at Delhi, and lingered on behind for the Durbar celebrations. Then they took the 'very long and very cold' railway journey to Peshawar – described by Headlam as:

> ... the advance post that guards India from the north, the mart wherein half India bargains, the British cantonment wherein, if you go out after dark without a lantern, you are likely to be shot first and challenged afterwards by a picket lurking in a ditch. It is a new India for you again here, and it gives you a new sensation. The rest of India is so astonishingly orderly and safe; here on the frontier you are on the confines of barbarism and unconquered lands, in the home of blood-feuds, rifle-thieves; face to face, if you are caught outside cantonments after sundown, with almost certain death.[36]

From Peshawar the Authentics took the overnight journey to Rawalpindi where they played and defeated the Northern Punjab, an all-British team. In Lahore, they played at the Gymkhana, a ground described by Headlam as 'one of the most charming in India.'[37] They faced a strong-sounding opposition – the Punjab – and here, for the first time since their arrival in northern India, they found themselves playing against a Muslim, Ahsan-ul-Haq.* Ahsan did not make much of a contribution in this match, a low-scoring game which the Punjab lost by 100 runs, but he is nevertheless a figure of fascination for the historian of Muslim cricket.

Ahsan-ul-Haq, born in Jullundur (stronghold of the Burki clan) was the first Muslim to play first-class cricket in England. A brutally effective right-handed bat and medium-pace bowler, in 1900 he travelled to study law in London. There he played club cricket for Hampstead alongside Australia's Fred Spofforth, 'the Demon bowler'. Ahsan made his first-class debut representing MCC against London County, WG Grace's team, in August 1901.[38] The following year he played three first-class matches for Middlesex,† with

---

*It is fair to stress that the Authentics did not confine themselves to British opposition during their Indian trip. In Bombay they played against a team of Hindus and also the Parsis, by whom they were soundly defeated. They also played the Muslims of Aligarh.

†During the 1902 season Ahsan completed five innings at an average of 10.80. He did not bowl. His batting was not included in *Wisden's* first-class averages for that year as he did not complete the necessary eight innings.

equal lack of success. He was then called to the Bar, returned to India, and vanished from cricket history for two decades.

In 1924 and at the age of forty-five, Ahsan enjoyed a remarkable comeback, making his Indian first-class debut while batting for Muslims v Sikhs (captained by the Maharajah of Patiala) at the Lawrence Gardens ground in Lahore. By now a judge and based in Dera Ghazi Khan, Ahsan travelled to Lahore by rail. His train was late, meaning that he only arrived at the ground in time to bat number 11. Ahsan slammed a century in 40 minutes.*

It is significant that this talented pioneer of Muslim cricket, in common with so many other early Muslim cricketers, was educated at the Mohammadan Anglo-Oriental College at Aligarh, now part of modern India. For this famous institution was to play a momentous role in the birth of Pakistan as a cricketing nation.

ALIGARH MUSLIM CRICKET

The search for the ethos, origins and defining characteristics of Pakistan cricket must start with Aligarh. The Muslim League – the political movement which brought Pakistan into being – has its roots at Aligarh, and so does Muslim cricket.

Aligarh, in turn, was born out of one of the darkest events of the nineteenth century, the so-called Indian Mutiny. This was an uprising which swept across Northern India in the summer of 1857, at one stage coming close to destroying British rule. Later many Muslims (including AH Kardar, Pakistan's first Test cricket captain) called the mutiny Pakistan's 'first war of

---

*He travelled with his twelve-year-old son Manzoor-ul-Haq, who later recorded that 'when we arrived at the ground, the last man was just about to go to the crease. He was stopped and my father went in (father had been nominated as captain of the Muslims). The not out batsman was Abdus Salaam whose score was 75. My father then hit exactly 100 in 40 minutes. The captain of the opposing side, that great patron of sportsmen His Highness Bhopindar Singh, ruler of Patiala, awarded my father a robe of honour made of gold thread for his performance.' (Letter to *Association of Cricket Statisticians and Historians Journal* (no. 58, summer 1987).) Upon reaching his century, Ahsan declared the Muslim innings at 559 for 9. His younger son Munawwar-ul-Haq (often known as MU Haq) also turned out to be a fine cricketer who played in the Quaid-e-Azam Trophy for the Punjab in the 1950s, narrowly missing selection for the 1954 tour of England. He would later have a role in the players' revolt against Kardar in 1976. Another son, Inam-ul-Haq, played for Muslims in India. Their sister married Abdul Hafeez Pirzada, AH Kardar's nemesis in the cricket politics of the Bhutto era.

independence'.[39] For the British, however, the mutiny represented an unforgivable act of collective treachery and disloyalty, and in response unleashed something close to ethnic cleansing.

Aware that the rebels had declared war in the name of Bahadur Shah Zafar, the last Moghal, the British annihilated the remains of Muslim power on the subcontinent. They ravaged the great centres of Islamic culture, Lucknow and Delhi. Muslims were forced, for a time, to leave Delhi, and the great Islamic libraries of the city were destroyed. For Muslims in India, these events marked the final destruction of everything they knew. A generation went into mourning, unable to decide on how to respond. Islam became synonymous with backwardness and barbarism. Muslims were behind other Indian communities – Hindus, Sikhs, Parsis, Christians – in every field. They were frozen out of power, and this impotence was all the more bitter for the knowledge that a great Islamic civilisation had ruled India for centuries.[40] This is how AH Kardar expressed his personal sense of desolation in his book *Pakistan's Soldiers of Fortune*:

> In order to understand and appreciate the genesis of Pakistan it is necessary to have a correct perspective of the social, economic and political conditions of the Muslims of the subcontinent of India. From the position of rulers of India (starting with the capture of Delhi by Mohammad Ghori in 1192 and the establishment of the great Moghal Dynasty of 1526 under Babur) the Muslims had become second-class citizens during the rule of the British in the aftermath of the Great Mutiny – the first War of Independence in 1857.

In the aftermath of the catastrophe there was an argument in the Muslim world about the relationship between modernity and faith, a dispute that had parallels with the debate in Victorian England, going on at the same time, where the ancient certainties of the religious establishment were being challenged by the discoveries of scientists like Charles Darwin and Sir Charles Lyell.

The Deoband seminary, which produced what is now known as the Deobandi School of Islam, was founded by Maulana Mohammad Qasim Nanautvi in 1867 in a small town northeast of Delhi. Concerned to find a way of enabling Muslims to survive as Muslims without power, the Deobandis focused the attention of believers on scripture and attacked all idea of intercession for believers at saints' shrines. From now on it was God's guidance and the individual human conscience which was going to fashion a Muslim society. Believers were encouraged to avoid the British courts and follow Deobandi legal advice. The Taliban represent a recent development of this school, modified by Pashtun culture.

A second school of thought, however, argued that there was no contradiction between Islam and modernity, and furthermore that Islam could only be rescued from paralysis and backwardness by coming to terms with the victorious British. The figure most closely associated with this point of view is Sir Syed Ahmed Khan, the founder of the Aligarh movement. Syed was forty years old when the Indian Mutiny occurred, and was on the side of the British. When the revolt was suppressed he sank into depression, and at one stage contemplated settling in Egypt. Instead he stayed behind, fired by a mission to urge his fellow Muslims to learn English and come to terms with Western arts and sciences. Syed declared that 'science shall be in our right hand and philosophy in our left; and on our head shall be the crown of "There is no God but Allah and Mohammad is his Apostle."'[41]

In 1875 Syed Ahmed Khan was the driving force behind the foundation of the Mohammadan Anglo-Oriental School at Aligarh. It was designed, says its historian David Lelyveld, 'to establish a private British-style educational institution that would make adequate room for the religion of Islam.'[42] Lelyveld says that 'it arose out of a dissatisfaction with British-Indian schools, government and missionary, as well as with Islamic madrassahs, which were supposedly giving the wrong kind of education to the wrong kind of people.'

The most significant achievement of the school, soon to be promoted to a college, and in 1920 to the rank of university, was to be the creation of an anglicised Muslim elite. The graduates from Aligarh, and its various offshoots, formed much of the leadership of the Muslim League in the first half of the twentieth century which led the fight for an independent Pakistan. They also provided many of Pakistan's finest cricketers. Just as Aligarh quite deliberately provided an alternative to the indigenous tradition of madrassahs, where teaching was normally carried out in Persian and subjects such as science played a marginal role, so its sporting curriculum encouraged Western enthusiasms. Traditional sports – kite-flying and *kabaddi* (raiding opponents territory) – were downplayed or ignored while football and (in particular) cricket became an essential part of the Aligarh culture.

Cricket at Aligarh started in 1878 when the mathematics professor, Rama Shankar Mishra, founded a cricket club, whose members were expected to wear a uniform of 'blue flannel, coat, shirt, knickerbockers and cap.'[43] The club did not at first thrive. An anonymous old boy, who entered the college in 1881, remembers cricket matches as 'occasional' events, adding that 'membership of the Cricket Club was not compulsory but optional.' He concludes that 'It was not till Mr Beck arrived in 1883 that real interest in cricket and sports began.'[44]

Theodore Beck, a Cambridge mathematician and a member of the Apostles, the intellectual secret society, was appointed principal of Aligarh the following year, in 1884. One of his first acts was to take the college on a cricket tour round the Punjab, including a match against Government College, Lahore. According to David Lelyveld, 'spectators could see what Aligarh was all about whenever a match stopped for prayers.'[45] Beck promoted muscular Islam, analogous to the muscular Christianity then fashionable in Britain. He also maintained that Aligarh's role was to foster the 'noble and manly game of cricket.'[46] Rudyard Kipling records that his eponymous hero, Kim O'Hara, 'played in St Xavier's eleven against the Alighur [sic] Mohammadan College.'* Kipling does not record the result, but probably St Xavier's were thrashed as Aligarh soon emerged as a very strong team.

When the Indian team toured England in 1911, three players came from Aligarh.† Some of the greatest names of Muslim cricket before Partition were

*Kipling, Rudyard, *Kim* (London: Penguin Classics, 2011), p.166. Since Kim was around fourteen when he played this cricket match this would imply that it took place around 1879, supposing Kim to have been born in 1865, as scholars have assumed. But cricket had only just started at Aligarh in 1879, and only took off from 1884 onwards. Kim's cricket match against Aligarh therefore lends weight to the theory, favoured by Peter Hopkirk and others, that Kipling's hero was born around 1875. If so, this raises enjoyable speculation that future British spy Kim O'Hara would have played cricket against Muslim League stalwart Shaukat Ali. Aligarh was about a four-hour journey by train from Lucknow, where the fictitious St Xavier's was based.

†They were Khan Salamuddin, Syed Hassan and one-eyed Shafqat Hussein. One observer said that the three Aligarh men were 'the youngest members of the party, learned and cultured, with an astounding knowledge of British politics ... They are new to travel, but are keen on knowing everything so that they may be of use when they return.' See Prashant Kidambi, 'The most extraordinary cricket tour', *Wisden*, *148th Edn, 2011*, pp.74–84.

educated there, including Wazir Ali,* Nazir Ali,† Mushtaq Ali,‡ Ghulam Mohammad§ and Jahangir Khan.⁴⁷ This intense connection between cricket and Aligarh meant that cricket became a central part of Muslim identity as the idea of Pakistan emerged.

For example Mohammad Ali Jouhar, a famous journalist and one of the founders of the Muslim League, was a keen follower of cricket while he was at Aligarh in the 1890s, and remained interested in the game all his life.⁴⁸ His elder brother Shaukat, remembered as a 'good, slogging player' was captain of the school team.⁴⁹ As the Aligarh movement spread up through Sindh and the Punjab, so did cricket. Many of the great cricketing colleges of the provinces which now form Pakistan were offshoots, either directly or indirectly, of Sir Syed Ahmed Khan's Aligarh movement. One of them – Islamia College in Lahore – was to provide no fewer than six players in the Pakistan team that pulled off the famous inaugural Test victory over England at The Oval in 1954.

This is a good time to pause and assess cricket in Northern India at the turn of the twentieth century. Most people would never have heard of the game. Those few who had would mainly have regarded it as a strange, pointless activity played by the British occupiers. Barring military cantonments, it was scarcely played at all in the mountainous tribal areas, or in the vast rural tracts where the great majority lived. The game had, however, established a slender foothold in Karachi and Lahore. Karachi was nothing like the great metropolis, teeming with millions of people, that we know today. Perhaps 100,000 lived there, and the town looked south towards the Arabian Sea and the adjacent trading centre of Bombay. Lahore, capital of the Punjab, looked north. This walled city stood on the Grand Trunk Road which since antiquity had linked the Indian subcontinent to Asia. It was a place of marvellous complexity and romance, and in 1900 cricket was only just starting to become a part of the Lahore story.

---

*Wazir Ali was one of the famous Indian cricketers of the inter-war era. He played for India in all its early Test matches, played for Southern Punjab in the Ranji Trophy and was a great figure for Muslims in the Bombay Pentangular. At Partition he migrated to Pakistan and died shortly afterwards, reportedly in poverty.
†Nazir Ali was the younger brother of Wazir Ali and played in India's inaugural Test match at Lord's in 1932 as a bowler. He had played before then in Sussex and in club cricket around London. In 1930, playing for the Club Cricket Conference against the visiting Australians, he achieved a unique distinction as the only Muslim who ever dismissed Don Bradman. After Partition he emigrated to Pakistan, where he served as a Test selector from 1952 to 1968 and, during 1953–54, as secretary of the BCCP.
‡Mushtaq Ali, one of the great early Indian Test players, and the first to score a century for India overseas.
§Ghulam Mohammad toured England in 1932 with little success, but was a power in pre-Partition domestic cricket in India for fifteen years as a left-arm medium pacer.

EARLY CRICKET IN KARACHI

Lahore and Karachi have long been competing cricket centres. At times one city has held the ascendancy, at times the other. In the early days of British rule, Karachi was ahead. The city was made capital of Sindh following British annexation under Sir Charles Napier. Development then began under the eye of Sir Bartle Frere, who wanted to create a new Karachi to 'match the best in the empire'.[50] By 1932 CW Haskell, a cricketing school master, noted in a memoir that Karachi appeared 'more English in appearance than any other city in India, except New Delhi.'*

The British brought Karachi under the control of Bombay, the great imperial metropolis 500 miles to the south. As a result, the progress of cricket in Karachi was faster than anywhere else in Pakistan, and followed the path already taken in Bombay. It has already been seen how the British were quick to play the game in Karachi after the conquests of the early 1840s. As in Bombay, Parsis (some of whom had made their fortune as contractors during the Afghan War) were the first non-British to join in. At one point a single Parsi family, the Dinshaws, were said to be able to turn out a full team.[51] By the end of the nineteenth century, numerous Parsi clubs, including the Karachi Rising Star CC, the Karachi Independent CC and the Karachi Parsi Gymkhana had been formed.[52] Three Karachi Parsis were members of the first Indian touring party to England in 1886. Parsis invested heavily in the game: Hanif Mohammad's famous 499 was scored at the Karachi Parsi Institute, built by Parsi businessmen and still in use today.

As in Bombay, Hindus were slower to take up the game, not establishing their first club, the Sahta Sports Club, until 1889.[53] Muslims were slower still, their Bohra Gymkhana not built until 1898.[54] Thereafter cricket fever spread fast. A vivid portrait of cricket as it was played in Karachi during the first half of the twentieth century is available thanks to BD Shankar, a

---

*CW Haskell, *A Sinner in Sind* (Wellington, NZ: Wright & Carman Ltd, 1959), p.39. The early development of cricket in Karachi would not have been possible without the establishment of cricket-playing schools: the Church Mission School founded in 1844, the Karachi Grammar School in 1854, St Patrick's School in 1861. CW Haskell served as headmaster of both the Church Mission School and Karachi Grammar. He recorded that 'when the boys of CMS High School learnt that I was keen on cricket, I immediately gained a measure of popularity which I could not have otherwise gained.' Of greatest importance was the foundation of the Sindh Madrassah in 1884. Established in imitation of Aligarh, it can count among its alumni Mohammad Ali Jinnah, the founder of Pakistan, as well as Hanif Mohammad, one of the founding fathers of Pakistan cricket. Baloch and Baluch, *Pakistan Cricket*, p.14.

Hindu. Shankar, who was born in Karachi to a poor family in 1900, was dedicated to Sindh cricket from the moment, aged fifteen, he scored 47 for NJV High School against the Church Mission School. 'My joy knew no bounds,' recorded Shankar, 'and this happy incident put me straight in the cricket stride for the rest of my life.'[55] For the next three decades, Shankar remained the heart and soul of Karachi cricket. He records how prior to the outbreak of World War One in 1914 'there were in all eight teams including the local Gymkhanas. They arranged Saturday Fixture matches amongst themselves and Sundays were allotted to the second grade matches played by members of the Young Cricketers' Association.'

The crucial year in the development of Sindh cricket was 1916. In this year, a so-called 'war Quadrangular' was held to raise funds for charity.[56] The competition was based on the communal model already well developed in Bombay, and with the same four teams: Parsis, Europeans, Hindus and Muslims. It was easily won by the Parsis.

This Quadrangular very soon became an annual tournament, organised by the Sindh Cricket Association (SCA), which seems to have been formed over the winter of 1923–24. This is the moment when CB Rubie* emerges as one of a small number of Englishmen (a select list which includes George Abell in Lahore and Brigadier Rodham in Rawalpindi) who played a guiding role in the creation of an organised cricketing structure in pre-Partition Pakistan.[57]

Before coming to Karachi, Rubie had lived in Ceylon (now Sri Lanka). There he had helped produce a constitution for the Ceylon Cricket Association. This model was used for the Sindh Cricket Association (and, a few years later, for the Indian Cricket Board). Shankar records that 'at the start

---

*Claude Black Rubie was born in Lewes in 1888 and educated at Lancing. Served with the Lancashire Fusiliers in World War One, mentioned in Dispatches 1917. Played for Northern India against AER Gilligan's MCC in 1926–27. Manager of Phipson & Co, Karachi. Appointed manager of the MCC cricket team that would have toured India in 1939–40, but for the intervention of war. The 'Rubie Shield', an inter-school trophy, was named after him. Hanif Mohammad, playing for Sindh Madrassah, scored 305 against CMS School in the Rubie Shield final of 1950–51. Anthony de Mello in his *Portrait of Indian Sport* wrote that Sindh was 'the first centre in India in which cricket became highly organised in preparation for our launching upon the world in the twenties. And much of this commendable organisation was in the hands of Rubie. Cricket, just after the First World War, was very strong in Sindh, largely because of the influx of the British Army from Mesopotamia. Rubie, at that time, was the President of Sindh European Cricket Club; he was a keen and far-seeing man, who thought of cricket as no less than a way of life. Call him a fanatic if you like – but there is no doubt that his enthusiasm and his support played a vital part in our later formation of the Board of Control. We were always appreciative of Rubie's advice, which was realistic, selfless and valuable.' The *Lancing College Magazine* records that Lt Col CB Rubie CBE, TD died suddenly, after an operation, in a nursing home at Hove on 3 November 1939.

14 clubs joined this Association, and the membership at the time of Partition was well over 44.'[58] The SCA took the leading role in arranging tours to neighbouring provinces, receiving visiting teams, and organising tournaments, of which the most important appears to have been the annual Quadrangular. This became a Pentangular from 1922, when the Europeans formed their own side. Previously they had played as part of The Rest. Revealingly, this team contained players who were Jewish, Goan and Anglo-Indian. Accounts of this tournament cover many pages of Shankar's book. 'We have read in papers and books, in the later years, that there were many followers of the game who were against this sort of communal cricket,' wrote Shankar. 'They said it bred bad blood and feelings. If at that time they were to see the Sindh Cricket and its Pentangular, *which was mainly on the Communal lines* [Shankar's emphasis], they would have certainly altered their opinions. If such tournaments are properly organised and managed, there can be no fear of race prejudice.'[59]

The Parsi victory of 1916 turned out to be their swansong. Thereafter the Muslims and Hindus dominated. The standard of cricket was high. In October 1926 a strong MCC team, captained by Arthur Gilligan, came to Karachi. The local teams gave a good account of themselves. When the SCA sent a side, under Rubie's captaincy, to play Quetta the following year, the opposition captain remarked that the Sindh team 'was as good as any of the best county teams in England.'[60]

Then came Partition. Shankar was working in Quetta on 15 August 1947 and sombrely records his decision to stay in Pakistan. 'People left their jobs and went back to India fearing there will be no safety for any Hindu to live in a Muslim country.' Shankar had earned a pension 'through long service with the company of about 25 years' and could not afford to lose it. However, when riots broke out in Quetta, he was forced to retreat to Karachi: 'Being the capital town of the newly-born state, it was considered a bit safe from riots and loots etc etc. But this was not to be.'[61] Shankar agonisingly records that refugees were crammed 'in Musafirkhanas, cheap resthouses, station platforms or on the footpaths of the modernised Karachi with all their families children and grandchildren, etc etc. The streets of Karachi became dirty, and it was no more the cleanest city of India.'[62] Then the killing began:

> With the exodus of the Hindus the charm of Karachi was lost. The refugees who were staying in the Maidans (open grounds) and such foot-

paths, etc, started stabbing the Hindus during the night-time, so that, they may leave their houses and go to India, and as such leave the houses for them. Some of them went inside the houses of the Hindus and occupied them by force, all over Karachi. The situation was uncontrollable. In the evenings it became dangerous for a Hindu to move out with his family etc. Hindu hotels also began to disappear, and it became a problem for a Hindu as to where he could take his meals.[63]

Shankar records that at this point he dispatched his family to India, but 'I was determined to stay in Pakistan, and not to leave it at the cost of my job.'[64] It was to no avail. In January 1948, rioters looted his house and destroyed all his possessions, including his cricket memorabilia. Shankar bowed to the inevitable, fled the city of his birth, and made his way to India, where he built himself a new life in Kanpur.[65]

THE ORIGINS OF CRICKET IN LAHORE

As already noted, cricket came to Lahore in the 1840s, brought by British troops. It was the British who built the key cricketing landmarks of the city, such as the exquisite Lahore Gymkhana cricketing ground and Minto Park, where the young Kardar went to practise outside the city walls. But as a rule the British military occupiers played their sport in a capsule, only among themselves, and with little or no interest or concern for the ambient population.

In order to trace the roots of cricket in Lahore, it is therefore essential to concentrate on the great schools and colleges that were constructed in the aftermath of the Indian Mutiny. The most famous of these establishments is Aitchison College, whose magnificent grounds and buildings still dominate the city. In the words of its founder Sir Charles Aitchison, the school was intended to educate 'the young nobility of the Punjab.'[66] The initial intake of just twelve pupils in 1886 included the Nawab of Pataudi, grandfather of Iftikhar Ali Khan, who captained the India side which toured England in 1946. Bhupindar Singh, the cricket-mad Maharajah of Patiala, was another local chieftain who attended the school. His heir, Yuvraj Yadavindra Singh, followed in his footsteps.

From an early stage Aitchison's turf wickets were the finest in Pakistan, and cricket was always at the heart of the sporting curriculum. As a result, it is often assumed that Aitchison played a major role in the creation of cricket in Pakistan. In fact, the school provided no players at all for the early national teams, and only a handful thereafter. Some of those who have played for Pakistan have been outstanding, and include Majid Khan and his son, Bazid, Imran Khan, Ramiz Raja and Wahab Riaz.* All these great players emerged during the post-independence era, when Aitchison was no longer the exclusive preserve of nobly born Indians and catered more indiscriminately for the wealthy middle classes.

The reason for Aitchison's irrelevance during the formative years of Pakistan cricket is easy to explain. Its early cricketing protégés came from an Indian aristocracy which believed in fundamental allegiance to British rule, rather than the Muslim League or Congress, as they fought their great battle for independence. This native-born aristocracy tended to be detached from the cricket culture which came to rule life in Lahore in the years that followed World War One, and was essentially the creation of two rival institutions, lower down the social scale.

GOVERNMENT COLLEGE v ISLAMIA COLLEGE

Government College came first, founded in January 1864 as an extension of Calcutta University. Like Aligarh its foundation was a result of the Indian Mutiny. In Delhi, the city college had been closed down. In 1864 it was re-established in Lahore (considered the more trustworthy centre) under the authority of Dr GW Leitner, an educationalist and diplomat.

Cricket seems first to have been played in the winter of 1867–68, when a team went to Amritsar.[67] However, RB Chuni Lal, who entered the College in 1874–75, recalled that 'There was no regular provision, in the College of my days, for physical exercise and outdoor games, and they were as good as unknown.'[68] The Cricket Club was an independent institution within the College, and was obliged to fund itself.[69]

There was no dedicated cricket ground on College land until the end of

---

*Imran Khan believed that the school failed to prepare most of its players for the intensity of competitive cricket. Personal interview.

the nineteenth century. From 1880 onwards, however, the College was playing other schools in the Punjab. The greatest competition of this period came
from irregular games against Aligarh. In 1884 Aligarh, under the leadership
of its principal, Mr Beck, sent a team to Lahore. It thrashed Government
College.[70] Smarting from defeat, the Government College team gathered
enough subscriptions to fund a revenge match. On arrival at Aligarh, the
Government College students discovered that their opponents had prepared
a soft wicket to nullify the effects of Government College's talismanic quick
bowler Faiz Rahman. Government College suffered a second heavy defeat in
front of a large crowd of spectators that included Sir Syed Ahmed Khan.[71]

Right from the start, Government College (as its name indicated) was
respectable. The *Ravi*, the school magazine, emphasised good sportsmanship.
After a triumph in a tournament in 1911, the *Ravi* announced: 'We are glad
we won; but, without any undue humbug, we are sorry our opponents lost, and
hope the same thing will happen next year.'[72] This display of the stiff upper lip
was typical. Two years earlier, losing out in the Punjab University Cricket
Tournament, the *Ravi* reported: 'The shield has been brought back to Lahore
from Delhi but not quite in the way we expected or desired. We take this opportunity of heartily congratulating our everlasting rivals, the Forman Christian
College, on their splendid performance in the Tournament.'[73]

But neither Aligarh nor the Forman Christian College opposition
loomed half as large in the Government College consciousness as Islamia
College. During the inter-war years, contests between these two great Lahore
institutions were attended by vast crowds. Islamia stood for everything that
Government College did not. Government College was built in the traditional imperial style. Its buildings are a grand mixture of neo-classical and
neo-gothic, very much what can be found at a British public school from
the same period. Islamia is a large, whitewashed building with wide, elab-
orate arches and decorative gardens in the traditional Moghal style.

Government College was trusted (up to a point) by the British, but
Islamia was viewed as a hotbed of subversion.* Unlike Government College,

*The principal of Islamia College, Professor AA Shakir, observes that, during the colonial period both
institutions fed the imperial bureaucracy. However, Government College produced the civil servants while
Islamia College produced the clerks. Professor Shakir argues that this allowed students of Islamia to follow
a more diverse curriculum, the result of which is a greater proportion of poets and journalists among its
alumni than at Government. Professor Shakir claims that cricket stunted rather than fostered the development of a culture of dissent. Interview with Professor AA Shakir, Lahore, 12 July 2012.

Islamia College was founded in the Aligarh tradition of self-help and supported by an Islamic foundation, Anjuman-i-Himayat-i-Islam.* British suspicion of Islamia was justified. During World War One, a group of College students had secretly fled the Punjab, escaping through Afghanistan to Central Asia to form a resistance movement against British forces.[74] Jinnah, the Quaid-e-Azam, openly favoured Islamia, visiting the college many times between 1941 and 1947 to address students and the wider public who assembled in the playing field at the back.[75] He is said to have ignored Government College. The only educational establishment which Jinnah visited on more occasions than Islamia is thought to have been Aligarh itself.[76]

It was natural that Fazal Mahmood's father, Ghulam Hussain, should have become a professor at Islamia once he abandoned his career as a revolutionary agitator. No longer as committed to the destruction of the British Empire, he rejoiced instead in the downfall of the Government College cricket team. Fazal's early memoir (published in 1954) shows how deep this passion went. 'About 28 years ago, on a pleasant February morning, I opened my eyes to this world. When I became conscious about my surroundings, I learned that Islamia College, where my father taught as a professor, was round the corner,' recalled Fazal. He then produced this extraordinary account:

> My father would display a very strange behaviour. Once or twice a year, in the middle of the night, he would abruptly get up from his sleep and start shouting: 'Jahangir, get hold of that catch and get Baqa Jilani out ... He is out!' He would then suddenly turn sides and shout loudly, 'We have won the match!'

Jahangir Khan and Baqa Jilani† – the subject of this nocturnal perturbation – were two of the best-known cricketers of the inter-war era. Both of

---

*Hussain, Dr Syed Sultan Mahmood, *56 Years of Islamia College Lahore, 1892–1947* (Lahore: Izharsons, 1992), p.2. This method of foundation directly echoes the advocacy of Sir Syed Ahmed Khan's third finding by his Committee Striving for the Educational Progress of the Muslims in the 1870s, advocating that, in the face of failures by government-maintained schools to provide an acceptable curriculum for Muslim boys 'the responsibility for educating its youth should also rest with the [Islamic] community itself.' Also, see Dr Mohammad Ali Shaikh, *Hasanally Effendi*, pp.21–23.

†Baqa Jilani, a capable bat and right-arm pace bowler who died tragically young, reportedly after an epileptic fit, aged around thirty, in 1941. He made his mark with a hat-trick for Northern India against Southern Punjab in the first Ranji Trophy tournament of 1934–35. Southern Punjab were dismissed for 22. He played one Test for India against England in 1936.

them played for India, and both were members of the astonishing Burki clan. However, during the passionate contests between Islamia and Government College of the 1920s, Jahangir Khan, who used to play for Islamia College wearing a *shalwar* (baggy trousers),* was on the opposite side to Baqa Jilani of Government College. Fazal continued:

After this, [my father's] breathing would revert back to normal and his face would look relaxed again as he would slide back into deep sleep. Next morning when we would narrate the story from the night and ask him for his outburst, we would learn that it was the time for the finals between the Islamia College and the Government College for the University Cricket Tournament. The background to this is that the Islamia College and the Government College were continuously locked in a fierce rivalry over cricket and both the teams wanted to surpass each other. Because my father was also the president of the Islamia College cricket team, it was his duty to maintain their motivation and pride. He would work for it day and night because of his own interest in the game. This condition of my father started registering on my mind when I was around six years old. Even though, his talk was almost incomprehensible to me, my father had started to train me. He would strongly advise me: 'Mahmood when you grow up, you should become a bowler and one day defeat the Government College so badly that they will run from the ground.'[77]

*Personal interview with Jimmy Rana, who says Jahangir was teased as a result of his clothing. See also interview with Jahangir Khan in *The Cricketer (Pakistan),* published July 1981. Asked how he came to play first-class cricket, Khan replied: 'I left Jullundur in 1927 and came to Lahore where I entered the famous Islamia College ... my maternal uncle was an Islamia old boy and had been captain of Lahore's Mamdot cricket club for 22 years. His younger brother played a lot of cricket in Aligarh's MAO College ... it was my display at Islamia College that selected me for the 1932 tour of England.' The Jahangir family combination of Islamia College and Mamdot cricket club is unusual. Islamia cricketers would more often play for Crescent. Baqa Jilani played first for Government College, then confusingly migrated to Islamia. (See SK Roy, *Indian Cricketers,* 1947.) Others who attended both colleges included Dilawar Hussain, Mohammad Nissar, Saeed Ahmed, Sultan Mahmud, SF Rehman and Shuja-ud-Din. Government College graduates included Jamil Rana, Saeed Ahmed, Mohammad Ilyas, Waqar Ahmed, Aftab Gul, Saleem Altaf, Shafqat Rana, Pervez Sajjad, Zafar Altaf, Dilawar Hussain, Mohammad Nissar, Fida Hassan, Baqa Jilani, Agha Ahmed Raza Khan, Mian Mohammad Saeed, Mahmood Hussain, Waqar Hasan, Salim Malik, Aamer Sohail, Inzamam-ul-Haq, Majid Khan, Agha Zahid, Sarfraz Nawaz and Shafiq Ahmed.

Islamia produced: Mohammad Nissar, Amir Elahi, Baqa Jilani, Jahangir Khan, Gul Mohammad, Kardar, Fazal Mahmood, Imtiaz Ahmed, Anwar Hussain, Murawwat Hussain, Nazar Mohammad, Khan Mohammad, Maqsood Ahmed, Agha Saadat Ali, Zulfiqar Ahmed, Israr Ali, Dilawar Hussain, Munawwar Ali Khan. I am grateful to Sultan Mahmud, SF Rehman, Jamil Rana and especially Najum Latif for compiling this list.

Thus the rivalry between Government College and Islamia was instrumental in forming the greatest player of the early years of Pakistan cricket. Fazal Mahmood would always carry the values of Islamia College with him. As a student in the early 1940s, he stood guard for Jinnah during the Quaid-e-Azam's visits to Lahore.[78] As a player for Pakistan, he took special pleasure in the destruction of English cricket teams. He was honest, dedicated to Pakistan and (as we shall see), much later in life, was plunged into despair at what he saw as the collapse of the values taught by the Quaid-e-Azam at independence.

To begin with, Government College was the stronger team and inflicted many wounding defeats on insurgent Islamia. But as British rule faltered, and the Muslim League gained in confidence, so Islamia turned the tables. In the 1940s the fortunes of Government College mirrored those of the British, as it went down to nine consecutive defeats to Islamia in the University championships.[79] By 1947, the year of independence, a cowed Government College had become resigned in advance to their annual humiliation, as the February 1947 edition of the *Ravi* shows. Its sports-writer, in his pre-tournament preview, was reduced to noting that, 'As usual we hope to meet Islamia College in the final. As usual we hope to . . . doesn't matter!'

When the result inevitably went against them, the *Ravi* put on a stiff upper lip: 'For the result we put a "ditto" to our last years.'[80] But Government College has no reason to feel ashamed. By the early 1940s Islamia College could produce what was probably the greatest schools team that has ever existed. As we have seen, at age thirteen Fazal Mahmood joined Islamia in 1940 (the year that the Muslim League launched the Lahore Resolution, whose call for separate Muslim states was a decisive moment in the creation of Pakistan). The following year, playing for the first XI, he scythed through Government College in the inter-collegiate final, taking five wickets for 13 runs.[81] The team he joined included a galaxy of future Pakistan Test players: Gul Mohammad, Nazar Mohammad, Abdul Hafeez (later to change his name to AH Kardar), Maqsood Ahmed, Imtiaz Ahmed, Shuja-ud-Din, Zulfiqar Ahmed.[82]

During the 1940s these players were members of a college which played what Fazal Mahmood called a 'vanguard role' in the Muslim League struggle for a separate Islamic homeland. Fazal, Imtiaz, Nazar Mohammad and others would take part in Muslim League rallies and processions. Sometimes they were baton-charged and tear-gassed.[83] A few years later they formed the core of the Pakistan teams which secured success against India and England.

This prodigiously talented squad was in part the personal creation of the Islamia College principal, Professor Sheikh Mohammad Aslam. Cricketers achieved hero status within the College, and were known as 'the Imperial Force'.[84] Aslam personally visited the families of his target cricketers in the manner of a modern football manager, determined to enroll them and keep them out of the hands of rivals.[85] Fazal records that he once harboured a plan of defecting to Government College. 'Colonel Aslam got to know about it. He cycled down to my house, took me to the college, and made sure that I stayed on at Islamia.'[86]

As the stars of 1940s Islamia cricket graduated to the national game, so did Professor Aslam. The first generation of players were his pupils and disciples, and he served as treasurer of the Board of Control for Cricket in Pakistan in the early years.[87] But Professor Aslam had fertile ground to work with. Something was in the air in Lahore between the wars. I walked through the old city of Lahore searching out the homes of old cricketers. Every quarter of the old city seems to have given birth to a Test player: Gul Mohammad, Nazar Mohammad, Imtiaz Ahmed and AH Kardar all lived close to Bhati Gate, within about 100 yards of each other. (Their legacy continues: I noticed that small boys are still to be found playing against every wall and by every street corner.) By the 1920s, a Lahore cricket culture had evolved, and it has deepened and widened ever since. Nothing shows this more surely than the story of Kardar's greatest rival, the Indian captain Lala Amarnath.

THE TWIN IDENTITIES OF LALA AMARNATH

Lala Amarnath is the most romantic figure of early Indian Test cricket. As a young tearaway, he scored a century on debut for India against England in Bombay in 1933, and was later sent home for indiscipline by his captain, the appalling Maharajkumar of Vizianagram, during the disastrous 1936 India tour of England. Only after World War Two was Amarnath at last granted his due and appointed Indian captain. Later two sons, Mohinder and Surinder, followed their father into the national team, creating a famous cricketing dynasty.

A third son, Rajender, has written his father's biography, *The Making of a Legend*. This work of filial celebration contains stories which present Pakistan and its leading sportsmen (in particular Kardar) in an unpleasant light. For example, Rajender Amarnath asserts that Kardar assaulted Lala Amarnath in a hotel lobby in Lahore during the Test match of January 1955.[88] I have found no corroboration for this story. All surviving members of the Pakistan team have assured me they never heard any word of such an incident at the time.*

Furthermore, Rajender Amarnath's book leaves out the single most essential and formative element of his father's early life: his adoption by a Muslim cricketing family from Lahore. This was the Rana family, whose wider connections include the controversial umpire Shakoor Rana, as well as the Test cricketers Shafqat and Azmat.† In the 1920s, the senior cricketing Rana was Tawakkal Majid, a leading light in Crescent, one of the big cricket clubs in Lahore. I arranged to meet Tawakkal's son Jimmy, now seventy-seven, over coffee in the Lahore Gymkhana Club. Jamil 'Jimmy' Rana, himself a fine cricketer in his day who played first-class cricket for the Punjab, told me the following story:

> On the way home from a match my father passed some boys playing in the street. One of them unleashed a most sublime cover drive. He asked him to play it again, and he did. He had a very good eye. The boy was Lala Amarnath. My father said: 'Take me to your family.' They turned out to be very poor people. He offered to take him into our house, and pay for him to learn how to be a cricketer. They were delighted. As a result Amarnath was brought up as a member of our family.‡

*I approached Hanif Mohammad, Waqar Hasan, Wazir Mohammad and Imtiaz Ahmed, all of whom played in that Test. Each one of them said that they never even heard talk of a fight. They would surely have done so had it taken place.

†Jimmy Rana's mother's cousin was the first wife of Shafqat Rana's father. Source: Jimmy Rana. It should be noted that the surname was not in use before Partition.

‡Interview with Jamil Rana, July 2012. Rauf Malik, now in his eighties, used to manage the People's Publishing House in Lahore. He recalls seeing Amarnath emerging every afternoon from Tawakkal's house wearing white cricket kit to go to practice sessions, adding that Amarnath used to live in the '*chubara*' (upper room) on the first floor. Rajender Amarnath told me that he could not comment on his father's connection with the Rana family because his father had never told him about it. In his autobiography, *From Dusk To Dawn*, Fazal Mahmood wrote that Lala Amarnath 'worked in the railways workshop in Lahore, on a salary of half a rupee a day.' (Op. cit. p.105.) Although fifteen years younger, Fazal played regularly against Amarnath in club cricket in Lahore.

So I asked Jimmy Rana to travel with me to the old city, and walk with me from Amarnath's childhood home (where he had lived with his paternal grandparents[89]) in the old Hindu quarter of Lahore to his new home with the Rana family in a side street near neighbouring Mochi Gate. The distance was scarcely 200 yards, and took us five minutes through crowded streets.

Amarnath's home (in what is now the flourishing Shah Alam market) no longer exists. Like almost all the buildings in the old Hindu quarter, it was burnt down at the time of Partition. Jimmy Rana told me that the Hindus were well-armed and held out for many days against the encircling Muslim mobs. Eventually, however, the killers broke in and inflicted terrible bloodshed, using cans of kerosene to burn down the quarter, including the house where young Amarnath had been raised. By then Amarnath was at his training camp in Poona, captain designate for the 1947–48 India tour of Australia.

All this lay in an unimaginable future when Amarnath went to live with his new patrons in the early 1920s. His new family resided in a distinguished town house: it is still there, though dilapidated and marked for demolition. Jimmy Rana showed me the first-floor room where his famous guest had entertained Lahore's cricketers, and kept his growing collection of cricketing trophies. 'Even though we were a Muslim family bringing up a Hindu, we never once urged him to convert,' Jimmy told me with pride. He added that at the time Amarnath arrived, Jimmy's grandfather had just installed electricity, one of the first Lahorites to do so. For many years, young students would cluster in the streets outside the windows of the house, so that they could continue their studies after dark. Perhaps 600,000 people lived in Lahore in those days, mostly in the walled city. There were no cars, no telephones and no secrets. The very rich travelled by tonga. Everybody else walked. If you wanted to leave a message you went to your local barber – *nai* – and he would pass it on (the *nai* would also carry out circumcisions).

Amarnath was not the only great cricketer sponsored by the Ranas. Jimmy Rana told me that the others included Amir Elahi, the leading leg-break and googly bowler of the inter-war era. He was to accompany Amarnath on the disastrous 1936 tour of England, and ten years later was a member of Amarnath's team that toured Australia. In 1952, aged forty-four, he played five Tests against Amarnath's India as a member of Kardar's touring party.

Naturally Amarnath played for Crescent, the Rana family club. Crescent was the most dynamic team in Lahore, a product of the city's bustling middle classes. Its bitter rival was Mamdot, a team built around princely power which included such great players as Jahangir Khan. Mamdot reflected the style of the feudal clubs which dominated in the earliest period of Lahori cricket, during the first decades of the twentieth century.* During the later stages of World War Two, Zulfiqar Ali Bhutto, future president of Pakistan, is said to have played for Mamdot.[90] Crescent was more urban, insurgent and allied to the rising Muslim League. Many of its players had studied at Islamia College.[91] Indeed the competition between the two great Lahorite clubs mirrored the epic contests between Government and Islamia College.

Like many other clubs, Crescent played at Minto Park, just outside the city walls. They would get to the ground early to prepare the wickets. Jimmy Rana told me how proud his father had been of Amarnath, how many trophies their young Hindu prodigy had brought in, and how Amarnath was friends with all the players. To illustrate the closeness he told me how, on the eve of an important final between Crescent and Mamdot at the Bagh-e-Jinnah, Mamdot planned to send a band of *goondas* (thugs) to beat up Amarnath with cricket bats with the intention of injuring him so badly that he would not be able to play. Crescent got word of this scheme and provided a bodyguard. 'The players covered him with their bodies so that he was not hurt,' Jimmy Rana told me.

---

*It is generally believed that the Mamdot Club was established by Nawab Shahnawaz Khan of Mamdot, ruler of a small princely state near Ferozepur in Punjab towards the end of the nineteenth century. Nawab Shahnawaz never allowed the collection of monthly subscription from the players of his club, while poorer players were also provided with free kit and playing equipment. The Club had its practice nets outside the Mochi Gate of old Lahore but in the early 1940s the nets were moved to Minto Park. Fazal Mahmood joined the Mamdot Club in 1943. Mamdot Club players were allowed to eat and take refreshments from vendors, with bills paid by the Nawab. Outstanding players included Dilawar Hussain, Baqa Jilani, Jahangir Khan, Mohammad Nissar, Gul Mohammad, Mian Mohammad Saeed, S. Wazir Ali, S. Nazir Ali, Khawaja Saeed Ahmed, Anwar Hussain, AH Kardar, Nazar Mohammad, Fazal Mahmood and the Nawab's cousin fast bowler Munawwar Ali Khan. Mian Salahuddin and Nawab Aslam Mamdot, who funded the BCCP with Rs. 5000/- each in its early stages, were also playing for the Mamdot Club. Rivalry brought an end to the Mamdot Club. It is said that the Punjab Cricket Association cancelled Mamdot's membership after it was accused of not paying its annual fee. The Club insisted it had paid its dues, and produced a receipt. Crescent refused to accept this and paid a famous bodybuilder (Mahmood Butt) to throw out Mamdot cricketers from the meeting. Nawab Aslam Mamdot sought help from Ayub Khan to revive the Club but to no avail. After the end of Mamdot Club some of its players moved on to the Universal Cricket Club. Others went to the Crescent Club and Ravi Gymkhana. For the information on Lahore cricket clubs above and on Crescent Cricket Club below, I am indebted to Jamil Rana, Javed Zaman, Sultan Mahmud, Afzal Ahmed and above all Najum Latif.

A different version of this story appears in Rajender Amarnath's biography. According to Rajender, his father later complained that, 'I had to perform better than all the other players, as I was the only Hindu playing for the predominantly Muslim club.' Rajender recounts that the attack on Amarnath took place on the eve of a match between Hindus and Muslims: 'That evening, Amarnath was strolling in the Anarkali Bazaar with his friends, when suddenly a group of supporters of the Muslim team attacked them with lathis shouting, "Break Amarnath's bones!" Since he was the fulcrum of the Hindu team, his friends fell on him, covering him and taking blows on their own bodies, till reinforcements in the form of Hindu supporters came to their rescue.'*

Crescent could not hold such a brilliant player as Amarnath for long. Frank Tarrant, an Australian who worked as cricket coach for the Maharajah of Patiala, saw Amarnath play and recommended him to his employer, thus introducing Amarnath to the alluring (and better remunerated) world of princely cricket. Jimmy Rana, however, insists that Amarnath was never to forget the kindness that had been shown to him. Standing outside the light-blue front door of his old family home, he told me:

> Whenever he came to Pakistan after Partition he used to call on my family. Once he brought two sons. He bowed down in reverence at the threshold of this house. He ordered his sons to do the same. One of them got some dirt from the floor on his forehead, and brought out a handkerchief to remove it. Amarnath told him, 'Put that handkerchief away and spread the dirt on your face. If this house hadn't been here you two would have been playing in the street.[92]

---

*Amarnath, p.8. Jimmy Rana's version was corroborated by the former Test umpire Munawwar Hussain in a memoir after Lala Amarnath's death published on 8 August 2000. Hussain remembered how, 'With his stunning performances both with bat and the ball, Amarnath dominated Lahore's cricket to such an extent that other clubs were scared of him. A cricket tournament called Yousuf Shah-Ramcharandas was played in December every year. Once Mamdot Club and Crescent Club landed in the final. Scared of Amarnath's ability to clinch the match single handedly, some miscreants from the opponent's group manhandled him an evening before the match to prevent him from playing. Some members from his club rescued him and prepared him for the encounter. Next morning, Amarnath scored a marvellous 50 against Mohammad Nissar, the fastest bowler of that era and helped Crescent Club win the final.' Munawwar Hussain's account differs in some details from Jimmy Rana's. For example, he records that one 'Ustad Gul, a prominent bowler of the early 30s' was responsible for luring Amarnath to Crescent Club (see http://www.espncricinfo.com/allrounder/content/story/84898.html).

So when, in 1952, Pakistan faced India at cricket in a Test match for the first time, the two captains – Lala Amarnath and AH Kardar – would have understood each other very well. They had been brought up in the same city, played as boys on the same streets, represented the same clubs and tested their skills against the same players. They spoke the same language, ate the same food, and wore the same clothes. But for an accident of religion and history, Amarnath and Kardar would have been on the same side.

In India, Lala Amarnath is understood as a Hindu who escaped Muslim prejudice and hostility to make a name for himself as a great Indian cricketer. But in Pakistan he is remembered as a product of the brilliant Lahorite cricketing culture of the inter-war period who would never have realised his prodigious sporting potential but for the friendship of Muslims. He carried the burden of his twin identities with him all his life. In one way or another, a version of this tragic conflict has haunted Pakistan and Indian cricket ever since.

INTIMATIONS OF A NATIONAL PAKISTAN CRICKET TEAM

Cricket was an evanescent and superficial presence in northern India at the end of the nineteenth century but grew fast thereafter. By the eve of independence, Lahore and Karachi were flourishing cricketing centres where the game was played at a serious level. New structures had emerged, and some talismanic players. Meanwhile the Parsis had lost their dominance. Partly as a result, Karachi, the epicentre at the start of the century, was gradually giving ground to Lahore.*

A cricketing consciousness was emerging by the 1930s, and slowly becoming part of an incipient national consciousness. However, one must be very cautious. Cricketing enthusiasm scarcely reached Baluchistan or the North-West frontier, let alone Bengal, while Karachi and Lahore had very

*The gradually increasing dominance of Lahore over Karachi is suggested by an analysis of players from present-day Pakistan who played for India in Tests from 1932 to 1936. Four Lahore-born players – Mohammad Nissar, Lala Amarnath, Dilawar Hussain and Amir Elahi – did so. Only Jeomal Naoomal from Karachi played for India. In addition four Muslim players from the Burki stronghold of Jullundur – Wazir Ali and his brother Nazir Ali, Jahangir Khan and Baqa Jilani – did so (the first three of these migrated to Pakistan at Partition, while Jilani would certainly have joined them but for his premature death in Jullundur in 1941). By contrast Karachi players had been well represented in nineteenth-century touring teams to England, Lahoris not at all.

different cricketing sensibilities. Karachi was more eclectic; Lahore had a negligible Parsi presence, and Hindus were less dominant.

Above all, any talk of a national consciousness runs the risk of anachronism. It must be borne in mind that the idea of Pakistan sprang to life at the last gasp of the British Empire. The name itself was not invented until 1933, when it was coined by a Cambridge intellectual named Choudhry Rahmat Ali,[93] author of a famous pamphlet where the name 'Pakstan' [sic] appears to have been used for the first time, and which started with the resounding assertion:

> At this solemn hour in the history of India, when British and Indian statesmen are laying the foundations of a Federal Constitution for that land, we address this appeal to you, in the name of our common heritage, on behalf of our thirty million Muslim brethren who live in PAKSTAN [sic] – by which we mean the five Northern units of India, viz: Punjab, North-West Frontier Province (Afghan Province), Kashmir, Sindh and Baluchistan – for your sympathy and support in our grim and fateful struggle against political crucifiction and complete annihilation.[94]

But in 1933 a state of Pakistan still seemed a remote and unachievable dream, and the idea did not come into focus until the Lahore Resolution, calling for independent states for Muslims, was adopted by the Muslim League in March 1940. This vision did not turn into specific national demands until the final months before Partition.[95]

So there is a grave danger of imposing a shape on events which bears no relation to the muddled and confusing reality. The cricketers of Lahore and Karachi in the 1930s were not driven by patriotism, held little grudge against the British occupation, and most of them had only the dimmest awareness of the great forces that were about to uproot their world and change it forever. Cricketers are rarely thinkers or political activists.

Nevertheless, with the advantage of hindsight, one may discern by the 1930s the formation of structures which anticipate the national team that emerged in Pakistan after Partition. There are two such intimations. One is the Northern India team which played in the inaugural Ranji Trophy in 1934, and intermittently thereafter until Partition. The Ranji Trophy competition was based on geography and the teams were inter-communal, mixing Hindus, Muslims, Parsis and other faiths as well as a number of Englishmen (although it should be noted that the Northern India side became progressively dominated by Muslims).

NORTHERN INDIA AND COMMUNAL CRICKET BEFORE PARTITION

The Northern India side has received far less attention from historians than the Muslim sides which played in the great communal tournaments of pre-Partition India, and whose importance has been beautifully established by Ramachandra Guha.[96] These sides are the source of legend and monopolise the collective memory of Pakistan cricket. In their time, they certainly had a greater following, both in live spectators and newspapers, than those which competed in the Ranji Trophy.

As we have seen, the first Muslim side to play first-class cricket competed in the Bombay Tournament of 1912–13, turning it into a Quadrangular, alongside the Parsis, Hindus, and 'Europeans' (English).* The Muslims opened their account in 1912 with a seven-wicket victory against the Europeans. However, they were then crushed by the far more experienced Parsis. The Muslims first won the Quadrangular Tournament in 1924–25, when for the first time they held trials for the representative side from outside Bombay. Their captain, Abdul Salam of Aligarh, was a proper cricketer who took 150 first-class wickets in 33 matches, including twelve in the final of the 1923–24 Lahore Tournament against the Hindus. The Muslim Students Union gave a dinner in honour of the winners at which the toast was proposed by MA Jinnah. He expressed confidence that 'even their Hindu brethren would rejoice in the Mahommedans' success in a spirit of true sportsmanship. The cricket field had many lessons to teach in other walks of life. The brotherly feeling that prevailed throughout the cricket field was no less remarkable.'[97]

---

*The Muslims were captained by Dawood Nensey, chosen because he was 'really at home with a knife and fork, for [in] those days lunching with the British Sahibs was of great moment.' AFS Talyarkhan in *Official Souvenir of the Silver Jubilee of the Bombay Cricket Association 1930–1954* (Mombay, 1954), cited in R Guha *A Corner Of A Foreign Field* (Picador, 2002), p.124. Batting number 10 he scored three runs in his two matches, did not bowl and did not take a catch. He set a precedent for later Pakistan first-class cricketers selected for social prestige.

At that stage the Quadrangular was still primarily a great social festival, as were its counterparts in Karachi, Lahore (which had first-class status) and Central Provinces, held in Nagpur.[98] By the late 1920s, however, the Congress party and the Muslim League had begun to clash over the future of India and there were inter-communal riots in many Indian cities. The Hindus boycotted the Bombay Quadrangular and the competition disappeared for four years, although communal tournaments continued without problems in Karachi, Hyderabad and Nagpur. Despite enduring political and communal troubles, and under pressure from players and fans, the Bombay Quadrangular resumed in 1934–35. The Muslims beat the Hindus in a final marked by a duel between the great fast bowlers Amar Singh and Mohammad Nissar for the Muslims.

The Quadrangular immediately re-established itself as a carnival, and when the following year's final was played between Hindus and Muslims 'the tents were fully occupied and the supporters of the rival teams were keyed up to the highest pitch of excitement.' Throughout the city, hotels and other public places with radio receivers were packed with people. The Muslims won, thanks to centuries from two brothers who had become established stars, Wazir and Nazir Ali, and a fine performance by a fast bowler, Mubarak Ali.

The Bombay Quadrangular became a Pentangular in 1937–38, when it added 'The Rest' (said to include Buddhists, Jews, Sikhs and 'non-European' Christians). However, the Hindus walked out of their match with the Europeans in protest against their seat allocation. The Muslims enjoyed united crowd support in the final when they defeated the Europeans by an innings, thanks to a century from their charismatic opener, Mushtaq Ali.

Support for the tournament kept it going throughout World War Two, despite worsening intercommunal tensions and a call from Mahatma Gandhi for a boycott.[99] The most dramatic Bombay Pentangular match, the 1944–45 final, was watched by over 200,000. The Muslims took a narrow lead on first innings. As the bowling creases were heavily pitted, Vijay Merchant, the Hindu captain, asked for the pits to be filled. The Muslim team wanted their captain, Mushtaq Ali, to refuse. He overruled them, saying that the game had to be played 'in the true sportsman's spirit.' Mushtaq himself was then injured so badly in the Muslim second innings that a doctor ordered him not to take any further part. It was the Hindu CK Nayudu (a spectator) who urged him to continue. Mushtaq Ali obeyed, scored a rapid 30 in support of the centurion KC Ibrahim, and the Muslims won by one wicket.[100] This match had a profound influence on Kardar (who played in it as Abdul Hafeez). He later wrote: 'Whenever things went against me as a captain, I took inspiration from this great match. It inspired me to fight until the last ball was bowled.'[101]

According to Shaharyar Khan, a former chairman of the Pakistan Cricket Board and Pakistan Foreign Secretary, these pentangular matches, 'especially between the Hindus and Muslims, had the intensity of an Ashes Test Match. As in England and Australia, cricket had entered the domain of mass public appeal in India. From there it was only a short step to the India-Pakistan matches that followed shortly after independence.'[102]

Khan was right to emphasise the excitement and emotion generated by communal cricket. However, there are more clues for the historian of Pakistan cricket in the (communally blind) Northern Indian team which competed in the Ranji Trophy. There were seven Muslims, two Hindus and two Europeans in the team when Northern India opened its campaign in the Ranji Trophy's first season with a match against the Indian Army at Lawrence Gardens, Lahore, in December 1934. With very few exceptions (which included an undistinguished English cricketer named Charles Hamilton Leigh Kindersley*) it represented the cream of the Lahore cricketing culture of the time.

Northern India reached the final that year where they lost to Bombay. They were to reach four more semi-finals in five seasons, but lost them all.† From 1941 to 1947, they played a total of twelve Ranji Trophy matches: two at Aitchison College, two in Lawrence Gardens, one at Minto Park, and the others away. During this period, their captains ranged from Jahangir Khan (Muslim), Ramprakash Mehra (the lone Hindu in that side), and Mian Mohammad Saeed (Muslim, soon to become Pakistan's first national captain). February 1947 marked the end of Northern India in the Ranji Trophy. They were due to play Holkar in the semi-final. But the communal violence and general chaos made it impossible for them to reach the ground at Indore. They conceded the match by a walkover.

---

*His first-class record was 33 runs from four innings.
†They did not enter the Ranji Trophy in 1939–40 or 1942–43.

Less than two years were to pass before the first team to play as Pakistan in a representative match walked out onto the field, against the West Indies in Lahore in November 1948. Nine of its members had gained first-class experience for Northern India in the Ranji Trophy before Partition. Clearly, Northern India was the most important supplier of future Pakistan cricketers. North-West Frontier Province appeared eight times in the Ranji Trophy from 1937–38 to 1946–47. They won only one of these matches and supplied no Test players to either Pakistan or India.* Sindh supplied four future Test players to India (including a future captain, GS Ramchand) but none to Pakistan.† Southern Punjab's sole graduates to the Pakistan Test side were Maqsood Ahmed and Israr Ali, although Mian Mohammad Saeed played most of his Ranji Trophy cricket for them. The Bengal team was drawn almost exclusively from West Bengal and all of its home matches were played in Calcutta. It produced no Pakistani players.

So the statistics scarcely bear out the claim that the Muslim sides that played before entranced crowds in the Bombay Pentangular were a precursor to the Pakistan national team which emerged following Partition. This claim has been an important part of the thesis that a simmering hostility based on communal resentment underlies Pakistan-India cricket. In truth, only five of the inaugural Pakistan team had played for the Muslims.‡

---

*Their lone century-maker was an Englishman, RL Holdsworth, who gained an Oxford Blue as far back as 1919.

†For quiz-setters, Sindh also had a future English Test star, Reg Simpson, who played for them during wartime service in India, while Denis Compton was playing for Holkar.

‡When Pakistan played its first official Test series, against India in 1952–53, it used four players who had appeared for the Muslims: the captain AH Kardar, the opening batsman Nazar Mohammad, Anwar Hussain and the veteran leg-spinner Amir Elahi. But all of these players had also played in the Ranji Trophy for Northern India – so had Imtiaz Ahmed, Fazal Mahmood, and Khan Mohammad. Maqsood Ahmed and Israr Ali had also played Ranji Trophy cricket, for Southern Punjab. Four newcomers had played no Ranji Trophy or Pentangular cricket before Partition: Hanif Mohammad, Waqar Hasan, Mahmood Hussain and Zulfiqar Ahmed. The touring party to England in 1954 had four former Muslim players: Kardar, Ghazali, Mohammad Aslam and a new opening batsman, Alimuddin. Six of that party had played for Northern India: Kardar, Imtiaz Ahmed, Fazal Mahmood, Khan Mohammad, the restored Mohammad Aslam and the slow left-arm bowler Shuja-ud-Din. Other former Ranji Trophy players were Maqsood Ahmed, Ghazali, who had represented Maharashtra, and Alimuddin, who had played for Rajputana and Gujarat. Nine other members of that eighteen-strong party had played no Ranji or Pentangular cricket.

4

THE GROUND BY THE GOOMTI RIVER

*'Before we left Lucknow I went out for a last look at the Monkey
Bridge and the cricket ground lying beyond it, where Pakistan had
gained her first Test victory in her inaugural Test matches.'*

– AH KARDAR, CONTEMPLATING THE SETTING
OF PAKISTAN'S FIRST TEST VICTORY

No one was in any doubt about the significance of the victory over
MCC in Karachi. Just over six months later, on 28 July 1952, the
country was elected to membership of the Imperial Cricket Conference
(ICC). India abandoned all resistance and proposed its northern neighbour,
with the MCC (representing England) seconding the proposal. Pakistan was
now eligible to play Test cricket, and once again it was India who led the
way, inviting her northern neighbour for a five-Test tour starting that
October. The significance of this series, one of the most important in the
history of Test cricket, was not widely grasped at the time, in large part
because India and Pakistan both ranked so low in the cricketing hierarchy.

The very name of the body which then controlled international cricket –
the Imperial Cricket Conference – betrayed an essential truth. World cricket
was still in the hands of the white nations which had invented Test matches
three-quarters of a century earlier. England and Australia stood at the apex,
in alliance with New Zealand and a South Africa which was starting to
introduce the formal apparatus of apartheid.

Wisden, the authoritative annual account of world cricket, reflected this balance of power. Its 1953 report of the ICC meeting, which admitted Pakistan, gave more space to the ICC's efforts to stop players' unseemly scramble for stumps at the end of Test matches. The same edition allocated the 1952 Pakistan–India series eleven pages at the back of the book. By contrast twenty-nine pages, more prominently placed, were devoted to the white-only South African tour of Australia and New Zealand the following year.*

Pakistan scarcely deserved this obscurity. She was not just facing her first-ever Test series but was also playing against the country from which she had traumatically separated only five years earlier, and against whom she had already fought one war, over Kashmir. By contrast, it was to take England nine years to play football against the Germans after the fall of Berlin in 1945, and it had taken until 1930 for an international football match between England and Germany after the conclusion of World War One in 1918.

Lord Mountbatten was later to claim that his vivisection of India had been a success because scarcely three per cent of the population had been caught up in the violence of Partition.[1] But the former Viceroy's three per cent rule did not apply to the rival India and Pakistan cricket teams. Almost all of the Pakistan cricket team had been caught up in the carnage of 1947, either directly or indirectly. Many of them had lost property and suffered the loss of relatives and friends.

CROSSING THE BORDER

Most Test teams are accustomed to journeys of several thousand miles at the start of a major tour. Before modern air travel these could last several weeks or even months. But AH Kardar's Pakistan cricketers faced nothing more

---

*In the Editor's Notes at the beginning of this *Wisden* edition, the arrival of Pakistan as a Test-playing country was greeted in a single sentence: 'Pakistan, newly elected to the Imperial Cricket Conference, began their official Test career with a tour of India, and later India went to the West Indies.' The tone of bored neutrality changed when (white-only) South Africa was mentioned in the same article: 'By drawing the rubber with Australia, JE Cheetham's men not only re-established South Africa's cricket reputation but showed the value of determination and aggression even when the cause looks hopeless.' Editor's Notes, 'Growth of World Cricket', *Wisden 1953*, p.83. Revealingly, *Wisden* from 1948 to 1952 headlined reports of Commonwealth and MCC tours as tours of India, even though they included Pakistan and Ceylon.

arduous than a two-hour bus journey from Lahore to neighbouring Amritsar, spiritual centre of the Sikh religion, for their 1952 series against India.

The thirty-five miles between these two cities was, however, laced with history. Until only five years previously Amritsar and Lahore had been part of the same easygoing and tolerant Northern India culture. Muslims, Sikhs and Hindus lived side by side in both towns, and had been accustomed to travelling to and fro. Now there were no Muslims in Amritsar, and no Sikhs or Hindus in Lahore. The Wagah border outpost between the two cities was now the only crossing point on the 1,800 mile long land frontier between West Pakistan and India. It had seen its share of bloodshed. In August 1947 the death trains, which would arrive at Lahore full of recently slaughtered Muslims, every carriage dripping blood, had passed through Wagah on their way from India. Eighteen years later, it would be the site of one of the major tank battles between India and Pakistan in the 1965 war.

The Pakistan national team was accompanied all the way to the border by a convoy of supporters in taxis, rickshaws and tongas, all hooting and cheering. Kardar himself went separately, having been ordered to travel in a car with Major General Abdur Rehman, Pakistan's deputy high commissioner in Jullundur. Rehman briefed Kardar about the political sensitivities of the forthcoming trip.

It was only necessary to read the newspapers as the cricketers embarked upon their tour to understand there remained a problem between India and Pakistan over Kashmir. Indian prime minister Pandit Nehru was in the *Ambala Tribune* on 11 October asserting provocatively (and inaccurately) that, 'Our position is correct from every point of view, whether it is judged legally, constitutionally, morally or from any other point of view.'[2] Meanwhile the *Dawn* newspaper in Karachi carried calls for a United Nations settlement. The following day's paper focused on the failure of Dr Frank Graham, a UN envoy, to arrange agreement between India and Pakistan. Throughout 1952 there were highly charged reports of troop movements along the borders.[3]

This cricket trip was meant to contrast sharply with all the suspicion and hostility. As the Pakistan team prepared to cross the border in October 1952, *Dawn* quoted from an article in the *Pakistan Times* which articulated the official point of view:

Our cricketers go to India not merely as the finest representatives of the game but also as ambassadors of goodwill. We hope the tour will tell a different tale [to that of recent history] and that on the cricket field will be forged new friendly ties that will help to bring two estranged neighbours closer together.[4]

The following day, *Dawn* reported the welcoming reception at Amritsar, quoting speakers who 'emphasised that a sense of fair play and sportsmanship transcended all boundaries and helped to strengthen friendship between countries.'[5] Wherever the Pakistan team went, it was guaranteed the same kind of welcome and the same kind of speeches. At times it must have become very wearying for the players, especially since they were obliged to put up with some four or five receptions a day.[6] What did they really feel? It is impossible to tell. I have spoken to four surviving cricketers who accompanied Kardar on this tour, and they all say it was a tour like any other. The wicketkeeper-batsman Imtiaz Ahmed was in Lahore throughout the summer of 1947, and lived through the mob violence at first hand. Waqar Hasan's family home in Amritsar was burnt down, with his grandparents incarcerated alive. Ten years ago Waqar Hasan wrote a memoir which tells his life story. It is a fascinating book, for after his spell as a Test cricketer he worked hard to become one of Pakistan's greatest industrialists. In the section of the book devoted to the tour of India, he records:

From Lahore we left in a bus for India for the eleven-week tour. The child-like enthusiasm of being a part of the first-ever team to tour as a Test playing nation was glaringly visible on everyone's faces. At the Wagah border we were warmly greeted by the local officials and the India cricket board entourage who profusely garlanded us before taking us to Amritsar, the holy city of the people who followed Sikhism, the teachings of Guru Nanak and Guru Gobind Singh. Pakistan were to start their tour here with a three-day match against the North Zone team. Sikh pilgrims from all over the country and from overseas came to Amritsar to pay homage to the Guru and to have a look at the Golden Temple, the holy shrine in the midst of a huge pond. They would queue up for hours to reach inside the main room of the temple to see the holy book of the Sikhs, the *Granth Sahib* which contains the sayings of the Guru. We visited the place. It was quite fascinating. For me especially it was sheer excitement to be in a city where I was born on September 12, 1932.[7]*

It was these very Sikhs – or rather, their followers – who murdered Waqar Hasan's grandparents. When I went to see him in his grand office in downtown Karachi, I asked him if he had visited his grandparents' house, and he replied not. Today, tearfulness is expected of the international athlete. Perhaps those who have endured genuine tragedy are more fastidious about conveying emotion, partly because they understand how dangerous it can be.

Upon arrival in Amritsar the Pakistan players noticed that little things had changed in the town that many of them had known so well. The match was played at the Gandhi Grounds. Before Partition it had been known as Alexandra Park. There were guards everywhere, and they were not allowed to take a step outside the hotel grounds.† This must have been especially tough for the three members of the Pakistan squad – Maqsood Ahmed, Waqar Hasan, Khurshid Ahmed – who had been brought up in Amritsar and were now unable to move freely in what had been their home town. The Pakistan team was carefully monitored by intrusive Indian security, Kardar complaining that they would even spy on him in his hotel room.‡ The Indian Army's commander-in-chief, General Cariappa, launched the first match of the tour by throwing a cricket ball at the captain of the North Zone cricket team.[8] This game of cricket petered out into a draw, but was notable for a century in each innings of the three-day match from Hanif Mohammad; at the time it made him the youngest cricketer to achieve this feat.§ Then, at the end of the match, a young Sikh approached Kardar and 'handed him a copy of the Holy Quran which had been left by Muslims' when they fled Amritsar at Partition.[9]

---

*A similar story emerges from Hanif Mohammad, who tells how, 'I was really excited about the whole thing. I am sure the others were too.' Hanif Mohammad, p.39.

† *Fazal Mahmood aur Cricket*, p.78. 'After personal introductions and warm reception, we were taken to the Imperial hotel. There were security arrangements at the hotel and an armed army person always at the gate. I must admit that they looked after us very well, but we couldn't visit Amritsar as we were under very strict observation. We were not even allowed to go out of the hotel and walk on the road outside for even few moments.'

‡ Kardar claimed to have been followed by Indian spies: 'I had just entered my hotel room and was about to take off my jacket that there was a knock in the door and on my beckoning the caller entered. When I looked at him quizzically he said he was from the intelligence and wanted to know my movements.' This incident occurred on the eve of the Lucknow Test. *MOAR*, p.157.

§ His record was taken from him in 1979–80 by another Pakistani, Aamer Malik, who lost it in 2002–03 to AT Rayudu of India.

The schedule, which had been hurriedly organised, did not help Pakistan. Most touring Test teams of the post-war era expected a decent run-up to the opening Test – three or four provincial matches, at least, in which players can find form and acclimatise themselves. But after the single warm-up game at Amritsar, Pakistan was plunged into its Test match debut at the Feroz Shah Kotla ground in New Delhi.

Once again the protocol surrounding the fixture was overpowering. Lala Amarnath, the Indian captain, was part of the delegation which met Kardar's Pakistanis at the railway station. Then the team went to pay its tribute to Mahatma Gandhi by laying wreaths at the marble platform on the bank of the Yamuna River, marking the spot where Gandhi was cremated at Raj Ghat. Then they made an offering at the tomb of the Sufi Muslim saint Nizamuddin Aulia.

When Kardar at last had a look at the Test wicket, he was perplexed: 'The top of the surface was a screen of soggy mud and it was evident that it would go after a few hours.'[10] He thought the wicket had been specially prepared to suit the Indian spinners. 'How important it was to win the toss,' Kardar revealed gloomily, 'was made apparent by Amarnath's jubilant gesticulation to the pavilion – an order to his openers to pad up.'

Before the start the two teams were presented to the Indian president Rajendra Prasad. Finally, the Test could begin. Khan Mohammad bowled the first official Test delivery for Pakistan. He soon found his rhythm and dismissed both Indian openers. When Amir Elahi had Vijay Manjrekar caught in the slips by Nazar Mohammad, the score was 67 for 3. Then it was Fazal Mahmood's turn, inducing a short-leg catch. His victim was Lala Amarnath – the same batsman he had claimed as his inaugural first-class victim.

By lunchtime – when the Indian prime minister Pandit Nehru and his daughter Mrs Indira Gandhi* paid a visit – India were four wickets down. The hosts slowly recovered from this low point, thanks to an attritional innings by Vijay Hazare. Even so at the close, with India 210 for 7, Pakistan could consider that the day belonged to them. One point concerned Kardar – as he and his team set off to yet another function that night, this

*Her husband was born Feroze Gandhy, but the spelling was soon changed to match the founder of India.

one at the Rashtrapati Bhavan, the official residence of the president of India – the poor wicketkeeping of Hanif Mohammad, who had dropped two easy chances.

Things could scarcely have gone worse for Pakistan on the second day. Catastrophe struck when Khan Mohammad broke down so badly that he never again bowled on tour. Just as bad, India rallied with a tenth-wicket partnership worth 109 runs. Hanif missed an easy stumping chance off Kardar's bowling to dismiss Ghulam Ahmed, the number 11 batsman. Ghulam Ahmed, a Muslim who had elected to stay in India, went on to score 50 in an Indian total of 372.

When Nazar Mohammad and Hanif scored 64 for the first wicket in the Pakistan reply, all seemed well. Then Nazar ran himself out and Vinoo Mankad's left-arm orthodox spin did the rest. On a pitch that seemed specially prepared for him, Mankad captured eight Pakistani wickets in the first innings and five in the second. Mankad's flight and length were perfect, the ball bit and fizzed, his delivery was so swift that his overs barely lasted a minute; he never gave the batsmen a rest. 'He melted our players with his terror-filled bowling,' said Fazal. 'Our players were very scared of Mankad and they lost their senses.'[11] Pakistan's Test history had begun in abject humiliation, with a defeat by an innings and 70 runs.

The officially sanctioned accounts of this game, including Kardar's own *Inaugural Test Matches*, suggest that the Pakistan team handled this defeat phlegmatically. But in his 1954 autobiography, written for an Urdu-speaking audience, Fazal Mahmood gives a version of events that is not found elsewhere. Fazal claims that:

> Hundreds of spectators were taunting me. 'Well … did you win the match?' asked someone. Another remarked: 'Well, son, the same way we will take back Kashmir.' On hearing this, I lost my temper. I jumped towards the fence and shouted back: 'If I do not avenge my defeat at Lucknow then my name is not Fazal Mahmood.' On hearing this, many spectators laughed at me and many girls shouted back, 'Wish you good luck boy, but you will never win the match.'[12]

At one stage, says Fazal, he felt so angry that he 'literally drank my own blood.' A chronically inexperienced side, Pakistan could easily have gone to pieces. Only two members of the team had played Test cricket before this series – Kardar and the veteran leg-spinner Amir Elahi, who had both represented India.* Even they could only muster four Test matches worth of experience between them. Kardar later reflected that, 'We knew it was critical to revive our spirit and fight back. We would have lost self-confidence, which would not only have affected the series but other tours as well. The immediate future of Pakistan cricket was to be influenced.'[13]

Several factors worked in the Pakistanis' favour before the second Test at Lucknow, the famous centre of Muslim civilisation and high culture, a factor which in itself must have raised the spirits of the visiting team. First, the unplayable Mankad dropped out.† Second, the match was played on a jute-matting wicket. Though he had never played on such a surface before, it suited Fazal Mahmood. Those taunts at Delhi inspired him to produce one of the most devastating spells Pakistan cricket has ever seen. Once again Amarnath won the toss. Once again he decided India would bat. This is how Fazal, writing for his Urdu fans, described events as they unfolded:

When I went onto bowl, it felt extremely difficult. As there was jute-matting on the wicket instead of coir matting. I had no prior experience to play on such a wicket and I had no inkling of differences between the two. As a result, when I threw my first ball, it felt as if I had bowled on a dead turf because the ball did not move fast nor did it swing. After hitting the ground it went straight and very slowly and Roy‡ stopped it very easily. I was surprised and looked at Roy. In this confusion I threw several balls but Roy was not impressed. I did not give him a chance to score, but he stopped my balls very easily, despite the fact that my length and direction was hundred per cent right. I threw three overs like this, but after continued failure to impress I thought I must do something

---

*Amir Elahi made his first-class debut in 1934–35 for Northern India in the Ranji Trophy, and represented Muslims with great success in the Bombay Pentangular. He was a member of the 1936 Indian touring party in England, but did not play any of the Tests. He was later chosen for the 1947–48 Indian tour of Australia, in which he played one Test. Though picked as a bowler, he was not put onto bowl. Elahi was forty-four when he made his debut for Pakistan in 1952. He was the first Pakistan Test cricketer to die, in 1980. Elahi, a natural entertainer, played cricket for enjoyment. But if the situation was serious he would walk slowly to the wicket with the words: 'Gentlemen, I mean business today.'

†So did Hazare and Adhikari, whose batting had proved so painful to Pakistan in the first Test. But it was the absence of Mankad which made the real difference.

‡The India opening batsman Pankaj Roy. He top-scored with 30 in this Indian innings before falling lbw to Fazal.

different. I decided that I should make use of the seams of the ball. Therefore in the fourth over when Manjrekar* came to face me I started using my new tactic. My happiness knew no bounds when the ball swung to my desire and went cruising towards Manjrekar, showing him the pavilion. After Manjrekar I bowled the same way to other players as well and started defeating them.[14]

By tea-time Pakistan had bundled them out for 106. 'Fazal bowled with demoniac grace. He was a man inspired to crush Indian batsmen,' recorded Kardar.[15] Kardar knew that he had a chance to secure Pakistan's first Test victory. He demanded dedication from his team in reply, and they delivered. The outstanding innings was played by Nazar Mohammad, who carried his bat in a stay at the wicket lasting eight-and-a-half hours. Nazar scored 124 out of the Pakistan total of 331.

In the second innings, Fazal took seven more wickets as India lost by an innings. This time it was the Indians who endured the hostility of the crowd. According to Fazal: 'After the match the crowd behaved so badly that it still scares me. They attacked the camp of the Indian players and set it on fire. They even broke the windows of the bus that was taking them back to the hotel and even pelted stones on the players. The players saved their lives by a hair's breadth.'[16]

Kardar later remembered:

Before we left Lucknow I went out for a last look at the Monkey Bridge and the cricket ground lying beyond it, where Pakistan had gained her first Test victory in her inaugural Test matches. The empty stands which envelope the ground and the resting place of Sarojni Naidu, the great Indian social worker, could not hide the slow moving waters of the Goomti river, on whose banks Pakistan's cricketers had managed to lower India's colours within six months of our Cricket Board's recognition by the Imperial Cricket Conference. I can never forget Lucknow and the ground by the Goomti river.[17]

*Vijay Laxman Manjrekar, one of India's finest-ever batsmen. He was bowled by Fazal Mahmood for 3 in the first innings, and fell lbw to Fazal for 3 again in the second.

It feels unfair to tear Abdul Hafeez Kardar away from the Monkey Bridge, the slow-moving waters of the Goomti River, and contemplation of his enormous achievement. Only fourteen months had passed since Cornelius had sent that letter of invitation to Kardar, and now he had led his country to a Test victory. Pakistan and Kardar had come a very long way. But the caravan was rolling towards the Brabourne stadium at Bombay, for many years cricket's headquarters on the subcontinent, where India was hungry for revenge and Mankad, with his terror-filled bowling, was back.

Many Pakistani cricket followers, exhilarated by victory in Lucknow, had made the journey down from Karachi and the atmosphere was tense with expectation as Amarnath and Kardar strode out to the middle to toss. Kardar was perhaps unfortunate to win it, for *Wisden* records that he 'faced the unenviable task of deciding whether to bat on a pitch affected by sun following early morning dew. He chose first innings and Pakistan made a bad start from which they never recovered.' Only Waqar Hasan, now coming into form following failures with the bat at Amritsar, prevented a complete rout. He scored 81 before being last out, stumped off Mankad, as Pakistan folded for 186.

In reply India dealt destruction, Hazare and Umrigar both scoring centuries, brutalising the leg-spin bowling of Amir Elahi and even treating Fazal with a certain contempt. In a daring move, with India 201 runs ahead, Amarnath declared towards the end of the second day and immediately got his reward when India picked up the wicket of Nazar Mohammad.

The third day of the match, however, belonged to Pakistan. 'I can still feel the tense atmosphere and the deadly silence that prevailed at the Brabourne stadium as Hanif, the little schoolboy, and Waqar went out to face the Indian attack,' Kardar recalled.[18] These two batsmen – Hanif just eighteen and Waqar, twenty-five – forged an extraordinary partnership. 'This was the fighting spirit of Pakistan,' enthused Kardar. 'This was the real Test to which the babes of Pakistan responded with maturity, skill and grace. Bombay belongs to the babes, this was the song of the Brabourne stadium crowd.'[19]

Only 25 minutes remained when Waqar was caught at short leg off Mankad. Hanif fell shortly afterwards, for 96, also to Mankad. Even so Kardar felt that Pakistan, 25 runs behind with seven wickets left, had a fighting chance of saving the game. It was not to be. To his utter mortification his team wilted (Kardar dismissed by Mankad for 3) and India romped to a ten-wicket victory. 'This day's cricket should not be written off Pakistan's record; for this should be remembered by all. The collapse that sealed the fate of Pakistan's batsmen on 16 November was heart-breaking for Pakistani cricket fans and humiliating for the players. Never again, I hope sincerely, shall our players put up such a rotten performance. There is no other word,' mourned a heartbroken Kardar, 'that can explain our batting debacle.'[20]

Yet the Pakistan Test team that now headed off towards Madras was still in the fight. Batting first, Pakistan subsided to 240 for 9 half an hour before the close when Lala Amarnath made a mistake. Not wanting to expose his own batsmen to a handful of overs in the fading light, he withheld his main strike bowlers, allowing Pakistan's tail-enders Zulfiqar Ahmed and Amir Elahi to bat out to the end of the day. They took full advantage, putting on 104 in 85 minutes for the last wicket. Then Pakistan grabbed control of the game, taking the top six Indian wickets for 175 runs before rain wiped out the last two days of the match. 'Everyone present on the ground was sure that Pakistan will win the fourth Test,' recalled Fazal. 'Suddenly the rain started and within no time the ground turned into a lake. A number of people got trapped in knee-length water. My heart was pained to see this treatment from God.'[21] Had weather not intervened, and play followed the pattern of the early matches, Kardar's team would probably have won.

Kardar used the stop for rain to present an inscribed silver salver to Vinoo Mankad, who had reached his Test double of 1,000 runs and 100 wickets in the Bombay Test. Mankad had needed just 23 Tests to achieve this feat. It would be the quickest Test double until Ian Botham achieved it in 1979 after 21 Tests. The inscription read: 'To Vinoo – on his great achievement from his admirers – members of the Pakistan Cricket Team – Wishing him a very happy career and every success.' This generous gesture demonstrated the good spirit in which much of the cricket on this tour was played.

In the final Test, played at Calcutta, Pakistan seemed at one stage in danger of defeat, but were saved by a defiant 97 from Waqar and a doughty defensive 28 not out from the indomitable Fazal. Pakistan had lost the series, but it did not feel like that. 'There can be no denying that our team made a fine showing in India,' was Justice Cornelius's verdict, adding that 'no praise can be too high for the magnificent spirit which the players, who were mostly very young, showed under the keen leadership of Mr Kardar, himself not quite 28 years of age at the time.'[22]

Crowds gathered to meet the team off the plane when it touched down at Karachi on 21 January 1953. The tour had generated goodwill on both sides of the border. It had established Pakistan as a Test-playing nation. No wonder that, on his return home, Kardar suggested that Test matches against India should be renewed annually. Meanwhile, the exultant national captain had something equally momentous to look forward to: MCC now extended Pakistan an invitation to play four Tests in England, the home of cricket, the following summer. This was another leap forward and Kardar, who knew English conditions better than anyone else in Pakistan, at once began to apply all his intelligence to the question of how to beat the English at their own game and on their own territory.

5

TRIUMPH AT THE OVAL

'There was a freshness about that Pakistan. No marks of weariness and cynicism. There was buoyancy; no sign of internal strife. It was an innocent Pakistan, free of collective guilt. The exuberance of the cricket of this period seemed intertwined with the task of nation-building. There were few things that Pakistan had achieved as a new nation. Cricketing success was one of the early bonds of nationhood.'[1]

– OMAR KUREISHI, PAKISTAN CRICKET
COMMENTATOR AND WRITER

At Partition, Justice Cornelius and the BCCP faced two intractable problems: how to ensure that Pakistan cricket had an international presence, and how to build a sound domestic structure. Against all expectations, Test match glory came first. Kardar's team defied logic. Kardar had created a successful Test team at a time when the domestic structures which went with it were still non-existent. There was no first-class game in Pakistan and very little support for the players.

The fundamental decision made by Cornelius and Kardar amounted to a rejection of the market model for the development of cricket in Pakistan. Kardar's economic and political beliefs amounted to a version of Islamic socialism. He believed in the ability of government to mould society and establish social justice.

The key achievement of Kardar and Cornelius was to establish cricket as a manifestation of Pakistan's national identity, therefore worthy of patronage either directly by the state or by state-owned institutions. Only international success could have brought this about. Once it had done so, national prestige was at stake and the resources of the state could be brought to bear.

This system worked both at a personal and a club level. We have already seen how Prime Minister Nazimuddin released Fazal Mahmood from police duties, so that he could attend an important cricket dinner. This intervention established the essential precedent that cricketers were understood to be servants of Pakistan. Kardar also benefited from this arrangement. He had been working for an oil company in East Pakistan when the call came through to captain Pakistan. This company seems not to have made it easy for him to take time off, and Kardar soon grasped that his duties as national captain were incompatible with his private-sector obligations. He soon left his private-sector company and became an instructor with the Pakistan Air Force in Karachi.

Probably Kardar was lured into the air force by Group Captain Cheema, who would later become secretary of the BCCP in 1954. Cheema also tapped up Waqar Hasan, one of the debutants on the 1952 tour of India, to train as a fighter pilot. In fact, Hasan never completed his training. 'Commitment to the game, training for it to excel at the top level and touring with the team in fact never allowed me to concentrate and train as an air force pilot,' he later remarked. 'Destiny has its own ways. I became a businessman instead and I never ever regretted that.'[2] By contrast Imtiaz Ahmed, who was recruited into the administrative branch, remained in the air force for many years. MEZ Ghazali, who played in Pakistan's famous defeat of the MCC in 1951, was another air force man. Not all the armed services were happy to provide sinecures to cricketers. The practice was disliked in the Pakistan army, which has never encouraged cricket.[3] Only one serving soldier, Lt Col. Shuja-ud-Din, played much Test match cricket for Pakistan; when he met Ayub Khan, the commander-in-chief accused him of being a 'waster'.[4] Cricket never entered the military sports curriculum in the way that other sports, in particular hockey, have done, though there were informal matches between regiments.

The military and police service were not the only employment for promising cricketers. The Pakistan Public Works Department (PWD) offered Hanif

Mohammad the post of roads inspector, though he never inspected any roads. Hanif's benefactor was Mr Kafiluddin, the chief engineer, and one of the crucial figures in early Pakistan cricket. 'My financial worries were now over. Due to his support and patronage,' Hanif recorded in his autobiography, 'I was able to pay undivided attention to cricket.'[5]

Pakistan at first depended almost entirely on foreign visitors or overseas tours to provide first-class experience for their players. This at last changed in 1953–54 when Cornelius pushed the Board to create a national championship. It was named the Quaid-e-Azam Trophy, in honour of Jinnah. With occasional intervals, fluctuating membership and frequent rule changes, it has been contested in Pakistan ever since, and remains the country's principal first-class tournament.

Under pressure from Cornelius, the rules were devised in a hurry. There were not very many of them – particularly on player qualifications. Nine teams were originally invited: East Pakistan, Baluchistan, Karachi, Bahawalpur, Punjab, Sindh, North-West Frontier Province, Services and Railways. The first two dropped out (thus setting a pattern of in-and-out participation by teams from East Pakistan), so that seven teams were left to play a knockout tournament of three preliminary matches, two semi-finals and a final.

The lack of residency qualifications gave opportunities for two remarkable patrons to assemble their own teams. Bahawalpur at this stage was an autonomous princely state within Pakistan – it had a cricket-mad Amir* and an even more cricket-mad hereditary chief minister, Makhdoomzada Hassan Mahmood,† who induced him to pour state

---

*Sadeq Mohammad Khan Abbasi V ruled Bahawalpur from 1907 to 1966, first as Nawab and later as Amir. Bahawalpur was never a British possession and until independence in 1947 was ruled by its own Nawabs. Only in 1955 was the state formally merged into Pakistan.

†Born in 1922 in Bahawalpur, brother-in-law of the late Pir of Pagaro, Makhdoomzada was one of the great early patrons of Pakistan cricket. Educated at Aitchison College, he was installed as chief minister of Bahawalpur after graduating. He made his first-class debut in November 1951 when he captained a combined Bahawalpur/Karachi side against Nigel Howard's touring MCC at Bahawalpur. Batting at number 9, he scored just four runs, but he claimed the wicket of Tom Graveney in the MCC second innings. He never again played a first-class match. Makhdoomzada oversaw the construction of Dring stadium and provided the sponsorship and administrative support which at one time turned Bahawalpur into the finest regional side in Pakistan. In 1954 he was chairman of the selection committee which picked the Pakistan team to play England. He served for several years as Board chairman in the 1950s. Kardar pays a generous and heartfelt tribute to Makhdoomzada in his *Memoirs of an All-rounder*, pp.190–94. His son, Ahmed Mahmood, served as Governor of the Punjab from December 2012 to August 2013.

revenues into cricket and cricketers. He built a showpiece modern stadium, originally named Dring after his predecessor, a popular Englishman who served as prime minister after Partition. The Dring stadium was also unusual in providing a turf wicket – at this stage one of only three in the whole of Pakistan.*

Makhdoomzada Hassan Mahmood recruited many of the best players in Pakistan with no birth or other connection with Bahawalpur, including the brothers Hanif and Wazir Mohammad, Pakistan's fast bowler Khan Mohammad, Alimuddin, Amir Elahi, Imtiaz Ahmed and Zulfiqar Ahmed.[6] Hanif records that the Karachi players were looked after, on the chief minister's instructions, by Mr Khawaja, an officer of the Bahawalpur Bank.[7]

The Pir of Pagaro – by coincidence the brother-in-law of Makhdoomzada – was an even more dramatic patron of the game. He was the clan and spiritual leader of the Hurs people of Sindh. His father, Pir Sabghatullah Shah, was hanged by the British in Hyderabad Central Jail in March 1943 for protesting against colonial rule, and he and his brother were sent to school in England. For a teenage boy, such an experience might have turned him against all things British, but the young Pir fell in love with cricket at his suburban school in Pinner, Middlesex.

On his return to Pakistan after Partition, he set up his own nets at his house opposite the Karachi Gymkhana, which were open house to the Mohammad brothers and other eager boys in the city. The hospitable Pir could, however, be a dangerous opponent. Playing in his nets one day, he was felled by a short ball from a future Test opening bowler, Mohammad Munaf. His Hur followers, who constantly accompanied him, assumed that he had been attacked and pounced on the unlucky bowler and the other boys, including Hanif. They were rescued from their religious revenge in the

*The importance of matting wickets cannot be overestimated in the early history of Pakistan cricket. Players learnt the game at school and club level on a playing surface which differs significantly from turf, especially in wet conditions. Matting offers great bowlers, such as Fazal, considerable sideways movement through cut or spin. The tension of matting can also be varied to suit bowlers: slack matting allows the ball to grip better when it lands and deviate more sharply, tense matting gives more bounce. However, in any conditions matting has more consistency of bounce than turf and batsmen once settled can play more confidently and aggressively. They can often get away with poor footwork or shot selection which would be fatal on turf. Matting wickets prevailed in Pakistan throughout the 1950s, and were widely blamed, by both domestic and visiting analysts, for holding back the development of Pakistani cricketers. As we shall see later, Richie Benaud had a major role in their replacement.

nick of time by the young Pir's secretary. A few years later, a visiting MCC team had a similar experience when they felled the Pir in a one-day match; this time the Pir himself came to their rescue by rising to his feet and resuming his innings.[8]

The Pir led out the Sindh team in the very first match of the Quaid-e-Azam Trophy, against Bahawalpur in the Dring stadium. He was sporting enough to include Mohammad Munaf, the player who had knocked him out in his own nets, and his team included another future Test player, the stylish batsman Wallis Mathias (one of the few Christians to represent Pakistan).[9] However, they were comfortably beaten by the Bahawalpur stars.

This initial Quaid-e-Azam Trophy set some patterns for the future. One, already noted, was the tendency of teams to withdraw. In later years, these withdrawals were often last-minute, after teams discovered who they were drawn against, and decided to avoid an expensive journey or possibly an expensive drubbing. Another was the system of declaring a winning team based on first-innings only, where there was insufficient time to complete a second innings.

Especially important and connected features were the freedom of players to play for teams willing to pay or support them, and the mix of regional and corporate teams. Services and Railways had the capability to put a first-class team in the field, which most regional centres lacked. They were needed to provide the numbers for a proper tournament. Railways and the Air Force (who made up most of the Services XI) were relaxed about releasing their members to play cricket for three days, and the regional teams also depended on those sorts of employers. As Wazir Mohammad recalls: 'We got paid nothing for appearing in the Quaid-e-Azam Trophy and we had to get leave from our offices to play in matches or attend training camps.'[10]

The Quaid-e-Azam Trophy was not perfect. But it was up and running. Six years after independence from Britain, Pakistan had her own system of first-class cricket. In years to come, the trials for Quaid-e-Azam Trophy matches were a vital passage for talented young cricketers to catch the eye of selectors and get their chance in first-class cricket. It did its immediate job of guiding the selectors for the 1954 tour of England; every single one of the touring party was a Quaid-e-Azam Trophy player.

THE EAGLETS

Apart from the Quaid-e-Azam Trophy, Justice Cornelius made another notable contribution to the long-term future of Pakistan cricket. Aware that Pakistan's cricketers lacked serious coaching of the kind that was available in rival nations, the judge formed the Pakistan Eaglets Society, which arranged for Pakistani cricketers to travel to England for coaching. In 1950, Cornelius sent over an advance party of four players: Imtiaz Ahmed, Khan Mohammad, Agha Saadat and Rusi Dinshaw.*

Two years later, Cornelius dispatched the first full Pakistan Eaglets team of fourteen members, under the leadership of Mian Mohammad Saeed. Once again it reflects well on Mian Saeed that, although deprived of the national captaincy, he was happy to lead what was in effect a Pakistan academy team on an educational journey through Britain. It is surprising that Kardar, now marked out as national captain, did not insist on doing the job himself. MJ Mobed† was the manager of the team.

Mian Saeed's Eaglets received useful coaching at the Gover-Sandham school for about a month and then played a number of matches in the South-West against Somerset, Devon, Gloucestershire and Dorset. They did not lose a match and introduced Pakistan to thousands of English people among their hosts.[11]

The great coach Alf Gover, who had accompanied Lord Tennyson on his tour of India in 1938, was one of the rare Englishmen who approached Pakistan cricket without bigotry and ignorance. Immediately grasping that Pakistan had 'an abundance of talent', his advice to his students was sparing and wise. After Hanif Mohammad had been in the nets for three days, Gover called him over to say that he was a 'natural player' and 'there was nothing I could tell him.'[12] He told Mian Saeed that 'everything is correct

---

*No Parsi has come closer to playing Test matches for Pakistan than Rusi Dinshaw, who toured India under Kardar. On that tour he played in only two first-class matches and in three innings scored only eighteen runs. His father Nadir Dinshaw was also a fine first-class cricketer.

†Minocher Jamshedji Mobed, a first-class cricketer from Karachi, represented Parsis in the Sindh and Bombay Pentangular from 1919 to 1947. He also played against Gilligan's MCC in 1926–27 and Jardine's team in 1933–34. Famous for his big hitting, he was called 'the Jessop Of Sindh'. After retirement, Mobed became an umpire and stood with Daud Khan at Karachi Gymkhana when Pakistan defeated MCC by four wickets in late 1951, thus opening the door to Test cricket. When questioned about controversial umpiring decisions, he replied: 'I am a Parsi.' According to KH Baloch and MH Baluch (*A Century of Karachi Cricket*, p.17): 'That was a simple way of expressing that his integrity was beyond question.'

with this little kid. Everything is already perfect.'[13] Hanif's team-mate Sultan Mahmud remembers Hanif's obsessive dedication to the game on this tour:

> We were playing Devonshire at Torquay, and in the morning when we went into bat the ball was moving in the sea-breeze. In the first over of the day he played forward, but the ball went through his defence and bowled him. Hanif was very quiet at lunch and did not say a word at tea. In the evening we went out to a party, there was dancing, but Hanif was nowhere to be seen.
>
> I was sharing a room with Hanif and got back after midnight. I assumed he would be asleep and went in very quietly. But the light was on. He was still up, with his full kit on, whites, bat, pads, boots, gloves. He was practising the shot he had been out to in the morning in front of the mirror.
>
> He turned to me and said: 'I am very upset. I don't know how I missed the ball.'
>
> I told him it was the movement caused by the sea-breeze.
>
> That was Hanif in the making.[14]

Fazal Mahmood missed out on the 1952 trip but toured with the Eaglets the following year. He always maintained that he gained important experience about British conditions on this three-month trip. Gover wrote later that:

> He had an unorthodox action: when his bowling arm was about to begin its upward swing from behind he would check and do a twirl of his hand and wrist and then go on with the upward swing ready to deliver the ball. Any alterations to his action would have ruined him, so I decided to improve his repertoire by teaching him away-swing.[15]

Before leaving, as his final preparation he went to The Oval to witness Len Hutton lead England to his famous Ashes victory over Australia. Fazal emerged from the ground resolved to 'offer any possible sacrifice' which might enable Pakistan to triumph over England in the Tests. It was an idea which, says his biographer Sheikh Inam Ashraf, 'caught him like a spear to the heart.'[16] On 26 August, he and his team of Eaglets caught the boat ahead of the long journey home to Karachi. Upon arrival, Fazal immediately set himself to practise, keeping in mind the instructions he had been given by Alf Gover.[17]

ENGLAND v PAKISTAN 1954

Kardar felt threatened both personally and professionally as he and his touring party assembled at Karachi for their long journey to Britain on the SS *Batory* on 12 April 1954. Just ahead of the tour, supporters of Mian Mohammad Saeed, led by Fida Hassan, then president of the Punjab Cricket Association, launched a determined bid to oust him as captain. Initially casual about the threat, Kardar was alarmed to learn that his opponents had gained a majority on the BCCP. He was advised to approach the Defence Secretary, Iskander Mirza. He gave Kardar an interview and resolved the issue very simply, by threatening that the team would be issued neither with passports nor foreign exchange unless Kardar was captain.[18]

England were the greatest cricket team in the world. The previous year they had captured the Ashes. The batting line-up contained Len Hutton, Denis Compton, Peter May and Tom Graveney, four of the best batsmen that England have fielded since the war. As captain, Hutton could choose a formidable bowling attack from Alec Bedser, Fred Trueman, Brian Statham, Jim Laker, Tony Lock and Johnny Wardle. (During that summer England would also find the out-and-out pace of Frank Tyson and the multiple variations of Bob Appleyard.) With Godfrey Evans as wicket-keeper and Trevor Bailey the all-rounder, this team was one of the finest England sides of all time.

Kardar had little to match this. Khan Mohammad was a good quick bowler. However, he was heavily involved in league cricket. He was therefore the only player in the team who claimed to be professional, and as a result got involved in a series of rancorous disputes about pay, probably the reason he missed two of the Test matches.[19] Kardar himself excluded another pace bowler of quality, Yawar Saeed, son of Mian Mohammad Saeed. He ended up playing against Pakistan on the tour, as an amateur for Somerset.

Fazal Mahmood was proven to be an outstanding performer on matting wickets but rather unkindly considered by Kardar (and some others) to be 'on turf wickets, essentially, a change bowler.'[20] With the exception of Hanif and Waqar Hasan, who had done well on the India tour, the batting was sketchy. In particular, the loss of Nazar Mohammad, centurion in Pakistan's first Test match victory, was a blow.[21]

Indeed the lack of first-class experience, let alone Test match calibre, in the Pakistan team was unnerving. For example Khalid Wazir, who had never even scored a first-class 50, played in two of the Test matches as a batsman, totalling fourteen runs across three innings.* There was no official scorer. Members of the team were expected to share out this duty.[22] Pakistan did not bring with it a single accredited newspaper or radio correspondent.[23] Apart from his other duties, the team captain found himself instructing members of his squad on quite rudimentary issues, like how to hold a knife and fork.[24] They were a cheerful, unsophisticated collection of young men driven by love of the game and simple patriotism. They stayed in modest hotels or bed and breakfasts, and did their own laundry because their allowance of only ten rupees a day was not enough to pay for such luxuries. Travelling to and from matches, they sang popular songs, recited poetry or folk melodies. They realised to their surprise that many British people did not know that Pakistan existed. For much of the tour, the team was accompanied by an official from the Pakistan High Commission whose task was to educate the British public about this.

Most observers wrote off Pakistan's chances. Vijay Merchant, the fine Indian batsman who had toured England in 1946, sent a message that 'if Pakistan draws ten and wins four or five county matches in England it should consider its tour a success.'[25] This message angered Pakistani cricketers, but it expressed the common perception. Faithful Alf Gover was one of the very few who disagreed. In advance of the series, this wise man warned in a newspaper column that 'Pakistan will win at least one of the four Tests.'[26]

By a piece of good fortune, CLR James, the greatest cricket writer of all time, was on hand to report Pakistan's opening match at Worcester. James, who established a reputation as a cricket correspondent in the 1930s, had

---

*Khalid Wazir was the son of the legendary Muslim cricketer Syed Wazir Ali, who toured England with India in 1932 and 1936. Khalid Wazir never played again for Pakistan, and indeed never returned there, settling in England.

been living in New York for fifteen years, where he spent his time writing books and developing theories about Marxist philosophy. However, in 1953 James was interned on Ellis Island, in due course was expelled from the United States and returned to the *Manchester Guardian* as a cricket writer.

Born in Trinidad, James was then brooding on the masterpiece that was to establish his reputation, *Beyond A Boundary*, a meditation on cricket and national identity in the West Indies. Writing of growing up as a lover of both cricket and of English literature, James noted that 'as far back as I can trace my consciousness, the original found itself and came to maturity within a system that was the result of centuries of development in another land, was transplanted as a hot-house flower, is transported and bore some strange fruit.' This observation also fitted Pakistan cricket very well.

James caught the Pakistanis on a happy day as they scored 374 for 8 on their first innings of the tour. Kardar won the toss and chose to bat, meaning that James had an opportunity to pay attention to Hanif Mohammad: 'He is short, like Bradman and Headley, with broad shoulders. His stance is not easy but concentrated, legs apart, left shoulder pointing directly at the bowler. He plays back strongly, but he moves his left foot well out to the pitched-up ball and slashes his bat at it late, beating the fieldsman to the boundary on either side of the bowler. The stroke is perfectly controlled and beautifully timed, and this in combination with his strong back-play is a sound foundation for many runs.' But the bulk of James's article was taken up with a description of a long partnership between two other Pakistan batsmen, Alimuddin and Maqsood Ahmed. They both scored centuries and James concluded that in a good summer Pakistan would score 'plenty of runs.'[27]

For the remainder of the match, as Pakistan bundled Worcestershire out twice, James had the opportunity to assess Pakistan's bowlers. He was encouraging about the sixteen-year-old leg-spinner, Khalid Hasan. Sadly Hasan would make no mark in his lone Test, and never played for his country again (making him the youngest player at the end of a Test career). His presence on the tour was widely attributed in Pakistan to favouritism by Kardar.*

Fazal, as so often, was the hero. 'At half past three this well-built and powerful man, whose every step both running up to bowl and walking back

---

*Khalid Qureshi was a far better slow bowler than Khalid Hasan, but his left-arm spin was similar to Kardar's. Many believed Qureshi was kept out of the team because Kardar did not want strong competition.

is charged with energy, was bowling as strongly as he had been doing at eleven in the morning. His eleven for 102 in this match, on a pitch which was consistently true and easy in pace, is a remarkable performance.'[28]

Sadly, the perfect weather conditions for the Worcestershire match were not repeated. Kardar's Pakistanis were drenched almost everywhere they went, and in particular in the most important matches. As a result, they were forced to play in conditions of which they had little or no experience. This was probably the biggest reason why so many of the most important players failed, and why until the very last Test, Pakistan was never more than an ace from disaster.

In the first Test, played at Lord's, the first three days of the match were rained off.* Play did not start until 3.45pm on the Monday, the fourth of the five days. Never before had the Pakistan batsmen had to cope with the consequences of uncovered pitches, and very swiftly they were bundled out for 87. The situation would have been worse but for Hanif. It was not the runs he scored that counted, it was the time he spent in the middle. He batted three hours for his 20 runs on an unplayable wicket, scarcely attempting a scoring stroke. Kardar maintained it was his best innings of the tour. Hanif batted with intense concentration, watching the ball with great care, making sure that his body was in line. It was on occasions like these when Hanif's lack of inches was such an advantage, enabling him to monitor the ball off the pitch and onto his bat.

When England batted they saw the chance to strike quick runs and give themselves a chance to bowl out Pakistan in the second innings. But Fazal and Khan Mohammad exerted great control, and shared nine wickets; Fazal with four for 55 and Khan Mohammad five for 61, including Len Hutton, for 0, with a swinging yorker (the first victim of what would become a major weapon of Pakistani fast bowlers). After 100 minutes' batting England declared at 117 for 9. When Alimuddin was bowled by Bailey off the eighth ball of the second innings, it appeared that England could seize control. But once again, Hanif steadied the situation. By the time that he was lbw to Laker off the final ball of the day, he had batted for five hours and 40 minutes in the

---

*The customary meeting between the Queen and the players was cancelled, and rescheduled for Buckingham Palace. When she met Fazal Mahmood the Queen looked into his eyes, but moved on. Once she had shaken the hands of all the players in the queue, the Queen returned to Fazal. 'You are a Pakistani. How do you have blue eyes while the others do not?' Fazal replied: 'Your Majesty, the people coming from the northern areas of Pakistan do have blue eyes.' *Fazal Mahmood*, p.37.

course of the match for just 59 runs. But these were priceless runs, hewn from the rock-face. Again and again, he would save his country with innings like these.

Pakistan felt optimistic that they had the skill and temperament to contain the England team. But this optimism was destroyed in the second Test at Trent Bridge, a match which caused Kardar to despair. Everything that he had feared at the start of the tour came about. Even today it is heartbreaking to contemplate what happened on Kardar's darkest day as cricket captain of Pakistan.

Kardar won the toss and batted on an easy wicket. For an hour all went reasonably well. Alimuddin was bowled by Statham, but Hanif and Waqar Hasan, the two stalwarts, saw off Bedser. The trouble started after an hour when Bob Appleyard, making his Test debut, came onto bowl.* Hanif, having scored 19 in reasonable comfort against Bedser and Statham, was lbw to Appleyard's second ball, playing for an off-break which straightened. Waqar was bowled playing back to Appleyard's in-cutter. Maqsood and Imtiaz followed very swiftly, and soon Pakistan were 55 for 5. Appleyard had taken four wickets for six runs in his opening spell in Test cricket. 'His mixture of in-swingers, off-spinners and leg-cutters, his variation of pace and flight, bore the stamp of a highly skilled craftsman,' noted *Wisden*. But this was little comfort to the Pakistanis who, despite a minor rally led by Kardar, were all out before tea.

England then made full use of the easy wicket that Pakistan had scorned. Compton, dropped by wicketkeeper Imtiaz off Fazal when he scored 20, advanced to a mammoth 278, his highest score in Test cricket. The Pakistani fielding collapsed. Close fielders, with the partial exception of Waqar and Hanif, were too slow to stop the singles, while those on the boundary were unable to prevent twos being run. In all, 496 runs were scored in the course of the day, 192 of them in a partnership of 105 minutes between Bailey and Compton. The batsmen would shout: 'Run two, he can't throw!'† Fazal

---

*To be fair to Kardar and Co., this quickish off-spinner was then at his peak. He would head the averages in the winter tour against Australia. In a career shortened by tuberculosis he took over 700 first-class wickets at an average of just 15.48.

†Kardar's account in *TSOT*, pp.40–3, well conveys the misery the Pakistan captain experienced during this innings. Majid Khan told me that until Pakistanis began to play county cricket the general standard of fielding was terrible and that players were actually discouraged from attempting hard throw-ins for fear of injury. Majid Khan: personal interview.

Mahmood broke down after bowling ten overs at normal pace, and thereafter came in off a shortened run. Eventually the Revd David Sheppard, captaining England in the absence of Len Hutton, called a halt to the carnage by declaring at a massive 558 for 6. Rain then fell, changing the nature of the wicket, which now became spiteful. It was impossible for the Pakistanis to hold out, and they subsided to defeat by an innings and 129 runs. It was at this point that murmurs, hurtful to Kardar, started to be heard that Pakistan had been introduced prematurely into Test match cricket.[29] At the end of the game, Kardar became involved in a row with Fazal in which he accused him of declaring himself fit, when actually he had not recovered from injury.[30]

The murmurs grew louder after the third Test at Old Trafford. England batted first and scored 359 for 8. Then a day's rain radically changed the conditions. *Wisden* recorded that 'sometimes the ball flew from a length, at other times it squatted, and all the time the spin bowlers were able to make it turn sharply.' Pakistan were bowled out for 90. Made to follow on, they were 25 for 4 when the rain came again. Between lunch and the close of play on the third day, the Pakistanis had scored 155 runs, while losing fourteen wickets. During this period, MEZ Ghazali came out to bat twice within the space of approximately two hours, being dismissed for a duck on both occasions, the quickest 'pair' in Test history. For the remainder of the match, the players sat in the pavilion singing Punjabi rain-making songs. These were successful and the final two days were washed away. 'The story of Pakistan's batting is full of sorrow on a cruel wicket,' recorded Kardar.[31]

The voices questioning Pakistan's capacity for Test match competition grew. Neville Cardus, doyen of cricket writers, wrote: 'I must say that, in my opinion, a mistake was made by those authorities who decided that the time was now ripe for Test matches between Pakistan and England.' Cardus brutally concluded that: 'to say the plain truth, the Pakistan team would scarcely hold its own in the English county cricket championship with Yorkshire, Nottinghamshire, Middlesex or Northamptonshire, not even in a fine summer.'[32]

This was the dark state of affairs as Pakistan approached the fourth Test match at The Oval: Kardar's job on the line, dissension in the camp, ridicule in the press, and Pakistan's position as a Test nation in question. In many teams everything would have fallen apart, but not Kardar's Pakistanis. 'It might sound incredible and even audacious to refer to the great optimism that prevailed at this stage in our camp,' wrote Kardar later. Fazal put pressure on Kardar ahead of The Oval game to issue a statement that Pakistan would win the Test.[33] 'I decided to fight for the honour of my country and the nation, even though I had to put my life in danger for it,' said Fazal.[34]

Kardar won the toss and defiantly chose to bat. In the first over, Hanif was lbw to Statham. 'This was the biggest blow for the Pakistan team,' recorded Fazal. 'It was as if a lightning bolt had struck my heart and, for a moment, our balcony was frozen into silence.'[35] Thereafter the pattern of events was familiar. Statham, Tyson and Loader demolished the Pakistan batting. Kardar, who put all his life and soul into his 36, managed some resistance, but the rest of the top order failed as Pakistan were bowled out for an ignominious 133.

The following morning a monsoon-like outburst turned The Oval into a lake and wiped out the day's play. This was Pakistan's first piece of luck from the weather, and it was one of the turning points of the match, in that epoch of uncovered wickets. Conditions were suddenly perfect for Fazal. Len Hutton was all at sea. First, he edged Fazal through the slips for four, then drove him expansively through extra cover for another boundary. In the next over, Hutton shaped to play a Fazal inswinger to leg. In fact it was the ball that went away, and he was caught by the wicketkeeper. This delivery gave exquisite satisfaction to a watching Alf Gover, because it was the one he had added to the Fazal repertoire in his indoor school the previous year. 'My loyalties were so divided,' wrote the former Surrey and England bowler, 'that I did not know whether to laugh or to cry.'[36]

Fazal took six England wickets for 53 runs in a spell of 30 consecutive overs. Among his victims were Hutton, May, Compton and Graveney, who was beaten five balls in succession by Fazal before offering a catch to Hanif at slip. Compton, dropped twice off Fazal's bowling, was finally dismissed for 53. At the other end, Mahmood Hussain played an excellent supporting role with four wickets.

Pakistan were back in the game, with a tiny first innings lead of three runs, but conditions were still dreadful. Hanif struck out for 19, and Kardar extracted 17 invaluable runs. The Pakistan captain was worn down by the agony of the situation. Determined not to get out and driven on by the weight of responsibility, he had been at the wicket for 70 minutes when he struck a Wardle full toss half-heartedly back to the bowler to be caught and bowled. Kardar, a proud man who felt so strongly the need to set an example as captain, did his best to hide the extremity of his disappointment. At this point, Pakistan had 76 runs on the board with seven wickets down. The match seemed to be over, and with it Kardar's captaincy and Pakistan's prospects of being taken seriously as a Test nation.

What followed was so unexpected as to seem miraculous. A partnership between two batsmen, who had not previously been taken seriously, nearly doubled the score. The leading role was taken by Wazir Mohammad, elder brother of Hanif. Seven years earlier the Mohammad family had entrusted Wazir with a perilous mission. As Indian tanks rolled into their home town of Junagadh, they sent him, just seventeen years old, on the long journey to Karachi to scout out whether it was safe for the family to move there.

In circumstances requiring equal coolness and sound judgement, Wazir spent half an hour at the wicket before scoring his first run. Wazir's determined innings owed much to an inspired piece of amateur dramatics, which he recalled with relish nearly fifty years later. 'I was hit on the front foot by an inswinging full toss from Statham. It was painful, but I could have carried on. However, I decided to stay on the ground, pretending that I could not get up. I had treatment and the game was held up for several minutes. I glimpsed the wicketkeeper, Godfrey Evans, from the corner of my eye and could see that he was taken in. He told Brian Statham to pitch it up because I would not be able to play on the front foot. In fact, I wanted the ball pitched up, because short balls on that wicket were much harder to face. Some kept low and some reared up. Statham and the other bowlers did pitch it up and I remembered to groan in pain and hop about when I used my front foot.'[37]

Wazir remained unbeaten at the end on 42, runs acquired over the course of nearly three hours, helped by partnerships with the off-spinner Zulfiqar Ahmed and the fast bowler Mahmood Hussain, which together put on 82 runs and doubled the score. According to Shuja-ud-Din, who himself played a valiant role in this match: 'The runs accumulated by these three gutsy players can without hesitation be termed the most precious in the foundation years of the new cricketing nation.'[38]

Even so, these batsmen had done no more than give Pakistan a slight chance. England needed 168 to win, in acres of time. Hutton, again all at sea against Fazal, was quickly dismissed.[39] But May and Compton batted well and shortly before the close of the fourth day England had 109 on the board, with only two wickets down. Fazal later claimed that Kardar wanted to take him off at this stage and that he was obliged to grab the ball from out of his captain's hands saying, 'Do you want to lose the match?'*

Fazal at once delivered a slower ball which produced a false stroke from May, well caught by Kardar at gully and a crucial wicket. Hutton then sent in Evans ahead of Graveney, hoping to knock off a win in the last hour of play. But Evans was bowled by Fazal at once, while Graveney fell to the left-arm spin of Shuja-ud-Din. Shortly before the close, Compton was dismissed by Fazal. Overnight, England were in need of 43 runs, with four wickets left.

Fazal was certain that Pakistan would win: 'I had that kind of a feeling, backed by determination, perseverance, application, concentration and motivation, and I knew we could turn the tables.'[40] England's main chance lay with Wardle, who was promptly dropped at second slip off Mahmood Hussain by Alimuddin, who was so upset that for a while he was incapable of saying sorry to his captain. Wardle and Tyson hung on for half an hour, and the game seemed to be turning, though extremely slowly, towards England. Wardle was dropped three times in consecutive balls – a nerve-wracking reverse hat-trick. The Pakistanis and their supporters in the ground† greeted every run with a groan of despair. Then Fazal removed Tyson, caught behind by Imtiaz who was claiming his seventh victim in the match.‡ The next over Kardar, having consulted with Fazal, recalled deep midwicket from the boundary in order to have a short leg. The following ball Wardle – the vital impediment to Pakistan's victory – turned the ball round the corner and was caught by Shuja-ud-Din.§ But it is Fazal who should be permitted to describe the final moments of this momentous Oval Test match:

> On the other end I started to bowl at McConnon. I had bowled five
> deliveries to him but this servant of God played very defensive. I was very
> unsettled by his attitude and felt troubled. I was eager to see the final

*Fazal Mahmood, p.45. Fazal's account suggests that Kardar had given up any hope of winning at this stage, and was hoping for rain.

†How many were there? Fazal says a crowd of 'only a few hundred' (Fazal Mahmood, p.46) turned up on the final day. But Shuja-ud-Din says 4,000. According to Wisden, 25,000 attended Saturday's play and 24,000 were there on Monday, the penultimate day of the match.

‡Imtiaz claimed 86 victims on the tour, 81 behind the stumps, which is still a record for a touring wicketkeeper.

§As so often, two contending versions exist. Fazal insists he was responsible for this field change (Fazal Mahmood, p.47) while Kardar (TSOT, p.83) says the decision was made after a 'consultation' with Fazal.

scene of this drama. I felt that only McConnon was now between the ground and the victor's balcony. To get rid of this last impediment, I bowled my sixth ball with full force. Perhaps McConnon was also bored with his lifeless play or maybe he wanted to show some fury like a dying candle. Therefore, he tried to hit the ball and score a quick run. The ball went straight to Hanif who promptly threw it on the stumps. McConnon was run out. On watching this I ran towards Hanif in frenzy, took him in my arms and started dancing. My dreams had been fulfilled. My desires had been satiated. England was defeated by 24 runs and Pakistan's name had come prominently on the map of international cricket. There was a commotion in the Pakistan stand. Everyone was jumping for joy.[41]

When Fazal Mahmood got back to the pavilion, he found that Alf Gover was jumping up and down shouting, 'We have won, we have won!'[42] General Ayub Khan, commander-in-chief of the Pakistan army and later to mount a military coup, was rather incongruously present and doubtless full of military good humour. With him was Lt Gen. Azam Khan, who would help orchestrate Ayub Khan's rise to power in 1958. He had already obtained experience administering martial law in the Punjab after riots had broken out the previous year.

There was one ugly touch. Mian Saeed, who could so easily have been captain, was watching at the ground with his son Yawar, but (says Yawar) was excluded from the post-match celebration by Kardar.* Justice Cornelius was in a state of wild excitement. He was striding around saying: 'Call Hutton, call Compton and tell them to learn from Fazal how to play cricket.' Outside the crowd shouted, 'Nara-e-Hyderi!', 'Pakistan Zindabad!' and 'We want Fazal!' Fazal went out onto the balcony to meet the calls from the crowd. When he found himself standing where Len Hutton had stood a year earlier, tears rolled from his eyes, and a shiver went up his spine.[43] After the tour ended, sixteen cricketers made the sea journey back to Karachi. But Fazal (so his team-mates would say) never again left The Oval.

---

*Interview with Yawar Saeed. According to Yawar Saeed, Kardar again displayed vindictive behaviour when the Pakistan team travelled to Somerset, for whom Yawar was playing. 'I went to receive the team,' recalls Saeed, 'but they never spoke to me.' He says the players had been instructed not to by Kardar.

INDIA IN PAKISTAN 1954-55

'If every cricket match between India and Pakistan can be played without a ring of machine guns and troops to keep the onlookers from rioting, then I feel the prestige attaching to the game is great.'

– WALTER HAMMOND[1]

Very few Test series have been expected so eagerly as the India tour of Pakistan which followed The Oval Test victory of 1954 – and few have disappointed so much. The Test series brought out the worst in Kardar. The Pakistan captain became overbearing and unpleasant off the field, and ultra-defensive on it. The Indian captain, Vinoo Mankad, responded with some of the same negative tactics.

The scoring rate rarely exceeded two runs per over, on a number of occasions plunging well below that. At the end of the five-match series the scoreline remained 0–0, the first time in history that such a thing had ever happened. This highly unusual result was to be repeated, however, the next occasion that Pakistan and India met, in 1960. After the fourth drawn Test in Peshawar in 1954–55, the *Ambala Tribune* published a match report entitled 'Match Saved But Cricket Killed.'[2] The writer commented: 'The trouble is that there is more than cricket at stake in these four-day Tests. Neither side can allow the other to win.' Yet the crowds flocked in throughout, and indeed there was a poignant contrast between the public goodwill felt for both teams and the morbid spirit in which the matches were played by the players themselves.

The first Test, the first ever on Pakistan home soil, was played at Dacca, the capital of East Pakistan, in a stadium that had been erected in just seven weeks. Kardar won the toss and elected to bat. When Vinoo Mankad led his team onto the field, he was met with an ecstatic reception by the packed crowd.

Although slow, the play was dense with meaning. Pakistan were all out for 257 halfway through the second day. India then collapsed for 148. Pakistan had the opportunity to use their very substantial first innings lead to create a winning position. But Kardar's team did not attempt this. Some 73 overs were bowled in the remainder of the third day, off which Pakistan scored 97 runs for the loss of one wicket. The following morning, however, everything changed. The moment Mankad brought on his leg-spinner Subhash Gupte, Pakistan's batsmen were all at sea. Gupte took five wickets in six overs, while Pakistan lost their last nine wickets for 42 runs. India needed just 267 runs to win, with almost a full day left. But this time it was India who played safe. At the end of the day, the score stood at 147 for 2 and the Test match was drawn, just 710 runs having been scored across the four days.

So much for on the field of play. Off the field, Kardar made what appears to have been an unforgiveable speech. The most damning reports have come from Indian sources, which have the ring of the truth, and there is some supporting Pakistani testimony as well. The fullest account is an article written some twenty years later by the Indian commentator Berry Sarbadhikary, headlined: 'When Kardar Nearly Ruined A Test Series.'[3] According to Sarbadhikary, the Pakistan captain made a speech at a reception during which he contrasted the Pakistan performance in that summer's series against England with India's collapse against English pace in 1952, when notoriously the top order Indian batting had been unable to cope with Fred Trueman. Sarbadhikary added Kardar's 'malignant stress on the word "Indians" could be matched for its venom only by the women news-readers from Radio Peking at the height of the 1962 Chinese aggression.' He claimed that Vinoo Mankad grew furious as he listened: 'Suddenly we saw the rival captains, Kardar and Mankad at a secluded corner of the vast Banquet Hall involved in an angry exchange of words and almost on the point of a scuffle.'

The existence of bad blood is confirmed in the account by the Pakistan Test player Shuja-ud-Din, who played in all the Tests. He recorded:

> Those were the days when memories of holocaust during the Partition in 1947 were still lingering in the minds on both sides of the border. That proved the central reason behind these encounters going beyond the traditional cricket rivalries and hence the atmosphere between the players also remained tense and strained. And it was not a great surprise when very few opportunities arose during India's 16-week tour for players from both sides to inter-mix on a social level.[4]

No version of this speech was reported at the time by a Pakistan and Indian press corps probably under some kind of official guidance to encourage a public mood of goodwill in what was still a very sensitive situation, with fears that the cricket could stimulate a return to communal disorder.

The second Test was played in the Dring stadium at Bahawalpur, the first and last Test match to be staged there. India scraped their way to 235, as Fazal bowled a mammoth 62-over spell in which he conceded 86 runs and took four wickets. Hanif Mohammad scored 142, out of Pakistan's reply of 312 for 9 declared, the boy prodigy's first Test century. But he took 468 minutes (not far under eight hours) to reach this objective, thus killing the match.[5] Umrigar, India's opening bowler, sent down 59 overs in Pakistan's innings, taking six wickets for 74. India plodded to 209 for 5 in their second innings by the close.

Notwithstanding the dullness of the first two Tests, the crowds flocked to the Bagh-e-Jinnah ground in Lahore for the third. Many thousands of spectators crossed the border just to see the match, the first time that the great majority of them would have made such a journey since Partition seven and a half years previously. The border was opened for thousands of Indian visitors and the normal stifling bureaucracy which attaches to visas was dropped. Two special trains went across the border each day, and permits for motor vehicles were handed out. Pakistanis invited Indians into their homes, while rooms in schools and hostels were set aside for Indian visitors.[6] The *Tribune*, a largely Hindu paper which had been based in Lahore pre-Partition before seeking refuge in Ambala, 'was surprised to see the Mall Road and Anarkali Bazaar crowded with Indians and Pakistanis greeting each other with embraces, some with tears in their eye, reviving all memories of their days together.' According to the *Tribune*, many Indians sought to visit the homes they had left in such a hurry amid the chaos of August 1947: 'Unlike some previous attempts after the Partition, this time the present occupants of Indian evacuee buildings welcomed visitors and entertained them to tea or meals.' For one returnee, it was all too much:

> One blind man visited his house in the walled city and wept bitterly when he touched the doors and walls of his former residence. He was pacified by occupants and was afforded shelter and meals there and was offered to be resettled if he preferred to live in Lahore but the laws of the two countries stood in his way and he returned in dismay.[7]

Once again, however, the cricket was petrifyingly dull. There was never much chance of a result after Pakistan laboured to 328, scored off 187 overs (Gupte bowled 73 of them, with 33 maidens, conceding 133 runs while taking five wickets). The Pakistan selectors chose the off-spinner Miran Bakhsh at the age of 47 years and 284 days, making him the second-oldest player to make his Test match debut.* The elderly Bakhsh bowled tidily enough, conceding 82 runs in 48 overs, and taking two wickets. He played in the following match but was allowed only ten overs without taking a wicket, and that was the end of his Test career. The highlight of this Test was 99 by 'Merry Max' Maqsood Ahmed. He was the first Pakistani to succumb at this score in a Test, and the mode of dismissal (stumped off the leg-spinner Gupte) was characteristic. The news was too much for one fan listening to Omar Kureishi's radio commentary in English: the poor man died of a heart attack.[8]

The fourth Test, played at Peshawar, was the most funereal of the lot. After Kardar won the toss and chose to bat, his team proceeded to the total of 188, scored off 146.3 overs. Once again, the Pakistan batsmen were

---

*James Southerton (49 years and 119 days) holds this record for England in the first-ever Test match against Australia in 1876–77. Miran Bakhsh learnt his cricket at Rawalpindi, where he learnt his trade by bowling in the nets to English batsmen in pre-Partition days. His father was the chief groundsman at the Pindi Club Ground, where Bux spent many hours helping his father in the preparation of wickets and ground maintenance while perfecting the spin bowler's art. After retiring as a player at the age of 51, Miran Bakhsh took on his father's role as groundsman at the Pindi Club, which he combined with coaching duties. At the age of 84 Miran Bakhsh, the oldest cricketer to make his Test debut in the twentieth century, died during his morning walk.

greatly troubled by the bowling of Gupte, who took five wickets for 63 in 41.3 overs. The leading Indian batsman Umrigar then took the match by the scruff of the neck to give his side the chance of a significant lead, but Kardar resorted to the negative tactics he had condemned at the start of the tour. He ordered his fast bowlers to bowl wide outside leg stump, with eight fielders on the leg side. As Shuja-ud-Din, who played in this poignant contest, recorded: 'This was simply not cricket, but it did not matter as long as you did not lose.'[9]

Pakistan collapsed to 70 for 4, including 21 from Hanif Mohammad, assembled in 195 minutes at the crease. 'The air was quite electric; the situation so crucial; the agony immense,' recorded the journalist Qamaruddin Butt.[10] Mercifully for Pakistan, Imtiaz Ahmed now played one of his finest innings. Kardar ordered Imtiaz to play safe. Instead he strode to the wicket and laid into the bowling.[11] Even so, India only needed 126 to win, with an hour remaining, after Pakistan were dismissed. To a modern team, the prospect of knocking off these runs would have been irresistible. Yet so entrenched was defensive thinking that Vinoo Mankad's team made no effort to do so. India faced nineteen overs during this final stage of the Peshawar Test, during which they took their score to 23. Now only the Karachi Test match remained. In an audacious move, Pakistan offered to play the match out to a finish regardless of time. But India refused.[12]

THE SPECIAL PATHOLOGY OF
INDIA v PAKISTAN CRICKET

It was becoming evident that Tests between Pakistan and India had developed a unique sensibility. Those who were normal became slightly mad. Those who were already troubled were temporarily blinded with a kind of insanity.

These Test matches were burdened with a weight of history, meaning and consequence which they could not sustain and beneath the pressure of which they buckled. No cricketing contests, not even the Ashes rivalry between England and Australia, have ever carried as much gravity. At some level, the knowledge of the events of 1947 surely persisted, and not just as a memory.

The conflict between the two countries has never ceased. Neither

Pakistan nor India has yet been able to deal with the past in such a way that it no longer presents an obstacle to the future. By the time the 1952 Test series took place, there had already been one war between India and Pakistan over Kashmir. Both the 1952–53 and 1954–55 Test series took place against the background of threats and sabre-rattling speeches by political leaders. Already Indian and Pakistani soldiers faced each other across the Kashmir heights. India–Pakistan Test matches must always be seen, therefore, in the context of past and future wars. This also helps to explain the contradiction between the humourless, unforgiving cricket played out in the middle, and the joyful attitude of the crowds. While the cricketers were paralysed by history, the humanity of the spectators demonstrated the belief among Sikh, Muslim and Hindu alike that cricket could somehow show the way to reconciliation and the end of hatred and war.

THE HUMILIATION OF
A PAKISTANI UMPIRE

Another chota peg boys
Let's have a go at Baig, boys
Goddam this steamy heat, chaps,
The climate of Peshawar
D'you think Baig's too hot, boys
He put us on the spot, boys,
He'd appreciate a shower,
In this stinking hot Peshawar,
Let's go and hunt for Baig, boys
A double berry peg, boys[1]

– ALAN ROSS, 11 MARCH 1956

Cricket against the MCC presented a different kind of problem. That winter's England tour of Pakistan, during which a Pakistan umpire was abducted by members of the England cricket team, anticipated many of the obstacles and misunderstandings which have continued to damage Anglo-Pakistani relations, on and off the cricket field, ever since.

Unusually, Pakistan faced two touring teams in the winter of 1955–56. The first tourists, from New Zealand, hailed from a country which has always been welcomed in Pakistan. This three-Test series, won 2–0 by the home side, showed that Pakistan were capable of playing beautiful and fluent cricket. The contrast with the rancorous and damaging series that started just six weeks later, against a touring party sent over by the MCC, is striking.

The full story of this MCC tour has never been told before. But now that the MCC records – five volumes of them in the Lord's library – have at last become available, it is possible to reveal exactly who did what to whom, name with certainty those involved, to set out their role, clear the innocent, and to describe the private agony of MCC officials as they attempted to save the tour from cancellation.[2]

The MCC's first mistake was to dispatch an 'A' team to Pakistan that winter, signalling that England considered that Pakistan only merited a second XI.* Yet only four years earlier, in 1951–52, India had been granted a full-scale tour with five Tests. In the light of the great triumph at The Oval in 1954, Pakistan felt that they deserved similar treatment. MCC disagreed.

The England captain, DB Carr, was quoted as stating on arrival in Pakistan that, 'I will not touch the shores of England until I avenge The Oval defeat.'[3] A public school and Oxford man, Carr reflected the apparently uncomplicated social and political outlook of post-war Britain. His opponent, Abdul Hafeez Kardar, another Oxford man, was a manifestation of the pride and moral earnestness of Jinnah's Pakistan. Few had realised up to this point that these two sets of values were in such sharp conflict.

The first serious fixture was a four-day match, at Karachi, against the Governor General's XI, which included ten out of the eleven Pakistan cricketers who had defeated England at The Oval. This was a tight contest in which neither side reached a total of more than 200. Tony Lock bowled MCC to victory. Practically unplayable on the matting, he delivered 78 overs in the match, including 50 maidens, recording the memorable match figures of 78-50-88-11.† At one point, Lock sent down seventeen consecutive maiden overs.‡

---

*The decision to send out an MCC 'A' team instead was explained in the carefully written *Wisden* match report: 'In order that some of the countries who seldom receive visits of full-strength sides from England should be able to keep interest alive in the intervening years, "A" tours were originated. To England it gave the opportunity of trying promising young cricketers and also of rewarding players for long and valuable service in county cricket.' *Wisden 1957*, p.791.

†Lock was the most successful bowler on the tour, recording figures of 557-296-869-81. His bowling average was 10.72, and he conceded well under two runs per over. It should be noted that Lock's quicker ball was almost certainly illegal, although rarely called.

‡Lock's seventeen consecutive maiden overs was bettered eight years later in the Test match between England and India at Madras, January 1964. In England's first innings RG 'Bapu' Nadkarni bowled

However, the bad feeling that dogged the tour began at a formal dinner following the match. In an attempt at humour, Donald Carr referred back to the period when he had played alongside Kardar for Oxford University. Back then, Carr disclosed, Kardar had been known as the 'mystic from the east.' There is no evidence that Kardar, who had a keen sense of his own dignity, had taken warmly to this kind of labelling even at Oxford. Seven years on, no longer as an undergraduate and installed after much effort and some fierce battles as the captain of the Pakistan cricket team, he was even less appreciative. It was therefore insensitive of Carr to use this epithet and stupid to develop the theme, saying that Kardar was also regarded at times as the 'mistake from the east', a remark which was reported in the local press.[4] Carr saw it as a 'harmless joke between old team-mates',[5] while Kardar took it as a serious insult. Had the situation been reversed, and Kardar openly mocked an England captain during a tour of England at a public dinner, it might not have gone down well either.

The MCC then went up-country, playing games against the Pir of Pagaro's XI at Hyderabad* and the Amir of Bahawalpur's XI at Bahawalpur, and forgot about the joke. Kardar, however, did not. He cut Carr dead when the two next met in the dining room of Faletti's Hotel in Lahore, where both teams were staying, on the eve of the first unofficial Test. When Carr asked Kardar for an explanation while walking out for the toss the following day, the Pakistan captain complained about 'that speech you made in Karachi. I've never heard anything so disgusting in my life.' Carr made no attempt to apologise: 'Well, if you want to take it that way, you'll have to take it that way.'[6]

Carr's team, like many England sides to follow, was locked into too narrow a set of social and moral parameters to be able to fully respond to Pakistan. They did not relish the warm local hospitality, and were churlish when local fans tried to garland them at railway stations.[7] Brian Close, in his autobiography, summed up the attitude of the MCC players to Pakistani hospitality: 'They showed us their new dams and their monuments to local heroes like Jinnah and Liaquat Ali Khan. They took us hunting. But their

---

21.5 overs (131 balls) without a run being scored. His final analysis was 32-27-5-0. FJ Titmus and JM Parks played in both matches. Forty years later, when I met him at a reception, Nadkarni was still angry that his sequence was ended by a misfield.

*The Pir had formed this team in 1953. Players were paid 'talent money' and, said the Pir, the purpose was to encourage young talent.

hotels were not yet up to western standards and the food was strange in the extreme to most of us.'[8]

This was the background to the first 'Test match' between MCC and Pakistan. Some 30,000 spectators crammed into the Bagh-e-Jinnah ground in Lahore, but, with the two sides scarcely on speaking terms, the cricket they witnessed was fractious and dreary. The MCC team might not have been a Test side, but it included some of the stars of the coming decade of Test cricket in Brian Close, Ken Barrington, Fred Titmus and Tony Lock. Batting first, the MCC took nearly 130 overs to crawl to 200. Fazal Mahmood bowled 46 overs for 55 runs, taking three wickets. Yet the Pakistanis were even slower. According to Shuja-ud-Din, who was playing in the Lahore match: 'In order to thwart Tony Lock's effectiveness, skipper AH Kardar had instructed his batsmen to dampen off the spinner's confidence by simply shutting up against him.'[9] Lock's bowling analysis tells its own story. In 77 overs, of which 44 were maidens, he gave away 99 runs. Crucially, he took only three wickets.

The *Wisden* analysis calls what followed 'one of the most boring days in the history of cricket.' Hanif Mohammad took 525 minutes to record his century, breaking his own recent record for the slowest Test hundred.* Eventually Hanif was dismissed for 142, compiled over ten and a half hours, out of a team total of 264 at the time of his dismissal. 'This seems to be tedious going,' Hanif later acknowledged, going on to make an important statement about his overall philosophy and approach:

> ... but the circumstances demanded that I curb my stroke-play and stay at the wicket, as my captain Kardar had instructed, because he wanted me to blunt Lock's spin and stall the effectiveness of his marauding spell during the tour.
>
> This seemed to be the beginning of a pattern, wherein I was entrusted with the task of keeping one end intact, stone-walling all types of attack, and despite possessing all the shots in the book, I was able to display my mastery over just the defensive ones. Anyhow, that is what my country required from me, and as far as I was concerned, that was always the first priority.[10]

---

*Hanif's 525-minute century was 'bettered' only a few years later by Jackie McGlew's 545-minute effort against Australia in 1957–58. The record was seized back by another Pakistani opener, Mudassar Nazar, with a 557-minute century against England, in front of another delighted Lahore crowd, in 1977–78.

A very rare photograph of Fazal Mahmood's father Ghulam Hussain (seated, middle row, second from left). Jahangir Khan is standing fourth from left. Islamia College, where Ghulam Hussain was vice-principal, was a major nursery of Pakistan cricket.

British soldiers playing cricket at Kohat near Peshawar on the North-West Frontier. This remarkable photograph was taken in the early 1860s.

The Burkis of Jullundur; the greatest sporting clan of all time.

Jahangir Khan (father of Majid and uncle to Imran Khan and Javed Burki) shakes hands with King George V, India v England, Lord's 1932.

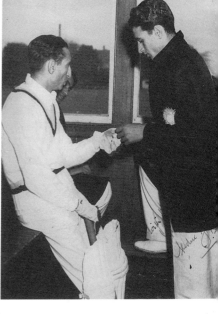

Emperor and retainer. Kardar helps Pataudi put on his batting gloves, Worcester 1946.

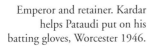

Imtiaz Ahmed and Maqsood Ahmed going out to bat during the unofficial 1951 Karachi Test match between Pakistan and the MCC.

Prime Minister Nazimuddin meets Pakistan cricket stars Fazal, Imtiaz and Nazar at the state dinner to commemorate the 1951 victory over the MCC which secured Pakistan Test status. Fazal is present on the personal orders of Nazimuddin.

Many great figures of Pakistan cricket are in this picture at the Lahore Gymkhana. Fida Hassan is speaking. Justice Cornelius is leaning forward on his right. The two boys behind are Majid Khan and his brother Asad, a future Oxford blue. On the left is Agha Ahmed Raza Khan, while at the front is Dr Jahangir Khan.

Mian Saeed, Pakistan's first captain, right, with West Indies counterpart John Goddard during the Lahore 'Test' of 1948.

Ameer Bee, cricket's greatest matriarch, with her own sporting trophies. Four of her sons, Wazir, Hanif, Mushtaq and Sadiq, played Test cricket, and the fifth, Raees, was unlucky to miss selection.

A unique photograph. Three sisters and mothers of three Pakistan cricket captains. From left to right: Shaukat Khanum (Imran Khan's mother), Iqbal Bano (Javed Burki's mother, seated), Naima (Majid Khan's mother). They are with their brother Agha Ahmed Raza Khan.

Pakistan take their first ever Test wicket. India's Pankaj Roy bowled by Khan Mohammad at New Delhi, 16 October 1952. Hanif is the wicketkeeper, Kardar is at silly mid-off.

The Pakistan cricket team for the 1954 tour of England, captained by Abdul Hafeez Kardar. Back row (left to right): Wazir Mohammad, Khalid Hasan, Shuja-ud-din Butt, Shakoor Ahmed, Zulfiqar Ahmed. Middle row: Khalid Wazir, Mohammad Aslam, Ikram Elahi, Mahmood Hussain, Waqar Hasan, Alimuddin, Hanif Mohammad. Front row: Ebbu Ghazali, Fazal Mahmood, Abdul Hafeez Kardar (captain), Imtiaz Ahmed and Maqsood Ahmed.

'At half past three this well-built and powerful man, whose every step both running up to bowl and walking back is charged with energy, was bowling as strongly as he had been doing at eleven in the morning' – CLR James reporting on Fazal Mahmood leading the Pakistan attack at Worcester, 1954.

Fazal Mahmood and his Pakistan side leave the field after their historic victory against England at The Oval in 1954.

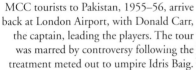

Shuja-ud-Din (a future army colonel and historian of Pakistan cricket), right, going out with Alimuddin to open Pakistan's second innings in the third Test at Lahore against India, 1955.

MCC tourists to Pakistan, 1955–56, arrive back at London Airport, with Donald Carr, the captain, leading the players. The tour was marred by controversy following the treatment meted out to umpire Idris Baig.

Two men in overcoats.
Kardar and Len Hutton.

Justice Cornelius, presenting a prize
to the Probables of Pakistan Women's
Cricket Team at the Gaddafi stadium in
the 1970s.

President Iskander Mirza watching
Pakistan defeat Australia in October
1956 (Fazal took 13 wickets). Mirza
(grey double-breasted suit) is sitting
next to his prime minister, Huseyn
Suhrawardy. Both men would die in
exile.

President Eisenhower and President
Ayub Khan enjoying a day's cricket
at the Karachi Test against Australia,
1959. Only 104 runs were scored on the
second-slowest day's play in Test history.

Saeed Ahmed rehearses his legendary cover drive in India, 1960–61.

Height of fashion: Majid Khan, Abdul Qadir and Imran Khan.

Brigadier 'Gussy' Haider towering over the 1962 Pakistan touring team. It returned home in disgrace after a series of humiliating defeats. Those standing, from left to right: Javed Akhtar, Munir Malik, Imtiaz Ahmed, captain Javed Burki, the Baggage Master, Brigadier Haider, Fazal Mahmood, Alimuddin, Mushtaq Mohammad and Nasim-ul Ghani. Crouching down at the front, from left to right: Wallis Mathias, Afaq Hussain, Asif Ahmed and Intikhab Alam.

Waqar, who had scored so freely against New Zealand, hit a four off his first ball, but did not get another run for 50 minutes, in total spending six-and-a-half hours reaching 62. At one point Lock bowled ten consecutive maidens, each one watched with fascinated concentration by an entranced crowd.[11] The match was drawn,[12] but Pakistan then won their second 'Test match' at Dacca by an innings and ten runs, against MCC batsmen unable to cope with Fazal Mahmood and Khan Mohammad, who took all twenty wickets, eight to Fazal and twelve to Khan.

Both teams now moved to Peshawar with the series still wide open. Pakistan were one–nil up, with two matches to play. MCC struggled to 188 in the first innings, unable to cope with the slow left-arm spin of Kardar, then in the best bowling form of his international career, who took six wickets for 40. But England still felt sore about the umpiring. Idris Baig stood at the end from which Kardar was bowling. He upheld three lbw appeals, each of which England regarded as unfair.[13] In the last minutes of the day, the sense of injustice increased when a Lock delivery struck the pads of the Pakistani opener Alimuddin, with the batsman pinned well back in front of his stumps. According to Brian Chapman in the *Daily Mirror*: 'The English "howzat" echoed down the rocky defiles of the Khyber Pass. But Idris preserved an aloof calm in the face of one of the most explosive appeals that has ever assaulted an umpire's eardrums.'[14]

But all was not yet lost. Brilliant bowling by Lock (33-23-44-5) enabled MCC to bowl out Pakistan for 152, a lead of 36. MCC then collapsed again to Kardar (31-22-26-5), and were all out for 111, setting Pakistan 148 to win. This turned out to be not nearly enough. Hanif and Alimuddin put on 67 for the opening partnership and by the close of the third day Pakistan needed only eight more runs, with only two wickets lost.

When play ended the England party took the short journey back from the cricket ground to Dean's, a hotel which would provide a base for western correspondents covering the Soviet invasion of Afghanistan some thirty years later.[15] The hotel has since been pulled down and converted into a shopping plaza.

The players took afternoon tea on the lawn, then returned to their rooms to change ahead of the Peshawar Cricket Association Dinner, where they were to be the guests of honour. This occasion, conveniently held at Dean's, was dry, meaning that those who wanted a drink needed to quench their

thirst beforehand. From about 6.45pm onwards several of the MCC players, wearing dinner jackets, gathered in the room belonging to Yorkshire's
Billy Sutcliffe, vice-captain, and the son of the great England batsman
Herbert Sutcliffe.* Spirits were high, and the plan to drench Idris Baig with
water was conceived over glasses of beer in Sutcliffe's room.[16]

This scheme needs to be placed in context. The touring MCC cricketers
had found time weighing heavy on their hands in between matches. They
had started giving one another what they called the 'water treatment'.
Sometimes they used water pistols, more often buckets of water. This sounds
juvenile today but back then was the 1950s, era of the student 'rag' and a
more innocent age.

Why was Baig their special target? It was not simply that MCC disliked his
umpiring decisions. Mirza Idris Baig was the type of umpire who liked to project himself into the centre of the action on the field. Once he was umpiring
in a match played in a Karachi public park when a bystander, who later turned
out to be a Pashtun from the tribal areas, walked across the pitch. Baig ordered
the Pashtun off the field, at which point the passer-by opened his jacket, took
out a knife, and pursued the terrified umpire round the outfield, in an episode
out of a Charlie Chaplin movie. Baig once told Geoffrey Howard 'you must
understand ... that a lot of the crowd come to watch me umpire.'[17]

During their stay in a Dacca hotel three weeks earlier, Idris Baig had
chanced to pass by while one of the water games was in full flow. He was told:
'You will get the water treatment one day.'[18] From then on, the thought of
soaking Baig lingered in the minds of the MCC players. Even leaving aside
what the MCC players regarded as his biased umpiring, there was something
uniquely provocative about his demeanour. As the cricketers drank beer in
Billy Sutcliffe's room, they worried that if Baig did not stand as umpire in the
final match at Karachi, they would never see him again.[19] Now was, possibly,
their last chance. The MCC players had no thought at this stage of kidnap-
ping the Pakistani umpire. They simply hoped to invite Baig to Sutcliffe's
room after the dinner 'for a friendly drink and a chat' and soak him there and
then. In preparation for this immersion, says Brian Close, 'two huge cauldron
like vessels were filled with water and placed high in the ceiling.'[20]

---

*Sutcliffe captained Yorkshire as an amateur for two years in 1956 and 1957. His second name was
Hobbs, in honour of the great Surrey batsman Jack Hobbs, with whom Sutcliffe's father Herbert joined
forces to form a famous opening pair for England between 1924 and 1930.

But when the invitation was extended at the end of the dinner, Baig declined, saying that he preferred to go back to his hotel. This forced a change of plan. At a council of war it was resolved to send a delegation of MCC players to seize Baig. Some seven team members travelled by tonga up to the Services hotel, adjacent to the cricket ground where both Idris Baig and the Pakistan team were staying.[21]

Donald Carr, the England captain, was the leader of this expeditionary force, which was made up of his vice-captain Billy Sutcliffe, Brian Close, Harold Stephenson, Ken Barrington and Roy Swetman.[*] Barrington and Swetman had both been given out lbw by Baig in the first innings. The England cricketers, who wore masks, sought out the umpire, who was still wearing his dinner jacket, and gagged him. According to one witness, the England players 'literally carried' Baig back downstairs, out into the street. Baig was taken in a tonga driven by an England player, legs dangling on the roadside, to Dean's hotel.[22]

The journey between the Services hotel and Dean's was not far – fifteen minutes on foot and perhaps five by tonga. Once at Dean's, Brian Close suggests that Baig tried to escape. 'Suddenly he made a bolt for it, pursued by our skipper Donald Carr and myself. The skipper it was who flattened Idris with a flying rugby tackle in the gardens.'[23] Although certainly a vivid description, this must be dismissed as false. No attempted escape is mentioned by any other account of the night, and Donald Carr has emphatically denied to me that he tackled the umpire.

Upon arrival, Baig was taken to Billy Sutcliffe's room,[†] the scene of the earlier drinks, and made to sit down in a chair under the skylight where the buckets of water awaited. By now, at least half of the MCC touring party had gathered.

In his autobiography, Ken Barrington clears two players of any involvement: Tony Lock, who was asleep in bed, and Maurice Tompkin, perhaps suffering

---

[*]The MCC obscured the names of the assault party at the time, but Donald Carr named them when he met the Lord's committee in a private session. According to the minutes of the meeting, Gubby Allen asked Carr, 'Who was implicated?' Carr replied, 'Those who went to fetch Idris Baig from his hotel were myself, Sutcliffe, Close, Swetman, Stephenson and Barrington.' Minutes of meeting held at Lord's, 17 March 1956, at 12.15pm. MCC Library Archive, MCC/CRI/5/1/62 (2 of 2).

[†]The host for the Baig water treatment was not named at the time. But a written statement delivered by Howard to Cheema on 28 February makes clear it was Billy Sutcliffe: 'They decided to ask Idris Beg [sic] to have a drink with them in one of the rooms – Sutcliffe's – and give him some ragging which they rather foolishly assumed that he would not take amiss.' G. Howard to Group Captain Cheema, 26 February 1956, MCC Library Archive, MCC/CRI/5/1/63.

from the onset of the illness that would kill him at the age of thirty-seven less than a year later.[24] A telegram sent by Geoffrey Howard to Ronnie Aird on 5 March provides further clues. It reads: 'Except Peter Hants, Tony, A Moss, Alan Welsh, Fred and Ian STOP Rest involved greater or lesser degree STOP Weather much improved now signs indicate today calm ahead.'

It can be deduced from this deliberately cryptic cable that Peter Sainsbury (a Hampshire player), Tony Lock, Alan Moss, Allan Watkins (Glamorgan), Fred Titmus and Ian Thomson (the Sussex fast-bowler who flew out as replacement for the injured Mike Cowan), among the fifteen-strong touring party, were innocent. If Tompkin is also exonerated, on the basis of Barrington's testimony, that leaves eight guilty men: Carr (captain), Sutcliffe (vice-captain), Richardson, Close, Swetman, Stephenson, Parks, Barrington.

Here Donald Carr, the England captain, can take up the story as the key eye-witness and participant:

> . . . we invited him to sit in a certain chair, so that Closey and Swetman could go round the back and hide behind the wall. 'Idris, would you like a drink?' I said. 'No,' he said. 'I do not drink.'
>
> There were two holes in the wall, and they each had a bucket. 'I will have nothing but water.' So I said, 'Well, here it comes.' And I must say, it was a marvellous bit of shooting. It plummeted down right on top of him, and he spluttered away.[25]

According to Carr, this 'was considered terribly funny by everyone who was there.'[26] Carr also claims that Idris Baig soon recovered from his shock and started to 'see the funny side of things.'[27]

The umpire's abduction had been witnessed by at least one member of the Pakistan team, and reports were now spreading.[28] A search party, which included Khan Mohammad, arrived at Dean's hotel, and burst into Sutcliffe's room.* Whether or not Baig was, as Carr later claimed in his defence, beginning to get the joke became irrelevant. The Pakistan players had witnessed

---

*Lock, *For Surrey and England*, p.119. Lock states that 'just at that moment, however, the Pakistan players Khan Mohammad, Shuja and Mahmood Hussain, looked into the room. On seeing Baig, they started to laugh. That did it . . . His own people had seen his dignity lowered.' Khan Mohammad and Shuja were playing in the Peshawar match, but not Mahmood Hussain, who did play in the following game at Karachi. His presence is therefore slightly mysterious. Probably he was twelfth man. Conceivably Lock was referring to Mohammad Hussain, Pakistan's manager.

Baig's humiliation and had 'roared in laughter at him.'[29] Baig stormed out of Dean's hotel in search of Group Captain Cheema, secretary of the BCCP.

He tracked Cheema down to the Air Force Officers' Mess, where he was drinking with Kardar as well as Jamsheed Marker* and Omar Kureishi,† Pakistan's two most famous radio commentators of the era. Cheema and Kardar went out to meet Baig, who looked 'greatly disturbed and agitated', listened to his story, then set off at once to Dean's hotel.[30] The Pakistan team manager Mohammad Hussain‡ accompanied them, as did the two radio commentators and a number of Air Force officers who had also been at the mess bar.

At Dean's the MCC players were having a party. Here Kardar takes up the story:

> Group Captain Cheema told me to bring Carr to him because he wanted to talk to him. Since I had known Carr in the University days at Oxford I went into the room and addressing Carr said: 'Donald come out with me I want to talk to you.' Donald Carr sharply replied: 'What about, talk to me here.' As we came out I told him: 'It is about something that concerns you, and you know you are in trouble. You had better talk to us about it.' Even then Donald Carr did not quite realise the gravity of the situation and held out the snobbish reply, 'Talk to my manager.' Cheema said: 'Yes, we will talk to the Manager also but you had better be there because you are the Captain of the team and implicated in the incident.'[31]

There followed a private meeting in Geoffrey Howard's hotel room; Howard, Carr and Sutcliffe representing MCC and Cheema, Kardar, Fazal and Mohammad Hussain for Pakistan. Carr and Sutcliffe for a time sustained the argument that nothing had gone so very wrong, adding that Idris Baig had enjoyed his ragging. Cheema, by contrast, maintained that 'when the MCC team kidnapped Idris Baig, gagged him and later maltreated him they had

---

*One of Pakistan's earliest and most memorable cricket commentators, later to have a distinguished diplomatic career, culminating as Pakistan's Ambassador to the United States.

†Later to become editor, well-known author and newspaper columnist.

‡Mir Mohammad Hussain, full back in the legendary Indian hockey team, which won the gold medal in the 1936 Berlin Olympics, beating Hitler's Germany 8–1 in the final. After Partition Hussain managed Pakistan's inaugural tour of India in 1952–53, and served as assistant manager during the 1964–65 tour to Australia and New Zealand. A useful cricketer, he made his first-class debut for Sindh against Bahawalpur in the first Quaid-e-Azam Trophy match in the 1953–54 season. Hussain cuts an invisible figure during the Idris Baig affair, with the running being made by Cheema and Kardar.

violated not only the code of decency but also they had violated the basic tradition of cricket, that is, to respect an umpire.'[32] When Idris Baig was called
in to give his story, he added to the confusion by threatening to sue the MCC
players 'for injury to his person.' By now it was past midnight.

Cheema lost patience and threatened the MCC: 'Chaps, I do not think
you realise what you have done, because in the face of the statement given
by Idris Beg [sic] you have kept on repeating that you have done nothing
wrong. Since you have shown that you are unwilling to acknowledge your
grave mistake, I suggest you pack up and go home.'[33] Geoffrey Howard
replied: 'You cannot do this to us.' But Cheema's reply was lethal: 'We can
invite you but when you misbehave by molesting an officer of the Board of
Control for Cricket in Pakistan we can send you back.' Carr at last agreed
to write letters of apology both to Umpire Baig and to the Board of Control
for Cricket in Pakistan. Carr's letter to the BCCP, dated 26 February and
written immediately after the meeting in Howard's room, explained:

> Some members of the MCC team including myself, after a somewhat
> hilarious party in our hotel, thought it would be amusing to offer Mr
> Idris Baig some slightly unusual hospitality. This was meant in the form
> of a 'rag' but most unfortunately the whole matter misfired in that he was
> manhandled to some extent and was unable to appreciate the spirit in
> which the whole matter was intended.[34]

When Howard and Kardar finally left their meeting, at around 3am, they
found the press waiting outside. Three British journalists were in Peshawar
covering the match: Crawford White of the *News Chronicle*,* Brian
Chapman of the *Daily Mirror* and Ron Roberts of the *Daily Telegraph*.† One
Pakistani journalist, Omar Kureishi, was also present.

What followed cannot really be called a press conference, rather an informal discussion between the press and the tour management about how the

---

*Cricket writer for the *News Chronicle*, *Daily Mail* and *Daily Express*, where he ghosted Denis Compton's
column. A fine cricketer who played for Lancashire 2nd XI, bowling right-arm fast, then an intelligence
officer in wartime bomber command before taking up cricket journalism.
†Ron Roberts, pro-establishment *Daily Telegraph* cricket writer who later found his vocation managing
international cricket tours. It was his International World Tour of 1962 which gave Basil D'Oliveira,
then an almost unknown Lancashire league professional, his first chance to play first-class cricket. Roberts
died tragically young of a brain tumour, aged thirty-nine.

Baig story should be handled. Media coverage of cricket tours was a far more intimate affair than today. There was, furthermore, a convention that off-the-field behaviour was a private matter.

Ron Roberts – who was later accused by the Pakistanis of being one of those who took part in the attack on Baig – advocated that the story should be suppressed.[35] Chapman replied that journalists had a duty to their newspapers. He was supported by Kureishi, who pointed out that 'there had been a lot of people at the hotel and that the story was bound to leak, and it was better that we wrote a controlled version rather than let the other press make up its own story.'[36]

This was sensible. Word that Idris Baig had been kidnapped was spreading quickly in the local, vernacular press. The *Nawa-e-Waqt*, a bestselling paper published in Urdu, reported that 'the terrible incident that took place last night will not only shake the world, rather, will defame the respected game of cricket.'[37] The report added that the England team 'abducted Idris Baig from Services hotel to their hotel and tortured him. It is told that MCC players forced him to drink whisky, which Idris Baig has been avoiding all his life; then water was thrown at him.'[38] In the days that followed, reports on other incidents of MCC misbehaviour, ignored up to that point, came to light. *Time Magazine*'s report the following week, entitled 'Just Banter, Old Boy', referred to some of them:

> Exporting British culture as energetically as Britons ever did in the playing days of Empire, cricketers for the staid old Marylebone Cricket Club began their tour of Pakistan this winter by roughing up some hotel servants in Karachi. 'A bit of tomfoolery,' said the diplomatic hotel manager. Then the ambassadors of goodwill moved to Dacca, where they squirted soda water over the hotel guests. Polite Pakistan laughed it all off as mere youthful enthusiasm. Last week the Pakistanis stopped laughing.*

---

*'Just Banter, Old Boy', *Time Magazine*, 12 March 1956, in Lord's Library Archive, MCC/CRI/5/1/62. This article prompted a letter to the MCC from RH Hadow, the British consul general, reporting concern 'among friendly Americans, particularly several extremely pro-British Rhodes scholars in this district' and demanding an explanation. See also Omar Kureishi's account in *The Times of Karachi*, 3 January 1957: 'There had been a general beating up of some bearers in a Karachi hotel, there had been a water-drenching prank at the Shahbagh hotel in Dacca where the management had threatened to call the police, two of the party, Sutcliffe and Ron Roberts, had run off with a rickshaw in Dacca and wrecked it, one of the touring party had thrown water at a Station Master at lala Moosa. There had been wild tonga races at Lahore and Peshawar.' All of these claims were denied by the MCC.

Geoffrey Howard and the MCC denied all these stories.* But no power on earth could stop them spreading. Pakistan was soon overcome by a national mood of anger towards the British. In Peshawar, the authorities provided the English cricketers with guards. Six armed soldiers accompanied Brian Close and other English cricketers as they played golf.[39]

In Lahore the *Nawa-e-Waqt* recorded that the Baig incident 'raised a fume among the residents of Lahore and the incident was talk of the town the whole day.' A rally was called to demand action against the England cricketers who had 'disrespected and tortured Mr Idris Baig', the protestors carrying slogans saying: 'Go Back MCC' and 'Long Live Pakistan Cricket Team'.[40] The British Deputy High Commission offices went into lockdown, and feared that their offices would be attacked.†

Back in Peshawar, angry students chanted 'Shame! Shame!' when the match began again after the rest day. Once Pakistan had won, crowds gathered outside the ground, shouting 'MCC, go home!' as a police escort hustled the England team to safety.[41] Meanwhile Idris Baig, his arm in a sling, had become a national hero.

From Belmont Park in Kent came a furious letter from Lord Harris, son of the famous Lord Harris who, when Governor of Bombay, was widely (although wrongly) believed to have introduced cricket to the Indian subcontinent. 'What my father would have said I tremble to think,' declared Lord Harris, 'but I have no doubt as to what he would have done, and this is to have ordered them [the MCC team] home forthwith.'‡

---

*DB Carr insisted they were false when tackled by the MCC Committee on return to England. Minutes of meeting held at Lord's, 17 March 1956, at 12.15pm. MCC Library Archive MCC/CRI/5/1/62 (2 of 2).
†DWS Hunt, Deputy High Commissioner to Lahore, to Brian Castor of Surrey CCC. Hunt complained that 'after two years or so of trying to improve relations between the British and the Pakistanis, an incident like this means a tremendous setback. As a matter of fact the day the full story was in the press – the 28th – we were threatened with demonstrations and the police sent eight men to guard us ... By a fortunate fluke it was a day of torrential rain so people did not feel like demonstrating, otherwise, I am afraid, we would have had some windows broken. I may say the British community here are unanimous and very violent in their condemnation. Certainly it will take some time to live down. The team behaved reasonably well while they were here in Lahore, but I have heard stories about Karachi and Dacca which suggested they needed a firmer hand at the helm.' Lord's Library Archive MCC/CRI/5/1/62.
‡Lord Harris to Aird, 28 February 1956, MCC Library Archive, MCC/CRI/5/1/62. Aird wrote back by return of post: 'I think your father would have taken no action about the incident in Pakistan until a full report had been received from the Manager and this is what we are waiting for.' This answer mollified Lord Harris: 'I quite understand the position. Obviously you could not do anything until you had a report from the other side.' For an account of Lord Harris's influence on Indian cricket, see Guha, *A Corner of a Foreign Field*, pp.53–55.

Other letter writers were more forthright still. 'Will this not remain as a stigma on the face of English civilisation and culture?' complained Mirza Sajid Ali Baig from Hyderabad. 'The English reputation of morality, tolerance and sporting spirit built during the last century have all been severely damaged by the handful of semi-cultured players.'[42] Many Pakistanis were infuriated by the MCC line, vigorously promoted by Ron Roberts in the *Daily Telegraph*, that Umpire Baig had been the victim of 'innocent mischief'. A special report in *Nawa-e-Waqt*, filed from London, highlighted this English hypocrisy:

> The newspapers have done wrong by representing the bullying act of MCC as 'ragging'. I don't consider Englishmen as 'sportsmen'. They think high about themselves if they win a match and if they lose, they start fighting, blaming the weather sometimes and sometimes the umpire. They fought with the umpire when they were beaten by Australia. Same was the situation in West Indies.*

This criticism carried more truth than many Englishmen liked to acknowledge. Nevertheless Geoffrey Howard, the tour manager, deserves sympathy. His daily letters back to Ronnie Aird, the MCC secretary, have been preserved. Sent back through the British High Commission diplomatic bag rather than normal mail, they reveal an extreme sense of isolation. Howard's first letter to Aird, written on 1 March, three days after the incident took place, starts: 'I just do not know how to start to write. My brain is reeling and every fresh track I try and along which I seem to make some progress always ends in frustration.'[43] The telephone system hardly worked in Peshawar, and cables were little better. He had practically no idea of the reaction to the story back in London or even in the Pakistan national capital of Karachi. Pakistani officials were hard to track down, and he was dependent on tongas to attend meetings. This meant that although the England team was at the centre of an international storm, events were being dictated from elsewhere.

---

*'Incident of Peshawar Test Match and Britain Press', *Nawa-e-Waqt*, 8 March 1956, p.2. Special report from Majeed Nizami, though the words quoted here are from Mr Noor Illahi Malik. The reference to Australia is mysterious. There were no umpiring controversies on England's Test series of 1954–55 (which England won 3–1) or 1950–51. England were very unhappy with the umpires in 1946–47, particularly when Bradman was given not out after an apparent slip catch in the first Test, but made no public complaint. England did show dissent against local West Indian umpires during their Test series in 1953–54, for which see *Wisden 1955*, pp.762 et seq.

LORD ALEXANDER AND ISKANDER MIRZA

The English, however, enjoyed one crucial piece of good fortune. Field Marshal Lord Alexander of Tunis, a hero of both world wars, was president of MCC.* During the 1930s, Alexander had conducted campaigns on the North-West frontier, while Iskander Mirza, governor-general of Pakistan and president of the BCCP, had served as a district officer. The two men were therefore bound by ties of honour and friendship.

Lord Alexander took his duties as MCC president seriously. Three months earlier, he had travelled to Liverpool to see the touring party off on their sea journey to Pakistan. He had delivered them a lecture about Pakistan and on how to conduct themselves in a foreign country. It was not his fault they ignored his advice. Unlike the many figures in the cricketing establishment who regarded the Baig incident as essentially comic, the Field Marshal grasped the importance of what had happened. He at once took control of the situation, despatching on his own initiative two cables to Pakistan. The first was an official message of 'regret and apology' to Iskander Mirza.

Lord Alexander also sent Mirza a personal message which read: 'I am greatly perturbed at the reports about the behaviour of our team in Peshawar. I have been waiting to receive our manager's report before writing to you, but since I have not yet received the report I hasten to tell you how much I deplore this unfortunate incident and to offer you, an old and valued friend, my own personal regrets.'[44] Then he picked up the phone to Mirza and offered to order the England team home, and make financial

---

*Field Marshal Lord Alexander of Tunis was renowned for his charm and diplomacy (see his biography *Alex* by Nigel Nicolson (Weidenfeld, 1973)). He fought on the Western Front in World War One, being awarded a Military Cross, Distinguished Service Order and French Légion d'Honneur. He left Dunkirk in June 1940 on the last destroyer, having ensured that all British troops were evacuated. As a Harrow schoolboy, he played in the legendary Fowler's Match at Lord's, on 8 and 9 July 1910. The match was named after the Eton captain, Robert St Leger Fowler, whose brilliant play rescued his school from an impossible situation. When their ninth wicket fell in the second innings, Eton, who had been made to follow on, led by four runs. They won the game. The future Field Marshal played a notable role. He took five wickets for 40 with his leg spin and was then at the heart of the action as the game reached its thunderous conclusion. Alexander, batting at number 11, came into bat with Eton needing 23 to win with just one wicket remaining. He remained at the crease while thirteen runs were added, but was then caught at slip. It was reported that the Etonian cheers which followed Alexander's dismissal could be heard as far away as Paddington Station. By my calculation, at least eight of the twenty-two boys who played in this immortal fixture were killed in combat during the 1914–18 war.

reparation to Pakistan. The MCC cricketers did not know about this, and the first they heard of it was over a crackling wireless set.[45]

This intervention was greeted with irritation within the MCC, as Trevor Bailey, the England all-rounder, later revealed. Bailey was present when Lord Alexander announced that he had offered to withdraw the England team. He and Gubby Allen, chairman of the England selectors, were appalled. 'Had I been out there, I might have enjoyed that moment of the tour. It was a classic case of boisterous, fairly juvenile horse, or rather water, play,' recorded Bailey, adding that, 'It was an occasion when Gubby Allen and I were in complete agreement and rather supported the theory that soldiers do not make the best diplomats.'[46]

But Bailey's judgement was hopeless. Alexander's immediate expression of contrition on behalf of the MCC was a masterstroke. It made it very much easier for Iskander Mirza to react in a generous way.* Mirza insisted that the tour must go on.[47]

The MCC was very fortunate that Iskander Mirza was in charge of the BCCP. A demagogic figure, such as Zulfiqar Ali Bhutto, would hardly have been able to resist the temptation to stir up maximum trouble. Mirza could not have been more pro British – or less demagogic. Thirty-five years earlier, he had been the first Indian to graduate from the Royal Military Academy at Sandhurst, where he proved himself not just a promising soldier but also an outstanding cricketer.† He was commissioned into the Indian army, before joining the Indian political service. After Partition he rose fast, being appointed interior minister, then governor of increasingly turbulent East Pakistan. In 1955, he succeeded Ghulam Mohammad as governor-general. This was the position (occupied by Pakistan's founder Jinnah from Partition in 1947 up to his death) Mirza held when the Idris Baig affair flared up.

So, thanks to Alexander and Mirza the tour was saved. Outwardly the

---

*Iskander Mirza, President of the BCCP from 1955 to October 1958, when he was replaced by Ayub Khan, both as President of the BCCP and also President of Pakistan.

†The RMA cricket records state that 'Sikander makes his own rules; in a faultless 163 not out at the Oval he only scored about 30 in front of the wicket, and he has played many other good innings of the same type, notably a priceless 80 odd not out against the Greenjackets. If he continues to play cricket as we all hope he will, the forcing shots will come, and he will wake up one day and find himself a famous cricketer.' Humayun Mirza, *From Plassey to Pakistan: The Family History of Iskander Mirza, the First President of Pakistan* (Lanham, Md: University Press of America, 1999), Appendix III. Alas, Mirza injured his back on his first military assignment, putting paid to cricket.

England players were contrite. Inwardly, many of them still did not believe they had done anything wrong.

On return to Britain the entire squad was summoned to Lord's for a meeting with Field Marshal Alexander and the MCC committee. The Baig affair was not mentioned.* The primary purpose of the interview appears to have been Alexander's warning to each player against discussing the tour with 'the Press, their friends or even their families in a way which may discredit Pakistan.'[48] This was sensible advice, which some of the MCC players were later to ignore.

Donald Carr and Geoffrey Howard then stayed behind to answer detailed questions. Carr said that 'the Test matches were played in a very tense atmosphere and hostile spirit.' However, he added that 'relations were good off the field except so far as the Pakistan Captain was concerned.'

The notes record Carr's parting remark to the Lord's committee: 'Quite honestly, when I look back on the Peshawar incident I think it was about the funniest thing I have ever seen in my life.'[49]

IDRIS BAIG: THE AFTERMATH

After his interview with the MCC committee, Donald Carr rang up Ronnie Aird and told him that he was happy to take 'full responsibility' for the incident in Peshawar. This sensible move gave protection not just to the MCC players but also to those above Carr in the MCC hierarchy. The MCC was now able to close the affair, with the announcement that 'the responsibility for the incident rests entirely with the captain and he has been so informed.'[50]

In the early weeks after the row, the MCC pondered some kind of financial penalty on the players. But Carr's acceptance of responsibility dispelled any idea of a fine. In the end, all the players involved received full bonuses on top of their tour fees.[51] Ronnie Aird told Yorkshire that 'the three Yorkshire cricketers who accompanied the MCC "A" Team to Pakistan received excellent reports from the captain and manager.'[52] These included

---

*There is no suggestion in the official record that it was raised, while Tony Lock states explicitly that 'the President did not even mention the umpiring incident.' Lock, *For Surrey and England*, p.129.

Brian Close, who flung a bucket of water over Baig, and Billy Sutcliffe, in whose room the so-called water treatment took place. In his letter to Surrey, Aird praised Roy Swetman – who threw the second bucket of water – for his 'excellent temperament for the big occasions.' Aird added that, 'Off the field he is stated to have shown much character and sense of fun.'[53]

By 20 March – three days after the team had returned to England – the MCC completed its investigation into the Pakistan tour. The key passage read as follows:

> The captain, who was present at the time, should have recognised at once that this 'ragging', although initiated by nothing more than high spirits and with no harmful intent whatsoever, might be regarded, as it was in many quarters, as an attack upon an umpire. The Committee are satisfied that this was not the case.[54]

This was a whitewash. By any standards Idris Baig had been the victim of a serious, premeditated attack.* Any court of law would have found in Baig's favour, had he chosen to press charges of assault, as he threatened to do at one stage.

MCC denied that the players who abducted Baig were 'under the influence of alcohol.'† Once again the official MCC account was false. The Peshawar Cricket Association dinner was dry, so it is reasonable to assume that the England players had had nothing to drink between approximately 8pm, when the pre-dinner reception started, and 10.30pm, the approximate time the dinner ended. But how much did they drink before the dinner?

Here we are helped by Geoffrey Howard's contrite private note to Group Captain Cheema, written two days after the abduction. Howard stated that there were approximately seven or eight cricketers in the room, and eighteen bottles of beer were delivered. Howard deduced from this that 'no one can have had more than two bottles of beer', making it sound as if no player

---

*Privately MCC acknowledged this, as Geoffrey Howard's private letter to Group Captain Cheema on 28 February shows: 'They went to his hotel and brought him back to their own in a tonga and against his wishes. I think but cannot be certain that the strained arm he sustained was done in attempting to get away and out of the tonga.' MCC Library Archive, MCC/CRI/5/1/63.
†Geoffrey Howard's statement of 17 March 1956 asserts that: 'Suggestions made in some quarters that the members of the team implicated in the affair were under the influence of alcohol are quite unfounded and completely untrue. In fact the majority of the team are either teetotal or persons who drink very little indeed.' Taken from *Wisden 1957*, p.793.

could have sunk more than two pints. However, these bottles would almost certainly have been the large quart bottles then generally available in Pakistan, retailing at 6 shillings each,[55] meaning that the players could have consumed four pints each, or in some cases more.[56]

What of the claim that it was 'initiated by nothing more than high spirits?' Here is Donald Carr accounting for his actions in a private letter to Ronnie Aird dated 28 February, two days after the drenching: 'I must point out that this was no vicious attack on an umpire, because he had given bad decisions against our team. This has been the line adopted, perhaps naturally, by the Press out here, and I gather it has also appeared at home. We know that Idris Baig is a very poor umpire, but so are many others who have stood in Pakistan; it was the fact that he is such an incredible caricature of an umpire. Pompous and very full of his known importance, that made him an ideal subject for our purpose.'[57] In other words, the attack on Baig was a bullying assault on a man who stood out from the crowd. Furthermore, the crucial MCC claim that the attack 'had no connection whatsoever with umpiring decisions made by Mr Idris Baig' is also open to scrutiny.

MCC had been grumbling about Baig ever since the first 'Test' in Lahore where, according to Geoffrey Howard's tour report, Baig 'not only gave bad decisions but also performed his duties in a most extraordinary way.'[58] Howard wrote to Cheema requesting advance notification about the choice of umpires ahead of the Dacca match. There was no reply, but Howard was given a private assurance by KR Collector, the former BCCP secretary, that Baig would not be standing as umpire. In the event, Baig was umpire once more, and once again there were, in the opinion of the England team, 'several glaring umpiring errors.'[59]

So Howard wrote a further letter, once again demanding a change of umpires for the Peshawar match.[60] There was no reply to this letter, and the England team only learnt on the morning the Peshawar game started that Baig was in charge. By the end of the first day's play three England players had been – unfairly in the opinion of the MCC – given out lbw by Baig off Kardar. That evening Geoffrey Howard expressed his anger in a private letter to Billy Griffith, MCC assistant secretary: 'the umpiring was by any standards I have seen outside village cricket between two rival teams with their own umpires, the worst I have ever seen.'[61] Howard was by now incensed and confided in Griffith that he was resolved to throw all caution to the winds: 'Whatever the result of the match I think we shall have to say that we will not accept one of the two now standing in the last "Test",' he wrote, in reference to Baig.[62]

On the evening of Sunday 26 February, by which time it was obvious that Pakistan would win, the English tour manager Geoffrey Howard wrote a letter home to his wife in which he again complained about 'some really shocking umpiring. It is such a pity that they allow these incompetents to do it – they are without doubt there to help the home side – because they are quite strong enough to at least avoid being beaten by us without this aid.'[63] He must have been writing this letter at almost exactly the moment that his captain Donald Carr and a group of England players were leaving Dean's hotel on their journey to seize Umpire Baig. Geoffrey Howard would later remember watching them leave and reflecting, 'What are they up to?'[64] The MCC line that there was no connection between the attack on Baig and the team's collective fury at his allegedly biased umpiring strains credibility.

IN DEFENCE OF UMPIRE BAIG

But what of Idris Baig himself? Born in Delhi in 1911, he was at his peak a decent right-hand batsman, dangerous right-arm medium-fast bowler, and a capable gully fielder. He made his debut for Delhi in the Ranji Trophy in the 1935–36 season, playing his last game some ten years later. This was an era when first-class matches were few and far between, and Baig played only seven. He took 23 wickets at an average of 13.60, while averaging a useful 22.46 with the bat. Baig's record as a player and length of time in the game is inconsistent with England claims that he was ignorant of the rules.

At the end of his playing career, Baig switched to umpiring. He met with such success that he was chosen to stand in the first-ever Test match on Pakistan soil, alongside Daud Khan,* at the Dacca stadium against the

*Daud Khan made his first-class debut for Sindh against Northern India Free Lancers at Karachi in 1936–37. He played for Sindh against Lord Tennyson's MCC at Karachi in 1937–38, scoring 49 and 10 and remained not out on both occasions. After Partition he played for Sindh against West Punjab at Lahore in the very first first-class match played on Pakistan soil. Later he took up umpiring and was on duty with MJ Mobed during the second unofficial Test against Nigel Howard's MCC at Karachi on the 1951–52 tour. From 1954 to 1973 he officiated in fourteen Tests. He was also the liaison officer for the MCC 'A' team in 1955–56.

touring Indians at the start of 1955. The Quaid-e-Azam Trophy player Qamar Ahmed recalls Baig as a 'very imposing figure, tall and upright and with a pleasant disposition. He chewed betel nut and paan leaf, and used to have a pouch in his pocket containing the leaf, nuts and *qawam* (chewing tobacco)'.[65] In the late 1950s, Baig was regarded as Pakistan's best umpire.

The evidence that he was biased is not as clear-cut as critics allege. Indeed it is easy to show that many of the charges made against Umpire Baig – and Pakistani umpires in general – lacked foundation. The MCC archives contain a record of a conversation between Geoffrey Howard and Vinoo Mankad, who captained the Indian team which toured Pakistan during the winter of 1954–55. This was part of Howard's preparation for the looming MCC 'A' tour of Pakistan, and Howard summarised Mankad's remarks as follows:

> It must be borne in mind that the Pakistan Board of Control is Government sponsored and Government controlled and it is not the policy of the Government to lose Test Matches! Apparently all the umpires are Government Officials, and in danger of losing their jobs if decisions are given which result in Pakistan losing a Test. Vinoo makes the point that, whilst it is impossible to get batsmen out lbw, and run outs and stumpings are practically unknown, it applies to both sides and the object is rather more to ensure that Pakistan does not lose rather than to use doubtful methods to see she wins . . . They found in Test Matches that they had either to catch out or bowl out the opposition and it was not particularly easy to bowl people out who stood in front of their wicket with absolute confidence and safety.[66]

Howard accepted Mankad's statements without question. But Vinoo Mankad was not a disinterested witness, and it is easy to prove that almost everything he told Howard was false. First of all, umpires were not simply government officials, as Mankad said. Daud (who stood at the other end during the India series) was a professional draughtsman. More importantly, the claim that it was 'impossible' to get batsmen out lbw was nonsense. In Mankad's India v Pakistan tour, five Pakistan batsmen were dismissed lbw. This was exactly the same number as the Indian lbw victims. However, Umpire Baig only stood in the first four Tests, during which period there were only two Indian lbw victims, against four Pakistani. So during Baig's period, a Pakistan batsman was twice as likely to be dismissed lbw than an Indian one.

Mankad's claim about run-outs and stumpings was also wrong. Far from being 'practically unknown', there were an unusually large number of these types of dismissal during the 1954–55 Pakistan-India series. Furthermore, most of these were given against Pakistan. Pakistan suffered eight run-outs and seven stumpings, while just four Indian batsmen were run out and none stumped. These figures are impossible to square with Mankad's claim that India were obliged 'either to catch out or bowl out the opposition.' Howard could easily have established all this by looking at the tour scorecards. Instead, he relied uncritically on a hostile witness.

Significantly the MCC also wrote to Henry Cooper, the tour manager during the three-Test New Zealand tour of autumn 1955, asking for advice. Cooper gave a wide-ranging survey of Pakistan conditions, adding the following postscript: 'The umpires we found quite reasonable. Idris Baig, though impossibly vain, was first rate. The others seemed pretty impartial on the whole, though I feel there was always a bit of national prestige to be upheld if possible.'[67] He received a sceptical response from Ronnie Aird: 'We have been warned about the umpires and your remarks about them are rather more favourable than I expected.'

In the light of all this, let us now study the evidence of Baig's alleged bias during the MCC 'A' tour of Pakistan. Once again it is lacking. We have seen that the MCC players felt strongly that Idris Baig was biased. The statistics suggest otherwise. Seventy-five MCC wickets fell in the four-match series, of which sixteen were lbw. Of the fifty-one Pakistan wickets, ten were lbw. So approximately one in five wickets fell to an lbw decision, a proportion which is roughly what one would expect. Crucially, the proportion of lbw decisions given against each team (20%) was identical. Furthermore, two Pakistani batsmen were given out run-out or stumped, against just one MCC player.

In 1957, a year after the water incident, Baig was appointed manager of the Eaglets tour of England. It passed harmoniously and highly successfully. Bolstered by Hanif Mohammad, the Eaglets won 23 of their 35 matches and lost only one.[68] There is no doubt Baig's umpiring career suffered as a result of the MCC complaints. He was not asked to stand in any of the three MCC teams that came to Pakistan after the notorious water-treatment series – not Ted Dexter's 1961–62 tour, Mike Brearley's Under-25 tour in 1967, nor Colin Cowdrey's in 1969. Yet he harboured no resentment. In 1970, Donald Carr managed the international side which went to Karachi to raise funds for the relief of cyclone victims in East Pakistan. Carr was in the changing room before the game when Idris Baig introduced himself with the announcement that he was in charge of the match organisation, and gave Carr a warm hug. As the two men ambled out onto the wicket, Carr felt a tap on the shoulder and it was one of the players, holding out a bucket of water, asking: 'Would this help?'[69] Idris Baig laughed as much as anyone else. This greatly reviled man emerges much better than most from the affair in Peshawar.

YEAR OF PRODIGIES

'You are the only hope to save Pakistan.'

– AH KARDAR TO HANIF MOHAMMAD

By the summer of 1956, Abdul Hafeez Kardar was at his peak. For the first time there was no challenge for the captaincy, the threat from Mian Mohammad Saeed (now in his late forties) having subsided. Aged thirty-one, Kardar was probably playing the best cricket of his life, frequently spearheading match-changing rearguard operations from the lower middle order, while his left-arm spin was capable of destroying a good batting side on a helpful wicket. He was a strong fielder, and superlative in his specialist gully position. There was, furthermore, no doubting Kardar's courage. For instance, he had taken ball after ball from Frank Tyson at The Oval on his body and he would do the same later in the West Indies against the rampant bowling of Roy Gilchrist.

Partly for these reasons, Kardar now had total domination of his team. As a captain he had a flair for field changes, for instance positioning Shuja-ud-Din at short leg to earn the critical wicket of Wardle on the final morning of The Oval Test. Kardar was an exceptionally good reader of the game. Jamsheed Markear recollects accompanying Kardar to the nets in Karachi where a batsman he had never seen before, England's Reg Simpson, was facing. Kardar watched Simpson deal with four or five deliveries then turned away. His verdict: 'Two slips, two gullys.'[1]

Kardar forged a personal style. Probably influenced by the Nawab of Pataudi, he acquired his suits and shirts from Jermyn Street in London's West End. Photographs of Kardar, with his saturnine good looks, often make him resemble the leading man from one of the classic Hollywood movies of the era. One of his friends was Keith Miller, the Australian war hero and cricketing idol, one of the most glamorous men in the world in the 1950s. Always punctilious about personal relationships, Kardar maintained a correspondence with Miller until he died.

Kardar was a paradox. He prided himself, sometimes to the point of absurdity, on his Oxford education and dressed like an English gentleman. He instructed his cricketers in English table manners and etiquette. For instance, when they came to stay, he would give them the money to place beside the bed to tip the servants.[2] He insisted on punctuality and good manners, and those who failed on either point risked being driven out of Pakistan cricket.

Yet at the same time as celebrating what he saw as English manners, he found himself increasingly in conflict with the MCC. After the Idris Baig episode, the English establishment regarded Kardar with suspicion. As Kardar became more mature and confident, he acquired a post-colonial sensibility. He disliked the way that England and the other white cricketing nations bossed the world game.

He was now a celebrated public figure: 'I cannot tell you how it feels to be a hero,' he wrote a few years later. 'I am shy and therefore I took all compliments – the most cherished of all these being recognised by young boys in the streets, in bazaars by grown-ups, in the shops by veiled ladies, by passengers on railway platforms, in such remote places as on all railway stations between Mymensingh and Rajshahi; on one such journey I was presented with guards of honour, civic receptions in East Pakistan – I took them all with very humble gratitude.'[3]

Kardar was as much at ease on these almost viceregal journeys across his native Pakistan as he was at high table at Oxford, at smart New York or London parties, in the company of businessmen and politicians, with film stars and actresses. He appreciated to the full the good things in life, yet retained an increasingly powerful set of political beliefs that were guided by his Islamic faith. Indeed, Kardar was gradually establishing himself as a political voice in his own right. He began to intervene in controversy by writing letters to *The Times* in London, often on recondite issues such as the level of the Pakistan rupee. Two future prime ministers – Zulfiqar Ali Bhutto of Pakistan and Alec Douglas-Home of Britain – were among his friends.

Kardar was now often called 'Skipper' or, in Urdu, *Captaan*. He did have a rival in the dressing room, however. He and Fazal Mahmood were wary of one another. Fazal complained to friends that his genius was responsible for all of Kardar's great achievements. When they were both young cricketers in the early 1940s, Fazal and Kardar had been intimates, walking through the streets of Old Lahore and out to Minto Park for net practice, and cycling together to games.

Fazal said that Kardar was a changed man when he came back from Oxford. Abdul Hafeez – known to friends as 'Feeja'[4] – of the easy-going early years had vanished, to be replaced by stiff-necked AH Kardar.[5] Yet there is no doubt that the Kardar-Fazal combination worked. Hanif Mohammad, who observed this relationship as closely as anyone, says today that, 'Kardar knew how to get the best out of a player. He was not very friendly with Fazal Mahmood. I don't know what he used to say to him but he used to get the best out of him.'[6] However uneasy their partnership, these two men steered Pakistan to its prodigious early success.

Even today Pakistanis love to reel off the victories – England defeated on home territory, victory at Lucknow against India, New Zealand massacred at home. And now came Australia.

KARACHI 1956

The Australians, on the way back home after being demolished by Jim Laker in the Ashes, stopped off on the subcontinent. Three Tests were scheduled against India, one against Pakistan.[7] Pakistan had asked to host two Tests, only for the request to be rejected. But this single Test turned out to be one of the most compelling in the country's history.

The Australian side was full of famous names – Neil Harvey, Richie Benaud, Alan Davidson, Ray Lindwall and Keith Miller, playing what turned out to be his final Test.* Batting first after winning the toss, they were unable to cope with Fazal's leg-cutters and break-backs on his trademark matting wicket. Fazal had prepared for the Australians' arrival by staying for a month at Sam's hotel at the Murree hill station north of Islamabad, which had served as one of the summer headquarters for the British Raj.† Every day he had gone on fast walks up the mountains, and returned to eat fresh fruit and vegetables.

Fortified by this bracing regime, he dismissed five of the top six batsmen, capturing six first innings wickets in all and never wavering in length or direction. Khan Mohammad accounted for the remaining four. Up in Murree, Fazal had boasted to the manager at Sam's hotel he would dismiss Australia for under 100. They scored 80. 'Khan Mohammad and I bowled unchanged for nearly four hours,' recorded Fazal. 'Ours was a sort of combined operation in which we did not allow the batsman any opportunity to relax. They had to play each and every ball.'[8] Fazal made a particular mockery of Miller who played and missed at five consecutive leg-cutters, and was then flummoxed by Fazal's break-back. This was masterly bowling.[9]

Pakistan then failed in their turn. 'Our batting was pathetic,' recorded an anguished Fazal. 'It seemed the achievements of the first day were wasted.' Miller dismissed Hanif for a duck, and by the close of the first day Pakistan stood at an uncertain 15 for 2. Only 95 runs had been scored in the day but, according to the cricket writer Jack Pollard, 'The Australians who played in that match still regard the first day as one of the most fascinating they ever encountered.'[10] This day of laborious and attritional cricket, in which runs were scored at a rate of 20 an hour, is proof that the game does not need to be played at a frenetic pace in order to make compelling viewing.

The following morning, Kardar led one of his smouldering rearguard acts. When he came to the crease at 70 for 5, the Australians were back in the game.

*This Test was notable for other milestones and significant events. Ray Lindwall took his 200th Test wicket; the brilliant twenty-four-year-old Queensland fast-bowler Ron Archer tore a muscle at the end of the game, and sadly never again played Test cricket. The day off to mark the killing of Liaquat Ali meant this was the only Test match in history to have two scheduled rest days. Gul Mohammad, who had previously played for India, was chosen for Pakistan, meaning that he joined the small congregation of players who have represented more than one country. It was one of the very rare Test matches where the winning team has been booed by the home crowd, dismayed by the crawl to victory on the final day. For this disturbance, see *Fazal Mahmood*, pp.59–60.

†Fazal had been asked to accompany the Pakistan team on tour to Kenya. But he had contemptuously dismissed East Africa as a 'dinner dance' trip. 'Kardar tried to persuade me, but I wanted to prepare myself for the Australians,' wrote Fazal later. See *Fazal Mahmood*, p.60.

He scored 69, sharing in a partnership of 104 with Wazir Mohammad. Wazir, who made 67, easily gets forgotten in comparison with his younger brothers. But again and again, Wazir would come to the rescue, as he did with his second innings 42 not out at The Oval in 1954, or later when he partnered his brother Hanif in his heroic match-saving 337 in the West Indies.

This stand, which gave Pakistan a lead of 119, put Pakistan in a match-winning position. Though Australia played better in the second innings, they were still unable to cope with Fazal. In 48 overs, he captured seven wickets while conceding 80 runs, finishing with thirteen for 114 in the match. Despite a fighting 56 from Richie Benaud, Australia were only able to set Pakistan 69 to win. After suffering the early loss of Hanif, Pakistan set about attaining this objective very slowly indeed. By the close of the third day's play, Alimuddin and Gul Mohammad[11] had advanced the score to 63 off 45.5 overs in front of a crowd of 20,000. Play was then suspended for twenty-four hours, to mark the fifth anniversary of the assassination of Liaquat Ali Khan, Pakistan's first prime minister. Nevertheless, the Australians were amazed when 6,000 spectators turned up to watch Pakistan score the remaining six runs. The aggregate runs amounted to 535 at an average of 29.41 per 100 balls.[12] Fazal, the hero of this contest, wrote later:

> The victory against Australia marked the end of the first chapter of Pakistan's cricket history. It was the end of its childhood. After beating the two giants of the cricket world – England and Australia – Pakistan successfully ended the so-called teething stage of a precocious child. The cricket toddlers of four years ago, who tumbled to an astonished elder at The Oval, were now full-grown adults. Though it remained, of course, the youngest cricketing nation, yet it had earned a place among the strongest.[13]

There was a great deal of pardonable exaggeration going on here. Certainly Pakistan had pulled off a series of improbable victories against the best sides in the world, and it is also true that in Hanif and Fazal they possessed two world-class players. But hard times lay ahead. Well over a year would elapse between the one-off Karachi Test of October 1956 and Pakistan's next series against the West Indies at the start of 1958. During this period Pakistan's Test cricketers were obliged to endure fifteen months of international frustration.

THE QUAID-E-AZAM TROPHY 1954–58
AND DOMESTIC CRICKET

During the fallow times for their international team, Pakistan's domestic
cricket continued making healthy progress, creating new opportunities for
young players. One such discovery was the sixteen-year-old Nasim-ul-
Ghani, who delivered 79 overs to take three for 184 for Karachi Blues in a
Quaid-e-Azam Trophy match against Karachi Whites. This marathon effort
earned him a tour of the West Indies. However, as a young prodigy he was
outdone by Mushtaq Mohammad (the fourth of the legendary brothers),
who made his first-class debut for Karachi Whites several weeks before his
fourteenth birthday. He top-scored 87 and took five wickets as his team
destroyed Sindh.[14]

By now, first-class cricket was becoming an attractive career for boys from
modest backgrounds in Pakistan, particularly in the major centres such as
Karachi and Lahore, even though appearances in the Quaid-e-Azam Trophy
were still unpaid. Playing first-class gave a young player contacts with good
employers, while the chance of reaching the Test team, or even its fringes,
brought a player into a higher social sphere. Omar Kureishi recalled: 'cricket
was associated with social mobility right from the start. I remember how
youngsters such as Hanif and Fazal suddenly became toasts of the town and
rubbed shoulders with the social elite in a manner which was unthinkable
for players in other sports. This has always been part of the attraction of
cricket.'[15] Wazir Mohammad recalls the scene at Jahangir Park in the heart
of Karachi during the 1950s: 'There would be eight to ten teams playing
matches or practising in the nets. Boys would turn up from all over, hoping
to get a chance to show somebody what they could do.'[16]

The celebrated journalist and author Qamar Ahmed gave me a vivid
account of playing in the Quaid-e-Azam Trophy during this period. He
made his debut for Sindh against Karachi Whites in 1956–57 – in the
match where Mushtaq Mohammad also made his debut. Qamar played
for seven seasons but still totalled only seventeen first-class matches.
Nonetheless, these brought him close to national recognition and he is
the only man to have dismissed all five of the Mohammad brothers in
first-class cricket. 'We were lucky to get a few hundred people, even if
top names were playing, such as Hanif or Mushtaq or Saeed Ahmed. We

were paid ten rupees a match and for away games we stayed in some "very marginal" hotels. There was no broadcast coverage, but there were extensive match reports in newspapers, particularly *Dawn* in Karachi and the *Pakistan Times* in Lahore, and the Urdu newspaper *Jang*. These could give players a following.'[17]

Quaid-e-Azam Trophy players could also get a following for non-cricketing reasons. One such was the left-arm spin genius Prince Aslam, heir to the Nawab of Manavadar, a noted patron of hockey and cricket. Many contemporaries volunteered memories of this outsize character – playing practical jokes, dating a series of movie stars, driving to matches (often late) in a Cadillac, firing revolver shots in the air in protest at an umpire's decision. They agreed on his talent and Keith Miller rated him the finest of his type in Pakistan. Mushtaq Mohammad remembers him as the true inventor of the *doosra*. His lifestyle, however, left him out of favour with Kardar and the Test selectors.*

RADIO VOICES OF PAKISTAN CRICKET

At Partition, Pakistan's radio inheritance was scanty: three medium-wave stations of limited range at Lahore, Peshawar and Dacca, all under-equipped and under-staffed. However, in July 1951 Radio Pakistan moved to modern and technically advanced headquarters in Karachi. By 1960 it was also broadcasting from Rawalpindi, Hyderabad, Quetta and Multan. During the 1960s, the advent of cheap transistor radios allowed millions of Pakistanis without wealth or education to discover cricket through commentary. They were helped by shopkeepers, who made space for people to listen and posted the score and major news on blackboards. Shazad Humayun, himself a cricket commentator, described the impact of radio in these terms: 'in the rural areas ... access to radio was always there ... they did not have too many radio sets but still it [cricket] continued to flow to the rural areas ... In the urban areas ... I remember when I was a child listening to radio commentary, and roaming round the streets of Lahore I could see the shops with

*Conversations with Majid Khan, Mushtaq Mohammad, Aftab Gul, Qamar Ahmed and his cousin, Nawabzada Abdul Khalik Nasiruddin.

scoreboards and blackboards with the latest scores written on them ... I would say that if radio commentary had not been there, cricket would not be where it is today in Pakistan.'[18]

Pakistan audiences heard two radio voices working in tandem: Omar Kureishi and Jamsheed Marker. They each broadcast in English and 'their knowledge of affairs wider than cricket, command over language and urbane sophistication set them apart in a largely illiterate society.'[19] Hanif Mohammad commented simply: 'they were superb. They served as the eyes and ears of cricket lovers.'[20]

Omar Kureishi had grown up in Bombay. He became a childhood friend of ZA Bhutto and also joined him at the University of California, where he learnt the art of radio broadcasting, in English, as a regular panellist on a programme where university graduates commented on global issues. Jamsheed Markear, on the other hand, had a high-flying career in Pakistan's diplomatic service, eventually becoming ambassador to the United States and to the UN, and then a UN Special Envoy. Later, the pair were joined by two other cultivated broadcasters, Iftikhar Ahmed and Chishty Mujahid.[21]

The commentators covered only Test matches and other important fixtures, such as competition finals or visiting tourist matches or prestigious charity events. They ignored the routine contests in the Quaid-e-Azam Trophy (and there was no radio commentary for Hanif's 499 against Bahawalpur).[22] Moreover, for the first thirty years of Pakistan cricket all the radio commentary was in English – a second or third language to listeners. The journalist Munir Hussain sought to introduce, or perhaps more accurately, re-introduce,[23] commentary in Urdu. Hussain's first Urdu commentary was broadcast (after initial resistance from authority) in the 1969 final of the Jang Gold Cup – which happened to be sponsored by a leading Urdu newspaper. It was not used for a full Pakistan Test series until that of 1978-79, against India, and was confined to ten minutes per hour. Munir Hussain was made to sit outside the commentary box until the English-language commentators such as Kureishi had vacated it. Kureishi himself strongly resisted Urdu, declaring that, 'I do believe that English lends itself to cricket commentary like no other language.' He had a point, as the early Urdu commentators struggled to render cricket terms. A googly was rendered as a cumbersome but descriptive *dhokay baaz gaind* (treacherous, deceitful ball) and they never coped with lbw. Eventually they settled for using the English terms.

To lift the status of Urdu commentary, Munir Hussain had to lobby Pakistan's military ruler. 'General Zia was more comfortable in Urdu and kept talking about the need to promote Urdu. My pleas were accepted. For eight years I was the only one in the field, but now we have a spate of Urdu commentators.'[24] Besides Munir Hussain, Hanif Mohammad praised the Urdu commentators Hassan Jalil and Mohammad Idrees. 'They got the people used to listening to the game.'[25]

THE IMPORTANCE OF FAMILY IN PAKISTAN CRICKET

So far in this book the analysis of the domestic structure of Pakistan cricket has concentrated on clubs, schools, universities and employer organisations. While they are important, no account of the development of the sport can be complete without an examination of the role played by family life. In his masterful recent study,[26] Professor Anatol Lieven has made the arresting argument that Pakistan is more stable than outside commentators realise, and therefore cannot be compared to failed states such as Somalia or the Congo.

At the heart of his argument is the recognition that the institutions imposed by the British before independence, such as parliamentary democracy and the rule of law, are indeed failing. But he maintains that the biggest, most powerful and most traditional forces in Pakistan – family and tribe – remain as strong as ever.

For instance, Lieven demonstrates that government ministers cannot escape obligations to family and friends, meaning that they are obliged to reward dependants and connections upon attaining power. The power of the family may seem corrupt to modern western eyes, but it also provides a deep and enduring stability.

An analogous argument can be applied to cricket. One of the first points that strikes the historian of the game is the exceptionally large number of cricketing families and dynasties. Consider the first-ever Pakistan Test team, the one which played against India at Delhi in October 1952.

Nazar Mohammad, the opening bat (who received the first ball ever faced by a Pakistani in a Test match) was the father of the all-rounder Mudassar Nazar, who played 76 Tests for the country. Nazar's eldest son Mubashir

Nazar also played first-class cricket.[27] In addition, Nazar's elder brother Mohammad Sharif had been a useful Ranji Trophy player (and Sharif's son Azmat Hussain would go on to play first-class cricket in Pakistan).*

Nazar's opening partner Hanif was famously one of the five Mohammad brothers, four of whom had very distinguished Test careers, as well as the father of the future Test cricketer Shoaib Mohammad. One of the other brothers, Wazir, was also a member of the touring party, though he did not play in the first Test.

The captain AH Kardar was the brother-in-law of another tourist, Zulfiqar Ahmed. Middle-order batsman Waqar Hasan's younger brother, Pervez Sajjad, would later play nineteen Tests for Pakistan, and is still remembered as one of Pakistan's finest spin-bowlers.† Fazal Mahmood, as we have seen, was the son-in-law of Mian Saeed, Pakistan's first international captain. Fazal's brother-in-law Yawar Saeed (son of Mian) was a fast bowler who played for Somerset, was unfortunate not to play for Pakistan, and much later on would manage the national team.

Kardar's vice-captain Anwar Hussain Khokhar was the cousin of Mohammad Aslam Khokhar, who later became a member of the 1954 touring party in England, playing in one Test.‡ Finally Ghulam Ahmed, a Muslim who played for India in that match, was the uncle of Asif Iqbal, who migrated to Pakistan in 1961 and went on to be one of the country's very finest players.

An identical analysis could be carried out on any Pakistan team during this period, with similar results. The exercise is worthwhile because it shows that the national team was not a collection of deracinated individuals but must rather be understood as a network of assorted family connections and friendships, with roots that extended far beyond the cricket field. Local

---

*Mohammad Sharif represented Northern India in the Ranji Trophy from 1935–36 to 1941–42, playing seven first-class matches. He scored 395 runs at an average of 39.50, highest score 118. Sharif's son Azmat Hussain played one first-class match, representing Lahore.

†A third brother, Iqbal Shehzad, was one of Pakistan's finest film directors. He began his career as a sound engineer, married Rehana, a star of Indian cinema, and worked with her on *Raat Ke Rahi*, the first film made by a new production house called Montana Films. Its success allowed Iqbal Shezhad to try his hand as a director, with *Banjaran* in 1966. It won a big audience, dazzled by daring camera angles, unusually powerful acting, good production values and inventive editing. Iqbal Shezhad also made *Beti*, *Badnam* and *Bazi* – all classics. AH Kardar had two cousins who were major film makers: AJ and the even more celebrated AR Kardar, a pioneer of the film industry in Lahore.

‡Aslam Khokhar represented Northern India in the Ranji Trophy from 1941–42 to 1946–47. After Partition, he scored the first century in the first-ever first-class match played between West Punjab and Sindh at the Bagh-e-Jinnah ground, Lahore in 1947–48. Later Aslam Khokhar took up umpiring and stood in three Tests.

cricket clubs must also be examined in this way, because very often brothers and cousins would all play together in one team. Thus families and clans, through their informal network of support and connection, were one of the main seminaries of cricket in Pakistan.

THE MOHAMMAD BROTHERS

The two greatest of these clans are the Mohammads of Karachi and the Burkis of Lahore. Both made the journey to Pakistan at the time of Partition. The Mohammads made the perilous trek by land and sea from Junagadh, in what is now the Indian state of Gujarat, to Karachi. The Burkis migrated from Jullundur, which involved a more straightforward trip up the Grand Trunk Road to Lahore. As we shall see later, the Burkis (a small, close-knit tribe which has produced some forty first-class cricketers in Pakistan, including three national captains) and their extraordinary rise to cricketing greatness came in the 1960s and beyond. This coincided with Pakistan's emergence as a first-rate power on the international sporting stage.

By contrast, the Mohammads belong mainly (though by no means entirely) to the earliest phase of Pakistan cricket. At least one of the brothers featured in Pakistan's first 89 Tests. The 90th broke the sequence but then it resumed for another 11 Tests, so that the Mohammads were represented in 100 out of Pakistan's first 101 Tests, spread across twenty-seven years.*

Their mother, Ameer Bee, was herself a very fine sportswoman, who excelled at badminton and carrom, a game which has been compared to billiards. She was so talented that it seems likely that in the modern era she herself would have won renown in her own right. Her historical importance is as cricket's senior matriarch. She outranks even such stiff competition as Martha Grace (who reputedly taught her son WG to play with a straight bat, and produced two other Test players in the shape of WG's brothers Edward and Fred) and Australia's remarkable Jeanne Richardson, mother to Ian, Greg and Trevor Chappell.†

---

*Pakistan's 90th Test, the third and last Test against England in the 1977–78 series played in Karachi, was the first without a Mohammad brother. Sadiq was dropped because of poor form, while Mushtaq was unavailable because of Packer commitments.

†Jeanne Richardson, mother of the three Chappell brothers, was the daughter of the famous all-round sportsman Vic Richardson, who captained Australia at the end of a nineteen-Test career.

Four of Ameer Bee's sons played Test cricket for Pakistan: Wazir, Hanif, Mushtaq and Sadiq. A fifth, Raees, was unfortunate not to do so, serving as twelfth man for his country on one occasion.* Her grandson Shoaib, son of Hanif, was a strong and under-rated Test cricketer, whose Test batting average of 44.34 was higher than either his father or any of his uncles. In all, eleven members of the Mohammad family have played first-class cricket in Pakistan.†

Their story begins in Junagadh, a princely state now in present-day India, not far from the birthplace of the great KS Ranjitsinhji at Sarodar, at the turn of the twentieth century, when the British Empire was at its zenith. Sheikh Ismail, father of the five cricketing prodigies, was a keen player, as his father had been before him. Ismail's wife, Ameer Bee, had four brothers (Bashir, Dilawar, Hameed and Shakir) who were all decent club players.[28]

So cricket was part of the Mohammad family culture. Hanif remembers today how in Junagadh before Partition 'cricket matches at club level or state level were well-attended affairs, and an occasion for the entire family to go out and cheer the players. My elder brothers Wazir and Raees were in the state team and so was my uncle Shakir, who was a useful swing bowler who took a lot of wickets.'[29] Hanif recollects that he used to 'accompany my elder brothers to the nets run by the Nawab of Junagadh, who used to invite the top-notchers of the time to practise whenever he returned home from Cambridge in England.'[30] Today Hanif recalls that 'my childhood memories are all of conversations between my father, brothers, our relatives and friends revolving around the game of cricket.'

*Wazir Mohammad, born 22 December 1929; Raees Mohammad, born 25 December 1932; Hanif Mohammad, born 21 December 1934; Mushtaq Mohammad, born 22 November 1943; Sadiq Mohammad, born 3 May 1945. In addition Ameer Bee had a son and a daughter who died in their teens. See *Cricket's Great Families*, by Kersi Meher-Homji, p.131. Raees's near-miss came in the Dacca Test against India, which started on 1 January 1955. The night before the game, New Year's Eve, captain Kardar informed Raees he was playing, but the following morning changed his mind, and Raees was relegated to twelfth man. Raees was the first of the brothers to make his first-class debut, in 1949–50 for Karachi-Sindh against the visiting Commonwealth team. In his first-class career he scored 1344 runs at an average of 32.78, taking 33 wickets at an average of 31.27. In his autobiography (p.266), Mushtaq paid Raees the following tribute: 'It was Raees who taught me to bowl leg-breaks. He would mark my run up and make me bowl from 18 yards as I was too small to manage the full 22. He was a genuine leg spin googly bowler and the biggest spinner of the ball. If I think back after all these years, out of us five brothers, who deserved to play Tests, Raees had the most natural ability as a middle-order batsman and was a very fine leg spinner.'

†Besides her five sons, they are: Hanif's son Shoaib; Raees's sons Asif, Shahid and Tariq; Sadiq's son Imran. The current generation is represented by Ameer Bee's great-grandson Shehzar (Hanif's grandson and son of Shoaib).

All free time, he remembers, 'was reserved for cricket. We played till we were really exhausted. Weekdays in the afternoons and evenings, we used to play "county" cricket with a tennis ball on the terrace of our house, which was perfectly located on Station Road on the main street of Junagadh. The tennis ball was used to practise batting against swing bowling. We played "Test matches" on Sundays from 10am till sunset.' Hanif attributes a great deal of his success to these early sessions: 'The rules we played by were that if the ball was hit in the air and the batsman was caught off a rebound from the trees, he was out. Therefore, all of us tried to keep the ball down. A tennis ball has a lot of bounce and it is difficult to control it, but with practice, I did learn to keep the ball down.

'In my years as a Test cricketer, that very practice of keeping the ball down helped me. To practise bowling fast, and to play a fast delivery, we even played with a cork ball soaked in water, on a cement surface. It skidded and whistled past the bat at great pace.'

This innocent and peaceful life changed for good in 1947. First of all, the family patriarch Sheikh Ismail, fell ill with cancer. After retiring from the Indian army with the rank of captain, he worked as manager of a salt factory, besides owning a motel and a petrol pump. Then, in September 1947, in the immediate aftermath of Partition, the cricket-loving Nawab of Junagadh made the decision to throw in his lot with Pakistan.

The Nawab was entitled to do whatever he wanted under the independence settlement. In practice, the decision was impractical because there was no common border with Pakistan, and unpopular, because approximately ninety per cent of the population was Hindu. India severed air and postal links and sent troops to the frontier. Tension simmered and in early November the Dewan of Junagadh (Sir Shah Nawaz Bhutto, father of the future Pakistan president Zulfiqar Ali Bhutto) bowed to the inevitable, inviting India to take over the country. The Nawab and his court sought exile in Pakistan.

It was a terrible period for the Mohammad family. They were members of a Muslim minority at a dangerous time of communal riots and massacres. The cricket games stopped. 'As a schoolboy I remember troops entering my city. There were tanks and soldiers with guns, marching in front of our house,' recalls Hanif. 'We were all very frightened and all the children were told to stay indoors and not to even open the windows.'

The Mohammads resolved to follow the example of the Nawab. Wazir, the eldest brother, travelled in company with two uncles to Karachi to find accommodation there. Concluding that it was possible to build a new life in Pakistan, they summoned the others. This is how Hanif, who was about fourteen at the time, remembers the journey:

We left the house in the middle of the night to avoid being seen and boarded a ship at a small port called Veraval on the south west coast of the Arabian Sea. It was one of many small ports like Porbandar in the Kathiawar Peninsula.

Leaving most of our possessions behind, we stepped onto the little ship and sailed to the unknown ... Karachi! As the ship left the port, there was a feeling of great relief that nobody could now catch and kill us. There were other migrants too on the ship and we all looked like lost people. I, as a child did not even know the destination of our journey. I had never even heard about Karachi. My younger brothers Mushtaq and Sadiq were too little to know about anything anyway. Four and a half days later we docked at Karachi to start a new life in a new country.

In all, some thirty members of the Mohammad clan made this journey.[31] Arriving in Karachi they hired two camel carts, piled themselves and their belongings on top, and headed to the Haji camp, whose normal purpose was as a temporary shelter for Muslims making the pilgrimage to Mecca but was now a refugee camp.

The Mohammads had enjoyed security and middle-class affluence in Junagadh. In Karachi, they had practically nothing and certainly not enough to buy a new house, even though plenty had been left vacant and were on the market as a result of Hindus fleeing to India. Eventually the Mohammads discovered a vacant Hindu temple. 'Our chosen abode', recalls Mushtaq, 'was a big hall with a huge idol of the Hindu goddess Kaali, black in colour, pot-bellied and with a menacing red tongue hanging out.'

The temple hall in which they lived served as a dormitory at night time. In the day, it served as a cricket pitch. Mushtaq remembers that when Raees came back from his office (Wazir and Raees had found jobs at Habib Bank), 'we'd give him a chair where he would sit down and just keep feeding us the tennis ball from about 15 yards and he would turn the ball sideways for hours and hours. He would set a field and make us think about where we needed to play the ball.'[32] In this way were the future Test stars formed.

These years were a time of sorrow, loss and hardship for the Mohammad family. In 1949 Sheikh Ismail died. 'However we never lost faith in God,' recalls Hanif, 'and worked diligently and honestly. I firmly believe that the honour bestowed by God on my brothers and me is the reward for this patience and strength of faith.'[33] Thereafter the boys were raised by Ameer Bee, called by Hanif 'our greatest inspiration for as long as she lived.'[34]

It was Hanif who was spotted first. He recalls batting well for his school and afterwards being approached by a stranger. 'He asked my name and asked me where I lived and who my parents were. I told him about myself and he said: "You are a natural cricketer. You must not play any other game. If you play only cricket, you will earn a name for yourself."'[35] The stranger was Abdul Aziz Durrani. 'Master Aziz', as he was known, was responsible for helping shape the careers of many Karachi cricketers. As a young man, the Afghan-born Aziz had been good enough to represent India in an unofficial Test against Jack Ryder's touring Australians in 1936. He fled India for Pakistan at Partition, but left his family behind, a separation which caused him intense distress. His son, Salim Aziz Durrani, had a distinguished Test career for India.*

Master Aziz coached with a self-sacrificing devotion. Recalls Hanif: 'He spent all his money on his students. He bought us shoes, gloves, bats and anything any of us needed. Sometimes he was left with no money in his pocket and then he would ask us to get him something to eat. For us, he was like a father figure and an angel. I have yet to meet anyone like him.'[36]

Aziz was cricket coach at the Sindh Madrassah, the famous Muslim high school in Karachi where Mohammad Ali Jinnah, founder of the Pakistan nation, had studied. Prophesying that Hanif would become a top-class cricketer, he arranged a free scholarship for him. Under the guidance of Aziz, Hanif blossomed. Along with Raees and Wazir, he would play cricket at the Polo Ground, an area of parkland in central Karachi. 'One could see

---

*Described by Christopher Martin-Jenkins as an 'erratically brilliant left-handed batsman who could hit courageously or defend dourly, Durrani was a slow left-arm bowler who, despite his rather lazy-looking action, could extract nip from the pitch and subtly vary changes of flight and line.' He played in twenty-nine Test matches, averaging 25.04 with the bat, and 35.42 with the ball. He later attempted a movie career. Hanif's autobiography, ghosted by Qamar Ahmed and Afia Salam, contains a moving portrait of Master Aziz. See pp.19–22.

hundreds of people, mostly youngsters, playing cricket there every day of the week. Whoever came first would choose his own spot and pitch his stumps for practice or for a match. Even the *maulvis* (clerics) from nearby mosques came and joined in.' Soon Mushtaq and Sadiq, the two youngest Mohammads, would join their elder brothers.

Mushtaq recalls how 'when we were still small Sadiq, my youngest cousin Iqbal, and my older cousin Nisar and I used to set out every Sunday at 7.30am with just two *annas* each in our pockets [a comparison of this amount is impossible in these inflationary times] and we headed for the Polo Ground, in the centre of the city, where many teams used to be playing matches, with intermingling field placings.'[37] At first they were tolerated rather than encouraged. 'I will not forgive or forget the fact that I was made the permanent twelfth man for the Sunday matches,' Mushtaq later wrote.

Meanwhile Hanif was becoming a mighty force in the inter-school tournaments. On a Sindh Madrassah trip to Lahore, he made such an impression that he was invited for dinner with Mian Saeed, then Pakistan's captain. 'Remember one thing,' Saeed told Hanif, 'never be boastful when you score runs. Never raise your collar and behave as if you are a gift from the gods. Always remain humble, respect people, respect the game, and keep on playing even harder.'[38] Hanif lived by this advice all his life.

It was not long before he was offered a job by Kafiluddin, chief engineer at the Public Works Department in Karachi and a famous sponsor of young cricketers. Hanif was hired as a road inspector, though his real task was to play cricket. 'My financial worries were now over. Due to his support and patronage, I was able to pay undivided attention to cricket, and was included in the team that played against the MCC in 1951–52.'[*] This sponsorship provided the family with the means to move out of their Hindu temple. The Public Works Department allocated its trainee road inspector a prestigious house on the Officers' Colony in Garden Road.

The Public Works Department also hired twelve-year-old Mushtaq as a 'cement clerk.'[39] A year later, at the reported age of thirteen years and forty-

---

*Hanif, p.25. Kafiluddin, one of the moving forces in early Pakistan cricket, was responsible for the building of the National Stadium in Karachi. Hanif recalls that it was Kafiluddin who alerted him and his brothers that Denis Compton, then one of the most famous cricketers in the world, was arriving in Karachi. Compton's plane crash-landed, leaving the cricketer stranded in Karachi for several days, during which he batted with the young Mohammads in the nets and gave them coaching tips. See Hanif, p.26.

one days, Mushtaq made his first-class debut for Karachi Whites against Sindh at Hyderabad. The schoolboy took five wickets and scored 87 as Karachi won the game. Hanif (captain of the Karachi Whites) promptly dropped Mushtaq, causing family resentment. Nevertheless, within two years Mushtaq was playing for Pakistan against the West Indies, making him at a reported 15 years and 124 days the youngest ever Test cricketer.*

Sadiq followed on soon after, making his debut in the 1959–60 season at the age of just fourteen years and nine months. He was the only left-hander among the Mohammad brothers.† He had to wait ten years to be selected in a Test match, against New Zealand in Karachi in 1969. Thereafter he established himself as a reliable Test match opening batsman, besides enjoying a successful county career with Gloucestershire in the English county championship.

PAKISTAN IN WEST INDIES 1957–58

Kardar held that domestic cricket was undemanding and did not provide enough information from which to choose a Test squad: 'Though the inter-provincial matches were played on a league basis, and a number of players got the opportunity of calling themselves first-class cricketers, the majority of these matches could not be judged as first-class.'[40] So ahead of the West Indies tour, he summoned the leading prospects to a national training camp so that they could 'show their worth'.

These pre-tour camps were beloved of both the Pakistan and Indian establishments. They were normally held at one of the great national cricket centres, with the players housed in tents outside the grounds. Players were expected to rise at 5am, then undergo a series of punitive physical exercises.

---

*But was Mushtaq really as young as fifteen? One hazard of the upheaval of migration was the loss of belongings and documents. 'Although I believe I was born in November 1943, it is possible it was November 1942,' he wrote in his autobiography, adding 'though there is every chance those records were legitimate there is also a chance they were not. My mother never had a birth certificate for me.

'My age became officially registered as such when Hanif enrolled Sadiq and me in school. Hanif told the school administrators my birthday was 22 November 1943 and ever since, that is the date that has stood.' Mushtaq, p.26. Mushtaq briefly lost his record as youngest-ever Test cricketer to another Pakistani, Hasan Raza. He told me of his delight at getting it back, when the latter's age was rejected by the PCB. See below, pp.385 et seq.

†Sadiq told me that he was compelled to be a left-handed batsman by his elder brothers because they thought it would improve his chances. Sadiq Mohammad: personal interview.

Later in the day, there would be fielding practice and tactical discussions. Finally, some cricket was played.

Kardar would invariably be the first to arrive at the ground, punishing anyone who turned up late. He interpreted the camps as fulfilling a broader role in adapting his unsophisticated players to the customs and practices of western civilisation. 'He would guide us how to eat,' recalls Nasim-ul-Ghani. 'We didn't know how to use knives and forks or our manners round the table.'[41]

Kardar was soon unhappy with the arrangements. The BCCP had insisted, against his will, on holding the camp at the Dring stadium at Bahawalpur. But – as normally the case with the Pakistan captain – there was a problem. Out in the West Indies the wickets were shiny, fast and perfect. Here the wicket was slow, the ball kept extremely low, and even bad bowlers could impart substantial spin on the ball. Kardar complained that 'whereas the bowlers found it easy to turn the ball considerably and therefore formed a wrong opinion of their own worth, thereby misleading the selectors, the batsmen failed to gain necessary confidence that the camp was designed to build up.'[42] Eventually he shifted the camp to his native Lahore.

New talent was at last showing itself. Ijaz Butt, later to make his name as a disastrous chairman of the Pakistan Cricket Board, emerged as a promising wicketkeeper-batsman. Two new spinners were being tried in the shape of Haseeb Ahsan and Nasim-ul-Ghani. Most important of all was the arrival of twenty-year-old Saeed Ahmed, the first major batsman to break through into the Pakistan Test team since the first series against India five years before. He arrived as the career of Maqsood Ahmed ended. Maqsood's attitude left much to be desired: 'Maqsood was dropped because he was completely unwilling to continue the morning physical training and gave up coming to the nets after a few days,' wrote Kardar. Maqsood – a popular figure – later took to journalism, which offered a style of life which he found more congenial. He had been at Karachi for the famous defeat of the MCC in 1951, in the opening match against India at Delhi, and at Fazal's match at The Oval. His departure was an early sign that Kardar's band of heroes was breaking apart.

It is hard to recapture today the magnitude of the journey upon which the Pakistan cricket team embarked to the Caribbean in December 1957. The cricketers were unpaid, but received an allowance equivalent to £1 a day for the duration of the tour, out of which they were expected to pay for meals, laundry, and other essentials.[43]

They travelled by air, a series of hops to London, and then by sea on the SS *Golfito*, a banana boat, to Barbados. Upon arrival the players went for net practice. 'This was our first contact with cricket after sixteen days of travel by air and sea, during which we covered nearly 13,000 miles,' recorded Hanif.[44]

This West Indian cricket tour cannot be fully appreciated without some understanding of its political and social underpinning. While Pakistan had achieved independent status a decade earlier, the struggle was still going on in the West Indian islands. Barbados, for example, would only gain her sovereignty in 1966, while the West Indian captain was habitually a white man. Gerry Alexander was chosen for this series.* This twenty-nine-year-old, Cambridge-educated wicketkeeper-batsman had not even played a first-class match in his native country until March 1957, nine months earlier, for Jamaica against the touring Duke of Norfolk's XI. He had only played two Test matches, making 0 not out, 11, 0 and 0 on the previous summer's tour of England. Far greater players, such as Everton Weekes and Clyde Walcott, were overlooked as captain.

The captaincy issue did not, however, prevent the West Indies playing some wonderful cricket. For the first half of the Barbados Test, played over six days at Bridgetown between 17 and 23 January 1958, Pakistan were obliterated. The West Indies were beginning to emerge as one of the finest teams in history. So much is obvious from a recitation of the first five in the batting order: Conrad Hunte, Rohan Kanhai, Garry Sobers, Everton Weekes, Clyde Walcott. Only the great Frank Worrell, who was taking time off to study for a degree in economics at Manchester University, was absent.

After Kardar lost the toss, this awesome line-up toyed with the Pakistan attack. Hunte, making his Test debut, blasted his way to 142, only to be surpassed by 197 from Weekes, then coming to the end of a magnificent career. Sobers hammered 52, Walcott 43. Faithful Fazal, maybe showing the first signs of age, conceded 145 runs for just three wickets.

---

*Gerry Alexander, the last white man to captain the West Indies. Alexander's native Jamaica was not to achieve full independence from British rule until 1962. Following a campaign led by CLR James, Frank Worrell would become the first full-time black captain of the West Indies, leading the team on its famous 1960–61 tour of Australia.

On the third day the Pakistan batting was blown away by the pace of Roy Gilchrist, a very fast opening bowler and one of the nastiest pieces of work ever to stroll onto a cricket pitch. He repeatedly beat the Pakistani batsmen for sheer pace. Shortly after lunch, Pakistan were all out for 106.

When Alexander asked Pakistan to bat again, they were 473 runs behind on first innings, with more than three and a half days left. 'Everyone was feeling it was a matter of formality to get Pakistan out,' noted Hanif. 'I must confess that we too did not feel that we could last for three and a half days to survive defeat.'[45] The West Indian bowling was fresh, having taken just 42 overs to skittle out Pakistan in the first innings. It was also very strong. Besides the lethal and wicked Gilchrist, Collie Smith with his off-spin was capable of being troublesome on a wicket that would soon start to break up.* He was partnered by the slow left-armer Alf Valentine, famous for destroying the England batting order in 1950. Eric Atkinson, Gilchrist's opening partner, was useful, while his older brother Denis was a very handy bowler of off-breaks. Finally there was Garry Sobers, who could bowl any kind of left-arm spin and would soon show himself equally capable as an opening bowler.

When Hanif and Imtiaz Ahmed went out to bat on the afternoon of 20 January, they were not facing an ordinary or a depleted attack. Many apparently great cricketing feats are attained against inferior opposition, but not Hanif's. Imtiaz eventually fell to a debatable lbw decision for 91. The ball was going wide down the leg side and Imtiaz had advanced several paces down the pitch. The famously knowledgeable West Indian crowd, who were relishing the Pakistani fightback, booed and shouted at the umpire.[46]

On the fourth day, Pakistan scored 178 runs in five hours for the loss of just one wicket, that of Alimuddin. Gilchrist was bowling very fast, short balls; Hanif was used to dealing with such deliveries and normally used his small stature to duck harmlessly underneath them. Gilchrist, however, was aiming directly at Hanif's head. Hanif responded by waiting until he could judge their trajectory, and swaying out of the way at the very last moment. He tried to hook one of them, but missed. At the end of the over, Clyde

---

*This fine all-rounder died in a car accident the following year, in which his friend Garry Sobers was also involved. Some 60,000 people attended the funeral in his native Jamaica. He had an excellent series against Pakistan in 1958, averaging 47 with the bat and taking 13 wickets. He had not yet reached his peak when he died.

Walcott strode over to Hanif with advice: 'Don't try to hook Gilchrist because he is too fast for you.'

By the close of play the Pakistan score was 339 for 2. That night, when Hanif went to his room, he found a note of encouragement from his captain in the bedroom he shared with his brother Wazir.[47] Kardar, a born motivator of men, would place such notes in Hanif's room every night. 'You are the only hope to save Pakistan,' read one. 'Hanif, you can save it. Just stay there,' read another.[48]

At the start of day five, Hanif arrived early at the ground for net practice. That day a further 186 runs were scored, for the loss of Saeed Ahmed for 65. Their team-mate Nasim-ul-Ghani recalls that 'at lunchtime Hanif would go into a corner, eat a small piece of chicken, relax, take a shower.'[49]

Hanif was profoundly exhausted, and in constant pain, yet he drove himself on and on. Batsmen did not use thigh-pads in those days and the quicker deliveries thudded constantly into Hanif's almost unprotected (he did try and use hotel towels) upper thigh. An indentation had begun to develop, caused by the repeated thud of cricket balls sent down at 80 or 90 mph on his already wounded flesh.

Hanif's upper cheekbones were black with burnt blood as layers of skin had peeled off. Hanif had a cap to mitigate the rays of the West Indian sun, but could do nothing to prevent them reflecting off the mirror-like wicket. Modern players smear their face with a white cream to protect against sunburn. It had not been thought of in the 1950s.

By this stage, recorded Hanif, he 'felt that I knew every particle of the wicket and every face on the ground. I found that the wicket had started cracking and certain holes were so big as to allow a pencil to find its passage through. There were certain balls I do not know how I managed to stop.' The score at the close of play on day five was 525 for 3, Hanif's score stood at not out 270. When Hanif got home to his room that night, the note from Kardar waiting for him on his dressing table read: 'You've got to stay till tea time. Then we will save the game.'[50]

By tea-time Hanif had advanced to 334. The game was now safe, but Hanif was dreaming of passing the 364 scored by Len Hutton at The Oval in 1938, then the highest innings ever scored in Test cricket. Shortly after tea, Hanif attempted to glide a delivery from Denis Atkinson past the slips and was caught behind.

His innings had lasted 16 hours and 39 minutes – 999 minutes in all.[51] It was then the longest ever played in first-class cricket.* At the time of writing, twenty-seven scores of 300 or more runs have been made in Test cricket, but only two have been made in the second innings.† Hanif's was the greatest defensive innings ever played, and beyond question the most heroic.

The second Test, played at Port of Spain, was a closely fought contest in which Pakistan were only defeated after a series of unhappy umpiring decisions at crucial moments. However, Pakistan's batting crumbled badly against Gilchrist. The turning point came in Pakistan's second innings when, chasing 355 to win, Hanif was brilliantly caught by Sobers at gully off Gilchrist. Hanif had scored 81, but his nerve had gone. He found himself backing away to leg against the West Indian paceman. Forty years later, Hanif owned up to his personal crisis:

> Gilchrist's fearsome and threatening pace had totally shattered my confidence. Thank God I had stopped hooking him. I will always remember a delivery from him. It pitched short and kept on coming at me. I swayed, tilting my small frame back, but was caught on the wrong foot, and didn't know which side to move. It whizzed past, barely missing me. I do not know how I survived it. If it had hit me on the face or head I would surely have died. That delivery still returns to haunt me in my nightmares.[52]

This is an honest description of the private nightmare often involved in facing real pace. Batsmen did not wear helmets until the late 1970s.‡ Every time Hanif faced a rearing ball from Gilchrist, he was forced into an instant decision, reached in a fraction of a second. One false judgement and Hanif was facing a serious injury, probably to the head, perhaps even death. Some believe that Hanif was never the same batsman after his moment of terrifying clarity against Gilchrist.

*In November 1999, Hanif's record was broken by Rajiv Nayyar who batted for 16 hours and 55 minutes on his way to 271 in a Ranji Trophy match between Himachal Pradesh and Jammu and Kashmir at Chambra. Nayyar occupied the crease for 1,015 minutes, faced 728 balls and hit 26 fours and a six. Hanif's 999 minutes (16 hours and 39 minutes) remains the longest innings in Test cricket.
†Brendon McCullum scored 302 in the second innings for New Zealand against India in February 2014.
‡Hanif's brother Sadiq was a pioneer, on Pakistan's England tour of 1978, a few years after sustaining a terrible head injury at short leg. (He also had a sponsorship offer from the makers, St Peter.) Sadiq Mohammad: personal interview.

The third Test led to crushing defeat for Pakistan, who batted first. Hanif, now useless as an opening batsman, was out to Gilchrist almost at once. But his opening partner Imtiaz scored a fine century, and Pakistan reached 328.

What followed was merciless slaughter of a nature rarely seen in top-level cricket. It was led by the twenty-one-year-old genius Garry Sobers. Sobers announced himself with 365, one run for each day of the year. He and Conrad Hunte, who scored 260, put on 446 for the second wicket. Though in statistical terms Sobers had reached a memorable total, it does not bear comparison to Hanif's epic 337 in terms of physical endurance, character, skill, application or even significance in terms of affecting the match result.

The Pakistan bowling attack was in ruins from the start. The fast bowler Mahmood Hussain broke down with a thigh strain after five deliveries. Nasim-ul-Ghani fractured his thumb. So Pakistan were without two of their four main bowlers. Fazal filled the breach by bowling 85 overs, taking two wickets for 247 runs.* Kardar was forced to use eight bowlers. Hanif, who had no bowling credentials, was bowling left-handed when Sobers scored the run that took him past Len Hutton's world record of 364. Immediately afterwards Gerry Alexander declared, with the West Indies score on 790 for 3.

Pakistan went down to an innings defeat. Hanif dropped down the order for the rest of the tour, a humiliation forced by the need to hide from Gilchrist. Pakistan played well enough in the fourth Test, and Saeed Ahmed announced himself as the coming force in Pakistan cricket with a majestic 150 in the first innings. But West Indies still won easily.

In the final Test, Fazal produced his old magic to bowl the West Indies out cheaply, and Pakistan won by an innings and one run. When Kardar announced his retirement, Fazal Mahmood was his natural successor.

*See *Wisden 1959*, p.814. 'Fazal Mahmood, who sent down a phenomenal number of overs for a bowler of his pace, and Khan Mohammad were left as the only two fit regular bowlers.' Khan Mohammad had no wicket for 259 in 54 overs. Given the calibre of the depleted Pakistan attack, Sobers's achievement was minor compared to the 375 and 400 not out made by his compatriot Brian Lara in 1994 and 2004, both times against powerful and fit England attacks. The 380 scored by the Australian opener Matthew Hayden against a poor Zimbabwe team in 2003, which temporarily held the world record, was meaningless.

9

FAZAL REPLACES KARDAR

'When war is not on, the best place for the promotion of team spirit is the sports field.'

– FIELD MARSHAL AYUB KHAN, RULER OF PAKISTAN 1958–69

AH Kardar was barely thirty-three years old when he retired. He had played only twenty-three Test matches, and could have persisted into the 1960s. Kardar, such a prolific writer, never came up with an explanation of why he quit so soon.

Shuja-ud-Din records that 'some of the cricket pundits were of the opinion that Kardar's step was a calculated plan to stage a comeback' in response to overwhelming public clamour.[1] This makes some sense. Throughout his career, Kardar entertained thoughts of retirement. As early as 1953, in the wake of the first tour of India, Kardar briefly gave up cricket, issuing a statement to Reuters stating that he had done so. This first resignation – described by Kardar at the time as 'a serious decision and a terrific wrench for me' – was a protest against what he regarded as Pakistan's chronically poor cricket administration. Details about this first resignation are sketchy, and Kardar must have been persuaded fairly quickly to change his mind.[2]

According to Khalid Qureshi, a friend of the Pakistan captain and part of the squad which toured India with Pakistan in 1952, Kardar once again toyed with resignation during the 1954 tour of England. Over a beer and a cigarette during The Oval Test, Kardar suddenly informed him that it had been a long tour and that he would quit when it ended.

At this point in the match, defeat looked more likely than victory, and Kardar doubtless felt a natural sense of impending disappointment. He must have feared that the 1954 tour would be seen as a disaster, and that he would be blamed. But this was before Fazal turned the tables and Pakistan won the match. When he spoke to the press in the aftermath of victory, he announced his determination to continue to lead Pakistan cricket.*

Kardar's regular flirtation with the idea of resignation shows that he found the captaincy of Pakistan far more of a nervous strain than he ever publicly acknowledged. Whatever his motive, Fazal Mahmood relished his belated chance to show after the West Indies tour that he was his own man, and was determined not to relinquish without a struggle a job he had coveted for many years.

A MILITARY COUP AND ITS CONSEQUENCES

The departure of Kardar from international cricket coincided with the collapse of the civil administration in Pakistan. In October, President Iskander Mirza proclaimed martial law, only to be overthrown himself a few weeks later by the man he appointed chief martial law administrator, General Ayub Khan.†

---

*Personal interview with Khalid Qureshi, son of AA Qureshi, a Test umpire and vigorous promoter of early club cricket in Lahore. Khalid played for Pakistan against the Commonwealth XI in 1949 in the calamitous Lahore fixture, and later toured India in 1952, playing in side matches but in none of the Tests. In 1962, playing for Lahore Gymkhana against the Punjab Club (not to be confused with the Lahore gentleman's club of the same name), a game which did not have first-class status but was nevertheless a highly charged contest, Qureshi took nine wickets for no runs. The Punjab Club was dismissed for the humiliating total of three. After the 1952 tour of India, Qureshi emigrated to England to train as an electrical engineer, witnessing all of the Tests and renewing his association with Kardar. When Qureshi asked Kardar to explain his sudden change of mind, Kardar laughed and said, 'Qureshi, my boy, this is politics. You should always keep the element of surprise alive that keeps you in the news.'
†Kardar's analysis of Ayub's rise to power: 'He had stepped noiselessly into the Cabinet as Defence Minister and had established contacts at the international level. Ironically, he had also made sure that it would be through his old friend, President Iskander Mirza, that he would work his way up. They had two things in common, a Sandhurst background and the belief that the people of Pakistan were not ready for democracy. They had worked out the power game together but finally it was the man in uniform, the soldier of fortune, who reached for the gun faster.' AH Kardar, *Pakistan's Soldiers of Fortune*, p.27.

After sending Mirza into exile in London,* Ayub moved quickly to remove power from Pakistan's provinces in favour of smaller, local units, and this was mirrored in cricket administration. The Punjab Cricket Association broke up into associations for Lahore, Multan and Rawalpindi, and the Sindh Association split between Khairpur and Hyderabad.

In 1958–59, East Pakistan withdrew from the Quaid-e-Azam Trophy (apparently on the grounds of expense) but Combined Services re-entered the competition, with the army especially busy after the coup, it became even more of an Air Force team. The competition that year was dominated by an extraordinary batting feat in the semi-final between Karachi and Bahawalpur, the defending champions. Winning the toss on the Karachi Parsi Institute ground, Karachi sent Bahawalpur into bat and dismissed them for 185. By the close of the first day, Karachi had replied with 59 for no wicket, Hanif making a controlled 25 not out. By close on the next day, he was on 255 not out, after adding 172 runs with Waqar (37) and 103 with his brother Wazir (31) Hanif's first century needed 160 minutes, the second only 102. He gave one sharp chance on 94 'but the fielder at point failed to dive and pick up the catch.' (Pakistani fielders were understandably reluctant to dive on their rough outfields.)

By the time he reached his triple-century, Hanif was very tired, and it was his brother (and captain) Wazir rather than he who wanted to push for records. By tea on the third day, Hanif was 17 short of Don Bradman's 452 (the unselfish Wallis Mathias meanwhile had scored an almost unnoticed century at the other end in a partnership of 259). Against a wilting attack, Hanif had managed to teach himself two new scoring strokes off the back foot on each side of the wicket. Bradman's record duly fell and towards the close of play Hanif was in sight of 500, in the company of the young wicketkeeper Abdul Aziz. With two balls to go in the last over of the day, and knowing his brother would want to declare at the end of it, Hanif looked at the scoreboard. It showed 496 against his name.

---

*Iskander Mirza fled penniless to Britain, where he is said to have lived in a small West London flat and worked as an accountant at Veeraswami, the Indian restaurant in Swallow Street, Piccadilly, and, for a time, as general manager at the Dorchester hotel. Neither the Dorchester nor Veeraswami can cast light on these reports. Ex-president Mirza was once seen strap-hanging on the London Underground by Qamar Ahmed, Quaid-e-Azam Trophy player turned cricket journalist. Qamar offered his seat to Mirza, who attempted at first to decline it. After Mirza's death in 1969, President Yahya Khan reportedly refused to allow his body back into Pakistan. Mirza, a Shia, was flown to Tehran and buried there. In contrast to many of his successors, he did not make an illicit penny out of public office.

'I hit Riaz Mahmood past point and took a single, and as the fielder Muhammed Iqbal fumbled, I went for the second run to be able to face the last ball to get two more runs. The next moment, I saw the throw coming to the keeper Tanvir Hussain from Iqbal. The throw beat me by a yard and a half and I was out. I thought that I had made 497. It was while coming back to the pavilion that I saw the scorer putting my score on the board as 499. I discovered that the boys running the scoreboard had erred. Instead of my 498 they had put 496 as I went for the run. I was really furious. Had I known that, I would have waited for the last delivery to get the required runs.'*

At the time and since, critics have carped at the standard of the Bahawalpur attack. It was short of pace, and was opened by an off-spinner and a leg-break bowler. However, the off-spinner in question was Zulfiqar Ahmed, an experienced Test performer, and all but 28 of the 200 overs Hanif faced were bowled by recognised bowlers, while Bahawalpur were after all the defending champions. Bradman himself sent a gracious congratulatory telegram at the fall of his twenty-nine-year-old record. Ayub Khan gave Hanif a specially struck Pride of Performance medal and Karachi Municipal Corporation handed him 10,000 rupees (in 1959, equivalent to about £750).

Hanif's innings lasted 640 minutes, four hours shorter than his matchsaving 337 twelve months earlier against the West Indies. When Bahawalpur were beaten by an innings the next day, Hanif joined the band of cricketers who have been on the field throughout a first-class match. He was watched by about a thousand people.[3] Hanif's record stood for thirty-five years, until it was overtaken by the great West Indian Brian Lara, playing for Warwickshire against Durham on 6 June 1994. The England batsman – and future Pakistan coach – Bob Woolmer was present at both innings.†

---

*Hanif Mohammad, *Playing For Pakistan*, op. cit. pp.114–18. Curiously, a scoring error marred another world record, the 555 scored by Yorkshire's openers Percy Holmes and Herbert Sutcliffe against Essex in 1932. Herbert Sutcliffe gave his wicket away, thinking the record had been broken, only to discover that the Essex scoreboard showed 554 after all. A previously unrecorded no-ball was added to the total after the event. See obituary in *Wisden 1994* of Charles Bray, the Essex captain. One feels that a similar unrecorded run might have been awarded to Hanif.

†Woolmer was Warwickshire coach in 1994 and thus played a role in the decision to delay the Warwickshire declaration so that Lara could break Hanif's record. In 1959 he was a ten-year-old prepschoolboy and had just flown out to Karachi (his BOAC Comet being forced down by fighters over Baghdad en route) where his father worked. Mushtaq Mohammad, who played in the Karachi match, was in Birmingham when Lara made his record score. He was tipped off by phone when Lara passed 450, and raced to Edgbaston cricket ground, but arrived too late.

Hanif made another century in the final, when Karachi beat Services by 279 runs. However, the most notable event of this match was the death of Abdul Aziz (Hanif's blameless partner when he was run out for 499). He was struck over the heart while batting, collapsed and died while being rushed to hospital.* The bowler was Dildar Awan, a slow off-spinner. Abdul Aziz, the son of a Muslim cleric, may well have been concealing a heart condition to fulfil his dream of becoming a cricketer.

WEST INDIES TOUR PAKISTAN 1958–59

Fazal at once asserted his authority as captain. In a move aimed directly at Kardar, who had been appointed chairman of selectors on his retirement, he insisted on making his own selection decisions.[4] His training camps were even more severe than Kardar's. The first of these took place in the Karachi National Stadium in preparation for the arrival of the West Indies. Fazal discovered that some of the players, finding their proximity to the city centre too much of a temptation, were skipping the curfew and coming back late at night to sleep in their tarpaulin tents. Outraged, he intensified the training schedule, leading them off on unfeasibly long twenty-mile runs. Ayub Khan, hearing of this camp, came to visit. He had never before displayed much interest in cricket, but may have felt he needed some publicity to soften his image as a ruthless military commander. Ayub watched the players practising for a while then called them together for some words of encouragement: 'When war is not on,' observed the general, soon to appoint himself field marshal, 'the best place for the promotion of team spirit is the sports field.'[5]

The West Indies reached Pakistan in mid-February, having defeated India 3–0 in a five-Test series. Once again their chief agent of destruction had been the fearsome Gilchrist, who had taken twenty-six wickets at an average

---

* *Wisden 1960* obituary. He was the second player to be killed as the result of a blow at cricket. The first was George Summers of Nottinghamshire, playing against the MCC on a poor pitch at Lord's in 1870. He was struck by a short delivery from John Platts, a fast bowler. He died in Nottingham a few days later. Platts was heartbroken and gave up pace bowling for spin. In 1993, Ian Folley, formerly of Lancashire, died of a heart attack following an unsuccessful hospital operation after being hit in the face while fielding at Whitehaven. In 1998 in Bangladesh the former Indian Test opener, Raman Lamba, fielding at short leg without a helmet, was hit in the head by a hard-hit pull; he died of a consequent brain haemorrhage.

of just over sixteen apiece, but Fazal benefited from a stroke of luck. At the end of the Indian tour, Gerry Alexander sent Gilchrist home for dangerous bowling.

This was a relief to Hanif Mohammad, who had been practising intensively against fast, short-pitched bowling in the nets in order to ready himself for Gilchrist's arrival. Hanif at once reverted to his usual role of opener, and in the first Test match at Karachi batted six and a half hours for 103. This innings – along with seven wickets from Fazal – was enough to ensure victory. The Pakistan second innings provided another example of Hanif's physical courage. His finger was fractured late in the day, but he remained at the crease in excruciating pain, so that an incoming batsman would not have to face the bowling at an awkward time. Hanif missed the remainder of the series because of his injury.[6]

The second Test match, played in the East Pakistan capital Dacca, turned into a memorable game. Alexander won the toss and put the Pakistanis into bat. With Hanif injured the fast bowling of Wes Hall, just as fast as Gilchrist but less evil, reduced Pakistan to a desperate 22 for 5. A courageous stand between Wallis Mathias, who scored 64, and Shuja-ud-Din rescued the side. Nevertheless, Pakistan were all out for 145. The West Indies fared even worse. The final six batsmen all scored nought as the team collapsed from a fairly respectable though wobbly 65 for 3 to a dreadful all-out 76.* The main agent of destruction was once again Fazal, who captured six West Indies wickets for 34 runs.

In the second innings the Pakistan batsmen collapsed again, and were once again indebted to Mathias who top-scored for the second time with 45. The West Indies needed 214 to win but fell 41 runs short. This time Fazal claimed six wickets for 66 runs. It was his final Test match-winning performance.†

'After winning two Tests in a row', concluded Fazal, 'I was a satisfied man.'[7] He was entitled to be. With or without Gilchrist, Alexander's team was a formidable side, as it finally showed in the third Test. Unlike the first two, it was played on turf rather than matting. The West Indies eased their

---

*This would remain the West Indies' lowest score until they were bowled out for 53 at Faisalabad in the first Test against Pakistan in 1986, Abdul Qadir taking 6 for 16.

†Fazal was the first Test bowler to take twelve or more wickets in a match against four different opponents. It took many more years until he was joined by Muttiah Muralitharan (who had the chance to bowl against nine other countries in contrast to Fazal's five).

way to 469, then bowled Pakistan out twice to win by an innings and 156 runs, Wes Hall and an emerging off-spinner called Lance Gibbs among the wickets. For the first time, Pakistan had been defeated on home soil. This match, the third in a series which had already been won by Pakistan, was the first Test match ever attended by the future Pakistan captain Imran Khan.[8] It was notable for a great innings from another rising West Indian star, Rohan Kanhai, who struck 217, made in just seven hours.

It was also the first appearance in Test matches of Mushtaq Mohammad. At 15 years and 124 days (if his age can be believed), he became the youngest-ever player in Test cricket, and the third member of his famous family to do so. Mushtaq performed nothing of note, but this was the start of a Test career which would span two decades, linking Fazal to Imran and Lindwall to Lillee.*

AUSTRALIA IN PAKISTAN 1959–60

Fazal's next challenge was Australia, captained by Richie Benaud, who had assessed Pakistan conditions and analysed lucidly and without rancour how they could be combated. Determined to learn the lessons of the 1956 defeat, he ordered his team to practise on matting before leaving home. According to Shuja-ud-Din, whose testimony carries extra weight because he played in this series, Benaud was so concerned that the matting would be tampered with that he would order his players early to the ground to check it.†

Benaud won the toss in the first Test, which was played at Dacca. He elected to bowl, perhaps conscious that Ian Johnson's Australians had been

---

*Mushtaq noted at the end of his career that, 'I was so young when I started out I almost played into the 1980s yet was still able to play against a star of the 1940s like Ray Lindwall.' Mushtaq Mohammad, p.39. Mushtaq played against Lindwall for the President's XI at Rawalpindi in November 1959.
†According to *Shuja*, pp.55–6, Benaud 'was aware of the tricks employed by the home team in laying the matting, i.e. by having it nailed rather loose when the visiting teams were batting, and keeping it tight to avoid any discomfort when Hanif Mohammad and the rest of the Pakistan batsmen were setting their stalls. During the Test matches, Richie Benaud would make sure that one of his team members actually spent the night in the ground, so that the batting strip was not tampered with in any form or shape. This in fact was taking the precaution a little too far. The left-arm spinner Lindsay Kline, whose services were only employed on the Lahore turf wicket, as a twelfth man for the other two Test matches was assigned to reach the ground at least two hours before the actual play got under way. And furthermore, he would make sure that the matting would be nailed in, in his very presence at the start of each day's play, and would request attention to the wicket whenever one or two nails lost ground grip.'

knocked over after batting first three years earlier. At first this tactic backfired, thanks to yet another defensive masterpiece from Hanif Mohammad, who scored 66. Fifteen minutes were left on the first day, and the score had reached a solid 145 for 3, when Hanif was bowled by 'Slasher' Mackay. Pakistan then collapsed to 200 all out.

Australia responded with 225 (Fazal, five for 71), fortified by a brilliant 96 from Neil Harvey. The Pakistan batsmen were completely unable to cope with Mackay's furtive medium pacers in their second innings. In 45 overs he claimed six wickets at a cost of 42 runs, with 27 maidens. Australia strolled home by eight wickets. In a total of 206.2 overs stretched over two innings, Pakistan had assembled 334 runs.

Fazal was injured in the second Test, and Imtiaz took over as captain. Shuja-ud-Din called Imtiaz a poor leader who 'had previously captained the Services in the domestic championship, but failed to inspire the troops.' Perhaps Shuja, a soldier, disliked playing under Imtiaz, an airman. Fazal's bowling was badly missed. Imtiaz, declared Shuja (one of the main strike bowlers and therefore in a position to know) 'was leading the thinnest bowling attack in Pakistan's cricket history.'[9]

This match was the first played at the new Lahore stadium, purpose-built for Test matches and completed in 1959. The days of the Bagh-e-Jinnah, perhaps the most beautiful ground ever used for a Test cricket match, were at an end. Pakistan enjoyed first use of the new turf strip, and were rolled over by the Australian opening pair of Alan Davidson and Ian Meckiff for 146. Made to follow on, a great innings by Saeed Ahmed of 166 forced Australia to bat again. Australia were set 122 to win in just under two hours and got home with twelve minutes to spare.

The third Test at Karachi was notable for the presence of Dwight Eisenhower.* Ayub Khan's decision to invite a visiting US president to the cricket was a reflection on the absence of rival entertainments in post-Partition Pakistan, but it also told a deeper story. Only a few months had passed since Ayub, with CIA support, had brought to an end eleven years of civilian rule, during which no US president had visited Pakistan. The

---

*This match also saw the Test debut of the all-rounder Intikhab Alam. He bowled the Australian opening batsman Colin McDonald with his very first delivery in Test cricket. According to Shuja-ud-Din, McDonald, going for a cut, was deceived by a 'perfectly disguised top spinner.' Shuja, p.58. However, Intikhab himself told me, with a demonstration, that it was a quicker leg-break, which gripped on the mat and hit McDonald's off-stump. Intikhab Alam: personal interview.

alacrity of the US president's visit signalled to the world that its most important democracy supported Ayub's military dictatorship. Only four US
presidents have ever visited Pakistan – Eisenhower, Richard Nixon, Bill
Clinton and George Bush Jnr – and never during periods of civilian rule.

Turning up on the fourth day, the president, who left early, watched some
of the most boring cricket ever played. Just 104 runs were scored as Hanif
Mohammad meandered towards one of his more pointless centuries. The
president also got an eyeful of Ijaz Butt, later to become a notoriously
incompetent chairman of the Pakistan Cricket Board, who stayed at the
wicket for 483 minutes while scoring 64 runs in the course of this match.
After play Ayub Khan was lobbied by Richie Benaud, who urged him for
the sake of Pakistani cricket to eliminate matting. The new president and
patron of the BCCP listened to him and issued an order for all first-class
grounds to install turf wickets. 'Thus Pakistan has Benaud to thank,' noted
Hanif drily, 'for the development of its cricket facilities.'*

Under Kardar, Pakistan, whatever her occasional misfortunes abroad, had
been impregnable at home. Now she had lost three consecutive home games.
Kardar began to toy with the idea of a comeback. Pakistan's famous 1–0 victory over India in the Rome Olympics of 1960, which had brought to an end
India's 32-year run of gold medals at Olympic hockey, stimulated Kardar's
appetite for a return. In late summer of 1960, he was in England for an operation to remove the cartilage from his knee.† Out of hospital, he went to the
Gover School for practice[10] and then, in a meaningful move, Kardar turned
down an invitation to become a selector for the forthcoming tour.[11] Two
weeks later, he declared himself fit. Speaking from London, he declared: 'A
victory against India should give our cricket as great a spur as our hockey victory against India at the Rome Olympiad will give fillip to hockey in

---

*Hanif Mohammad, p.131. Shuja locates this discussion to the second Test at Lahore, Hanif to the third
Test at Karachi. But was turf really such an improvement? Its initial effect was a shortlived boom for
Pakistan's fertile rural areas, who exported tons of their soil to Karachi and other centres. No voices were
raised against the Australian's lobbying and the president's decree; no one suggested that matting (with
its low maintenance costs and no demand for water) might be a better surface than turf for cricket pitches
in Pakistan. It was accepted by all that Pakistan must conform to the standards set by the (white) cricket
establishment. Hastily laid, the new turf wickets produced low bounce and extravagant spin – and consequent slow, low-scoring matches. Improvement or not, turf wickets remain Ayub Khan's lasting legacy
for Pakistan cricket.

†Kardar was operated upon on 19 September 1960 for the removal of the cartilage by surgeon JN
Wilson at the Royal National Orthopaedic Hospital. See *Dawn*, 20 September, p.14. Between 1928 and
1956 India won six gold medals and remained unbeaten in the Olympics.

Pakistan.'[12] Amid mounting speculation, Kardar was invited to attend a trial match for the impending India tour at the Bagh-e-Jinnah ground in Lahore.

Kardar flew the 8,000-mile journey from England to Karachi on 21 October, the day before the match[13] – billed as between the Kardar XI and the Fazal Mahmood XI – was due to start. It was a wearying flight at the best of times, and this one was seven hours late – poor preparation for a cricketer who had scarcely played since the West Indian tour ended more than two years ago. A harassed and tired Kardar caught the onward flight to Lahore the next day, travelled directly to the ground, and went almost straight in to bat, amid thunderous applause from spectators.

By no means did everybody want him to succeed. His three greatest critics were present that day: Fida Hassan, mastermind of an unsuccessful attempt to dump Kardar ahead of the 1954 England tour; Mian Mohammad Saeed, who had lost the captaincy to Kardar in 1951; and Mian Saeed's son-in-law Fazal Mahmood, who felt that he had lived for far too long in Kardar's shadow, and knew his former captain well enough to feel certain that he would make an intolerable subordinate.*

Kardar's play seemed listless: a great player fighting a cruel battle against time, exhaustion, and a chronic lack of match practice. Shafqat Rana was batting at the other end.† Fazal showed no mercy. He at once brought on Mohammad Farooq from the Gymkhana Club end. Farooq was a promising youngster and arguably Pakistan's best pace bowler of the time,‡ but at his peak Kardar would have handled him with relative ease. Now he struggled to see the ball. He slashed one boundary between the slips to the third man boundary. Then he lunged forward and missed hopelessly, to see his stumps shattered. His innings had lasted thirteen minutes. Spectators recall that Kardar walked back from the middle slowly, head bowed and

---

*By this stage Kardar knew – in theory – that he was simply playing for a place. Fazal was confirmed as India tour captain at the start of the game.

†Personal interview, Shafqat Rana. He recalls the match as follows: 'There was no sign of Kardar when the match started. Imtiaz Ahmed and Shakoor Ahmed opened the innings. After Imtiaz was retired at 54 Burki came in. I went in at number 4 after Shakoor Ahmed was bowled by Nasim-ul-Ghani for 37. In the meantime Burki retired at 51 and to my utter surprise instead of Duncan Sharpe I saw Kardar walking in. He looked a bit overweight but walked with his jaunty and erect gait with his neck stiffly tilted. He came to the wicket. Never looked at me as I stood on the other end and never exchanged a word. In between the time I was at the crease Kardar must have come to the ground. I heard that Shuja-ud-Din and Fazal had squeezed themselves and sat in a corner glumly as Shuja lamented that he was surely to be dropped if Kardar becomes the captain. Fazal too was very upset and worried for his captaincy.'

‡Mohammad Farooq had seven Tests for Pakistan as an opening bowler which produced 21 wickets at over 32 apiece. He broke down in England in 1962 after taking 4 for 70 in the Lord's Test.

crestfallen, and made no eye contact with anyone. He knew his days of big-time cricket were over.[14]

Several days later Ayub Khan, who had by now arranged to be promoted to field marshal, oversaw an investiture ceremony at Rawalpindi. AH Kardar received the Tamgha-e-Pakistan, one of the highest honours the Pakistan state can bestow. Fazal Mahmood received the president's medal for Pride of Performance. Everyone knew that it was Fazal who got the prize both men wanted: the captaincy of the Pakistan touring side to India.

PAKISTAN IN INDIA 1960–61

This was one of the dullest Test series in history, and no attempt will be made to describe individual matches in their suffocating detail.* The enthusiasm and expectation of the crowds contrasted with the boredom and ill-temper of the play. Shuja-ud-Din called this five-Test series the 'ultimate torture for a genuine cricket lover'.

Pakistan and India had agreed in advance to stretch the Test matches to five from four days in an attempt to ensure a result, but even this sensible precaution made no difference. The two teams played out their second consecutive 0–0 series draw. Indeed every single one of the fifteen first-class games played by Pakistan during their thirteen-week tour ended in

---

*However, Hanif's insanely brave innings in the first Test at Bombay cannot be allowed to pass without mention. Two weeks before the Test he had developed an infection of the feet. What followed is in Hanif's own words, as recorded by Noman, p.110: 'I was operated on and my toe-nails were removed. Naturally I thought I was out of the series. But such was the intensity of the Indo-Pak encounters that captain Fazal actually wanted me to play! I told him that I could not even put my shoes on. So I suggested that if the captain was so keen that he should get a special shoe made or cut the toe section of the cricket boot. The doctor said we were crazy and forbade me to play on the grounds that a yorker could destroy either foot. But the captain was insistent and worked on my mother, to whom he knew I could not say no. They bandaged my feet and got a shoe from Wallis Mathias, who had bigger feet than mine. I had a 45-minute net before the Test and at the end of it my socks were red with blood. But I played in the first Test in Bombay without toe-nails. My mother said I owed it to Pakistan ... Such were the passions which got aroused when the two neighbours met. The manager, Dr Jahangir Khan, did not want me to play. I played nonetheless. My innings in that Test was the finest I have played though the least remembered. It was like batting with nails piercing your feet. It was a cricketing crucifiction. But I got 90 runs and then had severe cramp. The Indian captain, Contractor, refused the request for a runner, probably because he thought this was a ruse and this was an injury sustained before the game. Technically he was right to refuse the runner. I was then in the odd position of not being able to run a single nor having the energy to hit boundaries. But I lasted to the end of the day and was taken to the hospital, where they worked on the cramp and my feet. I resumed my innings the next day and was run out for 160.' Hanif played the entire series without his toe-nails, which had only begin to reappear by the fifth and final Test.

stalemate. *Wisden 1962* recorded that 'the chief aim of the contestants appeared to be to uphold national prestige by avoiding defeat rather than to take the risk of trying to enforce a decision. Cricket was a secondary interest.' To his dying day Fazal Mahmood, who treated the series in the spirit of a football manager desperate to escape with an away draw in a local derby, would argue that the 0–0 result justified his defensive tactics.

He was turning out to be an unimaginative Test captain. The regime of the pre-tour training camp demanded that any fielder who dropped a catch in practice was forced to run round the ground. 'Our captain Fazal Mahmood, who was a Superintendent of Police in Lahore, pushed us beyond our limits with punishing fitness drills,' recalled Mushtaq Mohammad, who was only eighteen years old at the time. 'We would get out of bed at 5.30am each morning to go for a run, under the orders of a physical trainer from the army.' Mushtaq recalled that one 25-mile run left many in the side nursing injuries: 'Some of us had bruised heels, others had hamstring or groin injuries and I had blisters inside my thighs that were very painful.'[15] He said that Fazal was a 'crazy man' who alienated many of the senior members of the side. Much of the bitterness and negative play that marred the tour may have had its roots in this training camp, with its stress on hard work and discipline rather than a natural enjoyment of the game.

Pakistan scored their runs at 35 per hundred balls, India 39 per hundred balls. On only 11 of the 25 days' play did either side score more than 200, and on almost half of those occasions this faster scoring took place on the final day of what had already become a dead match. India's best bowler in the series, RG Nadkarni, sent down 191 overs at a cost of 219 runs, with 119 maidens.

Several months after the tour, the Indian press obtained a leaked copy of the tour report written by Jahangir Khan, the manager. He painted a picture of a Pakistan cricket team riddled by petty jealousy and indiscipline, with the rot starting at the top. Hanif, according to Jahangir Khan, 'had developed another bad habit of getting ready late. Special messengers had to be sent to fetch him every time we had to go to the ground or any other function.' The captain also came in for severe criticism: 'Fazal was never found in the hotel after the day's play. He had no longer any interest in his team after 5.30pm. He used to dress up and disappear.' Ayub Khan was furious, calling the players *goondas* (thugs) and insisted that in future army officers should be recruited to manage the tour and ensure discipline.[16] At the end of the tour, both Hanif and Fazal were fined 500 rupees – half their bonus payment – and Fazal was sacked.

KARDAR AND FAZAL: AN ASSESSMENT

Eighteen months later, at a moment of crisis, Fazal would respond to a national plea for help and make a final return to the national colours. But to all intents and purposes the Fazal-Kardar era had now ended, and with it the first heroic era of Pakistan cricket. The two great cricketers had emerged from the same culture, and shared many of the same ideals. As schoolboys they had cycled together to matches, and both made their first-class debuts in the same match for North India in early 1944.

Fazal was a much greater cricketer. Among Pakistani pacemen, only Waqar Younis, Wasim Akram and Imran Khan can be spoken of in the same breath. Fazal was the decisive match-winner in every single one of his country's great early victories – the vital win against the MCC at Karachi in 1951, India at Lucknow in 1952, England at The Oval in 1954, Australia at Karachi in 1956, and the West Indies at Port of Spain in 1957. But he was not just a destroyer. Fazal was unselfish, unfailingly stepping up to carry the burden of stock bowler in trying circumstances when his country needed him. Shockingly, Fazal did not even figure when the English cricket writer Christopher Martin-Jenkins compiled his list of the world's 100 greatest cricketers, a volume which displayed the Anglo-Saxon bias which has long dominated global cricket writing.

By contrast, the statistics announce that Kardar was mediocre. His batting average in the 23 Tests he played for Pakistan was 24.91, and his 21 wickets came at a cost of 45.42 each. But this does not reflect Kardar's contribution. With very few exceptions, the early Pakistan matches were dour and low-scoring affairs. Apart from Hanif, and (in his first Test series) Saeed Ahmed, most of Kardar's colleagues in the top six of the Pakistan batting order had a similar average, or worse. Even more to the point, almost every run Kardar scored for Pakistan was of value. He tended to come to the crease in circumstances of the utmost difficulty, and would remain there for long periods, extracting his team from trouble or leveraging it into winning positions. His bowling provided balance and extra options to the attack. Like Fazal, he willingly played the role of stock bowler at moments of need.

But his unique contribution was captaincy. His leadership provided the early Pakistan Test sides with ambition, discipline and a sense of mission. How badly this was needed can be measured by the rapid disintegration after he left. Kardar and Fazal can therefore be classified with a very small group of cricketers who were nation-builders as well as sportsmen. Other members of this select category include Frank Worrell* and Learie Constantine of the West Indies, and Don Bradman of Australia. It is not a coincidence that Constantine was the only hero Kardar acknowledged, aside from the senior Nawab of Pataudi.† Two great men had left the stage, and twenty years would pass before Pakistan experienced cricketing fulfilment again.

*Sir Frank Worrell was the first black man to captain West Indies through an entire series, and the first to be chosen to lead an overseas tour.
†Learie Constantine, West Indian cricketer and politician, one of the most brilliant West Indian cricketers of the inter-war era. He played a major role in the campaign for Trinidad independence, was a prominent supporter of the campaign for a black West Indian cricket captain, and campaigned for race equality in Britain. He was knighted in 1962 and raised to the peerage (as the United Kingdom's first black peer) in 1969.

IO

THE 1960S: THE LOST DECADE

'Cricket should be officially banned and the country saved from further bad repute.'

– MALIK FATEH KHAN, WRITING IN *NAWA-E-WAQT*, ON PAKISTAN'S
DISASTROUS PERFORMANCE ON TOUR IN ENGLAND IN 1962

Pakistan cricket was entering a period of abrupt decline. In the 1950s, Pakistan played 29 Test matches, of which they won eight, lost nine and drew 12. In the 1960s, Pakistan won just two Tests out of 30 played, both against New Zealand. Eight were lost, while 20 were drawn. Pakistan cricket was overcome by a morbid defensiveness. Avoiding defeat became the height of national ambition.

Kardar's team had reflected the hope, confidence and even the ebullience of Jinnah's newly created Pakistan. This had faded. Ayub Khan's dictatorship imposed a pattern of conformism on Pakistan society that found its way onto the cricket field and did not lift until the emergence of ZA Bhutto and his Pakistan People's Party at the start of the 1970s.

The key to Pakistan's victories in the 1950s had been pace bowling. No replacement was found for Khan Mohammad or Fazal Mahmood, leaving Pakistan without match-winners. Pakistan's best bowlers in the 1960s were spinners – Mushtaq Mohammad, Pervez Sajjad* and Intikhab Alam. But

*Pervez Sajjad is the brother of Waqar Hasan, a regular in Kardar's team of the 1950s.

Pakistan groundsmen, confounding their international image as cheats who would prepare their wickets to suit the local side, prepared pitches which favoured quicker bowlers.[1]

The finances of Pakistan domestic cricket faced permanent crisis. Cornelius and Kardar had worked hard to make sure that Pakistani businesses or government departments provided a livelihood for first-class cricketers. But ambitious cricketers moved out of Pakistan. Mushtaq Mohammad was one of the best players in the country, yet Pakistan was obliged to do without him from 1962 to 1967, because of his decision to develop his career as a county cricketer with Northamptonshire. Khalid Ibadulla (who could bat, bowl medium-pace or keep wicket and played for Warwickshire), was another case in point. Ibadulla, who was called up to join Kardar's Indian touring party as a seventeen-year-old as early as 1952, did not make his debut for Pakistan until the Karachi Test against Australia in October 1964, promptly making up for his twelve wasted years by scoring 166.

Pakistan found it very hard to obtain international opposition. For instance, the West Indies did not play against Pakistan between March 1959 and February 1975, a gap of almost sixteen years. Australia played only two Tests against Pakistan in the 1960s, one at home and one in Pakistan. Fourteen of Pakistan's 30 Tests during the 1960s were against England, but relations were awkward, with MCC teams slow to return to Pakistan after Donald Carr's catastrophic visit. There were no Test matches between India and Pakistan from Fazal's 1960–61 series until 1978–79. This left New Zealand, who accounted for nine out of Pakistan's 30 Tests in the 1960s. Finally, South Africa made it impossible for Pakistan to play against them because of apartheid.

A further problem was lack of government support. Today cricket is recognised as the national game, but that was not the case in Pakistan's early decades. It is possible to gain some sense of the priority attached to cricket by studying ministerial statements made in the National Assembly. Maddeningly these are erratic, but they do show that cricket was literally the poor relation.

In 1950–51, hockey and lawn tennis both received government grants of 15,000 rupees (then equivalent to around £1,600), while cricket got nothing at all. The following year cricket did receive 15,000 rupees (made to the BCCP and the first payment I can find for the sport) but the Pakistan Olympic Association received more, as did lawn tennis.[2] A longer and more continuous list of sports grants was published by Kazi Anwarul Haque, education minister in the late 1960s. This important table gives a record of government grants to all sports from 1958–59 to 1967–68. Hockey and athletics (Pakistan Olympic Association) come top with cricket running third, above wrestling and football.[3] This order of precedence was confirmed several years later when Haque's successor Abdul Hafeez Pirzada provided a list of all cricket and hockey Test players who 'are or have been' in government service since the formation of the Pakistan state. Pirzada produced 57 hockey players, and just 16 cricketers.*

On average the team would play just three Tests a year, and in both 1963 and 1966 there were no Tests at all. Pakistan reverted to the situation of the late 1940s, when she was starved of international cricket and therefore dependent on wandering sides, or series against non-Test-playing countries such as Ceylon or Kenya. No wonder some of Pakistan's star players walked away from the national game. Indeed there were times during this dire decade when there was reason to wonder whether cricket would survive at all as a spectator sport.

After the India tour, Fazal was written off by the selectors. That left just two members of Kardar's band of 1952 heroes in the national side – Hanif and Imtiaz, who was made captain. Keeping wicket, opening the batting and the captaincy overwhelmed Imtiaz, and he led Pakistan to defeat against Ted Dexter's England at Lahore in October in the first Test of their 1961 series.† Pakistan, for so long unbeatable on home soil, had now lost four out of their last five home Test matches, a situation viewed inside Pakistan with intense despondency.

In the remaining two Tests of the three-match series against England, Pakistan made certain that defeat would be avoided. Hanif scored a century in each innings in the second Test at Dacca. His 111 in the first innings was compiled over eight hours and 20 minutes, while his 104 in the second lasted six hours and 35 minutes. Overall he batted for almost fifteen hours in the match, more than half the game.

---

*The National Assembly of Pakistan (Legislature), Debates, Official Report, Saturday, 26 May 1973. The cricketers listed were: Javed Akhtar, Anwar Hussain Khokhar, Fazal Mahmood, Javed Burki, Gul Mohammad, Imtiaz Ahmed, A.H.Kardar, Munir Malik, Naushad Ali, Nazar Mohammad, Alimuddin; Waqar Hasan, Shuja-ud-Din, Maqsood Ahmed, Miran Bux, Sq. Ldr MEZ Ghazali.

†England, splendidly led by Dexter on his first appearance as captain, won by five wickets. They would not win in Pakistan again until Nasser Hussain's famous victory in semi-darkness in Karachi in December 2000.

After the Dacca Test the England squad travelled to Karachi where, following a six-hour flight and a 14-hour train journey, they played Bahawalpur and encountered Fazal Mahmood. Fazal, who had been dropped from the Test side, took six wickets for 28 as England were all out for 114. On the strength of this performance, Fazal was recalled for the third and final Test. The old stalwart sent down 63 overs for 98 runs, but took no wickets as England surged to 507, Dexter striking a superb 205. But steady Pakistan batting, fortified by two more defensive masterpieces from Hanif, ensured that the match was a draw.

JAVED BURKI AND THE 1962 TOUR OF ENGLAND

Pakistan now began preparations for the 1962 tour of England, a series which no lover of Pakistan can contemplate without subsiding into traumatised despair. Shuja-ud-Din called it 'the lowest and most depressing point in the history of Pakistan cricket.'[4] After the 1962 fiasco, Pakistan would not be allowed by Lord's to undertake a full five-Test tour of England for a quarter of a century.

The first problem was the captaincy, since Imtiaz Ahmed was deemed to have failed. There was no obvious successor and the selectors,* chaired by Cornelius, alighted on twenty-three-year-old Javed Burki. Although this appointment proved disastrous, Cornelius's choice looked sensible at the time. Burki had toured India with Fazal Mahmood's team in 1960 and performed well, scoring 325 runs at 46.42, and displaying an impressive temperament. He performed even better against Dexter's team in 1961–62, scoring two important centuries in three Tests.

Burki had just graduated from Oxford University, where he had been a Blue from 1958 to 1960. In his final year, he had come second in the English first-class batting averages, scoring 961 runs at 53.38. His Oxford University career had given him a great deal of experience in English conditions and placed him in the tradition of Kardar, whose time at Oxford had been an essential preliminary to his captaincy of the national team. Kardar

---

*The five-man selection committee comprised of Justice AR Cornelius (chairman), Agha Ahmed Raza Khan, Masood Salahuddin, IA Khan and Khan Mohammad. See *Pakistan Times*, 19 March 1962.

endorsed the choice of Burki, saying, 'I do not see any reason why given a piece of luck the team should not recapture the high standard attained on the previous tour of 1954.'[5] Finally, Burki's father, a general, had been one of three officers who had confronted Iskander Mirza late in the evening of 27 October 1958, insisting that he step down from the presidency and make way for Ayub.[6] In the military government that followed, Lt General Wajid Burki was made minister for health.

Many still allege that the elevation of the general's son to the captaincy was another reward from a grateful Ayub Khan. This is conceivable, though no hard evidence has ever been produced to prove this theory. The case for Burki was strong enough without the need to bring special pressure to bear.[*] Ayub Khan's influence could certainly be detected, however, in the choice of tour manager, Brigadier Haider (often spelt Hyder), and his assistant, Major Rahman. Haider, an officer who served during World War Two in Iraq, Italy, Libya and Greece,[†] was the beneficiary of Ayub Khan's decree that army officers should be installed to impose discipline. He was thus an early example of a large number of military figures who played a powerful role in the administration of Pakistan cricket over the following fifty years. According to Hanif Mohammad, Haider 'neither knew anything about the game, nor was interested in learning about it.'[‡] An expert polo player, before play started he would ask, 'When do we start the next chukka?' Nevertheless

---

[*]Javed Burki himself told me that he was very reluctant to assume the captaincy and would have preferred Imtiaz Ahmed. He had already declined the captaincy of Oxford University (AC Smith therefore led Oxford two years running). Javed Burki was then in the civil service academy. He was reminded of the rule that civil servants representing Pakistan at sport were considered to be on duty, and ordered to assume the captaincy.

[†]At the end of the war he was specially flown back to India on the orders of Auchinleck to get married. Haider came from a military family, attended the Indian military academy at Meerut before World War Two. In 1960 he was promoted to Brigadier and raised the 5th Armoured Brigade, from which he was seconded to run the national cricket team. In 1966 he was made Director General of West Pakistan Rangers, where he remained until retirement in 1971, Major Rahman (assistant manager in 1962) joining him as Superintendent. He was indeed, as his critics alleged, an outstanding polo player, playing regularly for the army for eight years and serving as president of Pakistan polo from 1966 to 1971. He spoke Italian fluently. His first name was Ghaziuddin but the British were unable to pronounce it, so it became Gussy and this stuck with him for the rest of his life. Gussy Haider is one of the most unfairly maligned figures in the history of Pakistan cricket. Even Shaharyar Khan, who ought to know better, fails to come to his defence, denouncing him as a 'polo-playing, tally-ho type cavalryman who knew absolutely nothing about cricket' (*Cricket Cauldron*, p.30. See also p.130). Interview with Brigadier Haider's sons Irfan and Anis Haider, and *Sportimes* special supplement on the 1962 tour.

[‡]The autobiographies of both Hanif and Fazal contain sulphurous stories about Haider's inability to understand elementary rules of cricket, such as the role of the nightwatchman or the difference between a bouncer and a googly. 'It was criminal to send such an official on a cricket tour. Such managers are no help to the team,' concluded Hanif. See Hanif, p.153.

Haider was a force for good, a cheerful and courteous presence who smoothed away many of the diplomatic difficulties on the tour.[7]

At no stage during 1962 was Burki's team competitive. In the opening Test at Edgbaston, England scored an effortless 544 for 5, then bowled Pakistan out twice to win by an innings. There followed a respite as Pakistan beat Surrey at The Oval. This was to prove the only victory over a county during the tour, and Burki's men promptly lost against Glamorgan and Somerset, thus vindicating Tom Graveney's unkind judgement that: 'If Pakistan became part of the English county championship, you wouldn't see them at the top of the table.'[8]

The second Test proved even more of a disaster than the first. Pakistan were bowled out for 100 halfway through the first day, Trueman claiming six for 31. In the second innings, Burki and Nasim-ul-Ghani added 197 for the fifth wicket, both scoring centuries. Nasim's was the first Test century by a Pakistani on English soil. Pakistan nevertheless lost easily. The team crashed once again to an innings defeat in the third Test at Leeds.

Back home, the situation was viewed as a national emergency. In the *Nawa-e-Waqt*, Rafiushan Qureshi declared that 'history will never forgive this', adding that the 'team lacks spirits and a desire to win.'[9] A despairing Sultan Arif sighed that 'the irresponsibility and disinterest with which our players played at Leeds is shameful. No justification can be presented for this.'[10] After the team lost seventeen wickets to lose the game on the third day of the Headingley Test, Arif despaired that 'this was a black day in Pakistan's cricket history. Pakistan played a game that has never been seen or heard.'[11] One writer in the *Nawa-e-Waqt* demanded the instant recall of the team from England, demanding in addition that 'cricket should be officially banned and the country saved from further bad repute.'[12]

The *Nawa-e-Waqt* claimed that the players did not care whether they won or lost. 'Every member of the Pakistani team is trying to get a new car and everybody wants his car to be the best among all. The moment our players arrived in London, they started visiting car dealers.'[13] It was now that the heavy insinuations began to surface that nepotism lay behind Burki's appointment.

Meanwhile the cry went round Pakistan: 'Bring back Fazal!' Newspapers' editorials demanded his immediate reinstatement, and an 'unending stream of letters' poured into newspaper offices calling for his return.'[14] Cornelius summoned Fazal to his chamber in the Supreme Court. Fazal, still seething at being dropped, played hard to get. At length Cornelius abased himself: 'Fazal, can you save Pakistan from utter humiliation?'[15] Fazal packed his bags, and went direct to the airport. On arrival in London he was greeted joyfully by Brigadier Haider: 'Fazal has come. Everything is going to be all right now.' Javed Burki was less enthusiastic. According to Fazal, he 'did not like my presence in England.'[16]

There was to be no repeat of The Oval triumph of 1954. Fazal was now, in cricketing terms, an old man. He was also out of practice. 'My fingers had become as soft as a pianist's,' he recorded. 'I could not rotate the ball.'[17] Nevertheless, being Fazal, he threw himself into the task. The fourth Test started just 48 hours after his arrival. Opening the bowling, Fazal bowled 16 consecutive overs, conceding just 17 runs. By the time England declared at 428 for 5 Fazal had delivered 60 of the 134 overs delivered by the Pakistan attack. His analysis read: 60-15-130-3. Sir Len Hutton wrote in his newspaper column: 'Burki, I feel, must have looked around his bowlers and wondered who he would bring on next. His answer always was Fazal – Fazal and more Fazal.'[18]

Partly thanks to Fazal, partly thanks to rain, and partly thanks to a century from Mushtaq Mohammad, Pakistan averted defeat. They were destroyed and humiliated in the final Oval Test however. Cowdrey (182) and Dexter (172) combined to place England in the invincible position of 406 for 2 at the end of the first day. Pakistan's batting then collapsed twice. An awful tour was over. Seventeen matches had now passed since the last Pakistan Test victory, against the West Indies in March 1959.

The team returned to face public anger, much of it aimed at Burki. It was not merely the spineless performance on the field that became an issue. The young captain was accused of insouciance off it. Fazal described his first net practice after arrival in England: 'This team had lost three Tests in a row, but he did not appear worried. He would come strutting out to the field, would whistle, and leave after a few minutes as if he did not care.'[19] Hanif Mohammad says that he was 'rude, raw and arrogant.'

The national revulsion against Javed Burki and his team became so great that Ayub Khan felt obliged to respond by setting up a National Enquiry, headed by the Attorney General. When I interviewed Burki for this book, he commented that the media were heavily censored in Ayub's time. He and his father both believed that their attacks on his captaincy were a proxy for attacking the regime through his father, known to be a close associate of Ayub.

The findings of the commission were suppressed, though it was understood that Burki had been heavily censured.[20] Nine of his side would never again play cricket for Pakistan. The 1962 tour marked the end of the road for Antao D'Souza, Ijaz Butt, Imtiaz Ahmed, Alimuddin, Wallis Mathias, Mahmood Hussain, Munir Malik, Javed Akhtar, Shahid Mahmood and Fazal Mahmood. Javed Burki continued to represent Pakistan, but never again as captain.

APRIL 1965: TEST MATCH SUCCESS AT LAST

At the start of the 1964–65 season Pakistan sent a touring 'A' team to Ceylon, a country upon which Kardar's team had been able to rely for bloodless victories. Pakistan, captained by Imtiaz, lost the 'Test' match at the Colombo Oval inside three days. Ceylon had probably improved over the previous decade, but Pakistan had got worse. Imtiaz, who had been recalled after the Burki disaster, was now sacked, leaving three rivals for the captaincy: Saeed Ahmed, Intikhab Alam, and Hanif, the one remaining player from Pakistan's first Test series against India in 1952.

The selectors chose Hanif, whose first task was to lead Pakistan against the visiting Australians. As ever, the circumstances were humiliating. Australia arrived on the way back from their summer tour of England, played one match against Pakistan, and left. There is a mystery about Australia and Pakistan during the quarter-century after Partition. The two countries contested just four Tests in the 1950s, each one of these on Pakistan soil. During the entire 1960s, this number shrank to two, both played in 1964.

Hanif's team included six debutants. Two of them, Asif Iqbal and Majid Jahangir (Javed Burki's first cousin, later to become better known as Majid Khan) opened the bowling.* This partnership was by no means Pakistan's deadliest attack, but over time both were to make a huge contribution to the rebirth of Pakistani cricket. Majid's father, Jahangir Khan, stepped down from the panel of selectors once it became clear that his son was a contender for the national team.

*The other debutants were Khalid Ibadulla, Shafqat Rana, Abdul Kadir and Pervez Sajjad.

Pakistan scored 414 in the first innings, thanks to Ibadulla's 166 on debut. He shared an opening stand of 249 with another debutant, Abdul Kadir, who was unlucky to be run out on 95.* On the fourth day, Pakistan should have forced the pace and given themselves a chance of bowling out Australia. Instead, both Hanif and Burki dawdled. Under Hanif's captaincy, Pakistan was invariably too cautious to create a real winning chance. Even Hanif's brother Mushtaq felt that 'Hanif was very defensive and was not creative or imaginative and would often go with the flow of the game.'[21]

Almost immediately after the drawn game in Karachi, Hanif led his team on a four-Test tour of Australasia – three matches against New Zealand, then the lowest ranked cricket nation in the world,[22] and one against Australia. There were two important absences from Hanif's squad, which was managed by Mian Saeed. Ibadulla, hero of the Karachi match, was not selected because he was already committed to play for Otago, the New Zealand first-class side, in the Plunket Shield.[23] Majid Jahangir did not tour because, so the Australians insisted, he threw the ball.[24]

Pakistan were again insulted by being given only one Test on their visit to Australia in 1964–65, although Australia had no other international commitments. Worse still, the Test, at Melbourne, was given only four days. Pakistan drew, thanks to two fine displays by Hanif Mohammad, who scored 104 in the first innings and 93 in the second before being stumped, an improbable end to a Hanif innings.[25] Mohammad Ilyas made an unsuccessful debut as an opener. His Test career would end, far more dramatically, also in Australia.[26]

The action now moved across the Tasman Sea to New Zealand, and an obscure three-match Test series (played, as then normal in New Zealand, over four days each) between the two weakest teams in world cricket. On the one hand, neither side was good enough to score many runs. On the other hand, neither side was good enough to bowl the other out. As a result, the second Test at Auckland produced what *Wisden* called 'one of the most uninspiring performances in all Test history.'[27] On the first day, Pakistan's batsmen played out 71 maiden overs.† Brian Yuile, the left-arm slow bowler,

---

*Abdul Kadir was the brother of Abdul Aziz, the tragic victim of a blow over the heart in the Quaid-e-Azam Trophy final of 1958–59. Another brother, Abdul Rashid, also played first-class cricket. They were the sons of Pesh Imam (a mosque cleric).

†At the end of the day the score was 152 for 8, 127 overs having been bowled.

bowled 47 overs while taking four wickets for 33 runs. Eventually the match was ruined by rain. All three Tests were drawn.

Two months later New Zealand returned to Pakistan, playing no preliminary matches and going straight into a Test at Rawalpindi, Ayub Khan's military headquarters. Pakistan won by an innings and 64 runs. Majid Jahangir, having resolved problems with his bowling action, was back in the team but Pakistan's match-winner was the slow left-arm bowler Pervez Sajjad, who destroyed New Zealand in their second innings with the figures of 12-8-5-4 as the New Zealanders collapsed from 57 for 2 to 59 for 9. The match was over in 12 hours and 40 minutes and 1,319 balls.*

New Zealand struck back in the second Test at Lahore when they removed half the Pakistan side for just 121 runs, but then Hanif Mohammad was joined by Majid Jahangir, who made his mark in Test cricket as the two added 217 runs for the sixth wicket. Hanif scored 203 not out, while Majid struck 80. The match was drawn, but Pakistan secured a fine victory in the third Test match at the National stadium in Karachi. Saeed Ahmed scored a majestic 172 (out of 307), Mohammad Ilyas made a fine century in the second innings and Intikhab Alam had a match analysis of seven for 92.

Thus Pakistan's two Test victories of the 1960s were both achieved within a single fortnight at the start of April 1965. There would be no chance to build on this achievement. Even as Saeed Ahmed and Javed Burki struck the winning runs against the modest New Zealand attack at the end of the third Test, the early skirmishes of the Second Kashmir War were under way.

The war started in earnest when Ayub Khan tried to infiltrate soldiers into Kashmir to foment an insurgency against Indian occupation. This manoeuvre was quickly spotted by India, who hit back hard, seizing a number of Pakistani positions. Ayub then ordered a full-scale military assault, which caught the Indians by surprise. India in turn widened the war by attacking Pakistan through the Punjab. Indian forces were on the outskirts of Lahore; in Zaman Park they could hear the thunder of guns and see the explosions along the border as the Indian army advanced towards the

---

*By comparison, the shortest completed Test match – Australia's victory over South Africa on a 'sticky dog' at Melbourne in 1931–32, lasted 5 hours and 53 minutes and 656 balls. This Test was supposed to be timeless. The Melbourne spectators did not even see Bradman bat, since he had been injured in a freakish dressing-room accident before Australia took the field. However, he took a brilliant running catch on the boundary in South Africa's second innings.

city.[28] A thirteen-year-old Imran Khan was distraught to be banned from joining the local militia. Finally, a ceasefire was agreed at Tashkent. Like so many of the recent cricketing encounters between the two countries, this military contest ended in stalemate. Both sides suffered heavy losses, and both sides believed (falsely in the case of Pakistan) that had time allowed they would have won. Imran Khan later remembered that 'everyone in the country was united in a desire to defeat the enemy. I don't think Pakistan has ever witnessed such unity. The nearest thing to it was perhaps when we won the World Cup in 1992.'[29]

This unnecessary war was followed by another long period of cricketing purdah. Between the culmination of the war on 23 September 1965 and the end of the decade, Pakistan would play only nine Test matches, six against England. More than three years would pass until Pakistan hosted another home Test, seven years before they next played Australia, ten years before they next played West Indies, and thirteen years before their next Test against India. As the Ayub Khan dictatorship tightened its grip, Pakistan was once more thrown back onto its domestic resources.

CRICKET IN THE SHADOWS OF WAR

'No English side ever started a game of cricket without having a cup of tea.'

– COLIN COWDREY

Pakistan's cricket was from this point overshadowed by armed conflict. President Ayub Khan became more autocratic, continuing to rule through emergency legislation. He sacked ZA Bhutto as foreign minister (and political heir apparent) in 1966. He also ordered, on charges of conspiring with India, the arrest of Sheikh Mujib, the new leader of East Pakistan's leading political movement, the Awami League.

Ayub's autocracy was especially unpopular in East Pakistan, where it exacerbated long-running political, linguistic and economic grievances.[1] East Pakistan had not shared the West's explosive growth under Ayub. The region had grown relatively poorer although it was still contributing a major part of Pakistan's export earnings from tea and jute. Bengalis resented the non-recognition of their language, Bangla, and the enforced use of Urdu, the first language of only a small minority. More and more Bengalis identified themselves as victims of colonialism and occupation.*

---

*As far back as 1955, Omar Kureishi commented on the Pakistan–India Test at Dacca and noted, 'East Pakistan was not a colony of West Pakistan. Why then did I leave it with the feeling that it was being treated as one?' (Kureishi O, *Home To Pakistan*, op. cit. p.59.)

These grievances were mirrored in East Pakistan's cricket. As we have already seen, East Pakistan teams were in-and-out participants in Pakistan's first-class tournaments. Not one East Pakistani cricketer played for Pakistan in the years up to 1966. MH Maqsood's generally optimistic survey, *Twenty Years Of Pakistan Cricket 1947–67,* contained a bleak passage by Badshah Shirazi: 'The review of 20 years of Cricket in East Pakistan depicts a sad picture of poor planning and lack of interest by those who ruled over the affairs of sports in the province for the last two decades.'

From 1966 onwards, East Pakistan's cricket received more attention from the authorities, particularly as the political situation deteriorated further. Several of their players were recruited into the powerful PWD team, one received Test selection, and a few more prestigious matches were directed to East Pakistan, notably the Dacca Test of 1969. But these scattered initiatives were engulfed by the political crisis and war which led to the total secession of East Pakistan.

A NEW TRIUMVIRATE FOR PAKISTAN

Almost two years passed since the end of the 1965 war before Pakistan was presented with another chance to impress in the Test arena. By now they were the forgotten team of international cricket. In England, where memories of Javed Burki's tourists had not been erased, Hanif's touring party was greeted with barely a murmur of polite interest.

The touring party nevertheless contained some substantial players. Saeed Ahmed remained a dominant middle-order batsman. Javed Burki, now reduced to the ranks, was only twenty-eight and still considered to possess potential. Hanif himself was incontestably a great cricketer. Mushtaq Mohammad and Intikhab Alam were two fine all-rounders, and neither had reached his peak.

Yet more important, the touring party contained three young players of incalculable promise for the future. Their impact over the next fifteen years was to be immense, as Pakistan moved from deferential third-raters to become one of the most feared teams in the world.

Wasim Bari, a nineteen-year-old from Karachi, would be the automatic choice as national wicketkeeper for the next seventeen years.* His story speaks volumes about the self-sacrifice that is essential for success at the top of any sport. His links with Karachi, where his grandfather ran a carpet-exporting business, stretched back well before Partition. His father had studied at Ludhiana College, near Jullundur, whose principal was Dr Jahangir Khan. Born in 1948, Wasim Bari attended St Patrick's College, Karachi (also alma mater of two of Pakistan's Christian cricketers, Wallis Mathias and Antao D'Souza). After school, young Wasim and his brothers and sisters would go over to watch the Test players in the nets, picking up loose balls and handing them to the bowlers. In this way he glimpsed Kardar, Hanif, Mushtaq, Mahmood Hussain and the Test wicketkeeper Imtiaz Ahmed.

The cricket coach at St Patrick's was Jacob Harris. 'When I was in the 6th class [aged 12–13] I said that I was going to be a cricketer', recalled Bari as I interviewed him in his office at Karachi's National Stadium. 'My class-mates laughed, I couldn't even get into the school team. Imtiaz Ahmed was my role model. I practised catching, non-stop. I threw myself thousands of catches alone and I recruited boys from the alleys to throw catches and bowl at me on local tennis courts. I asked them to swing the ball either way. I also played squash and practised with a squash ball.

'I emphasised glovework. Later my friend Alan Knott told me that glove-work is the quality by which wicketkeepers are judged. John Murray told me I had the hands of a pianist. I also skipped rope, on the advice of Master Aziz. He told me that wicketkeepers need strong legs like a boxer. I slept every night with my cricket bag and gloves. I didn't have any spikes. I played in rubber shoes on mat. Coir matting, made then in East Pakistan and Ceylon, is good for developing bowlers, because it helps cut, and young batsmen as well.'

Bari was finally spotted, aged sixteen, by Wazir Mohammad at trials for intercollegiate cricket: 'Wazir told the president of the Karachi Cricket Association that he had found "the best wicketkeeper in Pakistan".' Wasim Bari soon made his first-class debut in the Ayub Trophy, Karachi v Karachi University, under the captaincy of Waqar Hasan. Later that season, in the

---

*For his first Test match, at Lord's, he had no gloves in good condition. The reserve wicketkeeper, Fasihuddin, lent him a pair – Wasim Bari took three victims in them and went on to claim another 225. (One wonders if Fasihuddin ever regretted the loan.) Wasim Bari: personal interview.

Quaid-e-Azam Trophy final for Karachi Blues v Lahore Greens, he had seven victims in the match, aged seventeen years and one month – a record for any wicketkeeper in a Pakistan domestic final.

Another youngster on the rise was Asif Iqbal. A superlative natural athlete, Asif was a brilliant all-round cricketer. He and Majid Khan were the first of a new generation prepared to liberate themselves from the insecurity, paralysis and intense self-doubt which disfigured Pakistani cricket in the 1960s.* He belonged to that admirable class of cricketer, invaluable to their captains and worshipped by supporters, who tend to do best when it really matters. Again and again, when his team faced collapse or defeat, Asif would come to the rescue.

But even beyond that, Asif was to drive forward the commercialisation of the sport, secure better rewards for players, and play a significant role in the eventual destruction of Kardar. Later still, he would help pioneer the development of cricket in Sharjah, the first non-colonial expansion of the game.

Asif's personal story is one of the most fascinating in the history of Pakistan cricket. He was born in 1943, four years before Partition, in Hyderabad, South India. His uncle, Ghulam Ahmed, was himself an outstanding cricketer. He was one of the small band of Muslim cricketers, who remained behind and played for India after Partition, taking 68 wickets in his Test career at 30.17 and captaining the national side. Later he became secretary of the Board of Control for Cricket in India.

After independence Asif's family continued to live in Hyderabad, even after an attempt by the Nizam to remain independent was thwarted. Asif, coming from a middle-class family, was never allowed to play in the streets. Nevertheless, his uncle Ghulam Ahmed secured his entry to a local school by writing a letter to the principal stating that 'Asif is an outstanding cricketer and I have no doubt whatever that he will represent India.'² By 1959, aged sixteen, Asif was playing Ranji Trophy cricket for Hyderabad.

---

*Majid Khan: 'Our generation of players were in a sort of limbo. We had started playing our cricket under a very defensive inheritance. We had come in when Pakistan had a poor bowling attack and the captains typically had a siege mentality. But players such as Asif and myself were naturally attacking and wanted to change the mentality which we inherited. A move from an insecure, defensive side to a more aggressive, open one. It took a lot of time before we started believing that we could win.' Quoted in Noman, p.125.

Asif says today that he never encountered prejudice against Muslims in Hyderabad: 'It was a very mixed society. Muslims celebrated Hindu festivals and vice versa.' However, by the late 1950s the majority of his family had already migrated to Pakistan, and he joined them in Karachi. Within days of arrival he was approached by the umpire Idris Baig, who signed him to play for the Public Works Department at a fee of 120 rupees a month. Today Asif praises the support he received from Baig: 'He gave great encouragement to young cricketers. He gave me confidence and would say to me: "Nobody can stop you becoming a Test cricketer."' In 1963, Asif was sent on the Pakistan Eaglets tour of England, managed by Mian Saeed. At the end of the season, Saeed repeated Baig's message: 'Nobody can stop you playing for Pakistan.'[3] The following year he made his Test debut against the visiting Australians at Karachi. However, he was not to show himself as a world-class cricketer until Hanif's 1967 tour.

The third member of this brilliant young triumvirate was Majid Khan. 'All his movements were marked by natural grace,'[4] Wasim Bari later remarked. 'There was an air of princely laziness.' Khan was a product of Aitchison College, while his first-class debut, aged just fifteen, was a sensation. Playing for Lahore, he scored a century against Khairpur before mowing down the opposition with six wickets.[5]

Majid was the son of the legendary Jahangir Khan, while his cousin, Javed Burki, was also a member of the 1967 touring party. Today Majid Khan calculates that forty members of the Burki clan have played first-class cricket in India or Pakistan. With the arrival of both Javed and Majid in the Test team, the Burki story takes centre stage. To understand the true nature of their influence, it is necessary to go far back in time, and high up into Pakistan's remote tribal areas.

THE BURKI TRIBE AND ITS IMPACT ON PAKISTAN CRICKET

Like many Pakistani families or tribes, the Burkis can trace their history back for at least a thousand years. They believe they travelled from Turkish Kurdistan approximately eight hundred years ago and settled in the impregnable valley of Kaniguram, 7,000 feet high in the mountains on the border of modern Afghanistan and Waziristan.*

According to one plausible account, the Burkis were bodyguards for Mahmood of Ghazni, who conquered parts of modern Afghanistan and northern India in the eleventh century, and were rewarded with lands.[6] Having settled, they made a living as traders, taking horses and silks for sale in India.[7]

In approximately AD 1600 (or H978 in the Islamic calendar) there was a great drought in Kaniguram.[8] 'The elders decided that some people would have to leave in order for the others to survive,' reports K Hussan Zia, historian of the Burkis. 'It was thus that 40 families bade farewell to Kaniguram. The entire population walked with them for some miles and watched from the top of a hill till they were out of sight.'†

The forty caravans went to Jullundur, an area they knew well already – their horsetrading journeys to Delhi had long taken them along the Grand Trunk Road through Jullundur and Multan. Once in Jullundur, these Pashtun tribesmen established themselves in a group of fortified small towns and villages, called 'Bastis'. There they lived for almost three hundred and fifty years, until they were forced to leave at Partition. For all of this period the Burkis never married outside the tribe, and thus retained their solidarity. 'Theirs was a unique community – an island of carefully preserved Pashtun culture and civilisation in a sea of totally different indigenous India,'[9] says K Hussan Zia.

For many years the Burkis of Jullundur retained their trading links with Kaniguram. Towards the end of the eighteenth century, following the Sikh destruction of Moghal power, these were cut off. Only at this point did the Pashtuns of Jullundur cease to speak their tribal language of Ormuri, taking up Punjabi. The Kaniguram connection has not been entirely lost, however,

*K Hussan Zia, a member of the Burki clan, records that 'the history of my own paternal ancestors, as well as many other Pashtuns of the Bastis generally, can be traced to a scholar named Ibrahim Danishmand. The popular story is that he was educated in Baghdad or Damascus (some say Neshapur in Iran), and in recognition of his achievements was awarded the title of "Danishmand" – the wise one. On return, he called on the famous sage, Shaikh Bahauddin Zakria, in Multan. The latter advised him to preach among the Pashtuns who, apparently, were in need of enlightenment.' *The Pashtuns of Jullundur* (K Hussan Zia, Lahore, 1994).

†K Hussan Zia, p.24. The Burki culture is today under threat as never before, thanks to the war between the Pakistan army and Taliban in the tribal areas. Most of the inhabitants of Kaniguram have reportedly been forced to flee, taking shelter in Karachi, Islamabad and other major cities, while others are living miserable lives in camps for disabled people. According to Khan Zeb Burki, 'Before displacement, these people lived closely together, but now they are miserable, dispersed and cannot remain in touch. The language of Burki-Ormuri is taking its last breaths, and if no proper attention is given to the issue, will cease to exist.' See 'Blemished gem of Pakistan's tribal regions' by Khan Zeb Burki, *Asia Times*, 7 July 2012.

and until recently many Burkis (including Imran Khan and Majid Khan)[10] continued to visit their ancestral home.

The Burkis were sharp, alert and physically strong, excelling at traditional sports such as wrestling. In the second half of the nineteenth century a renowned wrestler from their tribe, Gul Mohammad Khan, had a maxim named after him – 'Zameen jumbad, na jumbad Gul Mohammad' (*tr*. 'The earth may move but Gul Mohammad won't'). As British sports spread across north India in the late nineteenth century, they excelled at football, hockey* and cricket, as well as producing crack shots.

One of the earliest first-class cricketers from the Burki tribe was Khan Mohammad Khan, son of the renowned wrestler. A right-hand fast-medium bowler, Khan played six first-class matches, taking 24 wickets at the useful average of 22.16. More significant was his kinsman Khan Salamuddin. Educated at Aligarh, he was one of just three Muslim members of the Maharajah of Patiala's cricket team which toured England in 1911.† Jahangir Khan called him 'uncle', but the phrase seems to have been used (as often in Muslim countries) out of respect. I can discover no close family connection.

Salamuddin's son Masood was also a fine player, good enough to represent All-India against Jack Ryder's touring Australian team of 1935.‡ However, Salamuddin (grandfather of Arif Abbasi, who did so much to repair the finances of Pakistan cricket in the 1980s and 1990s) moved away from Jullundur to live and work in Bhopal, and thus departs at a relatively early stage from the Burki cricketing story.

The key figure linking the Burki family to mainstream cricket in (at first) All-India and (after Partition) Pakistan is Ahmed Hasan Khan. The son of a

---

*At hockey they have produced numerous champions including Feroz Khan, who represented All-India at hockey in the 1928 Amsterdam Olympics. Niaz Khan and Hameedullah Khan Burki both represented and captained Pakistan in international hockey.

†Patiala's tourists provided the first India team to embrace Parsis, Hindus and Muslims – the three major forces in non-European cricket. Salamuddin, born in Jullundur in 1888, was an all-round cricketer who thrived in the years leading up to the outbreak of war in 1914. On the England tour he played 13 out of the 14 first-class matches, taking 33 wickets at an average of 32.81. He was a pace bowler, forceful bat, and brilliant slip-fielder.

‡Masood Salahuddin, born in Meerut 1915. Like his father he was a quick bowler and forceful bat. Made his first-class debut for United Province against Delhi 1934–35. The following year he played for India against Ryder's Australians. He opted for Pakistan at Partition, captaining Pakistan Railways in the inaugural Quaid-e-Azam Trophy of 1953–54. He was assistant manager on the 1954 tour of England, and managed the 1971 touring side, when (according to Imran Khan) he conducted himself like a *kala sahib* at the MCC dinner for the Pakistanis at Lord's: 'There we sat, squirming with embarrassment as our manager told the assembly that English cricket had taught us to behave properly. He got completely carried away, informing the MCC members that we owed it to the MCC and cricket for teaching us how to hold a knife and fork properly.'

civil servant, he was born in 1883 and entered Government College, Lahore, in 1900, where he was captain of the cricket XI for the unusually long period of three years. He entered government service, and wherever he was based throughout his long and peripatetic official career he would set up a cricket team. He ended up as District Commissioner at Mianwali (coincidentally the family home of the Niazis, and therefore Imran Khan's tribal base).

Ahmed Hasan Khan had four daughters, one of whom died young, and only one son. The son, Ahmed Raza Khan, born in 1910 and known to his family and friends affectionately as Aghajan, followed his father and grandfather into government, joining in the same batch of new recruits as Mian Mohammad Saeed, first cricket captain of Pakistan.

Aghajan played first-class cricket both in India and Pakistan: fifteen first-class matches, first for Northern India then for the Punjab, as a right-handed batsman. They brought him 597 runs at 28.42 with one century.*

Aghajan played alongside AR Cornelius as one of two non-Europeans for the British dominated Jullundur Cricket Club in the mid-1930s. He has left behind a journal of his career, a crucially important document for the historian of Pakistan cricket.† It records how, like his father, he loved to assemble a team of friends to play cricket wherever he was posted, thus evangelising the game. For instance, in the late 1930s he was based in the Punjabi town of Gujrat (close to the modern India–Pakistan border), where he started a team. 'The first match was played against Khunjah, a town about five miles away from Gujrat,' recorded Aghajan:

*Ahmed Raza Khan made his first-class debut for Muslims against Punjab Governor's X1 at Lahore in 1928–29. He also represented Northern India in the Ranji Trophy. He played for Northern India against Jardine's MCC touring team of 1933–34 at Lahore. MCC were bowled out for 53 and 58 in two innings. Aghajan scored 15 and 0 and did not bowl. After Partition, he played for Punjab against Nigel Howard's MCC touring side of 1951–52 and scored 52 and 24. He played his last first-class match in December 1960, when he led the Punjab Governor's X1 against Punjab University.

†*Reminiscences of an Officer, Aghajan's Service Diary*, ed Prof. Farrakh A Khan, who died shortly before this book was published, privately printed, February 2010. I am indebted to Prof Farrakh for allowing me to read this diary. The diary records (among much else) the role played by cricket in ensuring Aghajan's entry into the Punjab Civil Service: 'In February 1934, I appeared before the Board, which comprised of:

1 Mr Penny – Financial Commissioner (President).

2 Mr Puckle – Chief Secretary.

3 Dr Woolner – Vice Chancellor of the Punjab University.

When I entered the room for interview with the Board, Mr Puckle shouted "Good morning Raza, I saw you playing against MCC the other day." Evidently he did so in order to put me at ease. Mr Puckle then started asking me questions.

Mr Puckle: "Who do you think is the best bowler in India?"

Self: "I think, Sir, Nisar (played for the All-India Cricket Team) is the best bowler."'

The Khunjah team led by a medical practitioner objected to the matting being fixed on the pitch. However, they were persuaded to let it stay when they were convinced that the wicket would play better with the matting on it. I won the toss and elected to bat. As usual I put on pads and went into bat. The Khunjah team looked at my pads curiously and objected to my wearing them. With some difficulty they agreed to let me wear the pads and declared that they would also wear the pads ... When we declared the innings closed and the Khunjah opening batsmen came in we were astonished to see them wearing leg guards, upside down. We had to help them put on pads correctly.[11]

More significant than Aghajan, however, were his sisters. Three of them became mothers of Test captains, a unique record for Pakistan or any other nation. The oldest sister, Iqbal Bano, married within the clan to an army officer, Wajid Ali Khan Burki. Their second son was Javed Burki.

The next sister, Mubarak, married Jahangir Khan, also from within the clan. Their eldest son, Asad Jahangir Khan, won an Oxford Blue in cricket. Their second son was the great Test batsman Majid Khan. The third sister, Shaukat, married out of the clan to Ikramullah Khan, a civil servant, the union producing four daughters and one son, Imran Khan.

As independence approached, life grew precarious for the Pashtuns of Jullundur. Surrounded by Hindus and Sikhs, their proud and self-contained life was becoming impossible.[12] K Hussan Zia recalls that:

An uneasy calm prevailed in the Bastis. Everyone had waited with baited breath for 14th of August. It arrived and passed. Pakistan came into being as an independent state but we still did not know which districts would be included in it. Mountbatten still had to make the last minute changes. The final announcement was made one day before Eid that fell on 18th August in 1947. It was a disaster. No one celebrated Eid that year. The Sikhs went on a rampage, killing, burning and looting but they left the Bastis alone as they feared the Pashtuns. Muslim refugees began to pour in from the neighbouring villages and the city. They told harrowing tales of massacres of men, women and children alike. There were horrible mutilations of women with breasts cut off, spearing of infants and other unspeakable crimes. The core of the attackers were made up of army men from the local Sikh states, such as Patiala, Nabha and Kapoorthala, dressed in plain clothes. They would set fire to some isolated Muslim village at night and then set about their grisly bestial work as the hapless, unarmed inhabitants fled in terror. Places where there was a likelihood of meeting a determined resistance, like the Bastis, were left alone for the time being. Humanity was at its lowest, cowardly ebb.

K Hussan Zia recalls being trapped: 'You could see the glow of the fires burning at different places in the city and shuddered to think what was happening to the people there.' He says that a refugee camp was set up in the military cantonment, but 'the roads leading to the camp were unprotected from the bands of murdering Sikhs that lay in wait for anyone attempting to seek shelter there. The government had ceased to exist as far as the Muslims were concerned. They had suddenly lost their rights, including the right to remain alive.' This was confirmed when the Indian prime minister, Pandit Nehru, came to Jullundur and told the Muslim population it had no choice but to flee to Pakistan.[13]

Very reluctantly the Burkis, abandoning almost all their possessions and the lives they had lived for hundreds of years, left their home. Says Zia:

> The truck ride to Pakistan is etched clearly in my mind. All along the way there were long lines of bullock carts, human beings and animals, wearily trudging towards Pakistan in sultry heat. They remained bunched together as far as possible. Any stragglers were quickly disposed of by the Sikhs who were a constant menace. Sometimes, the dead remained unburied. The carcasses of dead animals were strewn all over the road. A great carnage had taken place near the crossing of Beas river. Bloated dogs and vultures still dotted the site amid broken carts and strewn belongings. Life had become very cheap. Diseases like cholera and dysentery took as much toll as the murderous Sikhs.

Not all the Burkis faced circumstances as terrible as this. Aghajan's family were holidaying in Kashmir, up in the hills to escape the summer heat, when the holocaust of Partition took place. They were able to make their way peacefully to Lahore (where Aghajan had gone ahead to supervise the evacuation of Sikhs and Hindus).[14] Meanwhile Jahangir Khan and his family, including the infant Majid Khan, were then living in Montgomery (since renamed Sahiwal), where he was principal of the local college. Montgomery, now part of Pakistan, was safe enough. Shaukat, Imran's mother, was already in Lahore when Partition took place.

But the Burki clan (in common with the estimated ten million Muslims who had fled from India) was now all but destitute. Individual clan members made do as best they could, moving in with family connections already established in Pakistan, occupying houses abandoned by Hindus and Sikhs, or finding temporary accommodation in camps. They had to cope with a profound sense of bereavement, not only for their loved ones who had been killed by marauding Sikhs but also for an entire way of life. 'The Pashtuns did not abandon the Bastis voluntarily,' records K Hussan Zia. 'The circumstances were such that they had no option but to leave. The fact that it happened so suddenly did not give them enough time to prepare themselves for the shock, either materially or psychologically. The sudden move was highly disconcerting, traumatic and unsettling.'[15]

For a period, all was chaos. Matters started to settle only after the Pakistani and Indian governments agreed a system of compensation, designed to ensure that Muslims, Sikhs and Hindus who had been obliged to start life afresh were awarded lands and properties of comparable value to the ones they had left behind. The Burki clan made a very good trade indeed, and one that was keenly resented. 'Lahore has been looted twice, once by the Sikhs, and once by the Pashtuns of Jullundur,' it used to be said.[16] Whatever the truth of this remark, it pointed to a transaction that would have immense consequences for the history of cricket in Pakistan.

In the 1930s Ahmed Raza Khan's uncle, Khan Bahadur Mohammed Zaman Khan (Zaman Khan),* had moved to Lahore, where he was appointed postmaster general for the Punjab, then undivided and a province about the size of present-day Finland, stretching from the North-West Frontier to Delhi. He settled with his family, building a comfortable house approximately two miles away from the Old City of Lahore and adjacent to Aitchison College.

---

*All three of Zaman Khan's sons became first-class cricketers. Humayun Khan was captain of Aitchison College and Government College, before playing for Lahore and Javed Zaman was another captain of Aitchison, going on to become vice-captain of Government College. He also played for Lahore, and captained the Lahore Gymkhana for sixteen years. The youngest son, Ahmed Fuad Khan, played for Combined Universities in the Quaid-e-Azam Trophy before embarking on a military career, ending up as Brigadier.

The area was wild and wooded, containing a few large houses lived in by prosperous Hindus. In those days, and for decades to come, it was possible to walk out of Zaman Khan's house into the surrounding fields and woods.

At Partition, Zaman Khan's extended family fled there for refuge. They filled up his house, camped in his garden, and occupied the neighbouring houses left empty by the fleeing Hindus. Jahangir Khan, his wife Mubarak and the infant Majid moved into a nearby house which had been vacated by a Hindu judge, where Majid lives to this day. It was not long before his brother-in-law Ahmed Raza Khan moved into another house which had been abandoned by its former Hindu occupants in such a hurry that it was still partially furnished.

Ahmed Hasan Khan, the patriarch of the cricketing dynasty, came to join his brother Zaman shortly before Partition, having suffered a heart attack. He brought with him his family, including Shaukat, the mother of Imran. At first they lived with Zaman. After Shaukat was married, she and her husband built a house just opposite her father's home. Possessing the air of a large, comfortable country rectory, it now belongs to Imran and he stays there when he is in Lahore today.

Javed Burki, the eldest of the three future Test captains, never lived in the area permanently. His father was in the army, served with the medical corps throughout World War Two, in North Africa, Iraq and finally the terrible Burma campaign. Javed was born in Meerut, in what is now north India, and his family was based in the garrison town of Rawalpindi. However, the young Javed came to stay with his grandparents frequently, first in the Bastis of Jullundur and, after Partition, with his cousins in Lahore.

It is hard to envisage a more idyllic place for children to grow up than this rural backwater of the great city. As memories of the Partition trauma receded, the Burki tribe would play cricket through the long, lazy, Lahori days, inventing their own rules, and playing in their back gardens and the fields. In the late 1950s, as the area became swallowed up by Lahore's suburban sprawl, these fields were converted into a residential zone based around a park. Named Zaman Park in honour of Zaman Khan (the first Burki to have moved there), it was ideal for organised sport, above all cricket matches. Javed Zaman (Zaman Khan's second son) was the driving force. He had been captain of Aitchison College, and a very fine cricketer. He would organise the Burkis into two teams.

This was one of the great seminaries of Pakistan cricket, at least comparable in significance to the Bhati Gate area of Old Lahore where Fazal and Kardar practised in the 1940s, or the abandoned Hindu temple where the Mohammad brothers endlessly practised the game in post-Partition Karachi. It is reasonable to guess that the world's highest concentration of first-class cricketers per square foot could be found in this exclusive Lahore suburb.

PAKISTAN TOUR TO ENGLAND 1967

There may have been two Burkis in Hanif Mohammad's 1967 team to tour England, along with the country's finest-ever wicketkeeper and one of its greatest all-rounders, but Pakistan had still not found a replacement for Fazal Mahmood. Without such a figure, the attack was toothless.

Hanif's touring team began as Javed Burki's had left off. In the first Test at Lord's England made a powerful first innings total of 369, mainly thanks to 148 from Ken Barrington. Soon defeat seemed inevitable. Matters were not helped when Saeed Ahmed, booked to go out to bat at the fall of the first wicket, locked himself in the washroom and refused to come out.[17] Saeed was showing an early sign of the temperamental instability that would bring his career to a premature end. But with the score at 139 for 7, Hanif Mohammad and Asif Iqbal came together to add 130. Asif scored 76 before falling to Illingworth, but Hanif carried on remorselessly to score an undefeated 187, out of 354, a knock which lasted more than nine hours and during which Hanif faced 556 balls.[18] This masterpiece of determination from Hanif, who was not considered an innovative or adventurous batsman, also contained one of the first examples of a reverse sweep in a Test match.[19] In the second innings the English top batting failed, only to be rescued by a stand between D'Oliveira and Close. Pakistan were set 257 to win, and a tight finish seemed likely, but most of the final day was lost to rain.

Pakistan emerged with credit from this match at Lord's and at the heart of this achievement were the performances of Hanif and Asif. Their partnership was a union between Pakistan's past and future, between expert defence and brilliant strokeplay, between experience and naivety, pessimism and optimism, the ego and the id. There were still bad days to come, but something was changing in Pakistan cricket.

The second Test, at Trent Bridge, was less happy. Pakistan were unable to cope with the bowling of Ken Higgs, Geoff Arnold and Derek Underwood in helpful conditions, and lost by an innings. The third Test was defined by Asif Iqbal. When he came to the crease in Pakistan's second innings, the score was 53 for 7, with 167 runs needed to make England bat again. 'I heard the PA system announce that they were talking to the Pakistan team to agree a 40-over match to be played that afternoon,' Asif remembers today. 'It made me angry that they made that announcement. Somewhere in my mind, that gave me a challenge.'[20] He and Intikhab launched into a brilliant partnership of 190, a world Test record for the ninth wicket.* When Asif reached his century, hundreds of Pakistani fans raced to the middle and hoisted him shoulder-high. When he was finally out for 146, Asif had made the highest score by a number 9 Test batsman.† Colin Cowdrey approached him after the game, telling him that 'you have just played one of the greatest innings I have ever seen', and asked him to sign for Kent. Pakistan still lost the match, but they left behind an aroma of joy and defiance.

ISOLATION DEEPENS

The central problem remained. Teams could not be found to play against Pakistan. Hanif's touring side returned home with a fair number of rising stars, but a blank Test match fixture list in a country where Ayub Khan was struggling to maintain his authority. Ayub's government had hit rock bottom in an attempt to re-establish the system of official and military governance which had kept the British in power. Like the British, Ayub and his Sandhurst-educated generals could not believe that Pakistan's illiterate masses were ready for democracy.

By the late 1960s, Pakistan was in the grip of two simultaneous revolutions. In the West, Zulfiqar Ali Bhutto launched his Pakistan People's Party, with an ambitious programme promising major land reform, which sought to take advantage of the growing revulsion against Ayub Khan's faltering

---

*It lasted until 1997–98, when Pat Symcox and Mark Boucher surpassed it for South Africa against Pakistan at Johannesburg.

†Clem Hill had made 160 in that position for Australia in 1907–08, but Hill was normally at number 3. Asif was overtaken by Ian Smith, the New Zealand wicketkeeper-batsman, against India in 1989–90.

dictatorship. One thousand miles away in East Pakistan, Sheikh Mujib's Awami League dominated the political scene and was raising its demands. It drew up the Six-Point Programme, which demanded almost total economic, fiscal, legislative and military separation. Serious clashes broke out between protestors and the police and army.

It was amid this environment of national instability, great danger and looming tragedy that the 1969 MCC tour took place. Pakistan was facing the greatest crisis of its short history, and it was by no means certain the country could survive. For the majority of MCC players, the tour would provide the most terrifying days of their lives.

It is astounding that the tour went ahead at all. MCC officials had been ready to despatch an England side to apartheid South Africa, despite warnings that an English cricketing presence would be mercilessly used as a propaganda weapon for Prime Minister John Vorster's apartheid government; hence the national outburst of revulsion that eventually brought about the tour's cancellation. In Pakistan, the MCC was also handing President Ayub Khan a valuable propaganda gift. In the eyes of MCC officials, the Pakistan tour was no more than a useful way of providing employment for contracted players during the winter months. In the eyes of the embattled president, the tour provided desperately needed legitimacy to his bankrupt regime.

There were also important differences. In the case of South Africa, the MCC was acting in direct defiance of the publicly expressed wishes of Harold Wilson's Labour government.[21] But in Pakistan, the MCC tour was actually sanctioned and encouraged by the British Foreign Office. Pakistan's military government had been established with the support of the United States and Britain; now the two Western allies were working flat out to ensure the survival of Ayub Khan. The tottering field marshal was seen in both Washington and London as a vital ally in the Cold War, while his democratic rival ZA Bhutto was viewed with distrust because of his links to the Soviet Union and China. Likewise, London and Washington viewed the independence movement in East Pakistan with disfavour because it threatened to weaken Pakistan and strengthen India, which was supported by Soviet Russia.

There was a second difference. Touring South Africa, however morally loathsome, had been unlikely to jeopardise the lives of MCC players.

South Africa's efficient state security apparatus could be relied on to keep protestors well out of reach. This was not the case in Pakistan, where parts of the country were rapidly falling outside the control of the state. There was no way on earth that anyone could feel confident that the team would be safe.

This is the political background to the story of how a naive clique of bungling and incompetent MCC officials, sanctioned by the British Foreign Office, made the extraordinary decision to send the England cricket team into a war zone.*

The preliminary weeks of the tour were safe enough. The MCC travelled to Ceylon (now Sri Lanka) for a handful of warm-up games. The players enjoyed golf, messed around on the island's beautiful beaches, and played a relaxed kind of cricket. Every day brought word of violence and horror from Pakistan. Right up to the last minute, frantic negotiations went on between the tour management in Ceylon, the MCC at Lord's, the BCCP and the British High Commission. The negotiations were hampered by a cable strike in London, which cut off the touring party in Colombo (and the BCCP in Pakistan) from Lord's.

There was uncertainty about where the Test matches would be staged, which up-country fixtures would be included, and where the players would stay. The original plan was for an initial first-class match to be played at Chittagong in East Pakistan, followed by an internal flight to the regional capital of Dacca for the first Test.[22] But as reports of violence in Dacca escalated, the MCC balked. Just a few days before the tour began, the BCCP conceded that the Eastern part of the tour should be abandoned.[23]

Armed with BCCP assurances, the MCC team flew from Sri Lanka into Karachi, only to find the city under a dusk to dawn curfew. The team stayed in a hotel close to the airport, ready to make a dash for a plane out of the country if the situation grew too dangerous.[24] By this stage Tom Graveney, the vice-captain, concluded that 'we had no right to be there playing cricket.

---

*It is not possible to tell the story of the England tour of Pakistan with total confidence because the relevant documents either do not exist, or cannot be found. There are, as ever, no records in the Pakistan Cricket Board. No files can be found in the MCC archive at Lord's. Despite earnest searching I have been able to track down no Foreign Office cables at the National Archive at Kew. I have therefore been forced to rely on testimony from Pakistan and England players on the tour, as well as newspaper reports. The full story remains to be told.

Literally, it was neither the time nor the place for it.'[25] According to Graveney, 'From hour to hour the situation altered. At no time was it known exactly where in the country we would be in twenty-four hours' time.'

With the itinerary of the tour still unclear, the three most senior members of the touring party – tour manager Les Ames, captain Colin Cowdrey and Graveney – were invited to meet the BCCP. This meant a flight to Rawalpindi, which Ayub Khan had made Pakistan's capital city in the wake of his military coup. Ayub's reason to change from the southern metropolis of Karachi, chosen by Jinnah, to the dusty garrison town of Rawalpindi was easy to decipher. He wanted to bring his country's civil government under military supervision. As part of this rearrangement the BCCP had been dragged north, and now occupied a small office inside the general headquarters.[26]

Fida Hassan, the Punjabi bureaucrat who fifteen years earlier had tried unsuccessfully to plot the downfall of Kardar as captain, was now president of the BCCP. He was rarely to be seen in this office. He doubled up as adviser to Ayub Khan, a post which made him an essential link between Pakistan's military and civilian government. Hassan's presence at the head of cricket, and the cricket board location inside Pakistan's military headquarters, left no reason to doubt that as far as Ayub was concerned, cricket counted for only one purpose: to serve his military dictatorship.

At that very moment, Ayub Khan needed a Test match in East Pakistan. The MCC touring party had made the cancellation of the Dacca Test a precondition for the tour going ahead. But this news had gone down badly in Dacca, where it had been seen as fresh evidence of East Pakistan's inferior status, and given rise to angry demonstrations.[27] In order to calm the situation in Pakistan's mutinous Eastern wing, Ayub needed Dacca restored to the Test programme. 'We had the meeting in Fida's office,' recalled a bemused Tom Graveney, 'and when it was over we had got Dacca, the place everybody had assured us we would not have to visit, back on our programme. It is an indication of how quickly things changed out there.' It was not just Ayub Khan and his lieutenant Fida Hassan who wanted the MCC touring party to go to Dacca. The British High Commission, eager to lend as much support to Ayub as it could, was also determined that the MCC make the journey. The English cricketers were reluctant, as Graveney confirms: 'Admittedly things had quietened down in the previous few days, but they already had a death toll that did not slip out of the memory easily. It did not suggest itself as a venue for a Test match.' Keith Fletcher later claimed that, 'We were no longer cricketers, it seemed, but ambassadors being paid a tour fee to keep the peace.'[28] Ultimately, the English players were pawns in a larger political game that had nothing to do with them. In condition for their compliance, they demanded a permanent police presence and the army within easy call. These were simple assurances for Fida Hassan to give, and they were soon to prove just as simple to break.[29]

The tourists' early games were held in Ayub's regional strongholds of Bahawalpur, Lyallpur and Sahiwal. Arranged in a great hurry, they presented logistical problems. The Bahawalpur fixture started the day after the Lyallpur game, forcing the MCC players to get up at 5.30am and board a specially chartered plane to reach the ground on time. The team arrived ninety min-utes late, provoking Colin Cowdrey into a fine example of English sang-froid. The captain informed panicking local officials that 'no English side ever started a game of cricket without first having a cup of tea.' The team stood its ground in the dressing room, regardless of the impatient crowd outside, and would not leave until tea was taken at leisure.[30]

These contests enabled the tourists to acclimatise to local conditions, although their more significant function may have been to reward Ayub Khan's supporters. It was three weeks after their arrival in Pakistan that England arrived in Lahore for the first Test match, and the first potential flashpoint.

Meanwhile the Pakistan cricketers were facing their own problems. Hanif Mohammad was stripped of the captaincy to make way for Saeed Ahmed. He was more socially confident than Hanif and, even as vice-captain, had played the role of leader at cricketing functions.* Typical of the man, Hanif did not sulk and remained a member of the team. This switch to the Lahori Saeed was, however, taken badly by Hanif's supporters in Karachi and became one of the excuses for the riots which later broke out.†

---

*As Hanif acknowledged. See Noman, p.127. According to Saeed himself, he enjoyed a private meet-ing with the Queen during the Lord's Test of 1967. He had the confidence to ask her what image she had of Pakistan and she replied 'cricket and horses'. Saeed also claimed that he had asked the Queen if he could meet her again at Buckingham Palace and that she had given him an open invitation to visit whenever he liked.

†Mushtaq Mohammad, however, attacked Saeed as a nervous wreck of a captain who agonised over field settings and bowling changes. Mushtaq Mohammad, op. cit. p.85.

The second problem was political. Ayub Khan, while welcoming the tourists as a political boon, was keenly aware that the impending Test matches would provide an ideal forum for his opponents to make mischief. While he wanted the matches to go ahead, he was also eager that they should last as short a time as possible. On his personal order, the Tests were cut short from five days to four.*

Ayub Khan also interfered in team selection. In Western Pakistan the key figure was Aftab Gul, a talented student organiser from Punjab University, and a lieutenant of Ayub Khan's enemy, ZA Bhutto. Two days before the Lahore Test, Gul met the England team at a reception, where the England player Basil D'Oliveira asked Gul whether the Pakistan team had yet been picked. 'No,' replied Gul, 'but I know I'm playing. If I don't play, there's no Test match.'[31]

But for the presidential edict that it should only last four days, the Lahore Test would have been a fascinating contest. Cowdrey scored an unruffled century amid the noise and hubbub as England struggled to 306 in their first innings. Pakistan then sank to 52 for 5, but a brilliant 70 by Asif Iqbal took the score to 209. England set Pakistan 323 to win, and the match ended tantalisingly poised with Pakistan needing 120 for victory with five wickets in hand. Thanks to Aftab Gul, there was little trouble from rioters. 'He just put up his hands like a gladiator and everybody sat down and kept quiet,' remembered D'Oliveira.[32] Aftab Gul opened the batting in both Pakistan innings, recording scores of 12 and 29.

Gul was stood down for the second Test at Dacca, where the problem was secessionist agitation rather than students protesting for democracy. Instead Niaz Ahmed, the only cricketer from East Pakistan who ever represented Pakistan, was brought into the team. There was no real cricketing case to be made for Niaz, who replaced Asif Masood as opening bowler.

The England team were reluctant to travel to Dacca. But manager Les Ames was assured, both by the Pakistan authorities and the British Foreign Office, that order had been restored.[33] Upon arrival, however, it instantly became clear that the Pakistan police and military had pulled out of the

---

*See Shuja, p.111: 'The duration of the Lahore Test had been changed from five days to four, under the direct orders of President Ayub Khan who after a decade long reign was no longer a popular head of state and was trying desperately to save his own political career.' Noman records that 'the first Test at Lahore was curtailed from five days to four as Ayub Khan wanted to curb the momentum of the student movement in the western wing of the country.' See also Hanif Mohammad, p.194.

capital, which was in the hands of rioters. According to the opening bowler John Snow, the touring party expressed a desire to leave, upon which they were informed 'in no uncertain terms that our coach would not reach the airport.'[34] Snow, the son of a country vicar, says that the week which followed was 'probably the most nerve-wracking in my life. Day and night we could hear gunfire – some of it only yards from our hotel as the students patrolled the streets armed with rifles, seeking out people they believed to be corrupt. When found some of these people were bound and gagged and tossed in the river to drown.' Ayub Khan's Pakistan state had lost all authority in East Pakistan, and the streets were in the control of armed groups. The moment the MCC cricketers flew into Dacca, they had become hostages to the students.

The MCC party felt betrayed – an emotion the team management unleashed when, on arrival in Dacca, they met Ray Fox, the Deputy High Commissioner. Tom Graveney describes the mood of the meeting:

> Immediately we went into close session with the High Commission representatives. The debate became heated. It was of little interest to us that we were supposed to be safer with the police and army out of the way as the sight of them only provoked violence among the students. We were told in Rawalpindi that we were going to have protection, yet the only people in uniform in the city were a handful of traffic policemen, men without any authority. Nor could we just turn round and go – God knows what would have happened had we done that. We felt we had been 'conned'.[35]

Graveney adds: 'The MCC party were let down over Dacca and nothing that was said at the time or has been said since alters the situation.' Keith Fletcher saw the situation clearly: 'Our preferences counted for nothing. We went, virtually on the insistence of our Foreign Office, who apparently feared recriminations against the English population of Dacca if we pulled out.'[36] Fletcher records that, 'On the eve of the Test match, Ray Fox gave the traditional cocktail party to celebrate the team's presence, and it was timed for 6.30 in the evening. Soon after 7pm we were ushered out, without explanation. Most of us were surprised, as these functions invariably occupy a couple of hours, but nobody would have felt offended if we had not met another group of white faces on the way into the building. They turned out to be the representatives of the British and European community and their purpose in being there was to discuss plans for evacuation! The entire city was under student law. There was no evidence of policemen and no troops.'[37]

The match itself belonged to Basil D'Oliveira, the only member of the touring party equipped to cope with the violence and disorder in Dacca, having been brought up in Cape Town at the height of apartheid. He knew from personal experience what it was like to cope with riots and police charges. D'Oliveira came to the wicket with England in deep trouble. Not long after his arrival, they plunged to 130 for 7, replying to Pakistan, who had scored 246 on a wicket of hardened mud. The surface had broken up by the time the England innings started. The batsmen could not cope in such conditions against Pakistan's four-man spin attack of Intikhab Alam, Saeed Ahmed, Pervez Sajjad and Mushtaq Mohammad. D'Oliveira, who had learnt his art on rough tracks like this one, played a match-saving innings. The Pakistan fielders clustered round him saying, 'You're not English, you're one of us. If you get out we can beat them.'[38] D'Oliveira, who regarded his performance as the greatest innings of his life, nursed England to a tiny first innings lead. As at Lahore, it was only Ayub Khan's instruction that the Test match should be confined to four days that prevented a gripping conclusion.

In the end, the High Commission's judgement proved correct. Despite constant mayhem in the stands, the Bengali students kept order well. Niaz Ahmed bowled only twelve overs in the match, and never played for Pakistan again.* The team made it out of Dacca safely.

Gul was back for the final Test, extended to five days, since the previous two had been drawn. But even his influence was not enough to control the crowds in Karachi. With England 502 for 6 at the start of the third day, a mob invaded the ground and the England team fled to safety. They left Pakistan that night.

The main action was now off the pitch. In worsening health, and shaken by a failed assassination attempt, reportedly remarking that 'the politicians are swine and won't listen to me', Ayub issued his last orders as president.[39]

---

*Niaz Ahmed, who was not a Bengali, had moved to Karachi in 1967. In the Dacca Test, Saeed Ahmed had suggested that he declare himself unfit on the night before the match so that he could pick Asif Masood as a replacement. Niaz agreed but then Saeed changed his mind and picked him after all. Niaz left cricket to pursue an engineering education. Information: Najum Latif.

An old and ill man, Ayub, who had ruled Pakistan for longer than anyone before or since, urged his commander-in-chief, Yahya Khan, to assume power and impose martial law.

THE SLIDE INTO CIVIL WAR

Yahya Khan was a heavy drinker[40] but in his sober periods a realist who made a genuine attempt to overcome Pakistan's political crisis. With the support of the Nixon administration in Washington, Yahya initially tried to crack down on protestors, but was forced to admit that Pakistan was ungovernable by the military. He prepared for elections and tried urgently to find compromise with and between Pakistan's civilian politicians. In 1970, he initiated a series of major land reforms and he ended the 'One Unit' status of West Pakistan which had been imposed by Ayub. The four provinces, Sindh, Punjab, Baluchistan and NWFP (renamed Khyber Pakhtunkhwa), which Ayub Khan had abolished, saw their regional assemblies, courts and other institutions restored. However, there were no matching relaxations in East Pakistan.

Yahya's promise of an election led to intense politicking in both East and West Pakistan, dominated by Sheikh Mujib and ZA Bhutto respectively. Meanwhile, Yahya ruled the country through military cronies. At least Pakistan cricket was spared this treatment. In succession to Syed Fida Hassan, Yahya appointed IA Khan as the new president of the BCCP.* His appointment might have been a gesture towards East Pakistan, since he had been very supportive of cricket there and had developed the Dacca stadium. However, he was only a part-time president, since his main job was to run the Water and Power Development Authority. (This improbable combination of roles has been repeated twice since, by Maj. Gen. Safdar Butt (1984–88) and Lt Gen. Zahid Ali Akbar Khan (1988–92).)

In Pakistan's domestic season, the Quaid-e-Azam Trophy had a crowded programme with thirty-two matches, three played by East Pakistan, captained

---

*IA Khan was the son of Nawab Ismail Khan, one of the most powerful figures in the Muslim League, wearer of the cap which was later favoured by the Quaid-e-Azam and came to be known as the 'Jinnah Cap'. Educated at Aligarh, where he excelled at cricket and passed into the ICS, he managed the 1967 touring team of England. He was Yahya Khan's appointee as president of the BCCP from 1969 to 1972. His first act was to bring back Kardar into national cricket by appointing him chairman of selectors.

by MA Latif. Reflecting the troubled situation in East Pakistan, all of these were played in the West, where the team did well to beat Hyderabad (a century for Latif) and Khairpur. The final pitted two employer's teams against each other, reflecting a new balance of power in Pakistan cricket. Pakistani International Airlines (PIA) beat the Public Works Department by 195 runs. PIA had managed to recruit more stars into their line-up, including Hanif and Mushtaq Mohammad, Asif Iqbal, Wasim Bari and Pervez Sajjad, but the star performer, with 95, was the youthful, as yet uncapped, Zaheer Abbas.

Amazingly the Ayub Trophy was restored – and under that name. Seven teams – including all four from East Pakistan – seem to have refused to play as a result.[41] The final was won by PIA over Karachi Blues in a typical attritional battle over first innings. For PIA, Hanif contributed 190 and Mushtaq 123 in a total of 524 scored in 240 overs. Karachi Blues just managed to avoid the follow-on, with 96 for Sadiq Mohammad, the youngest of the brothers, and 75 from the captain, Intikhab Alam.

Zaheer Abbas was the leading batsman in both competitions, despite a lapse in the Ayub final when, before scoring, he became only the tenth batsman to be given out for hitting the ball twice.[42]

New Zealand were unfancied visitors that year, the lowest-ranked Test team and one which had never beaten Pakistan. However, the series proved to be highly charged. This, surprisingly, had nothing to do with the still troubled political situation but with Kardar, whom IA Khan installed as chairman of selectors. He was determined to give priority to young players and to take a firm line against paying travel costs to established stars in England. The executive committee, under Kardar's influence, stripped Saeed Ahmed of the captaincy and gave it to Intikhab Alam. The decision had cricketing merit. Intikhab was a fine all-rounder with good captaincy skills, which had matured through his English county experience at Surrey. He was also a much more compliant character than the abrasive Saeed, who protested publicly against his sacking and was supported by demonstrators. He made matters worse when he manhandled IA Khan after meeting him by chance in the lobby of the Seventh Day Adventist Hospital on Bunder Road, Karachi, where Saeed's wife was then hospitalised.[43] In the light of this incident, the BCCP smacked an indefinite ban on him, Saeed delivered a written apology, and the BCCP rescinded the ban but decided not to play him against New Zealand anyway.[44]

The first Test, at Karachi, saw three Mohammad brothers, Hanif, Mushtaq and Sadiq, play together for Pakistan, matching the three Grace brothers in England's first home Test match in 1880 (and not repeated since). On a poor pitch, the new off-spinner Mohammad Nazir Junior took seven for 99 – at that time, Pakistan's best performance on Test debut. Another debutant was bespectacled batsman Zaheer Abbas, who failed in both innings and was promptly dropped. Zaheer would be back. Intikhab made a challenging second innings declaration and Pervez Sajjad took five cheap wickets, but New Zealand clung on for a draw.

The new opening partnership of Hanif and Sadiq worked. In both innings, the brothers did their job of seeing off the new ball. In the first innings they put on 55 (Hanif 22, which took two hours and twenty minutes). In the second they put on 75 (Hanif's contribution was 35, lasting two and a half hours). But Hanif was a marked man. Back in 1951 AH Kardar, as Pakistan captain, had brought seventeen-year-old Hanif into his national team. Eighteen years later Kardar, as chairman of selectors, spat him out.

This episode reveals Kardar at his least sensitive, and exposes Hanif in all his vulnerability. Through his heroism and determination, Hanif had turned himself into a sporting symbol of his country's implacable determination to survive in a dangerous world. During the eighteen years that he represented the national team, he had been easily his country's best batsman. The very least he deserved was to be treated with grace and respect.

At the start of the 1969–70 season, Kardar had invited Hanif to the Bagh-e-Jinnah cricket ground in Lahore to make a film for coaching purposes. In between filming sessions, the two men had a long conversation about the future. Hanif remembers that Kardar 'told me that I had at least three to four years of cricket left in me and that I should continue to play.'[45] Hanif in response told Kardar that 'the day I felt I didn't have it in me to survive at the top, I shall quit.' Hanif also communicated to Kardar that 'my preference was to be told in advance by the selectors, so that I could be mentally prepared to bow out with grace in front of my fans.'

According to Hanif, Kardar made no suggestion that he should retire at once. Hanif was on fine form for his PIA team in the Quaid-e-Azam Trophy. However, at the end of the Karachi Test just a few weeks later, the chairman of selectors started to drop heavy hints. It should be noted that Kardar's fellow selectors were handpicked. They were all, like Hanif and Kardar, heroes of the famous 1954 Oval victory over England – Imtiaz Ahmed, Mahmood Hussain and Wazir Mohammad.* Kardar held them in a psychological grip.

First of all, Kardar approached Wazir to ask Hanif to announce his retirement. 'Being my brother,' recalls Hanif, 'he refused to do that because he knew that Kardar was being unjust and unkind.'[46] Next, says Hanif, Kardar dispatched 'a group of journalists to me at the close of play on the last day to ask me if I was making an announcement.'[47] Hanif told them he had nothing to say.

Then, asserts Hanif, Kardar resorted to blackmail. He recalls that:

> Later he came himself and told me, 'Everyone has to retire one day. I think you should announce your retirement. Your younger brothers are in the team and you should think of them as well. I promise you that I will give you a benefit.' It was a sort of indirect threat that if I didn't retire, my brothers' careers would be affected. I was so shocked and upset that I did not say a word to Kardar. I had always had great admiration for the man and had always respected him. Suddenly he had gone down drastically in my estimation as he had broken his promise to me that he would let me know well in advance if the selectors planned to drop me.
>
> I had tears in my eyes and to hide them I took the back seat of the coach on our way to the Beach Luxury hotel where we were staying. There were many friends and well wishers who believed that I could continue for at least three to four years. They were very angry with Kardar and advised me to ignore his threat. 'Let him drop you,' they said.

Hanif was still only thirty-four, and had played in 55 of Pakistan's 57 Tests to date. Although he had slowed down in the field, he was by no means a spent force with the bat.† Eventually he surrendered. 'I was a lost soul,'

---

*These are the names given by Hanif (p.198). However, a different list is given in Baloch's *Encyclopaedia of Pakistan Cricket*: Fazal Mahmood, Imtiaz, Shuja and Wazir Mohammad. Their names also appear in the souvenir programme for the second Test against New Zealand at Lahore. The key point survives: the panel of selectors had all played under Kardar and, Wazir apart, were likely to take their orders from him.

†In five matches for PIA in the run-up to the Karachi Test, Hanif had scored 109,154, 1, 0, 114, 4, 59. In that year's Quaid-e-Azam Trophy he averaged 63.

wrote Hanif, 'after the announcement of retirement and moved about in a daze. Friends and fans commiserated with me and expressed anger at the forced decision, and the atmosphere at home was burdened with sadness. My mother, who had been overjoyed at the rare honour of having three of her sons playing for the country, felt cheated out of the happiness which proved to be so shortlived.' Still under contract to PIA, Hanif continued to play domestic cricket for several more years, without enthusiasm but with success. Talk of a comeback came to nothing because Hanif wanted Kardar to ask him publicly, and Kardar refused.[48] Such was the end of one of Pakistan's greatest players. As long as Test cricket is played, Hanif's patience, fortitude, single-mindedness, dedication, raw courage and extraordinary powers of concentration will always be marvelled at and celebrated.

The Hanif-less Pakistan side moved on to Lahore. They batted poorly against a very moderate attack and set New Zealand only 66 to win, which was achieved by five wickets. Shafqat Rana made a point to the selectors by scoring 95. Pervez Sajjad took seven for 74, the best figures of his Test career, which ended anti-climactically a few years later. A new talent, Younis Ahmed, received one of many shocking decisions by the umpires, then disappeared from Pakistan's Test ranks for the next seventeen years. He did not help his cause by playing in South Africa, and earning a ban.

In the final Test, on a poor pitch at Dacca, Glenn Turner batted for 681 minutes in two innings. Supported by an unbeaten century by Mark Burgess in the second innings, he earned New Zealand a draw and thereby his country won a cricket series for the first time against anybody. This proved to be the last Test played by Pakistan in Dacca. The brilliant teenager, Aftab Baloch, made a slow 25 on his debut and disappeared from the selectors' minds for years. Shafqat Rana added 65 not out to his previous 95 – and never played another Test match.[49]

THE EAST DISAPPEARS FROM PAKISTAN CRICKET

Shortly before Yahya Khan's scheduled election in December 1970, East Pakistan was struck by a cyclone. About half a million were killed outright, thousands of homes were destroyed and transport, infrastructure and essential services were devastated. The central government was widely blamed in

East Pakistan for an inadequate response and the waste or misuse of the international aid which poured in.

This resentment helped to propel the Awami League to almost total victory in the elections in East Pakistan. Sheikh Mujib's party won 167 of the 169 East Pakistani seats. Although they won no seats at all in the west, it gave them an overall majority in the 300-member assembly. In the west, ZA Bhutto's Pakistan People's Party surprised everyone by winning 85 seats on a socialistic programme summed up in the slogan 'Food, Cloth and Shelter'. Bhutto and the other parties in the West claimed that they remained committed to a unitary Pakistan.* Nevertheless, this commitment did not extend to allowing Sheikh Mujib, the outright winner of the national elections, to become prime minister, as he was fully entitled to do thanks to his victory in the ballot box.

Although the prospects for political compromise were poor, Yahya Khan pursued it doggedly. He gave the new assembly a deadline of one hundred days to produce a new constitution and pinned his faith on a power-sharing agreement in which Bhutto and Mujib would serve under the senior Bengali politician Nurul Amin, who was chairman of the unitary Pakistan Muslim League. Yahya travelled to Dacca to sell this idea to Mujib, but he and the Awami League held out for near-total independence: East Pakistan would run all its own affairs, including trade and defence, with the sole exception of foreign policy. Bhutto rejected this proposal totally and induced Yahya Khan to break off talks.

In March 1971, Yahya Khan suspended the National Assembly with no date for its restoration. Sheikh Mujib called for civil disobedience and strikes, which were supported by most of East Pakistan's government workers and caused paralysis. A new conference in Dacca between Yahya, Mujib and Bhutto broke up without result. Yahya denounced Mujib as a traitor and ordered the Pakistan army to reconquer East Pakistan. He fatally underestimated the Awami League's will to resist and the support it would receive from the great majority of the population. With the launch of Operation Searchlight (followed by Operation Barisal by the Pakistan Navy), East

---

*Bhutto's conduct and motives in this phase are still much debated. Bennett Jones suggests that his prime motive was to secure power for himself and his party in West Pakistan, and was indifferent to the fate of the East (p.142 et seq). Sir Morrice James takes a more favourable view of Bhutto, as a man resisting an impossible set of demands from Sheikh Mujib (pp.173–6).

Pakistan fell into civil war. Mujib and some of his lieutenants were arrested and interned in West Pakistan; others escaped and fled to India, along with millions of non-political refugees. Guerrilla resistance forces, the Mukti Bahini, harassed the Pakistan army, who retaliated more and more fiercely and indiscriminately against the civilian population. The Indian prime minister, Indira Gandhi, gave the Bengali resistance public support and Major Ziaur Rahman (ironically a veteran of Pakistan's 1965 war against India) proclaimed East Pakistan's independence as the new nation of Bangladesh.

Against this momentous background, the Punjab Governor's XI played its traditional fixture against Punjab University. This match had remained the pinnacle of the social calendar, but it disappeared from the first-class list after this final fixture. An era had passed and Dr Nauman Niaz mourned the end of the values which it embodied. Pakistan's cricket administrators, he wrote later, 'had little time for the old game ethic. Cricket was too much identified with an outmoded social division in the country, with a powerless but still affluent class which did not reflect the general outlook of the country in its perpetual half-strangled appeals for proper behaviour and good form and the rest of it.'[50] This could well be an Englishman mourning the disappearance of the amateur in 1963.

The Governor's XI won a low-scoring match. A well-connected schoolboy from Lahore played for them in his third first-class match. Opening the bowling he took five wickets cheaply. More was to be heard of Imran Khan.*

The Ayub Trophy was restored under the more sensitive name of the BCCP Trophy and East Pakistan teams appeared for the last time. Playing in Dacca, East Pakistan Greens were beaten by an innings by PIA's A XI. The Whites fared even worse against PIA A on the same ground. Propelled by Zaheer Abbas's 196, PIA A scored 513 for 4 declared off 94 overs (then thought an electric rate of scoring in Pakistan). In reply, East Pakistan Whites collapsed to 34 all out. This game, played at the end of January 1971, was to be the last, inglorious, first-class appearance of any East Pakistan team, and of MA Latif (out for 4).†

As Pakistan slid into civil war, the BCCP made a series of last-minute

*The game was played 27–29 November 1970, days ahead of the elections. Imran took his five wickets across both innings.

†Niaz Ahmed, East Pakistan's Test representative, continued to play in the West for several seasons in the Public Works team, and captained them several times. PIA A eventually won the trophy by beating Karachi Blues in the final.

efforts to conciliate East Pakistan on the cricket field. It arranged a new Under-19 tournament, which involved three East Pakistan teams. The outbreak of war brought proceedings to a sudden close; an eighteen-year-old Imran Khan 'was on the last flight out of East Pakistan before the army went in.'[51] Of greater importance was the special series of three fixtures against an International XI, captained by Micky Stewart of Surrey and England.

The first of these matches was held at Karachi, where the International XI collapsed to the leg-spin of Intikhab Alam (6–30) and Pakistan won. The second match took place in Dacca where, in an attempt to appease East Pakistan, the BCCP unearthed a Dacca University student, Roqibul Hasan. Unlike Latif and Niaz Ahmed, Roqibul was a Bengali and the BCCP may have had some idea of using him as a poster boy. The previous year, on the evidence of a handful of first-class appearances, the selectors had made him twelfth man in the final Test against New Zealand. Whatever their intentions, Roqibul refused to comply. He opened the innings with a map of Bangladesh on the face of his bat, and informed his fellow team members that the next time they came to Dacca they would need a visa.[52]

Roqibul Hasan failed (scoring 1 in each innings) as the Pakistan batting collapsed. On the fourth day Pakistan were in deep trouble, eight wickets down, Sarfraz Nawaz and Wasim Bari in the middle, and only 128 ahead. News came through over the radio that negotiations had collapsed and Yahya Khan had announced the postponement of the National Assembly.

This was the moment when all hope of a settlement was abandoned, the government lost control over East Pakistan, civil war began, and the nationalist insurgency embarked on its final phase.

Rioting students at once invaded the pitch, and the following exchange took place:

> Student leader: There's no danger to you or your players. But we wish the game to be abandoned. We're protesting because Bhutto has called off a meeting with our leader.
> Micky Stewart: Can't you just wait till we get these two wickets and knock off the runs?[53]

The International team captain was told this would not be possible. His team repaired to their dressing room, from where they listened as gun battles broke out. After two hours, a military vehicle drove them to an army camp, navigating its way around dead bodies lying on the road, and, later that night, they made it to the airport.

For the Pakistan team it was more terrifying. Sarfraz Nawaz recalls facing the Australian seamer Neil Hawke when the mob invaded. He urged a soldier to fire on the crowd before the Pakistan team were lynched; the soldier pointed his gun instead at Sarfraz.

The players huddled for cover in the dressing room for several hours. They were not told when the International players were whisked away.* Eventually the Pakistan team were taken by military truck to the Purbani hotel in the town centre. 'We were told not to move about, not to go anywhere,' recalls Intikhab, 'just stay in your rooms. There were no communications.'

After several futile attempts to get help, Intikhab tracked down a well-disposed senior officer. Intikhab says this turned out to be Brigadier Haider, polo-playing manager of Javed Burki's 1962 Pakistan team. Although mocked for his ignorance of cricket, Haider had been a notably calm head amid the metaphorical carnage of that 1962 tour, and amid the all too real physical devastation and horror of 1971 he once again rose to the occasion: 'OK, not to worry, tell me how many of you there are.'†

Intikhab says that the journey from the Purbani hotel to the airport would normally have taken fifteen minutes. 'It took us three hours because of the burnt trees lying on the roads.' Intikhab recounts how he sat in the front of a military jeep with a machine gun in his hands, halting to clear the road blocks every few yards. 'I can't ever begin to describe the scene at the airport,' recalls Intikhab. 'Millions of people there trying to get onto that flight. Now, I had about fifteen tickets with me and there was an army presence all over.' Somehow they escaped.

Now the team was involved in a race against time. The third match was due to start at Lahore on 4 March. Indian airspace was barred to Pakistan overflights so they were forced to travel via Colombo in Sri Lanka. As the plane landed, the front wheel burst. This held them up for several hours.

---

*According to both Sarfraz Nawaz and Shafqat Rana, Micky Stewart invited Intikhab Alam (his Surrey team-mate) to join the International X1 on their flight out, but he refused.
†But was it really Haider? I have found no evidence that Haider was in East Pakistan in 1971, and his family say he retired as Director General of the West Pakistan Rangers in Lahore later that year. Perhaps he masterminded the team's escape from there; more likely another officer came to the rescue.

'They put on extra speed on the aeroplane to bring us to Lahore for the Test,' remembers Intikhab.

The BCCP assumed they would be late, and had arranged an alternative XI to play the International team. However, it rained in Lahore that morning, and Intikhab's team arrived just in time for the delayed 2.30pm start. Sarfraz still remembers the 'hanging faces' of the alternative XI when the first team arrived.

Batting first, Pakistan not surprisingly collapsed. Imran Khan, representing his country for the first time, came in with the score at 80 for 7. He made 51 not out as he steered the team to 153, then took three wickets, opening the bowling with Sarfraz Nawaz, the first occasion these two great bowlers opened for Pakistan. Imran's performance earned him a place in the Pakistan touring party to England that summer, as well as an offer of a county place for Worcester.

For another youngster, Roqibul Hasan, the Dacca Test was his last first-class appearance – at age seventeen. In an interview years later, he recalled his appearance for the BCCP XI: 'After lunch on the last day, the student processions came, there were a lot of bonfires and the stadium was invaded.' He added: 'I knew that it was the end of my Test cricket career. During that period I was involved in freedom fighting. I was called up by the Bangladesh government-in-exile to form a cricket team like the soccer team we had playing all over India and creating awareness for our cause.'[54]

When the Quaid-e-Azam Trophy resumed – in March 1971 – all the East Pakistan teams withdrew and handed their opponents a walkover.* The focus now turned to the tour of England, scheduled for the summer.

British media were reporting the Pakistan army's repressive tactics and the growing number of refugees gave out accounts of the deliberate murder of sympathisers with the secessionist movement. Public opinion in Britain turned against Pakistan. The Pakistan High Commission in London grew nervous about the team's reception and even safety, and urged a postponement of the tour, but IA Khan, Yahya Khan's choice as BCCP president, would not hear of it and lobbied the MCC successfully to continue as planned.[55] The selectors gave up on Roqibul Hasan, Niaz Ahmed (the East

---

*The tournament was remodelled yet again into a knockout tournament and a 100-over limit was put on first innings. PIA A were upset by Punjab University, who lost the final to Karachi Blues, on first innings.

Pakistan player who had toured England in the calmer days of 1967) and MA Latif. Their one gesture towards East Pakistan was to include two of its administrators in the selection committee. At this stage, it is hard to believe that they seriously imagined this would placate public opinion in East Pakistan, and the two men never showed up.[56]

The selectors made several controversial decisions, particularly the omission of Mushtaq Mohammad and Majid Khan, supposedly because of their respective commitments to Northamptonshire and to Cambridge University and Glamorgan. IA Khan claimed that Mushtaq had made excessive financial demands on the Board of Control. The media and the public took the players' side and they were hastily reinstated. The selectors were also attacked for dropping Mohammad Nazir but then recalling him to replace the injured Pervez Sajjad. They placated opinion by taking both. These events resulted in Pakistan acquiring a party of nineteen players for a short tour – an example of overprovision which was to be repeated in later years.

In the end the tour passed by with relatively few political problems, although the team faced a sustained demonstration outside Edgbaston.* One incident had an element of farce. The team's most argumentative players, Saeed Ahmed and Aftab Gul, went out with Mohammad Nazir to an Indian restaurant in Portsmouth. The owner was a Bengali and refused to serve them. Saeed responded 'in unsophisticated language' and a highly public shouting match developed. The tour management responded by banning visits to Bengali-owned restaurants, although it was never clear how the players were supposed to ascertain ownership in advance.†

Another incident was potentially more serious. During the first Test, it was announced that the Pakistan players would autograph a bat for the Lord Mayor of Birmingham, in aid of Oxfam's appeal for East Pakistan refugees who were victims of cholera. The players had not been consulted in advance, and Aftab Gul, the most politically connected of them, refused to sign. ITN on 19 June reported his belligerent claim that India had used 'the bogey of cholera' to blacken Pakistan and that the relief appeal was an excuse to provide money for India.[57] Other players dug in their heels. The Bishop of

---

*In an era of regular campus protests, most British students ignored the East Pakistan war unless they had a personal connection. South African apologists, smarting from the successful protest against South Africa's tour the previous year, often accused them of double standards.
†Zakir Hussain, *The Young Ones, 1971*, pp.5–6.

Liverpool, former England captain David Sheppard, a leader of the movement to break cricketing links with South Africa, threatened to organise a
boycott of the tour. The Pakistan manager, Masood Salahuddin, ordered the
players to sign. Aftab Gul continued to refuse, vocally, and was disciplined.
The others complied although Aftab Gul claimed that most supported
him.[58]

There were numerous other off-the-field dramas which were not political in origin but were to recur many times in the future. In the opening
match against Worcester, Saeed Ahmed refused to occupy the number 3 slot,
apparently not relishing the prospect of facing Worcester's West Indian
opening bowler Vanburn Holder on a green wicket. Zaheer Abbas came to
the rescue and scored a century. It was the moment that Pakistan's premier
middle-order slot irrevocably changed hands. Saeed Ahmed tried to secure
himself a Test berth lower down, was refused, and went AWOL on a shopping spree with his wife.[59] Earlier he had induced younger players to visit
nightclubs and then reported them for waking him up when they returned.
Meanwhile Saeed Ahmed's brother-in-law, Sarfraz Nawaz, announced that
he was unfit to play in the first Test but performed energetically in Second
X1 and Sunday League matches for his English county, Northamptonshire,
while Pakistan were playing the third Test without him. All the players complained about tour payments (especially the meal allowance of 75p*). The
junior players resented the much higher allowances and other privileges
given to the seniors.

After all of these disturbances, the first Test opened with one of the greatest performances in Pakistan's cricket history. British cricket reporters had
given little chance to Pakistan against an England team which had just won
the Ashes. In particular, they suggested that Pakistan's top order would be
brittle against England's express bowler, Alan Ward. Nonetheless, when
Intikhab Alam won the toss at Edgbaston he had no hesitation in batting.
Ward did strike early, quite literally, when Aftab Gul missed his third delivery and was hit in the face. He was taken off the field† and Pakistan's
number 3 had to come in – bespectacled, apologetic, unrated Zaheer Abbas.

*This had been held at the established level of 15 shillings, which would not buy much of an evening
meal. 1971 was the first year of decimal currency in the UK; prices edged up and 75p was soon worth
less than its pre-decimal equivalent.
†The BBC's *Test Match Special* commentator Brian Johnston assured listeners the next day that 'the
doctor inspected his head and found nothing in it.'

It was his second Test match and he had managed only 12 and 27 at home to lowly New Zealand in his first. After some early uncertainties, Zaheer's innings simply got better and better. He lost Sadiq Mohammad at 68, but then added 293 with Mushtaq Mohammad, stroking the ball effortlessly to all parts of the field. Mushtaq left after scoring exactly 100, but Zaheer put on another 82 with Majid Khan. Finally, to his fury, Zaheer fell to Ray Illingworth attempting his least beautiful stroke, the sweep. He had scored 274 in 550 minutes with 38 fours. Asif Iqbal took over, ending the second day on 98 not out, despite a broken jaw. In pursuit of his century, he ran out the debutant Imran Khan. Intikhab Alam carried on into the third day to let him complete it, before declaring on 608 for 7. It was Pakistan's highest score to date against England.

When England batted, another little-rated Pakistani came to the fore. The opening bowler Asif Masood had a curious sidestep at the start of his action, likened by John Arlott to Groucho Marx chasing a pretty waitress. On that day, it helped him to swing and seam the ball prodigiously. He dismissed John Edrich second ball, on his way to five for 111, and reducing England to 148 for 6, supported by Pervez Sajjad and Intikhab Alam. Despite Alan Knott's 116 and Basil D'Oliveira's 73, England had to follow on for the first time against Pakistan. Asif Masood then hustled out another four batsmen. Pakistan were on the edge of a famous victory, but rain and bad light interfered heavily with the last two days and the match was abandoned with England five wickets down and 26 behind.

The second Test at Lord's was wrecked by rain but the third Test match at Leeds was a dogfight. Pakistan made one change: Saeed Ahmed got back into the side because Majid Khan was captaining Cambridge in the Varsity match at Lord's.* England won the toss and batted in perfect conditions. Wasim Bari took three good catches to reduce them to 74 for 3, but Boycott made another century, D'Oliveira a belligerent 74 and England made 316. Pakistan laboured to a lead of 34, batting for more than 209 overs. Zaheer Abbas needed over 40 overs to make 72, Mushtaq Mohammad needed almost as many to make 57. Pakistan looked like falling behind but Wasim Bari squeezed 94 from the last three wickets, of which he scored 63. He then

---

*Although Cambridge University were having a revival under his leadership, the traditional match had generally declined sharply in standard in the past decade. It revealed much about English and (even more so) Pakistani social attitudes that it should still take priority over a deciding Test match for Pakistan.

caught Brian Luckhurst off Asif Masood's first ball, to complete a four-ball pair for Luckhurst. He then had Boycott brilliantly caught at short leg by Mushtaq Mohammad. As so often, D'Oliveira saved England in adversity. Playing late on a now difficult wicket he made 72. Supported by a fifty from Dennis Amiss and 45 from Illingworth. The other opening bowler, Saleem Altaf, then produced figures of four for 11 in 14.3 overs, and England set a victory target of 231. Wasim Bari equalled the then Test wicketkeeping record with eight catches, three of them brilliant. With no great alarms, Aftab Gul and Sadiq Mohammad knocked off 25 without loss in the rest of the day.

However, the next morning Aftab played a foolish shot against Illingworth, and departed without further score. Zaheer (first ball), Mushtaq Mohammad and Saeed Ahmed followed quickly, watched by a composed Sadiq Mohammad. At 65 for 4, Asif Iqbal came in and gave him the support he needed. They added 93 with little worry as Illingworth shuffled a six-man attack. Then, unaccountably, Asif Iqbal decided to charge the slow left-armer, Norman Gifford. He missed and gave an easy stumping. Sadiq was unruffled and he and Intikhab made 24 slowly, with time not a factor. Finally, Ray Illingworth turned to England's regular partnership breaker, Basil D'Oliveira. His first over removed both batsmen. Pakistan needed 46 from the last three wickets and in the first innings they had made double that. Wasim Bari and Saleem Altaf added 16. Now Illingworth made his second inspired decision, by summoning his only bowler of real pace, Peter Lever. Because of injury he had not bowled yet in the innings. He responded by shooting out the last three in four balls. Pakistan lost by 25 runs, a result which still causes heartbreak to survivors over forty years later.

In spite of the defeat and all the off-field problems, this short tour represented a coming of age for Pakistan. Intikhab had captained shrewdly, held together a fractious team with little intelligent support from the official management and worked himself hard as a bowler, taking 72 first-class wickets on a short tour. *Wisden 1972* summed up the tour as one which had established Pakistan as 'a real force in world cricket' and quoted Intikhab Alam's own modest statement: 'I said at the start that we were good enough to win at least one Test. But for the rain on the last day at Birmingham I am sure we would have done so. Of course I was disappointed that we did not beat England, but I am sure that we did enough to justify a full tour.'[60] Many English supporters agreed with him but this would not happen until 1987.[61]

END OF AN EPOCH

Pakistan's Test cricketers returned to a nation confronting mortal threat. As Indian forces gave first covert and then open support to the Mukti Bahini guerrillas, Yahya Khan's army began to lose control of East Pakistan. Like many armies in such a position before and since, the Pakistan army stepped up repression, with no result except to increase resistance. India declared war and its army marched into East Pakistan, where it overwhelmed the already exhausted Pakistan army in barely two weeks. On 17 December 1971, the Pakistanis surrendered and nearly 90,000 soldiers became prisoners of war, including Lt Col. Shuja-ud-Din, one of the heroes of The Oval in 1954. While in prison, Shuja was to organise regular cricket matches for his companions, and appealed to the MCC to send out kit.[62]

Amid local and international celebrations, including a string of major rock star performances, the state of Bangladesh came into being, with Sheikh Mujib as its first prime minister. It was under-resourced and deeply scarred by war. There is still no reliable estimate of Bengali civilian deaths during the conflict. An official Pakistani commission came up with a figure of 26,000, Indian and Bengali sources came up with three million. Contemporary American estimates were around 300,000.[63] Not surprisingly, in this year of war, no overseas cricket teams came to Pakistan and the BCCP had to rely on domestic competitions to keep the game alive and perhaps also to create a sense of normality. The new season began in September 1971 with a new knockout competition between six local teams for the Punjab Governor's Gold Cup. Punjab University beat Rawalpindi by an innings in the final, despite a heroic bowling effort of eight for 140 in 64 overs from yet another slow left-arm bowler, Abdul Wahab. For the University, Wasim Raja scored over 150 as did Shafiq Ahmed, yet another 'nearly man' who would have a career of six scattered Tests.

A one-off match produced a thrilling eight-run victory for a Pakistani XI against the Punjab, despite two half-centuries by Wasim Raja. Pervez Sajjad and Mohammad Nazir shared fourteen wickets for the Pakistani XI. There was no Quaid-e-Azam Trophy tournament but the BCCP Trophy attracted two teams each from Karachi, Lahore, PIA and Railways, the Public Works Department, the National Bank, Punjab University and seven teams from other cities in West Pakistan. There were fewer mismatches than in some other seasons, although Multan collapsed to 59 all out against Railways A, but the form book held good and two of the strongest teams contested the final: Karachi Blues and PIA A. This had some familiar performances. Hanif Mohammad made 186 for PIA A as they scored 402 in 162 overs, Pervez Sajjad bowled 77 overs for them in two Karachi innings. There was no hope of a result in five days and PIA A won the trophy on first innings.

Halfway through the season, Yahya Khan at last resigned and stepped down as commander-in-chief. He entrusted the surviving state of Pakistan, in the west, to the civilian politician with the largest following, ZA Bhutto, who promptly ordered his arrest, stripped him of his military decorations, and cut his pension. Pakistan had entered a new era. For the next six years the country and its cricket were to be run by men with powerful minds, strong personalities and a reform agenda at home and overseas, but also with a gift for making enemies: ZA Bhutto and his old friend and new political follower AH Kardar.

KARDAR'S APOTHEOSIS

'Had Bhutto gone straight to Oxford instead of spending three years at Berkeley in the United States, he would have played first-class cricket not only in England but also later in Pakistan. But those three years in California were to turn him into a political person.'

– AH KARDAR[1]

Pakistan's worst national humiliation was followed by its most hopeful moment since Partition. ZA Bhutto now led the country's first democratically elected government, and he held out the prospect of national rebirth. He and his Pakistan People's Party represented far more than a domestic rebellion against military rule. They were a local manifestation of a movement that was shaking the world.

Bhutto, just forty-three when he took office, was one of a small number of young leaders and resistance fighters who took on the post-war establishment and sought to forge a new world in the 1960s. Che Guevara, John F Kennedy and Bhutto's friend Colonel Gaddafi had blazed the trail; now in the early 1970s, Bhutto was one of the most exciting politicians on the planet. He possessed vision, flair, brilliance and charisma. He was the first civilian leader of Pakistan with the self-confidence to take on the country's military rulers. Bhutto sacked the armed forces chiefs, having many officers court-martialled for war crimes or incompetence.[2]

Bhutto's purges inevitably extended to Ayub and Yahya Khan appointees in the civil service and public corporations, including sporting bodies. He was determined to open up his administration, partly to bolster its loyalty to him, but also in a genuine search for new talent. In 1973, a new constitution was approved which for the first time formally established Pakistan as a parliamentary democracy. Bhutto became prime minister. His rule would become increasingly authoritarian, but there was a heady period when there were high hopes that democracy would succeed.

From the start, he faced serious international problems. In his view, supported by a great majority of Pakistanis, the American alliance had done nothing for Pakistan in its hour of need. The United States, such a faithful ally of the military dictatorships of Ayub and Yahya Khan, withheld the hand of friendship from democratically elected Bhutto. Ayub Khan had been able to rely on lavish US aid, at its peak worth more than $50 per capita. American aid to Bhutto's Pakistan never even reached $10 per capita.* To run the government, Bhutto needed to find new sources of capital. This was the prime motive for a wave of nationalisations, particularly of banks and construction companies, although these were also a means of transferring power from the elite families who had dominated the Pakistan economy into the hands of the people (and of Bhutto supporters).

Having given up on the Americans, Bhutto also decided to sever some of his formal links with the United Kingdom. In January 1972, he took Pakistan out of the Commonwealth. Under the old rules of international cricket this would have meant Pakistan automatically forfeiting her membership of the ICC, and therefore losing her status as a Test-playing country. Ironically, Pakistan benefited from the precedent set by South Africa's departure from the Commonwealth in 1961. According to the rules, South Africa should have been barred, but (thanks to the support of England, New Zealand and Australia) she continued to play against the other white Test-playing countries.†

*At its peak in 1962, under Ayub, total US aid to Pakistan per capita was $55. In 1973, Bhutto's best year, total US aid per capita was $10.3 (adjusted for inflation). Source: www.ips.org.pk/security-and-foreign-policy/1080-us-aid-to-pakistan.

†In theory the Tests played by South Africa after 1961 had no standing. In practice England, Australia and New Zealand ignored the ICC rules. Cricket statisticians continue to treat South African matches post-1961as full Tests and count them towards career averages etc. There remains an impeccable argument that these matches should be struck off the official record. In 1965 the ICC (renamed the International Cricket Conference) ended the link between Commonwealth membership and Test status.

Bhutto worked actively to win new friends and financial support for his government, especially among Arab and Islamic nations. He developed an especially warm relationship with Colonel Gaddafi, which left a lasting legacy to Pakistan cricket – the renaming of the Lahore stadium after the Libyan leader. The new name was announced at a mass public rally in February 1972.[3] In 1974, he hosted an Islamic summit in Lahore. It boosted his regime both internationally and domestically, helping him to win national assent to his recognition of Bangladesh and the other concessions he had made to secure the release of Pakistan's prisoners of war.

At this summit, Gaddafi visited his eponymous stadium and spoke there to a hand-picked audience of Bhutto loyalists.* The handsome young Libyan leader informed the crowd of nearly 100,000 that Pakistan was the 'citadel of Islam in Asia' and promised that Libya was 'ready to sacrifice its blood' if Pakistan was threatened.[4] The new name of the Gaddafi stadium survived even Gaddafi's fall and death in the Libyan revolution in 2011, because of failure to agree on a replacement.

All of the developments described above had a strong influence on Pakistan sport, which played a key role in Bhutto's political ambitions at home and abroad. He set up the ZA Bhutto Institute of Sports and Culture 'on essentially political grounds', according to the analyst Shahid Javed Burki, to develop 'a political rapport between himself and the people.'[5]

Bhutto appointed a reliable ally and professional politician, AH Pirzada, in overall charge of sports. Bhutto hoped to win new friends in the Third World through international sport, which had become a major diplomatic forum (as evidenced by the ping-pong diplomacy preceding Nixon's dramatic rapprochement with China). Bhutto was particularly active in support of the sports boycott of apartheid.

Inheriting from his military predecessors the role of patron of cricket, Bhutto was determined to put the role to good use. Yahya Khan's man, IA Khan, was stripped of the presidency of the Board of Control. For his replacement, Bhutto stretched out a hand to AH Kardar, an appointment which combined merit and political expediency. Kardar had already gained

*Sir Morrice James, op. cit. p.192. Gaddafi enjoyed his trip to Pakistan so much that he stayed on for four days after the conference was over. Bhutto always had a high personal regard for Gaddafi, and in his final days hoped that the Libyan leader might spring him from his prison cell. I am grateful to Bhutto's confidant Aftab Gul for this information.

a reputation for clear-mindedness, integrity and administrative ability. He was still hugely popular with the fans. Bhutto hoped that his former national captain would restore his country's cricketing greatness and offer the prospect of escape from the failures of the 1960s – as Bhutto himself intended to do for Pakistan on the international stage. But the appointment was also an acknowledgement of a friendship that stretched back to boyhood.

Zulfiqar Ali Bhutto and Abdul Hafeez (as Kardar had then styled himself) first met thirty years earlier, during World War Two, when Hafeez would travel down from Lahore to Bombay.[6] Bhutto was a cricket-mad youngster who loved to be near cricket stars, such as Mushtaq Ali, the popular Muslim cricketer who scored India's first Test century overseas, or the precocious Alimuddin.[7] He was coached by Mushtaq Ali, and also by the brilliant Vinoo Mankad.[8]

But Bhutto was more than a star-struck fan. He was also a useful right-handed batsman, who played for the Sunder Cricket Club in Bombay, where he was occasionally used as opener.[9] In his autobiography, Kardar asserted that the future president was a good enough cricketer to have earned a Blue had he attended Oxford first, and then the University of California at Berkeley, rather than the other way around.[10] Be that as it may, Bhutto was certainly a decent player, probably ranking among Pakistan presidents in cricketing talent second only to Iskander Mirza. According to Kardar, his 'interest in cricket was that of a scholar. He knew the history of cricket, including such technical developments as the introduction of the third wicket and the sightscreen.'[11]

Kardar's link with Bhutto was reinforced in the early 1950s when he met Bhutto's friend Omar Kureishi, a newspaper columnist, author and radio commentator. His book, *Once Upon a Time*, provides a charming and (for the historian of Muslim cricket) important recollection of a cricketing childhood in wartime Bombay. In 1979, Kureishi recalled: 'We had been schoolboys together at The Cathedral School in Bombay. We had played cricket, indeed that had been the bond. We bunked classes to watch the Muslims play in the Pentangular, celebrated their triumphs and agonised over their defeats. I think our foremost ambition then was to become first-class cricketers.'[12]

Kureishi later travelled to study at the University of California, where he was soon joined by Bhutto. They shared lodgings and played cricket together at Griffith Park for a club called the Corinthians, for whom Bhutto opened the batting.* Kureishi became one of Pakistan's earliest cricket commentators upon his return. As we have seen, he was on duty in that capacity when he became witness to the events surrounding the Peshawar 'Test match' against MCC in 1955. Throughout the 1950s and 1960s, he would probably have acted as a link between Kardar and Bhutto.†

At first Kardar, as national cricket captain, would have been a more glamorous figure than the future prime minister and president as he slithered up the greasy pole. Kardar stepped down as captain just after Bhutto had become the youngest member of Ayub Khan's cabinet in the aftermath of the 1958 coup, with responsibility for power and water (a duty, as we have noted, often combined with the chairmanship of the national cricket board, though not in Bhutto's case). Then Kardar struggled for a new role (he attempted to establish himself as a jute trader, moving to East Pakistan to set up a business which failed[13]) while Bhutto soared. By 1963, aged just thirty-five, he was Ayub Khan's foreign minister, the equivalent of foreign secretary in Britain, and used his status to become the dominant presence in government and at overseas gatherings. He pushed a cautious Ayub, against his better judgement, towards war with India. When the peace treaty was negotiated at Tashkent in 1965, Bhutto made a public display of anger and disappointment, exploiting his exit from Ayub's government soon after and setting up his Pakistan People's Party in 1967.

From this moment, Bhutto assailed Kardar with demands that he join his PPP. Kardar was sympathetic. More than any politician since Jinnah, Bhutto represented what Kardar believed. Kardar's political identity has been misunderstood, partly because his aloof demeanour helped to propagate the myth that he was some kind of aristocrat or feudal lord, partly because of MCC hostility.

He was never a supporter of Pakistan's religious zealots. He was a worldly figure who enjoyed the pleasures of the flesh, yet at the same time a socialist

---

*Omar Kureishi recalled, 'On Sundays we played cricket at Griffith Park. The standard was poor and he and I were the super-stars of our team The Corinthians. It was fun cricket and we toured around California.' http://www.bhutto.org/article55.php.

†According to Kardar, having first met Bhutto in 1942, he corresponded with him 'when he was at Berkeley and I was at Oxford' and met him in Karachi 'before he joined Ayub Khan's cabinet.' AH Kardar, *Pakistan's Soldiers of Fortune*, p.142.

who believed in equality and the redistribution of wealth. He had a romantic attachment to English values and tradition, which expressed itself in a
snobbish pride in his Oxford education, and yet at the same time he was a
fierce partisan for Pakistan, who hated British arrogance and officialdom.
Important to his political formation was a bruising personal experience of
Western arrogance at the hands of a blinkered English cricketing establishment. Had he been British, Kardar might well have found a home for his
complex, contradictory beliefs inside the smarter cadres of the Hampstead
Labour Party.

No political leader could ever embrace each one of Kardar's attachments,
foibles and ambitions. But Bhutto, who shared so many of Kardar's personal
weaknesses, came much the closest to granting lucidity and coherence to
Kardar's outlook on the world. Much later, Kardar would explain his decision to join the PPP in the following terms:

> The first reason for joining the PPP was the fact that I had known Bhutto
> since 1942. In fact, I believe I am the only Pakistani politician with such
> long acquaintance with Bhutto. I admired his intellectual capacity and
> firmly believed that Bhutto had no match in our political life except per-
> haps Wali Khan from the NWFP. The second reason was the progressive
> Manifesto of the Party. No political party, except the underground, com-
> munist Party, had ever before raised the issues of poverty, ignorance,
> hunger, privation and disease affecting the teeming millions of Pakistan.
> All those who believed in improving the lot of the poor joined the PPP.
> I was one of them.[14]

The passage above was written in 1988, almost twenty years later. It con-
centrates on Kardar's idealistic reasons for joining the PPP. Other
considerations caused Kardar to procrastinate. In 1969 – two years after the
formation of the PPP – he accepted the post of chairman of selectors, a job
which would hardly have come his way had he been out of favour with the
military regime.

Kardar was to pay a price for this indecision. In all political movements,
special weight is attached to early supporters – the classic example concerns
the so-called 'gaullistes de la première heure' who came to the aid of General
de Gaulle's free French in 1940 – who risk all to join what looks to many

outsiders like a doomed or dangerous cause. Kardar jumped on board the PPP only in the spring of 1970, once its bandwagon was well and truly rolling. Bhutto was delighted, inviting his new acquisition on a tour of the clubs of Karachi to show him off.[15] Privately, however, Bhutto held Kardar's cautious attitude against him.*

Bhutto allowed Kardar to run on the PPP ticket in the Punjab provincial assembly elections of December 1970. Kardar was duly elected for a seat in Lahore, where his Arain caste was well-represented.[16] There then followed a lull of almost a year, while the country remained under Yahya Khan's martial law and the future of East Pakistan was resolved.

Kardar's first public act during this nebulous post-election period was to go on hunger strike in sympathy with striking Lahore journalists who were in dispute with their owners. This was an early, telling example of Kardar's political naivety. He almost certainly expected that he would please Bhutto by taking this pro-worker stand, but in fact the PPP leader was infuriated. Bhutto had used socialist rhetoric to win votes during his election campaign. Now that power was within his grasp, the last thing he needed was to fall out with newspaper proprietors. This kind of complexity was far beyond the comprehension of the honourable, literal-minded former Pakistan cricket captain.

Conscious that Kardar had lived in East Pakistan for many years, Bhutto used him as a PPP envoy, dispatching him on three missions into what had become hostile territory, to try and establish the facts on the ground, and the possibilities for peace.[17] Kardar travelled fearlessly around the country. He received at least one death threat, by telephone through to his hotel room from a fanatic, and experienced some of the tragedy at first hand.

After the indiscriminate slaughter of students and professors at Dacca University that followed the army crackdown, Kardar rang an army acquaintance to ask after the safety of a friend, only to receive the reply: 'Hafiz [sic], do you want anyone to be disposed of?' Kardar angrily replied that 'my mission was a mission of enquiry and peace and not of getting people murdered.'[18] It was a strange and horrible period of military terror

---

*For evidence of this lingering sense of presidential disappointment, see R Rafi Raza's letter to Kardar on 24 August 1972. Raza, Bhutto's special assistant, pointedly reminded Kardar that 'you joined the Party in September, 1970. On the eve of the general elections, and prior to that, you were not in the political field. The exact extent of your contribution … is not unknown to the President.' AH Kardar, *Pakistan's Soldiers of Fortune*, p.159.

and political paralysis, which came to an end only with the resignation on 20 December 1971 of Yahya Khan, after the abject humiliation of Pakistan's military surrender.

KARDAR IN POWER

Kardar's entry into government was by no means a simple matter. His appointment as Punjab's minister of health was announced in the newspapers, but he refused to accept on the basis that 'while I considered the portfolio of Health as extremely important yet without any background of the subject I did not feel I could do justice to it.'[19]

In protest, Kardar vanished for three days 'while the entire staff of the Department of Health, including the Health Secretary,* were telephoning and looking for me.'[20] He later recorded that 'the rest of the Cabinet members looked [on] in bewilderment at a colleague refusing to be a Minister, whereas they had begged days and nights for such appointments.'[21] Eventually, he agreed to take the portfolio of 'food and co-operatives'. The Punjab needed to increase its wheat imports by around 40% in short order, and he relished the challenge. His secondary responsibility of 'co-operatives' was filial tribute by Kardar to his father's leading role in the Punjab co-operative movement.

According to Kardar's own account, he was fully occupied and reluctant to accept when Pirzada approached him with the offer of a fresh responsibility: the presidency of the BCCP. Pirzada then explained that Bhutto was insistent he should take the job, and that both of them would face trouble if he refused. Kardar gave in.[22]

The new president was wise to insist. Kardar used his period in charge of Pakistan cricket to galvanise decisive change. Almost all of the previous holders of the post had been political figures (including presidents Iskander Mirza and Ayub Khan, for the first five years of his incumbency) who lacked the time and energy to devote to cricket administration. Kardar was the first serious cricketer, the first to bring energy and vision to the post, and one of the few with irreproachable personal integrity. Ghulam Mustafa Khan, who

*Roughly equivalent to the permanent secretary at the Department of Health under the British system.

served as a senior official for forty years at the headquarters of Pakistan cricket, says today that Kardar 'was the best president the cricket board ever had.'[23] It is difficult to dispute this judgement. In England Lord Harris, the Yorkshire (and England) cricket captain, politician and colonial governor, is still regarded as the most influential administrator in English cricket. Kardar, who shared many of Harris's autocratic instincts and singularities, was his equivalent in Pakistan.

Ghulam Mustafa recollects that Ayub Khan 'never came' into the office and that even his successor Syed Fida Hassan 'was too big a boss. We used to go to him.' Kardar, by contrast, would come in person – always immaculately dressed and always on time – after lunch, direct from his ministry. Ghulam Mustafa recalls that he would 'see all the files, issue instructions, ring people up. The entire control was his.' Just as he did in 1951, Kardar grabbed Pakistan cricket by the scruff of the neck. He ruled like an absolute, and by no means always benevolent, monarch. He was arbitrary, dictatorial and utterly unforgiving and ruthless with anyone who crossed him. He launched Pakistan cricket into a new era.

His first priority was to give the Board a permanent headquarters and a well-staffed secretariat. It had led a peripatetic existence for over twenty years, shuttling between Karachi, Lahore and latterly Rawalpindi to suit the convenience of its leaders.* Records and accounts had been stored in different homes and offices of executives, and even in cars and on the bicycle of an early Board member, Professor Aslam. At times, there were no designated staff to prepare for meetings and record and execute decisions, let alone carry out any long-term planning.

Kardar moved the Board out of Rawalpindi to the newly built stadium in Lahore.† Bhutto accused him sternly of land theft, but then added 'any theft of land for good purposes is all right'. Kardar had a good relationship with the Australian Cricket Board and he hoped to set up a Cricket House on Australian lines, with nets, dining areas and accommodation for cricketers, to become a central development agency for all Pakistan cricket.[24] (Inertia and rivalries frustrated this ambition; in 1997 Majid Khan, who had

---

*The head office did revert to Karachi during Air Marshal Nur Khan's period in charge (1980–84).
†ZA Bhutto made a speech inaugurating the new BCCP offices in Lahore, on 23 October 1972, in which he alleged that 'there is a great deal of similarity between cricket and the great game and art of politics.'

become chief executive of the renamed Pakistan Cricket Board, called it a millstone.[25]) Kardar begged furniture and heaters for the new headquarters from wealthy friends of Pakistan cricket.

As honorary secretary, he picked one of his favourite young cricketers, Zafar Altaf, who had proved his administrative ability in the Punjab Civil Service. Zafar earned wide respect internationally as well as domestically. Kardar instituted a policy of training other young cricket players and enthusiasts in posts within the new secretariat: one of the most successful, Khalid Mahmood, arranged Pakistan's (much fuller) international programme over the next decade, although with mixed success.[26]

Finally, Kardar created a testimonial fund to reward retired Pakistan cricketers. Their efforts on behalf of the national team, though wholehearted, had been effectively unpaid. Fazal Mahmood, Khan Mohammad, Maqsood Ahmed, Imtiaz Ahmed, Mahmood Hussain, Hanif Mohammad, Alimuddin and Intikhab Alam all received the sum of 20,000 rupees each (then equivalent to around £725). With this fine gesture, Kardar rewarded some of the major players who had followed him so loyally in the previous two decades.

Others received a smaller amount. Waqar Hasan, by now one of Pakistan's most prominent businessmen, donated his sum to flood relief. Kardar's brother-in-law Zulfiqar Ahmed asked the BCCP to share his donation between the veterans Miran Bakhsh and Amir Elahi, who he felt deserved (or perhaps needed) the money more than he did.[27]

Zafar Altaf provides some vivid memories of Kardar's habits and style. 'I continued to work as a civil servant and went to the Board after office hours. Kardar would arrive after lunch and work until 7.30. Then we would have a cheap meal at a restaurant (he would never take food at work, only tea). However, he was an early riser for prayers and I used to get regular telephone calls at 5.30am. I always knew the caller and would answer automatically "Hello, skipper." Very few people were mad enough to ring about work at 5.30.'

Zafar Altaf emphasised that Kardar was simultaneously a Pakistani, a Punjabi and an Oxonian. 'All three had to be understood to work with him.' He had strict standards of integrity, and would not give the slightest pretext for people to suspect favouritism. When his son Shahid wanted to play first-class cricket, he said that he would have to resign as BCCP president. In exchange for a first-class career, he offered his son five years at Oxford.[28]

Kardar's key ambition was to find new sources of finance for Pakistan cricket, to build new stadiums and practice facilities and refurbish decayed old ones, and to offer a living wage and a potential career for players and coaches. He turned to Pakistan's banks and other major companies, particularly but not exclusively those nationalised by Bhutto. He created new first-class and later one-day competitions for them on condition that they would raise teams, give jobs to talented cricketers, and invest in stadiums. He also promoted their representation on the Board of Control, and with it their participation in the Quaid-e-Azam Trophy.

At this point, the historian of Pakistan cricket runs into difficulty. No one has attempted a complete narrative of all the new competitions in the Kardar years. I do not propose to offer such a narrative myself, but will pick out some features and individual highlights which illustrate the new developments in Pakistan cricket.

The first is simply to note the names of some of the new teams: the Commerce Bank, the National Bank, Pakistan Customs, Habib Bank, Dawood Industries, Income Tax Department, Water and Power Development Authority, United Bank, Servis Industries. Employers' teams had been around in Pakistan for a long time, but Kardar sought a much deeper relationship between patrons and Pakistan cricketers. He expected the cricketers to be given real jobs with career possibilities, rather than sinecures, and in turn he expected the cricketers to take these seriously. When confronted by the players' revolt over money he wrote acidly: 'The banks were obliged to look for leading and promising players to enrol them. My objective was served. Players got jobs with handsome salaries and benefits. Later I was grieved that with a few honorable exceptions players would neither attend office to learn the banking profession, nor, in some cases, even make themselves available for the bank's team.'[29]

Kardar's five years saw a huge expansion of domestic cricket in Pakistan. His first season began modestly with a new Sikander Ali Bhutto Cup (named after Bhutto's step-brother, who had died tragically, aged only seven). The following year saw the arrival of the National Bank of Pakistan Challenge Cup and a Kardar Summer Shield and a Punjab tournament; there was also a restored Universities Championship. Most important, in that same season the BCCP Patron's Trophy began (replacing the old Ayub Trophy and its politically neutral successor, the BCCP Trophy). It was dedicated to patrons' (i.e. employers') teams and timed to allow players to join local, regional and other teams competing in the regular Quaid-e-Azam Trophy later in the season. Finally, the most successful Patrons and Quaid-e-Azam Trophy teams met in the Pentangular Cup, a name that revived memories of communal cricket to packed crowds in pre-Partition India.

In 1974–75, Pakistan saw its first one-day competition, the Servis Cup, with six matches. There was also a new one-off Abdul Sattar Pirzada Memorial Trophy, named after the father of the sports supremo. However, Kardar himself barely mentions the new competitions, or the new plenitude of first-class matches, in his memoirs, which devote far more attention to his energetic cricket diplomacy.*

Kardar was the first Pakistani to play an active role at the International Cricket Conference (as the Imperial Cricket Conference had been renamed in 1965). He claimed that one of his predecessors fell asleep at the ICC when Sir Donald Bradman was speaking on the vital issue of illegal bowling actions.[30] Kardar brought a different style: 'the time for snoring had ended and roaring had to start.'[31]

He took the lead at the ICC on a wide range of issues, some purely cricket-related, others with wider global significance. Invariably he found himself in confrontation with Gubby Allen, the MCC grandee (and spiritual descendant of Lord Harris) who governed English cricket for much of the post-war period. Kardar and Allen did not get on, but resembled each other far more closely than either would have cared to acknowledge.

Kardar first set out a distinctive agenda by proposing neutral umpires at Test matches; it earned him a contemptuous dismissal from Allen.† With the help of Zafar Altaf, he won over Clyde Walcott to support a limit on

---

*Imran Khan was and remains a scathing critic of Kardar's expansion of commercial and departmental teams, which (in his view) eroded player and spectator loyalty and reduced the standard of play and, especially, facilities and grounds. He regards season 1974–75, when the five best teams in Pakistan dominated the first-class programme, as the last satisfactory season in Pakistan's domestic cricket. He himself abandoned domestic matches in 1981, when he found himself sinking in sand in his run-up on an inadequately prepared pitch. Imran Khan: personal interview.

†Shahid Kardar, Kardar's son, remembers accompanying his father to Lord's on a mission to press the case for neutral umpires to an unimpressed Gubby Allen (interview with the author). However, neutral umpires did appear first in Pakistan, in the home series in 1986–87 against the West Indies, on the personal initiative of Imran Khan. See also Kardar, op. cit. p.227–29.

bouncers in the World Cup in 1975. With West Indian backing, and English benign neutrality, the proposal was carried.*

On wider issues, Kardar's prime objectives were to maintain the ban on South Africa and boost Asian representation on the ICC. He foiled an attempt (promoted in his fierce words by 'Asian quislings') to re-admit South Africa to the ICC (and the 1975 World Cup) on condition that it was represented internationally by mixed-race teams. The proposal, which was in direct opposition to Bhutto's foreign policy, was a red rag to Kardar, who had a long record as an anti-apartheid campaigner. He wrote later 'the quislings did not realise that by this time the issue had moved from purely sports exchanges to a very high political plane, and that Third World countries had taken an unambiguous and irrevocable stand against the racist policies of South Africa.'[32]

He refused point-blank to visit South Africa on behalf of the ICC to report on 'the progress of gradual transition in the relations between white and non-white cricketers.' When England's Freddie Brown urged him to go with a hackneyed plea to 'keep politics out of cricket' Kardar had a stinging and satisfying put-down: 'It is those whites in South Africa who have brought racist politics into cricket, and not us.'[33] Zafar Altaf was present when he told the full ICC: 'if they cannot value human beings irrespective of colour, caste or creed, then they have no business in international cricket.'[34]

On Asian representation at the ICC, Kardar experienced frustrations which led him to tackle a fundamental issue – the veto power of the (white) foundation members, England and Australia. He pushed hard for full membership for Sri Lanka, where he remains revered, and for affiliate status for Bangladesh. This was granted in 1977, sadly just after Kardar's embittered resignation from his post in Pakistan cricket. Sri Lanka had to wait for full membership until 1981.

However, Kardar did secure the admission of Singapore as an associate, and he invited Singapore to join his newly formed Asian Cricket Conference, in December 1974, with headquarters at the Gaddafi stadium.† This initiative alarmed the ICC. The secretary Jack Bailey (who doubled as

*Kardar, op. cit. p.206. Kardar admitted that the rule should have helped Pakistan in the World Cup and was furious at Majid Khan's captaincy for throwing the 'advantage' away.
†Strictly speaking, this was a revival. An Asian Cricket Conference was instigated by Anthony de Mello, of India, in January 1949, with a membership of India, Pakistan, Ceylon, Burma and Malaya. It met again in 1950 and then disappeared.

MCC secretary) asked Kardar to rename it the Asian Cricket Council, to avoid any suggestion that it was claiming equal status with the ICC. Bailey and his master, Gubby Allen, were especially anxious that year about an assertive approach from Pakistan on Asian representation; they thought it might embarrass that year's ICC chairman, the Duke of Edinburgh.[35] This was a foolish worry; the Duke was already experienced in sporting politics and even more experienced in robust language.

Kardar now decided that the time had come for a full assault on the England and Australian vetoes, the ultimate safeguard of white power in the ICC. According to Zafar Altaf, the Duke had some sympathy with Kardar, describing the veto as a 'very colonial' arrangement.[36] Kardar proposed its abolition in a fundamental reform of the ICC constitution. A series of preliminary meetings convinced him that the ICC would try to bury this deep in the agenda, so he decided to forestall this by raising his proposal through a point of order before the formal agenda began. The upshot was predictable. The ICC set up a special committee to review the constitution and present a range of proposals the following year. With almost no support elsewhere in the ICC, Kardar accepted that this was the best he could achieve.

After the matter was put to the vote, Kardar could not resist, says Zafar Altaf, asking the Duke who were the forty Englishmen sitting behind him. Informed that they were there to keep the minutes, Kardar said, 'Mr President, I have my secretary here, he will take the minutes and send them to you tomorrow.' The forty departed, one repeating an offensive description of Kardar from his first Oxford-Cambridge match as a 'mystic from the East.'[37] Later Kardar put down the Australian representative, Tim Caldwell,[38] who was unwise enough to defend the status quo to him at a reception at the Sri Lanka High Commission. Kardar gave a vehement defence of equality of representation and concluded: 'Mr Caldwell, send Don [Bradman] and I will give him two vetoes. He is great. He is the master of the game. But here, comparing my cricketing background to yours [Caldwell had played three state matches in Australia] I cannot give it to you. I cannot yield to a mediocrity.'

The put-down gave Kardar much satisfaction and led Gubby Allen to gulp down his drink.[39] It did not help his cause. The veto power remained until 1993. However, Kardar had put the issue on the agenda and initiated the long process which led to a permanent change in the governance of international cricket. MCC and the British establishment never forgave him. Unlike many other eminent Pakistani cricketers[40] he was never offered honorary membership of MCC, let alone the honours which were offered to the leading cricketers from former British colonies or dominions, for instance Lord (Learie) Constantine and Sir Don Bradman.

TEST CRICKET RESUMES

We have seen above how Pakistan became cricket's pariah nation during the 1960s, a metaphor for the parochialism of the Ayub Khan years. Just as Bhutto rebuilt the country's international reputation in the 1970s, so Kardar restored Pakistan as a major Test-playing nation.

The re-emergence of Pakistan on the international stage is a story of progress amid perennial power struggles and pantomime passages. Recurring ingredients in the story are inexplicable collapses in prosperity and heroic rallies in adversity, complex minuets and manoeuvres over the captaincy and vice-captaincy, capricious selectors and their real or imagined victims, managers or media in a fury, crowd disturbances, 'bad boys' who have to be punished but sometimes come good with a big performance, and new or fringe players who become overnight sensations. Sometimes the pitches become the main story – the stage itself moves centre stage. Over all of it looms the stern, unforgiving, dictatorial figure of Kardar.

The story begins with a tour to Australia over the winter of 1972–73, eight years after Pakistan had last played a Test against Australia. The tour began with the selectors quarrelling amongst themselves and excluding Hanif Mohammad, although he had reportedly made an effort to return from England in time to take part.[41] The Pakistanis were not helped by the Australian Board of Control, so often contemptuous of Pakistan, who gave them a very poor advance programme in which to prepare. Few of the team had ever played on Australian pitches. It took a long time for the bowlers particularly to adjust.

Partly as a result, Pakistan lost the first Test at Adelaide by an innings. The second Test at Melbourne started almost as badly. Australia batted first and rapidly and Ian Chappell made a challenging declaration at 441 for 5.

Then Pakistan's batting came good. Sadiq Mohammad and Majid Khan scored fluent centuries and four other batsmen reached fifty, including Saeed Ahmed, a very reluctant opener. The Pakistanis were especially severe on a new Australian fast bowler who had not told the selectors he had broken a bone in his foot; unfortunately for England, the wicketless Jeff Thomson was given a second chance two years later. Intikhab Alam declared on 574 for 8 in protest against a volley of bouncers from Dennis Lillee, who hurled the ball away in indignation, and set up a lasting personal feud against Pakistan players.

Australia scored another 400 in their second innings. Richie Benaud's brother John scored a fast century the day after he had been discarded by the selectors. He never played another Test in Australia, proving that selectoral caprices were not confined to Pakistan. Australia gave Pakistan a plausible victory target of 293 in 325 minutes, but all the main batsmen succumbed to the pressure exerted by Lillee and another new Australian bowler, the 'tangle-footed' Max Walker. There were foolish run-outs of Zaheer Abbas and Mushtaq Mohammad. Pakistan were reduced to 138 for 7. Intikhab Alam hit out for 48 but no one could stay with him and Pakistan were all out for 200.

The third Test at Sydney was preceded by Pakistan's struggle to find an opening batsman to face Lillee. Saeed Ahmed made it clear that he did not want the job and claimed to be injured. The tour management, MEZ Ghazali and Zafar Altaf, did not believe him and sacked him outright from the rest of the tour, ignoring a last-minute appeal from Saeed to Pirzada, Pakistan's sports supremo. It was written in red ink and Saeed asked Pirzada to imagine that it was his blood.[42]

They punished another reluctant opener even more severely. Mohammad Ilyas had been hit in the face earlier in the tour. According to Zafar Altaf, he incurred the injury after spending a night out and not going to bed. For a month he was a passenger, unable to see the ball, and when the party was due to go on to New Zealand, the tour management decided that he was still unfit to play. He too was sacked. Zafar Altaf insists that Kardar had nothing to do with either decision, but I believe that they would not have taken either without consulting him. It was a bitter way for a Pakistan cricketer to gain overseas experience.

The eventual choice of opener was the veteran Nasim-ul-Ghani, whose primary trade was as a slow left-arm bowler. He did not bowl in this match but scored 64 in Pakistan's first innings. Asif Iqbal scored 65 and Mushtaq Mohammad a century as Pakistan squeezed a lead of 26. Salim Altaf and Sarfraz Nawaz had learnt how to bowl in Australian conditions. After bowling out Australia for 334 in the first innings they did even better in the second, as four wickets apiece reduced Australia to 101 for 8, but Pakistan could not remove two tailenders, Bob Massie and a one-cap spinner, John Watkins.

Australia eventually set a modest target of 159. Pakistan lost their openers but stood at 48 for 2 when bad light stopped play. On the last day, the Pakistani batsmen were strangled by Max Walker and Dennis Lillee. They fell to a mixture of limp shots and desperate ones, one great catch and a debatable lbw, and were all out for 106.

EXIT SAEED AHMED AND MOHAMMAD ILYAS

Kardar now intervened to punish the players who he believed should take the responsibility for Pakistan's 3–0 drubbing. First in the firing line was Saeed Ahmed. Kardar refused to believe Saeed's excuses for his failure to play, and announced that he was being sent home to Pakistan, citing 'his continued irresponsible behaviour and sub-standard performance during the tour.' Upon his return home, Kardar, after a meeting of the BCCP executive committee, imposed a life ban.[43]

This marked the end of the Test career of a very fine batsman, who for fifteen years had been the mainstay of the Pakistan top order; the only batsman besides Hanif Mohammad to have started out in the 1950s and to have averaged over 40. (He was also a tidy off-break bowler.) Fazal Mahmood called him the 'bravest batsman Pakistan ever had.'[44] In the fine words of Omar Noman, 'the abiding cricketing memory of Saeed is of a dashing number 3 batsman who brought colour and joy to a rather dull batting side.'[45]

After his sacking, Saeed Ahmed's marriage and business ventures failed. He pondered a political career, becoming one of a small group of supporters of Mustafa Khar, governor of the Punjab, after he fell out with Bhutto. For a time, he lived in a caravan at the bottom of Khar's drive. In September

1975, he was arrested for taking part in a political demonstration on behalf of Khar in Lahore, spending two nights in a lock-up.[46] Saeed fought a long lawsuit against the BCCP to clear his name and resume his cricket career.[47] At the age of forty, in 1977–78 he was chosen for the North-West Frontier Province Governor's XI against Mike Brearley's English tourists. He managed only 0 and 3 with the bat, but had the satisfaction of bowling Derek Randall with his last ball in first-class cricket.

In due course, Saeed Ahmed's departure marked the start of a powerful religious mission. In 1982, he became the first former Test cricketer to join the Tableeghi Jamaat, the mass religious movement which can attract crowds of more than one million people to its annual gatherings. Today, Saeed wears a *shalwar kameez* (a traditional Pakistani outfit), sports a beard, lives a devout life, and has become a preacher. He helped to recruit other Test players to Tableeghi Jamaat, notably Saeed Anwar. He now attends to deeper truths than cricket is capable of expressing.

Kardar next turned his attention to the errant Mohammad Ilyas. He was just twenty-seven, and still trying to establish his Test place. Interviewed today about the events of thirty years ago, Ilyas says that there had been tension between him and Kardar since before the tour began. During the tour itself, the two men had a row, and Ilyas says that he punched Kardar. The response was terrifying. 'When the touring party left for New Zealand,' remembers Ilyas, 'they left me behind. They took my wallet with them, my passport, my bags, everything. I was left with just the clothes I was standing up in.' For several days, Ilyas slept on a Sydney park bench. Then he was fortunate to bump into, by chance, the Ceylonese cricketer Gamini Goonesena, a fine all-rounder who had played for Cambridge University and Nottinghamshire in the 1950s. 'He gave me food and shelter,' recalls Ilyas, 'I am most grateful.' At the time Goonesena was playing for Waverley District Cricket Club (now Eastern Suburbs) in Sydney. Goonesena listened to Ilyas's story, and alerted the authorities. Ilyas says that before long Gough Whitlam, the Australian prime minister, personally intervened, ordering that he should be given an Australian passport and $4,000. By the end of the season, Ilyas had joined Goonesena playing at Waverley and later he moved, still on his Australian passport, to England.

However, he could not go back to his native Pakistan. 'My grandfather died, and I could not attend his funeral. My sister married and they would not give me a visa,' he recollects, his eyes filling with tears. Only when Bhutto was displaced in a military coup by General Zia could Ilyas return. He wrote a letter to Zia, and received a prompt reply from the Pakistan High Commission in London, which issued him once more with a Pakistan passport.

Ilyas had risen to become chairman of the national selectors by the time I interviewed him, and he said of Kardar: 'He was a great captain. He was a great ambassador for the nation. He was a very decent man. It was written what was going to happen. I am not a religious man but my God created me and he will provide for me.'[48]

CAPTAINCY TURMOIL

Even a troubled Pakistan were far too good for New Zealand in 1972–73. Although they won only one Test (at the world's southernmost international ground at Dunedin) they generally outplayed their hosts. In the win at Dunedin, Asif Iqbal scored 175 and Mushtaq Mohammad 201 in a record fourth-wicket partnership of 350. Mushtaq then turned to his wrist spin to help Intikhab Alam (then probably the best leg-spinner in the world) bamboozle the New Zealanders. It was the first time in his Test career, already over thirteen years long, that Mushtaq had finished on the winning side. Fittingly, Mushtaq himself played a huge role in the victory, becoming only the second player in history to score a double-century and take five wickets in the same Test.[49]

Sadiq Mohammad and Majid Khan were century makers in the drawn Tests, Wasim Raja impressed as an attacking left-hand batsman and right-arm wrist spinner, Wasim Bari kept wicket brilliantly – almost everyone did something good on a happy tour, although Zaheer Abbas missed out as a reluctant opening batsman in the Tests.[50]

Then came yet another Kardar bombshell. As the last day of the third and final Test started, Kardar cabled Intikhab to inform him that he had been dropped as captain. The new captain, Majid Khan, was as surprised as anyone. 'Is this a joke?' he asked. Majid (described by the late Christopher Martin-Jenkins as a 'dignified, intelligent and amiably sleepy cricketer'[51]) was still in the process of establishing himself as a Test batsman. He had been a successful captain of Cambridge University during his time as an undergraduate, and this swayed Kardar's thinking. Nevertheless, other cricketers, above all Asif Iqbal (Intikhab's vice-captain) and Mushtaq, were more senior and experienced. The sudden elevation of Majid brought back memories of the appointment of his first cousin, Javed Burki, ten years earlier. It smacked of nepotism and privilege, besides making heavy demands on one of Pakistan's most talented young batsmen. The decision was also cruel to Intikhab, who had performed as well as anyone, did not deserve the blame for the series defeat in Australia, and had just led his team to their first-ever overseas series victory in New Zealand. In the poetic phrase of cricket writer Zahid Zia Cheema, Intikhab was 'winnowed out like unwanted husk.'[52] Perhaps Kardar's apparently irrational conduct was the result of other pressures. His position as minister in the Punjab government was precarious, and his relations with ZA Bhutto were coming under heavy strain.

Majid, meanwhile, had to captain a home series against England. He and the England captain Tony Lewis were both Cambridge Blues who had been team-mates at Glamorgan since 1968. Played on slow pitches, the Tests produced three draws, mainly of interest to statisticians, who were delighted when three batsmen (Majid Khan, Mushtaq Mohammad and Dennis Amiss) were each out for 99 in the third Test. Apart from that statistic, the Test was memorable mainly for a crowd riot, caused by gate-crashing students and schoolboys who invaded the pitch to congratulate Majid on reaching 50. He fled and the Karachi police charged the boys and gave several of them serious head wounds; this provoked a general round of stone throwing and arson.[53]

Majid Khan was sacked, becoming the fourth Pakistan captain after Imtiaz Ahmed, Javed Burki and Saeed Ahmed to be removed after just one series in the top job. Intikhab, inexplicably demoted the year before, was reinstated, equally inexplicably, for the return tour of England in 1974. Omar Kureishi, friend of both Bhutto and Kardar who had become one of Pakistan's most celebrated journalists, was appointed manager.

The first Test at Leeds was dominated by seam. Pakistan's opening pair of Asif Masood and Sarfraz Nawaz outbowled England in the first innings, and secured a lead of 102. But the Pakistan batsmen were strangled in their second innings and set a target of only 282. John Edrich, Mike Denness and Keith Fletcher got England close with four wickets left, but rain then cut the match short. Rain also played a major role in the Lord's Test, which became infamous for the failed covers. Sadiq Mohammad and Majid Khan* gave Pakistan a flying start before a storm drove them off. Water leaked onto the pitch and turned it into an early Christmas for Derek Underwood. He proved unplayable and took five for 20 in short order. These included Wasim Raja, sensationally caught off a mighty straight drive by a leaping Tony Greig at long off. Eventually, Intikhab declared on 130 for 9 to get the use of the damaged wicket for his own team. Thanks to late resistance from Alan Knott and Chris Old, England got a lead of 140. Pakistan lost three quick wickets, but Mushtaq Mohammad and Wasim Raja launched a counter-attack; the latter's straight six off Underwood is still remembered fondly by friend and foe. They added 96 and put Pakistan 33 ahead at the close of the fourth day.

More heavy rain fell overnight, and again leaked through the covers. The two overnight batsmen resumed as if nothing had happened. Wasim Raja was then caught, at 53, off Underwood, who dismissed the next three batsmen without scoring. Mushtaq holed out for 76 and Pakistan were eventually all out for 226. Underwood took eight for 51, his best figures, to finish with thirteen for 71 in the match.

Fortunately for Pakistan, rain had left England only 65 minutes to score 87 for victory on the fourth day. Today that would seem highly achievable, especially by a team that could not lose, but the past is another country and England's openers, Dennis Amiss and David Lloyd, did not attempt it. When the last day was abandoned, Pakistan got the draw which most observers thought they deserved. Even so, Omar Kureishi was moved to issue a furious complaint against the MCC's 'appalling show of negligence and incompetence in not covering the wicket adequately'; the MCC secretary, Jack Bailey, made a long reply full of excuses for a failure which had been unfair to spectators as well as the tourists.[54]

As if in compensation, the third Test at The Oval produced a benign pitch on which Pakistan made 600. Majid Khan flayed 98 before missing a ball from Derek Underwood, while Mushtaq Mohammad scored a comfortable 76. Zaheer Abbas, however, dominated the stage, after failing in the

---

*This was the match in which Majid Khan turned Test opener. The move transformed Majid's own batting and also, by opening up a space for the all-rounder Wasim Raja, transformed the balance of the side. Majid formed an opening partnership with Sadiq Mohammad which ranks among the finest in the country's history. The elevation of Majid was the idea of Omar Kureishi. For an illuminating discussion of the background to Majid's shift up the order, and its consequences, see Noman, p. 151.

previous Tests. On the easy Oval wicket, he scored 240, raising questions, which were to dog him for the remainder of his career, about why he could not score more runs when it really counted.[55]

The whole innings was scored at the then electric rate of 3.64 an over, but still it was not quick enough. With centuries from Amiss and Fletcher, England replied with 545 at the much more sedate tempo of 2.41 an over. Intikhab wheeled out five batsmen, but Imran Khan toiled through 44 wicketless overs for 100 runs. In his long Test career, he had only two more spells which yielded 100 runs without a victim. That more or less ended the entertainment, although Pakistan managed to fritter away four wickets before the match died of inanition.

Pakistan had now drawn six Tests in a row against England, but more importantly demonstrated equality at least in virtually every position. They emulated Don Bradman's 1948 Invincibles by being unbeaten in first-class matches on tour. The comparison is flattering since Bradman's was a full tour – but Pakistan were the first to achieve this on any tour since, long or short.

They also had the satisfaction of beating England in their first one-day international series. In the first, at Trent Bridge, a Majid Khan century had a strike rate of 117.2 – a statistic invented for the new form of cricket. Pakistan attained England's 244 with seven overs to spare. In the second, they dismissed England for 81 and Zaheer Abbas supplied a not-out fifty when they overhauled it. Their performance left Pakistan confident about their prospects in the following year's inaugural World Cup.

HEROICS FROM SADIQ MOHAMMAD AND WASIM RAJA

Before that, they were due to play two Tests against West Indies at home in 1974–75. Pakistan had not played a Test match against them since the 1950s. The West Indies had not yet assembled their pace battery of the late 1970s and 1980s, but Clive Lloyd brought over an attack led by Andy Roberts, backed by Keith Boyce, Bernard Julien and the veteran off-spin-ner Lance Gibbs, soon to annoy Fred Trueman by breaking his then record of 307 Test wickets. Besides Lloyd, their batting line-up included Roy Fredericks, Gordon Greenidge, Alvin Kallicharran and a youthful Viv

Richards. In short, they were a very good side, who had just won a thrilling series against India 3–2, with a thumping victory in the final Test.

Intikhab Alam was reappointed Pakistan's captain and most of the England tourists reappeared, except for Imran Khan, who had remained in England, and Sadiq Mohammad, who did not return in time from playing grade cricket in Australia (which was becoming a new outlet for Pakistan players). A new opener, Agha Zahid, replaced him and there was a long-delayed Test return for Aftab Baloch, who had been a prodigious performer in domestic cricket.

In the first Test at Lahore, the two first innings had a similar pattern. Andy Roberts was too good for most of the Pakistani batsmen, who were all out for 199, but Sarfraz Nawaz was in turn too good for the West Indians, other than Kallicharran, who was left stranded on 92. West Indies led by only 15 runs. Agha Zahid completed a miserable and solitary Test, lbw to Roberts before the arrears were knocked off. However, the pitch had eased, and Mushtaq Mohammad scored a patient century, supported by all the other batsmen, especially Aftab Baloch, whose not out 60 was admired by everybody except Kardar.[56] Intikhab's declaration was too cautious to allow any result, although there was time for the left-handed Guyanese opener Leonard Baichan to complete a century on debut and Viv Richards to be out for 0.* At one stage, just after tea, it looked as though West Indies might have a chance of winning. Pakistan responded by bowling 7.5 eight-ball overs in an hour.

For the second Test in Karachi, Sadiq Mohammad† was back as opener and Aftab Baloch was replaced by the left-arm fast bowler Liaquat Ali. Pakistan batted first. Majid Khan scored exactly 100 in coruscating style, but most of the top-order batsmen failed and Pakistan were badly placed on 246 for 6. Wasim Raja characteristically counter-attacked and reached his first century, adding 128 with Wasim Bari, who made a fighting fifty. Wasim Raja's century produced a crowd invasion which delayed matters for two and a half hours.

---

*It made little difference. Baichan played two more Test matches, Richards another 115.

†Sadiq was then playing grade cricket in Tasmania. Kardar asked him to come back to play two Tests against the West Indies. Sadiq pointed out that this would cost him $800, and asked Kardar for this sum as compensation, and a return ticket. Kardar refused this, and told him that Pakistan should come first, and he was not picked for the first Test. Two days later, Kardar phoned and told him that Pakistan needed him. He dropped the request for compensation and settled for a return ticket. He arrived just in time for the second Test and he had very little rest after the flight from Australia. Source: Sadiq Mohammad, personal interview.

Intikhab Alam promptly declared overnight on 406, to exploit moisture on the pitch, but few of the West Indians seemed to notice it. Centuries from Kallicharran and Julien, and seventies from Fredericks and Lloyd propelled them to 493. In fact, the only victim of the pitch was Wasim Raja, who sprained his ankle badly while bowling.

The other major casualty was Sadiq. 'Towards the end of the West Indian innings, Intikhab asked me to go to short leg. I said that I was not needed there, since the West Indies were about to declare.' But Intikhab pressed him. He took up the position and Intikhab promptly bowled a full toss. The batsman, the tailender Vanburn Holder, whacked it and hit Sadiq behind the ear. 'I fell on the pitch and was taken to hospital. The brain specialist Dr Jummah operated on me. He told me that another two centimetres and the blow would have killed me. I was released and given painkillers. Not feeling any pain, I drove my fiancée and her mother to go shopping for jewellery for our forthcoming wedding. But when the painkillers wore off, I was barely able to drive home. I collapsed into bed and was woken by morning prayer.'

Pakistan had lost five wickets while Sadiq was in hospital, and were struggling to save the match. Still in great pain, he came in to partner Asif Iqbal. They had a stabilising partnership but when Asif Iqbal was stumped for 77, Pakistan were only 61 runs in front with only three wickets to fall, since Wasim Raja by now had a foot in plaster and was not expected to bat. Sadiq now had to nurse the tailenders. He rose to the task, taking four balls an over, especially from the West Indies fastest bowlers, Boyce and Roberts. Sarfraz stayed with him for two hours, contributing 15 to a partnership of 64. Liaquat Ali, unrated as a batsman, also hung around in a partnership of 40 and finally Pakistan were safe. There was no need for Wasim Raja to come in – but he did, with his foot in plaster, to give Sadiq Mohammad, not out 98, the chance of a hundred. Zaheer Abbas was his runner. 'But I miscounted the balls in the over, and sent Zaheer back. As a result, Wasim Raja had to face a full over from Lance Gibbs. He was bowled by a full length turning ball.'[57] Poor Sadiq was left high and dry.

Years on, this brief partnership is still taught to children as one of the heroic episodes of Pakistan's cricket history.[58]

WORLD CUP 1975 TEARS

After Intikhab Alam's restoration in place of Majid Khan, Pakistan had held their own against two strong England and West Indies sides. They had thumped England under his leadership in two one-day internationals. Intikhab had extensive experience of one-day cricket in English conditions with his county, Surrey. But still the selectors deposed him as captain for the Prudential World Cup – and did not even include him as a player in the fourteen-man squad.

Asif Iqbal became captain, Majid Khan his deputy. Mushtaq and Sadiq Mohammad, Zaheer Abbas and Wasim Raja were the frontline batsmen and there was a berth for the teenage prodigy Javed Miandad. The bowling looked problematic. Asif Iqbal was no longer a frontline bowler. Imran Khan was restored but was yet to achieve greatness. Asif Masood, with a run-up as eccentric as ever, was over the hill, and only Sarfraz Nawaz looked capable of running through an opposing team. Nonetheless, Pakistan were still confident and many punters chose them as dark horse winners, even when they were drawn in a 'group of death' against Australia and West Indies, with Sri Lanka the predicted punchbag.

Their first match was against Australia at Leeds, in the unaccustomed heat of the first of two blazing summers. It began well enough. Naseer Malik, one of the makeweights of 1974 in England, took two wickets economically, helping to reduce Australia to 124 for 4. However, a not out 80 from Ross Edwards, with belligerent support from the tail, brought Australia to 278 off their 60 overs. For Pakistan, only Majid with 65 got anywhere near the asking rate. Asif Iqbal mustered a fifty and Wasim Raja 31, but no one else managed double figures against an attack led by Max Walker and Dennis Lillee, who took five for 34.

This was not a disaster if Pakistan could beat West Indies at Edgbaston. Asif Iqbal had to undergo a hospital operation* and Imran had to sit an exam in Oxford. They were replaced by Javed Miandad and a workmanlike seamer, Pervez Mir. Majid Khan, the replacement captain, scored 60 off the main West Indian bowlers, only to edge a catch behind off the fill-in

---

*According to Kardar, for piles (Kardar, op. cit. p.206); according to Nauman Niaz, for a hernia (*Nauman Niaz*, vol. 2, op. cit. p.1144). Neither is an emergency operation and the tour management should have known about them in advance.

bowling of Clive Lloyd. Mushtaq Mohammad made a composed fifty and Wasim Raja scored one at over a run a ball, a rate then considered electrifying. Pakistan finished with an adequate but not overwhelming 266.

Sarfraz then shot out the top three West Indians with just 36 on the board. Naseer Malik again took two cheap wickets and Pakistan got a bonus when Javed Miandad, an occasional bowler, supplied twelve cheap overs and dismissed Clive Lloyd after he had scored a rapid fifty.* Pakistan had West Indies at 166 for 8. Deryck Murray, the wicketkeeper, was a competent batsman but he had only the tailenders Vanburn Holder and Andy Roberts to accompany him, with 101 to make. Sarfraz had some overs in hand, but Majid held him back, and Holder and Murray added 35 quite comfortably. Eventually, Sarfraz was brought back and dismissed Holder. Andy Roberts came in. The last-wicket pair needed to make 64, the biggest partnership of the innings, in 14 overs. Sarfraz stayed on to finish them off, but Murray and Roberts were unruffled. Murray took elegant boundaries, Roberts smacked anything well pitched up. Sarfraz ran out of overs and 29 were needed off six more. The unsung Pervez Mir bowled a maiden, but Asif Masood was wayward. The score advanced. Murray survived a run-out opportunity with ten needed. Suddenly Majid had run out of frontline bowlers. He had lost count of the overs. With five needed to win, he had to give the final over to Wasim Raja, and to make matters worse, instead of his normal and often penetrative wrist-spin, Wasim Raja elected (or was instructed) to bowl at medium pace. The batsmen took a risky leg-bye. There should have been a run-out, but instead there was an overthrow. Then Roberts scored two off the bat. The scores were level on the fourth ball. Roberts pushed it calmly to midwicket and Pakistan were beaten.[59] Javed Miandad and many of his older colleagues were numbed: 'It was a terrible, devastating loss. Our team was in a state of shock. I was overwhelmed by grief and cried for hours.'[60]

Kardar, who was watching the match, was furious at Majid's 'inept and unimaginative handling of the team' but Nauman Niaz later claimed that Kardar himself had sent out instructions to Majid.[61] The post-mortems on the terrible defeat continue to this day. Pakistan had to play out, for them, a meaningless match against Sri Lanka. There were easy runs for Sadiq (74),

---

*Lloyd was furious to be given out caught behind, and accused both Javed Miandad and Wasim Bari of cheating. Another lasting feud had begun.

Majid (84) and Zaheer (97) as Pakistan cruised to 330 for 6. Then there were easy wickets for seven different bowlers, as Sri Lanka were dismissed for 138. Ironically, it was Pakistan, Sri Lanka's biggest advocates, who did most harm with this result to their claims for Test recognition.

Pakistan may have exited in anguish from the first World Cup, but there was plenty of domestic cricket to console fans in the subsequent season. This 1975–76 season represented the apogee of Kardar's system, with 63 domestic first-class matches. The Quaid-e-Azam Trophy, once Pakistan's premier tournament, had been eclipsed. Of the 31 first-class teams, 17 were regionally based, five from companies or public corporations, four from banks, four from the armed forces or government departments and one from combined Universities.

The Kardar system produced a marginal increase in the number of first-class cricketers, but it largely failed to provide a training ground for Test cricket. Very few of the players who topped the averages in the Kardar years forced their way into the Test team, which continued to rely heavily on Pakistan's stars from English county cricket.

MUSHTAQ MOHAMMAD: A NEW STYLE OF CAPTAIN

Kardar's ambitions suffered a fresh blow after the 1975 World Cup setback. He had hoped to resume cricketing relations between Pakistan and India that winter after a lull of fifteen years, with each country staging three Tests.[62] It was the last of Kardar's visionary ideas. Had it come off, it would have been a contest of historic importance, and caused huge excitement and interest in both countries. But it came too soon after the 1971 war, and Pakistan was left with an empty international timetable.

The gap was filled with a tour of Sri Lanka, and Intikhab Alam was restored as captain.[63] Pakistan lost both one-day internationals and the first Test, while Sarfraz Nawaz consolidated his reputation as a trouble-maker by kicking down the stumps, apparently in protest against umpiring decisions.[64] He was sent home. According to Shuja-ud-Din, 'Intikhab Alam and Imran Khan were lucky not to have met the same fate', adding that 'at one stage it seemed difficult to envisage whether there was any point in continuing the tour.' The embarrassed cricket administration in Pakistan were forced to pass on their regrets over the unfortunate episode and promised to hold an enquiry, in a telegram to the prime minister, ZA Bhutto.[65]

Pakistan won the second match to square the series, so the tour was not all a disaster. It gave the emerging generation – Javed Miandad, Mudassar Nazar, Haroon Rashid and Imran Khan (who took thirteen wickets in the two 'Tests' at an average of 15.61 each) – the chance to feel their way in the international arena. The most important outcome, however, was to hasten the long overdue recognition of Sri Lanka as a full member of the International Cricket Conference, and thus as a Test-playing nation.*

In the short term, however, the tour did for Intikhab. When New Zealand arrived in Pakistan in the autumn of 1976, he was replaced by Mushtaq Mohammad. This move would be heavy with consequence.

Mushtaq had been a first-class cricketer since 1956. He had made his Test debut in March 1959. Yet he was still (officially) only thirty-three and – as events were soon to show – had not quite reached his peak as a Test cricketer.

He immediately established himself as a more assertive kind of captain. Intikhab Alam was a pragmatist who rarely sought to challenge the men who ran Pakistan cricket.[66] Mushtaq insisted on getting the players he wanted and then stood up for them in ways that had been unimaginable before. Under Mushtaq's leadership, Pakistan was soon to turn from a second-rank team into one of the best in the world. His role has been underrated;[67] Pakistan's subsequent achievements under Imran Khan meant his own contribution has been overlooked. The world should know that Mushtaq counts, alongside Kardar and Imran, as one of his country's three greatest national captains.

The selectors announced their decision to appoint Mushtaq in early October 1976, less than a week before the first Test match in Lahore.[68] Though given virtually no time to prepare, Mushtaq at once asserted himself with a brave confrontation with the selectors, chaired by Imtiaz Ahmed, on the eve of the Test.

Imtiaz wanted to drop Asif Iqbal and retain Intikhab. Mushtaq insisted on keeping Asif and replacing Intikhab with Sikander Bakht. When the team was announced, and Mushtaq learnt that he had not got all his own way, his reaction was remarkable:

*Sri Lanka played their first Test match in 1982.

I won the toss and elected to bat at the Gaddafi Stadium, but while we were batting, I wrote my resignation and at lunch I marched up to the room where the selectors were sitting and resigned from the captaincy because I had not been given the side I wanted. I intended to give it up after the match. They did pick Asif, which should never have been a talking point in the first place, but they also picked Intikhab instead of my preference Sikander Bakht, and backed up Imran and Sarfraz with Asif as the third seamer. Although I got most of the team I wanted, I didn't like the balance of the side, which meant a great deal to me. I wasn't happy that the selectors wanted to send a captain out with a bowling attack he didn't want. I always felt the captain should have the last say on selection and be wholly accountable if things go wrong.[69]

No captain had made such a nuisance of himself since Kardar. At tea-time, Mushtaq was summoned back to see the selectors: 'They informed me that they didn't like the way I tried to resign on the first morning of my first Test as captain and I said I was sorry but added that I did not like the way they tried to make me their puppet, as Intikhab had been so long.'

However, the Test was chiefly memorable for the arrival of a cricketing genius. Pakistan batted first and were in trouble at 55 for 4, the top order mowed down by Richard Hadlee. Then Javed Miandad – only nineteen years old and playing in his first Test – came together with Asif to add 281 in an electric partnership for the fourth wicket. Miandad took less than three hours to score his century and was eventually dismissed for 163. Afterwards, the New Zealanders collapsed, and Pakistan won by six wickets.

Although this Test was significant with hope and consequence, the action now shifted to off the field. A chain of events unfolded that would change cricket in Pakistan forever.

THE REVOLT OF THE PLAYERS

Kardar had always prided himself on being a conscientious 'shop steward' for his country's cricketers. As captain, he had protested to the Board about the dismal match fees, accommodation and transport arrangements for Pakistan's international players.[70] As we have seen, he believed that the new patrons he brought into Pakistan cricket had dramatically improved the rewards and career prospects of domestic cricketers.

But he also held the view that Pakistan's cricketers should count it a privilege to play for their country, and be ready to forego personal gain when they were selected. He expected them to subordinate their personal ambitions, and their outlook and methods, to the interests of the Pakistan team, to accept decisions from authority with no public dissension, and to behave, on and off the field, as representatives of Pakistan. As captain, selector and administrator, he took severely against players whom he judged to have violated those standards.

Kardar never realised how far the leading players' expectations had been changed, particularly on finance. Those who had played professional cricket in England had earned far more money than Kardar's generation of Test players, and been exposed to a very different set of values. They had played with other overseas cricketers who had looked after their professional careers (or even had them looked after by professional agents, something then unknown in Pakistan cricket). Even run-of-the-mill English county professionals had become better rewarded and much more assertive than those Kardar had known as a county amateur after the war. Hanif Mohammad warned Kardar of this when he was asked to 'talk some sense' into his brother Mushtaq. 'You have to remember that most of these players have county contracts and play in professional set-ups. You have to listen to them.'[71]

It is therefore fair to say that Kardar was socially and psychologically unprepared for the players' demands for money. He was also unprepared for the support they would receive in the media and among the cricket public.

The issue of money was already simmering in advance of the home Tests against New Zealand. I have heard different recollections of the sums involved from players concerned. Wasim Bari said simply that senior players wanted their allowances re-examined.[72] Sadiq Mohammad told me that the leading players were seeking a daily allowance of $15 a day, and extra payment for laundry. Mushtaq confirmed that a small laundry allowance was a key demand. 'On the last Australia tour we had to spend each evening in, washing our kit.'[73]

Majid Khan provided a more detailed picture. 'In 1976 we were having a visit from New Zealand, followed by a tour of Australia and West Indies.

In the last home series against West Indies in 1974–75, the players were paid 1,500 rupees per Test.' (Then equivalent to about £83.) 'For the New Zealand visit, this was cut to 1,000 rupees.' (Roughly £56. By contrast, in 1976 English players' Test fees were increased from £180 to £200.[74]) 'The players complained about the pay cut, but Kardar told us that the Board was paying 4,000 rupees a month to bring back the players from England.'

While negotiations were in progress, Kardar tried to get the players to sign a contract for the forthcoming Australia and West Indies tours which cut their living allowances from $35 a week, set during the last Australian tour in 1972–73, to $25 a week. The players called for $50 a week. Majid Khan was scornful about Kardar's next move, sending Khalid Mahmood, 'then a lowly tax official', on the PCB's first-ever fact-finding mission, tracing the players' travel itinerary, to justify the $25 per week allowance, including their transit across the United States. 'He must have stayed in bus shelters,' observed Majid.[75]

Majid was one of six leading players to seek better fees and allowances: the others were Mushtaq and Sadiq Mohammad, Asif Iqbal, Imran Khan and Wasim Bari. Mushtaq was originally their leader, but in his absence in London, Asif Iqbal took over from him. Asif sensibly rejected an offer of mediation from Kardar's old friend Keith Miller (now fifty-seven, and in Pakistan to lead a somewhat motley international team). He told the other players that he had engaged a professional negotiator on their behalf. This was MU Haq, current president of the Karachi Cricket Association, and son of the Ahsan-ul-Haq who scored a century in forty minutes, batting at number 11 for Muslims v Sikhs at the Lahore Gymkhana in 1924. Significantly, MU Haq may have had a long-standing resentment against Kardar over his non-selection for the 1954 tour of England.[76]

The issue of pay came to a head just before the second Test match at Hyderabad. As Mushtaq explains:

We were supposed to fly out of the country en route to Australia three days after the third Test match, and so tour contracts had to be signed in advance. These contracts, though, were rejected by the players on a number of issues. One such sticking point was the players were expected to clean their own cricket whites; the Board could not even allow us a $10 laundry allowance and it didn't go down well with the senior players.

Kardar claimed that the Board could not obtain the $10 per man out of its benefactor, the State Bank of Pakistan.[77]

On the eve of the second Test against the New Zealanders at Hyderabad, the six staggered everyone when they announced they would boycott the match. Kardar's initial response was white-faced anger. He denounced the cricketers as mercenaries, then called up replacements.[78] Intikhab Alam was lined up as emergency captain. The players were persuaded to withdraw their threat only after a late-night meeting between Kardar and Mushtaq in the captain's hotel room, in which Kardar promised to do all he could to ensure that the players' demands were met.* Final agreement was only reached at 9.20am, forty minutes before play was to begin.[79]

On the morning of the Test match, there were two Pakistan teams (both congregated in a very crowded Pakistan dressing room), and two Pakistan captains. 'Who's coming to toss with me, Mushy or Inti?' asked the New Zealand captain Glenn Turner.[80] Once the cricket started Mushtaq, who must have been under massive strain, steadied himself to score a century. Sadiq managed one too, in the second example of two brothers scoring a century in the same Test innings,† as Pakistan tore New Zealand apart with a ten-wicket victory.

Mushtaq notes in his autobiography that despite the two Test victories 'there were no congratulations or hint of a bonus from the Board; it was almost as if they wanted us to fail, so they could drop all of us and bring in this new team like they had threatened at Hyderabad.'[81]

This bitter contractual battle did not, however, affect Pakistan's performances on the pitch. On the opening day of the third Test at Karachi, Majid blasted his way to a century before lunch, the first Pakistani ever to achieve this feat, and the first in forty-six years to do so on the first morning of a Test match.‡ Once Majid was dismissed after an innings, according to *Wisden*, 'packed with imperious hooks and fluent, effortless cover drives',

---

*But what was agreed? Kardar claimed that the players 'merely wanted an assurance that the Board would consider their demands.' (*Cricket Conspiracy*, p.14). But Asif Iqbal believed that Kardar had 'specifically assured that the weekly allowance of $25.00 would definitely be increased to $50.00 as demanded by us.' (*Cricket Conspiracy*, p.55). Majid Khan agrees: 'Kardar was very benign,' he recalls. 'He said he had accepted the players' demands for the $50 weekly allowance. Tell them to go and play.' (Majid Khan: personal interview.) This misunderstanding was to cause great trouble later.

†The first pair were Ian and Greg Chappell, also against New Zealand.

‡The others were Victor Trumper (1902), Charlie Macartney (1926) and Donald Bradman (1930).

Javed Miandad then motored into action, scoring 206. Captain Mushtaq also plundered a century, as Pakistan piled up 565 for 9.

This time, however, New Zealand put up stout resistance, and managed to hang on for a draw, greatly helped by a series of dropped catches by wicketkeeper Shahid Israr, who was playing in his first and, as it turned out, only Test.* Once the Test match was over, attention at once reverted to the forthcoming Australian tour, now less than six weeks away. Majid Khan takes up the story:

> Zafar Altaf, the PCB Secretary, came to the team hotel after the match, met the players in Mushtaq's room, and handed out tour contracts on official paper for signature. The others did not read them carefully, and relied on Kardar's word about the tour payment, but Asif Iqbal read it right through. He asked why the contract had set the allowance at $25 per week after Kardar had agreed $50. Zafar Altaf said that he did not know.
>
> Asif then offered to sign the contract on plain paper (not official paper), and only as a goodwill gesture, because they believed that Kardar had been guilty of bad faith.

Kardar saw this refusal to sign full contracts as a declaration of war. He warned the strikers against pressurising the Board of Control, adding if they persisted they would not only lose their Test careers but their jobs with departments and banks. In press briefings, he accused the players of being 'unpatriotic' and behaving like 'mercenaries'.[82] Then he sacked Mushtaq as captain, while the ever pliable Intikhab was brought back, with Zaheer Abbas as deputy.[83]

THE HUMILIATION OF KARDAR

For a quarter of a century, Kardar had been the most powerful figure in Pakistan cricket. He was used to getting his own way, and must have

---

*Why was Israr picked? He was nowhere near as good a wicketkeeper as Wasim Bari. Bari believes he was being punished for his involvement with the rebels. In two long interviews this memory alone stirred the equable wicketkeeper to anger. 'It spoilt my chance of a run of 50 Tests. It was nothing to do with my performance in the previous two Tests. No explanation was given, but I think that Kardar, who had been close to me, felt that as a PIA boy I should not have stood with the rebels. My replacement Shahid Israr dropped eight chances.'

calculated that this time would be no different. But he had made one fatal mistake; he had fallen out with ZA Bhutto, prime minister of Pakistan and the patron of Pakistan cricket.

A year previously, Kardar had done something unforgiveable; resigning from the Punjab Government over an issue of principle.[84] Although unwise, his action had been thoroughly in character. He was exceptionally scrupulous about how he conducted himself in office, for example never allowing his ministerial car (a grey Fiat) to be used unless for official purposes. Throughout his years as a minister, the former national cricket captain always carried, whatever the circumstances, a letter of resignation in his pocket, signed but undated. His Jermyn Street shirts, suits and tie were changed every day. But always the letter remained.

For Kardar it was rather like carrying a loaded gun, and the temptation to use it became too great when he was called to a meeting with the Punjab chief minister, Hanif Ramay. Kardar attached great importance to punctuality, and indeed would always go to extreme lengths to ensure that he arrived at exactly the right time to any meeting. On this occasion Ramay (a short-lived chief minister who would soon himself develop differences with Bhutto, and later still go into exile under Zia) kept Kardar waiting. After an hour, Kardar dated his pre-signed letter and walked out. Doubtless other factors were involved, and Kardar was growing disenchanted with Bhutto for a number of reasons. But the immediate motive for the resignation was Ramay's timekeeping.

This action infuriated the despotic Bhutto because he insisted on sacking his ministers, rather than allowing them to resign. At a time of increasing domestic political opposition, the prime minister had no remaining motive to support Kardar against the media and the cricketing public, who were on the players' side. He pulled the plug on Kardar by ordering Abdul Hafeez Pirzada, education minister and (more relevantly) president of the Pakistan Sports Board, to side with the players.* According to Sadiq Mohammad, the six 'rebels' were taken by Pirzada to Bhutto's house in Rawalpindi. The prime minister heard the players' demands and ordered Pirzada to settle with them. 'It was all over in five minutes,' recalls Sadiq.[85]

---

*Pirzada's father, Abdus Sattar Pirzada (a former chief minister of Sindh), had been an early BCCP president, from 1951 to 1953. The Bhutto and Pirzada families have been allied for more than a century.

Pirzada had been a founder member of the PPP and one of Bhutto's most trusted lieutenants. He was to follow his master into jail (and, following Bhutto's death, go into exile) after the coup d'état the following year. For Pirzada (who today insists he remained on good personal terms), Kardar had been a boyhood hero.* In 1951, he had watched Kardar's gritty undefeated 50 against MCC at the Karachi Gymkhana that secured Pakistan her Test status. In 1954, as a young man studying for the bar, he had taken time off his work to attend the great Fazal-inspired victory at The Oval. 'To me, these men were gods,' he recalls today. 'They were great names.'[86]

Now it was his task to cut down his childhood idol. 'I thought Kardar was being too autocratic and imposing himself on the players. The prime minister was patron-in-chief. His advice could not be ignored.' Pirzada forced Kardar to accept a new selection committee for the Australian tour, with Hanif Mohammad (who had been sacked by Kardar seven years previously) as chairman. Pirzada further deposed Kardar's supporter, Imtiaz Ahmed, as tour manager, in favour of Shuja-ud-Din. Intikhab, who had sided with the management and was Kardar's choice as captain, was also dumped in favour of Mushtaq Mohammad. Kardar had never experienced such public humiliation.

Kardar's role in the Pakistan cricketing story was nearly over. Though barely fifty years old, by 1976 he was a man out of time. For a quarter of a century he had been the public voice, private conscience and directing intelligence of Pakistan cricket. As a player and as an administrator, he had brought the national game he loved with such passion to hitherto unimaginable heights. From this moment on, his role would increasingly be reduced to impotent observer rather than architect of great events.

---

*But the feeling was not reciprocated. Kardar later accused Pirzada of handing out 'sledge-hammer treatment' to cricket. He said that he 'chose to settle old scores. What he achieved was an emasculated institution and rampant indiscipline. Hafiz [sic] Pirzada's legacy still haunts Pakistan cricket.' MOAR, p.189.

PART TWO

THE AGE OF KHAN

1976–92

INTRODUCTION

Omar Noman, historian of Pakistan cricket, has identified five stages in the evolution of the game of cricket.[1] The first, which lasted until the early nineteenth century, was rural, bucolic, occasionally violent and patronised by the elite. There were few nationally established rules, if any.

The second coincided with the codification and standardisation of the sport, along with prodigious technical innovation. The sport remained essentially English, and was dominated by the awesome figure of WG Grace.

Stage three embraces the first half of the twentieth century, and was notable for the steady globalisation of the sport. However, to most intents and purposes this concerned just two countries. By far the most important international contest throughout the period was the Ashes rivalry between England and Australia. The great Sir Donald Bradman scored nearly three quarters of his Test runs against one team alone, England.

The fourth stage in cricket's evolution, suggested Omar Noman, took place during the 1950s and 1960s. He called this a 'period of transition, as newly liberated countries started emerging as a major force.' The most successful of these emergent nations were the exhilarating West Indies teams under Frank Worrell and Garry Sobers, which asserted themselves on the international stage to become the greatest and most brilliant force in world cricket.

Nevertheless, cricket remained tied to its amateur origins during this early post-war period. Rewards for players were negligible, the white cricketing nations were very much still in charge, while nobody bothered much about the mass audience. Something had to break and it did. 'Cricket entered its fifth phase in the 1970s, ushering in a golden era of innovation and expansion,' says Noman. 'The international game lost its amateur ethos and was replaced by professional management. International referees, neutral umpires and television replays were introduced to remove distortions of bias and to address disciplinary problems. The World Cup became an international event, and regional venues such as Sharjah made a successful appearance on the circuit.'

Noman calls the post-1970s era a new golden age, thus appropriating a phrase which had hitherto been applied by cricket writers to the period before World War One, when English and Australian cricketers carried out superlative feats, inventing the game anew as they did so.

The bold and even impertinent phrase was completely justified. In the last quarter of the twentieth century, the new cricketing countries exploded onto the international scene, bringing with them waves of extraordinary and wonderful talent. New forms of the game were developed, while the traditional five-day Tests attained a quality never approached before. At the same time, some of the uglier aspects of world cricket vanished. White-only South Africa, supported for so long by the English establishment, was driven out of world cricket, replaced after two decades in exile by a successful multi-racial team which sought to represent Nelson Mandela's vision of a rainbow nation.

Pakistan was at the heart of this revolution in world cricket. In the 1960s, the nation's cricket had been characterised by defiance, dullness, deference and defensiveness. But the sport woke up in the 1970s, with a surge of great players and ebullient personalities. Pakistan embraced the world, bringing fresh forms of expression, a love of experiment, an amazing exuberance and a novel national assertiveness.

For Pakistan, this change can be dated precisely. The witching hour, when history suddenly began all over again, was 1976. The national side, hardened to defeat for so long, suddenly became capable of beating any other team in the world. There is no question that the revolt of the players and the challenge to AH Kardar's authority marked the transition. Kardar's principled opposition to professionalism, though honourable, meant that he was an insuperable impediment to change.

Even admirers of Kardar must acknowledge that Pakistan emerged as a front-rank cricketing nation only after he had been driven to the shadows. But the rising generation could take advantage of his legacy – Pakistan cricket was more popular than ever before. More first-class cricket was being played, and grounds and training facilities had improved. Cricket was beginning to spread out beyond the twin centres of Karachi and Lahore and turning into a mass sport across the entire country. The national cricket team was suddenly stronger, angrier and more motivated than ever before.

PAKISTAN CONFRONTS THE WORLD

'What Packer is doing is prostituting cricket.'

– PRESIDENT ZIA TO MUSHTAQ MOHAMMAD

Let us now turn our attention to the team that Mushtaq Mohammad led to Australia in 1976–77. The most striking point is that the captain, and the majority of the players, came from Karachi. Pakistan cricket had been shaped by Lahore ever since Partition, and this was no longer the case. The younger, more dynamic city was emerging as a real force.

The second striking point was the balance between youth and age. Mushtaq's team contained most of the outstanding players who had emerged in the late 1960s – Majid Khan, Asif Iqbal, Wasim Bari, Zaheer Abbas, Sarfraz Nawaz. But they were now being joined by a new generation, of whom Javed Miandad and Imran Khan were soon to turn into giants.

In the first Test at Adelaide, the Pakistan batting crumbled to 157 for 6, and it seemed as if nothing had changed. Zaheer Abbas, hitherto criticised for scoring only easy runs, then accumulated 85 against Dennis Lillee and Jeff Thomson as the team recovered to 272 (Imran 48). Pakistan then yielded a big first innings lead to Australia, for whom Ian Davis and Doug Walters scored centuries.

Pakistan fought back. Thanks to a century from Zaheer and a magnificent 152 not out from Asif Iqbal (half of these in a last-wicket stand worth 87 with Iqbal Qasim, who contributed 4), they set Australia 285 to win. When Australia reached 201 for 3, victory seemed theirs for the taking. They were then choked by Qasim, who bowled 30 eight-ball overs which produced four wickets for 84. Australia were left 24 runs short with four wickets left. Their not-out batsmen, Gary Cosier and Rodney Marsh, were savaged in the local media for not having a thrash in the final hour.

At Melbourne, Australia smashed 517 for 8 declared at over four an over. None of the Pakistani seamers took a wicket, in rapid time. In reply, Majid Khan made 76, Sadiq Mohammad a patient 105 and Zaheer 90. At 241 for 1 Pakistan looked safe, but after Sadiq was out the rest of the innings was blown away by Dennis Lillee.

Australia led by 184 and added 315 swiftly in their second innings (Imran Khan taking five wickets in a Test match for the first time). In pursuit of 497 to win, Pakistan crumbled to 151.

Imran's performance was a portent. At Sydney, he unleashed a legendary spell of fast bowling. With an improved action (which was later re-modelled), he shot out six Australians, supported by three wickets from Sarfraz Nawaz, and Australia fell to 211 all out. Pakistan in turn were in trouble at 111 for 4. With the match in the balance, Asif Iqbal came to play what Omar Noman has called 'the most-important match-winning innings of his career, and certainly one of the major innings in the evolution of Pakistan cricket.' Supported first by the debutant Haroon Rashid, who made 57, and then by Javed Miandad (64), Asif scored 120.*

So Pakistan had a lead of 149 – and Imran took a further six wickets to win the match. No Pakistan seam bowler had taken ten wickets in a Test since Fazal Mahmood in the 1950s. It was Pakistan's first victory in Australia. To quote Noman again: 'The emergence of Imran had qualitatively shifted the level and capacity of Pakistan to win Tests. Here was an outstanding strike bowler around whom an attack could be shaped. This was the first time that Miandad and Imran had contributed to a win, but this pattern was to be repeated to telling effect over the next decade and a half.'[1]

---

*Haroon was one of seven brothers to play first-class cricket, equalling the record of the Walkers of Middlesex and the Fosters of Worcestershire.

The national team now set off to face the formidable West Indies.* It was the first Pakistan tour of the Caribbean since Hanif Mohammad's great achievements in 1957–58. None of their current players had any experience of local conditions. As in Australia, the Pakistanis proved themselves equal to the challenge.

The first Test, at Bridgetown, was one of the greatest played by Pakistan. Thanks to a brilliant 88 from Majid and an enterprising century from Wasim Raja, they managed 435 against an attack including two new and especially hostile fast bowlers, Joel Garner and Colin Croft. Clive Lloyd's 157 took West Indies (struggling at 183 for 5) to virtual parity.†

In the Pakistan second innings, Andy Roberts shared the spoils as Pakistan collapsed to 158 for 9. Wasim Raja was joined by Wasim Bari – and the two Wasims achieved a tenth-wicket partnership of 133: Wasim Raja made 71 with five fours and two sixes, Wasim Bari made 60 with ten fours. The stand put pressure on the West Indies and they conceded the world record total of 68 extras in a Test innings (added to 35 in the first).

West Indies were set 306 to win, and Imran, Sarfraz and Saleem Altaf took nine of their wickets for 237. Unfortunately, they were frustrated by the tailenders Roberts, Holder and Croft, who survived for 90 minutes. West Indies clung on and were 251 for 9 at the finish.

Pakistan were dismissed for 180 in the second Test at Port of Spain, unable to cope with Croft who took eight for 29. Wasim Raja once again nursed the tail with 65. Roy Fredericks scored a century as West Indies led by 136. Mushtaq Mohammad took four wickets and Intikhab Alam two – in what turned out to be his last Test. Pakistan batted better in the second innings. Majid Khan and Sadiq Mohammad made 54 and 81 in an opening stand of 123, and Wasim Raja hit seven more fours and two more sixes while adding 76 with Imran. However, West Indies had little trouble with a target of 205.

---

*Between the Australian tour and the visit to West Indies the Pakistan team visited Fiji. In theory an idyllic visit, it turned into a fiasco. Only a handful of senior players stayed in hotels, the remainder being billeted with local people. Khalid Mahmood got the blame. See Shuja (p.161), who was tour manager, for an informed account. He wrote that, 'Some of the top players even openly shouted that the two-week trip was only a ruse to probe and project the marketability of Servis Shoes.' Servis Industries were a major supporter of Pakistan domestic cricket.

†According to Imran, Mushtaq erred fatally by taking the new ball. The old one was reverse-swinging for him and Sarfraz Nawaz and they begged him to keep it. But Mushtaq was not aware of the new phenomenon (for which, see below, chapter 19), and assumed that the new ball would be a more attacking weapon. Instead 'Lloyd carted it all over the place'. Imran Khan: personal interview.

In the third Test at Georgetown, Pakistan once again could not cope with Roberts, Garner and Croft, and were all out for 194. West Indies replied with 448, which would have been worse without a cheap four wickets from the back-up bowling of Majid. Pakistan seemed certain to lose their second Test in a row. Majid then led the way with 167 as Pakistan fought to 540 in their second innings, the greatest Test innings of his career. Zaheer Abbas, who had missed two matches, made a comeback with 80 and Haroon Rashid scored 60. West Indies needed 287 but there was time only for Gordon Greenidge to thrash 96 at over a run a ball. The match was saved in yet another example of the fighting spirit which Mushtaq had instilled into his team.

So far, however, Mushtaq himself had made little impact. This changed during the fourth Test at Port of Spain. Coming in at 51 for 3, Mushtaq made 121 in six hours and eleven minutes. He added 158 with Majid (92) and 55 with Wasim Raja, before being ninth out. He then took five for 28, supported by four for 64 from Imran, as West Indies collapsed to 154.

Pakistan scored 301 in their second innings. Mushtaq got a fifty, Wasim Raja 70 (with three sixes) and the contrarian Sarfraz Nawaz chose this time to score his second Test fifty. The same trio shared nine wickets equally as West Indies lost by 266 runs. The series was now level with one match to play.

In the first innings of the deciding Test, Imran had another six-wicket haul but Gordon Greenidge scored exactly 100 and West Indies made 280. Haroon Rashid (72) alone made any impact in Pakistan's reply. Wasim Raja smashed two sixes off the leg-spinner David Holford and then holed out attempting a third – off the last ball before lunch. This sort of dismissal contributed to his treatment by the selectors.* Wasim Bari was hit in the face by Colin Croft. Helmets were still a few years away and he was badly injured.

First Mushtaq and then Majid substituted behind the stumps in West Indies' second innings. Greenidge and Fredericks scored over 80 apiece in an opening partnership of 182, before the stand-in stumper Majid took two fine catches to remove each of them. Pakistan's least-regarded bowlers,

---

*Wasim Raja played 57 Tests in no fewer than twenty-three different series. This was one of the few in which he played all five matches, in which he scored 517 runs at 57.

Sikander Bakht and Wasim Raja, took three wickets apiece, but West Indies set a target of 442. Pakistan subsided to 138 for 5 before Asif Iqbal scored a century and Wasim Raja made his last contribution to the series – 64 with another two sixes.* They salvaged pride, but Pakistan lost by 140 runs.

Despite this loss, Pakistan were now established as one of the best Test teams in the world, and a top draw for crowds. Of huge importance for the future, their overseas victories in Australia and West Indies were watched by viewers in Pakistan for the first time, through satellite television.[2]

Intikhab Alam had faded away (he was an isolated figure ever since he broke with Mushtaq over pay[3]) but the rest of the side was intact and reinforced by a world-class performer in Imran Khan. Javed Miandad had been eclipsed in Australia and West Indies but was still only a teenager at the end of the Caribbean tour, and clearly a major force for the future. There was enough other talent around for the selectors to enjoy the luxury of excluding Wasim Raja. Wasim Bari was the world's top wicketkeeper.

Although most of this team had been at odds with Kardar, and ultimately driven him from office, the status they earned for Pakistan cricket must have given him satisfaction. It was left to his successor to deal with Kerry Packer.

THE PACKER REVOLUTION

Two grave crises faced Pakistan cricket in the wake of the climactic Test series in Australia and West Indies. On 5 July General Zia, chief of the general staff, ordered the arrest of Prime Minister Bhutto and his cabinet, declared martial law across Pakistan, and promised elections within ninety days. As so often with a change of regime, this event would in time lead to drastic changes in the management and outlook of Pakistan cricket.

The coup d'état in Islamabad was accompanied by revolution in world cricket. In May 1977, news broke that the Australian businessman Kerry Packer was to stage a breakaway competition in defiance of the national authorities. Although his initiative proved short-lived, Packer changed cricket forever.

---

*Wasim Raja's fourteen sixes remains a record for a Test series, although equalled five times since.

He challenged virtually every single assumption held by the establishment. For the establishment, cricket was a sport; for Packer it was a business.
For the establishment, cricket was mainly about the team; for Packer it was
exclusively about the individual. For the establishment, cricket was a way of
life; for Packer it was another form of entertainment.

It is easy to forget that many of the aspects of the modern game which
are now taken for granted were invented by Packer: day-night matches,
white balls, coloured kit, floodlights. The brilliance of the Packer package
permanently changed the way the game has been shown on TV, and sold to
the public.[4] For Packer – and this was his most heretical idea of all – the
paying customer came first.

The first Pakistan player approached by Packer was Asif Iqbal. He had no
hesitation. 'This is what I have been fighting for all my career,' he said.
'When I put it to the rest of the team, not a single player said he didn't want
it.'[5]

For Asif, the Packer offer brought to a head the same issues as the revolt
of the players the previous year. 'Playing cricket was our passion,' he says
today. 'If we had had to pay money to play cricket we would have done that.
But if money was being made, why should we not be part of it? We wanted
to play the game as a profession.' Majid Khan suggested to me that experience of English county cricket had changed the outlook of Pakistan players
and made Packer's offer to them attractive. 'We realised that we were enter-
tainers, whom crowds came to see, but we were not getting the returns which
other countries' players were getting. The English were the highest paid, then
the Australians. The rest were nowhere, and treated like amateurs.'*

One immediate effect of the Packer initiative was a reconciliation
between Pakistan and the world cricket authorities. Throughout the 1970s,
the BCCP and the International Cricket Conference had been at odds. Now
suddenly, all could agree on the menace of Packer. The BCCP's first act after
the Packer announcement was to defy modernity by outlawing professionalism from Pakistan cricket.[6] This perverse act of mordant conservatism was
announced, after a six-hour meeting, on 14 July – Bastille Day. The *ancien
régime* was still in charge in Lahore.

---

*Majid Khan first heard about Packer's initiative in the last Test of Pakistan's 1976–77 tour of the West
Indies. 'Tony Greig arrived and called me and Imran and Mushtaq and Asif to a meeting.' Personal interview.

The new BCCP president, Chaudhry Mohammad Hussain, had been treasurer during the Kardar years, and treated his old boss with deference. More important still, Abdul Hafeez Pirzada, Kardar's nemesis, had been locked up at the same time as Bhutto. As a result of Pirzada's incarceration, Kardar re-emerged as a potent force and made a determined effort to restore the status quo. Through his acolyte Chaudhry Mohammad Hussain, he wasted no time in reversing Pirzada's changes. Hanif Mohammad was fired as chairman of selectors. Most of the panel who had stood by Kardar during the revolt of the players – Imtiaz as chairman, alongside Mahmood Hussain and Zafar Altaf – were restored.[7] Mushtaq was fired as captain and replaced by Wasim Bari.

The next problem was how to handle the Packer players. Even though the High Court in London had just declared the ICC ban on Packer players unlawful, Imtiaz made sure that not one of them was selected in the pre-tour camp assembled before the looming tour by England.*

Kardar was not to have matters all his own way, however. The Packer players had many influential allies, above all Omar Kureishi. During the early years of Pakistan cricket, Kureishi and Kardar had been bosom buddies, fighting the same battles and believing in the same things. More recently a shadow had fallen between them.† Kureishi took the side of the Packer players and his influence was a constant factor in the battles that lay ahead.

ENGLAND v PACKERLESS PAKISTAN 1977–78

As so often, the touring team (playing as England for the first time rather than as MCC) arrived in Pakistan at a delicate moment. General Zia-ul-Haq was trying to consolidate his grip on the country, the most urgent problem being what to do about deposed Prime Minister Bhutto.

---

*None of the four available Test players – Mushtaq, Majid, Zaheer, and Imran – were chosen. By now Asif had announced his retirement from Test cricket, a decision he was later to rescind.

†According to Henry Blofeld (p.154) the breach occurred when Kureishi managed the Pakistan side in England in 1974: 'Kardar liked to watch the game from the balcony in the players' dressing room. The presence of the chairman of the board made the players uneasy, and when they told Kureishi this he spoke to Kardar and asked him if he would mind watching from elsewhere. Kardar took this as a personal attack on him by Kureishi and they ceased to be friends.'

Bhutto had been released from jail three weeks after the coup, but immediately took the opportunity to address large public meetings, giving the generals the by no means misleading impression that he was plotting a political comeback. He was incarcerated once again at the start of September 1977, released two weeks later, then imprisoned for the final time on 16 September. The following month he was charged with conspiracy to murder Ahmed Raza Kasuri, a political opponent, whose father had been killed in an ambush. In Bhutto's absence, his wife, Nusrat, became president of the Pakistan People's Party and co-ordinated his defence.

These momentous events had a direct bearing on the England touring party. Pakistan was under martial law, which meant that public meetings were forbidden. Cricket matches provided an excellent surrogate venue for political expression. The England tour therefore featured a number of riots, the most dangerous of which was arranged by the PPP in an attempt to unsettle Zia's military government.

Throughout, confusion reigned over Packer (though not in the dogmatically Packerless English team, arguably the dullest ever to leave Britain's shores). Shuja-ud-Din noted that, in the absence of the Packer players, Geoffrey Boycott 'was the star attraction of the touring side.'[8] This was not an exaggeration in a top-order batting line-up that read as follows: Boycott, Mike Brearley (captain), Brian Rose, Derek Randall, Graham Roope and Geoff Miller.*

However, Chaudhry Mohammad Hussain, the new Pakistan cricket chief, found it hard to hold the line against Packer's influence. A campaign was mounted to bring back the Packer players (Majid Khan, Zaheer Abbas, Imran Khan and Mushtaq Mohammad; Asif Iqbal had announced his retirement from Test cricket).[9] According to *Wisden*, 'The first intimation that practical steps had been taken to include the Packer men – aptly dubbed Packerstanis – for the first Test at Lahore came briefly on the radio when the touring team were in faraway Peshawar.'[10]

Contact was made with Mushtaq, and some twenty-three names were announced for the first Test. The spectre of a return for the Packer rebels was not dispelled until the opening day of the Test. In their absence, what

---

*First innings top order, opening Test at Lahore. A young all-rounder named Ian Botham was in the squad, but not picked.

followed was desperately dull. Mudassar Nazar, son of Pakistan's first Test centurion Nazar Mohammad, reached 100 in only his second Test. He took 557 minutes to do so, thus recording the slowest Test century of all time, twelve minutes longer than South Africa's Jackie McGlew's effort against Australia at Durban in 1958.[11]

Mudassar's century arrived late on the second afternoon. Spectators invaded the pitch in a premature celebration when he reached 99, leading to a riot. Henry Blofeld, who was commentating, claimed that 'it made marvellous running commentary for listeners in England.'[12] Four rioters sought refuge from the police in the English dressing room. When order was restored, records *Wisden*, 'the rioters voluntarily cleared the ground of debris.'

More serious riots took place the following day when Nusrat Bhutto and her daughter Benazir, who had recently stepped down as president of the Oxford Union, attended the game. Neither was known as a cricket enthusiast and their attendance had the air of an attempt to mobilise the crowd. 'The trouble started in the stand at square leg,' recorded Blofeld, 'where the ladies all sit together making a colourful splash in their Punjabi clothes.'[13] Police fired tear gas to dispel rioting spectators, and play was brought to an end 55 minutes early. Nusrat Bhutto left the stadium with blood flowing from her forehead, which she claimed to be the result of a blow by a police baton. Boycott, who reached his half century in twenty minutes longer than Mudassar, looked on course to overhaul the Pakistani's new record for the slowest century. However, he was bowled by Qasim for 63, accumulated over 332 minutes.

The game left two positive memories. The first was a rare act of sportsmanship in Anglo-Pakistan cricketing encounters. Mike Brearley recalled Qasim after he had been given out caught. He signalled that the catch had not carried, an act of integrity which deprived the England spinner Geoff Cope of a hat-trick on his Test debut.

Second, the leg-spinner Abdul Qadir made his debut. Blofeld described him as a 'beautiful bowler who really spins the ball.'[14] Though his figures were not remarkable (32 overs, one for 87) he was soon to emerge as one of the greatest and most influential players in all Test cricket. The team then moved on to Sahiwal for a one-day international, a thrilling encounter in which England secured victory off the final ball of the match with a four struck by the still little-known Ian Botham.

Qadir made an impact in the second Test at Hyderabad, taking six for 44 to skittle out a Bothamless England for 191 and set up Pakistan with a winning chance. Statistically, this was the best performance by a Pakistan bowler against England, improving on Fazal's six for 46 at The Oval in 1954. A tardy declaration by Wasim Bari gave England the chance to escape with a draw, Boycott recording a not-out century in England's second innings.

Meanwhile events off the field were out of control. Sarfraz Nawaz had teamed up with Aftab Gul, who had retired from cricket and was now building a career as a lawyer. On his own, either man was a handful. Together, this union of the two most seditious and intractable characters in the history of Pakistan cricket created chaos. The trouble started after the Lahore Test.

Sarfraz, who was Wasim Bari's vice-captain, flew back to England complaining that he had not been paid. He also complained that Wasim Bari took little note of his advice. Once in London, he refused to come back unless the Board gave in to his financial demands. Eventually, Sarfraz was given an assurance that he would get the money he wanted, and the opening bowler was back in Pakistan in time for the third Test.[15]

The Sarfraz affair, however dramatic, was essentially a sideshow. Omar Kureishi, Hanif Mohammad and others were pressing for the return of the Packer players, a campaign that prompted the first intervention of General Zia-ul-Haq into cricket. Perhaps it gave him the taste, for within months of ousting Bhutto he made the game one of his major concerns, often intervening at critical moments, and using it as a weapon both in domestic and foreign policy.

I have discovered no record of Zia having any interest in cricket before becoming chief martial law administrator in the wake of the 1977 coup. In so far as Zia liked playing any sport, it was golf. General Zia nevertheless was popular with cricketers. The BBC *Test Match Special* team took a particular delight in him, with his upright bearing and bushy moustache. 'We thought he looked just like Terry-Thomas,' recalls Henry Blofeld.[16] General Zia's demeanour indeed had something of the 1950s character actor, who specialised in playing disreputable members of the English upper middle classes, and was famous for catchphrases such as 'dirty rotter' and 'a complete shower'.

The general called in his top cricketing brass on the rest day of the first

Test at Lahore to discuss the Packer problems.[17] It has never been completely clear what, if anything, was decided at this meeting, which took place in the conference room of the general headquarters at Rawalpindi,[18] four hours' drive from Lahore. All of those present, apart from Kureishi and Hanif, were against Packer.

However, in the wake of the Rawalpindi summit, Kureishi felt confident enough to contact Australia, asking about the availability of the Packer players.[19] Several days later, Zaheer, Imran and Mushtaq flew into Karachi, Kerry Packer himself having gone with them as far as Singapore. On arrival in Karachi, the rebels joined the other Pakistan players in the nets. At this stage, they seemed certain to play.

With two days to go before the Test started, Zia called a further meeting, this one at the state guest house in Karachi, where the Test was to be played. Kardar (who held no official position), his follower Chaudhry Mohammad Hussain (Cricket Board president) and Imtiaz Ahmed (chairman of selectors) were at this meeting. Kardar used his full influence to blacken the Packer players.[20] He informed the president that it would be disastrous for the reputation of Pakistan cricket if the Packer players were chosen, and that it was very likely that England, who were intransigently opposed to Packer, would refuse to play. Zia was convinced. This was Kardar's last intervention in Pakistan cricket politics and, ironically, one where he and his old enemies in the English cricket establishment saw eye to eye. Mushtaq, Imran and Zaheer were put on the plane back to Australia.[21]

But before they took off, Mushtaq requested a meeting with General Zia, which was witnessed and recorded by Henry Blofeld:

The General spoke first. 'Why do you want to see me?'

'We were brought back to play in the Test Match,' Mushtaq answered. 'Why are we not playing?'

'That is your bad luck,' the General replied. 'Why are you not available to play cricket for Pakistan all the time? I have raised the fees of Test cricketers and I will guarantee that you will get good jobs.'

'We are professional cricketers, and have lived abroad for a long time. And Packer is promoting cricket.'

'What Packer is doing,' the General said quietly, 'is *prostituting* cricket.'[22]

The Karachi Test was locally called the 'Packer funeral'.[23] Batting first, England (captained by Boycott after Brearley withdrew with a broken arm) crawled to 266 off 124.1 eight-ball overs. It ended up as the eleventh consecutive Test match between the two countries staged in Pakistan to end in a draw. During one period in the second innings, Boycott played 18.7 eight-ball overs with just one scoring shot, a two.

Sadiq Mohammad was dropped. For the first time in 90 Tests, Pakistan's team had no Mohammad brother. At lunch on the third day, President Zia attended the match, and presented both teams with gold medals. The tedium reinforced Pakistani resentment of England's stance. This was succinctly expressed by Javed Miandad: 'Common sporting etiquette demanded that England should have been ready to face the best side we could put together. The English team and management didn't quite see it that way and in the end the match went ahead without the Packer stars. I thought it was all a bit childish of the English, especially their captain Mike Brearley.'[24]

Much worse was to come. Wasim Bari's Packerless Pakistanis were humiliated during their return tour to England in the summer of 1978. They were unable to cope with Ian Botham, who grabbed his best Test figures of eight for 34 but was later to prove less effective against full-strength Pakistan sides. They lost their first two Test matches by an innings, the scale of the defeats drawing comparisons with Javed Burki's 1962 debacle. Sadiq was the only Pakistan batsman to pass 50 in the series, and the failure of Javed Miandad (57 runs at an average of 13) was unexpected and depressing. Their best bowler, Sarfraz Nawaz, was injured. He managed only six overs in the first Test and missed the second. Finally, in the rain-sodden Test at Leeds, he took five cheap wickets as England subsided to 119 for 7 in reply to 201. Throughout the series, Wasim Bari protested repeatedly but unsuccessfully at English players running down the pitch – a charge regularly applied since then to Pakistani cricketers. It was a desperate tour for him as captain, but he excelled again as a wicketkeeper and did not concede a bye in the three Tests.[25]

The touring party returned to Pakistan in disgrace, the management flying back to Islamabad rather than Karachi in order to avoid a hostile reception.*

*It was, even by Pakistan's heroic standards, a very large management team. According to Shuja, 'the military ruler also authorised a large number of cricket officials of various organisations to accompany the team for the whole duration of the tour ... In fact the touring party on its arrival in England gave the semblance of a wedding party as numbers of officials had decided on taking their wives and children.' Shuja, pp.181–2.

Chaudhry Mohammad Hussain resigned as Board president the day after the Test series finished. He was replaced by a military man, the inevitable answer to any Pakistan problem, Lt Gen. KM Azhar.* Waqar Hasan and Javed Burki were brought in to help him.[26]

General Zia had learnt his lesson and the objective was clear: restore a strong national team, even if that meant bringing back the Packer players. This was all the more urgent, because he planned to resume cricketing relations with India. General Azhar asked Arif Abbasi to handle negotiations with Packer's right-hand man, Linton Taylor. An able protégé of the future PCB president Air Marshal Nur Khan, Abbasi began in this way a long, sometimes controversial, and often interrupted career of service to Pakistan cricket. Abbasi would transform his country's cricket over the coming years by embracing corporate sponsorship and commercialisation.

Abbasi at once made it clear that the PCB had no further interest in banning Packer players. He explained that there was no difference between playing for Packer and playing for an English county or league side, as so many Pakistanis had done for years. So long as there was no clash with Pakistan's domestic season or international commitments, Pakistanis were free to play for Packer. In return, Taylor not only agreed to release Pakistani players on demand but also set up a scheme for three to six young Pakistani players to play Australian grade cricket. This scheme had several notable beneficiaries, including future Test players Mohsin Kamal, Aamer Malik, Salim Malik, Shoaib Mohammad and Iqbal Sikander, before it became another victim of an ad hoc administration in the PCB.[27]

CRICKETING RELATIONS RESUME WITH INDIA

More than seventeen years had passed since Pakistan had played India at cricket. During this period there had been two wars on the subcontinent (1965 and 1971), the second of which had caused the secession of East

*Born in Aligarh, Azhar had attended the All-India Muslim League in which the Pakistan Resolution was adopted in 1940. Responding to Jinnah's call to fight for the British, he fought on the Burma front during World War Two, and later in Kashmir in 1948. During the 1965 War he conquered 1,300 square miles in Rajasthan. He was injured while commanding Pakistani forces on the Rajasthan front in 1971 during his tenure as the NWFP governor. He also served as president of the Pakistan Hockey Federation.

Pakistan. ZA Bhutto had been too closely involved with these tragic events to rebuild Pakistan's relations with India. General Zia, encouraged by the United States, which, true to form, regarded his military regime with far greater favour than the elected Bhutto government, moved fast to do so. The fall of Indira Gandhi's Congress Party in 1977, its replacement by Morarji Desai's Janata Party, and the consequent ending of the state of emergency in India may also have helped.

India, managed by the former Maharajah of Baroda, Fatehsinghrao Gaekwad,* arrived for their two-month tour in late September 1978. The Indian players were received at Karachi airport with a mighty fanfare, and both sides attended a host of public and private social functions.[28] The Pakistan public were signalling their delight at the resumption of cricket relations and perhaps also their desire for peace with India. *Wisden* commented: 'The warmth and enthusiasm with which the Indians were received, plus the cordial relations between the players, made it plain enough that the renewal of cricketing rivalry between the two neighbouring countries was long overdue.'[29]

Nor was there any doubt about the personal cordiality between the captains, Mushtaq Mohammad and Bishan Singh Bedi, who had been county colleagues in England at Northamptonshire.[30] However, Bedi later remembered 'extreme hostility from the public and the media – and the umpires.'[31] His memory may have been coloured by the battering he took as a captain and as a bowler. Zaheer Abbas punished India's brilliant spinners – Prasanna, Chandrasekhar and Bedi himself – amassing 583 runs for just three times out, although India did discover a fast-bowling all-rounder called Kapil Dev. Of India's batsmen, only Sunil Gavaskar could cope with Pakistan's pace attack of Imran Khan and Sarfraz Nawaz, who took fourteen and seventeen wickets respectively on generally unresponsive wickets.

The first Test, played at Faisalabad, was a dull draw and the thirteenth in succession between the two countries. Matters looked up when the teams reached Lahore. Lala Amarnath, invited to be a commentator by Pakistan television, received a hero's welcome on his return to his native city. A large Mercedes met him at the airport. When the Indian tour manager, His

*Full name: Lt Col. Farzand-i-Khas-i-Daulat-i-Inglishia, Shrimant Maharaja Fatehsinghrao Prataprao Gaekwad, Sena Khas Khel Shamsher Bahadur, Maharaja of Baroda. An attacking right-handed batsman, Gaekwad represented Baroda in the Ranji Trophy and was a well-known cricket commentator.

Highness the Maharajah of Baroda, sought to board it, he was firmly barred from 'Lala Saheb's' car and ordered into the bus.[32]

On the cricket field, the courtesies ended. The second Test at Lahore was preceded by astute planning from Mushtaq Mohammad and his brother Hanif, who had been put in charge of preparing the pitch. At their behest, the first-day wicket was green and assisted Pakistan's pace attack. Mushtaq planned to field first if he won the toss, and he expected India to bat first if he lost it.[33] In fact, he did win it and Sarfraz and Imran took four wickets each to destroy the Indian batting for 199. A double-century from Zaheer Abbas helped Pakistan to 539 for 6 declared. When India batted again, Gavaskar and Chauhan put on 192 in their opening partnership, and appeared to have secured a fourteenth consecutive draw.

They were then out (according to the Indian writer Shashi Tharoor) to 'umpiring decisions that defied belief.'[34] India were able to set Pakistan a modest 126 to win, a task accomplished with ease, Zaheer hitting the match-winning six. He was watched from the VIP enclosure of the Gaddafi stadium by Nazar Mohammad and Fazal Mahmood, the joint heroes of Pakistan's only previous Test win over India, at Lucknow in October 1952. Zia declared a national holiday and took care to meet the team.* Shashi Tharoor noted with disdain: 'It was almost as if the results of the wars on the battlefield had been reversed on the cricket pitch.'[35] In the third Test at Karachi, the fourth innings target was rather more daunting – 164 at more than six an over; now a routine task, then almost unprecedented. Asif Iqbal and Javed Miandad made a mockery of the Indian bowling before Imran, promoted for the slog, struck 19 off a Bedi over. Pakistan had won the Test series 2–0.

Pakistan also won two out of three one-day internationals. India were comfortably placed in the third, but Sarfraz denied them by bowling unreachable bouncers. None were called wide by the umpires and Bedi protested by walking off the pitch and forfeiting the match.[36] On another occasion Mohinder Amarnath was struck on the head by a bouncer from Imran. When he bravely returned to the middle after a visit to hospital, he was greeted by another bouncer from Sarfraz.[37] This series transformed

---

*But not Majid Khan, who told me, 'I was on holiday all the time, so it did not affect me.' Majid Khan: personal interview.

cricket in Pakistan. 'Used to a diet of placid, meaningless matches,' recorded Omar Noman, 'the national audience witnessed for the first time the entertainment and passion that the game was capable of generating.'[38]

After the triumph over India, Mushtaq Mohammad led his team overseas against New Zealand and Australia. New Zealand were at full strength (Packer had not called on any of their players) but Richard Hadlee had yet to reach his peak and the rest of their attack was no match for Imran, Sarfraz and the reliable third seamer, Sikander Bakht. Pakistan took the Test series 1–0 with two draws.[39] Mushtaq demonstrated a flair for public relations by encouraging his team to let young spectators bat and bowl to them during intervals. But his captaincy was surprisingly cautious, and allowed New Zealand to escape with a draw in the second Test. Both sides complained about the quality of the umpiring (still in the hands of the host country).[40]

The short Australian series was packed with brilliance and controversy. At Melbourne, Australia were cruising to victory (at 303 for 3 they seemed on course for a victory target of 382) until Sarfraz produced a sensational spell of seven wickets for just one run with an old ball. In total, he took nine for 86 in Australia's second innings – then the best performance in Tests by any Pakistan bowler, and still the best overseas.* Later this performance would be ascribed to the fiendish Pakistani invention of reverse swing, but Sarfraz himself insists that he simply bowled straight and exploited inconsistent bounce.[41]

This superb Melbourne Test produced the first of several incidents which *Wisden* described as 'unsportsmanlike and completely opposed to the best traditions of the game, even if they technically complied with the Laws of Cricket.' In Australia's first innings, Rodney Hogg played a successful defensive stroke and then left his crease to inspect the pitch. Javed Miandad, who had walked over from short leg to pick up the ball at silly point, then turned, flicked off the bails and appealed successfully for a run-out. Mushtaq Mohammad diplomatically tried to recall the batsman but the umpire upheld his decision and Hogg smashed the stumps on his way back to the pavilion.

Javed defended himself vigorously: 'I was portrayed as having done something crafty or underhand, but as far as I was concerned Hogg was out of

---

*It was overtaken at Lahore in 1987–88, when Abdul Qadir took nine for 56 against Mike Gatting's England side.

his ground and that was the end of it.'* Television replays confirmed Javed's defence that he could not see why Hogg had left his ground, and that he had pulled off a smart piece of fielding. He also had distinguished historical precedent on his side. In the 1882 Oval Test which gave rise to the Ashes legend, WG Grace ran out a batsman who had stepped out of his crease to pat down a divot. Nevertheless, the incident marked Javed's card with Australian fans and players, and helped to set up a far more serious encounter in a later series with Dennis Lillee.[42]

In the second Test at Perth, there was a tit-for-tat incident when the Australians ended a troublesome last-wicket partnership by running out the non-striker, Sikander Bakht, for backing up too far. His not-out partner Asif Iqbal, who had made 134, smashed the stumps in his turn. In Australia's second innings, the non-striker Andrew Hilditch picked up the ball after it had come to rest and handed it politely to the bowler, Sarfraz, who then appealed successfully for 'handled the ball'. Only two other wickets fell (both to uncontentious run-outs) as Australia easily chased down 236 to level the series.[43]

WORLD CUP 1979: MORE MISERY FROM THE WEST INDIANS

Pakistan's next venture was the 1979 World Cup in England, for which Asif Iqbal replaced Mushtaq as captain. According to Javed, Mushtaq was the victim of a plot by senior players who wanted to supplant him; the official excuse was that he was no longer agile enough for one-day cricket.[44] So ended Mushtaq's superb, unforgettable era as captain. He had led his team through six Test series, three of which had been won, and one of which is regarded as among the most memorable of all time. He had fought out two competitive drawn series against Australia, and his team had come within one wicket of levelling a series in the West Indies, then the greatest team in the world.

In England, Pakistan began with easy wins – one predictable, against the

---

*Imran Khan was another to come to Javed's defence: 'Javed was brought up in the type of highly competitive street cricket in which this sort of thing was commonplace – every rule in the book was stretched to get people out. Fielders would tell a batsman that he had dropped something on the pitch, and when he went to retrieve it they'd run him out.' *ARV*, p.38.

minnows, Canada, the other less predictably against a still Packerless Australia. Majid Khan flayed the Australian bowling in a rapid opening stand of 99; Asif smashed 61 at the close, when Pakistan scored 47 from the last five overs. Although Asif now rarely bowled in Tests, he produced a tight spell, and astute captaincy, as Australia never got on terms with their target of 288.

However, in the third group match, Pakistan 'choked' after reducing England to 118 for 8. Bob Taylor, a modest batsman and Bob Willis (even more so) were allowed to put on 43. After reaching 27 for 0 in reply, Pakistan suddenly collapsed to 34 for 6 against the late swing of Mike Hendrick, in ideal conditions for him at Headingley. Omar Noman recalls that 'the match was being broadcast live but had to take a break, to cover a horse race, with Pakistan at 27–0. By the time the race coverage was over, Pakistan had lost six wickets.'[45]

Asif Iqbal, Wasim Raja and Imran Khan dug them out of the pit, but when Asif was eighth out for 51 Pakistan were still 41 short of their target of 166. But Wasim Bari proved a reliable partner for Imran and they added 30 without much difficulty. Mike Brearley now produced his master stroke by throwing the ball to Geoff Boycott. It was a long, long time since Boycott had been a front-line seam bowler for England, but to the delight of his home crowd he induced fatal strokes from Wasim Bari and the last man, Sikander Bakht, whose slog was brilliantly caught at mid-off by Hendrick, with a furious Imran at the non-striker's end.

Pakistan were still through to the semi-final. Unfortunately, this was against West Indies. In perfect batting conditions at The Oval, Asif Iqbal surprisingly elected to field first. Gordon Greenidge and Desmond Haynes opened with a partnership of 132 in 107 balls; Imran yielded nearly five an over and Sarfraz nearly six (this, in the era before fielding restrictions). Asif took four wickets, but at over five an over, and only the gentle and rare off-spin of Majid Khan checked West Indies' progress to 293.[46]

Sadiq Mohammad was out early in Pakistan's reply, but Majid (unusually, in a helmet in place of the battered hat which had once been his father's) and Zaheer then added 166 in 36 overs off the best pace attack in world cricket: Andy Roberts, Michael Holding, Colin Croft and Joel Garner. But both then fell to Croft (as did Javed Miandad first ball). Then Viv Richards, a part-time spinner, dismissed Asif Iqbal, Mudassar Nazar and Imran Khan in quick succession. Pakistan were all out for 250 with nearly four overs to go.

DEFEAT AND DISQUIET IN INDIA

Asif Iqbal had been Pakistan's most consistent player in the World Cup and it was not a great surprise when he was retained as captain for the forthcoming tour of India, beating off a comeback bid from Mushtaq Mohammad. It was argued that if Mushtaq was not agile enough for one-day cricket, he would not cope with a five-day Test. Cruelly, the selectors rejected his plea to tour India as an ordinary player; according to Javed this decision reduced him to tears.[47] Asif says today that, for him, to be appointed captain of Pakistan on a journey back to his native India 'was a dream come true.'[48]

Another key absentee was Sarfraz Nawaz. He was not injured and the decision 'undoubtedly stemmed from a clash of personalities' according to *Wisden*. Asif told the chairman of the BCCP to 'make someone else captain if you want Sarfraz to be part of the team.'[49] His replacement was Ehteshamuddin, a worthy performer in Pakistan's domestic cricket, but already twenty-nine years old. He did not let Pakistan down, with fourteen wickets in the six-Test series at just over 19 apiece, while the unassuming Sikander Bakht managed twenty-four, including eight for 69 in the second Test. Imran broke down with a persistent rib injury, but came back brilliantly.* Abdul Qadir failed to mystify anyone and took only two wickets.

Pakistan lost the six-Test series 2–0. The weakened attack never bowled out India twice and India escaped several times from losing positions. But the real weakness was the batting. Mudassar Nazar, in the first Test at Bangalore, scored their only century. Only Wasim Raja, with a Test average of 56.25 and Javed Miandad (42.50) managed any sort of consistency and they were often out when well set. The Pakistanis were aggrieved and demoralised by umpiring decisions, especially lbws; Javed was so determined not to be hit on the pads that he took to practising without them in the nets.[50] In the third Test at Bombay, the Pakistanis accused the Indian authorities of doctoring the pitch, and in the fourth at Kanpur, Asif Iqbal threatened that Pakistan would abort the tour in protest at the umpires.[51]

By then, Asif was a detached leader of a quarrelling, underperforming

---

*In a sarcastic attack on press reporting, Imran noted that 'there was little sympathy for my muscle injury, which I had evidently contracted while performing debauched calisthenics with Indian actresses.' *ARV*, p.43.

team – literally so, when after Kanpur the Pakistanis were asked to leave India for ten days during the national elections.* They arranged to tour Bangladesh – the first visit since independence – but Asif was not with them. Majid Khan, his vice-captain, learnt that he had decided instead to visit his family in Bangalore and Hyderabad. Majid tried to persuade him to change his mind. In a long talk, he told Asif that he was needed to restore morale and help the team to regroup in Bangladesh. He thought he had succeeded, but when the Pakistanis took off for Dacca, Asif was absent.

The Pakistanis, under Majid, got a warm reception at Dacca airport, but they were victims of local politics when they moved to Chittagong to play a one-day match against Bangladesh. Chittagong was a major centre of support for Bangladesh's founder, Sheikh Mujib, who had been overthrown and killed by the army in 1975. As previously in Pakistan, opponents of the military regime saw the chance to use a major cricket match as an outlet for protest.

At the ground the Pakistan team became aware of a group of demonstrators in the general stand at the far end of the pavilion. They were chanting in Bengali, which the Pakistanis could not understand. Majid asked what they were saying and the local district commissioner smoothly told him that they were complaining about discounts for students.

The situation worsened when Pakistan took the field. More protestors invaded the stadium, armed with clubs and iron bars. Majid shouted, 'Let's go!' and led the team back into the dressing room just ahead of a full-scale riot. The police used tear gas and even bullets as the players hunkered down in the dressing room all afternoon and evening. A few were eventually sent back, under heavy escort, to the team hotel to pack for all the rest. Normally, there were no flights into Chittagong but a special aircraft was sent in to take the Pakistanis back to Dacca, where their next match was cancelled. It was all horribly reminiscent of the riot in 1971 when Pakistan played Micky Stewart's International XI.[52]

This unhappy tour saw the first rumours of a problem which has plagued Pakistan cricket ever since – relations with illegal bookmakers. Both Majid Khan and his cousin, Farrakh Khan, who was team doctor for the early part of the tour, told me of their alarm when a mysterious stranger, 'a big fat chap', appeared regularly on the team bus. Majid did not know him, but Dr Farrakh

---

*None of the Indian political parties wanted to risk association with an Indian defeat by Pakistan.

recognised him as a Bombay bookmaker. Majid objected to his presence on the way to practice sessions, but he now says that Asif overrode him, and told him that the man was helping him with his benefit season for his English county of Kent. Majid did recognise another bookmaker – this one a young man – who had greeted the Pakistanis at Delhi airport. Majid thought that he came from Delhi, but in Bombay he shadowed the team bus in an expensive BMW and tooted his horn in greeting. Majid thought that he was a friend of Imran's and Zaheer's, and says that he later attached himself to Asif. His disquiet grew when Javed Miandad reported (from his family in Ahmedabad) that there had been a huge volume of betting on the final Test at Calcutta.

This was the setting for the much-discussed coin-tossing incident. Gundappa Viswanath stood in as India's captain for his brother-in-law Sunil Gavaskar and walked out with Asif Iqbal for the toss. In those days, there was no match referee at the toss, nor any television cameras or reporters. Viswanath flipped the coin, Asif called, the coin fell on the ground. Then (allegedly) before Viswanath could see the result of the toss, Asif snatched up the coin and told him that he had won. If this is true it is suggestive, because under the normal etiquette of cricket, the visiting captain would not touch the coin.[53]

Be that as it may, this Test, in a dead rubber, produced the best cricket of the series and Asif's most positive captaincy. Viswanath elected to bat and India made 331 all out: four wickets to Imran, fully fit again, four to the toiling Ehteshamuddin. Pakistan reached 272 for 4 on the fourth morning of the five-day Test. Asif declared 59 runs behind. Imran shot out two Indian batsmen; supported by Ehteshamuddin and Iqbal Qasim, he then reduced India to 92 for 6. But the Indian tail, led by Kapil Dev and the left-arm 'bits and pieces man' Karsan Ghavri, squeezed out another 113 runs over a long time, and Pakistan had to make 265 runs in 280 minutes on a worn, slow pitch against a mean over rate. Javed and Asif raised hopes briefly with a partnership of 43 in eight overs, but when both were out, Imran and Wasim Bari saved the game – Bari making 0 not out in 43 balls.

It was Asif's last hurrah. He had announced his international retirement and was soon committed to a new enterprise – establishing cricket in Sharjah. It would bring riches and glories to Pakistan cricket, but also charges of scandal and corruption.

A FALSE START WITH JAVED MIANDAD

'We were after all only Pakistan and he felt he could take liberties with us.'

– JAVED MIANDAD ON DENNIS LILLEE

By 1979, General Zia had consolidated his military regime. After the Soviet invasion of Afghanistan, the US Carter administration resumed military and economic aid to Pakistan, which served as a base for the anti-Soviet Mujahadeen fighters in Afghanistan. This aid figure rose eventually to $3.2 billion.[1] However, it also forced Pakistan to care for 2.7 million refugees (mostly old people, women and children), housed mainly in makeshift camps near the Afghan frontier.

Pakistan's economy performed well under Zia, despite his penchant for appointing military cronies to important economic posts. The resumption of economic aid, and the revival of private investment as Zia reversed Bhutto's experiments in nationalisation, helped to propel average economic growth of 6.6% a year, the best performance of any Pakistan regime. However, the biggest contributor was the growth of remittances from Pakistanis working overseas. These rose from $578 million in 1976–77, Bhutto's last year in power, to $2,886 million, over 10% of GDP in 1982–83 under Zia.[2] As these fell away in later years, growth slowed and Zia became less popular.

Domestically, Zia sought support from religious parties and factions, continuing a policy initiated opportunistically by Bhutto in his last years. However, he went much further than Bhutto in enforcing Islamic laws and promoting Islamic content at every level of education. In his final year, Zia announced that the Sharia would become Pakistan's paramount source of law and would override any other. (One result of his policies was the eclipse of women's cricket in Pakistan, which had formed its first association in the late 1970s.)[3] Zia's programme was deeply unpopular with Pakistan's Shi'ite minority and provoked clashes in all of Pakistan's major cities. Karachi was also increasingly troubled by conflict between Mohajirs (emigrants from India at Partition) and Pashtuns, whose migration to Karachi had been accelerated by the fall-out from Afghanistan.[4]

AFTERMATH OF DEFEAT

Defeat by India in 1979–80 was viewed in Pakistan as a national disaster and led to changes at the top. Asif Iqbal's career as one of the great talismanic players of Pakistan was over. Next to go was the BCCP president, General Azhar Khan. Appointed by Zia, Khan paid the price of all defeated generals and was sacked and replaced by Air Marshal Nur Khan.

Nur Khan had a record of achievement in the Pakistan Air Force, Pakistan International Airlines and most relevantly as a superb administrator at the Pakistan Hockey Federation. His first move was audacious: Javed Miandad, at twenty-two, was made the new captain of Pakistan. Mushtaq Mohammad had been restored by the outgoing Azhar Khan but on his first day in office, Nur Khan asked him to step down, offering him instead the role of coach. After expressing some displeasure, Mushtaq accepted.

Nur Khan asked Mushtaq's advice on a successor; he unhesitatingly volunteered Javed Miandad,[5] despite the rival claims of three senior players, Wasim Bari and Majid Khan (both former captains) and Zaheer Abbas. Nur Khan explained: 'There were many pleas to bring Mushtaq back, since he had been an outstanding winning captain, but I wanted to look forward to the future.'[6]

Javed had played twenty-seven Tests and scored 2,252 runs at an average of over 62.* He had captained Pakistan at Under-19 level and in domestic cricket had led Habib Bank to victory in all of Pakistan's first-class tournaments – a unique grand slam.[7] Unfortunately, he was to be unable to overcome the resentment of senior players.[8]

Javed's reign began well with a win over the visiting Australians by seven wickets, on a spinners' track in Karachi. Iqbal Qasim took eleven wickets for 118 and Majid Khan anchored Pakistan's first innings with an unusually patient 89. But the headlines were stolen by Pakistan's new off-spinner, Tauseef Ahmed. There are many stories of unknowns breaking through into the national team, but his remains incomparable.

Javed Miandad later claimed that Tauseef 'had walked into the Pakistan Test side literally as a nobody off the street.'[9] This is an exaggeration, but only slightly. Tauseef, aged twenty-one, had played one first-class match the previous season for the Public Works Department against a powerful PIA side, picking up five wickets at low cost. He had then disappeared back into club cricket. According to Javed, Tauseef was recommended to him by his friend Riaz Malik, a successful businessman 'who was managing a competent club side' in Karachi, and Javed agreed to let him bowl at the Pakistan team in the practice nets. However, others suggest that the recommendation was made to Mushtaq (by now the Pakistan coach).[10]

At any rate, Tauseef took the bus from his home to the National stadium with some rudimentary kit and began to bowl at Pakistan's top order in the nets. His sharply spun off-breaks regularly beat Zaheer, Majid and Javed himself. Instantly, he was drafted into the Pakistan team, displacing the unlucky Ilyas Khan, who had originally been selected as the off-spinner.†

Tauseef took seven Australian wickets in the match for 126, helping spin Pakistan to victory. He would play another thirty-three Tests and seventy one-day internationals, alternating with another off-spinner, Mohammad Nazir.

The remaining two Tests were high-scoring draws. The Australians

---

*Among cricketers who played more than twenty Tests, Javed Miandad shares a distinction with Herbert Sutcliffe: their Test batting average never fell below 50.
†Ilyas Khan was a seasoned performer in Pakistan domestic cricket; in four previous seasons he had taken eighty-one first-class wickets at less than 22 apiece. Thanks to Tauseef Ahmed, he never played a Test for Pakistan.

scored 617 (Greg Chappell 235) at Faisalabad, batting into the fourth day in protest against Pakistan's refusal to make up for time lost to rain on the rest day. In Pakistan's reply, there was time for the wicketkeeper-batsman, Taslim Arif (a short-term replacement for Wasim Bari) to score a not-out double-century, which was the highest Test score by a wicketkeeper until overtaken by Zimbabwe's Andy Flower against India in 2001. In the third Test at Lahore, Allan Border became the only batsman to score over 150 in each innings of a Test, and Majid Khan posted his final Test century.

Javed's next series was at home to West Indies in 1980–81. His team gave a reasonable account of themselves, but the opposition had too much fire-power for most of his batsmen. Zaheer Abbas, in particular, was given a torrid time by Malcolm Marshall, Colin Croft and the volatile Sylvester Clarke.

The first Test was drawn, thanks to Imran Khan's first Test century. Supported by Wasim Raja (76) and Sarfraz Nawaz (55), he rescued Pakistan from the depths of 95 for 5. He became the second Pakistani (after Intikhab Alam) to complete the Test 'double' of 1,000 runs and 100 wickets.[11] Sarfraz was incensed by the pitch, claiming that it had been doctored to suit Pakistan's slow bowlers, then took off for London saying that he needed treatment for a groin strain.[12] He therefore missed the next Test, on an underprepared pitch at Faisalabad where West Indies won by 156 runs. Pakistan's spinners, Abdul Qadir, Iqbal Qasim and Mohammad Nazir, took all twenty opposition wickets, but the West Indian batsmen coped better against them than Pakistan's batsmen did against pace.

Marshall's four for 25 destroyed their second innings. It was Pakistan's first home defeat since 1969. Taslim Arif broke a finger and that was the end of a Test career which gave him a batting average of over 62. He was replaced by a better wicketkeeper, Wasim Bari.

Javed was grateful for Bari's support in the next Test at Karachi, when he helped him to revive Pakistan's first innings from the depths of 68 for 6, with Zaheer retired after being struck on the forehead by Croft. In the innings of 128, six Pakistani batsmen failed to score, a Test record. West Indies squeezed out a lead of 45, despite Javed's unorthodox but inspired decision to have Iqbal Qasim open the bowling with Imran.

Pakistan were in trouble again in their second innings, but Wasim Raja (77 not out) nursed the tail to 204 for 9. The match was saved – with a little help from an umpire who delayed the start of the final day by twenty-three minutes after leaving his kit behind. More would be heard of Shakoor Rana.[13]

The final Test went to a new venue, Multan – a sign that popularity of the game was spreading beyond the long-standing centres, a development which Nur Khan was anxious to encourage. The crowd did not live up to Multan's reputation as the 'city of saints'. A spectator threw an orange peel at Sylvester Clarke, who retaliated by hurling back a brick. It struck one of the leaders of the students union, causing a furious crowd reaction. Play was halted for twenty-five minutes, and peace was only restored after the West Indian batsman Alvin Kallicharran made an appeal on bended knee for play to resume.[14]

Sarfraz Nawaz had returned from England to partner Imran, who took five for 62. An unusually patient century from Viv Richards (his first against Pakistan) took West Indies to 249. However, this was enough for a lead of 83, as only Majid, Javed and Wasim Raja put up much resistance to the pace quartet. The match petered out as a draw amid torrential rains as the West Indies laboured to 116 for five. It was enough for them to take the Test series 1–0.

One unintended consequence of this series was to strengthen Pakistan's case for neutral umpires, a cause promoted by Nur Khan. While it was in progress, one of Pakistan's most respected umpires, Khalid Aziz, made a public protest against pressure from officials to make decisions in favour of the national team. Suffering the fate of most whistleblowers, he was sacked and banned for life. His colleague, Ghafoor Ali Khan, resigned as secretary of the Pakistan Umpires Association, also in protest against official interference.[15]

MUTINY BREWS IN AUSTRALIA

In the low-scoring series against West Indies, Javed had batted better than most (with an average of 32.85, second only to Wasim Raja). His captaincy nevertheless faced simmering criticism,[16] and matters moved towards a head during the winter.

The side Javed took to Australia in 1981–82 was underpowered in batting and bowling, and blighted by the hostility to him of senior players, especially his vice-captain Zaheer Abbas.* Zaheer's tour began unhappily when Jeff Thomson broke one of his ribs in the state match at Brisbane; Mohsin Khan flew out as a replacement.

The team was in no state to begin the Test series on Australia's paciest pitch at Perth, although Javed's decision to bowl first appeared to pay off when Pakistan's seamers, led by Imran Khan's four for 66, dismissed Australia for 180.

In reply Pakistan made their worst ever start – 28 for 8 – against Dennis Lillee and the expert swing bowler Terry Alderman. A few blows from Sarfraz Nawaz took them to 62. Australia then cruised to 424 before declaring. Pakistan batted better in their second innings, led by Javed's 79, but the off-spin of Bruce Yardley removed six batsmen on a wearing pitch and Pakistan lost by 286 runs.

This second innings saw the infamous confrontation between Javed and Dennis Lillee. As Javed ran a single, Lillee, the bowler, took a kick at him, thus becoming, almost certainly, the first player in Test history to kick another while a match was in progress. It was a gentle kick but still a kick, and Javed then raised his bat at Lillee, as if in threat. Lillee claimed that Javed had abused him, which Javed denied (and the Pakistan players had received regular 'sledging' throughout the Test without retaliating physically). The Australian team fined Lillee AUS$200 (then equivalent to around £120) and asked Javed to apologise, which he refused to do. The umpires thought the fine too light and at their insistence Lillee was banned for two one-day internationals.† Javed agreed with the umpires: 'We were after all only Pakistan,' he commented later, 'and he felt he could take liberties with us. Had I been captain of England, I wonder if the idea of retaliating with a kick on the pads would even have entered Dennis's mind.'[17]

---

*Majid Khan recalls a stand-up row between the two men in the dressing room at Melbourne during the state game before the first Test. Javed accused the injured Zaheer of leaving the ground without permission as the game headed for a draw and exclaimed melodramatically, 'I'll see to it that either you play for Pakistan or I play for Pakistan!' The row was ended only by a warning that journalists were approaching. Majid urged Javed to initiate disciplinary action against Zaheer, or else forfeit all authority within the team. However, Javed took no further action. Majid Khan: personal interview.

†Noman, op. cit. p.191. Javed Miandad defended himself strongly in *Cutting Edge*, op. cit. p.246, but made the remarkable allegation that some Pakistan team members wanted him to be punished as well. If true, it indicates how far his personal relationships with team members had fallen into disrepair. *Wisden 1983*, p.975, criticised Javed for not apologising, but pinned most of the blame on Lillee, and considered even his revised punishment too light.

In the second Test, Lillee had the satisfaction of dismissing his good friend Javed among five victims. On his return to the side, Zaheer hit a courageous 80 but Pakistan's 291 in excellent batting conditions was not enough. Australia replied with 512 for 9 declared on the back of a masterful double-hundred by Greg Chappell. Mohsin Khan and Mudassar Nazar gave Pakistan an opening partnership of 72 in the second innings and the game should have been saved on a placid pitch, but other batsmen, including Zaheer and Majid in the same Yardley over, were out playing carelessly or irresolutely, and Pakistan left Australia only three runs to win. Javed angered other players, especially Imran, by hinting that they had not tried.[18]

To general surprise, Pakistan rallied in the last Test at Melbourne. Six batsmen made fifties as Pakistan reached 500 for 8 declared. Australia's three fast bowlers (Lillee, Thomson and Alderman) failed to take a wicket. Imran bowled some fierce spells and Iqbal Qasim strangled the Australians in their reply, and forced them to follow on. In their second innings the same bowlers, with help from Sarfraz Nawaz, shot out an unresistant Australia for 125, and Pakistan won by an innings and 82 runs.

REVOLT AGAINST JAVED MIANDAD

Nur Khan and his board were determined to stick by Javed Miandad as captain for the home series against Sri Lanka, newly promoted to Test status. This was more than reasonable. Pakistan had shown fighting spirit in Australia to come back to win after two defeats, and Javed hardly deserved the blame for the series loss. Overall, Javed's captaincy record was respectable. He had led Pakistan to a famous home victory against Australia, lost a closely fought series to the West Indies (then the best team in the world), and defeated Australia by an innings at Melbourne. However, the senior players viewed the matter differently.

The arrival of Sri Lanka as a Test match nation (the first nation to be given Test status since Pakistan thirty years earlier) meant that the four largest world religions (Christianity, Hinduism, Islam and Buddhism) could claim representation at the top of international cricket. This did not, however, lead to any increase in love and tranquillity in the Pakistan dressing room. Two days before the Sri Lankans arrived, ten senior players put their names to a letter refusing to serve under Javed: Majid Khan, Imran Khan, Mohsin Khan, Mudassar Nazar, Sarfraz Nawaz, Sikander Bakht, Wasim Bari, Zaheer Abbas, Wasim Raja and Iqbal Qasim.[19]

Nur Khan told Javed: 'We'll leave them out, the lot of them.'[20] The Air Marshal refused to back down or even speak to the rebels, and like Kardar before him he picked a replacement Pakistan team. (Later Wasim Raja, Iqbal Qasim and Mohsin Khan were forced to abandon the rebels by their bank employers.) One beneficiary was the eighteen-year-old Salim Malik, who became the third Pakistani (after Khalid Ibadulla and Javed himself) to score a century on Test debut. Another was Haroon Rashid, recalled after two years, who rescued Pakistan from a first-innings crisis with a superb 153. Sri Lanka's inexperience at Test level was evident in their second innings of 149 – scored in only three hours, as batsmen went for their shots against the miserly Iqbal Qasim.

For the second Test, four of the remaining rebels, Majid, Zaheer, Imran and Mudassar were included in the squad, but then omitted when negotiations broke down.[21] Sri Lanka performed much better in this Test, and with more positive captaincy might have forced a win. A new wicketkeeper, Ashraf Ali, rescued Pakistan twice with the bat.

After this drawn Test, there was serious anxiety that Pakistan might have to tour England with an inferior XI, as in 1978. At this point a remarkably graceful Javed Miandad cleared the air by volunteering to step down after the Sri Lanka series. He took this step against the express wishes of the Pakistan Cricket Board, which urged him to stay in his job. 'Divisions had developed within the team,' Miandad wrote later, 'and had I continued, Pakistan cricket would have been the ultimate victim.'[22] His final act was to recommend Imran Khan as his successor; there is some doubt whether Miandad would have played under Zaheer.

Mudassar, Majid, Zaheer and Imran at once returned; Ashraf Ali kept his place although Wasim Bari was now available. Imran celebrated with eight for 58 (his best Test figures) in Sri Lanka's first innings, and a further six (also for 58) in the second. Zaheer celebrated with a century, and there was another by Mohsin Khan as Pakistan won by an innings and 102 runs.

Zaheer Abbas hoped to succeed Javed Miandad, but once again Nur Khan had his own ideas about captaincy: 'Imran Khan's name was suggested but many people were opposed to him. Some felt his performance would suffer while others thought he was too irresponsible. But I called him in England and had a long chat with him, after which I was convinced that the responsibility would do him good.'[23]

Zaheer was bitterly disappointed: 'I felt insulted and humiliated at not being asked. Everybody else seems to have been given at least one chance and now this young boy was appointed.'[24] Zaheer was named vice-captain. Nur Khan gave Imran a gift he did not want but soon learnt to appreciate: Intikhab Alam as cricket manager. Intikhab's diplomacy and bureaucratic skills were a valuable foil to Imran and for many years helped to ensure that Imran got what he wanted on and off the field.

In fact, Imran was not, as Zaheer scornfully claimed, a 'young boy'. He was twenty-nine years old and a veteran of thirty-seven Test matches. Pakistan's new captain was to dominate the international stage for the next ten years, and lead the national team to undreamt of achievements. For impact on the wider game of cricket, only two players bear comparison: WG Grace, who turned cricket into the English national sport; and Sir Donald Bradman, whose great batting feats came to express Australian identity during the depression years of the 1930s.

IMRAN AND THE REVOLUTION
IN WORLD CRICKET

'Watching my two elder cousins play in Test matches, I imagined myself striding out, performing great feats with the bat, and pulling Pakistan out of a tight spot. Such childhood fantasies are common enough, but in my case they had the force of reality.'[1]

– IMRAN KHAN, IN HIS AUTOBIOGRAPHY *ALL ROUND VIEW*

Imran Khan was portrayed by some English cricket writers as a gorgeous manifestation of the Indian princely tradition. This was essentially an attempt to domesticate him for an English audience. In truth, Imran had no princely connections and was not aristocratic. His family had never, like the cricket-loving Indian princes, become apologists for British rule.[2]

Imran's father, Ikramullah Khan Niazi, an architect who had been educated at Imperial College London, was involved in the independence movement before Partition. Imran describes him as 'fiercely anti-colonial', remembering how he used to tell off waiters at the Lahore Gymkhana Club who tried to speak to him in English.

However, much the greatest influence on the young Imran was his mother, Shaukat. She was born into the extraordinary Burki clan, who played a powerful and formative role in the history of cricket in Pakistan, and whose exploits flow through the nation's cricket like a great river. Imran Khan was a manifestation of this Burki cricketing culture.

A twelve-year-old Imran was taken by Ahmed Raza Khan, his uncle and by now a national selector, to watch Pakistan play New Zealand at Rawalpindi in March 1965. His two cousins, Majid and Javed Burki, were both playing. As uncle and nephew watched Pakistan gain an innings victory (without any notable contribution on this occasion from the Burki cousins), Ahmed Raza Khan told his friends that one day Imran Khan too would play for Pakistan. 'I never forgot that moment,' Imran later recorded. 'For me, his words were gospel.'

By the age of fourteen, Imran was the youngest member of the Aitchison College school team, where he was opening batsman. Aged sixteen, he was selected for Pakistan Under-19s against a touring side of English schoolboys from Middlesex and Surrey, which included two future Test players, Bob Willis and Graham Barlow and several future county players.[3] 'To begin with, I was treated with a certain amount of hostility. My team-mates thought I did not deserve a place in the team and was there on the basis of my connections,' recalled Imran.[4] This point of view was not unreasonable. At the age of sixteen, Imran was first selected to play first-class cricket for Lahore. The chairman of the selectors was his uncle, while the team captain (and some senior players) were his cousins. 'Some called this nepotism. I of course preferred to regard it as pure coincidence,' remarked Imran later.[5]

Imran opened the batting for Lahore A against Sargodha, scoring 30, caught at the wicket off the fast-medium Sherandaz Khan.* Imran was the seventh bowler used in Sargodha's innings; he took two tail-end wickets but they cost him 43 in only seven overs. It then rained. Rather than hang around the ground, Imran went home for a sleep, returning to discover the game had already resumed. When he got to the wicket, he was promptly run out for 0. He was not called on to bowl in Sargodha's second innings, when they scored 51 to win, nervously, losing five wickets. It was an inauspicious debut, recalls his older cousin and team-mate Javed Zaman. 'Imran had a slinging action and opened the innings. He didn't take any wickets [the two tail-end victims obviously left no impression] . . . and was run out in his first over.'[6]

---

*Curiously, the first bowler to dismiss Imran in first-class cricket was a Burki cousin. Sherandaz Khan's uncle was Baqa Jilani, brother-in-law of Jahangir Khan, who played one Test with him for India on the 1936 tour of England.

Imran also played under the captaincy of his cousin Javed Burki. 'He used me intelligently, shielding me when things were going badly and encouraging me at the appropriate times.' At the age of eighteen, as we have seen, Imran was chosen to represent a Pakistan XI against Micky Stewart's touring International XI, and did well enough to be selected for the 1971 Pakistan tour of England.

Before the England tour, he was approached by Wing Commander William Shakespeare, chairman of Worcestershire. Shakespeare arranged that Imran should attend Worcester Royal Grammar School as a boarder, where he would take his A-levels and try for Oxford or Cambridge. A year later, Imran was on his way to Keble College, Oxford.

This intervention from Wing Commander Shakespeare changed Imran's life, and thus the history of Pakistan cricket. His studies at Oxford kept Imran away from the Pakistan domestic game. His cricket was therefore confined to the summer months, when he played for Oxford University (where he opened the bowling, batted at number 4, and eventually captained) and for Worcestershire in the county championship after university term ended.

This Oxford experience may have slowed Imran's development as a cricketer,* but he developed a broader perspective and gained experience of leadership. When he finally emerged as a top-ranking Test player, Imran was in his mid-twenties. But he was unusually well-equipped as a human being for sport at the highest level. Proud, highly intelligent, disciplined, hard-working and charismatic, this remarkable cricketer was about to shape one of the greatest cricket teams the world had known.

PAKISTAN CRICKET COMES OF AGE

Imran Khan took charge at a vital moment in the evolution of Pakistan cricket. From the late 1970s onward, the game was exploding in popularity and significance. New forms of cricket were invented, and old forms

---

*Oxford cricket was not strong in this period. In all, Imran scored 1,306 first-class runs for Oxford University at an average of 32.65, with three centuries. He took 85 wickets for them at a cost of 27.37 apiece. In two matches for Oxford & Cambridge combined he scored another 370 runs, and took another 11 wickets at 26.18 apiece. Oxford University won only two first-class matches during Imran's three years there; in both he was a major contributor.

adapted in ways that no one could have predicted. The sport spread to new areas in which it had never existed before, where it discovered it could attract all classes and unify the entire country. Pakistan cricketers were no longer patronised by the dominant white cricketing nations. Instead, they came to be feared and resented. The balance of power tilted. All these changes took place during Imran's period of dominance, and he came personally to represent the cricketing consciousness of the new era.

Suddenly the game was followed with the same undiluted fervour and passion with which Brazilians play football. Indeed cricket came to fill the same role in Pakistan society as football does in Brazil. It represented, in an untrammelled way, the national personality. A new generation emerged which played the game with a compelling and instinctive genius. Many of these new players came from poor backgrounds, and some from remote areas. These superlative, new players did not simply change the Pakistan game. They reinvented global cricket. Untrained and self-taught, they did not accept the rules of the game as they were interpreted in the rest of the world. They imposed their own personalities, with the result that cricket went through a period of inventiveness and brilliance comparable to the so-called golden age before World War One.

Two discoveries stand out. The first was reverse swing, which changed cricket as profoundly as over-arm bowling did in the Victorian period. Reverse swing is a phenomenon of such importance that I have allocated it a long chapter of its own in Part Three (see p.349). As with all new discoveries, reverse swing (which is now accepted as a legitimate part of international cricket) was greeted by a mixture of technical fascination and bitter resentment. Even more than arguments about umpiring, it became the primary cause of estrangement between Pakistan and the white cricketing world in the 1990s.

The second was not a discovery but a rediscovery: the emergence of wrist-spin bowling, which had been all but extinguished by the 1960s. During this era, cricket administrators and captains, especially in the dominant white nations, attributed a special importance to conformity. Cricket came to stand for the suburban, middle-class values that were triumphing across the industrialised world in the wake of World War Two.

In Britain, seam-up bowling was the dominant component of any serious bowling attack. Off-spin, whereby the bowler causes the ball to revolve in the air following a flick of the fingers, was also a very important, if secondary, element. Off-spin was orderly, controlled, reliable and in the hands of an accomplished practitioner almost guaranteed not to give away more than 2.5 runs an over. For John Emburey, England's leading off-spinner at the time, spin-bowling was above all the art of containment. He sought to restrict scoring more than he wanted to take wickets. In all these respects, this cautious method fitted well into the ordinary bourgeois sensibility of post-war Britain, New Zealand and Australia.

Leg-spin required more than a flick of the fingers, but mobilised the wrist and upper arm as well, thus opening up a new universe of wicket-taking deliveries. It was chaotic, unpredictable, unruly and utterly subversive of the values promoted throughout the cricketing Anglosphere. Leg-spin was at the heart of Pakistan's cricketing revolution.

ABDUL QADIR: PORTRAIT OF AN ARTIST AS A GREAT CRICKETER

The story of this patriotic and deeply religious cricketer embraces the two greatest themes of recent Pakistan cricket history: the technical inventiveness of a new generation and their sudden emergence from outside the middle-class elite. When Abdul Qadir told me his story in the upstairs office of his independent cricket academy in Lahore, he spoke at the pace of an express bowler rather than a loopy spinner. His right hand, which propelled 60,885 leg-breaks, googlies and flippers in first-class and major one-day cricket matches, constantly twisted and whirled, as if he wanted to bowl them all over again.

Abdul Qadir was one of four children, raised in a tiny house in Dharampura, a poor and crowded district of Lahore. He is proud of his Pashtun family origins; his father migrated to Lahore and earned a tiny salary reading prayers at a local mosque. He also taught the Holy Quran to local people for nothing. It was barely enough to raise a family, and they sometimes missed meals. His father had no sporting interests, and there were no other older relatives to inspire and teach his second son to play cricket. 'But he did pass on my cricket values – excellence, honesty, respect for opponents,' says Qadir.

He was entirely self-taught, practising hard in the nets and experiment-ing continually – even in his dreams. 'I used to go to bed with a cricket ball and as I was falling asleep I used to imagine various grips and what the ball would do.'* This method helped him discover three or four different ways to produce the standard deliveries in the leg-spinner's repertoire.

At one game near the Fortress stadium, he was spotted and recruited by the best local club, the Dharampura Gymkhana. As often happens in Pakistan, the newcomer had to watch the seniors and prepare nets and pitches for them before he even had a chance to practise, let alone play a match. When they finally put him into the first team, he obliged them with a century and five wickets.

His all-round performances gained him a place in Government College, Lahore. From there, he went to work and play cricket for the Water and Power Development Association at 230 rupees a week (around £10 at the then exchange rate), and then an even better offer came from the Habib Bank – 750 rupees a week (around £32). Qadir was thus an early benefici-ary of AH Kardar's system of commercial teams – his father was amazed that cricketers got paid at all. At Habib Bank, he was number 7 in a powerful batting line-up including Mohsin Khan and Javed Miandad. This led him to concentrate on bowling, a decision reinforced on his first-class debut, aged twenty, against the United Bank in the SA Bhutto Cup (another prod-uct of the Kardar-Bhutto era). Batting number 7, he received a shocking lbw decision on the front foot. 'I went to the toilet and wept and decided never to put my pads on again.' When Habib Bank took the field, the regular bowlers, including Test opener Liaquat Ali, were unable to break through. When finally given the ball, as the sixth bowler, Qadir took six for 67. His photograph appeared in *Dawn* newspaper over the caption: 'Abdul Qadir Wrecks Opponents.'†

The novelty of Qadir was his aggression. Pakistan had maintained a tradition of leg-spinners – including Mushtaq Mohammad and Intikhab Alam – but Qadir alone viewed wrist-spin as an attacking art. His philosophical doctrine was attack, and his overriding objective was wicket-taking. For Qadir,

---

*Abdul Qadir: personal interview. He told me he did not play at all until he was around twelve years old, in a pick-up game, where he was out first ball in two attempted innings. 'It was the worstest [*sic*] ever debut,' he said, struggling to convey its depths.
†I have not traced this historic headline, but rely on Abdul Qadir's word.

leg-spin was like fast bowling, in the sense that each delivery contained ultimate menace, intensity, ambition and personal commitment.

He wrecked twenty-five other first-class opponents in that first season and sixty-seven in the next, which earned him a Test debut in the home series against England in December 1977. His figures were modest (the wicket of number 11 batsman Bob Willis at a cost of 82) but he was retained and captured six for 44 in the next Test in Hyderabad, and ended up as leading wicket-taker for Pakistan in that series. Nevertheless, for the next few years, Qadir struggled to keep his place in the team. By 1982, when Imran became captain, his confidence was low after a run of poor performances, and he was contemplating retirement at age twenty-seven.[7] Imran backed him unconditionally (unlike Javed Miandad, who had favoured the skilful left-arm spinner Iqbal Qasim) and insisted on his selection for the 1982 tour of England. Under Imran, Qadir was given the scope and confidence to fulfil his destiny.

PAKISTAN IN ENGLAND 1982

Just as Kardar had defined Pakistan cricket in the 1950s, so Imran Khan set his seal on the great Test team of the 1980s. To begin with, the materials were unpropitious. Mushtaq Mohammad's admirable side was in eclipse. Most of its great players were either retired (Mushtaq himself, Asif Iqbal) or a little past their best, such as Wasim Bari, Majid Khan and Sarfraz Nawaz. The team was also beset by internal argument and jealousy.

It is hardly surprising that some of his closest friends urged Imran not to take on the captaincy. But Imran immediately imposed his personality. Two immediate decisions stand out. The first, discussed above, was the choice of Abdul Qadir. The second was Imran's brutal personal decision, announced without warning, to drop his first cousin, Majid Khan. This was done on the opening day of the first Test at Edgbaston. Majid had been Imran's hero since he was a young boy. It felt 'like dropping my elder brother', remembered Imran. 'It was dreadful, but there was really no justification for including him in place of one of the younger batsmen who had been making runs.'[8] Majid did not speak to Imran for twenty-five years.[9]

If Imran felt any guilt, he took it out on the English, reducing them from 168 for 2 to 272 all out. His seven wickets for 52 included Botham, bowled by a searing yorker. At the other end, Imran's protégé Abdul Qadir (deliberately hidden in the preceding one-day series) mesmerised every English batsman except the left-handed David Gower. He took only one wicket; he and Imran believed that English umpires could not detect his googly and top-spinner any better than their batsmen. According to his friend and rival Iqbal Qasim, Qadir took to announcing them to umpires before he delivered them.[10]

Pakistan ought to have taken a first-innings lead but irresponsible batting left them 21 behind. In England's second innings, the makeshift opener Derek Randall somehow scored a century despite being completely at sea against Qadir. Nonetheless, England were 188 for 8, only 209 ahead, after a superb spell of five for 40 by the unsung seamer Tahir Naqqash. Then the Pakistan bowlers lost the plot as the wicketkeeper Bob Taylor scored 54 and squeezed over 100 runs from the last two wickets. In a heavy atmosphere, Botham shot out Mudassar Nazar (for a pair) and Mansoor Akhtar before a run had been scored. He bowled 21 overs unchanged, taking four wickets as Pakistan crashed to 77 for six. Imran resisted with 65, and Tahir completed a fine match with 39, but Pakistan still lost by 113 runs.

In the second Test at Lord's, a beautiful double-century by Mohsin Khan, supported by fifties from Zaheer Abbas and Mansoor Akhtar, lead Pakistan to 428 for 8 when Imran declared overnight on the second day after long interruptions for rain. The crowd could then enjoy him bowling in tandem for long periods with Qadir, who destroyed England's lower order with four for 39. In the follow-on, Imran and Qadir failed to make much headway, as Chris Tavaré plodded towards the second slowest half-century in Test history, including 67 minutes before getting off the mark, and later, an hour without adding a run. Sarfraz and Tahir were both unfit and for lack of any alternative, Imran tossed the ball to the part-time medium-pacer Mudassar. He was rewarded with a spell of three wickets in six balls for no runs. Bad light (capriciously handled by the umpires) threatened Pakistan's victory bid, but on the last morning Mudassar added another three victims, including Botham for 69 (to a long hop), while Imran dismissed Tavaré for 82, which had occupied 407 minutes. Unusually, he delayed taking the new ball until

112 overs had gone, before at last handing it to Qadir who ended another irritating last-wicket stand. Pakistan were left with a target of 76 in a maximum of 18 overs as dark clouds gathered. Imran sent in Javed Miandad to partner Mohsin Khan. The pair countered England's widely spread fields by brilliant running between the wickets. With four overs to spare they gave Pakistan their first victory in England since 1954 at The Oval, twenty-eight years earlier.[11]

Pakistan's victory set up a great finish to the three-match series (Pakistan had not been permitted a full five-Test series since Javed Burki's fiasco in 1962). However, the third Test began on a farcical note, when the former opening bowler Ehteshamuddin was called up from league cricket to partner Imran, in the continued absence of Sarfraz Nawaz and Tahir Naqqash. The poor man was seriously overweight and after lumbering through fourteen reasonable overs in England's first innings, he pulled a muscle and was unable to make any further contribution.

Pakistan batted first and made 275, with fifties from Mudassar, Javed and Imran. Restored to the side, but in the middle order, Majid made only 21 but had the satisfaction of becoming Pakistan's leading Test run scorer. Gower (74) and Botham (57) brought England to 256. They blunted Qadir, but the spinner was furious when umpire David Constant refused a caught-behind off Gower early in his innings.

The Pakistanis were even more angry with Constant in their own second innings. Despite another half-century from Javed, Pakistan were only 128 for 7 when Qadir joined his mentor Imran. They added 41 and then Imran found another resolute partner in Sikander Bakht. They added another 30 runs, before Sikander was given out by Constant, wrongly, to a bat-pad appeal. This proved the turning point. With no faith in Ehteshamuddin, the last man, Imran was then caught attempting to hit Botham for the boundary which would have given him a second fifty.

England had to make 219. At 168 for 2 (Fowler 86), it looked like a stroll. With Ehteshamuddin absent, Imran threw the ball again to Mudassar. The new 'golden arm' of Pakistan cricket then took three wickets and England were tottering at 189 for 6 when Botham accepted an offer of bad light. Mudassar dismissed him the next morning, but Vic Marks and Bob Taylor eked out the remaining 20 runs for victory by three wickets.[12]

In post-match interviews Imran complained bitterly about Constant's umpiring, but the tour had made his reputation as captain. Despite Pakistan losing the Test series 2–1, Imran had won the respect and loyalty of his team, and he had led from the front. Personally, he had contributed 212 runs at an average of 53 and 21 wickets at 18.6, some of the best all-round figures ever produced on a short tour. He had shown himself at his best in adversity.

AUSTRALIA WHITEWASHED

The next test for Imran's captaincy was not much easier; the winter tour by Australia. Crucially Imran stuck with Abdul Qadir. His selection was criticised heavily in some media, particularly in Karachi. The leg-spinner, for all his mystery, had achieved a return of only ten Test wickets in England at a cost of over 40.

The first Test at Karachi was preceded by a row over Zaheer Abbas; some of his supporters promised a bomb blast (no idle threat in Karachi) if he was not selected. He was, and his 91 led Pakistan to a healthy first-innings lead of 135. The Pakistan innings was interrupted by spectators throwing fruit and stones and then invading the pitch; Kim Hughes led his team off the field. Qadir made his first major contribution of the series with five for 76 in the second innings, baffling the Australian batsmen. Pakistan needed only a handful to win.

At Faisalabad, Pakistan posted 501 for 8 before Imran declared. There were centuries for Zaheer Abbas and Mansoor Akhtar. This was the only century of Mansoor's stop-start Test career and he hovered on 99 for twenty-five nervous minutes. The wicket, which did nothing for Australia's leg-spinner, Peter Sleep, became malign when Abdul Qadir took it over; he took four for 76 as a dazed and confused Australia were all out for 168. Following on, they resisted with a century from Greg Ritchie (in his second Test) but Qadir took seven more wickets for 142 with his googlies, flippers and leg-spinners. These were his best figures to date and helped Pakistan win by an innings and three runs.

Pakistan completed their first whitewash of any opponent in the next Test at Lahore.[13] Javed scored his first century for thirty months and there was another from Mohsin Khan, before Imran declared with a lead of 151.

Imran then took four more wickets to add to his four in Australia's first innings, Qadir dismissed Hughes and Border, and Pakistan needed only 64 to win.*

Pakistan's cricketers, particularly the captain, reached new heights of popularity after this series and General Zia decided to share some of it by hosting a gala dinner and presenting gold medals to the players.

TRIUMPH AGAINST INDIA

Imran Khan now faced the ultimate challenge for any Pakistan captain: a home series against India. This was one of those rare relatively happy periods in Pakistan-India diplomatic relations and this new tranquillity was finding its expression in regular contact on the cricket field.

This Test series was a grand contest.[14] India could boast conceivably the best batting side in the world: Sunil Gavaskar, Gundappa Viswanath, Dilip Vengsarkar, Mohinder Amarnath, Sandeep Patil, Yashpal Sharma, Ravi Shastri and Kapil Dev. By contrast, Pakistan's greatest strength lay in a bowling attack led by Imran, who was now thirty years old and at his superlative peak as an attacking fast bowler.

At this stage of its history, cricket was graced by a quartet of brilliant all-rounders: Imran, Kapil Dev, Ian Botham and Richard Hadlee. Every time they met, there would be a personal duel: Kapil Dev had won when Pakistan toured India. But even though Kapil was to take twenty-four wickets in the series, this time Imran would emerge the victor.

The first Test was a high-scoring draw at Lahore, memorable for two personal milestones. Zaheer Abbas followed Geoff Boycott in scoring his 100th first-class hundred in a Test match, but went one better by making it a double. Mohsin Khan with 94 and 101 not out became the first Pakistani to score 1,000 Test runs in a calendar year.

Pakistan crushed India by an innings and 86 runs in the second Test at Karachi – her biggest victory over India. Kapil alone resisted Imran and

*Imran told me that he rates his second innings' bowling as the best performance of his career, on a wicket which had lost its early life. He furiously berated the groundsman who had received an instruction to insert some fine gravel into the wicket on the fourth day to make it break up, and was glad when this stratagem failed. Imran Khan: personal interview.

Qadir in India's first innings of 169. Zaheer made another huge century (he loved Indian bowling) and Mudassar made one too as Pakistan reached 452.

Imran always enjoyed the sea breeze at Karachi. In India's second innings he produced one of his greatest spells; eight for 60 as India were dismissed for 197. Two Imran deliveries, the break-back which bowled Gavaskar when well set on 42 and the searing break-back which bowled Viswanath second ball (and secured Imran's 200th Test wicket) are endlessly replayed on video.

In the next Test at Faisalabad, Imran had the personal satisfaction of matching Botham's ten wickets and a century in a Test match. He took six wickets in the first innings and five in the second. As a centurion he was joined by Javed, Zaheer (again) and the young Salim Malik, in a Pakistan innings of 652, giving them a lead of 280. He was supported by four wickets from Sarfraz in India's second innings, where Gavaskar became the first Indian to carry his bat, in an innings of 127. Pakistan needed only ten for victory.

The fourth Test produced another innings victory. Pakistan piled up 581 for 3 declared. There were double-centuries for Mudassar and Javed as they equalled the world-record stand of 451 set by Bill Ponsford and Don Bradman against England at The Oval in 1934. Imran took six wickets again in India's first innings of 189. Sarfraz, with four, was the main destroyer in their second innings of 273.

These events were overshadowed by controversy about Imran's declaration, on the third day, which left Javed high and dry on 280 not out. Most of the Karachi press attacked Imran for not giving Javed the chance to press on to overtake Garry Sobers's then record of 365 (against Pakistan). Javed himself devoted an entire chapter to his grievance in his autobiography, claiming that Imran had given him no warning, pointing out that India were eventually beaten with plenty of time to spare, and hinting that Imran might have been jealous of him.[15]

Imran's most recent biographer, Christopher Sandford, noted that Javed was scoring at 30 runs an hour at the declaration. He would therefore have needed another three hours to overtake Sobers. He quoted Imran as saying that the wicket was 'stone dead' and that it was time to bowl at the demoralised Indians, adding 'if you have your enemy down, you must never let him up.'[16]

By now, Imran was experiencing recurring pain in his left shin. Although unable to bowl properly, and at times sporting a visible limp, Imran toiled through another 66 overs in the remaining two drawn Tests (plus eight in a one-day international). The fifth Test in Lahore was hit by thunderstorms, which cost the last two days. There was time for Mudassar to emulate his father by carrying his bat for 152. Mudassar made the same score in the final Karachi Test, which was hit by crowd demonstrations. They had a mixture of motives, including protests against the high price of tickets (the series rights had been sold to a private businessman), but they also turned on the 'Lahorite' captain, Imran.[17] At one point, Imran uprooted a stump to defend himself against a potential intruder.[18]

The five painful wickets he took in this Test gave him 40 in the series at less than 14 apiece. This is still a record series haul for a Pakistan bowler. He had also scored 247 runs at an average of 61.75 (against Kapil Dev's 178 at 22.25). At the top of the Pakistan batting order, Zaheer had scored 650 runs in the series, Mudassar 761 and Javed 594, each averaging well over 100. They set a record for the highest series contribution by any trio of batsmen.[19] Pakistan had utterly dominated their rivals. It soon turned out that the triumph had come at an intolerable cost.

IMRAN CUT IN HALF: WORLD CUP 1983

Imran had first noticed that something was wrong after the opening day of the second Test against Karachi.[20] He had bowled well to secure three wickets at a cost of just 19 runs as India collapsed. The following morning he woke up feeling a pain in his left shinbone.

He felt no discomfort while batting, but when he opened the bowling at the start of India's second innings the pain reappeared. He soon forgot about it in the evening Karachi breeze as the Indian batting melted from 101 for 1 to 114 for 7, and Imran (bowling fast inswingers) seized eight wickets for just 60 runs.

During that Indian tour of 1982–83, Imran was bowling better than ever. He was still young and fit, but thanks to a decade of experience and hard work he had acquired a veteran's mastery of his trade. During this period, he was one of the greatest fast bowlers the world has known. The third Test was at Faisalabad, normally a bowlers' graveyard. Against a very fine Indian batting side, Imran was utterly destructive, bowling 55 overs of immense pace to take eleven wickets for 181 runs. He also scored 117, including a gratifying 21 off a single over from Kapil Dev. For the first time, however, Imran started to feel pain while batting.

He travelled on to play in the fourth Test at Hyderabad, where on the third day he bowled what he considers to be his fastest ever spell, destroying the India batting (Gavaskar, Viswanath, Vengsarkar, Kapil Dev, Kirmani) with lethal, controlled pace. From this moment on a lump appeared on his shinbone, and he now needed to spray the area before bowling. 'Even so the agony was intense,' recalled Imran, 'I kept bowling until I had crossed the pain barrier, but as soon as I stopped I could hardly stand.'[21]

Imran should have rested after this. He was suffering from a stress fracture of the left shinbone, hardly surprising when one reflects that he was pounding in to bowl 90-mph deliveries for 20 overs or more a day. At this stage, the technology to identify the problem did not exist in Pakistan. Imran did have some X-rays taken at the end of the fifth Test, but they found nothing wrong. During these final two Test matches, Imran bowled a further 66 overs, and at times he was visibly limping in his run-up. Nevertheless, he took seven more wickets.

Pakistani doctors diagnosed nothing worse than bruising at the end of the series, a crucial error, for Imran's injury might have healed comparatively easily had he taken complete rest at this stage. It was only three months later that fresh X-rays shockingly revealed a huge crack on the shinbone. The specialist told him that he was amazed the bone had not shattered entirely under the pressure being put on it, adding that it would take up to a year to heal.

Imran needed a long period of rest and recuperation, well away from cricket. That was exactly what he was not going to get. By now Pakistan cricket had become dependent on Imran. The thought of doing without the team's greatest asset for the 1983 World Cup, to be held in England, was unbearable. It was accepted that Imran could not bowl. But the selectors insisted on keeping him as captain for his batting, his leadership and his experience of one-day cricket in English conditions.[22]

The decision left Pakistan short of quality in their bowling. Imran, however, insisted that Abdul Qadir should be employed in one-day matches. He and Pakistan were to be rewarded for this (at the time) very bold decision.

Pakistan stumbled through the qualifying round, in which Sri Lanka gave them a fright with a spirited attempt to score 339 to win. Then followed defeat against New Zealand, despite Qadir's man-of-the-match performance of four for 21 and 41 not out.*

In spite of Zaheer's 83 not out, Pakistan posted only 183 against England and lost with ten overs to spare. Sri Lanka gave them an even worse fright in their second group match. Pakistan were 43 for 5 before Imran rallied them with an undefeated century and found help from the inexperienced Shahid Mahboob, who made 77. Pakistan's final total of 235 looked in easy reach when Sri Lanka made 162 for 2. Qadir then induced several batsmen to self-destruct in a spell of five for 44, but the Sri Lankan last-wicket pair took them to just 12 runs from their target before Sarfraz struck. Against England, Pakistan made 232, thanks largely to Javed's 67, but it was undefendable.

To qualify for the semi-final, Pakistan needed to beat New Zealand and with a good run-rate. A masterful century from Zaheer and Imran's 79 not out brought Pakistan to 261. New Zealand lost seven wickets for 152 but their frequent saviour Jeremy Coney found reliable partners to launch a final assault which nearly undid Pakistan. However, the fielders, often their weak link, rose to the occasion. There were two fine catches in the deep, by Mohsin Khan and the substitute Mansoor Akhtar, and finally Imran ran out Coney. Pakistan won by just 11 runs and, crucially, edged out New Zealand on run rate by 0.08 runs per over.

The victory took Pakistan to a semi-final against their regular nemesis, West Indies. Their poor prospects were diminished still further when Javed had to stand down through influenza. Mohsin used 57 of their 60 overs in scoring 70 to anchor their innings, but no one took on the West Indian pace attack or even their fill-in bowlers, Larry Gomes and Viv Richards. Pakistan set a target of only 185 and West Indies strolled to it for the loss of two wickets.

Imran drew fierce criticism for Pakistan's performance, although his team had performed to its full capability. The criticisms were sharpened when India were the surprise winners of the tournament. They scored only 183

*Shane Warne pays a fine tribute to his predecessor in *My Autobiography* (Hodder and Stoughton, 2002): 'all of us spin bowlers owe a lot to Abdul Qadir because he was the first leggie to be dangerous in one-day cricket.' (p.175). He enjoyed visiting Qadir at his home in Pakistan in 1994, where they would flick deliveries to each other across his living room floor (p.230). This would have been the greatest masterclass in history in the art of spin bowling.

against West Indies in the final – one fewer than Pakistan's total in the semi-final – but managed to defend it with some unrated bowlers and take home the trophy.[23]

After the tournament, Imran played county cricket for Sussex. After taking specialist advice, he bowled a few overs. The stress fracture opened up yet again, and Imran was back to square one.*

A DRAB SERIES (WITH NO IMRAN) AGAINST INDIA

Pakistan cricket was now in confusion. Imran was forced to declare himself unavailable for Pakistan's short tour of India in the autumn following the World Cup and Zaheer Abbas finally achieved his dream of captaincy. Pakistan lost their other main strike bowlers before the series began. Sarfraz Nawaz criticised the BCCP over its handling of Imran's injury, and was banned from first-class cricket for six months as punishment. He took legal proceedings to quash the penalty, was invited to the training camp and then not selected, apparently on medical grounds. Abdul Qadir was excluded after having the temerity to seek a loan of 300,000 rupees from the Board to finance his new house in Lahore.[24] In the absence of his patron Imran, Qadir found it hard to get into the side.

India were unable to press home their advantage and all three Tests were drawn, with much time lost to rain. The first Test at Bangalore saw a spat between Javed Miandad and the gentle Indian slow left-armer, Dilip Doshi; to the crowd's delight Javed was brilliantly caught by the substitute fielder Kris Srikkanth for 99. In the second Test, at Jullundur, Javed battled fever to score 66 and Wasim Raja made a composed century, but Pakistan were frustrated by a new record: the slowest Test double-century, scored by India's opener Anshuman Gaekwad over 671 minutes. Pakistan had their best chance of victory at Nagpur in the third Test, when a second-string off-spinner, Mohammad Nazir, took five for 72 off 50 overs. A new generation from the Mohammad dynasty came into the Pakistan side: Hanif's son Shoaib, along with a left-arm pace bowler, Azeem Hafeez. Azeem had a congenital deformity: a fore-shortened right arm ending in a hand missing four

*Imran's own account of this mistaken decision is in *All Round View*, op. cit. p.61.

fingers. To be on the pitch at all was a massive achievement. Shoaib was to turn into a high-calibre Test batsman, with a higher batting average than even his famous father.[25]

IMRAN'S DARKEST HOUR

Zaheer Abbas proved a dull, defensive captain, a reversion to a previous era. He was nevertheless reappointed for the forthcoming tour of Australia, but then the interventionist BCCP president, Nur Khan, overrode his selection panel and reappointed Imran as captain on his own authority, even though he could not bowl and was ill-advised to play at all.

The appointment put intolerable pressure on Imran, who was expected to justify his presence in the side through batting alone. It unbalanced the side, and led to a great deal of bad blood. Imran then made things much worse by blocking the selection of Hanif Mohammad's son Shoaib, claiming that he was too young. This was perverse. Pakistan had always benefited from an adventurous youth policy, with Imran himself one such beneficiary.*

Angry at being over-ruled on so many fronts, chairman of selectors Haseeb Ahsan now very understandably resigned, shortly to be followed by Nur Khan, though the air marshal's departure was related as much to political differences with President Zia as to cricket.

This was the shambolic situation which prevailed when Imran's team arrived in Australia in late 1983. Imran now took his wounded shin off for a second opinion from a specialist in Brisbane (he would have done better to have done this before accepting the captaincy). The advice was unequivocal: Imran must not bat, far less bowl, for two months. When Imran told the BCCP about this, he was instructed to stay with the team 'and take my place in due course'.[26] Zaheer Abbas was appointed stand-in captain. He at once issued a statement that he would have chosen a different team, and was only a caretaker.

Pakistan now went into the first Test on the bouncy track at Perth. Yet again they were unprepared. Imran was a much-criticised spectator as

---

*Imran came to realise Shoaib's worth. He told me with particular enjoyment: 'I was the only captain of Pakistan to resign twice, the first time because Shoaib was chosen and the second time because a new selection committee dropped him.' (Imran Khan: personal interview.)

Pakistan lost by an innings. Seventeen batsmen were out to edges somewhere behind the wicket, but a newcomer, Qasim Omar, born in East Africa, won admiration for courage when he top-scored in both innings.[27] (His Test career included two double-centuries but ended in 1985–86 after he accused a number of fellow-players of drug taking). The players denied his charges, which were not investigated, and he was banned for seven years.[28]*

In the second Test at Brisbane, Zaheer elected to bat first, but no one supported his innings half-century and Pakistan were all out for 156. Centuries by Allan Border and Greg Chappell took Australia to 509 for 7 declared. Pakistan had lost three cheap wickets when they were saved by torrential rain.

For the third Test at Adelaide, Pakistan were strengthened by Sarfraz Nawaz, whose ban had been suspended by a judge in Lahore. Early on, he had an Australian newcomer dropped on the boundary by his handicapped opening partner Azeem Hafeez. Kepler Wessels, a South African exile who had qualified by residence, celebrated his reprieve by scoring 179. Azeem tried to make amends by taking five for 167 but Australia totalled 465. Pakistan put up their best batting performance in reply: centuries from Mohsin Khan, Qasim Omar and Javed Miandad, followed by 77 from a jet-lagged reinforcement Salim Malik, produced a total of 624. Kim Hughes's century saved Australia from a possible defeat.

Imran now defied doctor's orders by returning to the team as a batting-only captain. His decision, brought about by Imran's belief that somehow he must justify his presence on tour, made little sense. He replaced a bowler (the admittedly ineffective Mohammad Nazir), thus leaving Pakistan with an attack of Sarfraz Nawaz, Azeem Hafeez and Abdul Qadir, whose wiles and confidence were being blunted by an Australian team packed with left-handers.

Imran revealed later: 'I have never felt so nervous going into a Test match.' Yet he made a crucial 83 in the first innings, and a match-saving 72 not out in the second. These runs meant that he joined the small band of all-rounders to score 2,000 runs and take 200 wickets in Tests.

Despite Imran's heroics in the fourth Test, his presence had weakened an

---

*In 2001 Qasim Omar re-emerged into the limelight with claims that a ring of prostitutes had been organised by bookmakers during the mid-1980s as a reward for match-fixing by international players from several countries. He had a long interview about his claims with the ICC's Anti-Corruption Unit, under Sir Paul Condon, but Condon was unable to substantiate them in his report. (See 'Call girls to be questioned in cricket scandal', *Observer*, 21 January 2001; Radford, Brian, *Caught Out* (John Blake, 2001).)

already underpowered and divided team, and he won no gratitude from the Pakistan public for aggravating an already serious injury; new X-rays revealed the stress fracture had opened up again. Imran returned to Pakistan, facing a barrage of media criticism and, following the departure of Nur Khan, friendless in the cricketing bureaucracy. Zaheer, who had made no secret of his criticisms of Imran's leadership, was now officially appointed captain. Imran at last paid his leg the attention it deserved. 'In March 1984,' he wrote later, 'another round of X-rays suggested that my career was indeed over. I was to get out of cricket, like so many other great Pakistani players of the past, abandoned and abused. The prospect of never playing again was depressing, but even harder to face was the fact that I had been humiliated and would never get the chance to redeem myself.'[29]

At this stage, the Burki family connection came to the rescue. One of Imran's maternal cousins, Professor Farrakh Khan, was a cricketing doctor. We have already met Farrakh (son of Ahmed Raza Khan, who took Imran to the Rawalpindi Test match in 1965) as the team medic who became suspicious of the presence of a bookmaker on board the team bus during Asif Iqbal's tour of India.

Now Farrakh told the Punjab health minister, Hamid Nasir Chattha, about Imran's leg.[30] Chattha convened an emergency conference of Lahore's top orthopaedic surgeons: 'One of the participants suggested a form of treatment which was still at an experimental stage, whereby the healing process was hastened by means of electrical cycles passed through the leg.' The treatment was very expensive, and needed doing in London, but General Zia guaranteed that the government would supply the money. So in the spring of 1984, Imran travelled to the Cromwell Hospital in London for a six-month course of treatment, during which his leg was put in a cast. Neither he, nor anyone else, knew whether he would play cricket again.

PAKISTAN BEAT ENGLAND AT HOME

Like it or not, Imran was not the only one to miss the home series against England in March 1984. So did Javed Miandad, who suffered a serious, career-threatening head injury in a charity match – from a bouncer by Dennis Lillee. Javed had been too proud to wear a helmet.[31]

At Karachi, Abdul Qadir rediscovered his magic and took eight wickets in the match. Supported by Sarfraz, Wasim Raja and the restored Tauseef Ahmed, he dismissed England for less than 200 in each innings. The Pakistanis panicked against England's slow left-arm spinner Nick Cook when they had to chase only 65 to win, and he took another five cheap wickets. For victory, they needed a calm innings from their new wicket-keeper, Anil Dalpat, the first Hindu to play for Pakistan.[32] Remarkably, it was Pakistan's first home victory over England in an official Test.

An injured Ian Botham went home before the second Test.[33] It was a high-scoring draw on a sedate pitch, with centuries for Malik and Wasim and a glorious 152 from David Gower, helped by Vic Marks, who made his highest Test score of 83. However, Gower was lucky to survive a confident bat-pad appeal off Qadir – this was refused by a much-criticised Pakistani umpire, Mahboob Shah.

Pakistan were heading for a second victory in the third Test, until another largely self-inflicted crisis. Zaheer, with a runner for a serious leg injury, rescued their first innings, with much help from Sarfraz, who enjoyed himself hugely with his highest score of 90, as Pakistan's lead swelled to 102. After another brilliant century, Gower declared and set Pakistan 243 to win. Mohsin scored a rapid century, Shoaib 80 and Pakistan reached 173 without loss. Then followed another panic, this time against the pace bowler Norman Cowans. Six wickets fell for 26 and Ramiz Raja and Sarfraz had to block for the draw to give Pakistan their first series win against England.[34]

ACRIMONY AS INDIA RETURN

India returned to Pakistan in October 1984 after only a year. Nur Khan and the BCCP had hoped to milk the India connection with an annual 'Ashes' series, but this idea was abandoned after two drawn Tests full of dull batting on dead pitches in disturbingly empty stadiums. More defensive than ever, Zaheer Abbas asked for his teams to be packed with batting. The Faisalabad Test was so boring that the city's mayor called the pitch 'that barren and wretched piece of earth.'

Qasim Omar occupied it for 685 minutes in scoring 210, the longest Test innings ever played in Pakistan.[35] Mudassar Nazar spent 555 minutes at the crease before being dismissed for 199, becoming the first batsman to be dismissed one short of his double-century in a Test. The Indians abandoned this tour and went straight home on the assassination of Indira Gandhi, so that a one-day international and a Test in Karachi were never played.

A New Zealand side without Richard Hadlee and their most experienced batsman, Geoff Howarth, followed the Indians for another short Test series. In their warm-up match, a teenage pace bowler was drafted into the BCCP Patron's XI when Sarfraz and Tahir Naqqash dropped out at the last minute. He promptly took seven wickets for 50 in his second first-class match. More would be heard from Wasim Akram.

Pakistan took the Test series 2–0 with one draw. The matchwinner was Iqbal Qasim, recalled to the side in the early hours on the morning of the first Test at Lahore. He ended the series with eighteen wickets at just over 22 apiece, supported by Abdul Qadir, with twelve. Mudassar was pressed into service with the new ball.

In the second Test, Javed followed Hanif Mohammad in scoring a century in each innings, as Pakistan completed their second victory. Statisticians rejoiced that this was the 1,000th Test match, but the New Zealand captain, the normally affable Jeremy Coney, complained bitterly about the umpiring of Mian Mohammad Aslam and Khizar Hayat.*

Coney was even angrier in the final Test, in which New Zealand were on top thanks to their left-arm spinner, Stephen Boock. When a replacement umpire gave another reprieve to Javed, Coney led his fielders off the pitch and had to be persuaded to return. The replacement was Shakoor Rana. The new BCCP president General Safdar Butt made his mark by appointing an independent inquiry into the umpiring, headed by Hanif Mohammad. It identified six questionable decisions, four in Pakistan's favour.[36]

WASIM'S FIRST GREAT PERFORMANCE

Pakistan had a return trip to New Zealand only weeks later. Javed replaced Zaheer as captain and his first move was to insist on the inclusion of Wasim

*Omar Noman hints that the change of regime at the BCCP lay behind the new set of allegations against Pakistan umpires: 'It is worth pointing out that the phase of acrimony and tension with umpires occurred after Air Marshal Nur Khan, an upright and well-respected figure, had stepped down from the chair of BCCP. He had been replaced by General Safdar Butt.' Noman, p.210.

Akram in the touring party, replacing the luckless Tahir Naqqash, who had already been selected.[37] Wasim knew so little about international cricket that he did not even realise that he would be paid.[38]

For New Zealand Geoff Howarth returned and so, crucially, did Richard Hadlee. He took sixteen wickets at less than 20 apiece and New Zealand got their revenge with a 2–0 series win. The first Test at Wellington was drawn through heavy rain with Pakistan poorly placed. New Zealand won the second at Auckland by an innings, as only Mudassar (89 in the second innings) put up any resistance. The third Test produced the first great performance by Wasim, in only his second match. He took five wickets in each innings but it ended in heartbreak.

Chasing 278 to win, New Zealand lost their eighth wicket on 228, with Lance Cairns concussed by a Wasim bouncer. One of the world's worst batsmen, Ewen Chatfield, came out to join New Zealand's last specialist batsman, Coney.* Amazingly, they put on 50 and snatched victory. Javed was criticised for allowing Coney easy singles, but Chatfield actually took more of the strike and contributed 21 to the partnership with no apparent difficulty.[39] Wasim choked back his disappointment, and endeared himself to television viewers with a modest post-match interview with Mudassar as his translator.[40] Pakistan were without Qadir for this match. He had a row with Zaheer over his slack fielding in a provincial match and was sent home.[41] He muttered threats of retirement, but some of his greatest days were still ahead.

---

*Chatfield had nearly died in 1975, when hit over the heart by England's Peter Lever.

RETURN OF THE KHAN

'It took us hours to wend our way home through a singing, dancing multitude of over 200,000 that lined the roads in celebration of Pakistan's first victory over India on their soil.'[1]

– IMRAN KHAN, ALL ROUND VIEW

Meanwhile Imran Khan endured his expensive, government-funded, course of treatment. He later recorded in his autobiography, *All Round View*, that at first he felt 'extremely depressed and bitter about the way I had been treated by the cricketing community in Pakistan.' Confined to his London flat, he 'did nothing but read and wallow in self-pity.' But over time, even his anger against Zaheer began to fade: 'In the past I could not easily have forgiven anyone, a very typical Pashtun characteristic. Now I learnt how to look through other people's eyes and understand them better.' For the first time since his Oxford days (and supported by his friend, the painter Emma Sergeant), he mingled with people outside cricket. When Imran emerged from his confinement he had a broader perspective on life.[2] Seen in retrospect, it was perhaps the beginning of Imran's discovery of a new spirituality and devotion to Islam.

After six months, X-rays showed that his leg had healed completely. Imran went running in Hyde Park, where he felt 'like a bird freed from its cage.'[3] The first time he bowled the pain returned, but Imran told nobody. He concluded that if his wound opened up again, his career would be over.[4]

Imran returned to the national team in a tournament to celebrate the 150th anniversary of the Victoria Cricket Association, where he partnered Wasim Akram for the first time. He said: 'Wasim is going to be the best left-arm fast bowler since Alan Davidson.' Thus began the second great bowling partnership of Imran's career.

Pakistan's next engagement was a short home series against Sri Lanka. Imran reappeared as a bowler in the first Test at Faisalabad, under Javed's leadership. He found himself bowling at a Sri Lankan prodigy who hooked him for six to complete a dazzling century.[5] The batsman was Aravinda de Silva, sharing a fighting stand with another future giant of Sri Lankan cricket, Arjuna Ranatunga.

Replying to 479, Qasim Omar and Javed helped themselves to double-centuries against a weak attack.[6] In the second Test, at a new venue in Sialkot, centre of Pakistan's sports goods manufacturing industry, Sri Lanka posted their best bowling performance to date, as swing bowler Ravi Ratnayeke took eight for 85. Pakistan still built a lead of 100 and when Imran went back to his full pace, he took five for 40 and Sri Lanka could set only 99. Pakistan won by eight wickets.

Zaheer announced his retirement from Test cricket, having become the first Pakistani to score 5,000 Test runs. There were hints that he had been pressurised to stand down and like many great Pakistanis he was denied a farewell Test. The selectors dropped him for the final Test in Karachi in favour of Ramiz Raja (whose brother Wasim had his own vivid international career ended by the selectors the previous year).

Abdul Qadir, Imran and the restored Tauseef Ahmed bowled Pakistan to victory by ten wickets in the Test, despite another beautiful century by de Silva.[7] Throughout the series, the Sri Lankans complained about the Pakistan umpires. They paid back Pakistan in their own country the fol-lowing winter. Before that happened, Imran was restored to the captaincy, Javed standing aside voluntarily for a second time in what Shuja-ud-Din called 'one of the most amicable transfers of power in Pakistan's cricket his-tory.'[8] As in 1982, Javed put the team first. In his autobiography he gave the reasons: 'I had the choice of continuing as captain following that series, but decided against it. I did so because Imran didn't give me his full co-operation in that [Sri Lanka] series, and it was a great disappointment to me.

'As captain I would tell Imran to bowl a certain way, ask him to pitch one short or to mix in a slower one, but instead he said he was not able to control the ball or was afraid of getting hit about. I thought this was laughable because in 1985–86 he was at the peak of his craft as a fast bowler and had acquired impeccable control over the ball.'[9]

Imran, like Kardar before him, was not prepared to serve under a rival. He was appointed captain despite protests over his dictatorial style (he had lost friends on the BCCP by banning their secretary, Col. Rafi Nasim, from the players' dressing room and then refusing to attend a disciplinary hearing).[10] Imran's team were received sullenly in a country which had been plunged into civil war, and the atmosphere got worse in the first Test when the local umpires gave some shocking decisions, refusing one Pakistani appeal with the loaded comment 'this is not Pakistan.'

'The hostility was unrelenting and unanimous,' Imran recorded later. 'Even the waiters in the hotel and the people in the streets were rude to us. It was as though the entire population was united in its determination to beat us at all costs, and be thoroughly unpleasant as well ... I think the civil war in Sri Lanka was responsible for a heightened patriotic fervour which, on the cricket field, was transmuted into a blind hatred of the opposition.'[11]

Imran wanted to abort the tour, and a message from General Zia himself was needed to persuade him to stay. Tensions grew worse in the second Test, when Javed received a terrible decision and was then hit by a stone on his way back to the pavilion. Javed waded into the crowd to find the offender.

Sri Lanka's seamers used the conditions well and they beat Pakistan by eight wickets. Weather, poor fielding and more contentious umpiring ruined Pakistan's chances of winning the final Test. Pakistan's ill-humour was deepened when they stayed on for the four-nation one-day Asia Cup and the concurrent John Player Gold Leaf Trophy. Pakistan were the hot favourites, but when Imran was prevented from bowling by a batting injury, Sri Lanka easily beat them in the final. It was Sri Lanka's first tournament victory, and their grateful president followed General Zia's example and declared a public holiday.[12]

THE MOST FAMOUS SHOT IN CRICKET HISTORY

From this low point, Pakistan and Javed Miandad in particular, bounced back instantly into glory. Under Imran Khan, they travelled to Sharjah for a new five-nation trophy, the Austral-Asia Cup, with Australia, New Zealand, Sri Lanka and India.

Although without Imran, Pakistan won easily against Australia who were strangled by Abdul Qadir and Tauseef Ahmed (by now Qadir had over-turned the orthodox wisdom that leg-spinners were too expensive for one-day cricket; as in other ways, Shane Warne would become his benefi-ciary). Qadir was again the destroyer, this time in partnership with Wasim Akram, as Pakistan brushed aside New Zealand.

Omar Noman estimates that a billion people watched the televised final between Pakistan and India, the reigning World Cup champions. They wit-nessed India begin with a rapid partnership of 117 from Gavaskar and Srikkanth, after which Gavaskar and Vengsarkar added 99. However, Imran and Wasim throttled them back to 246. Pakistan lost wickets steadily and their sheet anchor, Javed, resolved simply to bat through the remainder of the 50-over innings to prevent humiliation. After good partnerships with a promoted Qadir and Imran, Pakistan reached 211 for 6, needing 31 off the remaining three overs. The first was to be bowled by the paceman Chetan Sharma. Javed's partner, Manzoor Elahi, was caught off a skier. Wasim came in but the batsmen had crossed and Javed was facing. He hit the next ball for six over long-on. He and Wasim added four more off the next three deliveries. Sharma bowled what should have been the last ball of the over to Javed; instead it was a no-ball, square cut for two to bring up Javed's cen-tury. A single then gave Javed the strike for the next over to be bowled by Kapil Dev. Two overs, 18 to make.

Kapil's over produces seven runs, helped by an overthrow when the bowler takes a misguided shy at the stumps at the batting end. Javed to face the last over from Sharma, 11 needed. First ball. Javed slogs to long-on; one run taken, Wasim is run out at the bowler's end attempting a second. The young wicketkeeper Zulqarnain comes in.

Second ball: Javed, on-drive, four runs.

Third ball: Javed pulls from outside off-stump towards backward square leg, brilliant stop by Roger Binny restricts him to single.

Fourth ball: Zulqarnain instructed to slog. Bowled. The Pakistan number 11 walks out to receive the fifth. It is the hopeless Tauseef Ahmed. Javed instructs him to tap the ball and run a single.

Fifth ball: Tauseef duly taps to short cover, hurtles to non-striker's end, scrambles home as throw from India's best fielder, Azharuddin, misses stumps. Four now needed.

Sixth ball: Sharma tries for a yorker, not noticing that Javed has walked a long way in front of his crease. Full toss. Javed hits it out of the ground.[13] Pakistan have won their first major one-day trophy with the most famous shot in cricket history.*

NEUTRAL UMPIRES AT LAST

Pakistan now faced what would become the most important and exhilarating year in the nation's cricket history. First, a home series against the mighty West Indies, the greatest team in the world. Then they toured India, and spent the summer in England. Finally came the 1987 World Cup, after which Imran planned his retirement. 'I knew that I was about to embark on a cricketing journey that would make or break my reputation as a player and as captain,' he wrote later.[14]

The first Test of the West Indies series, at Faisalabad, was a gripping struggle and the scene of Abdul Qadir's greatest performance. On the opening day, the Pakistani batting collapsed against West Indian pace to 37 for 5, at which point Imran came to the wicket. The first ball he received was a rearing delivery that struck him on his shoulder, which swelled up and became stiff. Imran carried on, knowing that if he went off, Pakistan would collapse completely. For a time he steadied the innings with Salim Malik, but then Courtney Walsh broke Malik's arm. Imran was last out for a heroic

---

*It would be interesting to calculate the number of times Javed's shot has been viewed in the following twenty-seven years. If one accepts Noman's original estimate of a billion viewers when it happened, the subsequent audience could easily be 10 billion, considerably more than the world's current population. The shot may have saved a large sum for the notorius Dawood Ibrahim, the underworld leader, now a fugitive. (See www.interpol.int/notice/search-wanted/1993-14193 and 'Profile: India's fugitive gangster', news.bbc.co.uk/1/hi/world/south-asia/4775531/stm; see also 'Dawood was at his daughter's marriage', *Times of India*, 30 July 2005.) According to Dilip Vengsarkar, he had offered each Indian a Toyota car in the event of victory: see *Dawn*, 29 October 2013. Ibrahim's daughter later married Javed's son.

61 out of 159. West Indies took a lead of 89 on first innings, despite Wasim's six wickets.

In Pakistan's second innings, Salim Yousuf, as nightwatchman, occupied 46 overs in scoring 61, Mohsin Khan and Qasim Omar made forties and Javed grafted 30 in three hours. But Pakistan led by only 135 when Wasim came out at number 9 to join Imran, with Malik in the pavilion, nursing the arm broken by Walsh.

Wasim put on 34 with Imran. Tauseef Ahmed came to join him and kept his wicket intact while Wasim whacked sixes off the West Indies fast bowlers. When Tauseef was finally bowled by Courtney Walsh, they had added another 38 – at which point Malik came out with his arm in plaster, and hung on for another 32 runs, while Wasim completed his first Test half-century.

West Indies needed 240 in four sessions. The first was enough to destroy them. Imran took four wickets, and Qadir grabbed the other six for just 16. The West Indies were skittled out for 53, then their lowest score.*

In the second Test at Lahore, West Indies took revenge with an innings victory – even though they totalled only 240. Malcolm Marshall took six wickets, Walsh seven, and the less familiar Tony Gray four, in an irresistible combination of pace bowling on a suspect wicket. Qasim Omar, struck in the face by Walsh, joined Malik on the casualty list.

The third Test at Karachi was a draw earned by late heroics. Viv Richards's 70 took West Indies to 240. Pakistan replied with 239 thanks to gritty fifties from Ramiz Raja and Javed. Imran enjoyed the Karachi sea breeze again in the West Indies second innings, with a burst of five wickets for 11. Desmond Haynes carried his bat for 88 and Pakistan were set 213 to win. By tea on the last day, Pakistan were 95 for 7 with Imran still at the crease. Again, Tauseef served Pakistan as a batsman, and was still there when the umpires called off the match for bad light. They were Indian umpires, on Imran's insistence; at last Pakistan had achieved their objective of neutral umpires. They contributed to a far more harmonious series than usual.[15]

---

*Since then, lowered to 47 against England at Kingston, Jamaica, in 2003–04.

INDIA CONQUERED ON A 'RESULT' PITCH

India did not return the compliment of neutral umpires when Imran took Pakistan on a five-Test tour in 1986–87, lasting two months in blistering-hot weather. This was a difficult series because of renewed border tensions between the two countries, leading to occasional crowd troubles, in which Pakistan boundary fielders were hit by stones and fruit. In the fourth Test they took to wearing helmets in the deep to protect themselves. The fifth and deciding Test match at Bangalore, in which India chased 221 for a fourth innings victory, was one of the greatest in history.

The Pakistanis took the one-day series 5–1. India's one win came fortuitously from Abdul Qadir, who ran himself out when the scores were level off the last ball. In the excitement, he had forgotten the rules. Pakistan would have won if he had kept his wicket intact.[16]

The first four Tests conformed to the recent pattern and were high-scoring draws. In the first, at Madras, Shoaib Mohammad scored a painstaking maiden century, Javed Miandad was run out six runs short, and Wasim Akram smashed 62 with five sixes and six fours. Imran, at number 8, scored an unbeaten 135 (5 sixes, 14 fours), sharing an unbroken partnership of 81 with – yet again – Tauseef Ahmed. India made 527 in reply to 487, with a spectacular hundred from Kris Srikkanth, and Pakistan batted out the remainder of the match with only three wickets down.

Pakistan were in trouble in the second Test at Calcutta, despite Sunil Gavaskar's mysterious withdrawal for 'personal reasons'.[17] They narrowly avoided following on to India's 409 thanks to Salim Yousuf, the first of many wicketkeepers after Wasim Bari whose batting was more useful than their keeping. India batted too slowly in their second innings to give themselves a chance of victory.

Test cricket came to Rajasthan for the first time when the third Test was held at Jaipur. Gavaskar returned and was dramatically dismissed by Imran's first ball, which was edged onto his pad and caught at slip by Javed. On the second day, the main drama was the surprise visit of General Zia, attempting 'cricket diplomacy' with the Indian prime minister Rajiv Gandhi. The background to Zia's initiative, which took Gandhi by surprise, was an Indian military build-up in the Rajasthan desert which had provoked an alarmed response. Zia was seen by millions of Indian television viewers, talking affably with Indian players and fans. He hailed a century by India's Mohammad Azharuddin, tactfully not mentioning his Muslim faith. Zia said: 'Cricket for peace is my mission ... My sole purpose was to come and watch good cricket and in the process meet with the prime minister and see how we could solve our problems.' Zia had a public relations success, getting a friendly reception from fans and players. Former Indian captain Bishan Bedi called him a 'warm-hearted man' in his syndicated newspaper column. The visit did help to secure a reduction in the military confrontation in Rajasthan, but Zia won no concessions on the main issue of Kashmir.[18]

As for watching good cricket, India plodded to 459 for 8 and declared after adding six more meaningless runs the next morning. Pakistan were in some danger of following on, until Imran scored 66 not out – yet another productive last-wicket partnership with Tauseef. The only other drama was the mysterious sawdust which appeared on the pitch after thunderstorms. Imran claimed that it had been applied illegally; the Indians said that it had been blown there by accident. The match petered out to a draw, as did the fourth Test at Ahmedabad.

The last Test was at Bangalore. Worried by vanishing crowds, the authorities left the pitch underprepared to produce some kind of result. As a consequence, Pakistan's selectors made a crucial last-minute decision, with Iqbal Qasim coming in for Abdul Qadir. Imran was pressed to make the crucial change by Javed, Mudassar and, unselfishly, by Qadir himself, who had managed only four wickets in the series at over 60 apiece.[19]

India's young left-arm spinner Maninder Singh drew first blood, taking seven for 27 as Pakistan were dismissed for 116. Iqbal and Tauseef came on for Pakistan after a few wicketless overs from Imran and Wasim. A composed half-century from Vengsarkar took India to 126 for four. However, when he was dismissed, the two spinners cleaned up the remaining five wickets for just 19 runs and India led by only 29. Ramiz and Javed, astutely promoted to open by Imran, cleared the arrears and more importantly put pressure on Maninder Singh. Salim Malik scored 33 and Imran 39 as he faltered and attempted too much spin. Nonetheless, Pakistan led by only 159 when the eighth wicket fell. Tauseef now took part in another crucial stand, this time 51 with Salim Yousuf. Pakistan eventually set India 221 on a now spiteful pitch. They almost got there as

Gavaskar gave a masterclass in footwork and timing against the Pakistan spinners.[20] He had reached 96 when Qasim produced a ball which bounced violently and had him caught at slip. Withstanding a late desperate charge from Roger Binny (compared by Imran later to the 'death throes of a landed fish'[21]), Pakistan won a gripping match by 16 runs. It was only Pakistan's third overseas series win, and on return the team received extravagant public congratulations.[22]

Imran called it 'the sort of reception that makes a whole career worthwhile. The crowd that came to welcome us in Lahore stretched from the airport to the heart of the city.' However, for one player the homecoming was heartbreaking. Imran told his matchwinner, Iqbal Qasim, that he did not want him on the forthcoming tour of England. He still preferred Abdul Qadir. Poor Iqbal was devastated and stumbled out of the room, unconsoled by the offer of a post as a playing assistant manager. Later he wrote: 'I was never sure why Imran did not have much confidence in me. I admired him greatly. He was an exceptional man. I particularly admired his dedication to keep improving . . . I was not a great bowler but I did take 172 wickets and played a role in several victories outside Pakistan.'[23]

ENGLAND 1987

Pakistan's visit to England in 1987 was their first full-season tour since Javed Burki's calamitous visit in 1962. Imran had a clear objective – to lead the first Pakistan team to overcome England in England. However, for the Pakistanis the tour got off to an ugly start.[24]

Arriving at Heathrow the team was humiliatingly held up and made to stand aside, with other passengers looking on, while sniffer dogs went through their luggage. Meanwhile Pakistan's request to have David Constant – who had been criticised for poor decisions in the 1982 series – removed from the umpires' panel was rejected by the Test and County Cricket Board. Pakistan pointed out in reply that India had objected to Constant on a previous tour, and that he had been withdrawn from the Test series.[25]

Pakistan lost the one-day Texaco Trophy narrowly, by two matches to one, in spite of a century and two fifties from Javed. The third match at

Edgbaston was snatched by England by one wicket, when Pakistan missed a run-out. There were ugly clashes in the crowds, provoked by drunken National Front supporters abusing Pakistanis on the field and off.[26]

In the first Test at Manchester, the Pakistan attack was without Imran (injured weightlifting) and Abdul Qadir (still in Pakistan, caring for his wife after a mystery illness). Rain washed out the match with Pakistan five wickets down and still 307 behind England's first innings of 447. Qadir arrived just in time for the second Test, at Lord's, which was also washed out after England completed a first innings of 368.

Imran was fully fit and fired up for the third Test at Headingley. He chose to bowl first, and took three wickets, as did Wasim Akram and a third, rather under-rated seamer, Mohsin Kamal. England were all out for 136. Pakistan stumbled to 86 for four but were revived by a 99 from Salim Malik which was faultless until he drove a full toss to cover. He was supported by a dashing 50 from the young Ijaz Ahmed and a bludgeoned 43 from Wasim.

Imran produced one of his greatest spells of controlled late swing in the second innings, which earned him seven for 40, added to three wickets in the first. It was marred only by a ridiculous claim for a catch off Ian Botham by the wicketkeeper, Salim Yousuf, when the ball had bounced in front of him. Botham reacted and umpire Ken Palmer had to separate the two men. Imran reprimanded Yousuf, whose appeal had embarrassed his colleagues.

Some English tabloids made a meal of the incident but later David Gower wrote a telling comment about double standards, recalling a similar incident involving the England wicketkeeper Bob Taylor: 'Because it was Bob Taylor, it did not develop into an issue, but when a Pakistani player becomes involved in something similar, he is labelled a cheat.'[27]

After the atmosphere calmed down, Pakistan completed a satisfying win by an innings. The fourth Test at Edgbaston appeared to be meandering to a draw after two high-scoring first innings on the first four days, interrupted by rain. But then Pakistan inexplicably collapsed against Botham and Neil Foster. More rain and a stubborn innings of 37 by Imran kept England in the field most of the day, but Pakistan set a final target of only 124 in 18 overs. Now it was England's turn to panic as Imran and Wasim bowled unchanged. This being a Test match they could use deep-set fields and bowl wide of the stumps. They took two wickets apiece and there were three run-outs. Bill Athey was involved in all of them, and he became a national villain when he used seven overs to score 14.[28] England finished 15 runs short on 109 for 7, and the Pakistanis celebrated this result as joyfully as a victory.

For some years, Javed Miandad had been accused of underachieving in Test matches in England. In fifteen Test innings there, he had managed 355 runs with an average of 25.36. At The Oval he made up for lost time. He came in at 45 for 2 and when he left the score was 573 for 5, of which he had made 260. He wrote later: 'I remember that innings as one of my most pleasurable. I got my hundred and ended the first day not out on 131. I came out the next day feeling in total command and set my mind towards a big score.' Still seething over Imran's declaration against India which had strangled him on 280 not out, he began to dream again of breaking Sobers's record of 365 not out. 'I got to 200 and then 250 with no trouble at all. With my score at 260 I played an over from [fast bowler] Graham Dilley during which Dilley injured himself and decided to finish his over off a short run. My concentration finally lapsed and I handed him a low return catch, which he eagerly took. We ended up walking back to the pavilion together.'[29] Centuries from Salim Malik and Imran brought Pakistan to 708, then their record score.[30]

Abdul Qadir was another star who had been criticised for underperforming in England. His reply came in England's first innings, when all his tricks finally came off. He had his best Test figures to date of seven for 96 and England followed on. He added another three in the second innings but Pakistan were handicapped by Wasim's absence (for an emergency operation for appendicitis). England were saved by a long stand of 176 between Mike Gatting (150 not out) and an unusually restrained Botham, who scored his slowest Test fifty, in 252 minutes.[31]

With this 1–0 series victory, Imran was now at his zenith. He was indisputably the world's best all-rounder. In the Test series his figures were 191 runs at 47.75 and 21 wickets at 21.66, compared to his rival Botham's 232 runs at 33.14 and 7 wickets at 61.85. He had total authority over his team and he got what he wanted from Pakistan's administrators. He had silenced his critics in the media and among fans, even in Karachi. Everyone expected him to lead the team to victory in the forthcoming World Cup – the first to be held on home soil.

CRICKET WORLD CUP 1987

Before a ball was bowled, the 1987 World Cup was a massive victory for Pakistan. In alliance with India they wrested the competition from English hands and shifted it to the Indian subcontinent. Both countries had to overcome deep-seated prejudice about their ability to finance and organise a major international tournament.

The capture of the World Cup was built on a personal alliance between Nur Khan, then president of the BCCP, and his Indian counterpart NKP Salve. This was sealed over lunch the day after India's victory at Lord's in the 1983 World Cup final – when Salve was seething over the rejection of his request for four tickets for his party. Salve speculated what would have happened if the final had been held in India. Nur Khan picked up the cue instantly: 'Why can't we play the next World Cup in our countries?'[32] Salve took up the idea, realising instantly the strength of an Indo-Pakistan alliance. It would require delicate handling at governmental level but both men were well placed. Nur Khan was then on good terms with General Zia, who had appointed him, and Salve was actually a minister in Rajiv Gandhi's government.

Salve and Nur Khan then revived an idea of Kardar's and formed the Asian Cricket Council, in association with Sri Lanka, newly admitted as a Test-playing country. Bangladesh, Malaysia and Singapore were the other founder members and Salve became the first president. It signalled the arrival of a new voting bloc in world cricket.

Nur Khan and Salve worked successfully on their respective governments to release foreign exchange for the World Cup project and to invest in stadia and infrastructure. Salve used his connections to secure a lavish Indian business sponsor, Reliance Industries.[33] They put up 70 million rupees (equivalent to about £4.7 million at the official exchange rate) and enabled Salve and Nur Khan to promise 50 per cent more prize money than their English rivals. Shrewdly, they promised that the additional prize money would be shared equitably among all the ICC members.

The English put up one other major objection. The early twilight in India and Pakistan would make it impossible to complete 60-over matches (there were then no floodlit matches). Salve and Nur Khan had a simple answer: cut the matches to 50 overs (a reform which would also keep players fresher and produce more tight finishes).[34]

The Indo-Pakistan bid won by 16 votes to 12 at the ICC and both countries confounded their critics by a rapid improvement in infrastructure, logistics and ticketing arrangements, with Pakistan's marshalled by Nur Khan's lieutenant Arif Abbasi. Pakistan were allocated 10 of the 27 scheduled matches: three in the (revamped) National stadium in Karachi, two at the Gaddafi stadium in Lahore, one each in Peshawar, Rawalpindi, Gujranwala, Hyderabad and Faisalabad.

Since the southernmost Indian venue was Madras (now Chennai), the 1987 World Cup had the greatest geographical span of any single sporting event in history. Scyld Berry noted in *Wisden* that 'it was the equivalent of staging a tournament in Europe, barring only the Soviet Union, without quite the same facility of transport and communications.' Berry remarked that the Sri Lankans had to travel from Peshawar to Kanpur to Faisalabad and then to Pune for their group matches. However, he summed up his account: 'The fourth World Cup was more widely watched, more closely fought and more colourful than any of its three predecessors held in England.'[35] Significantly, it used neutral umpires.

In Pakistan expectations were immense. Led by Imran, they had their best-ever one-day side. Pakistan played all their group matches at home, gaining five victories out of six. One was especially satisfying. At Lahore against the West Indies, the last pair of Abdul Qadir and Saleem Jaffer needed 14 to win off the final over from Courtney Walsh. Qadir hit 13 of them, including a straight six, Saleem got the other and Pakistan were home. Off the last ball, Walsh could have run out the non-striker, Saleem, for backing up too far. He declined to do so and became a hero to the crowd of 50,000.[36]

Qadir and Imran were the main forces in Pakistan's early victories. Against England in Rawalpindi, Qadir took three wickets in his final over to strangle England's pursuit of a modest target. In the return match against England at Karachi, he again (with Imran) choked England's early bid for a giant total. Pakistan's lone blemish in the group matches was their last, meaningless match against the West Indies in Karachi, when the police used tear gas against protesting students.[37]

Amid overpowering national expectations, Pakistan faced Australia in the semi-final at Lahore. Australia batted solidly, until Imran's second spell produced three for 17. Pakistan had a setback when Salim Yousuf was hit in the mouth and Javed took over behind the stumps for 30 overs. He later prided himself on achieving a stumping and a run-out (and allowing no byes), but it made him exhausted when he came to bat. Another crucial misfortune was a misleading message to Imran on the field that Pakistan would have to bowl only 49 overs. He gave them all to his frontline bowlers, himself, Wasim, Tauseef and Qadir. But in the event, Pakistan had to bowl their full quota, and Imran, perforce, gave the last over to the fifth bowler, the inexperienced left-arm seamer Saleem Jaffer. Steve Waugh took 18 off it, lifting Pakistan's target to 268.

In reply, Pakistan lost three quick wickets for 38. Imran and Javed steadied things with a partnership of 112 in 26 overs, before Imran was given out by Dickie Bird, caught behind off the part-time spin of Allan Border. Pakistan needed seven an over. Salim Yousuf and Wasim struck a few blows but Javed was simply too tired to maintain the necessary momentum. Eventually on 70 he attempted a desperate shot against Bruce Reid and was bowled. The last three wickets found the task of scoring 56 beyond them, despite some blows by Qadir. The final margin of Australia's victory was the 18 runs scored off Jaffer's fatal last over.[38] 'I have never seen the Pakistani public so disappointed as they were after our semi-final defeat,' noted Imran afterwards. 'I had underestimated the depth of feeling about the World Cup; most of the people leaving the stadium had tears in their eyes.'[39]

The Pakistan fans turned on their idols, and there was a good audience for the charges laid by Sarfraz Nawaz (by now a member of parliament) that the match had been thrown to facilitate a betting coup. Javed was one of the players directly accused. Sarfraz also pointed the finger at Abdul Rahman Bukhatir, of Sharjah. They took Sarfraz to court, but the action eventually died of delay in the judicial system. It set a pattern for the future, in which Pakistan defeats were assumed to be the result of match-fixing.*

It was not the perfect moment but Imran nevertheless chose to retire from cricket. He was now thirty-five years old, a substantial age for a modern cricketer, and elderly for a strike bowler. He had enjoyed a fine

---

*Javed Miandad claimed that he received a tearful plea to drop the case from Sarfraz's movie-star wife, Rani. Javed Miandad, op. cit. pp.160–1.

career, even though the World Cup victory had eluded him. The death of his mother Shaukat, from cancer in 1985, had had a profound effect on him, and already he had received intimations that his life was to involve more than cricket. As was now customary, Javed Miandad became captain in Imran's absence.

THE SHAKOOR RANA INCIDENT

'I am sure there is a general view that with a coloured umpire it is often a question of integrity; with a white-skinned man the same mistake is called human error.'

– MIKE COWARD, AUSTRALIAN CRICKET WRITER AND HISTORIAN

The Palestinian literary theorist Edward Said famously noted that western writers and theorists were able to come to terms with the east only through stereotypes. He asserted that even those texts which claimed to be objective were undermined by a bias which western scholars have been unable even to recognise. In essence, Said's central thesis asserted that western scholarship had appropriated eastern art, history, politics and culture in order to create a narrative which validated external political and economic domination. 'Very little of the detail, the human density, the passion of Arab-Muslim life has entered the awareness of even those people whose profession it is to report the Arab world,' wrote Said.

Said maintained that western study of Islam was primarily an act of self-affirmation by the west. Under the guise of objective reporting, something more sinister was going on – religious and racial discrimination as a tool of imperial domination. Western scholars, asserted Said, had got hold of the rich history and culture of Islam and placed European values at the heart of the story. Western scholarship, considered Said, presented the east as irrational, weak and feminine. By contrast the west was rational, strong and male. The east could therefore be portrayed as an unhappy deviation from the virtuous and dominant west.

In his presentation of this argument, Said concentrated on literary and academic texts, thus overlooking one interesting resource – western involvement with Muslim sport. The history of Anglo-Pakistani cricket offers a vivid illustration of many of the themes explored by the late Edward Said, and in an especially crude form. I have already examined British condescension in the context of the abduction of Idris Baig in 1955–56. Three decades later, history repeated itself.

ENGLAND IN PAKISTAN 1987–88

Even before it began, the England tour of Pakistan looked like a mistake. It attracted little interest from Pakistani fans, coming so soon after the disappointment of the World Cup. Without the resting Ian Botham, the England team was lacklustre, and England captain Mike Gatting's temperament was not equal to the stresses of this tour.[1]

As is often the case with England tours of Pakistan, the players were surly. 'The siege mentality settled in on us early,' remarked Graham Gooch later.[2] The batsman Bill Athey put it more succinctly: 'The sooner we get home, the fuckin' better.'[3] The trouble began with the first Test in Lahore at the end of November.

England, batting first on a pitch which had been specially prepared to suit Pakistan's spinners, were bowled out for 191 by Abdul Qadir, who took nine wickets for 56, still the best analysis by a Pakistani in a Test match. Pakistan, assisted by one of Mudassar Nazar's remorseless centuries, made 392.

When England batted again Chris Broad, the England opening batsman, was given out caught at the wicket off Iqbal Qasim. He remained at the wicket. 'I didn't hit it, I'm not going,' he declared. 'You can like it or lump it, I'm staying.'[4] After the best part of a minute had passed Graham Gooch, Broad's batting partner (who later announced he had heard 'a noise of some sort as the ball passed the bat') persuaded him to walk off.

A well-run cricket team might have despatched Broad on the first flight home. Instead, the England tour manager, Peter Lush, hitherto a public relations man,[5] let Broad off with a 'stern reprimand'. At the end of the match, which England lost by an innings and 87 runs, Gatting accused the Pakistan umpires of cheating: 'We knew roughly what to expect but never imagined it would be quite so blatant. They were desperate to win a Test match, but if I was them, I wouldn't be very happy about the way they did it.'[6]

Before the second Test, England played a Punjab Chief Minister's XI. It did not give them much respite, because they encountered a seventeen-year-old copy of Qadir, who took six for 81. Mushtaq Ahmed had announced himself.

Chris Broad's petulance in the first Test set the tone for the events of the following Test at the Iqbal stadium, Faisalabad in early December. Here England got off to a fine start. Thanks to a patient 116 from Broad and a sparkling 79 (off 81 balls) from Gatting, they reached 292. Pakistan then collapsed, and with three deliveries left for play at the end of the second day their score stood at 106 for 5 and they were in danger of defeat. This was the stage when Gatting's infamous confrontation with umpire Shakoor Rana took place.

Shakoor Rana was one of four brothers to play first-class cricket. His brothers Shafqat and Azmat won Test caps, but Shakoor toiled in club and domestic cricket.* In eleven first-class matches over fifteen years, he managed a total of 226 runs and 11 wickets. However, his brother Shafqat remembers him as a courageous player and a tough-minded captain at the City Gymkhana club. He feared no one as a player or later as an umpire. 'He always gave his decisions quickly and stuck by them. When Mohsin Khan once questioned one of his lbws, my brother gave him outrageous decisions in the next two matches when they met, until Mohsin Khan apologised.'[7]

Shakoor Rana had stood in fourteen Tests since 1974–75, which made him Pakistan's senior Test umpire. Three had produced controversies. In his very first Test, the West Indian Lance Gibbs made a rude protest against his no-ball call (Gibbs was a veteran off-spinner with a model action, who had almost never been no-balled). Shakoor was angered, and after a rest day meeting between him, Gerry Alexander (the West Indian manager) and

---

*His two sons, Mansoor Rana and Maqsood Rana, both gained ODI caps for Pakistan.

Clive Lloyd (their captain), he settled for an apology, by Lloyd. During the 1978–79 Indian series, there was a flare-up between Shakoor, Sunil Gavaskar and Bishan Bedi, when he tried to warn the Indian captain about one of his bowlers running on the pitch. This was settled by an apology from the Indian manager, the Maharajah of Baroda.[8]

Then there was the Jeremy Coney incident in the series against New Zealand in 1984–85. Coney led his team off during the third Test at Karachi after an appeal for caught behind against Javed Miandad had been rejected by Shakoor Rana. Coney's anger is especially noteworthy because he was one of the most affable men to captain any Test side.[9]

Shakoor Rana had not been in charge during the first Test of the England tour, and was not therefore implicated in the earlier allegations of bias. Indeed the umpiring seems to have been fair up to this point in the second Test. The thirty-eight-year-old English spinner Eddie Hemmings was bowling against Salim Malik. Before Hemmings came into bowl, Gatting had called up one of his fielders, David Capel, from the deep to prevent a single being taken. As Hemmings started his run-up, Gatting signalled to Capel that he had come close enough. Shakoor Rana, who was standing at square leg, halted play in order to inform Malik of Capel's new position. This is how *Wisden* summarised the situation: 'Shakoor claimed that Gatting had been unfairly moving the fielder behind the bowler's back; Gatting informed the umpire that he was, in his opinion, overstepping the bounds.* The language employed throughout the discourse was basic.'†

The two at once engaged in their famous face-to-face, finger-wagging confrontation, photographs of which were flashed around the world. Later Gatting claimed that Shakoor Rana swore at him first, as well as calling him a cheat. Shakoor made similar claims against Gatting, and demanded an

---

*There was nothing in the laws that explicitly prevented Gatting moving a fielder around as the ball was being bowled. However, there is an argument that Gatting was in breach of convention. For an invaluable discussion of that convention, see Berry, op. cit. p.146.

†For the English point of view, see Stephen Chalke, *Micky Stewart and the Changing Face of Cricket*, pp.250–9. Stewart claims that Shakoor Rana called Gatting a 'fucking cheating bastard', and that 14 of the first 30 wickets to fall to Pakistan in the series were 'victims of umpires' errors.' Stewart also asserts that the entire Pakistan cricket team were called for a secret meeting with General Zia: 'They had all been lined up in front of the President and ordered to win the match.' Whatever the veracity of Stewart's claims, Chalke's book strongly conveys the mood of martyrdom in the English camp. Stewart's assertion that General Zia was the *eminence grise* behind Pakistan's questionable umpiring decisions gains support from Berry, pp.109–10.

apology before play could be restarted.* This Gatting refused to do without a reciprocal apology.

The third day's play was therefore abandoned. Matters were made yet more complicated by Ijaz Butt, secretary of the BCCP. We have already met Butt as a young wicketkeeper-batsman selected for the Pakistan tour of West Indies in the late 1950s. We shall meet him again as the baffled and irate chairman of the Pakistan Cricket Board unable to cope with the spot-fixing affair of summer 2010. Butt had an instinct for being the wrong man in the wrong place at the wrong time.

On the afternoon of the abandoned third day, with the situation still completely unresolved, Butt suddenly left Faisalabad for Lahore, forcing Peter Lush, the MCC manager, to follow him. Once he had reached Lahore, Lush sought to meet the BCCP president Lt Gen. Safdar Butt (no relation to Ijaz), but was told that he was out to dinner.[10] It was the following morning before Lush could make contact with either Butt, and by then a full day's play had been lost.

England had been in a potentially match-winning position when the Gatting-Shakoor episode took place at the end of the second day. By the time it restarted, the match was to all intents and purposes dead. Rain and bad light further truncated proceedings.

The third Test at Karachi was another draw, though noteworthy for Qadir's match figures: 104.4-31-186-10. Virtually no spectators attended the game, and a sordid Test series came to a joyless end.

There was one final twist. It emerged that Raman Subba Row, chairman of the Test and County Cricket Board, agreed to pay £1,000 to each England player as a 'hardship bonus', thus appearing to endorse the England captain's behaviour.

England would not play another Test series against Pakistan for five years, and would not visit the country again for thirteen. Just over two years later Mike Gatting, the main protagonist, was to lead the 1990 rebel tour of South Africa. Four other members of the 1987 touring side (Athey, Broad,

---

*See Javed Miandad's account; 'It is often claimed that I was the one who urged Shakoor Rana to demand an apology from Mike Gatting. This is absolutely true. "You must insist on an apology," I told Umpire Rana when he asked for my opinion on the situation. I wanted the apology not as the opposing captain but as a Pakistani. Gatting's audacity in yelling at Umpire Rana was an insult to Pakistan. Can you imagine what the English would have demanded had I berated an English umpire the way Gatting had Shakoor Rana?' Miandad, p.251.

John Emburey and Neil Foster) would join Gatting on that disreputable enterprise. It is hard to come to grips with the set of values which led the England cricket captain to take such a strong stand against allegedly poor Pakistan umpiring, yet be relaxed enough about apartheid to take a rebel squad to South Africa.

In addition, two members of the side had taken part in the earlier 1982 English rebel tour of South Africa. They were Gooch, who captained the team, and Emburey, who was thus a member of both rebel tours. It was this morally troubled England team that faced a dismal future in the wake of the Shakoor Rana affair. Pakistan, on the other hand, were going from strength to strength, and greatness lay ahead.

GUIDANCE FROM A HOLY MAN

While England were touring Pakistan, Imran Khan went on a shooting trip with two friends 100 miles north of Lahore. After the shoot, the host suggested that they should go and visit a holy man, Baba Chala, who lived in a village just a few miles away from the Indian border.

The host asked Baba Chala how Imran should spend the rest of his life. But Chala looked at Imran and said that he had not yet left his profession. All three sportsmen answered that Imran had retired. But Chala replied: 'It is the will of Allah; you are still in the game.'[11] Pressure was indeed mounting on Imran to return. The Pakistan Cricket Board formally asked him; he declined. There were public demonstrations, while, according to Shuja-ud-Din, 'some even went to the extent of a hunger strike in front of his house begging him to come out of retirement.' A series was looming against the West Indies and General Zia uttered a personal plea. Eventually Imran was unable to resist.[12]

Javed Miandad resigned, once again showing extraordinary grace, self-knowledge and understanding: 'I had long ago come to terms with having to vacate the captaincy whenever Imran was available. His retirement had been premature and emotionally motivated, and I think he also realised that his campaign for a cancer hospital in Lahore would be better served if he continued in international cricket.'[13]

Imran's return began dreadfully as the West Indies whitewashed Pakistan

5–0 in the one-day series. In the second match, Imran earned huge credit from West Indian fans by recalling Desmond Haynes after a successful lbw appeal; he accepted Haynes's plea that he had hit the ball first.[14]

Team morale was low before the first Test in Georgetown, but Imran laid his own anxieties to rest with one of his outstanding bowling performances, seven for 80, despite a bruised toe. West Indies were all out for 292. In reply, Javed Miandad anchored the Pakistan innings with a six-hour century, coming in at 57 for 2. He faced a barrage of bouncers and bad language, and Winston Benjamin deliberately bowled some balls from far beyond the bowling crease in order to make them more physically terrifying. But according to Javed, 'It was just the stimulus I needed to raise my game. I started taunting the bowlers. I pointed my chest at Ambrose: "try and hit me and I'll show you," I told him when he dug another one near his feet.'[15] Javed was supported by Salim Yousuf (62), Shoaib Mohammad (46) and above all, by Mr Extras, who made his record score of 71 in Tests, with 38 no-balls. Pakistan got a lead of 143. Imran took four for 41 in West Indies' second innings, there were three wickets for Abdul Qadir and two for the rarely seen off-spin of Shoaib Mohammad. Pakistan needed only 30 and won by nine wickets. It was the West Indies' first home defeat for a decade.

The second Test at Port of Spain began with West Indies dismissed for 174, again by the tandem of Imran (4–38) and Qadir (4–83). Pakistan subsided to 68 for 7 but were revived by Salim Malik (66) and Salim Yousuf (39), to take a lead of 20. Centuries for Viv Richards and Jeff Dujon allowed West Indies to set a big target. The West Indies were tottering at 80 for 4 when Richards survived an lbw appeal. Salim Yousuf expressed anger and the two were heading for a brawl when they were separated by Imran and umpire Clyde Cumberbatch.[16]

Pakistan needed 372 for victory. Victory seemed unlikely at 67 for 3 but Javed set himself to make another long hundred. He assembled 102 in seven hours and 16 minutes, supported by Ijaz Ahmed (43) and, again, Salim Yousuf (35). Pakistan needed 80 off the last 20 overs and the feared West Indian attack seemed a spent force. Richards then turned to his own very occasional off-spin. He dismissed Ijaz and Salim, and the last man, Qadir, had to block the last five balls to secure Pakistan a draw.

After this performance, Pakistan felt confident of taking the series at Bridgetown. The sides were evenly matched on first innings, 309 to

Pakistan, 306 to the West Indies. Pakistan set 268 as a victory target. Shoaib made a second composed fifty before falling to the fatal part-timer, Viv Richards. Mudassar Nazar made 41, Imran a patient 43 and Salim 28 despite a broken nose. Then Wasim Akram bowled faster than the West Indian battery, and added four for 73 to the three wickets he captured in the first innings. When Pakistan reduced West Indies to 207 for 8 they had victory in their pockets, but the umpires then gave two contentious decisions against the not-out batsmen. One reprieved the tail-ender Benjamin (given not out lbw against Imran), the other saved the last recognised batsman Dujon (given not out caught silly-point off Qadir). This upset the bowler so much that it led him into a brawl with an insulting spectator.* The batsmen could not be parted, and West Indies scraped a two-wicket victory to level a brilliant series.

Later Qadir would reflect more calmly on these scintillating Tests. 'We won the series and under neutral umpires these doubts about who really won would not continue to linger. But the level at which the game was played was a great credit to both sides. This was almost as good as cricket can get.'[17]

DEMOCRACY RESTORED

On 17 August 1988 General Zia was killed in an air crash, along with the American ambassador to Pakistan, Arnold Raphel, the head of the US military mission to Pakistan, General Herbert Wassom, and a number of Pakistani generals. The origins of the crash are mysterious to this day,[18] although it was all but certainly sabotage.

Zia's authority had already been weakened by the growth of the ethnic violence in Karachi. It was further shaken by the return of Benazir Bhutto and her subsequent series of public speeches, by an explosion at an army ordnance depot near Islamabad which killed hundreds of people, and his dismissal of the independent-minded prime minister, Mohammad Khan Junejo. Under pressure from all the banned opposition parties, Zia had

---

*Arif Abbasi arranged for him to be paid $1,000 out of court to get Abdul Qadir home without facing charges. Arif Abbasi: personal interview.

promised nationwide elections in November. These duly took place, without the restrictions on political parties planned by Zia. Benazir Bhutto's PPP won the largest number of seats, 94, in the National Assembly. It left her short of an overall majority. However, the new acting president, Ghulam Ishaq Khan, a former civil servant who had served her father as defence secretary and then served Zia as finance minister, invited her to form a government. In the provincial elections, the Muslim League under Nawaz Sharif and his brother, Shahbaz, took power in Punjab. This inaugurated a long period of two-party dynastic politics in Pakistan.[19]

CORRUPTION AND PATRONAGE

As the first woman to rule Pakistan, or indeed any Muslim state, with a magnetic personality, educated at Harvard and Oxford, Benazir Bhutto benefited from 'a sustained love affair with Western politicians and journalists.'[20] They gave her the image of a decisive moderniser and Mrs Thatcher's nickname of Iron Lady. In practice, her first administration was notably cautious and pre-occupied by placating Pakistan's vested interests, particularly the armed forces and the religious parties. In spite of her progressive rhetoric, she left Zia's Islamist laws in place. Alone among Pakistani governments, in her first premiership she failed to pass a single piece of legislation.[21]

Its main feature was a spectacular rise in patronage and kickbacks, spearheaded by Asif Ali Zardari, whom she had married for dynastic reasons in 1987. Zardari quickly became known as Mr Ten Per Cent (although he has been frequently accused, Zardari has yet to be convicted of corruption in any court).[22] The new government inaugurated a borrowing spree, continued by her successor, which doubled Pakistan's foreign debt from $13 billion left by Zia to £26 billion in 1999. Most of this money was totally unaccounted for.[23]

Pakistan's cricket administration was unaffected by the new regime. In spite of Arif Abbasi's successful commercial initiatives, and the success of the 1987 World Cup, Pakistan cricket was not a major source of income or patronage when Benazir Bhutto first took power. Partly for that reason and partly for fear of confronting the armed forces, she left in place Zia's nominee as chairman of the cricket board, General Zahid Ali Akbar Khan. He remained there even when she clashed with him over his administration of Pakistan's atomic weapons programme and forced his retirement from the army.[24]

In 1990, her political fortunes waned sharply. The economy worsened when the United States imposed sanctions against Pakistan over its nuclear programme, while she and her husband were tarnished by revelations about corruption and incompetence of their appointees. She clashed repeatedly with the conservative president Ishaq Khan, who eventually dismissed her and her government in favour of Nawaz Sharif's Muslim League.[25]

WHINGEING AUSSIES

Later in 1988, it was the turn of the unhappy Australians to tour Pakistan. The series was scheduled, for reasons connected with the domestic Australian season, for boiling-hot September. Imran boycotted the tour because of that.

As ever, Javed Miandad stepped in as captain. He scored a double-century in the first Test in Karachi, and then Iqbal Qasim came back into the picture by taking nine for 84 in 64 overs straddling both Australian innings. With support from Abdul Qadir and the restored Tauseef Ahmed, Pakistan won by an innings.

The Australians complained about almost everything: the state of the pitch, the heat and, above all, the umpiring of Mahboob Shah. They protested demonstratively at the Pakistan officials' room in Karachi and at a press conference – called exclusively for Australian journalists. Like Mike Gatting before him, the Australian captain, Allan Border, threatened to go home.[26] In reply, Arif Abbasi gave a strong defence of Mahboob Shah: 'he is one of the best in the world and his impartiality is well recognised.' He had stood in the World Cup final in Calcutta in 1987, which Australia won; Arif suggested tartly that the Australians could not catch (they dropped thirteen in the first two Tests) and could not play spin.[27] In a public show of solidarity, Mahboob Shah was retained for the second Test, at Faisalabad, which was drawn.

The comparison with the performance by Mike Gatting's England a year earlier is unavoidable. Afterwards the Australian cricket writer Mike Coward wrote a troubling account of the tour.[28] He said that 'with few exceptions, the behaviour of the [Australian] team was so irrational and the prejudices so deep that it became impossible for journalists to distinguish between events just and unjust.' Coward added that the Australians were, at the least, 'guilty of elitism, behaving as they would not have behaved elsewhere in the cricket world and condoning behaviour they would not have condoned elsewhere in the cricket world.'[29]

A CRICKET-LOVING PRIME MINISTER

When Nawaz Sharif succeeded Benazir Bhutto as prime minister in November 1990, he continued her regime of patronage, with different beneficiaries. However, he differed from her in having a genuine love of cricket. He was proud of his first-class record, one appearance as a batsman for the powerful Railways team against PIA B in 1973–74. Opening the batting, he was out for a duck, one of just three first-class victims for the seam bowler, Shahid Ahmed Etemad. Nawaz Sharif did not bowl or take a catch, and he did not get a second chance at the crease because his team won by an innings. He was a little more successful in 1987, by then chief minister for the Punjab, opening for Lahore Gymkhana in a warm-up match against England before the World Cup. He notched a single before being bowled by Phil DeFreitas.

Three days earlier he had appointed himself captain of Pakistan's team to play the West Indies in another warm-up match. Imran, the man he displaced, was taken aback, but assumed that this would be an honorary role and that he would watch the match from the dressing room. To Imran's greater amazement, after tossing up against the West Indies captain, Viv Richards, Nawaz Sharif decided to open the innings again against one of the fastest attacks in history. His partner, the experienced Mudassar Nazar, wore full protection, 'while Sharif simply had his batting pads, a floppy hat – and a smile ... I quickly asked if there was an ambulance ready.'

The first ball, from the giant Patrick Patterson, hit the wicketkeeper's gloves before Nawaz Sharif could raise his bat. 'Mercifully, the second was straight at the stumps and before he could move his stumps lay shattered.'[30]

However, Nawaz Sharif met with greater success at club level. As prime minister he would represent the Lahore Gymkhana in weekend matches, flying down from Islamabad with an entourage. Fellow players and spectators have recalled to me a solid but strokemaking batsman, but added that the prime minister was undoubtedly helped by the choice of umpire – usually a political ally. More often than not, the following day's newspapers would hail another sparkling hundred.

In spite of his cricketing interest, Nawaz Sharif, like Benazir Bhutto, kept his hands off Pakistan's cricket administration. He too left General Zahid Ali Akbar Khan in place. This in itself was good news for Imran, since the general was a cousin of his. Even better, Nawaz Sharif gave him the important and lucrative job of chairman of the Water and Power Development Authority. This basically ensured that Imran got his wishes in Pakistan cricket without interference from above. On the rare occasions when this was threatened, he was ably protected by Javed Burki, as chairman of selectors, and Intikhab Alam, his team manager.[31] In many respects, the general was an ideal choice as chairman and he completed four years under three different governments. He may have had other pre-occupations, as was suggested over twenty years later, when he was detained in Bosnia on a request by Interpol. Pakistan's National Accountability Bureau claimed that he owned assets valued at 267 million rupees (equivalent to around £1.75 million), rather more than could be explained by his combined official salaries from cricket, water and power.[32] He was later released because Pakistan had no extradition treaty with Bosnia.[33]

CORNERED TIGERS

'We should go out there and fight like cornered tigers.'

– IMRAN KHAN

Pakistan were in disarray going into the 1992 World Cup held in Australia and New Zealand. Waqar Younis was injured, and missed the event altogether. Imran was obliged to drop out of the opening games because of injury, and in any case his days as a great bowler were over. Then there was the Javed Miandad problem. His form with the bat was so poor that he was originally omitted from the squad. This left him aggrieved, since he had received promises of selection from Imran and the tour manager, Intikhab Alam. Large sections of the media were on his back and he was convinced that he was the victim of a dark plot.[1]

Only at the last moment did Javed convince the selectors that he was fit and that his back would stand up to the stress of the tournament. According to Arif Abbasi, 'they announced Javed Miandad as vice-captain without the knowledge of either Imran Khan or Salim Malik, who thought *he* was the vice-captain. When he [Javed] was put on the plane to Australia, Imran did not know about his departure.'[2] It was an inspired decision – Javed's consistency under pressure took Pakistan into the later rounds and steadied them in the final itself. His selection gave him a joint record with Imran as the only men to have played in every World Cup.[3]

Pakistan's start was abysmal. Despite Ramiz Raja's century, they went down by ten wickets to the West Indies, Imran missing with a shoulder injury. An easy win over Zimbabwe (Aamer Sohail 114) was followed by a dismal all-out 74 against England, destroyed by the usually amiable seam of Derek Pringle. Rain reprieved Pakistan, so they came out of the game with a precious point. Against their arch-enemy India, they fell well short of a gettable 216, despite 62 from Sohail. Against South Africa they could not manage to overhaul 211, reduced by rain to 194 in 36 overs. Ramiz was missing with a shoulder injury and Javed was down with gastritis. Everything seemed to be against Pakistan. With three points from five games, they needed to win all their remaining group matches to survive.

It was at this point that Imran gave the team the speech of his life. 'We have nothing to lose. We should go out there and fight like cornered tigers.'[4] It produced a revival against Australia, dismissed by Mushtaq Ahmed and Aaqib Javed while pursuing a modest Pakistan score of 220, in which Sohail made 76 and Javed 46 despite still feeling weak from illness. Characteristically, he remembered 'one brawl of a match with tempers flaring on both sides.' The revival continued with a win over Sri Lanka, but Pakistan still needed to defeat the hitherto unbeaten New Zealanders to have a hope of survival. Even then, their fate was not in their hands. They also needed Australia to beat West Indies.

Pakistan completed their task against New Zealand, crushing them in the last group match by overhauling a paltry total of 166, with the loss of three wickets. Ramiz scored a fine unbeaten century and Javed contributed 30. Australia obliged them by defending a total of 216 against West Indies.

In their unexpected semi-final, Pakistan faced the well-organised New Zealanders in front of their home crowd at Eden Park, Auckland. Their captain Martin Crowe made 91. Luckily for Pakistan he was overcome by cramp, and then run out by his runner. In Pakistan's reply, Ramiz and Imran each made 44 but when Malik was out at 140, Pakistan had only 15 overs left to score 123. To Javed's surprise, Inzamam-ul-Haq was sent out to join him. 'He seemed nervous and overawed and looked like he had seen a ghost.'[5]

His young partner had been ill before the semi-final. His manager, Intikhab Alam, had given him some sleeping pills but they had made him throw up seven times and he had got little sleep. Inzamam had actually told Imran that he was too ill to play, but Imran (showing great faith) insisted,* and found a doctor who treated him on the massage table. Inzamam missed the opening overs of New Zealand's innings and went off the field several times.

Javed spoke to the young man reassuringly, and Inzamam soon found the middle of his bat. He recalls 'with God's guidance, I was able to play a great innings, although I was still feeling weak.'[6] He made 60 off 37 balls, most of them from the supposedly unhittable New Zealand containment bowlers, Chris Harris and Gavin Larsen. Javed, who had come in on 84 for 2, was unbeaten with 57 in the winning score of 264.

In the final against England, played on 25 March at the Melbourne Cricket Ground, Pakistan again suffered early blows. The opening batsmen Sohail and Ramiz fell early, thus bringing the old masters Imran and Javed together. 'We had been here before,' wrote Javed Miandad later. 'Both of us knew the loss of another wicket would trigger a batting collapse. The plan was simple. We absolutely had to bat out our full fifty overs.'† Scoring, in front of an almost completely silent crowd of 87,182 at the MCG, was slow. At one point just four runs came from the bat in 60 balls. Many watching wondered whether Imran and Javed had got their strategy wrong. At the halfway point of the innings, Pakistan had made only 70, at which point Imran walked down the wicket to Javed and said he would go for his shots. Then followed a gradual acceleration, and by the time Javed (who was suffering intense stomach pains in the second half of his innings) fell to Richard Illingworth for 58 they had put on 139 in 31 overs. Imran was then dismissed for 72 from 115 balls. He and Javed had done their job by creating a platform for the later batsmen. Inzamam hit 42 off 46 balls and Wasim Akram 33 off 21 as Pakistan reached 249.

This total looked a bit more defendable when Ian Botham, as a pinch-hitting opener, was caught behind off Wasim. He showed resentment at the

---

*Imran made Inzamam consider his own circumstances; he was having a cortisone injection into a damaged shoulder cartilage. 'Even if you have to be carried on the field in a stretcher you're playing,' he told him. Imran Khan: personal interview.

†Javed Miandad, op. cit. p.205. Imran has also pointed out to me that for this World Cup alone the bowlers *at each end* were given a new ball, so that early batsmen had to face a ball which kept its bounce and movement for longer than usual. Imran Khan: personal interview. The rule has been restored for the next World Cup in 2015.

decision; Sohail sent him on his way with a jibe about his mother-in-law.*
Aaqib Javed and Mushtaq Ahmed (used daringly by Imran) made further
inroads. But a partnership of 72 between Neil Fairbrother and Allan Lamb
left England well placed at 141 for 4.

Imran then called Wasim back for his second spell. Javed here describes
what happened next: 'In one of the defining moments of our cricket history,
Wasim took the ball and in the space of two unplayable deliveries all but
secured the World Cup for Pakistan.' The first swung late and bowled Lamb;
the second, immediately after, swung in viciously and cut in half the all-
rounder Chris Lewis for a first-ball duck. Fairbrother gave England some hope
by adding 39 with Dermot Reeve, but Pakistan finished off England 22 runs
short. Imran had the satisfaction of dismissing the last man, Illingworth.

Many players prostrated themselves to Allah on the MCG turf.[7] Javed,
who had been sick in the pavilion, ran onto the ground to celebrate. In his
autobiography he recorded how, when he picked out Imran, 'I patted him
on the shoulder so he could turn around and see me, and we locked in a
long embrace. There was so much to say, but neither of us spoke. I suppose
it was the kind of moment too great for mere words.'[8]

Pakistan won a tournament which had been played during Ramadan. It
seemed that a nation's prayers had been answered. Shuja-ud-Din noted that
'even the dacoits in the interior of Sindh failed to hide their delight, while
still in their hideouts, by firing their weapons.'

It was the greatest triumph in Pakistan's cricketing history, which their politicians quickly tried to exploit. The president, Ghulam Ishaq Khan, who was also
the BCCP patron, gave each member of the squad a gold medal, while the
prime minister, Nawaz Sharif, handed each one a cheque for 200,000 rupees
(then equivalent to around £4,500) and a plot of land in Islamabad worth
around £67,500.†

---

*But did Aamer really say this? The story was put about by Qamar Ahmed, who was asked in the press
box by colleagues to decode Aamer's remark as Botham walked off. He suggested that Aamer had told
Botham to send out his mother-in-law (in response to Botham having previously said that Pakistan was
a good place to send your mother-in-law on holiday). However, Aamer never disavowed the comment
and repeated the story to me himself. Qamar Ahmed and Aamer Sohail: personal interviews.

†Noman, op. cit. pp.267–71; Shuja-ud-Din, op. cit. pp.345–6. I have not been able to find figures for
the television viewership in Pakistan of the 1992 final. However, the World Bank estimated that at that
time 28% of Pakistan households had a television set. Watching important events on television was a
communal experience in Pakistan with as many as thirty or forty family members and neighbours clustered round the set, as many photographs attest. At the time, television was still a state monopoly. When
Brazil first won the football World Cup in 1958, there were only 78,000 black and white television sets
in the entire country (source: Sérgio Mattos, *A Brief History of Brazilian Television*).

Imran himself could and should have handled victory better. In his emotional acceptance speech, he unforgiveably failed to pay tribute to the performance of his players.[9]

IMRAN KHAN AND JAVED MIANDAD: AN ASSESSMENT

Sadly this speech marked the beginning of an estrangement between Imran and many of his team, who believed that he was intent on milking the World Cup success for his own purpose. Claiming a shoulder injury (the same excuse Kardar used to make), Imran bowed out of that summer's tour of England, and that autumn he retired from cricket, this time for good.

How does one assess Imran Khan's achievement? He was not an especially gifted cricketer. Javed Zaman, Imran's cricketing mentor, told me that, as a young man, 'Imran was a very sweet boy, not arrogant. He was a very, very average player. My opinion was that he wouldn't make it as a cricketer.'[10]

Imran's success is first and foremost a triumph of will and intelligence. Javed Zaman tells how when he first played top-class cricket he had an ugly, slinging action: 'Through hard work and dedication, he changed this.' Imran devoted himself to a strict, punishing regime of physical training. 'He would run and perform his demanding aerobics daily, with no exceptions,' recalls Javed Miandad, who played cricket with Imran for Sussex as well as Pakistan. 'Every day he would bowl 6–8 overs without fail. He wouldn't be bowling to any batsman but would just be on his own, bowling at a single stump. There would be a popping crease and 22 yards away there would be the solitary stump. In that setting Imran would bowl ... just Imran and the craft of bowling, with the rest of the world completely blocked out.'[11]

The slinginess noted by Javed Zaman was still in evidence when Imran made his first, disastrous Test appearance in 1971. When his cousin Javed Burki asked the seasoned professional Khalid Ibadulla to assess Imran, Ibadulla said he had a 'young man's action' and would not last long.[12] Colin Cowdrey told Imran to focus on batting, while Worcestershire tried to model him into an English county third seamer.

Imran refused to comply. He received, by modern standards, very little coaching and was essentially self-made as a bowler.* He turned himself into one of the greatest fast bowlers the world has known through hard work, determination and high intelligence, allied to magnificent physique.

So he followed the opposite trajectory to another great all-rounder to whom he was often, at the time, compared. Ian Botham burst onto the Test match scene as an astonishing talent, but got steadily worse, both as a batsman and a bowler. Imran was the opposite – always learning, always seeking to improve himself and always seeking out responsibility.

Imran would miss out on weak opposition, even though such encounters offered the chance of cheap, average-enhancing runs or a glut of wickets. He relished the fight against the greatest teams. Here was another contrast with Botham, who consistently failed against West Indies.

The national captaincy is a burden which has overcome many players, with Botham again the textbook example. Imran became a far better player as captain. Before his appointment as captain in 1982, Imran played in 40 Tests, scoring 1,330 runs at an average of 27.14. Thereafter he played 48 Tests, scoring 2,477 runs at 50.55. Before the captaincy, he took 158 Test wickets at 26.56. As captain, he added 204 at 19.90 apiece.

Imran was the only captain in Pakistan's history, apart from Kardar and Mushtaq Mohammad, with the strength of character to stand up to the cricketing bureaucracy. Again like Kardar, he was autocratic. Like Kardar (who greatly admired Imran)[13] he made his own selection decisions. Both came from Lahore. They were both individuals of unassailable personal integrity. Both were educated at Oxford, an experience that gave them an intricate understanding of western culture which enabled them to know their enemy. Both of them remained proud Muslims and patriotic Pakistanis. They viewed British and American foreign policy always with suspicion, and sometimes (in the case of Imran) with disgust. In their political careers, both Kardar and Imran sought to revive the virtue and independence of Pakistan.

---

*This point is well made in Javed Miandad's highly intelligent autobiography: 'In those days there was not the cricketing culture that developed in the 1990s and later. There was very little guidance and you had to seek help on your own. In his own writings, Imran has downplayed this aspect of his cricket education, but it needs to be acknowledged that he largely taught himself. He had complete confidence in his own physical abilities and mental skills, and it paid him great dividends. It takes a very strong mind to be able to teach yourself to become world-class at anything. This side of Imran's personality sometimes gets mistaken for arrogance, but it is really just strength of mind.' *Cutting Edge*, p.215.

Finally, both had the self-confidence and flair to captain in their own way. Unconstrained by selection panels, Imran's captaincy was marked by a series of brilliantly intuitive decisions. The most notable of these concerns Abdul Qadir. Imran gave Qadir the unqualified support and loyalty that all leg-spinners must have if they are to perform at their very best. For several years, the most enthralling sight in cricket was Imran, one of the greatest fast bowlers of all time, operating alongside Qadir, the re-inventor of wrist-spin bowling as an art form, and as an attack weapon. Again and again this pair would dismantle world-class batting orders. In his recent history of spin-bowling, Amol Rajan noted that 'cricket has yet fully to service its debt to Abdul Qadir.'[14] Imran played an important role in the Qadir story.

Towards the end of his time as captain, Imran showed similar faith in Inzamam and Mushtaq Ahmed, a faith that was rewarded in the 1992 World Cup. Imran's hunches did not always pay off. The batsman Mansoor Akhtar was kept in the Test side after a long run of disappointing performances, while others felt frozen out. Nevertheless, Imran was a great leader who brought out qualities in his players that they hardly knew they possessed.

Any serious consideration of Imran, however, demands an accompanying assessment of Javed Miandad, whose role has rarely been properly understood. Javed has been misrepresented, in particular by the white, western press, as morally inferior, a lower-class cheat, unreliable and untrustworthy. For these reasons, it has been assumed that Javed was never a great captain.

All these assumptions need to be corrected. Like so many other Karachi-born players, Javed's family came to Pakistan at Partition. His father, Miandad Noor Mohammad, had been an intelligence officer in the police department in Baroda before 1947.[15] Upon moving to Karachi, his father worked as a grader at the Karachi Cotton Exchange. In his spare time, he was a keen cricketer and sportsman, secretary of the Muslim Gymkhana, and an office-holder in the Karachi Cricket Association. In cricketing terms, Javed was born into the purple almost as much as Imran.

Javed attended the Christian Mission School, whose alumni included Mohammad Ali Jinnah, the founder of Pakistan, and (more relevantly) Intikhab Alam. Javed's schooldays were dominated by hours and hours of street cricket, still a permanent feature of Karachi, where passing cars weave in and out of cricket matches without apparently disrupting the games.[16]

He was spotted early, Mushtaq Mohammad telling Javed's father that one day his son would play for Pakistan. Mushtaq also gifted the young Javed a cricket bat. Javed made his first-class debut during the 1973–74 cricket season, aged sixteen, and scored 50, playing for Karachi Whites against Pakistan Customs at the Karachi Gymkhana ground.

The following year, batting for a Sindh youth team, Javed was watched by Kardar, then president of the BCCP. Kardar summoned the young man and congratulated him. The following day, Kardar was quoted in the newspapers saying that Javed was 'the find of the decade.'

So Javed was hardly the dangerous, half-educated street urchin relentlessly portrayed in the western press. He was well-educated, with a grounded set of values. It is certainly the case that he was a classic product of Karachi – urban, bustling, with a chip on his shoulder and an eye for the main chance. 'I have always had a militant approach to cricket,' he said. 'To me it is not so much a game as it is war.'[17] But this did not mean that Javed was a cheat, as detractors claimed.

Let us now consider Javed's record as a captain. Javed would take up the reins whenever Imran was unavailable, then willingly step down when Imran came back. This can be put in another way. Imran was almost always able to call on Javed, who played in 46 out of the 48 Tests when Imran was captain. By contrast, Imran played in only 13 of the 34 Tests when Javed was in charge. In other words, Imran could rely on the loyal presence of Pakistan's star batsman, while Javed was normally without Pakistan's star all-rounder.

Both men led their side to victory in an identical number of Tests: 14. Strikingly, Javed's percentage of victories was higher than Imran's. Javed Miandad deserves to be taken very seriously as one of the finest captains of Pakistan.

As Javed was always the first to acknowledge, Imran Khan was magnificent: 'I was fortunate to have seen Pakistan become a world class team during my playing career; it would not have been possible without Imran,' wrote Javed in his fine autobiography. 'Imran is no ordinary cricketer; he is one of cricketing history's greatest.'[18] The same can be said for Javed Miandad himself, and he played almost as significant a role as Imran in forging the great teams of the 1980s and early 1990s. Pakistan's success would not have been possible without Javed Miandad's acumen, forbearance, grace, grit – and superlative batting prowess.

PART THREE

THE AGE OF EXPANSION

1992–2000

INTRODUCTION

In the wake of the 1992 World Cup triumph, the historian of Pakistan cricket begins to feel sympathy with Edward Gibbon as he came to terms with the final centuries of the Roman Empire. It becomes necessary to deal with a succession of short-lived rulers, installed, deposed, and occasionally reinstalled after regular revolts from the legions. While the army remains full of soldiers of the highest quality, still capable of famous victories, too often it is fatally undermined by indiscipline and corruption. There are welcome intermissions of strong and competent leadership, but none in place for long enough, or with the necessary moral and constitutional authority, to bring about wholesale reform.

Gibbon would have relished the regular episodes of melodrama and farce in Pakistan cricket after 1992. But he would also have looked more deeply, and seen the problems of Pakistan cricket as a reflection of those which beset the Pakistan state itself: crime, terrorism, foreign intervention, a refugee crisis, abuse of power, entrenched corruption and clientalism, environmental degradation, a population explosion and millions more people to feed, house, educate and employ. As he watched the parade of Pakistan governments, civil and military, grappling with such problems with limited success or even making them worse, Gibbon might well have marvelled at the enduring power of Pakistan's cricketers to bring joy and hope to their followers.

So, for the following two decades, I shall partially abandon the generally chronological approach of the years before. Instead, I shall be focusing on the dominant issues which shaped Pakistan cricket in the modern period. The chapters will deal with Pakistan's invention of reverse swing, which changed fast bowling across the world; the persistent scourge of match-fixing; cricket's explosive expansion beyond its roots in the urban middle-class; the spectacular rise of Pashtun cricket; the dramatic story of women's cricket in Pakistan; the financial revolution in the sport; and the consequences of Pakistan's recent international isolation.

One crisis has succeeded another, and lurking behind all of them has been the perennial failure of leadership, on and off the field. I will do my best to give meaning to the 'churn' of captains and administrators, and the baleful influence of national politics which has left Pakistan cricket unable to cope with the fallout from problems which confront the whole nation.

But I will also celebrate the extraordinary expansion of the game of cricket in Pakistan. I will show how it was embraced by the mass of working people, urban and rural, in a way that was unimaginable before 1980. I will also tell the story of how, at last, women took up the national game in a purposeful way, and describe the problems they have been forced to overcome. The game even escaped the dictatorship of daylight. The arrival of electric light meant that a great deal of Pakistani cricket, down to the lowest club level, is now played at night-time and thus out of the heat of the day. I will show how, again and again, the sport of cricket gave meaning and common purpose to a nation in other ways at war with itself.

The direct narrative will therefore be intermittent, and linked to one or more of these themes. This looser structure will, however, reflect the exuberance and chaos of Pakistan cricket itself.

REVERSE SWING

'Your ball is moving but mine won't.'

– IMRAN KHAN TO SARFRAZ NAWAZ

Throughout its history, cricket has seen dramatic innovations in technique which shocked the establishment and changed the nature of the game for ever. Round-arm bowling was the first, followed not long after by over-arm. In batting, WG Grace astonished contemporaries by playing equally well off the back foot as off the front. At the end of the nineteenth century, Ranjitsinhji's leg glance, and then, in Australia, the hooks and pulls of Clem Hill and Victor Trumper, opened up half the field for batsmen to score in (Ranji's friend and contemporary, CB Fry was expected to apologise at school if he scored from a leg-side hit).[1] In the same era, BJT Bosanquet's casual invention of the googly, experimenting with a tennis ball on a billiard table, gave a new weapon to spin bowlers.[2] Before the Great War, SF Barnes, the greatest bowler of all time, discovered how to spin the ball sharply at medium pace (although this technique has proved too difficult for almost any bowler since).

The next surprise in bowling was the 'chinaman' – the mirror image of a leg-break, the stock delivery of a left-arm wrist spinner. It entered the cricket lexicon in 1933 after a racist complaint by one of its early victims. 'Fancy being done by a bloody Chinaman,' grumbled England's Walter

Robins, stumped in 1933 off a rather ordinary West Indian bowler called Ellis 'Puss' Achong.[3] In the late 1930s another practitioner, the eccentric Australian Chuck Fleetwood-Smith, acquired many fans, helped by his resemblance to Clark Gable. Garry Sobers bowled the chinaman in his early career, and more recently Paul Adams of South Africa beguiled batsmen and spectators with his unique 'frog-in-a-blender' action.

The 1950s produced a couple of 'mystery' bowlers – Jack Iverson of Australia and Sonny Ramadhin of West Indies, but they did not leave a legacy for others.[4] The next great bowling inventors were Pakistanis. For spinners, Saqlain Mushtaq introduced the 'doosra'[5] (meaning 'the other one' or 'the second'), a concealed leg-break. This has had its share of controversy, but nothing has caused more agitation, accusations and ultimately imitation, than Pakistan's re-invention of fast bowling through the phenomenon of reverse swing. Its mechanics figured in two celebrated court cases and excited an enduring scientific debate.

This made-in-Pakistan technique upset long-established theory and practice in the art of swing bowling. In doing so, it dramatically tilted the balance of power from batsman to bowler, in three different ways. In conventional swing, the shine on the ball gives a warning to the batsman of how the ball will deviate in the air. When a right-handed batsman sees the shine on the right side of the ball, he or she expects an outswinger which moves away from him or her. In reverse swing, the ball suddenly moves into the right-hander although the shine is still on the right side of the ball on release. In conventional swing, the ball swings most when it is new. Reverse swing happens – unpredictably – when the ball is old. In conventional swing, bowlers face a trade-off between swing and speed. In reverse swing, the ball actually swings more at higher speeds, particularly when the bowler achieves a yorker length. A Test batsman has to cope with a ball at 85 mph or more which at the last moment spears in at his feet or the base of his stumps. This is hard enough now, when reverse swing has become familiar. In the 1980s it seemed devilish – and its origins gave some of its victims another opportunity to display their prejudices against Pakistan and its cricketers.

One of Pakistan's great trio of reverse swingers, Wasim Akram, described the technique as a response to Pakistani conditions, in which conventional swing was quickly negated by the dry atmosphere and pitches. 'We started to avoid the usual method of keeping one side polished, hoping that would aid the swing. Instead we kept one side smooth and the other rough. The idea is to weigh down one side of the ball so that it acts as a bias against the other, leading to unexpected and late swing. *We would weigh down the smooth side with sweat and spit, earth or mud* [my italics; the use of earth or mud to alter the condition of the ball became illegal in 1980, see below p.359] so that it would be heavier than the dry rough side. With the ball hitting the boundary boards or the bat or the rough parts of the square, it's bound to show wear and tear, and that's why we could get reverse swing after 40 or 50 overs.' Wasim emphasised the control and effort required for reverse swing: 'you can't coast ... every ball needs to be up there in yorker territory, although you slip in the occasional orthodox swinging delivery just to keep them guessing.'[6]

Those interested in the science of reverse swing which supports Wasim Akram's description should study Bob Woolmer's analysis of 'The Science Of Swing' in his masterly but sadly posthumous *Art And Science Of Cricket*. Broadly speaking, a cricket ball reverse swings because of differences in the air flow when one side is very rough and the other kept smooth.[7] As we shall see shortly, the condition of the ball is all important and can be achieved both lawfully and unlawfully. Woolmer wrote with the authority of a great cricket technician and as Pakistan's most successful coach. In his book he strongly defended Pakistan's bowlers and suggested that the accusations of ball-tampering against them owed much to racial stereotyping.[8]

THE INVENTOR: SARFRAZ NAWAZ

The name most often cited as the inventor of reverse swing is Sarfraz Nawaz, the tall, often idiosyncratic but always thoughtful opening bowler who took 177 wickets for Pakistan in a 55-Test career from 1969 to 1984. However, as with Bosanquet and his googly, there are other claimants. Several sources mention the name of Farrakh Khan, a leading light of the Lahore Gymkhana in the late 1950s and 1960s, and suggest that he passed the secret to the young Sarfraz.[9]

Professor Dr Farrakh Khan, who sadly died just before publication of this book, was yet another member of the Burki clan and a cousin to Javed Burki, Majid Khan and Imran Khan. He was a promising opening bowler and a batsman with sound technique, who was good enough to be chosen on the Pakistan Eaglets tour of England in 1959 under the captaincy of Saeed Ahmed. Competition from other opening bowlers and lack of Test match opportunities for Pakistan in that era led him to give up regular cricket and follow a distinguished medical career, which (as I described on p.305) proved vital to the career of his cousin Imran.[10]

Farrakh Khan shared his memories of the 1959 Eaglets tour with me. His main success was as a batsman, who watched his colleagues, including Saeed Ahmed, fail repeatedly on English wickets by trying to force the ball off the front foot. He thought it better to stay on the back foot. He passed the tip to his captain, who promptly invited him to prove it by opening the batting in the next match against Derbyshire. He scored 80 out of 120 and kept his place for the rest of the tour.[11]

Competing with six or seven other seam bowlers, Farrakh Khan decided he needed more variety in his bowling and sought out Alf Gover, who had long been a mentor to young Pakistanis. 'I met him at the Richmond Club nets and said I could only bowl the outswinger. He taught me how to bowl the inswinger as well.' His first victim with the new delivery was an august one – Lala Amarnath, player-manager of the Indian Starlets visiting Pakistan in 1960–61. 'I clean bowled him.' His delight was still there, over fifty years later, and he demonstrated the grip. He continued to use the inswinger with success in Lahore club cricket, and in 1966, in the Lahore Gymkhana nets, he showed it to a seventeen-year-old Sarfraz Nawaz. 'I think he made some further developments.'[12]

It would be piquant to think that Gover was the ultimate source of the bowling technique which destroyed so many English batsmen in the 1980s and 1990s. However, what Farrakh Khan described and demonstrated to me appeared to be conventional inswing, and this was confirmed by Sarfraz when I spoke to him at the cricket academy he has created at Islamabad.

Somewhat stouter than in his playing days, Sarfraz Nawaz has a bear-like quality. He speaks softly (Wasim Bari told me that on his first England tour he needed a throat operation before he could appeal. He whispered his 'Owzat?' and had to gesture to ask his team-mates to support him).[13] He has an engaging catchphrase, 'and all that kind of thing', which sometimes emerges in curious places ('the crowd were charging us with sticks and steel bars and all that kind of thing').

Sarfraz was a late developer as a cricketer. He never played at school before matriculation and did not take up the game until his late teens when he began working for his father's construction company in Lahore. His conversion to cricket was a result of Pakistan's 1965 war with India over Kashmir. It led to the suspension of a major civilian contract for his father's company. The construction workers who were made idle invited the tall (6 ft 4 in) son of their employer to join their pick-up cricket matches. He proved a natural, and soon he got a trial at the prestigious Government College, Lahore and regular club cricket. He confirmed that he did learn in the nets with Farrakh Khan but added 'he did not bowl reverse swing but in-cutters. He did not know about reverse swing, or he would have bowled it himself.'

Always an analyst, Sarfraz discovered reverse swing by bowling with balls of all conditions, new, semi-new and old. He began on matting wickets, where he could cut the ball. 'One day I shone one side of a very old ball and it swung. It was rough on both sides but I shone one side and it swung towards the shine – it should not have done this.' In that Eureka moment, reverse swing was born.

He refined the new technique at the Mozang Link Cricket Club in Lahore. His opening partner Saleem Mir also knew how to reverse swing, but they kept it a secret from other bowlers.[14]

Like other talented teenagers, Sarfraz moved rapidly through the ranks of Pakistan cricket. In 1967 he made his first-class debut in the socially important annual match between Punjab University and the Punjab Governor's XI. He went wicketless and did not bat for the Governor's XI, but he played a major role for Lahore in their first-innings win over Karachi in the Quaid-e-Azam Trophy final of 1968–69.

Sarfraz's big break came in that season when he was asked to bowl in the nets at Lahore against the visiting MCC tourists. Roger Prideaux became the first English batsman to be surprised by reverse swing.* He was impressed enough to invite Sarfraz to join his county, Northamptonshire.

He made his Test debut in the Karachi Test against England, toiling through 34 wicketless but economical overs in the long England innings

---

*This was confirmed by Wasim Bari (personal interview), who also rated Sarfraz Nawaz Pakistan's greatest fast-medium bowler after Fazal Mahmood.

which was ended by riots. Injuries, county commitments and selector dis-favour made him wait for his next Test until the Australia tour of 1972–73, but he then became established as Pakistan's opening bowler while enjoy-ing a successful county career with Northamptonshire.

For years, he kept the secret of reverse swing from everyone except his old opening partner in Pakistan, Saleem Mir. (It did not help Saleem Mir very much; in eight first-class matches he took just eight wickets at an average over 40. Reverse swing has always required high-quality bowling, which is why Wasim Akram and Waqar Younis stood far higher than other expo-nents.) The technique was not much use to Sarfraz in England, where the ball did not get as rough as in Pakistan, and he usually employed conven-tional swing there. His Northamptonshire team-mate and future captain, Mushtaq Mohammad, was aware of reverse swing but rarely saw it and had no idea how it was achieved.

Finally, Sarfraz gave the secret to another Test player. During a one-day match in Guyana on Pakistan's 1976–77 tour of West Indies, he reverse-swung the old ball, and mystified his partner, Imran Khan. 'He complained, "Your ball is moving but mine won't." He did not know that I was rough-ing both sides of the ball on the last ball of my overs – so that it could not swing for him!' Sarfraz is still delighted with his ruse over forty years later. 'I told him I would show him in the nets, not in a match.' The next day he kept his word. The secret was to keep the ball rough on one side and make it heavier on the other with spit and sweat. It would make the ball move sharply towards the shine and unlike conventional swing the effect could be achieved at speed. 'I only told Imran because he was not then playing domestic cricket in Pakistan.'

I asked him if he used reverse swing for his greatest spell of bowling – seven wickets for one run which destroyed the Australians at Melbourne in March 1979. It gave him innings figures of nine for 86, the second-best Test performance by any Pakistani bowler and the best away from home. 'No. It was conventional swing and line and length.' There were also some mis-judgements by Australian batsmen. 'I bowled Dav Whatmore round his legs,' Sarfraz gloated. (Whatmore, who opened that day, later became Pakistan's coach.) I have watched low-quality recordings of his great per-formance and there are no signs of reverse swing. Most of the Australian batsmen were undone off the pitch.

Sarfraz was adamant that he obtained reverse swing by legal methods – exploiting dry pitches, especially in Pakistan, to create the required condition for the ball, and that he coached his bowling partners and fielders in how to shine the ball (legally) and how to return it. 'It is not necessary to gouge or scrape the ball, as English people claim. They did not know that a ball can do this when it gets older.' However, he was also frank about illegal methods. He mentioned Imran Khan's admission that he had used a bottle top in an English county game, but also reeled off a number of other leading players. Unfortunately, Sarfraz's conversation is regularly defamatory. 'X, who played under me, was the first to use the bottle top. He passed the secret to Y and Z, and the ball started to go every way. They needed help. There are many methods to work on the ball illegally. X had a zip with iron teeth in his back pocket. One umpire asked him to remove his trousers. Sometimes players put glue on the ball.' X, Y and Z are all Pakistan Test players.

THE INVENTOR'S HEIRS: IMRAN KHAN, WASIM AKRAM AND WAQAR YOUNIS

As often happens, the heirs to the inventor obtained more profit from his invention than he did.

Imran Khan told his biographer Christopher Sandford that he first used reverse swing against Australia in the Melbourne Test of 1977. In the first innings, with conventional methods, he had no wickets for 117 in 22 eight-ball overs. In Australia's second innings 'the pitch had got so hard it began to take lumps out of the ball, which then behaved like a boomerang.'[15] He took five for 122 (his first five-wicket haul in a Test innings), three bowled and one lbw. A characteristic of successful reverse-swing spells is a high concentration of bowled and lbws. Few commentators noticed the arrival of the new technique, since Australia crushed Pakistan by 348 runs. Reverse swing was not mentioned in his brilliant performance in the next Test, where he took 12 wickets. Every single one was caught (four by the wicketkeeper Wasim Bari, one a caught-and-bowled, two at deep square leg by the debutant Haroon Rashid, the others in the close catching cordon). Geoff Boycott, who was playing in Australia at the time, highlighted Imran's lightning pace, stamina and resistance, rather than any special effects with the ball. He cited Rodney Marsh, Imran's caught-and-bowled victim: 'He just didn't get tired. You'd hit him for four and he'd come back at you faster than ever.'[16]

Imran's greatest spell of reverse swing came against India in the second Test at Karachi in December 1982. Trailing by 283, India were making a fight of their second innings as Sunil Gavaskar and Dilip Vengsarkar had a long second-wicket partnership of 74 which took them to 102 for 1 on a flat wicket. Imran then returned for his second spell with the ball around 40 overs old. In the next 25 balls he took five wickets for eight runs. The normally impregnable Gavaskar was bowled through the gate. The experienced and accomplished Gundappa Viswanath was bowled shouldering arms to a late-reversing ball he expected to pass outside his off-stump.[17] Imran went on to claim eight for 60, his second best performance in a Test innings.* Five were bowled and two lbw – a marker of reverse swing. He was watched by his mentor, Sarfraz, by then Pakistan's third seamer.

The next great exponent of reverse swing, Wasim Akram, had the kind of debut that makes Pakistani teenagers dream. As a left-handed all-rounder he had not even been able to make the first team at Islamia College, Lahore. However, in November 1984 he was spotted in an Under-19 practice net by Javed Miandad who recommended him immediately for a trial match against the visiting New Zealanders. At Rawalpindi (one of Pakistan's least friendly surfaces for fast bowlers) he took seven for 50 in the first innings. He was swept into the party for the return tour by Pakistan of New Zealand, displacing the unlucky Tahir Naqqash who had already been selected.† He did nothing special in his first Test at Auckland but took ten wickets in the next one at Dunedin. There is no mention of reverse swing in accounts of this performance. Wasim's own account is tempered by his frustration at failing to break the epic ninth-wicket partnership between Jeremy Coney and Ewen Chatfield which won New Zealand the match and the series.[18]

---

*He edged it narrowly with eight for 58 in 1981–82 against Sri Lanka at the Gaddafi stadium, Lahore.
† *Wisden 1993*, p.20. According to Javed Miandad, Wasim Akram asked him how much money he should take to New Zealand, since he was not aware that Pakistan cricketers were paid on tour. O Samiuddin, 'Left Arm Explorer,' www.espncricinfo.com/magazine/content/story/457209.html.

Imran was his mentor. By now Sarfraz Nawaz had retired, and Imran had become the keeper of reverse swing. He certainly passed its secrets to his protégé, but Wasim's autobiography focuses more on Imran's basic lessons: sorting out his run-up, bowling conventional late swing, achieving yorkers at will and above all, stamina. He told him 'You have to work like a dog, Wasim.'[19]

The third of the great Pakistani exponents of reverse swing – Waqar Younis – was yet another teenage prodigy to be fast-streamed into the international team. He was discovered on television. Imran Khan watched him in the Super Wills Cup (between the best domestic teams in Pakistan and India) in 1989–90 and was impressed enough to go to the ground the next day and pick him for Pakistan's forthcoming series against India.[20] He made his Test debut one day before his eighteenth birthday – and dismissed another teenaged debutant, Sachin Tendulkar.[21] High pace earned him four wickets and he soon consolidated a place in the side.

The historian of reverse swing now encounters two major problems. First, its three great exponents were masters of every weapon in fast bowling. They could 'work over' batsmen with sheer speed, they could bowl bouncers and yorkers at will, and above all, they could make the ball swing fast and late by conventional means. Most of the great innovations in cricket are evident to the observer – such as overarm bowling, Ranji's leg glance, Bosanquet's googly – although the method used to produce them may be a mystery. Reverse swing does not announce itself so obviously. Without the aid of close-up analysis it might be conventional swing bowled exceptionally well. Second, its three great exponents said relatively little about it. Most of cricket's bowling innovators were not shy about their discoveries. Bosanquet was happy for Australians to call his delivery a 'bosie' before the more exotic name of 'googly' became established. In the modern era, Saqlain Mushtaq exploited the mystique of his 'doosra' and even claimed a further invention, the 'teesra', matched by Shane Warne's announcement of the 'zooter'.[22] Imran, Wasim and Waqar let their wickets speak for themselves. They rarely, if ever, attributed their victims to reverse swing.

Of the three, Wasim Akram has written the most about it. However, in his autobiography his proudest reverse swing performance is not from a Test match but in the 'Roses' match for Lancashire against Yorkshire in his second English county championship season, in 1989. His thoughts could serve as a template for the reaction of all Englishmen to being overtaken by a foreign innovator – and not just in sport.

> [This was] the first time that the English public saw what reverse swing was about ... I understand that Fred Trueman was amazed at the amount of late swing I was getting. It was no great secret as far as I was concerned. In the nets I'd worked hard at perfecting late swing from around the wicket, making my body turn more into a sideways position so that I could get the ball to move in the air. I'd told my Lancashire team-mates about the ideal conditions to get the ball to reverse: dry, hot, with the ball roughed up one side after about 40 overs' use – and yet I was the only one using that technique at the time in English cricket ... I was surprised that my colleagues didn't try to experiment with reverse swing when it was obviously working for me, but during that period they kept talking about line and length, about bowling in the 'corridor of uncertainty' on or about off stump. That was all very well against average players on wickets that helped the bowler, but when you come up against batsmen on flat wickets they'll just whip such deliveries through mid wicket all day ... Six of my ten victims were clean bowled in that match and it was simply a case of utilising ideal weather for reverse swing. A few more years were to pass before English bowlers began to see the value of this technique.[23]

It is fair to say that the cricket world did not really take notice of reverse swing until its victims started to complain about it.

A BRIEF HISTORY OF BALL-TAMPERING

Cricket is the only major ball game where the condition of the ball is crucially important. Unless it is lost or seriously damaged, the same ball is used for long periods of play and becomes more or less useful to different types of bowler. Essentially, fast bowlers like a ball which is hard and shiny and spin bowlers prefer one where the shine has gone which they can grip. Since the beginnings of organised cricket, bowlers have attempted, often with the co-operation of their wicketkeeper and other fielders, to get a ball in their desired condition. Often their methods are illegal, or if not actually illegal, judged to be unethical by their victims, with consequent changes in the laws or practices of the game.*

The commonest illegal method is 'lifting the seam'. A raised seam helps pace bowlers to control its direction, make it swing and, above all, achieve sharp bounce off the pitch. The great Australian fast bowler, Keith Miller, was a self-confessed exponent and when detected in 1953, bowling in a crucial Ashes Test match against England, he cheekily blamed the raised seam on the 'cheap balls we are getting nowadays'.[24] As Imran Khan argued forcefully in defending Pakistan's methods, 'lifting the seam' has been rife at all levels of cricket for years. (I have encountered it myself from superannuated trundlers in English social cricket.)

Other illegal methods of changing the state of the ball include gouging one side of it, with strong thumbnails or a small sharp instrument, splitting the stitches of the seam, or applying illegal substances to the ball. Legally, bowlers and fielders can use their own sweat and spit (unlike baseball pitchers) and until 1980 they could rub the ball in the ground. Illegal substances have included sawdust, resin, birdlime (on wicketkeepers' gloves), and hair oil – Keith Miller (again) was taught this art by George Pope, a Derbyshire seam bowler who had almost no hair.[25] In England's 1976–77 tour of India, the opposing captain, Bishan Bedi, accused John Lever of using Vaseline after he engineered an Indian collapse. The English authorities rejected the accusation, saying that Lever and other bowlers were using Vaseline to keep the sweat from their eyes.[26]

As already mentioned, reverse swing depended so critically on the condition of the ball that victims readily assumed that this must have been procured illegally. This charge first appeared in 1983 when Imran took six wickets for six runs in 23 balls, including a hat-trick, for Sussex against Warwickshire in the county championship. One victim, Chris Old, told the *Daily Mirror* that the ball 'looked as though a dog had chewed it.' The

---

*There is an interesting study waiting to be written about the inspiration and beneficiaries of changes in the laws of cricket. Many bowlers have complained that batsmen predominate among cricket administrators, and that most modern rule changes have helped batsmen, including covered wickets, shorter boundaries (coupled with heavy bats), fielding restrictions and the front foot no-ball rule, a special bête noire of the late Fred Trueman. They tend to be silent about the Decision Review System, which has increased the number of lbws. See the remarks of Dave Richardson, then ICC General Manager, in 'DRS has affected the game more than we thought it would', www.cricinfo.com, 14 February 2012.

umpire, Don Oslear, reported to Lord's that one side of the ball was scratched and torn and that some of the stitches had been cut, allowing a triangle of leather to be pulled away from the ball. He sent a report to the Test and County Cricket Control Board, but nothing was done. Oslear would play a crucial role in the controversies of Pakistan's tour of 1992; this early incident may have helped to shape his attitude to Pakistan fast bowlers and English cricket authorities.[27]

The first of Pakistan's opponents to protest against reverse swing were New Zealand during their tour of the subcontinent in 1990–91. Wasim Akram and Waqar Younis shared 40 of the 60 New Zealand wickets to fall in a 3–0 whitewash by Pakistan. New Zealand's captain and best batsman, Martin Crowe, complained at Lahore that the ball was totally shiny on one side and badly gouged on the other.[28] New Zealand made a practical protest in the third Test at Faisalabad, a notoriously easy wicket where results are hard to obtain, giving rise to the bowler-friendly remark: 'there's bad, very bad, and Faisalabad.'[29] The workaday seam bowler, Chris Pringle, and his fielders gouged the ball themselves with the top of a soft drinks bottle. Pringle gave an interesting account of this tour, which is generally fair to Pakistan and its cricketers. With the deliberately tampered ball, Pringle took seven for 52 in Pakistan's first innings, in which they were dismissed for their lowest score against New Zealand of 102. He claimed eleven wickets for 152 runs in the match. Interestingly, he was not able to achieve reverse swing, but the scratchings on the ball helped him keep the seam upright and move the ball off the pitch. (In Pringle's other thirteen Tests, with an untampered ball, he managed nineteen wickets at over 65 apiece.) He claimed that he showed the gouged ball frequently to the umpires, who ignored its condition, afraid that New Zealand would reveal Pakistan's methods.

Pakistan's next visitors were West Indies. Under Imran's captaincy (he had given himself a rest against the inferior New Zealanders) Wasim and Waqar took fifteen wickets between them in the first Test, which Pakistan won. The West Indies manager, the great off-spinner Lance Gibbs, protested against the condition of the ball. However, according to the PCB (then having another spell of ad hoc rule under General Zahid Ali Akbar Khan), Gibbs later agreed that 'the ball used by the West Indians was in a much worse condition than the one used by Pakistan.' Mudassar Nazar (then a Pakistan coach and a firm opponent of ball tampering) said that West Indians had admitted to him that they had tampered with the ball during their last two home Tests against England the previous year.[30] This protest fizzled out.

Wasim achieved one of his greatest performances in this match – four wickets in five balls. His account does not mention reverse swing in any of the dismissals, but records his annoyance that Imran dropped a dolly catch at mid-on which would have produced a hat-trick.[31]

BRITISH MEDIA STEREOTYPES OF PAKISTAN

For the first four decades after Partition, the country's cricketers were as a whole viewed with warmth in England, though from time to time they were also treated with what might be called patronising contempt. This basic goodwill was based on the premise that Pakistan did not assert herself, either on or off the pitch.

The emergence of the great teams of the 1980s, more than capable of defeating England, started to change this. So did Pakistan's more belligerent stance in international cricket politics. The petulance displayed by English players during the Gatting tour of 1987–88 was in part a response to this changing state of affairs. However, matters came to a head only during Pakistan's tour of England in 1992.

This produced the most serious allegations that Pakistan's match-winners, Wasim Akram and Waqar Younis, achieved their devastating performances by cheating. Before narrating the events of this tour, it is important to step back and study some of the British media narratives of Pakistan cricket.

By 1992, British tabloid media especially had established the idea that Pakistan cricketers were representatives of an alien and barely civilised country. None of England's other cricket opponents have ever been so constantly vilified. Not surprisingly, Pakistan's cricketers and commentators developed a counter-narrative of England (and its cricketers and umpires) – arrogant, hypocritical, and incurably prejudiced.[32]

The *Sun* newspaper led the way after the Gatting–Shakoor Rana confrontation with the offer of a 'Sun Fun Dartboard' which bore the image of Shakoor Rana. Lucky readers could hit him right between the eyes if they threw a double top.[33] The *Sun*'s fantasy violence followed a summer of real violence in England's home series against Pakistan in 1987, in which a Pakistani supporter at Trent Bridge had his throat slashed.[34] After the one-day international at Edgbaston in 1987 the editor of *Wisden Cricket Monthly*, David Frith, denounced the '*hordes* of Pakistan "supporters" [who] came not merely to watch the cricket but to identify – with a fanatical frenzy and to the embarrassment of Imran and his players – with "their team". Our enquiries have revealed that hundreds of them gained entry without paying and that *a battle plan was actually drawn up among them*.' The italics are mine. However, he did also mention white supporters 'with shaven heads and large boots' had been 'lurking in anticipation of confrontation.'[35]

In 1990 the former Conservative Party chairman Norman Tebbit cranked up the hostility to Pakistan cricket supporters with his infamous 'cricket test'. Referring to Asian spectators at England's international matches against Pakistan or India, he asked, 'Which side do they cheer for? Were they still harking back to where they came from or where they were?'[36] He invited listeners to believe that such supporters were still aliens, who had never learnt loyalty to Britain. Tebbit did not apply his test to white supporters of visiting teams, for example the Britons with New Zealand roots who cheered the All-Blacks on rugby tours.

In 1992, the *Daily Mirror* launched a double attack on the Pakistan touring team and its supporters. Its sportswriter Mike Langley warmed up by calling Javed Miandad, the team captain, 'Cricket's Colonel Gaddafi'. He then surpassed this by naming the team 'Javed's Brat Pack' and describing Javed as a 'wild man with a face you might spot crouched behind rocks in an ambush along the Khyber.' (Javed came from a middle-class family in Karachi, a thousand miles away geographically from the Khyber and as far removed culturally.) He accused Javed of 'arousing the always excitable Pakistani supporters.' Langley added a new layer of stereotyping to those supporters – being humourless. Referring back to Ian Botham's would-be comic quip about Pakistan as a place to send one's mother-in-law, Langley commented, 'I thought they'd laugh their curly slippers off and retort, "Well, what about Scunthorpe?" *Laugh, not them, they're too prickly and nationalistic ... Pakistanis being even hotter on apologies than they are on vindaloos*.'[37] Once again, the italics are mine.

Such articles were not confined to the tabloids. The political columnist Simon Heffer called Pakistan 'The pariahs of cricket' in a sulphurous article in the *Sunday Telegraph*. He puffed, 'No team has ever more merited the opprobrium of the international cricket community than our current visitors.' He suggested that Pakistan teams never let sportsmanship impede their pursuit of victory, that their umpires turned a blind eye to unfair play by them at home and that Javed Miandad's 'ethical deficiencies make him the last man to captain his country, *even if it is only Pakistan* [my italics again].' In a tasteless exordium, Heffer suggested that the only fair play on show in Pakistan's cricket stadia came when they were used for public floggings.[38]

The 1992 tour began smoothly enough. England gained partial revenge for the World Cup defeat by winning the first two one-day internationals. The first Test at Edgbaston was a rain-hit draw. It was memorable only for a stand of 322 between Javed Miandad and Salim Malik, and the TCCB's denial of a refund to spectators on the Friday of the match because three balls were bowled. The second Test at Lord's was a thriller. Seventeen wickets fell on the final day, before Wasim and Waqar won the game for Pakistan – for once as batsmen.

The Old Trafford third Test was a high-scoring draw. Aamer Sohail made a double-century, and David Gower (recalled if not forgiven after his aerial joyride on England's recent Australian tour) became England's leading run-scorer. When the match was completely dead, umpire Roy Palmer maintained the family tradition of annoying Pakistan[39] when he warned Aaqib Javed for intimidating England's number 11 Devon Malcolm. The Pakistanis considered this warning unfair, since Aaqib was not bowling bouncers and Malcolm had received no warning for his own short deliveries against their batsmen. They were already angry with Palmer for a decision against Ramiz Raja in their innings after a half-hearted English appeal. Aaqib reacted angrily and Javed, instead of calming his young bowler, ran over and supported him vocally with a wagging finger. Then came the famous incident when Palmer, in *Wisden's* carefully neutral words, 'returned Aaqib's sweater with more emphasis than usual, probably because it was caught in his belt.' Intikhab Alam, the team manager, claimed that Palmer had insulted his players by throwing the sweater at Aaqib.

The ICC response to this incident satisfied nobody. Match referee Conrad Hunte, deputising for the original appointee, Clyde Walcott, on the fourth and fifth days, fined Aaqib half his match fee. He gave Intikhab a severe reprimand for his remarks, and he was then fined for repeating them without apology. Javed was not punished and England were infuriated when Hunte called on both captains to ensure that their teams played within the spirit of the game. This incident sparked Simon Heffer's diatribe and the *Daily Mirror*'s description of Javed as a wild man of the Khyber. *The Cricketer*'s editor Richard Hutton, described Palmer being 'besieged by another fuming horde.'[40]

The *Daily Mirror*'s attack on Javed also warned him to 'bear in mind England's incurable curiosity about how Pakistan's bowlers can swing a worn ball on days when new ones won't deviate.' It was the opening of a media-generated campaign against Pakistan's two strike bowlers, who showed a sinister ability in the Test series to engineer England collapses for no apparent reason.

At Lord's, England had lost their last six wickets for 42 in the first innings and for 38 in the second. At Headingley in the fourth Test, they subsided from 270 for 1 to 320 all out in the first innings, but still managed to level the series with a six-wicket victory. There were more umpiring controversies in this Test as Ken Palmer and Mervyn Kitchen refused many plausible lbw appeals and Palmer mistakenly refused to rule Gooch run out as England were struggling to reach a small target for victory. At the deciding Oval Test, England lost seven wickets for 25 in the first innings and five for 21 in the second.

Afterwards, the England manager, Micky Stewart, told the press, 'The ball suddenly started to swing', and added archly, 'I know why', without further explanation. After England's defeat by ten wickets and the series lost 2–1, he answered the inevitable media questions. 'I know the method Wasim Akram and Waqar Younis use to make the ball swing so much but that is all I wish to say. It has been discussed in the dressing room and we know how they do it ... I am not being mysterious at all ... I have said a lot but nothing improper.'[41]

If Stewart and his team suspected ball tampering by the Pakistanis during the Tests, they had remedies. He could have complained to the umpires or the new match referees from the ICC. He could have directed his batsmen to take opportunities to examine the ball, or ask the umpires to do so. He might have arranged for observers to film the Pakistanis at matches and for analysis of television footage. He could even have raised the issue privately with the Pakistan team manager, Intikhab Alam, whom he had captained at Surrey. Instead, he made his insinuation to the media after the Test series was lost. He was rewarded by the tabloids. 'NAILED – Waqar caught in new ball tampering row' said the *Sun*, and the *Daily Mirror* asked 'Champs or cheats?'[42]

COVER-UP AT LORD'S

A fresh set of charges were levelled against Pakistan when the ball was replaced on the second day of the rain-affected one-day international at Lord's. Following a complaint by Allan Lamb, the on-field umpires John Hampshire and Ken Palmer conferred with the third umpire, Don Oslear. He informed the ICC match referee, Deryck Murray, that the ball should be replaced because of 'clear and obvious ball-tampering.'[43] Murray met the umpires and Javed and Intikhab during the lunch interval and the ball was replaced. However, all this was done in secret and neither spectators nor the media were informed at the time. Ironically, the replacement ball helped Wasim and Waqar much more than the previous one. They blasted out four English batsmen for ten runs to snatch victory for Pakistan.

Briefings from the England camp about ball-tampering unleashed a new media storm against the Pakistanis led by a provocative interview by Allan Lamb in the *Daily Mirror*. With its rival, the *Sun*, it called for Pakistan to be thrown out of world cricket.[44] Meanwhile, the Pakistani tour management put out that the ball had been replaced at *Pakistan's* request because it had gone out of shape.[45] Despite the media furore, both the TCCB and the ICC maintained a policy of silence on the reasons for the replacement – an inept decision which satisfied no one.[46] Still more ineptly, the TCCB turned Lamb into a martyr by fining him £5,000 for his interview while fining Surrey only £1,000 for a proven case of ball-tampering the previous season.[47]

PAKISTAN'S DEFENDERS

Nonetheless, the tour ended happily. Wasim and Waqar were regularly mobbed by autograph hunters – Pakistani and English supporters alike – and Pakistan delighted the spectators at their final festival match at Scarborough by joining them in pick-up games during the rain intervals.[48]

They had some forthright defenders in the media, notably David Gower (who called for restoration of the old law which allowed bowlers to rub the ball in the ground)[49] and Geoff Boycott. He called the Pakistanis 'exciting, attractive and talented ... they were magicians not cheats.' He told England to 'stop squealing. These two [Wasim and Waqar] could have bowled us out with an orange.'[50]

Jack Bannister would later collaborate with Don Oslear on his book *Tampering With Cricket,* but in *Wisden 1993* he hailed reverse swing as the first genuine bowling innovation since over-arm bowling. He too favoured relaxation of the law to allow limited 'treatment of the ball' by bowlers.[51] The editor of that year's *Wisden,* Matthew Engel, named Wasim Akram one of its Five Cricketers of the Year.[52]

AFTERMATH

Led by Wasim and Waqar, reverse swing established itself in the 1990s as a mainstream weapon for fast bowlers, with no taint of illegality.

Apart from Darren Gough for England, Allan Donald was able to achieve it for South Africa, as did a New Zealand bowler, Heath Davis, during a short Test career.[53] Later exponents included Zaheer Khan for India and the round-arm slinger, Lasith Malinga, of Sri Lanka, whom millions of children across the world have tried to mimic.

In 2005, England's Simon Jones became a national hero for using reverse swing in the winning Ashes series against Australia, as did Jimmy Anderson in the 2009 Ashes series. Both used it much earlier in an innings than Pakistan's great bowlers were able to do in the 1980s and 1990s. The England team in the field included a specialist ball custodian and polisher.

An interesting final take on reverse swing and its future came from Aaqib Javed, another practitioner who had been one of Imran Khan's disciples. In 2004, as a successful coach of Pakistani teenagers, he told Indian journalist Rahul Bhattacharya: 'It's very easy, honestly. If you go to our nets you see even a 16-year-old boy, who has played cricket for six months, [doing it]. There is a reason for this. Our cricket grounds are so rough. At our clubs you have to make a new ball last for one month. In those circumstances, it made sense to take care of a match ball to make it produce reverse swing. The main art, I'm telling you, is to get the ball into shape. I was a bit of a specialist at that!' Aaqib faced regular accusations of gouging the ball, in county and Test cricket in 1991 and 1992, but he passed over them in the interview. Like Sarfraz Nawaz when he spoke to me, he emphasised the importance of bowling and returning the ball – legally – in the right ways by all the bowlers and fielders.[54]

Another interesting point made by Aaqib was the importance of tapeball cricket – another great Pakistan invention, which introduces thousands of children and young people to cricket and has national championships in its own right. The ball is a tennis ball covered in insulating tape, except for one little slit. If positioned correctly, the slit generates tremendous late swing on the ball (which is a good preparation for the art of reversing) and learning to bowl a light ball at speed is a brilliant preparation for young pace bowlers when they pick up the real thing.[55]

If Aaqib is right, and any teenager can bowl reverse swing with the right kind of ball, then Pakistan can truly be said to have reinvented cricket.

THE CURSE OF MATCH-FIXING

'The commission felt a lot of the time that most of the people appearing before it were not telling the truth, or at least not the whole truth.'

– JUSTICE QAYYUM

Our study of reverse swing and its consequences has taken us right up to the twenty-first century, by which time the practice had become respectable. One other controversy, far more wounding and ugly, had meanwhile engulfed Pakistan cricket: match fixing. To understand its background it is necessary to go back two decades and pick up the narrative at the end of Javed Miandad's Test series victory in England in 1992.

In retrospect it seems obvious that Javed, who had been such a superb understudy to Imran, should at this point have been confirmed as Pakistan's long-term captain. It was not to be. He had just one more Test in charge before falling victim to a revolt by senior players.

Javed scored 92 in this one-off Test against New Zealand. Pakistan trailed by 48 on first innings and lost five wickets clearing the arrears. Inzamam-ul-Haq made his first Test fifty and he was supported by Rashid Latif, but Pakistan set a target of only 127. New Zealand were cruising to victory at 65 for 3 and Javed was thinking of relieving Waqar Younis with Mushtaq Ahmed. At this point, Asif Mujtaba took an astonishing catch at short-leg.

Waqar was rejuvenated and with Wasim took the remaining wickets for just 28.[1]

This thrilling victory gave Javed fourteen wins as captain. It equalled Imran's record in fewer Tests; thirty-four against forty-eight. It did not save him from being deposed by the Board, in favour of Wasim. 'The origins of this move could ultimately be traced to Imran,' Javed later claimed in his autobiography. 'Imran was close to all the top Board officials, including the chairman and the secretary, and had formally been retained as a Board adviser.'[2] Javed accused Imran of inciting younger players to reject his leadership, but his man-management skills were always poor and it did not need Imran to encourage Wasim to seek the captaincy in his place.

The PCB had recently acquired a new chairman, Justice Nasim Hassan Shah. Very short and very fat – indeed almost circular – he had no cricket background and was clearly a political appointment by the prime minister Nawaz Sharif.[3] Nasim received a post-mortem on the recent Australasian tour which blamed Javed for the team's poor showing. 'It was thought that he could no longer command the respect of his undisciplined and unruly bunch of youngsters.'[4]

Arif Abbasi fought a rearguard action for Javed but he was outvoted. Javed confronted Justice Nasim and the Board secretary Shahid Rafi and told them, 'Today you have destroyed Pakistan cricket.' Wasim, he said, was not ready for the captaincy, and the stability of the team would be fatally undermined.[5] Events would show the wisdom of this judgement.

WASIM'S UNHAPPY DEBUT TOUR

Wasim Akram's reign began with victory in a low-key one-day series in Sharjah against Zimbabwe and Sri Lanka. He was man of the match in the final against Sri Lanka, with four for 24. Then Pakistan reached the final of a triangular tournament in South Africa, losing to West Indies. Aamer Sohail was man of the match; however, it was a portent of future weakness that the Board sent him out as a replacement even though he was serving a ban for indiscipline in domestic cricket.[6]

Then Wasim led Pakistan for a Test and one-day series in the West Indies, in February–March 1993, with Waqar Younis as vice-captain. The deposed

Javed went as a player, but the selectors, with little apparent reason, rejected the experienced Salim Malik and Shoaib Mohammad. The one-day series saw a dramatic comeback by Pakistan and was shared two-all, when the crowd at Georgetown invaded and prevented Wasim from achieving a run-out on the last ball.*

The Test series was calamitous before it even began. In Grenada for the last warm-up game, Wasim, Waqar, Mushtaq Ahmed and Aaqib Javed were arrested on a beach, marched to a police station, and accused of 'constructive possession' of marijuana. Two English girls were also arrested, fuelling rumours of sexual adventures. To his great satisfaction the deposed Javed was asked to use his connections and influence in the West Indies to help bail out his new captain and vice-captain.[7] All those concerned denied the charges strongly and claimed that they were framed. The case was dropped.[8]

The Test series was lost 2–0 and in truth Pakistan hardly competed. The defeats were massive and the third Test was drawn after rain. Wasim had a terrible time with the bat (averaging eight) and ball (paying nearly 40 for his nine wickets in the series) and lost confidence in himself. Mushtaq Ahmed and Aaqib Javed were injured and there was no one else to support Waqar, who took nineteen series wickets. Javed's recurrent back complaints returned, and he could not manage a half-century in the series. Inzamam-ul-Haq failed until a crucial century in the final Test and the one consistent batsman was a newcomer, Basit Ali, who scored 222 runs at an average over 55. He was hailed as the next Javed, but in just a few years he would be a disillusioned failure, sick of international cricket.[9]

Basit maintained his good impression in Sharjah with a century in the final against West Indies the following autumn. Wasim was injured and a half-fit Waqar could not prevent Brian Lara hitting 153 to help West Indies chase 285 to win with five overs to spare.

Wasim was still injured when Pakistan received Zimbabwe, on their first overseas tour in December 1993. Waqar was stand-in captain, and enjoyed

---

*The tie was awarded by the match referee, Raman Subba Row, who had offended Pakistan in 1987–88, by giving Mike Gatting's England party a tour bonus of £1,000. Subba Row was appointed referee when the Pakistanis objected to Tom Graveney, who in 1987 had claimed that, 'Pakistan have been cheating for 37 years and it is getting worse and worse.' Shuja-ud-Din, op. cit. p.369, and *Wisden 1994*, pp.1095–6.

himself by taking thirteen wickets for 135 in the first Test – characteristically, five were bowled and six lbw. Crowds were poor throughout and the Karachi Test was switched to the small Defence Housing Authority stadium. Pakistan struggled against their weak opponents, who twice took a first-innings lead. After winning the first two Tests, Pakistan nearly lost the last one and were glad to draw thanks to a 315-minute fifty by Shoaib Mohammad.[10]

Javed supported him with 31 in what turned out to be the last of his 124 Tests. He had fought a long battle to prove his fitness to a hostile board of selectors, which included a manager he had once warmly admired, Haseeb Ahsan. In his autobiography he claimed that the selectors ordered the fast bowlers to bowl non-stop bouncers at him in practice. When Javed was then dropped from the touring party for New Zealand, he gave an emotional press conference, complaining of his 'humiliating treatment' and denouncing the mismanagement of Pakistan cricket. In the heat of the moment he announced his retirement from international cricket. That unleashed a wave of protests, not only, as he had expected, in his native Karachi, but throughout Pakistan. The Gaddafi stadium in Lahore, home of the Board, was picketed daily and protestors threatened to set fire to themselves.[11] Javed eventually announced his return after a personal plea from Benazir Bhutto, restored as prime minister.

WASIM DEPOSED: ENTER SALIM MALIK

Perhaps fittingly, Wasim Akram, who had come to power through one player revolt, was deposed after another led by his deputy Waqar Younis. No fewer than ten Pakistan players joined his protest against Wasim's 'domineering attitude'. However, Waqar's gracious offer to replace him was not accepted by a new panel of selectors. They had been appointed after a coup against Justice Nasim by the triumvirs of Pakistan cricket, Javed Burki, Arif Abbasi and Zafar Altaf.[12] The new selectors turned instead to Salim Malik.

On figures it was a logical choice. He had been around a long time, and was a consistent performer in Pakistan's middle order, with ten Test centuries, including one on debut in 1981–82 against Sri Lanka. He had been a *Wisden*

Cricketer of the Year in 1988 and had performed successfully for Essex in county cricket over two seasons. But somehow he had never been on anyone's radar as a captain. His one experience in the job, deputising for Javed in the ODI series against England at Trent Bridge in 1992, was unhappy, and later became viewed as sinister; he allowed England to pile up 363.

Like Javed Miandad, Salim Malik was often characterised as a poor boy made good, who had learnt his cricket as a street urchin.[13] In reality (again like Javed) Malik had a middle-class background. His father had a linen-export business in Lahore, and he learnt his cricket at the well-regarded Victorious Club.[14] In view of later events it is important to realise that match-fixing and corruption involved middle-class and educated cricketers as much as those from poor backgrounds with limited education. In his recent book Shaharyar Khan makes this point forcefully in relation to the disgraced Salman Butt, 'the young captain from a middle-class, educated family who represented for the nation a modern image of an erudite, well-spoken and articulate leader.'[15]

For the tour of New Zealand the selectors gave Malik a strong management team: Intikhab Alam, for team matters, and Majid Khan as tour manager 'to clean up the "nasty-boy" image of Pakistan cricketers.'[16] The Test series was won 2–1. Wasim was revived as a bowler and took twenty-five wickets in the series. He wrote later, 'There were days when I was hardly speaking to anybody in the team but I was fired up on the pitch.' He and Waqar shared fifteen wickets in the first Test, helped by a record nine catches by the wicketkeeper Rashid Latif, who also hit a six for victory. In the process, Wasim took his 200th Test wicket, and Waqar his 150th in fewer Tests than anyone except SF Barnes. There were eleven more wickets for Wasim in the second Test, and centuries for Malik, Inzamam and a first one in Tests for Saeed Anwar, who was becoming a fixture as opener.

Pakistan lost the third despite a maiden Test century from Basit Ali and bright opening stands from Saeed Anwar and Aamer Sohail. They set New Zealand 324 to win, a task that seemed impossible. Yet two relative unknowns, Bryan Young and Shane Thomson, shared a match-winning stand against the hitherto invincible Wasim and Waqar. This result later came under suspicion.

The one-day series was won 3–1 by Pakistan. However, the fifth match at Christchurch, which produced New Zealand's consolation win, was later to become the subject of investigation.

There was one curious incident, when Malik claimed to have won the toss in the first Test after making a call in Urdu. He then picked up the coin before the home captain, Ken Rutherford, had the chance to look at it, or ask for a translation.[17] Nevertheless, it seemed a wonderful start for Malik and the team showed fine spirit and discipline.[18]

SALIM MALIK'S GREAT START CONTINUES

Pakistan's next success under their quiet captain came in Sharjah, when they won the Austral-Asia Cup. India had re-entered after a two-year boycott of the tournament for the 'organisational bias' against them. Pakistan won the final against them with a fine all-round performance by Aamer Sohail, including a brilliant catch to dismiss Sachin Tendulkar.

Pakistan then triumphed in Sri Lanka. Javed Miandad should have been among them. He had cancelled his retirement after Benazir Bhutto had begged him to return and complete 10,000 runs in Test cricket under her premiership.* He worked hard on fitness and scored a century in a trial match before the tour. Unfortunately, he snapped a knee ligament in an impromptu football match.[19]

Even without him, Pakistan were far too good for Sri Lanka. They won the first Test by 301 runs, despite a wonderful century by Aravinda de Silva, which arrived with a six. Saeed Anwar and Wasim Akram were Pakistan's match-winners. A Sri Lankan spinner with a curious action toiled through 53 overs in the match but took just one wicket for 165 – Muttiah Muralitharan. The second Test was abandoned because Sri Lanka was under curfew in a highly troubled election campaign. In the third Test an Inzamam century helped to set up an innings win. Wasim and Waqar routed Sri Lanka even though by now they were hardly on speaking terms. Pakistan were the first visitors in a decade to win a one-day series in Sri Lanka.[20]

These successes were followed by a surprisingly dismal performance in the four-nation Singer Cup, also held in Sri Lanka. Pakistan finished last

---

*Javed had scored 8,832 by then. Even if he had maintained his customary average of 50 an innings he would have needed at least 24 more Test innings; Benazir Bhutto was clearly hoping for a long stay in power.

with no wins against India, Sri Lanka and Australia. Against Australia, Pakistan had stood at a comfortable 77 for 1, chasing 151, before sensationally collapsing to give the Australians victory by 28 runs.

Rumours reached Pakistan that some team members were involved in betting. Salim Malik denied it furiously, but Javed Burki (now 'cricket adviser' to the newly installed president of Pakistan, Farooq Leghari) set up an administrative inquiry. Sarfraz Nawaz (as would become his habit) denounced this step as inadequate, and demanded a full judicial inquiry instead.[21]

PAKISTAN'S MOST DRAMATIC WIN

These events were soon eclipsed by the first Test in Karachi, in September–October 1994, against the visiting Australians under Mark Taylor. This turned out to be one of the most exciting Test matches in history.

Wasim, Waqar and Mushtaq Ahmed took three wickets apiece in dismissing Australia for 337. Despite 85 from Saeed Anwar, Pakistan trailed by 81 runs on first innings. Only David Boon, with a century, and Mark Waugh, with 61, had much answer to Wasim and Waqar in Australia's second innings of 232, but Pakistan still needed 314 to win. Despite 77 from Anwar, the cause looked lost at 184 for 7, although Inzamam was still in. Not for the first time, Rashid Latif was a staunch partner, actually outscoring Inzamam with 35 in a stand of 52. But when Shane Warne took his fifth wicket Pakistan were 258 for 9. The last man Mushtaq Ahmed rose to the occasion, keeping Warne and McGrath at bay as Inzamam scored a careful half-century. When Pakistan needed only two more runs to win Inzamam had an inexplicable red mist and decided to charge Warne. He missed and the wicketkeeper, Ian Healy, had an easy stumping chance. Even more inexplicably the normally immaculate Healy missed the ball and it ran through for four byes to win the match.[22]

There was almost as much drama in the remaining Tests. Pakistan had to follow on at Rawalpindi. Despite seventies from Saeed Anwar and Aamer Sohail (who had also made 80 in the first innings) Australia were still on top, when Malik was dropped on 20 by Taylor in the slips. He went on to play one of Pakistan's greatest Test innings, 237, in 443 minutes. Supported by Aamer Malik (who had a fitful career of fourteen Tests with a respectable average of over 35) and, again, Rashid Latif, he made the game safe. Latif was injured for the third Test at Lahore, and his replacement Moin Khan seized the chance of a Test hundred. Nonetheless, Pakistan were in trouble again until Malik scored another hundred, as did Sohail despite a badly injured neck.

The draw gave Pakistan the rubber through the dramatic win at Karachi. Malik was man of the series, with 557 runs in six completed innings. He had led Pakistan to victories in three consecutive series, something no predecessor had achieved.[23] The future looked bright. But at this high point, Salim Malik's world fell apart and Pakistan cricket passed into a shadow which has not yet been lifted.

MATCH-FIXING: VILLAINS AND VICTIMS

At 6am Mohammad Amir and two of his brothers picked me up from my Lahore guesthouse and drove me to their family village of Changa Bangyaal, a four-hour journey north towards Rawalpindi. We arrived in time to be served a delicious breakfast (cooked by Amir's sister) in the courtyard of the compound where Amir was brought up.

Then Amir and his brothers went to a large walled-off area just outside the village. This was where, until he was around fourteen years old, Amir played all his cricket – improvised games with a soft ball, wrapped in tape.[24] A game was in progress when we arrived and Amir at once joined in. I felt slightly mortified when nobody invited me to do so, but kept this to myself, and it was suggested that I umpire instead.

So there I was, stood behind the stumps at the non-striker's end, as Amir ran in to bowl. It was one of the most sublime experiences of my life, watching the beautiful fluent left-arm action that has bemused some of the greatest batsmen in the world. The members of the other team showed less respect to Amir (who they had known since childhood). Some of them were also very skilful, and this six-a-side tapeball cricket was vigorous and exciting.

It is the nearest that Amir, who is serving a five-year ban, can come to playing the game. He ought to be out there playing for his country. The heart-breaking story of Mohammad Amir reveals a great deal not just about villains and victims in Pakistan cricket but also about Pakistan itself.

There are six brothers and one sister (another sister died young and lies, along with Amir's grandparents, in the village graveyard). Amir's father was a sepoy in the Pakistan army, who served in the 1971 war. When he retired he went to work as a watchman in the local school. Amir, the second youngest in the family, told me how he first picked up a ball when he was six or seven, and was eleven when he started playing in village games.

Then he got his huge opportunity. He was spotted by a cricket coach called Asif Bajwa and invited to join his cricketing academy in Rawalpindi. He was taken on as a boarder, with academic lessons in the morning and cricket in the afternoon. At the age of fifteen he was sent for trials for the Pakistan Under-19 team at the National Academy at Lahore. Here he met Salman Butt, the future Pakistan captain, for the first time. At first Butt gave Amir a great deal of encouragement, and Amir soon joined Butt's first-class team, the National Bank.

Amir suffered some fitness and injury problems, but he overcame these. He was seventeen years old when he was first chosen for Pakistan. He made an immediate impact and was soon the youngest-ever cricketer to reach 50 wickets in Tests. It was a dizzying rise – but the fall was just as dramatic.

During the 2010 Lord's Test between Pakistan and England, Amir was caught up in a sting organised by the *News of the World*, at that time Britain's best-selling Sunday tabloid newspaper. Amir was one of three Pakistan crick-eters – the others were Salman Butt and Mohammad Asif – who were paid to manipulate the game through what is called 'spot-fixing'.* Amir was banned for five years, and later pleaded guilty in a British court to con-spiracy to obtain corrupt payments, and was sentenced to spend six months in a young offenders' institution.

The story of Amir is hideous. From the moment he entered the Pakistan

---

*Spot-fixing is a form of cheating where a specific part of the game is fixed. It may refer to an agreement for a bowler to deliver a certain type of delivery or a batsman to play out a maiden over or secure his own dismissal. It can be distinguished from match-fixing, where the result of a match is determined in advance. The emergence of Twenty20 cricket has made spot-fixing far more difficult to detect. Amir was found guilty of fixing two no-balls. The Qayyum Report defined match-fixing 'as deciding the outcome of a match before it is played and then playing oneself or having others play below one's/their ability to influence the outcome to be in accordance with the pre-decided outcome.' Importantly, spot-fixing can be achieved by individual players. Match-fixing (as Imran Khan suggested to the Qayyum Commission) requires the collaboration of five to seven players as a minimum.

dressing room this brilliant youth was approached by bookmakers and others offering him money to cheat. He was also suborned by fellow cricketers, who were more difficult to resist. By far the best account is by Michael Atherton, cricket correspondent of *The Times*, and a former England cricket captain.[25] In a long, detailed, well-informed and sympathetic article, Atherton suggests that Amir was a foolish victim rather than an evil perpetrator of events. To simplify a very complex story, Amir was approached by a bookmaker named Ali, who tried to induce him to cheat. Amir refused but under the official Code of Conduct should have reported this approach. He did not do so, although he did tell his captain, Salman Butt. This turned out to be a terrible mistake. Instead of help and sympathy, Butt passed Amir onto a corrupt businessman called Mazhar Majeed. Majeed told the young fast bowler that he was in 'big trouble' and that his name was now known to the authorities. Mazhar told Amir that he could help him out of his difficulties, but only on condition that he complied with his request to bowl two no-balls in the Lord's Test.

This was the scam which Mazhar was carrying out, set up by the *News of the World* undercover reporter. It was soon exposed and quickly led to Amir's disgrace and imprisonment.

There is no denying that he was naive. But he was just a teenager at the time, and not equipped to deal with the difficult issues with which he was confronted. While Salman Butt's conduct was wholly repellent and disgusting, Amir's is tragic and more understandable. As Atherton wrote: 'I thank God that I did not, at seventeen years of age, find myself in the kind of dressing room that Amir walked into. In my 25 years playing and watching international cricket, I cannot think of a story that has sickened me more.'

HOW MATCH-FIXING GREW

There was no match-fixing in the early days of Pakistan cricket. Almost all accounts agree that bookmakers first became involved with cricket during Asif Iqbal's disastrous tour of India in 1980. We have already seen how Dr Farrakh, the tour doctor and a cousin of Majid Khan, was disturbed by the presence of a bookmaker on the tour bus.

This is how Shuja-ud-Din, a veteran of the Kardar years, described the atmosphere: 'Discipline in the Pakistan team under Asif Iqbal did not seem a priority in their agenda as many lucrative commercial offers and social functions served as major distractions. Besides it was openly alleged that Asif Iqbal had joined hands with the top Indian speculators and gamblers, and that some of his team-mates were found too weak to resist similar sort of temptation.'[26] According to the Justice Qayyum Report, the most authoritative official investigation into match-fixing allegations:

> For the Pakistan Cricket Team, the allegation of match-fixing seems to have started when Asif Iqbal was the captain of the Pakistan team in 1979–80. Asif was accused of betting on the toss. G Viswanath, an Indian cricketer in his book has written that when he went for the toss with the Pakistani skipper, the latter without completing the toss said 'congratulations' to the former, saying that the Indian skipper had won the toss.[27]

This allegation is denied by Asif, and weakened by the fact that Viswanath, the Indian captain, never wrote a book.[28] Simon Wilde, whose book on match-fixing is the most scrupulous and reliable study of the subject, asserts that the losses endured by bookmakers were so substantial that bets were cancelled.

Match-fixing was not confined to Pakistan. The problem has been every bit as significant in India, one of whose greatest players, Mohammad Azharuddin, was destroyed by corruption allegations. In South Africa, Hansie Cronje's career was ruined when it was proved that he was part of a match-fixing racket. Bookmakers have gained a grip on players from most of the Test-playing countries over the last thirty years.

This form of cricketing corruption has been a manifestation of the rise of big money, live cricket on TV and the collapse of moral standards. It has been made easy thanks to a surfeit of meaningless matches, owing to the rise of one-day cricket. Many observers assert that the spread of the game to Sharjah under the sponsorship of the entrepreneur Abdul Rahman Bukhatir created conditions where corruption could flourish.[29] Bukhatir was one of only three people who failed to respond to invitations to be interviewed for this book. However, he has frequently defended his record and Sharjah's.[30]

From a practical point of view, a major contribution to the problem was that betting on cricket was illegal in the two countries where cricket has the largest following: India and Pakistan. India allowed betting on horseracing, but this remains a minority interest and steep government taxes on wagers and winnings above 2,500 rupees made horse betting unattractive to punters. Pakistan had no legal betting of any kind. As with Prohibition in the United States, the attempt to ban something millions of people wanted generated gigantic opportunities for criminals, who were assisted by the growth of mobile telephones. An estimate cited in *The Times of India* in 2000 put the value of betting on each one-day match at US$ 227 million, and gave a range of US$ 6–9 billion for the value of total betting on Indian cricket matches in a year.[31] In short, enormous sums of money were involved.

Two former Pakistan captains, Majid Khan and Aamer Sohail, have called for the legalisation of some form of cricket betting. Both cited the same reason – legal betting allows for inspection of abnormal bets and patterns of betting, for example heavy bets on an underdog. Majid suggested to me that legalised betting might allocate 25% of its revenues to cricket. Aamer Sohail thought that legalised betting might end the control of the 'big fish' who set the odds and other conditions of the illegal betting market for the 'little fish' in Pakistan. In addition to legalised betting, Aamer Sohail attached high priority to raising players' salaries in Pakistan. He believes that the combination of low salaries, uncertainty over first-class selection and Test selection, and the disparity between the earnings of top players and the rest makes Pakistan cricketers especially vulnerable to approaches to fix matches.[32]

As with bootlegging during Prohibition in the United States, illegal betting contributed to the strength of organised crime on the subcontinent. Through their control of racketeering, prostitution, drugs, people-smuggling and arms trafficking, criminal gangs, like multinational businesses, spread across borders and could afford to be contemptuous of national governments. They could suborn officials, judges and law-enforcement agents – and were far better financed and better armed than the agents they could not bribe.

The presence of these gangsters means that it is too simple to conclude that all of the cricketing cheats were brought down by greed. Often they were subject to physical threats (sometimes to their families), blackmail and other forms of intimidation. The response of national cricketing authorities has been feeble, with Pakistan not much worse than the rest.

Allegations that match-fixing was part of Pakistan cricket never went away after 1980. They resurfaced, as we have seen, when Pakistan lost traumatically to Australia in the semi-finals of the 1987 World Cup. Claims that cheating was a systematic part of the national game started to gain a horrifying plausibility in the mid-1990s, when a spate of accusations followed the Pakistan captain, Salim Malik.

PAKISTAN CRICKET FACES MORAL COLLAPSE

Rumours about match-fixing under Salim Malik's captaincy began to build up in 1994, especially during the Australia–Asia tournament final against India in Sharjah in April, despite Pakistan's victory. They prompted the team manager, Intikhab Alam, to assemble the players and ask them to take an oath on the Holy Quran.[33]

The rumours redoubled after Malik's strange decisions in the Mandela Trophy, a hurriedly organised one-day tournament. Pakistan reached the finals with the hosts, South Africa, ahead of Sri Lanka and New Zealand who were eliminated. Ignoring almost universal advice to the contrary from his team-mates, Malik elected to bowl first in each final when he won the toss. Pakistan lost both matches heavily. Shuja-ud-Din described how 'in the first final in Cape Town, Pakistan threw away a perfect opportunity to gain the upper hand in the best-of-three finals. Asked to get 216, they slipped from a comfortable 101 for 2 thanks to two run-outs that paved the way for a self-destructive 37-run loss.'[34] Batting second in the second final, Pakistan slipped to 42 for 6. Malik was challenged by Wasim Akram and his vice-captain, Rashid Latif, could barely speak to him. A team meeting on the eve of the one-off South Africa Test, in January 1995, dissolved into acrimony. Rashid Latif claimed that Salim Malik refused to swear on the Holy Quran that the second Mandela Trophy final had not been fixed.[35]

When the Test was played South Africa won the toss and batted. Latif was injured (sparing him the need to speak to his captain) and was replaced by Moin Khan. Astonishingly, Malik insisted on playing a replacement fast bowler, Aamer Nazir, whose plane landed just an hour before the scheduled start. Not surprisingly he collapsed several times with cramp. He did manage two wickets at lower cost than Wasim, who bowled twenty-one no-balls. No one made much effort in the field, and South Africa's all-rounder, Brian McMillan, helped himself to a century, supported by fifties from Gary Kirsten, Jonty Rhodes and the number 10, fast bowler Fanie de Villiers. South Africa totalled 460, and Pakistan made exactly half of that, with Malik falling for 99. South Africa's captain was Hansie Cronje – then thought to be a godfearing Mr Clean.* He chose not to enforce the follow-on and eventually set Pakistan 478 to win. Inzamam-ul-Haq alone resisted with 95, beginning a rich vein of form, De Villiers added four more wickets to the six he took in the first innings, and Pakistan lost by their second-largest margin of runs – 324.[36]

Worse followed in Zimbabwe. The newest and weakest Test country beat Pakistan by an innings and 64 runs. The match began with another controversial, retaken toss, after the West Indian match referee, Jackie Hendriks, refused to accept Malik's claim that he had won it.[37] Zimbabwe won the second toss and batted. The Flower brothers had a stand of 269, and then Grant Flower put on over 200 more with the all-rounder Guy Whittall. Malik's brother-in-law, Ijaz Ahmed, made 65 in Pakistan's first innings, and Inzamam-ul-Haq made 71 then 65 in the follow-on, but otherwise Pakistan disintegrated and lost with a day to spare. Not surprisingly, this match performance was much analysed as match-fixing rumours thickened.

Pakistan rallied to take the Test series 2–1 but it brought no confidence in Malik's leadership. He could not buy a run as a batsman, and team discipline broke down. He made an extraordinary and unsupported allegation that a local umpire had tampered with the ball, and the Zimbabweans were also offended by racist sledging and the style of Pakistani complaints against their first African bowler, Henry Olonga.

By the time the Tests were finished, two Pakistan players had had enough and walked out on the tour, Rashid Latif and the out-of-form Basit Ali. It was soon rumoured that they were disgusted by corrupt behaviour in the

*This was the only Test in which the two most notorious modern captains, Malik and Cronje, played together. They faced each other in the 1996 World Cup, by which time Malik was an ordinary player.

team, led by the captain. Meanwhile Aamer Sohail was reported as condemning players for taking bribes. 'It is getting so bad that it is also getting all the guys who don't do it a bad name.'[38]

SALIM MALIK DEPOSED

This was the worst possible background for an accusation in Australian newspapers that 'a prominent Pakistan cricket personality' had tried to bribe Shane Warne and Tim May, the Australian spinners, to bowl badly in the Karachi Test in the previous autumn (which had produced Pakistan's dramatic one-wicket victory).[39]

Javed Burki (by now cricket adviser to the president of Pakistan) flew to London, met David Richards of the ICC and promised swift action on the newspaper allegations. After an eight-hour board meeting Salim Malik was suspended indefinitely and given seven days to reply to the charges of match-fixing. Intikhab Alam was sacked as manager. Rashid Latif and Basit Ali were judged 'in serious breach of contract' for walking out on the team. Imran Khan demanded stern action against Malik and other match-fixers (some sources quoted him calling for hanging) and then had a renewed spat with Sarfraz Nawaz.

The Board met again and confirmed Malik's suspension, but after a few days they met yet again and rescinded it. Malik and his lawyers argued that he was innocent until proved guilty and should be allowed to confront his Australian accusers. He gained support among the cricket public and the media, who resented the Australians for waiting five months to make their charges and then refusing to come to Pakistan.[40] These arguments eventually prevailed in a court in Lahore, when Judge Fakhruddin Ebrahim threw out all the charges against Malik for lack of evidence.[41]

Before that happened Ramiz Raja was appointed captain for the forthcoming home series against Sri Lanka. He had not been to South Africa and Zimbabwe (which might have been a major recommendation). He won the first Test by an innings at Peshawar, with eight wickets from Wasim and 95 from Inzamam. However, Wasim and other seniors never settled to his leadership. Sri Lanka levelled the series and then beat Pakistan in the final Test when Wasim joined Waqar on the injury list. Losing at home to Sri Lanka was too much for the public and the selectors and they restored Wasim to captain the forthcoming tour of Australia.[42]

By now, Malik had been cleared by the judge. The selectors added him to the tour party and in a spirit of reconciliation, Rashid Latif and Basit Ali also came back after paying fines of 50,000 rupees apiece (equivalent to around £920). Intikhab Alam was also restored as manager. Majid Khan protested against the Board's decisions, and resigned his post on the organising committee for the forthcoming World Cup matches in Pakistan.[43]

Wasim's second spell of leadership began as unhappily as the first. Pakistan were clueless against Shane Warne in the first Test. He took seven wickets for 23 in the first innings, his best figures. Most of them were gifted, although he missed out on his enemy Malik, unable to bat with a damaged hand. He did claim him (fourth ball for 0) in the second innings, in which Aamer Sohail's 99 could not stave off an innings defeat. Pakistan lost the second Test by 155 runs, but nine wickets in the match for Mushtaq Ahmed did give the tourists some hope. Mushtaq managed another nine wickets in the final Test, and bowled Pakistan to a 74-run victory. The crucial innings in this low-scoring game was an uncharacteristically long, grafting century by the restored Ijaz Ahmed, while his brother-in-law, Malik, contributed 36 and 45 in each innings. Ijaz and Mushtaq were the main contributors to Pakistan's victory in the one-off Test in New Zealand, which followed. Ijaz supplied another gritty hundred and Mushtaq grabbed seven for 56 in New Zealand's second innings. Pakistan split the one-day series 2–2, with good batting performances from Inzamam, Sohail, and Malik, recovering from the Australia leg of the tour which he spent mainly alone in his room, watching television.[44] Wasim had cordial relations with his opposite numbers Mark Taylor and Lee Germon of New Zealand. There were no untoward incidents (although some of the Pakistan fielding was so horrible that it was made into a comic television compilation) and none of the matches excited any suspicion of fixing.

WORLD CUP 1996

This happy interlude was ended when Pakistan crashed out of the World Cup in 1996. Playing in front of their home crowds, Pakistan cruised through their group matches, with only one defeat against South Africa. There was a last hurrah for Javed Miandad, recovered after a successful medically advanced operation in England on his knee. He had the satisfaction of being the only man to appear in every World Cup since the beginning, but in his own words, 'I felt like an unwanted member of the team. I was being sent in to bat at number 5 or number 6 even though I had played at number 4 all my life. The captain, Wasim Akram, and the team management knew that they were under-utilising me but they didn't do anything about it.' Thanks to Arif Abbasi, who had pressed hard to have World Cup matches played in Karachi under heavy security, Javed was able to say an emotional farewell to his home crowd after seeing Pakistan through to a comfortable victory against England.[45]

The quarter-final pitted Pakistan against India in Bangalore. At the last minute Wasim Akram withdrew, citing a side strain. The captaincy passed to his deputy, Aamer Sohail. It was the first time he had led Pakistan, but he ignored the vastly more experienced Javed, who seethed at third man as Sohail lost control of the game. The Indians reached 287, powered by 93 from Navjot Sidhu and 45 in just 25 balls from Ajay Jadeja, who carted Waqar Younis all over the park.

Javed seethed again down at number 6 when Pakistan replied. Sohail and Saeed Anwar smacked the Indian bowling in an opening stand of 84, but the Pakistan fans responded silently to a flood of boundaries. Sohail rashly taunted India's seamer, Venkatesh Prasad, and was promptly bowled by him next ball. Javed's composed 38 might have consolidated the innings at number 3 but was futile at number 6 when Pakistan had fallen behind the required run rate. In the end, they were all out 39 short of their target.[46]

Javed later claimed that he alone of Pakistan's defeated team watched Sri Lanka win the final against Australia in the Gaddafi stadium in Lahore; the remainder were too scared about their reception. A rumour circulated that Wasim's injury was spurious and that he had taken money from bookies to miss the match against India. He was forced into hiding as his effigy was burned and his home in Lahore was pelted with garbage by an angry mob.[47] Wasim denied the rumour at the Qayyum Commission, which acquitted him.[48]

A FALSE DAWN

After the World Cup defeat, Pakistan cricket had what proved to be a false dawn. It began with more upheaval at the Board, as Majid Khan replaced Arif Abbasi as chief executive. He immediately removed Intikhab Alam as manager of the forthcoming tour of England; he was replaced by Yawar Saeed (the son of Pakistan's first captain before Test status).[49]

Yawar had a trouble-free tour. The two captains, Wasim Akram and Mike Atherton, were county colleagues at Lancashire and they maintained an easy relationship between the teams in spite of Imran Khan's court case, defendant in a libel action brought by Ian Botham and Allan Lamb, in which Atherton was a witness.[50] On the field, Pakistan simply outgunned England and had easy wins in two out of the three Tests. England looked safe in the Lord's Test until inspired bowling from Mushtaq Ahmed and Waqar Younis induced a collapse from 168 for 1 to 243 all out. The drawn Test at Headingley was marred by racist abuse from a section of fans; Wasim kept his team calm. After a thin time with the ball he took six wickets in the match at The Oval to seal an easy victory. Despite intense scrutiny from umpires, he and Waqar produced reverse swing when needed without incident or complaint, but they were both outbowled by Mushtaq, who had seventeen wickets in the short series. On the batting front, no fewer than five Pakistanis averaged over 60, including an apparently rehabilitated Malik.[51] There followed an extraordinary period, even by the standards of Pakistan cricket.

In a four-nation Sameer Cup one-day tournament held in Nairobi, Kenya, Shahid Afridi was called into the side as an emergency spin bowling replacement for the injured Mushtaq Ahmed. He came from the Afridi tribe in the North West but learnt his cricket in Karachi. He was only sixteen and a half (officially at least). In his first international innings he hit a century – in 37 balls – off the new World Champions, Sri Lanka, including 28 off one over from Sanath Jayasuriya.* It was the start of an explosive career, in which he would be regularly discarded for indiscipline and restored by popular demand.

Back home for the first Test against Zimbabwe, allocated to the new

---

*It stood as the fastest one-day international century for 17 years, until New Zealand's Corey Anderson reached his with a six in 36 balls against West Indies on New Year's Day 2014.

stadium in provincial Sheikhpura, Pakistan slumped to 183 for 6. At this point, Wasim gave evidence of the frequent claim that he could have become a world-class all-rounder. He hit 257, with a record 12 sixes, in 363 balls. He was partnered by Saqlain Mushtaq, aged nineteen, in only his fifth Test, in a record eighth-wicket stand of 313.

In the next Test, at home to Zimbabwe, Pakistan gave a first cap to Hasan Raza – then assumed to be fourteen. He scored a composed 27 as the Pakistanis won by an innings but then had to wait another two years for his next Test appearance as an apparent veteran of sixteen.

THE FOUNTAIN OF YOUTH

Astonishing teenagers are a recurring theme in Pakistan's cricket history. Of the 33 players recorded as making their Test debut before the age of eighteen, 15 are Pakistanis.[52] For nearly forty years the list was headed by Mushtaq Mohammad, at 15 years 124 days in the third Test at Lahore against West Indies in 1958–59.

Hasan Raza displaced him in 1996–97, when he appeared against Zimbabwe at Faisalabad at the declared age of 14 years 227 days. However, within weeks of his debut Majid Khan, the PCB chief executive, ordered him to submit to forensic bone age tests, alongside the current members of Pakistan's Under-15 and Under-19 squads. The tests (which were carried out at the hospital created by Imran Khan in memory of his mother) disqualified a number of over-age members of the squads. These did not include Hasan Raza, but his age was reassessed at 'around 15'.[53] However, the Board's own website continues to show his birthday as 11 March 1982[54] (consistent with a Test debut at fourteen), as do many other sets of statistics.

Other sensational debuts include Shahid Afridi, who allegedly blasted his record-breaking ODI century in 37 balls against Sri Lanka at the age of 16 years 217 days. Aaqib Javed made his Test debut at the alleged age of 16 years 189 days, but this entails believing that he made his first-class debut for Lahore Division against Faisalabad – *as an opening bowler* – aged 12 years 76 days.*

*That would have left him just three days older than the official record-holder as youngest first-class debutant – Pakistan's early Test opening batsman Alimuddin. He allegedly appeared for Rajasthan in the pre-Partition Indian Ranji Trophy aged 12 years 73 days (see above, p.25).

There is a simple reason behind the uncertainty over the ages of Pakistan's cricket prodigies. The British left many worthwhile legacies to the Indian subcontinent, but these did not include an effective system of birth registrations. Pakistan's problem is shared with India, Sri Lanka and Bangladesh, who between them supply another 13 of the 33 players recorded as Test debutants before eighteen. Independent Pakistan has not rectified the problem. In 2011 a UNICEF report found that only 27 per cent of all births in Pakistan had been registered between 2000 and 2009. Even in Pakistan's best-recorded province, Punjab, the figure was 77 per cent (leaving nearly a quarter of all births unregistered). In Sindh and Khyber Pakhtunkhwa the figure was 20 per cent and in Baluchistan and the Federally Administered Tribal Areas (FATA) only 1 per cent of births were registered.[55] The Islamic faith offers no equivalent of baptismal certificates (which can provide a marker of age in Christian societies), and the ages of cricketers, and indeed other Pakistanis, are frequently established some years after birth, from other official papers, particularly school records, or by personal or family declaration.

Pakistan's cricketers have multiple motives to make themselves appear younger than their true ages, particularly since Under-19 cricket, and latterly Under-16 cricket, have become such important passageways to senior recognition. In the later stages of their careers, losing a few years helps senior players keep a place in the Pakistan team or win a contract overseas. Of course, personal pride is also a factor, and they may also want to inspire other teenagers after them.

For over forty years, the administrators of Pakistan cricket accepted players' own assessments of their ages, backed up by whatever documents they could produce – usually a school leaving certificate. The first official to impose reform on the system was Arif Abbasi, during his tenure as chief executive of the PCB in 1995–96. He told me that his aim was to preserve the integrity of Pakistan's domestic Under-19 championship, in which PIA had been accused of fielding an overage player. Abbasi told the team manager – Hanif Mohammad, no less – that he had 'mucked up' and had PIA disqualified. He also introduced a new system in which players' ages would be based on their certified age at entry into primary school, which officially was compulsory at five years old.[56]

Although this was much more reliable than the previous system, it could not give certainty about players' ages, because many Pakistani children miss out on primary school, or enter it late, particularly in rural or outlying areas. In 2007, a UNESCO report on the Pakistan education system, based on official Pakistan statistics for 2005–06, found that, 'Over 35% of the population 5 to 9 years of age is not in school. Given a population of 5 to 9 years old of some 19.5 million, this means that about 7 million children aged 5 to 9 are out of the education system.' The net enrolment rate was highest in Islamabad and the Capital Territories, but over 20 per cent of local children aged five to nine were excluded. In FATA and Baluchistan over half of primary school-age children were outside the system.[57]

Pakistan, like all ICC countries, now has to apply a double test for cricketers entered in any under-age tournament. The PCB has to inspect players' documentary evidence of age (still usually a school entry certificate) and conduct a physiological examination.[58] These are based on bone X-rays (the method which displaced Hasan Raza) and they have excluded a number of over-age players from domestic and international Under-19 competitions.[59]

However, Pakistan is still a country where teenage cricketers can dream of representing their country with the minimum of experience. The tradition is still alive in which the brilliant junior (such as Inzamam-ul-Haq or Waqar Younis) reveals his talent at the right time and place to astonished seniors and selectors, and is rushed into the international team.

Aaqib Javed and Hasan Raza were beneficiaries of that tradition. Interviewed by the Indian writer, Rahul Bhattacharya, Aaqib Javed was scarcely aware that he had made a first-class debut aged twelve. '*First class?* That was a first-class match? Are you sure? I remember playing one match when I was in school but . . . ' While at college, he turned up for some trials under Wasim Raja for a national training camp at the Gaddafi stadium. It was almost a joke, and he had never been to the stadium before. Each boy bowled only two deliveries. Aaqib thought that his two were better than most and boldly asked Wasim Raja to look at him again. He bowled three or four more. 'They were good balls, outswingers.' Wasim Raja picked him for the month-long camp. He rated him the most talented player and recommended him for the preparatory camp for the Under-19 World Cup in 1988. There he caught the eye of Imran, who took him on a charity tour of India – and then insisted on taking him on the Test tour of Australia.[60] Aaqib later became a notably successful coach of Pakistani teenagers.

In a 2005 interview about his debut, Hasan Raza showed no bitterness at his displacement as the world's youngest Test cricketer and some rough treatment by the selectors thereafter. He began (like so many local boys) playing tapeball cricket in the crowded streets of Karachi, where the ball has to be placed carefully to avoid being lost. Then he had success for Government Boys School, which encouraged him to try out for Pakistan's Under-15 World Cup squad in 1996. He made it and performed well, and then scored nine centuries in Karachi's Under-19 league. Zaheer Abbas, then chief selector, gave him his first-class debut (aged no more than fifteen) in a trial match against the visiting Zimbabweans, and he made 58. A ninety followed for Karachi Blues against Karachi Whites in the Quaid-e-Azam Trophy – whereupon Zaheer stuck him in the team for the second Test. 'I didn't really have any experience at all. I was very surprised. My goal was to play at the Under-15 World Cup that year first and then eventually for Pakistan. But so early I just couldn't believe it.'[61]

Mushtaq Mohammad, the man restored to pride of place as the youngest Test cricketer, still believes in his official birthday, 22 November 1943, as does his brother Sadiq.[62] However, by comparison with Hasan Raza, he was a seasoned veteran on his Test debut as a fifteen-year-old, with nine first-class games behind him. In the first (aged barely thirteen) batting number 9, he scored 87 for Karachi Whites against Sindh and took five wickets for 28 in Sindh's second innings. Mushtaq has said that he felt no pressure on his Test debut, and treated it as just another game. He has always been a firm believer in Pakistan's traditions of surprise selections, for players of any age, and maintained it himself as a national selector. He told the BBC in 2000, 'When you see a talent you must have the confidence to put him in the team.'[63]

MORE MARVELS

To return to the narrative, the next marvel in this phase of Pakistan cricket was Mohammad Wasim's century on debut at Lahore in the first of two Tests against New Zealand, after a duck in the first innings, although it did not save Pakistan from defeat. Pakistan levelled the series in Rawalpindi thanks to a debutant pace bowler, Mohammad Zahid, who took eleven wickets, using a new ball which (due to administrative incompetence by the PCB) had to be purchased hurriedly from a local sports shop. Mushtaq took eight of the remaining wickets as Pakistan won by an innings.

Saeed Anwar then produced an astonishing one-day innings at Madras against India in a special tournament to celebrate fifty years of independence for south Asia. He scored 194, then the highest one-day score, in 147 balls with 22 fours and 5 sixes. A slight man, who had been ill for six months, Saeed relied on exquisite timing. The opposing captain, Sachin Tendulkar, called it the greatest innings he had ever seen and the home crowd gave him a standing ovation.[64] After this exquisite effort, it is sad to see Saeed in the list of players tainted by match-fixing allegations.

Pakistan now had a year with five different captains. Saeed Anwar was at the helm for the 1996–97 home series against New Zealand. Ramiz Raja was restored for a short away series in Sri Lanka; two dull draws. Saeed was back for the 1997–98 series at home to South Africa; one defeat and two draws. It is worth noting that Salim Malik played in six of the Tests concerned, scoring 427 runs in eight innings, including a big hundred against Sri Lanka.

Wasim Akram then had the satisfaction of sweeping the West Indies at home, winning all three Tests. It was a weak West Indian side, led by an ageing Courtney Walsh with no bowling support and Brian Lara miserable, but it was still an excellent and disciplined Pakistan performance. Inzamam-ul-Haq, Aamer Sohail and Ijaz Ahmed piled up runs. Wasim led well and was the leading wicket-taker, although Saqlain Mushtaq led the averages with nine wickets at less than nine apiece.[65]

Pakistan's next engagement was a tour of South Africa and Zimbabwe. Perhaps remembering the previous disaster under Salim Malik, the selectors, now chaired by Saleem Altaf, made Pakistan's leading cricket campaigners against match-fixing captain and vice-captain: Rashid Latif and Aamer Sohail. Malik was not included, nor was Wasim Akram, officially for fitness reasons. If the Board and the selectors hoped for a new start from a young team, they were disappointed. Relations between the two sides were poisoned before the first Test, when Saqlain Mushtaq and the pace bowler, Mohammad Akram, claimed to have been mugged in the street; the South Africans claimed that they had been brawling in a nightclub.

Latif had a neck injury, so Sohail took over for the first two Tests. The first was a drab draw, the second brought Pakistan's first victory against South Africa. The stars were the young all-rounder Azhar Mahmood, who added a second century to one in the first Test, and Mushtaq Ahmed, who took six wickets in South Africa's second innings. Yousuf Youhana, the fourth Christian to play for Pakistan, made a low-key start to a long career. Pakistan failed to build on this victory. Team spirit was damaged when Khalid Mahmood, the new chairman of the PCB (Majid Khan remained chief executive) insisted on sending Wasim to join the team. This provoked the resignation of the chairman of selectors, Saleem Altaf. Wasim took three wickets in the first innings but looked less than match-fit and was out-bowled by Waqar Younis (still his strong rival), who took ten in the match. Latif took over the captaincy but his first outing was disastrous; he bagged a pair and kept wicket poorly. Pakistan crashed to defeat by 259 runs.[66]

Wasim was sidelined by fever in the first Test against Zimbabwe, which was a tame draw, but returned for the second, which Pakistan won through a massive hundred from Mohammad Wasim. Latif was in charge for both matches.[67]

THE QAYYUM COMMISSION

Throughout this period there was a continued swirl of rumours about match-fixing and corruption. The Board, under the leadership of Majid Khan, set up an administrative inquiry under Justice Chaudhry Ejaz Yousuf. It made a preliminary finding that Salim Malik, Ijaz Ahmed and Wasim Akram had been involved in match-fixing – but the Board then decided that the allegations required a full judicial inquiry, and that the players should be eligible for selection until this was completed. Majid pressed for this course with the president of Pakistan, still patron of the Board, the Muslim League politician, Mohammad Rafiq Tarar.[68]

It was entrusted to Justice Malik Qayyum, a respected judge and once a decent club batsman, to lead the full inquiry.[69] Qayyum began work in September 1998. He took evidence from fifty-three witnesses, including current and former players, officials, journalists and even bookmakers, some cheerfully admitting criminal offences. He took evidence from the Australians Mark Waugh and Mark Taylor, on their country's tour of Pakistan. Their evidence was then thrown into doubt by the public admission by Waugh and Shane Warne, the original accusers of Salim Malik, that they had taken money from an Indian bookmaker for information on the 1994 Singer Trophy match between Pakistan and Australia. The Qayyum Commission took fresh evidence from Waugh and Warne in Australia.[70] The Pakistan cricket public were incensed to learn that the ACB had fined Waugh and Warne but covered this up for several months.[71]

The Qayyum hearings produced a feast of allegations, beginning, as already noted, with Asif Iqbal's coin toss with Gundappa Viswanath, as far back as 1979. The other principal stories were as follows:

1) The claim that Salim Malik offered bribes to Shane Warne and Tim May to bowl badly in the Singer Trophy of 1994;

2) The Qayyum Commission confirmed Latif's protest against Malik's conduct during the one-day Mandela cricket tournament in South Africa;

3) Ata-ur-Rehman, a young fast bowler, came forward with allegations that he had been paid 100,000 rupees by Wasim Akram to bowl badly in the one-day match in Christchurch, New Zealand in 1993–94. There were, however, problems with Rehman's testimony, mainly that he repeatedly changed his story (he claimed under pressure from criminals). Latif also claimed that this match was fixed. He told the Qayyum Commission that before this match Malik called him to his room and tried to bribe him to play badly. Latif stated that four other players were present in the room – Inzamam, Waqar Younis, Akram Raza and Basit Ali. (The first three of these players denied this, while Basit Ali was suffering from jaundice and did not comment on the allegation.) Latif also alleged that when he took a catch to dismiss the New Zealand opener Bryan Young, Malik reprimanded him, saying that 'we have to lose the match';*

4) It was alleged that Pakistan, captained by Salim Malik, had thrown the third and final Test match against New Zealand at Christchurch in February 1994. Witnesses included Intikhab Alam,† whose evidence

---

*Qayyum, Part V, 19. Qayyum also noted that 'this is the same match which Ata-ur-Rehman says Wasim Akram had fixed with Ijaz Ahmed and Zafar Ali Jojo in Pakistan.'

†Qayyum, Part III, 29. Intikhab, according to Qayyum, 'maintained that betting and match-fixing had taken place during his tenure as manager.'

had special weight not just because he carried with him a wealth of experience but because he was team manager during this tour;

5) A former first-class cricketer turned bookmaker, Saleem Pervez, claimed that he had bribed Malik and Mushtaq Ahmed the sum of $100,000 to throw the one-day match between Australia and Pakistan in the Singer tournament in Sri Lanka in 1994.*

During the course of Qayyum's work, Khalid Mahmood and Majid Khan† left their roles at the PCB, which passed into the hands of two short-term caretakers, Mujeeb-ur-Rehman and Zafar Altaf.

Qayyum submitted a meticulous report to the Nawaz Sharif government in October 1999. Almost immediately afterwards, this government was overthrown by General Pervez Musharraf in a coup. This brought fresh change to the PCB when Musharraf installed his man, General Tauqir Zia, as the new chairman. He and the new government then sat on the Qayyum Report for several months. When finally published in May 2000 it made withering criticisms of many famous players but punished them relatively lightly.‡

In the introduction, Justice Qayyum stated that match-fixing was 'the most serious threat the game has faced in its life.'[72] He found Salim Malik guilty of match-fixing and recommended a lifetime ban and a fine of ten lakhs (1 million rupees, then equivalent to around £13,000). Wasim Akram was found not guilty of match-fixing 'on the ground of insufficient evidence.' Nevertheless the judge stated bluntly that, 'Wasim Akram is not above board. He has not co-operated with this Commission. It is only by

---

*Qayyum examined in detail claims that the following matches were fixed: the third Test between New Zealand and Pakistan, Christchurch, February 1994; the fifth one-day international between New Zealand and Pakistan at Christchurch, 16 March 1994; the Singer World Series match between Australia and Pakistan at Colombo, 7 September 1994; and Pakistan v England at Sharjah, 15 December 1997.

†Qayyum suggests that the investigation would never have taken place without pressure from Majid Khan, then chief executive of the PCB. According to Qayyum, Majid requested that 'a judicial inquiry be conducted into the allegations of betting and match-fixing, as he felt that only a judicial commission would be able to find the truth. Ordinary domestic inquiry officers had no power vested in them to either summon any person, nor to compel their attendance or to make them give statements on oath and in case they perjured, to be able to deal with them.' Qayyum, Part I, 9.

‡The Qayyum report arrived just when match-fixing scandals were erupting across the world. A month earlier, Hansie Cronje had confessed to match-fixing and in the same month the great Indian all-rounder Kapil Dev was accused of corruption by his former team-mate Manoj Prabhakar. Indian tax authorities had also mounted raids against Kapil Dev, former captain Mohammad Azharuddin and the Indian Cricket Board chief Jagmohan Dalmiya. Piesse, op. cit. p.265; Rae, op. cit. p.272.

giving Wasim Akram the benefit of the doubt after Ata-ur-Rehman changed his testimony in suspicious circumstances that he has not been found guilty of match-fixing. He cannot be said to be above suspicion.' He recommended a fine of three lakh (300,000 rupees). I approached Wasim for an interview for this book and was sorry to receive no reply.*

In a devastating conclusion, Qayyum stated that Wasim Akram should be 'removed from the captaincy of the national team' on the grounds that he was 'too sullied to hold that office.'

Waqar Younis got off more lightly, though the judge was suspicious of his testimony, and was particularly scathing about Waqar's breezy statement to the commission that he 'had not even heard of anyone being involved in match-fixing.'[73] Qayyum concluded that 'Waqar Younis has been reluctant to help this commission and even when prompted was not fully forth-coming.' He recommended a fine of one lakh (100,000 rupees), then equivalent to around £700. Qayyum was more brutal on Inzamam and Akram Raza, whom he accused of developing 'partial amnesia', adding that 'this commission believes that these players probably knew more than they revealed.' For Saeed Anwar, who fell under suspicion for his role in the Singer Trophy match against Australia, he also recommended a fine of one lakh. The judge felt that 'Saeed Anwar has by his actions brought doubt onto himself. Further, this commission felt that Saeed Anwar was with-holding some evidence from the Commission.'[74]

Mushtaq Ahmed was found to have 'brought the name of the Pakistan team into disrepute [by] associating with gamblers.' Basit Ali, who (accord-ing to Intikhab Alam) had actually owned up to involvement in match-fixing, was spared serious censure from Qayyum only because he had by then retired.[75] He recommended a fine of three lakh. In a sweeping judgement, Qayyum pronounced:

> This Commission felt a lot of the time that most of the people appear-ing before it were not telling the truth, or at least not the whole truth. Even more regretful was the attitude and statements of those who said

*However, Wasim Akram has answered Qayyum in his autobiography: 'I have never attempted to throw a match, and have never even considered such a thing for a second. I also have no knowledge of any Pakistan cricketer taking money to influence events on the field. That is a slur that just won't go away in Pakistan cricket, and it claimed Salim Malik when he was sacked as captain. Salim has always protested his innocence and I have no reason to doubt him.' *Wasim: The Autobiography of Wasim Akram*, p.4.

they had not even heard of match-fixing. Some appeared tutored, while others seemed unwilling to blow the whistle. Mr Waqar Younis, for one, initially said he had not even heard of anyone being involved in match-fixing. Inzamam-ul-Haq similarly seemed to suffer from amnesia. They both needed stern prompting to speak true and even then it is doubtful they spoke the whole truth.[76]

Ever since there have been rumours that the punishments would have been tougher but for political intervention to rescue the careers of some of the most senior cricketers. General Musharraf, who became president and (crucially) patron of Pakistan cricket when the Qayyum Report was published in 2000, did not discourage this suggestion when I interviewed him in his London flat.[77]

To sum up, the Qayyum Report amounted to a devastating condemnation of the culture of Pakistan cricket in the 1990s. It was morally sick, and many of the greatest players were criticised. They included: Wasim Akram; Waqar Younis, Mushtaq Ahmed, Saeed Anwar, Salim Malik, Inzamam-ul-Haq. All this is too heartbreaking for words.

CODA: THE 1999 WORLD CUP AND THE BHANDARI REPORT

While the Qayyum inquiry was in progress, Pakistan cricket continued as normal with all the main suspects in place. Under Wasim Akram, and with Salim Malik, they toured India in 1998–99 under tight security, following threats from Hindu extremists. A thrilling two-Test series was shared 1–1. In the first Test, Pakistan snatched victory by 12 runs, thanks to a blazing century from Shahid Afridi and ten wickets in the match from Saqlain Mushtaq, who produced a 'doosra' to dismiss Sachin Tendulkar for 136 in India's second innings. India's easy victory in the second Test was made memorable when Anil Kumble took all ten wickets in Pakistan's second innings.*

This fine series excited no suspicions but earlier, in 1998, the South Africans accused the Pakistani, Javed Akhtar, of taking bribes when standing

---

*His friend Javagal Srinath deliberately bowled wide of the stumps in the closing stages of the innings.

as 'neutral' umpire in England's Test series against South Africa. (He gave England seven lbws against one for South Africa in the close-fought deciding Test.)[78]

Pakistan's performance in the 1999 World Cup excited a fresh wave of suspicions, led by Sarfraz Nawaz and Majid Khan. These centred on Pakistan's shock defeat in the group matches by Bangladesh. Wasim bowled badly, conceding two extra overs in wides and no-balls. The normally immaculate Saqlain conceded six wides. Afridi was out to a rash shot. Saeed Anwar was run out by Inzamam-ul-Haq, who then got out to an awful shot himself. Mushtaq Mohammad was in agony as he watched this defeat. He was an emergency appointment as team coach – replacing the abrasive Javed Miandad, who had confronted the team over rumours of wrongdoing after an inept performance in Sharjah just before the tournament.[79]

A very different personality, Mushtaq was determined to keep a good relationship with his players. He suppressed his doubts about the Bangladesh performance, although he wrote later that the circumstances (Pakistan could afford to lose and still qualify for the next stage) made the match 'custom-made for fixing with the odds stacked so firmly in Pakistan's favour.'[80]

Sarfraz and Majid also focused on irresponsible shots which brought defeat in a group match against India. Then followed Wasim's obstinate decision to bat first in the final. Mushtaq argued strongly before the match in favour of bowling first. Lord's always favoured seamers first thing (as Wasim knew well from his one-day finals with Lancashire) and the pitch had sweated under covers for two days. Besides helping Pakistan's attack (packed with swing bowlers), fielding first would help calm the team members who were newcomers to Lord's. But Mushtaq could not overcome the resistance of Wasim, Ijaz Ahmed, Saeed Anwar and Salim Malik (in the tour party but on the skids as a player; Wasim thought he had lost his nerve against fast bowling). Pakistan batted first, crashed to 132 all out against Australia and lost the most one-sided final in World Cup history.[81]

Years later, Mushtaq remains haunted by this experience but he maintains his code of loyalty to the players. He told me: 'I felt at times that some things were wrong, but I had no awareness of match-fixing and I couldn't accuse anyone because of my suspicions. I had no knowledge of gambling to assist any investigation. I told the PCB I would report anything fishy but I did not want to be questioned about it afterwards.'[82]

All of these issues arrived too late for Justice Qayyum, so yet another inquiry was set up, under Justice Bhandari of Lahore. Abdul Qadir was its cricket expert. When Bhandari reported, in June 2002, he dismissed all the allegations. The players involved could not be condemned on the basis of inference and opinion, even from eminent cricketers. He also acquitted umpire Javed Akhtar,* and was scathing about the South African Cricket Board's failure to co-operate with his inquiry. He also had harsh words for the new Anti-Corruption Unit, set up by the ICC under former Metropolitan Police Commissioner Paul Condon, which had offered him no evidence except for a copy of an article in *Wisden*.[83]

In fairness match-fixing is a global problem, by no means confined to Pakistan. Shock results do happen; victory for an underdog gives meaning and exhilaration to sport. It should not automatically be cause for suspicion. Yet the body of evidence is there. The Pakistan dressing room during this period was squalid and rancorous. Those involved betrayed the game of cricket, tens of millions of passionate supporters and their country. Either through their actions, or through their reticence, they disgraced their families, and themselves. They have left a permanent and ineradicable stain on Pakistan cricket. To this day a cloud of suspicion still surrounds any Pakistan cricketer who goes out to play for his country, especially if (as happens to all cricketers) he has an off-day or makes a bad decision. The damage they have caused is boundless. It is astonishing that enthusiasm for the game has remained so high in view of the cynicism and corruption of so many of the greatest players.

---

*After his acquittal Akhtar sued his accuser, Dr Ali Bacher, head of the South African Cricket Board, for libel, seeking damages of 100 million rupees (then equivalent to around £1.2 million). Bacher refused to appear in court in Pakistan, and the umpire received no reward except to restore his good name (source: www.espncricinfo.com, 'Bacher refuses to appear in Pakistani court', 2 February 2001).

THE GROWTH OF PAKISTAN CRICKET

'Like everywhere else in the Indian subcontinent, the popularisation of the game among the masses took place in lanes and bylanes in non-descript towns and mundane village grounds, orchards, or grazing fields.'

– MURTAZA SHIBLI, BRITISH KASHMIRI AUTHOR AND POET,
ON THE GROWTH OF CRICKET IN KASHMIR

In Britain since World War Two, football has displaced cricket as the dominant national sport, the latter having receded in the national consciousness, losing its popularity among the masses, its appeal concentrating in a narrow middle-class base.

The opposite process has taken place in Pakistan. Even in the late 1970s cricket was still an elite activity, mainly restricted to the middle classes of Karachi and Lahore. As elsewhere on the subcontinent, the three decades since 1980 have witnessed an incredible expansion of the game, both socially and geographically. Cricket is now played with fanaticism in distant hamlets and among the poorest people.

The game has spread to rural villages, to obscure towns, to remote valleys, and in due course over the border to Afghanistan. It is played on riverbanks, on mountain plateaux, in graveyards, on barren earth – basically anywhere with a flat surface. It is played with rough-hewn planks, with wooden balls, with tennis balls, with compressed melted footballs, with anything that can bounce. It is increasingly played by women as well as men. This explosion of interest has thrown up some of the greatest cricketers the world has known.

One way to illustrate this extraordinary new cricketing consciousness is through personal narratives. We have already told the story of the wrist-spinner Abdul Qadir. That of his student and successor, Mushtaq Ahmed, is of special symbolism and importance.

MUSHTAQ AHMED: LABOURER'S SON AND CRICKETING GENIUS

Abdul Qadir was the prototype for a new generation of cricketers, for whom the game was a method of social and economic advance as well as a recreation. One of ten children (two of whom died in childhood), Mushtaq Ahmed was the son of a labourer. 'My father, Shamsudin, had to work all the hours under the sun to support us,' his son recalled in his autobiography. 'He would often start at five o'clock in the morning, and not return before midnight, as he was labouring in a cotton factory but was also responsible for getting the other labourers that the factory needed – for this he earned the equivalent of £1 a day.'[1]

Mushtaq was brought up in the Punjabi district of Sahiwal (formerly Montgomery), about two hours from Lahore. 'We kept three buffaloes in our yard,' he recalls. 'We had to feed them with hay and straw and they supplied us with milk each day. Our house only had three rooms and all the children would sleep in one of them. We relied entirely on my father's work at the cotton mill for money.'[2]

As a child Mushtaq would endlessly play cricket in the street. He recalled that:

Gradually cricket became my passion. Although we did not own a TV I would watch cricket whenever I could and was quick to imitate the players I admired. I would never be without a cricket ball in my hand and would happily bowl a ball at a poplar tree for hours on end. I imagined I was Imran Khan bowling medium pace or Abdul Qadir bowling his leg-spin. For me the tree was the stumps and I was in a Test match. If I

missed the tree I had to run after the ball before going through the
motions again – so it taught me to be accurate! All I wanted to do was
play cricket. I would be late for meals and as soon as I finished school I
would throw my books in the house to go out and play. I even used to
sleep with a cricket ball. My mum could not understand it and some
people said I was unstable. I should tell you the 'cricket' balls we used at
this time were not the kind of ball I am used to using now. If we managed to get hold of a tennis ball we would use that, but they were very
expensive. Sometimes we would put a cheap plastic football into very hot
water until it melted and shrank to the size of a cricket ball. These balls
had a lot of bounce and could be bowled with some pace. That was the
kind of ball I bowled at the tree.[3]

This account by Mushtaq describes with complete accuracy the experience
of literally millions of young Pakistani boys over the last two or three
decades. Of course, for most their dreams remained unfulfilled. Only a
minute fraction of them escaped to play first-class, let alone Test cricket.
Even today these young men remain a massive and very largely untapped
ocean of cricketing potential. If Pakistan had the organisation (and the
vision) to marshal them, it would overnight become the greatest cricketing
nation.

Also typical was the hostility of Mushtaq's family. His father would beat
him for bunking off school and playing cricket. He would tell his son that
if he failed to get a decent education he too would be forced to live his life
as a labourer. Furthermore, his father's true enthusiasm was for *kabaddi*, a
traditional South Asian wrestling game. 'This is a proper game,' his uncles
would tell young Mushtaq. 'You should play it. This is a man's game.'[4]

There appears to have been no cricket coaching in the rural area where
Mushtaq lived, so he learned off the television. 'We did not have a television at home, but fortunately one of our neighbours had a set and I would
go to his house to watch cricket whenever I could. They were quite happy
with the arrangement because they would send me on errands, going to the
cleaners or collecting the milk and I would run as fast as I could to finish
the job and get back to the game.'

Young Mushtaq studied all the great players. He taught himself to imitate Imran Khan but concentrated on Qadir's action. 'Abdul Qadir was my

bowling hero,' recorded Mushtaq. 'I just loved seeing him bowl and mar-velled at the way he would mesmerise batsmen. At that age I was already observing cricketers very closely and analysing their movements. I would watch him produce his variations and then go out and try them out for myself. By copying what I saw and practising for hours I found that the other boys in the street could not play me and I was getting them out.'[5]

Eventually Mushtaq's leg-spin got noticed. He was chosen for his Muhmuddiah High School. It was a very poorly resourced school, and Mushtaq's big break came when Muhmuddiah played their much better-equipped local rivals, the Comprehensive School. After the game, in which Mushtaq played well, he received an offer to play for the opposition. Since the school was four miles away, he was offered, as an inducement, a bicycle.

At the Comprehensive School, Mushtaq made the connections that were to take him to the top. He was invited to play for Montgomery Cricket Club, a major club owned by a biscuit manufacturer, Basharat Shafi, who paid him 500 rupees a month, which he was able to spend on cricket gear. Shafi was also president of the Multan Cricket Division. On his debut for Multan, Mushtaq scored 75; an unknown youngster, Inzamam-ul-Haq, scored a century. Another emerging player was Waqar Younis.

Such was Mushtaq's background. It was a very different trajectory from the cricketing educations of earlier generations, who rose through the con-ventional route of school and university. Essentially Mushtaq was self-taught on the street. Once again, it is worth quoting from his autobiography at length:

> The 1980s was a time of massive passion and enthusiasm for cricket among the poorer people of Pakistan. Ninety per cent of first-class crick-eters in Pakistan could not afford a bag or whites, so they relied on the patronage of their clubs: if not, they had to borrow clothing and equip-ment. I know that Inzamam, Waqar, Saeed Anwar and myself owe our enduring success with Pakistan to our upbringing. We were not playing at being cricketers like some of the rich people who managed a couple of seasons in the first-class game before going back into business. We were fighting for survival and developed the strong character and resolve needed to stay at the top once we managed to get there.[6]

For players like these hard work and passion were essential, but they shared these qualities with thousands of others. They also needed superlative skill and the essential lucky break. Great cricketers emerged overnight, like some volcanic eruption. This happened with Mushtaq in 1987, when the English tourists came to Sahiwal to play against the Chief Minister's X1. Mushtaq's sponsor Basharat Shafi asked him to be the 'waterboy'. Mushtaq remembers that, on the morning of the match, he was looking at the England team, 'with all their smart equipment, spikes and sunglasses.' Then Salim Malik, captain of the Chief Minister's XI and already a superstar, wandered up: 'Mushtaq, young fellow, you are playing today.'[7]

On that 1987–88 tour England were already experiencing terrible difficulty coping with the wrist-spin of Abdul Qadir in the Tests. They must have been looking forward to a reprieve on their trip to sleepy Sahiwal. Instead they were presented with what was in effect a Qadir clone. Mushtaq swept them aside with six first-innings wickets, and was called up for the Test squad in Karachi.

Trouble lay ahead. This country boy had never been in an aeroplane before, and had to be shown how to put on a seatbelt. At the hotel it emerged that he had never used a lift, and had to be rescued, along with his luggage.[8] He did not know a word of English, or how to use a knife and fork. All these skills would soon be learnt. The brilliant country lad from Sahiwal was launched on an international cricket career.

SHOAIB AKHTAR: NIGHTWATCHMAN'S SON

We now turn to the most elemental force of nature that Pakistan cricket has yet produced: the fast bowler Shoaib Akhtar, sometimes known as the 'Rawalpindi Express'. Shoaib turned himself into the fastest bowler in the world, the first to breach the 100mph speed barrier, unpredictable, merciless, terrifying to face. Some cricket writers have dismissed Shoaib as brilliant but inconsistent. This profoundly misunderstands the man. From an early age Shoaib possessed a knowledge of his own destiny that is more usually associated with statesmen or artists. This sense of mission gave an extraordinary integrity and lucidity to a magnificent cricketing career.

Shoaib hardly ever saw his father, Mohammad, who worked as a nightwatchman at a petrol station. He would be asleep when Shoaib got up, and at work when his son went to bed. The most powerful guiding force in Shoaib's life, therefore, was his mother Ammi, by whom he was raised in Mahalla Jaadi, one of the poorest neighbourhoods in the old British army base of Rawalpindi.

One of Shoaib's keenest childhood memories was the arrival of the land-lady seeking rent, and his mother's agitation.[9] His family had been so short of money that his mother had been given away for adoption when five years old to a childless English couple, from whom she had run away after sev-eral months. They came looking for her, but her family pretended not to know where she was.

Shoaib's mother Ammi, like so many unknown Pakistani matriarchs, deserves the gratitude of all lovers of Pakistan cricket. She had five sons (one of whom died in infancy) and one daughter. Somehow she paid for the edu-cation of the children. A *baba* (saint) predicted that she would have many sons, 'and one of them will make a big name for himself in the world.' She long assumed that that child was Shoaib, her youngest son, noting how his forehead would glow in the dark.

Shoaib taught himself as a schoolboy, excited by Pakistan's 1992 World Cup victory and seeking to emulate the action of Imran Khan. As so often in Pakistan, he was spotted by a coach, Shahid Bhaijan, who took him to play at the Rawalpindi Club. Shoaib was approached by Majid Khan, who asked his name: 'Shoaib. Very soon everyone will know my name.' Majid rebuked him: 'Son, I hope you have your head screwed tightly on your shoulders.'[10] The remarks of both men were equally prophetic. One evening Shoaib passed the Pakistan team practising at the Rawalpindi Club. 'I decided then and there', he later recalled, 'that I would play in the national team with these greats, come what may. Of course, I had no idea how to go about it, not even how to get into first-class cricket.'[11]

Shaoib went to Lahore for trials with PIA. Unable to pay for a bed for the night, he convinced a tonga driver to give him some bedding, telling him that one day he would play for Pakistan and come back to meet him when he did so. '*Naam yaad rakhna*' ('Remember my name') were Shoaib's part-ing words.

Shoaib was chosen to play for PIA, which meant living in Karachi, at that point (1994–95) convulsed by civil war between rival parties fighting for

power. On his salary of 500 rupees per month (then equivalent to around
£11) Shoaib could only afford the cheapest lodgings at the centre of the
fighting. He had to pick his way through dead bodies on his journey to the
National stadium. In Karachi during this period it was too dangerous to play
cricket in open ground for fear of bullets. 'The army had been given shoot-
at-sight orders and I survived bullets flying past me as I sat next to my
window. I saw people being blown up by rocket launchers,' he recalled. 'I
lived in a constant state of fear. I was still in my teens and had already spent
many nights on the roadside.'[12]

Eventually Shoaib left Karachi. It wasn't the gunfire. He wasn't given the
chance he craved. He failed at the PIA. Shoaib wrote later that he confronted the big shots in the PIA office:

> *Kameenon,* you rascals! You didn't give me a chance to play. Now you just
> watch what happens. Within a year I will be playing for the Pakistan
> team, try and stop me. I will be the star of the Pakistan team. Write this
> down so you won't forget it. I handed over my resignation letter saying,
> *laat bhejta hoon is naukri par* – I wipe my feet on this job, I spit on this
> job, I spit on you people and I spit on this sports body.[13]

Shoaib returned home filled with a sense of mission. He reports that for an
entire year 'I woke up early every morning and ran from 3am to 5.30am . . .
There were others who were definitely better than I was but not as hard-
working. They did not have the *junoon* – that obsession, the kind of
passion and belief that is needed to succeed.' This was a lonely and desperate period of Shoaib's life. Once he turned his head to the skies and
asked: 'Boss, are you there? Is someone going to talk to me, advise me?'[14]
Eventually Shoaib got his second chance with the Agricultural Development
Bank of Pakistan, and he took his revenge when they played PIA: 'When
the ball was handed to me, I probably had a terrible smile on my face, a true
reflection of my inner feelings. I got two of them on the helmet and in all,
injured five.'

After the game Shoaib stood outside the PIA dressing-room window and
yelled: 'How many of you did I get? Did you see what I can do?' Shoaib says
that 'the past had taken control of my mind and I couldn't help myself. I just
kept shouting and swearing at them till my team-mates dragged me away,

saying, "*khuda da vasta*, for God's sake, come away or you'll get into real trouble."[15]

A year later Shoaib was playing for Pakistan. He received a cheque for 8,000 rupees. He records in his autobiography that he 'gave his first cheque to his mother, and received her blessings.' Nor did Shoaib forget the tongawallah who had helped him out in Lahore. After a long search Shoaib found him sleeping on a street corner. 'I kept trying to push some money into his pocket but he wouldn't let me. Aziz Khan was a poor man in the eyes of the world, but to me he was rich with self-respect and dignity.'[16] Thus began the extraordinary Test career of the fastest bowler the world had known.

THE NORTH WEST: A NEW FRONTIER FOR PAKISTAN CRICKET

As this brand-new cricketing passion spread through the masses there was a most remarkable change in Pakistan's remote North West. The tribal people had refused to play cricket before independence, because they associated the sport with foreign occupation. This antipathy vanished after 1980. This is a phenomenon which cries out for greater explanation, and several factors were at work. The most important may have been the emergence of a number of cricketing stars of Pashtun heritage, of whom the most famous were Imran Khan and (later) Shahid Afridi. Television was crucial; it spread the sport at a time when the national team was enjoying unprecedented success, culminating in the 1992 World Cup, that moment of national triumph and exultation.

I travelled to Peshawar, capital of Khyber Pakhtunkhwa and administrative centre for the war-torn and lawless tribal areas.[17] These Federally Administered Tribal Areas (FATA), bordering Afghanistan in north-western Pakistan, are mountainous, inaccessible and governed by their own legal and moral codes. Almost entirely inhabited by Pashtuns, they were never tamed by the British, stand apart from the rest of Pakistan and have rarely consented to rule from the centre. Taliban influence has been strong ever since the invasion of Afghanistan in 2001, since when many parts have been devastated by civil war and drone attack.

Certain common themes emerged from my meetings and discussions with cricketers from the tribal belt. The first was their willingness to endure any hardship to play the game of cricket, and the second is the bleak reaction of tribal elders who tried to stop the game catching on. In some cases I talked to these players directly, but for safety reasons (it is folly for a western reporter to travel around the tribal areas) I also asked Abdur Rauf Yousafzai and Syed Irfan Ashraf, Peshawar journalists, to carry out interviews on my behalf. Abdur found Rehan Afridi, a twenty-year-old wicketkeeper-batsman from Landi Kothal on the Khyber Pass. Rehan started playing cricket with homemade bats aged about nine, and recalls being thrashed for doing so:

> My grandfather was a tribal elder and a very rigid, old-fashioned man. I did not know why he hated cricket but he would beat us just for not obeying his orders. And that order was quite simple: that we will not play game. In case of violation, my dictator grandfather would beat us with a stick, which he would spend time to cut from a branch of a nearby tree and prepare it for this special task.

Rehan says that the reason for his fascination with cricket was watching it on television. But there were no regular matches, no league, and no organisation in the tough and mountainous area where he was reared. Just once a year there would be a tournament on the Tatara ground, the nearest thing to a pitch in Landi Kothal. 'So we have to wait round the year for that event to come and let us display our abilities with bat and ball. If we failed to show our talent, the only available option was to wait for another year.'

Rehan started to look further afield. From the age of thirteen he would take the Bara bus to Peshawar, a one and a half hour journey in ancient vehicles driven at hair-raising speeds by hashish-smoking drivers. 'Two days in a week I used to come to Peshawar and I continuously adopted this regime for about five years,' remembers Rehan. Whenever his grandfather got to hear of these journeys he would make one of his special sticks and beat him.

Then one day, as so often happens in Pakistan, young Rehan was spotted. 'There is one Nanakpura School in Peshawar,' he recalls. 'The principal of that school, Sohail Khan, was an umpire at club level and a diehard lover of cricket. He saw me playing in Jinnah Cricket Club. He invited me to his school and told me that he will arrange for my studies if I am willing to play for their school side.'

Rehan was school captain. Soon he started to get paid for his cricket and made his first-class debut, aged seventeen, for Multan in 2009. Since then he has played in Bangladesh, in Karachi and when we spoke to him he had just received an offer to play for a team in Hong Kong. Rehan is making a living of sorts but complains of a dearth of first-class matches: 'My ideal is to play for the Pakistan cricket team, my spirit is high but my support system is weak.'

The lack of cricket is crippling the game on the North West frontier. Mohammad Sohail, a schoolteacher and an expert on cricket in the tribal areas, took me to the Peshawar Gymkhana. Here was a sight to bring contentment to any cricket lover. It was late afternoon, the sun was fading, and the light was gentle. Out in the middle a match was in progress, and the situation was tight (the Peshawar Club needing just nine runs to win with one wicket left). All around the ground were cricket nets, in all about twenty, each one filled with busy cricketers. I guessed that a total of about four hundred were practising.

This ground had been built by the British more than a hundred years ago. In the far corner, I came across the original two-ton roller, still very much in use, an engraving recording that it had been manufactured by Burn & Co in Bombay in 1902. Sohail took me to the Iskander Pavilion, named after Iskander Mirza, the cricket-loving Pakistan president who had played such a statesmanlike role during the Idris Baig affair. Mirza had opened the pavilion, said a notice, on 10 November 1957.

Each of these nets, Sohail explained as Peshawar lost its final wicket and ruefully walked off, was owned by a different club. These clubs often had up to a hundred members, who each paid a small fee to belong. Often twenty or thirty cricketers would turn up for practice, and a batsman would be lucky to get more than five or six minutes facing the bowlers, while the bowlers would bowl just a handful of deliveries. Despite all the obstacles, he told me that one net alone, used by the Peshawar Cricket Club, had produced eight Test cricketers.

He pointed out another, where the young Umar Gul had finessed his talents. Yet another net, with large holes and in a wretched state, was for Afghans. No visa is required to cross the border and tens of thousands make the journey every day. Among them were some who came in search of opportunities to play in domestic Pakistan leagues.

It was clear from talk among the other players at the ground that their presence is greeted with complex feelings. 'You must understand,' Sohail told me, 'people in this part of the world have two cricket teams – Pakistan and Afghanistan.' On the other hand they added to the pressure on resources, and these are very great. Approximately forty clubs – representing some four thousand players – were registered at the Peshawar Gymkhana. Only two of them can play on the ground at the same time.

Furthermore the cost is penurious. The Gymkhana Club is run by a private owner who charges rent of around 3,600 rupees – approximately £25 – for a game. Once the cost of balls and lunch has been added in, each of the young players has to find around 200 rupees (about £1.50) for a day's cricket. Since the majority of them are students or unemployed, this is more than they can afford. The lucky ones play, at most, one or two games a month. Many do not manage to get proper games at all.

In a Peshawar roadside café I met Ihsanullah Wazir, a mad-keen cricketer from South Waziristan, a mountainous region in the North West, who was forced to give up the game because of lack of opportunity. A well-organised young man with longish, jet-black hair, he was studying computer science at university: 'I will play cricket again once I am done with my degree.' He told me of his joy when at the height of the fighting in 2008, South Waziristan beat Khyber Agency in the FATA Gold Cup. 'Had we been provided opportunities the same as the rest of Pakistan,' said Ihsanullah, 'cricket in the FATA is the most fertile game to change identity of the tribal belt. The rest of the world at present sees us as terrorists, but this mindset is going to lose what little strengths we have in the FATA.'

Ihsanullah told me that the rhythms of cricket where he lives are completely different. In the Punjab and Sindh the game is played in the winter months, starting out in September to avoid the debilitating heat and monsoon rain of high summer. But in the mountainous tribal belt the game can only be played in the summer.

In Waziristan, it starts from 1 June and is played continuously for three months. During this period, it attracts many students on summer vacation. 'They find themselves eager to go back to their native towns in South Waziristan, where sports, particularly cricket, are their main source of entertainment,' says Ihsanullah. 'Their grounds in the rest of the country wear a bleak look due to the scorching summer heat; pleasant weather in the mountainous Waziristan awaits native youths studying outside the agency.' Ihsanullah says that during this time many tribal Pashtuns who work the rest of the year in the Gulf states arrange their schedules so that they can come back to Waziristan to play and watch the game.

The highlight is the Badshah Khan tournament, played in Shakai Tehsil for the last two decades. Three matches are played every day, fifteen overs a side with a locally made cork ball. Players do not play in cricket whites but the baggy dress of the tribal areas. One year the players experimented with the coloured kit used by one-day cricketers on television. This was severely discouraged by local elders. 'The first time proved the last time,' says Ihsanullah.

These games at Shakai draw huge crowds in a society where most modern means of entertainment are unavailable. Cricket integrates naturally into tribal structures. The teams arrive on the morning of the match on tractors, trolleys, cars, motorbikes, buses and carts. The players lead the convoy and they reach the ground to the beat of a drum. It is said that vendors earn more on the day of a big match than in the rest of the year. Victory is celebrated in the traditional fashion, with animals slaughtered and fellow tribesmen invited to join a feast.

'Following the drum beats,' says Ihsanullah, 'the winning party moves to a traditional place in the mountains where they stay overnight to celebrate their win.' I yearned to attend one of these cricket matches, and witness the celebrations that followed, and would have given almost anything to do so. Despite making many enquiries, I was unable to find a way that would not have been absurdly dangerous.

The zest for cricket is so great, Ihsanullah says, that it even continues during the many battles that rage across the tribal areas. He recalls an early military offensive against the Taliban, who were being punished for providing shelter to Arab and Uzbek fighters. 'On the western side of the Gulshan-i-Shakai ground the Pakistan jets were pounding the nearby Sleer mountain, while quite close by cricket matches were continuing in Shakai almost in a three kilometre radius.' The government jets were targeting the Taliban faction led by Nek Mohammad in the mountains. Meanwhile Maulvi Nazir, another Taliban leader, known to be pro-government, was providing security for the cricket tournament.

TALIBAN ATTITUDES TOWARDS CRICKET

There are conflicting reports about the attitude of the Taliban towards cricket. In theory the Taliban movement, driven by a puritanical hostility to sports and games, would be affronted by a sport with western connections such as cricket. And in some parts of Pakistan that is the case. In the early summer of 2012, two years after government forces had liberated the area from Taliban occupation, I travelled up the Swat Valley. Everywhere I went I saw cricket games in action – on the sides of hills, in side streets, high up in the most remote mountain valleys. There is very little level ground in this rugged and mountainous area, yet every piece seemed to have been colonised by cricketers. In the village of Null, in middle Swat, I found a game in progress beside a river, flowing fast with glacial melt.

The terrible floods of 2010 had rearranged the landscape (Swat, like Pakistan, has endured much more than its fair share of disaster in recent years) and the cricketers were playing on land that used to be orchards and rice fields. Now it was sand, gravel and boulders. The cricketers had salvaged a flat surface area for the wicket, but the outfield was another matter. Fielders would set off erratically over treacherous terrain after the taped ball as it bounced from rock to rock. The stumps were made of steel bars welded to a rectangular base. The players had no pads, no gloves and no box. A ten-year-old boy, Anwar Ali, kept score in a school exercise book.

Yet the standard in this ten-overs-a-side game, played in the shadow of the Swat mountains, was very high. The batsmen struck the ball cleanly, with cuts, hooks and lots of lovely, wristy shots against bowlers who were hostile and accurate. The teams told me that they practised every day, and played matches against rival villages two or three times a week.

The parents of the boys were daily wage workers, and many of their fathers had been forced to leave their families and travel to Saudi Arabia for work. The coach, Khauta Rehmann, who held a BA in computer science, told me that 'we want a proper ball and proper bats.' He might have added that he needs a proper ground as well. For all of their enthusiasm and talent, it is highly unlikely that any of these cricket fanatics will ever play the kind of game which most people reading this book take for granted, with proper equipment, a leather ball and a grass outfield.

The Taliban put an end to cricket round here. When the fundamentalist leader Maulana Fazlullah took over five years ago with a mission to
impose strict Sharia law, the moral code and religious law of Islam, he condemned cricket as a frivolous activity that distracted from Jihad. His fighters
came to the village of Null and said: 'Stop this nonsense. It's a waste of time
to do these sports. Pick up your gun.'

This bleak, ideological hostility to cricket seems not to prevail in other
areas. The young men I spoke to from Waziristan and Khyber told me that
Taliban commanders loved the game. They said that Taliban forces sometimes provided the security at matches, that Taliban commanders would
come to watch their games, and even told me of the existence of Taliban
teams. They wore traditional costumes which could interfere with their
stroke play (try playing a leg glance in a *shalwar kameez*) and were not very
good. 'They take defeat well. They are very sporting.' I was told by cricket-
loving tribesmen that army commanders would come down to distribute
prizes and awards. On the rare occasions that Taliban teams won there
would be much celebration, with guns fired in the air and feasting.

Taliban fighters are also passionate supporters of the national cricket
team. One tribal cricketer said he was in Miranshah, North Waziristan,
during the 2011 World Cup. He told me how the Taliban made sure that
they tuned their television sets to watch cricket matches. 'They loved to see
Shahid Afridi [who comes from one of the fiercest Pashtun tribes, notorious for their reckless brave resistance to British forces] cracking shots,' he
told me, 'and also loved Pakistan cricket. Though they are fighting against
the Pakistan Army they love to see the Pakistan cricket team winning
matches.' According to the *Express Tribune* newspaper, Taliban cricket fans
go to considerable lengths to provide themselves with generators so they can
watch the game through the power cuts that are an endemic part of Pakistan
life. 'These days a majority of our clients who ask us to arrange for a TV
connected to a generator are the Taliban,' said one Waziri electrician.[18]
Pakistan victories are met by riotous celebrations.

So cricket is one of the rare things which can bring the Pakistan military
and the Taliban together, in what amounts to a temporary ceasefire. For
example, it is not unknown for army bulldozers to clear the wicket of debris
at the start, and for the Taliban to provide security while tournaments are
under way. My informants told me that the Al-Qaeda, by contrast, never

played cricket and favoured volleyball. They also liked football – but never cricket.

THE GROWTH OF FIRST-CLASS CRICKET ON
THE NORTH-WEST FRONTIER

At Partition Pakistan inherited a North-West Frontier Cricket Association with a first-class ground in Peshawar. It had competed intermittently at first-class level in the pre-Partition Ranji Trophy, but its teams were weak and this pattern continued in the 1950s in the Quaid-e-Azam Trophy (when teams competed either as NWFP or as Peshawar).

Early players made little impact. The first Peshawar player to be picked for Pakistan was the controversial off-spinner Haseeb Ahsan, whose 12-Test career was ended when he was no-balled and sent home during Pakistan's disastrous 1962 tour of England. He later became the outspoken manager of Pakistan's 1987 tour of England. During the 1960s and early 1970s the major force in NWFP cricket was the all-rounder Maazullah Khan. But his efforts were normally in vain. In ten Quaid-e-Azam Trophy matches for Peshawar or NWFP he was only once on a winning side, and all of the last six were heavy defeats.[19] Selected for the 1974 tour of England for regional balance, he managed (on his last outing) to take one wicket and holds the melancholy record for the worst tour bowling average by any player: 183. However, as captain and later as administrator he was credited for encouraging two generations of North-West cricketers.[20]

One of Maazullah's protégés, Farrukh Zaman, became Peshawar's second Test player in 1976. A slow left-armer, he was given only ten overs by Mushtaq Mohammad at home to New Zealand; they were cheap but wicketless and he never got another Test, although he took over four hundred wickets in a domestic career of twenty-four years. He and Iqbal Butt, another slow left-armer, gave Peshawar a steady attack in the 1980s but the team made no impact in domestic competition until 1997–98, when they surprised everybody by reaching their first Quaid-e-Azam Trophy final, which they lost on first-innings to Karachi Blues. Their stars were two pace bowlers, Sajid Shah and seventeen-year-old Fazl-e-Akbar, who was a member of the same Durani clan as the Mohammad brothers' legendary coach, Master Aziz and his son, India's charismatic all-rounder Salim Durani.

This was the moment when Peshawar cricket truly began to take off. The team again made the Quaid-e-Azam Trophy final in 2001–02, with Fazl-e-Akbar again the spearhead.[21] He was one of four members of that side to play Test matches for Pakistan; the others were two batsmen, Yasir Hameed and Wajahatullah Wasti, and Arshad Khan, a tall, nagging off-spinner. Fazl, Wajahatullah and Arshad were in the Peshawar side in the Quaid-e-Azam Trophy final of 2004–05, which they won on first-innings over a Faisalabad side led by Pakistan's future captain, Misbah-ul-Haq.[22]

Suddenly Pakistan's North-West was producing a series of wonderful players: Shahid Afridi, born in the Khyber Agency; Younis Khan,[23] born in Mardan; and Umar Gul, born in Peshawar. Afridi and Younis migrated as children to Karachi.

An obvious indicator of the growth of cricket in the North-West is the number of first-class grounds. For years, there was only the Peshawar Club ground, which staged first-class matches from 1938, and a lone Test match, against India, in 1954–55. In 1984 it was joined by two grounds in Peshawar University. In 1985 Peshawar got a new Test venue, the Arbab Niaz stadium. This also staged a one-day international on the 'goodwill' tour by India in 2004–05, during which the Indian tourists were able to walk around the markets and bazaars with minimal security and buy carpets.[24] The year 2004 also saw first-class cricket at the Abbottabad cricket stadium. In 2010 first-class cricket reached the Sports Complex at Mardan and the Gohati stadium at Swabi.[25] Cricket at last was on the march.

KASHMIRI CRICKET*

A few hundred miles from Peshawar to the east lies the former princely state of Kashmir, a mountainous area which has been fiercely disputed between India and Pakistan since independence. Soon after Partition, Kashmir became a disputed territory between the two countries and their competing

*I have not travelled to Kashmir. This section relies in large part on a report carried out by Murtaza Shibli, a British Kashmiri, born and raised in Kashmir.

narratives of new nationalism. As a result, India and Pakistan have fought wars both for and on the territory, leaving Kashmir, once known as a paradise on earth, scarred and divided. The 'Line of Control' which separates territory controlled by India and Pakistan continues to witness regular fighting, causing death to soldiers and civilians on both sides.

Cricket in Kashmir, as on the North-West frontier, began as an elite sport. The country was never formally under the control of the British, though there was a British Resident, who made sure that British interests were safeguarded, and kept an eye on the Maharajahs, some of whom liked to play cricket. Very few ordinary people played the game, though it was introduced by Christian missionaries in their schools.

After 1947 Kashmir, against the will of its largely Muslim population, 'acceded' to India. It did have a Ranji Trophy cricket team, which first took part in 1959–60, but this was not very successful. At this stage very few Kashmiris took much interest in cricket, regarding it as an elite sport associated with what they viewed as an Indian occupation. Cricket only took off with the revival of Indian–Pakistan cricket in the late 1970s after the fall of Bhutto.

Kashmiris took an extraordinary interest in these matches in which – to the fury of the Indian authorities – they mainly supported Pakistan. On one or two occasions India hosted home matches against foreign teams in the region. Muslim Kashmiris attended in their thousands. The first match, in October 1983, was played between India and West Indies in Srinagar's Sher-i-Kashmir stadium, named in honour of Sheikh Abdullah, the famous Kashmiri leader who was pro-India in his leanings and had played a huge role in Kashmir's accession to India.

This match generated protests from activists who were pushing for freedom from India. They advanced to the stadium carrying thousands of green Pakistani flags and large posters of Pakistani players. Once in the stadium they set up chants of 'Pakistan Zindabad!'[26] A massive poster of Imran Khan was hung from one of the large maple trees (locally known as *Chinars*) on the flanks of the stadium. Every Indian wicket was jeered while every West Indian run was greeted with exultation by the crowd.

Sunil Gavaskar, in his book *Runs and Ruins*, describes his experience in Kashmir as the worst he had seen in his life:

As the Indian players came into the arena to loosen up and do their physical exercise, they were booed by some sections of the crowd ... This was
unbelievable. Here we were in India and being hooted even before a ball
had been bowled. Being hooted at after a defeat is understandable, but
this was incredible. Moreover, there were many in the crowd shouting
pro-Pakistan slogans which confounded us, because we were playing the
West Indies and not Pakistan.[27]

The opposing captain Clive Lloyd said that the West Indies 'had felt as if
they were playing at home.' The match had turned into a political spectacular. India batted first and, perhaps shell-shocked by their reception,
folded to just 176. Then, after 22 overs, the West Indies innings was halted
by a dust storm, Kashmiri youths invaded the playing area and dug up the
wicket thus bringing the match to an end.* Perhaps wisely, the match was
then awarded to the West Indies, on the grounds of faster run rate.

The victory was celebrated very widely across Kashmir, and those who
had dug up the pitch became heroes. Several of them went on to play a
significant role in the Kashmiri insurgency movement. For instance
Mushtaq-ul Islam would head a militant group, Hizbullah, as its chief commander. Showkat Bakshi rose to become a top commander of the Jammu
Kashmir Liberation Front (JKLF). Shabir Shah – Kashmir's 'Nelson
Mandela' and one-time Amnesty International 'Prisoner of Conscience' –
was also among those accused and arrested.

It was not until November 2011, after twenty-eight years, that a court in
Srinagar acquitted twelve of the accused men, two of them posthumously,
citing 'lack of evidence'. Showkat Bakshi told Indian newspaper the
Telegraph that he suffered immensely because of the case. 'I was a kid then
and we were simply protesting against holding the match here. I was arrested
and put behind bars for four months initially and booked for waging a war
against the country. For the next six years I was continuously harassed, so
much so that I picked up the gun.'[28] In his guise as a JKLF commander,
Bakshi was again arrested in 1990 and spent the next twelve years in
prison.[29] A quarter of a century later this cricket match is viewed as a milestone in what Kashmir separatists view as their 'Azadi struggle'.[30]

---

*According to some reports, the ground was dug up first.

From approximately the time of that cricket match, the Kashmiri cricket craze began. I asked my friend Murtaza Shibli, a British Kashmiri poet and writer, who was brought up in Kashmir in the 1980s, to write me a memoir. His report is so powerful, and so haunting, and parts of it so beautiful, that I will quote it at great length:

I remember large-size posters of Pakistani players – Majid Khan, Zaheer Abbas, Imran Khan, Iqbal Qasim, Javed Miandad, Wasim Akram and others adorning shops, schools, homes and even some government office buildings.

One of the biggest shops selling these posters was in the heart of Srinagar in Lal Chowk, just below the offices of the Press Information Bureau, or PIB, the central Indian propaganda and publicity department.

There was never any mention of the Indian players, except when they were discussed as underdogs, to be thrashed by the Pakistanis in every department of the game – bowling, batting as well as fielding. In this ever emotionally filled political narrative of the sport, the Pakistani players were always the heroes. Kashmiris always prayed and waited for the spectacle of India's defeat and humiliation; and when it came, they celebrated it with almost a religious fervor.

Murtaza described a childhood playing cricket:

Like everywhere else in the Indian subcontinent, the popularisation of the game among the masses took place in lanes and bylanes in nondescript towns and mundane village grounds, orchards, or grazing fields. *Idd Gahs*, the grounds where Muslims pray their Eid prayers twice a year also became favourite grounds for cricket matches, mainly on Sundays, when most of the people were at home. I even remember playing cricket in graveyards (*Qabristan*), funeral grounds (*Jinaz gah*) or even crematorium grounds of the local Hindu populace. One of my fondest childhood memories is playing cricket at Latoo Mazar, the biggest graveyard in my town. The length of the wicket was decided by the ground between the two large gravestones. There was no need to have proper stumps, as headstones would suffice.

Those days, for most of the people, a proper bat was not affordable.

Therefore, a basic version, made out of one plank of rough wood without a separate handle was the norm. Similarly, a proper leather ball was either not possible to get or too expensive. People would often play with a soft plastic ball or stronger *beara*, a solid wooden ball that was almost half the size of the standard leather ball but cheap and therefore popular and affordable.

It was very heavy, made by local wood carvers from the heavy and dense woods from almond, cherry or local berry tree called *brimuj*. As there was no concept of pads, helmets, gloves etc., it was dangerous to play with the wooden ball. The *beara* would cause injuries when it hit a batsman or a fielder. I have personally had several accidents with it, having bruised my legs, scarred shin bone or fingers while fielding. In extreme cases, people would end up with severe injuries. We even heard stories of children dying from it. But in our madness for cricket, everyone ignored the threats and the pain to carry on playing.

This cricket mania persists. During the last twenty-five years of turmoil, several cricket grounds have been destroyed or occupied by the Indian army, less because of malice than a need to house a large number of Indian forces that are present in Kashmir (it is the most militarised place on earth, with more than half a million soldiers for about six million people). Nevertheless, Kashmiris continue to play cricket with passion, in small courtyards in dense old towns and villages, on main roads during *hartals* and during shut-down calls given by the pro-freedom separatists.

Over time the game has lost some of its rustic trappings. Protective equipment is now almost mandatory for every match, even the local ones. The wooden ball, *beara*, ubiquitous only a generation or two ago, is almost extinct. A well-developed local bat industry supplies ever increasing demand and most of the people can afford a decent willow.[31]

Today there are hundreds of teams in every corner of Kashmir, regularly playing in proper cricket whites. Murtaza Shibli recalls that 'this is diametrically different from playing in my youth, when we would deliberately play wearing a *pheran*, a long gown like local attire, that would often stop the ball hitting the stumps, if one missed a ball.'

The Indian government now sees cricket as a soft-tool to 'de-radicalise' Kashmiris or to 'Indianise' them. The Indian Army and the police have started their own cricket tournaments, supporting local teams.[32] The army top brass are skilful at exploiting the game for counter-insurgency purposes: 'It is the endeavour of the army and the state police to encourage the local youths to hone their sportsman skills,' Maj. Gen. Sarath, the General Commanding Officer (GOC) of Kilo Force, a counter-insurgency force, told Indo Asian News Service.[33] Relative calm in Kashmir and the popularity and the prospect of finding a place in the Indian Premier League has strengthened the relationship of the Kashmiri players with mainland India and brought them closer.[34]

But one thing has not changed – Kashmiris still and very fervently support Pakistanis and not Indians. This became evident during the 2011 World Cup matches. At the quarter-final stage, when Pakistan won against the West Indies, it was widely celebrated with fire crackers. 'But India's win against Australia passed without a murmur'.[35] In the run-up to the semi-finals between India and Pakistan in Mohali, the police in Srinagar imposed a Section 144, an order that prohibits any gatherings of more than four people. This was enacted to ban large groups from watching the match together. The police also banned large-screen TVs at public places, road sides and even outside the shops. 'We fear there might be [a] law and order problem if Pakistan loses,' a police officer was quoted in *Greater Kashmir*.[36]

Nevertheless, the firecracker sellers in Srinagar reported (literally) booming business. 'I have almost exhausted my entire stock and the demand is still unending,' said Sameer Ahmed, a firecracker seller, to the *Greater Kashmir*.[37] More than half a million Indian paramilitary forces were put on high alert in order to prevent any sign of support for Pakistan. Luckily for India, they won the match, plunging Kashmir into a collective mourning. As a result, there were no celebrations or embarrassing public displays of pro-Pakistan enthusiasm, just mute despair.

In March 2014, 66 Kashmiri students were expelled from their college in Meerut for cheering Pakistan's victory over India during the televised Asia Cup match, after initially being charged with sedition.[38]

BALUCHISTAN CRICKET

I tried very hard to get to Baluchistan, but repeatedly failed to obtain the necessary 'No Objection Certificate'. The province has been wracked by insurgencies for many years, and I failed to find reliable first-hand accounts of cricket.

Official records, however, suggest that the game has (for understandable reasons) never made much headway. No Baluchi cricketer has ever won international honours. Aftab Baloch, whose family has its roots there, achieved two scattered Test caps in 1969 and 1974, but he was born in Karachi, and never played for any Baluchi team.*

The present captain of Quetta in domestic cricket, twenty-two-year-old Taimur Ali, played two Under-19 Test matches for Pakistan in England in 2007, aged (officially) sixteen, but this was before he joined Quetta and he was born in Jacobabad, Sindh. Ali Asad is another current Quetta player who has played Under-19 Tests, but he too is a transplanted talent, from Karachi. Baluchistan's long-serving representative on the board of selectors is Asif Baloch, 57, born in Quetta. His first-class career figures may say something about the weakness of Baluchi cricket: 27 matches which produced 628 runs at an average below 15 and 52 wickets which cost over 52 apiece. Mr Baloch is also a senior customs official; in December 2012 he was severely injured in a gun attack, possibly by smugglers, while on duty in the troubled Panjgur district of Baluchistan.[39]

Baluchi teams have played in domestic competition either as Baluchistan or more commonly Quetta. Neither has any record of first-class achievement. Baluchistan made one appearance in the Quaid-e-Azam Trophy in 1953–54, then did not re-enter the trophy until 1972–73, while Quetta competed in the BCCP Patron's Trophy. From 1972–73 to 1978–79 both teams played only three matches between them in Quetta.† There was a serious insurgency in Baluchistan from 1973 to 1977, which tied down 80,000 Pakistani soldiers.

The two teams continue to divide first-class responsibility in the present era. Baluchistan competed in the Faysal Bank Pentangular Cup in 2011–12,

---

*Ironically, it was *against* a very weak Baluchistan team that he scored his (little-known) quadruple-century in 1973–74 as part of Sindh's record score of 951 for 7 declared.

†One of these home matches was in 1974–75, in another Quetta ground which was still, curiously, known as the Ayub national stadium. Quetta beat the Customs team in a thrilling finish by 11 runs. The only other victory in this period came for Quetta against another weak team, Sukkur. Usually Baluchistan or Quetta were whipping boys. Apart from Aftab Baloch's 400 against Baluchistan, Karachi A's openers scored the world record partnership of 561 when they beat Quetta by an innings and 294 runs in the Patron's Trophy in 1976–77. Mansoor Akhtar scored 224 not out and his partner Waheed Mirza 324. Amazingly, they opened the bowling in both of Quetta's innings. Mansoor Akhtar played in eleven Tests, averaging 25, with one century, but Waheed Mirza never played a Test and scored only one other century in a first-class career with a batting average of 26. This is a similar pattern to Pervez Akhtar, scorer of the triple century for Railway in 1964 in their record victory of an innings and 850 runs against the hapless Dera Ismail Khan. He too managed only one other first-class century.

in which they managed one win against Federal Areas, which left them third in the table. None of these matches were played in Quetta. In the complicated structure of the Quaid-e-Azam Trophy in 2012–13, Quetta played eight matches, none at home. The Ayub national stadium staged its last first-class match in 1993–94. In 1989 Quetta's Racecourse stadium was renamed the Bugti stadium. Neither ground in Quetta ever staged a Test match. The Ayub saw two one-day matches against India: one won by India in October 1978 and one won by Pakistan in October 1984. The Bugti's lone one-day international was against Zimbabwe in October 1996, won by Pakistan. Quetta has not seen a first-class match since October 2008. The fate of the Quetta and Baluchistan teams can be compared to the Pakistan national team. In both cases, for tragic reasons beyond the control of the cricketers themselves, the teams are condemned to play away from home.

DEVELOPMENT OF WOMEN'S CRICKET IN PAKISTAN

'Fundamentalist newspapers carried daily threats, such as stoning our house down. They were opposed to any new activity for women. We even had death threats.'

– SHAIZA KHAN, CREATOR AND CAPTAIN OF PAKISTAN'S FIRST WOMEN'S REPRESENTATIVE CRICKET TEAM

Women's cricket has a long history in most of the countries which play it. In England the first recorded women's game dates from 1745, between Bramley and Hambledon, near Guildford, in Surrey.[1] Two years later the Duchess of Richmond promoted a women's match near her husband's estate at Goodwood.[2]

In 1822 a young English woman changed cricket for ever. Bowling at her brother John, and finding that her long skirt interfered with under-arm, Christina Willes delivered the ball with a round-arm action. Her brother John admired the technique and adopted it himself in a men's game. He was promptly no-balled and walked away in disgust, but round-arm was legalised a few years later.[3]

The first organised women's club was the White Heather, founded in 1887. One of its leading players, Lucy Ridsdale, won the heart of a future prime minister, Stanley Baldwin. She held a meeting of the club at Number 10 Downing Street, during the General Strike.[4] That same year, 1926, saw the formation of the Women's Cricket Association, representing mainly the south of England, while the north had the English Women's Cricket Federation.[5]

In Australia women were playing interstate matches before the Great War.[6] In 1934 England toured Australia and played the first women's Test series. They lost two and drew the other match, but went on to thrash New Zealand.[7] There were scattered series post-war between the three countries and then in 1960–61 England toured (white-only) South Africa, Rachael Heyhoe made her debut.

The first women's World Cup was held in England in 1973 – two years ahead of the men's, with teams from England, Young England, New Zealand, Australia, Jamaica and Trinidad & Tobago. Invitations to white-only South Africa were withdrawn and an International XI, of spare players from England, Australia and New Zealand, played in their place.[8] In 1976 the West Indies played their first Tests against Australia and India sent a team to New Zealand.[9]

The first organised cricket for girls or women in India is credited to an Australian teacher, Miss Ann Keleve, who introduced the game to her pupils at a school in Kottayam, Kerala, in 1913. Then the historians are silent until the 1950s, when women's cricket was thriving in Delhi. In the 1960s there were strong clubs for women cricketers in Madras, Bombay and Calcutta. In 1969 the Albees Club was founded in Bombay, with the support of Vijay Merchant and Polly Umrigar. The wicketkeeper, Tina Lalo, was a cousin of Farokh Engineer, and another of the club's stars was Nutan, sister of Sunil Gavaskar.

The Women's Cricket Association of India was founded in 1973, which saw the first National Women's Tournament, in Poona, although this involved only three teams, from Uttar Pradesh, Maharashtra and Bombay.[10] In 1975 the Australian Under-25 women's team toured India and played three Tests. These saw the debut of a sixteen-year-old wicketkeeper Fouzieh Khalili and a nineteen-year-old all-rounder, Diana Edulji, who gave long service to Indian women's cricket. During the same year, the Indian WCA was able to pay the fares of a touring New Zealand team. Indira Gandhi was a strong supporter of Indian women's cricket, which she saw as a means of emancipating Indian women.[11] By contrast, the history of women's cricket in Pakistan has a silence which lasted for almost fifty years.

THE BIRTH OF WOMEN'S CRICKET IN PAKISTAN

Five women's World Cups were held without a Pakistan team. Ireland, the Netherlands, and Denmark (which have no first-class cricket for men) all took part in the women's World Cup before Pakistan.

Women have appeared in this narrative so far only as nurturers or companions to Pakistan's great male cricketers. As already noted, the mother of the Mohammad brothers, Ameer Bee, was a notable sportswoman – but not at cricket. She was a champion at carrom and badminton – games which were socially acceptable for women.

In the Burki clan, packed with high-achieving cricketers and other sportsmen, the girls and women played cricket in the early family games but not beyond. According to Javed Burki, those who excelled at sport at school or college, did so 'as runners and things, not in ball games.' No Burki women achieved international sporting honours: 'they were very conservative then and they were not encouraged to pursue these things.' Organised sporting life for them ended after school and college.[12] If the Burki women found it hard to play organised cricket, one can imagine the problems for women without their resources and connections.

Mrs Bushra Aitzaz, chair of the women's wing of the PCB, gave me an interesting account of cricket for girls in her schooldays in the late 1960s. 'We played cricket with the boys at school. There was never an issue about us playing. Our mothers might say "you'll break a leg" or "the ball will hit you in the face" but there was no pressure from parents or families [not to play cricket]. But I really don't think there was such a great desire of girls to play cricket. They would play hockey, and at college we would play basketball, netball, tennis and badminton.' She said that during the 1970s the real barrier to girls' cricket in Lahore was the shortage of cricket grounds, and the lack of opportunity for girls to play after college.[13]

During the 1980s, when General Zia courted Islamic interests, the problems for Pakistan's female cricketers were heightened by conservative attitudes and restrictions. Ayesha Ashhar, manager of the current Pakistan women's team, recalls that during that period girls' matches at school and college tournaments could not be watched by single men, only by women, or men accompanied by their families, and it became harder for girls to play cricket outside Karachi or Lahore.

But the key issue was still the lack of opportunity. 'During the 1980s, maybe two per cent of girls, all with the right sort of family background, played cricket. Other girls needed transport to inter-district matches, which they could not afford. I played at school but I also played for the love of the game, in pick-up matches in open spaces [in Lahore] shared with kite flyers.' Like many talented teenaged sportswomen at this time, Ashhar opted for hockey when she was selected to play for the Pakistan team. Hockey gave women international and professional playing opportunities, but in cricket, 'after school and college there was no future then.'[14]

A women's cricket association came into being in Pakistan in 1978, based on the Lahore College for Women. One of its founder members, Azraa Parveen, then organised the Universal Women's Cricket Clubs with branches in major cities.[15] These early efforts foundered due to factional rivalries, lack of opportunity, and religious and cultural hostility.[16] The story of women's cricket was all but silenced in the 1980s, but when it resumed in the next decade it was thick with drama, which echoed many of the themes of Pakistan men's cricket, and indeed of Pakistan itself. We will again witness the rivalry between Karachi and Lahore, incompetent or negligent bureaucracy, accusations and counter-accusations, intrigues and protracted legal disputes. But we will also see heroism and achievement against powerful social and religious forces. Finally, we will see, amid enduring problems, a scene of opportunity and growth for Pakistan's women cricketers.

THE KHAN SISTERS

Although their role is disputed by their rivals, Pakistan's long-delayed entry into international cricket was undoubtedly the work of the remarkable Khan sisters of Karachi.[17]

Shaiza and Sharmeen Khan were the daughters of a successful carpet manufacturer, who sent them to study in England during the 1980s. They played cricket there at school and university, for the well-regarded Gunnersbury club in south-west London, and at county level for Middlesex. They say they came close to selection for England before the 1993 women's World Cup, but at the last minute they dropped out because they were not British nationals.

At that point they resolved that they would compete in the next World Cup with a Pakistan team, and wrote to the International Women's Cricket Council (then in charge of worldwide women's cricket, while the ICC was men-only) to seek representation for Pakistan and check the rules of entry for the next World Cup in 1997. They were invited to the World Cup final dinner at Lord's, where IWCC officials told them that they would be welcome to send a team in 1997, if they had been resident in Pakistan for a full year, if they had completed any necessary local formalities, and if they had managed to complete at least three international matches before the World Cup began.

Breaking away from university studies in England, they returned to Pakistan in 1996. With the help of Arif Abbasi, then chief executive of the PCB, they formed an association based in Karachi which was registered as a limited company and had it recognised by the PCB. It took the somewhat provocative title of the Pakistan Women's Cricket Control Association (PWCCA).[18]

They now had a limited time to find a team and organise the necessary three qualifying international matches. To put their new organisation on the map they placed newspaper advertisements inviting girls from all over Pakistan to come to trials for the World Cup, and they tried to organise an exhibition match between their side and an all-male team made up of former Test stars.

This initiative sparked a backlash. Shaiza Khan told me: 'Fundamentalist newspapers carried daily threats, such as stoning our house down. They were opposed to any new activity for women. We even had death threats.' The Karachi police commissioner was afraid of riots and urged them to call off the match and eventually they played a girls-only match behind closed doors, with no single men admitted – apart from a police presence of 8,000, including the police commissioner. 'We had to promote our match somehow,' Shaiza Khan told me. 'If we had just called it off, we would have died for ever.' To secure privacy and protection against fundamentalist threats, her father converted part of his carpet factory and its grounds to a dedicated private cricket centre. It had two proper pitches, a tennis court became a practice net with a bowling machine, and there was a gym and a swimming pool. Most important, there was accommodation for the players.[19]

The newspaper advertisements elicited several hundred responses, of whom around twenty, mostly hockey players, had some potential. (Shaiza and Sharmeen Khan confirmed to me that it was easier for girls to play hockey than cricket at the time, because women's hockey was an Olympic sport. 'Pakistani men were strongly against women cricketers. They said we couldn't hit a six and would only take singles.')

An especially promising recruit was eighteen-year-old Kiran Baloch. Her father had played for Baluchistan in the Quaid-e-Azam Trophy, and had encouraged her in family matches against her cousins. 'He taught me off-spin and leg-spin, and how to play forward and back.' But it was a different matter when she proposed to chuck her college exams and join the team on its pre-World Cup qualifying tour of Australia and New Zealand. With help from Arif Abbasi, she was able to persuade him that it would be a unique adventure to be part of the first Pakistan women's team.[20]

The qualifying tour (according to the Khan sisters) was the first ever, outside the Olympics, by any Pakistan women's team. 'No one had been before, not even the hockey and badminton teams. We opened the gate. The hockey team travelled six months later.' The new team was completely outgunned. As often happens at all levels of cricket, the hosts in New Zealand overestimated their visitors. In their first international match, the Pakistani women were all out for 56 in 33.3 overs (Baloch top-scoring with a 44-minute 19). The next day they conceded 455 to their hosts and went down to a record defeat of 408 runs. Against Australia they plunged to 23 all out and lost by 374 runs. 'We did not get out of bed for two days.'

In spite of the calamitous results, the team had won many new friends and, above all, fulfilled the qualifying conditions for the forthcoming World Cup in India.

DISPUTED TITLE

Not surprisingly after these results, some of the touring party felt discouraged and dropped out of the Khan sisters' squad. The sisters continued with the training camp in their father's factory grounds in Karachi, but were barely able to put together a team for the World Cup. They also suffered two other setbacks. First, their patron, Arif Abbasi, was replaced as chief exec-utive of the PCB by Majid Khan. The sisters described him to me as 'an ungodly chauvinist Pathan', who totally discouraged their efforts. They were denied the use of stadiums and the prices of practice nets and pitches quadrupled. They could not make use of any domestic coaches, and hired their own Australian women's coach, Jodie Davis.[21] Majid Khan's memory was rather different, when I mentioned the issue to him. He threw up his hands and said, 'I didn't want to get involved. I was having enough trouble handling my own cricket people!' – meaning the men.[22] In fairness, they were giving him a host of problems, including multiple changes in the captaincy, personal disputes, disciplinary problems and the first major allegations of match-fixing (see Chapter 20).

Majid also faced strong lobbying against the Khan sisters from a power-ful faction in Lahore, who disputed their right to represent Pakistan. In 1978, as mentioned, a body named the Pakistan Women's Cricket Association was founded in Lahore, led by Mrs Tahira Hameed.* It began to organise cricket tournaments for women, but then split into two factions, each claiming to be the true PWCA. By 1997, Mrs Hameed's faction was dormant, and the tournaments were being organised by the faction led by Mrs Shirin Javed.[23]

Mrs Javed was an important figure, well-connected in politics and cricket. Her brother-in-law was Ijaz Butt, the former Test cricketer who would later lead the PCB in its most troubled era. In 1988 she acquired a powerful ally in Mrs Bushra Aitzaz, whose husband was then the inte-rior minister. Together they began to lobby the PCB and national and provincial governments on behalf of women's cricket, which at that time had no official support at all. Mrs Bushra Aitzaz told me: 'We were pres-surising them and they were laughing at us – all these women want to play cricket for Pakistan. They were saying okay, okay, but no one was taking it seriously. Anyway, we went ahead . . . We established chapters in the four provinces. We had political women, known women to lead these chapters so that women could gain confidence, and we started to have four teams in Pakistan.'[24]

---

*She had been a leading athlete and tennis player, but not a cricket player. Her father was the first sec-retary of the Pakistan Olympic Association; her brother and a first cousin were Test cricketers. See www.dawn.com/2011/08/14/profile-in-a-league-of-her-own/.

Under Shirin Javed and Bushra Aitzaz, the PWCA objected fiercely to the Khan sisters' initiative. They themselves were beginning to organise trials for a Pakistan women's team, which had included Ayesha Ashhar. They regarded the Khan sisters as moneyed usurpers, who had stolen a march on them. Ashhar told me of her heartbreak at the time: 'We had practised for so long, I remember like six months and we were just kept standing there while someone else just went and played as a Pakistan team. Basically, that was the time when I left cricket.'[25]

The two contending factions fought a bitter duel. In the shocked words of the PCB Scrutiny Committee, later established in a vain attempt to resolve the issue, 'The national press carried statements and counter-statements of the representatives of these Associations criticising each other and claiming to be the true and sole body in charge of and controlling women's cricket in Pakistan. This war of words between the various Associations surpassed all norms of decency.'*

In this bitter struggle, the Khan sisters' organisation had the major advantages of a team in being (although depleted) and formal recognition by the PCB and the IWCC, which rebuffed the Lahore group's objections. The Lahore group went to the High Court to block the Khan sisters, and lobbied Majid Khan and the Sports Committee of the National Assembly.[26]

As a result, the Khan sisters and their team were put on 'exit control' by the immigration service, and denied permission to leave the country for the World Cup. To get round this, they split into small groups, hid their kitbags in cartons, and departed from Karachi on separate aircraft – changing into their Pakistan uniforms mid-flight.[27]

According to the Khan sisters, their team was now reduced to a bare eleven, and when they needed substitutes in their World Cup matches they had to beg them from their local Indian hosts. They had no official support or commercial sponsors, and their father met the entire cost of around $100,000 for their World Cup excursion.

Not surprisingly, they were overwhelmed by five far more experienced and better-resourced teams. They lost by eight wickets to Denmark, after being dismissed for 66 in 30 overs. Against England their batting improved,

*Report on Scrutiny of Women's Cricket Associations, January 2003. According to Mrs Bushra Aitzaz, actual fighting broke out between players from each association during a cricket match at Lahore College. The principal then banned women from playing there.

with 146 for 3 off 47 overs. Sharmeen Khan made 41, Kiran Baloch 22, and Shaiza Khan was not out 35 – but England had already made 376 for 2 off their 50 overs. Their nadir came against Australia – all out 27 in 82 balls. Australia reached their target (with one run-out) in 37 balls plus three wides. Against South Africa they restricted their opponents to 258 for 7 but inexperience showed in a contribution of 46 wides. Pakistan were then all out for 109 after an opening partnership of 84, in which Sharmeen Khan scored 48. Against Ireland, Shaiza Khan took three for 42 with her leg-spin as Ireland made 242 for 7, but Pakistan could reply with only 60 all out in 30.3 overs.

However, as in the qualifying tour, they won a host of friends, and all their opponents told them 'you won by being here.'

RECRIMINATION – AND RECORDS

After that first World Cup, the power struggle in Pakistan women's cricket endured for almost a decade, ping-ponging between the courts, the PCB, the National Assembly and the media. The Khan sisters continued to be the 'tenants in possession' of the Pakistan women's team, with the support of the International Women's Cricket Council, which maintained its refusal to get involved in Pakistan's domestic disputes.

In 1998 the Lahore-based PWCA, under Mrs Javed, lobbied the PCB and the Pakistan Sports Board, which set up a scrutiny committee to determine who should represent Pakistan's women cricketers. The Khan sisters boycotted this committee, which backed Mrs Javed, but the full PCB rejected their report because it 'failed to address the fundamental issues.' The PWCA then tried to enforce the Scrutiny Committee's recommendation in their favour through the High Court, which bounced the issue back to the PCB in June 2002. The PCB, now chaired by a Musharraf nominee, General Tauqir Zia, appointed a new Scrutiny Committee. It was chaired by Javed Zaman Khan, a senior member of the Burki clan and a doyen of Lahore cricket. The other members were Ijaz Faqih, an international cricketer from the 1980s, and Farooq Rana, a leading advocate.

Meanwhile, under the Khan sisters, the Pakistan women's team played its first two Test matches and a succession of one-day internationals. The first

Test, in April 1998, was in Colombo against Sri Lanka. It ended in defeat by 305 runs, but there were several fine Pakistani performances. Sharmeen Khan took 3 for 23 in Sri Lanka's first innings, Shaiza Khan had six wickets in the match and Kiran Baloch made 76 in Pakistan's first innings. The Sri Lankans swept all three one-day games but there were some other good moments for Pakistan, including four for 46 by Shaiza Khan and 60 by the teenaged wicketkeeper (and former hockey goalie) Asma Farzand.

The team visited Ireland and England in 2000. They crashed to 53 and 86 in an innings defeat in the sole Test against Ireland (Isobel Joyce, sister of Ed Joyce of Middlesex, Sussex, England and Ireland, took six for 21 in the second innings) and the Irish swept the four one-day matches. However, in England they managed to defeat an MCC side and received a congratulatory letter on behalf of HM the Queen.*

Pakistan missed the 2000 women's World Cup in New Zealand, but at home in Karachi to the Netherlands in 2001 they grabbed their first international victory, by one wicket in the last over. They were helped by 45 wides from their opponents but the all-rounder Sajjida Shah, officially only thirteen years old, anchored the innings with a not-out 28. The Dutch women handed them 67 wides when they won the second one-day match, but Shaiza Khan was still the architect of victory with five for 35 in the Dutch innings. She then took four for 33 and scored 28, and Sajjida Shah claimed four for 22 as Pakistan took a 3–0 lead. The Dutch staged a comeback, but Pakistan still claimed the series 4–3. However, their return to Sri Lanka in 2002 produced another six one-day defeats. In the fifth one-day match they managed to bowl out Sri Lanka for 119, but the batting was too frail for a quality opposition attack. It did not manage 100 in any of the one-day internationals.

None of these matches received any official or commercial financial support and the Pakistan team was financed entirely by the Khan carpet factory.

In January 2003 the Scrutiny Committee reported to the PCB. It praised the Khan sisters' facility in Karachi and their training methods, which it found generally superior to the standards of infrastructure, kit and training at the school and club matches under the PWCA in Lahore. It also noted that the PWCA had no formal constitution or legal status or an independent office or proper records.

---

*Musharraf, patron of the PCB, sent one too.

However, the Khan sisters' operation had the character of a single club rather than an association, and could not therefore be the authority for women's cricket in Pakistan. Accordingly, the Scrutiny Committee found against both rivals and recommended that the PCB itself should take over women's cricket, and establish a women's wing under 'a well-reputed lady.' It softened the blow for both rivals by recommending that the Khan sisters' organisation should take the lead in establishing new women's cricket associations in Sindh and Baluchistan, while the PWCA, under Mrs Javed, would do the same for Punjab and NWFP. Crucially, it suggested that the PCB should appoint a neutral selection committee and team management to take over the national team.[28]

The Scrutiny Committee's recommendations pleased nobody very much. The Khan sisters refused to yield to a PCB which had never supported women's cricket, or to share power with the PWCA. In their submission to the Scrutiny Committee they had attacked its lack of international experience and recognition, or legal structure, and its record in developing women cricketers. For their part, the PWCA were equally averse to a PCB takeover. One of their members organised a procession against the PCB. Mrs Bushra Aitzaz told me: 'She actually put the Chairman of the Board's name on a donkey and paraded him in front of the press club.'[29] Litigation resumed, as did the media war.

Meanwhile, the Khan sisters' organisation, still recognised by the IWCC, organised the team for the qualifying round, in the Netherlands, of the next women's World Cup, due for 2005 in South Africa. There they crushed lowly Japan. Sajjida Shah, officially now fifteen, took seven wickets for 4 runs, a record unlikely to be broken, while Khursheed Jabeen grabbed the other three wickets for two runs. The Japanese reached 26 only with the help of 17 wides. Pakistan also won a low-scoring game against Scotland, but defeats by the Netherlands, West Indies and Ireland knocked them out of the World Cup.

At home in Karachi, in 2004, Pakistan entertained West Indies. They grabbed their first two one-day victories against a Test-playing side, and produced their greatest performance in the only Test match. The PCB, now chaired by the former diplomat Shaharyar Khan, did not want to style this a Test match, although it was recognised as such by the IWCC and the National stadium at Karachi was leased on that basis to the Khan sisters' organisation. According to Arif Abbasi, Shaharayar Khan insisted on billing the match as Sindh versus West Indies. Abbasi advised the team simply to go to the ground at night and paint Pakistan in place of Sindh on the scoreboard.[30]

Under the banner of Pakistan, Kiran Baloch and Sajjida Shah opened the batting with a stand of 242 – a record in women's Tests and more than Pakistan had ever scored in an entire international innings before. Shah was out, cruelly, on 98, but Baloch batted on and on. She approached a double-century and the world record of 214 not out.*

Her partner was her captain, Shaiza Khan, who kept her calm and focused. She let her continue to 242, to make it harder for anyone to take the new record away from Pakistan. It was scored in 584 minutes, the longest innings ever played by a woman. When the West Indies replied to Pakistan's 426 for 7 declared, Shaiza Khan took a hat-trick on her way to seven for 59. Following on, the West Indies occupied 146 overs in scoring 440. Shaiza bowled no fewer than 55 of these, in taking another six wickets for 167, but Pakistan did not have enough time to score 162 for victory.

Shaiza's thirteen wickets were another record in women's Tests, but her achievements and Kiran Baloch's were marred by their conviction that their Board did not want them to win – and had warned the umpires accordingly. This cannot be established but I quote the allegation to show the depth of hostility between the Khan sisters and their team† and the PCB.‡

THE PCB TAKE OVER

This great performance turned out to be a last hurrah for the Khan sisters. The following year the ICC took over responsibility for international women's cricket from the hitherto independent IWCC. This deprived the

*Set in 2002 by Mithali Raj for India against England.

†A curious feature of this team was the selection of numbers 10 and 11, Mariam Anwar and Shabana Latif. Neither of them bowled or kept wicket, and neither reached the crease in either Pakistan innings. Anwar scored three runs in seven one-day appearances, and Latif scored none at all in three innings in four one-day matches. Like so many players in social cricket, it looks as though they were making up the numbers.

‡Shaiza Khan and Kiran Baloch told me that the umpires rejected countless appeals in the West Indian second innings. Shaiza did not let the umpires know about Kiran's approach to the world record, for fear that she would be 'triggered'.

Khan sisters' organisation, the PWCCA, of its biggest asset, international recognition, and it facilitated the takeover of Pakistan women's cricket by the PCB.

As the first head of the new women's wing, Shaharyar Khan, the chairman, appointed a distinguished educator. Mrs Mira Phailbus, the long-serving principal of Lahore's prestigious Kinnaird College.[31] He hoped she would give women's cricket fresh leadership with the support of both factions. Unfortunately, Mrs Phailbus had no experience of cricket, either as a player or an administrator. This lost her the respect of both rival associations. The Khan sisters refused to be 'put under a schoolmistress' and on their behalf Arif Abbasi protested that the PCB (still under an ad hoc committee) had no constitutional authority to remove the Khan sisters' PWCCA.

The sisters and Kiran Baloch disappeared from the new set-up and never played again for the national team. They now play their cricket in England. Without passing any judgement on the parties concerned, it is sad that Pakistan women's cricket has lost the contribution of these pioneers and achievers.*

The PWCA, through Mrs Bushra Aitzaz, also objected to Mrs Phailbus's appointment, and later claimed that she never showed up to meetings.[32] This is strongly denied by Najum Latif, curator of the Lahore Gymkhana Cricket Museum, who suggested that she was unfairly maligned and a victim of factional rivalries. He told me that Mrs Phailbus was an active chairman, and credits her with putting Pakistan women's cricket on the right track. She brought in a strong team, with the veteran former captain Imtiaz Ahmed as her adviser, and Shamsa Hashmi, a leading all-rounder from Lahore Women, as her administrator.

In short order, Shamsa Hashmi organised a National Women's Cricket Championship, contested by nine provincial sides, and won in its first year by a Karachi team of apparently new faces.[33] Both she and Imtiaz were ejected when Mrs Phailbus was replaced in 2008 by Mrs Shirin Javed (see page 435).[34] Her successor, Ayesha Ashhar, praised her energy to me but

---

*Shaharyar Khan suggests, ibid, that the PWCCA withdrew Kiran Baloch's services, but that is not what she told me. The other leading members of the Test team against the West Indies – Sajjida Shah, the wicketkeeper Batool Fatima, Khursheed Jabeen, Urooj Mumtaz and Nazia Nazir – continued to play international cricket for Pakistan after the Khan sisters left.

suggested that her administrative skills were diluted by her continued commitments as a player, national selector and manager.

Internationally, the new regime had a big success when Delhi Women became the first Indian women's side to visit Pakistan. They won all five matches against a new-look Pakistan side led by a Lahori, Sana Javed. This tour's success allowed Pakistan to host its first international tournament, the second Women's Asia Cup, from December 2005 to January 2006, involving Pakistan, India and Sri Lanka. Pakistan were heavily beaten in their first full international against a seasoned Indian team, and lost all their matches in the tournament. Their next international venture was a tour of South Africa; four one-day internationals lost and one no-result.

Pakistan were then awarded the right to host the qualifying tournament, in early 2008, for the next World Cup. However, political turmoil as the Musharraf regime tottered led the ICC to switch it to South Africa, where Pakistan won through to the World Cup itself. They dismissed Scotland for just 26 and also thrashed Zimbabwe; crucially they beat Ireland for the first time. In Australia for the Cup, in 2009, victories over West Indies and Sri Lanka ensured a sixth-place finish, in spite of a crushing defeat by the beaten finalists, New Zealand.

A GOLD MEDAL – AND THREATS IN INDIA

In 2010, the Pakistan women's team won its first international tournament when it claimed the 20-over women's cricket gold medal at the Asian Games in Guangzhou, China. In truth, their opposition was not formidable; with no India or Sri Lanka to face, Pakistan restricted Thailand, China and Japan to scores of 61 or less before meeting Bangladesh in the final. All-rounder Nida Dar took three cheap wickets as Bangladesh managed only 92, and then scored 51 not out as Pakistan won by ten wickets. It was the first gold medal ever gained by Pakistani women at any Asian Games, and significantly it had a big television audience. Pakistan's President Asif Ali Zardari, widower of Benazir Bhutto, found it worthwhile to associate himself with the team. He hailed their victory as 'a gift to the nation riding on a series of crises.'[35]

Pakistan qualified for the 2013 World Cup in second place in the preliminary tournament in Bangladesh, with an historic win over South Africa in a low-scoring match.[36] However, their visit to the Cup itself in India was marred by threats from Hindu extremists, which induced the organisers to move all their matches to Cuttack and accommodate them in a compound at the stadium. Pakistan's young captain, Sana Mir, graciously commented: 'We don't mind the accommodation. We are not here to stay in five-star hotels. We are here to play cricket and we are comfortable in the club-house.'[37]

The world's media ignored this story. One wonders how they would have reacted to the news that Pakistan could not guarantee the security of a visiting team and had forced them to stay in a stadium. The team's manager, Ayesha Ashhar, pointed out to me that several grounds in Pakistan could meet the same standards for visiting teams as Cuttack had given to hers.

Possibly unsettled, the Pakistan women's team were heavily beaten in all their group matches, where their highest total was 104. In the somewhat meaningless seventh place play-off, a not-out 68 from Nida Dar enabled them to reach 192 for 7 in their 50 overs, but this was eclipsed by an unde-feated century from Mithali Raj (holder of the world Test record which was broken by Kiran Baloch), which took India to a seven-wicket victory. Despite Pakistan's disappointing results, the matches had an enthusiastic fol-lowing on television.

THE PRESENT

Going back to the narrative off the field, in 2008 Mrs Shirin Javed took over as chair of the PCB women's wing from Mrs Phailbus. It was a long-held ambition, and she brought to the post high energy and excellent network-ing and lobbying skills, deployed not only on her brother-in-law Ijaz Butt but also on business leaders and politicians from all parties. As administra-tor, and manager of the national team, she appointed Ayesha Ashhar. Shirin Javed was not afraid of controversy, and was personally responsible for the sacking of Urooj Mumtaz as women's captain, despite Pakistan's good cam-paign in the 2009 World Cup.[38] Ill with cancer, she handed over at the end of her two-year contract, to her long-standing ally Mrs Bushra Aitzaz, the present chair.

As with the men's game, Pakistan's women's cricket has continued to attract its share of rivalries, controversies and alleged scandals.* But there is no question that it has made a huge advance since its silent pre-history before the 1990s.

In season 1991–92 there was not a single organised cricket match involving girls or women in Pakistan.[39] In the last full season 2011–12 there were thirty matches in the National Women's Cricket Championship, firmly established since its inception in 2004. These involved eleven regional sides, representing Islamabad, Abbottabad, Quetta, Peshawar, Multan, Sialkot, Rawalpindi, Faisalabad and Hyderabad, besides Lahore and Karachi, and three employers' teams, the Pakistan Education Board, the Higher Education Commission, and ZTBL†, the winners.

The participants were a sign of an established regional infrastructure (perhaps the most solid achievement of the new regime), while ZTBL's involvement as a sponsor stemmed from its former boss, Zaka Ashraf, transferred to the PCB by his patron, President Zardari.‡ None of these matches faced any special conditions on clothing or spectatorship, as religious and conservative groups have been able to impose in the past. Significantly, they were shown on television.§

In June 2013, I saw the present and future of Pakistan's women cricket at the ECB's facilities at Loughborough University. The national women's team was on a short tour of England and Ireland – their first overseas venture since the 2013 World Cup in India.

The players had arrived late the previous night after a long flight and a further onward journey, but they were having a hard practice session at the

*See for example 'Five women cricketers banned for making false sexual harassment claim', *Express Tribune* (Pakistan), 25 October 2013.

†The Zarai Taraqiati Bank Limited (ZTBL) (formerly known as Agricultural Development Bank of Pakistan) claims to be the largest public-sector financial-development institution in Pakistan.

‡Reported in *Dawn*, 8 March 2013. That year, ZTBL also won the new Shaheed Mohtarma Benazir Bhutto 20-over challenge trophy, in which the other participants were Punjab Women, Sindh Women, Federal Capital Women, Baluchistan Women and Khyber Pakhtunkhwa Women. They won it again in March 2013, sharing prize money of 200,000 rupees (around £1,330). The beaten finalists, Punjab, shared 100,000 rupees, and the player of the tournament, Bismah Maroof of ZTBL, collected 25,000 rupees.

§Mrs Bushra Aitzaz: personal interview. Both Ayesha Ashhar and Mrs Bushra Aitzaz emphasised to me that they had received no complaints or protests about women playing cricket from any religious or community group. Mrs Bushra Aitzaz told me a delightful story of the power of television to change attitudes. One of the current stars of the national team, from a provincial city, had a long struggle against her elder brother who did not want her to play cricket. Then the brother saw the team on television. 'He came up to me and said she'd had an offer to promote some commodity, so would we allow her to be put up on a billboard?'

nets, particularly the batters, working under a specialist coach, Basit Ali, to eliminate technical weaknesses. I spoke briefly to two of the players before they were whisked away to the gym.

Nahida Bibi is a batting all-rounder who made her international debut against Sri Lanka in 2009. She was then twenty-six, and comes from Quetta, in Baluchistan, where, as we have seen, cricket had little following for most of Pakistan's life as a nation. She has been studying at Baluchistan University for an MA in sports science.

She played many sports at school and college but committed herself to cricket at age twenty. 'When I started there were difficulties for me, because there are people in Quetta who didn't want kids to play cricket, and there was interference. Most of my family were opposed to me playing cricket, but my father supported me. Things have got better in the last six years, because the women's team has made progress, and television has shown this to people.' She also told me that improved financial rewards have given many more girls and women an incentive to get involved in cricket. They can hope to make a career from it. 'I am going to play on after I take my degree.'

The other player was the team's debutante, Iram Javed, twenty-one and a student of Urdu at the prestigious Kinnaird College in Lahore. Like Nahida Bibi, she is another batting all-rounder, who played many sports in childhood but took up cricket alone, her real love, at the age of seventeen. Her family had no background in cricket, but were very supportive. She has never faced any opposition to her playing cricket and she benefited from a strong local structure of school and age-group cricket. She told me, 'We have too much cricket in Lahore!'

Iram Javed is another who believes that television coverage brought a big change of attitudes to women's cricket, 'now everyone knows what we can do.' At a very early stage of her career she has appeared in several televised matches at Under-19 level and in the Benazir Bhutto T20 trophy. Like Nahida Bibi, she has a clear career plan after her degree. 'Nothing but cricket! I love cricket.' Her confidence would have been unthinkable twenty years ago. It is a sign of the huge journey made by Pakistan's women cricketers.

THE FINANCIAL REVOLUTION

'I played for the fun of it.'

– IMTIAZ AHMED, WHO PLAYED IN PAKISTAN'S FIRST 39
TEST MATCHES FROM 1952 TO 1962, IN CONVERSATION
WITH THE AUTHOR, 2011

Pakistan cricket has received revenues undreamed of by its pioneers and early heroes as a result of changes which were largely unplanned by its administrators. Essentially, it has become part of a world entertainment industry, supplying television viewers (and increasingly, viewers through personal information technology) with a product they are willing to pay for. Pakistan, with other cricket nations, became a beneficiary of simultaneous major changes in the governance and financing of international cricket in 1993. As we shall see, the resulting system depends crucially on the continued goodwill of India, which is far and away the biggest source of viewer revenues, and Pakistan cricket in particular exists in the financial shadow of her mighty neighbour.*

* I am immensely indebted to those who dedicated many patient hours of their full schedules to enable this chapter to be written. In particular I would like to thank Ehsan Mani, Arif Abbasi and Zahid Noorani (of Ten Sports), without whom the financial revolution itself would not have occurred. At the PCB, Subhan Ahmed and the finance team, led by Badar M Khan and Mubashir Manan, were endlessly helpful. At the ICC, the chief financial officer, Faisal Hasnain, and his team provided essential and detailed factual guidance. Between them they supplied all the figures in this chapter, unless otherwise stated.

To explain how Pakistan cricket reached this state, it pays to investigate its three phases in terms of finance and governance before the financial revolution of 1993. These are: the amateur phase from 1947 to 1972; the 'state socialism' phase under ZA Bhutto and Kardar; and the first commercial phase guided primarily by Arif Abbasi during the 1980s.

THE AMATEUR PHASE OF PAKISTAN CRICKET

For its first twenty-four years, Pakistan cricket was sustained by willing amateurs. Its administrators, notably AR Cornelius, combined their work in cricket with other major responsibilities. The players derived meagre remuneration from domestic matches and not very much more from international ones. They were expected to play for the honour of representing their country and establishing its credentials as a Test nation. When Imtiaz Ahmed, the great wicketkeeper-batsman, helped Fazal Mahmood destroy England at The Oval to earn Pakistan's great victory in 1954 his Test match fee was £5. By 1962, this sum had risen to just £7 10 shillings.[1]

For cricket to be played successfully at all in this period, it depended entirely on two sources of income: gate receipts and patronage. Gate receipts alone were insufficient in Pakistan first-class cricket to pay cricketers any more than the most basic expenses. Patronage came in many different forms; from state and regional authorities, from wealthy patrons and from educational institutions.

The early patrons were cricket enthusiasts with minimal commercial or political ambitions. This could even be said of the supreme Patron – the head of state to whom Cornelius had deliberately linked the Board of Control. Pakistan's early rulers made fitful attempts to identify themselves with Pakistan's cricketers when they were successful and to punish them, and their administrators, when they were not. As we have seen, one of these rulers, the generally undistinguished Khawaja Nazimuddin, made one vital directive for Pakistan cricket when he ruled that public servants remained on duty when they played international cricket matches, and therefore had to be released.[2] Otherwise, Pakistan's early rulers had strikingly little impact on the game. In that first era, before Pakistan's cricketers were achieving regular international success and acquiring a following on television, cricket was a low priority for its government.*

Cricket was financed by a combination of feudalism, charitable giving, and club receipts, plus a small state subvention. But it was in a noble cause; sport fulfilled its function if it could prove a national purpose. This was achievable with an amateur structure because the institutions that supported the development of first-class cricketers in the 1950s and 1960s, the great schools and colleges, pre-dated Partition, embraced the new Pakistan, and attracted financial support and large gates.

The annual fixture of Government College v Islamia College attracted crowds of up to 6,000 to the Old University Ground, and was covered by radio. It was considered a Test trial.

Cricket was a passport to fame but not fortune for its players. But the game that could barely afford its players a living wage was not awash with funds to invest in cricket grounds, practice facilities, coaching and competition levels consistent with producing a sustained winning international team. Test status was maintained. But the early promise of 1954 was unfulfilled.

Cricket was played on a shoestring. Its regional structures were underfinanced, gate receipts were distributed in mysterious ways, and there was virtually no outside income.

CRICKET UNDER STATE SOCIALISM

When ZA Bhutto was elected president of Pakistan from 1971 to 1973, and prime minister from 1973 to 1977, his mission was to transform Pakistan's society and its economy on socialist principles. His programme included nationalisation of major banks and industries designed to limit the power and influence of the dozen or so most economically powerful families in Pakistan. He appointed AH Kardar to head the BCCP. Together, Bhutto and Kardar directed the major companies and nationalised institutions to form first-class cricket teams, paying their cricketers as employees.

Bhutto's motives were to improve the morale of a country reeling from humiliation at the United Nations and the loss of East Pakistan to Indian

*See the budget figures mentioned above, on pp.171–2.

forces in 1971. Pakistan cricket lagged behind hockey (still the national game) and squash, as centres of excellence, yet the reach of the game across the regions and, above all, classes was broader. But the new system had a political purpose as well. As part of his broader project of social radicalisation, Bhutto sought to break the domination of elite universities in first-class cricket and broaden his own political power base in student bodies.[3]

Bhutto courted the non-aligned movement of the early 1970s, and his new structure of cricket fitted within the prevailing development model of Third World economies through closed statist structures. But it is striking that Bhutto decided to develop *cricket* within this framework. A different kind of populist politician could have abandoned the sport to its fate, as a relic of the colonial past, and a bastion of class privilege to be destroyed. Luckily, Bhutto himself was a cricket-lover. Instead of turning on cricket, he simply ousted its elite supporters and directed its economic survival, supported by the widest possible dissemination through (state-controlled) broadcasting.

Bhutto and Kardar's system of department salaries provided modest underpinning of the livelihood of cricketers similar to that provided to Olympic athletes in communist countries by paid positions in the state administration or armed forces, or to English 'amateur' athletes by paid off-season jobs from sympathetic employers.

Although an enthusiast for the new model, Kardar, as we have seen, retained strongly many attitudes from the amateur era, especially the idea that Pakistan's international stars should accept financial sacrifice to play for their country.

This attitude and the new model were challenged by the top players themselves – who had discovered a new market value for their individual services with the opening of the English county championship to overseas players in 1968. The great majority of players in Pakistan's successful international teams in the 1970s – notably Asif Iqbal, Intikhab Alam, Mushtaq Mohammad and his brother Sadiq, Sarfraz Nawaz, Majid Khan, Zaheer Abbas, Imran Khan and Javed Miandad – all played regularly for first-class English counties. Through their experience, they widened the gulf in skill between themselves and players who played only in Pakistan, and acquired new expectations about their earning power while becoming far less dependent on Pakistan's domestic employers.

Meanwhile, Pakistan's international successes were becoming much more accessible to cricket followers, partly through live coverage on television (which most viewers watched communally in public places) and through cheap transistor radios.

The Packer episode temporarily removed Pakistan's stars from the transistors and communal television screens. It gave them the opportunity to earn the kind of money which their best contemporaries could command and to free themselves completely from the control of their own cricket authorities. It also heralded a new model of cricket viewership – in which the best players would no longer be available for free.

THE FIRST COMMERCIAL PHASE OF PAKISTAN CRICKET

The settlement with Packer restored Pakistan's cricket stars to free public service broadcasting, at home and abroad. However, it had opened up awareness of their commercial value, and showed that their aspirations were unattainable under the state socialist model, which in any event was in full retreat after the fall and execution of ZA Bhutto.

Arif Abbasi was the first of Pakistan's cricket administrators to realise that Pakistan cricket needed new streams of revenue – and could be sold as an entertainment product to commercial sponsors. He came from a rich cricketing heritage. He was a grandson of the Aligarh-educated all-rounder Khan Salamuddin, one of the successes of India's pre-Test tour of England in 1911, and related to India's Pataudi dynasty. He had played first-class cricket for Pakistan Universities. But Abbasi was first and foremost a smart entrepreneur from Karachi, a protégé of Air Marshal Nur Khan who brought him into Pakistan's cricket administration when he took over the Board of Control in 1980.

Arif Abbasi's first move was a dramatic break from the Bhutto era; he told the Islamabad government that the Board no longer wanted its small annual subsidy. It would find its own financial resources. He also ended another Bhutto hangover – the practice of giving away Pakistan cricket matches to the state broadcasters. At times, the Board had actually paid the broadcasters to cover them.

His first commercial venture was modest by modern standards – offering a guarantee to a touring West Indian side, under Clive Lloyd. The guarantee was comfortably met from ticket sales and ground advertising, with a minimal contribution from television, and the tour earned Pakistan, as hosts, a surplus of around \$400,000.[4] The success whetted Pakistan's appetite and helped to inspire its successful joint bid with India for the 1987 World Cup.[5] That was another major marketing success, although again television income was a minor factor.

Significantly, Arif Abbasi pulled in major commercial income to support the domestic game. With no inhibitions about tobacco sponsorship, he secured major support from the Pakistan Tobacco Company for the Patrons Trophy, a new one-day Wills Cup and the historic Quaid-e-Azam Trophy. The Pakistan Automobile Corporation (the state-owned holding company for Pakistan's motor manufacturers) sponsored a new PACO Cup and formed a domestic team of its own. A crucial innovation was an Under-19 tournament, sponsored by Pepsi Cola, concentrated exclusively on the regions. Such deals resulted in a huge expansion of domestic cricket in the 1980s. Several seasons saw over 100 first-class matches (compared to seven in 1953–54, the first season of the Quaid-e-Azam Trophy, and 63 in 1975–76, at the peak of the Bhutto-Kardar system).[6]

These domestic successes were achieved largely without television income. If anything, television followed cricket's success rather than the other way round, when, in 1989–90, Pakistan television decided to televise Quaid-e-Azam Trophy matches for the first time.[7]

THE TRANSFORMATION IN 1993

Pakistan cricket had therefore become aware of its attractions as a commercial product by 1993 and was enjoying significant new streams of income which were independent of the state. But its subsequent commercial fortunes were shaped almost entirely by developments in international sport which were largely outside its control.

To understand the meaning of these developments it is necessary to go back to 1965, when the then Imperial Cricket Conference (originally founded in 1909 by England, Australia and South Africa) changed its name to the International Cricket Conference. But while it had lost the term 'Imperial' in its name, the two dominant forces in world cricket, England and Australia, (known as 'foundation members') still had the power of veto. As we have seen, Kardar had railed against this without success in the 1970s.

On 7 July 1993, his ambition was at last fulfilled. England and Australia lost their veto power and the ICC lost 'Conference' from its title, substituting the word 'Council'. The International Cricket Council came into existence based not at Lord's but in Dubai. In 1997, Jagmohan Dalmiya from India became the first Asian president of ICC, completing both symbolically and practically the loss of the domination of world cricket from Lord's.

The 1993 version of the ICC, which I refer to as the ICC settlement, survives with modifications to this day. It is the International Olympic Committee, or FIFA, of world cricket and has presided over a revolution in the development of cricket, being responsible for the global organisation of the game, with the exception of its 'Laws'.*

The ICC settlement had been born of a sense of frustration among the playing members that the domination by England (and Australia) of the governance of the ICC and of its principal function of organising fixtures and tour programmes was inequitable. The reluctance of England to accept Zimbabwe as a full member until 1992 exacerbated this feeling.

It was thus a political not economic settlement. Remarkably, the ICC settlement did not disturb the underlying economic arrangements of cricket to a major extent. The amounts changed, but the underlying ownership rights and percentages did not. The consequences of this decision were unforeseen and far-reaching.

The ICC budget in London in 1993 (when Colin Cowdrey, last of the amateurs, was president) was approximately £100,000. By 2007 the ICC had grown into a global business, generating revenues over the 2001–07 period of US $550 million and a surplus (after expenses) of approximately US $320 million. This surplus was distributable among its members in exactly the same proportions as the costs were shared in 1993, i.e. 75% to full members (Test-playing countries) and 25% to associate members. The ICC had been transformed, from a modest cost-centre funding the orderly administration of international fixtures, to a global entertainment business. This was brought about by ICC's ownership of the sports rights to international cricket competitions, and international cricket competitions only.

*The Laws of Cricket remain the responsibility of the MCC at Lord's. This role, important as it is, is similar to the role in golf played by the Royal & Ancient Club at St Andrews, and is the only remaining power of the founding imperial nation. The MCC has no responsibility for ICC match conditions and discipline, which have become close to a separate corpus of laws. Before the ICC settlement, the MCC had provided the secretary and president of the International Cricket Conference.

For in the same way that the ICC in 1993 took over the cost basis, ICC inherited the ownership of the World Cup.

Equally importantly, it left the ownership of the domestic and bilateral international competitions, principally Test match and ODI tours, in the hands of the domestic cricket boards. In 1997, the ICC members re-organised the fixture-setting commitments into the Future Tours Programme, a supposedly binding commitment by the ten full members to play each other twice in five-year cycles on each other's territory, in series consisting of at least two Test matches and three one-day internationals. Remarkably, the economic arrangements for these bilateral commitments were similar to those that existed before the ICC settlement; namely the revenues and costs of the tours were enjoyed and borne by the host nation.

Thus, crucially, the ICC settlement did not disturb the underlying economic structure of the game, in particular the ownership of sports rights, principally TV and sponsorship rights. The ICC owned the rights to international competitions; the members' cricket boards were free to own the domestic rights (if permitted by their governments) of the bilateral competitions, and, equally importantly, of existing or future domestic competitions.

The economic power of these rights and the transformation of the finances of sport were not fully appreciated in 1993, except by a group of far-sighted entrepreneurs led by Rupert Murdoch* and Subhash Chandra,† and the IMG Corporation of Mark McCormack.‡

These entrepreneurs in turn were enabled by revolutionary legislative changes in the two most important TV markets for cricket: the UK and India. The UK Broadcasting Act of 1990, in addition to allowing a fifth analogue TV channel, allowed the growth of multinational satellite TV. Coupled with an equivalent measure in India in 1991, this enabled the nascent satellite and cable TV industry in the UK to consolidate and develop strategic plans for televised sport in both the UK and India. In 2002 President Musharraf similarly liberated the market in Pakistan to equally dramatic effect, allowing the entry of Pakistan-based entrepreneurs, such as GEO TV of the Jang Group, to compete successfully.

---

*Rupert Murdoch, founder of News Corporation and Sky TV in UK and owner of Star TV in India.
†Subhash Chandra, founder in 1992 of Zee TV in India.
‡The American lawyer, Mark McCormack (1930–2003) founded the International Management Group (IMG) in the 1950s to represent leading golfers. It became the leading sports marketing agency in the world.

The four vital elements of cricket's big bang were in place by 1993 – these were: the ICC settlement and the end of the foundation members' veto; the acceptance of ownership of sports rights (especially TV rights) among and between the members with the ICC owning the international rights, the national boards the bilateral rights; the legislative foundation for dedicated pay-to-view sports broadcasting; and the arrival of a generation of global media entrepreneurs in the TV and satellite industries willing to invest stellar sums to obtain stellar returns.

The risk these entrepreneurs and their successors were willing to take, namely the massive investment in cable and satellite technology required to enable viewers to watch sport independently of the monopolistic terrestrial analogue broadcasters, was based on one big gamble. They bet that TV viewers of sport, known today by the unromantic but accurate description as 'consumers of content', would be prepared to pay by subscription to TV channels to watch sport in sufficient numbers at a subscription price which enabled the TV companies both to recover their investment in technology, and at ratings levels which commanded attractive and therefore lucratively priced advertising slots for manufacturers of consumer products.

The investment required was huge, and start-up losses were inevitable. The biggest of all, News Corporation, nearly went down in the process, suffering huge initial losses. It recovered only after the spectacular success of its investment in the rights of the English football Premier League, the first demonstration outside the USA of the value locked in the wallet of the 'consumer of content'.*

THE BIG BANG OF 2000

The first unlocking of the potential of TV rights came during the successful bid by India-Pakistan and Sri Lanka for the 1996 World Cup, organised in India by Pilcom under the leadership of Jagmohan Dalmiya. In 1993, Arif

*Sky first won the rights to broadcast the English football Premier League in 1992–93. Its subsequent success, through globalisation, made Sky TV one of the most successful channels in modern broadcasting. Without its initial success, it is inconceivable that its subsequent investment in televised cricket in 2003 would have occurred. It is no exaggeration to say that the English football viewer paved the way for the explosion in revenues that cricket has enjoyed. There is a fine analysis of Murdoch's capture of the Premier League in Bose, Mihir, *Game Changer* (Marshall Cavendish, 2012).

Abbasi and a fellow Pakistani, Ehsan Mani, a financial maestro,* secured a guaranteed price of $1.5 million from TWI (part of IMG), the first international sale of Pakistan cricket rights. They repeated the process for 1998–2003, securing a bid from TWI of $6.4 million plus a profit share, with $8.8 million eventually received from this arrangement. The sums seem modest now, but they were milestones in their time and whetted Pakistan's appetite for financial self-sufficiency.[8]

In his own words, Mani had 'stumbled into cricket administration', but it was he who advanced the concept which changed the universe of cricket administration throughout the world.

For all its commercial success, the 1996 World Cup had demonstrated the limitations of the existing system for the sale of cricket rights. So too had the 1999 tournament in England. Both were sold as 'one-off' events by the host nations. In the practice of the time, the host kept the lion's share of income and afforded the ICC and its members a profit share. But profits in England in 1999 had been modest.

Mani's remedy was for the ICC to sell rights in a bundle to all the competitions under its control over a period.

With the active support of Dalmiya and the head of the England and Wales Cricket Board, Lord MacLaurin, who had previously built Tesco into Britain's largest supermarket chain, Mani overcame resistance from reluctant ICC members, especially the future World Cup hosts, South Africa and the West Indies. In 2000, the ICC offered TV and sponsorship rights to all its forthcoming international tournaments by competitive tender, including the World Cups of 2003 and 2007.

He and the ICC were rewarded by a fierce competition, principally between Subhash Chandra's Zee Corporation and the Murdoch Group. The bundled rights were sold for $550 million, a staggering sum at the time.

This was cricket's big bang – and the cricket universe created by the big bang of 2000 continues to expand. For the successor ICC commercial tender, for the period 2007–15, the ICC bundled the tournament commercial rights for the ICC Cricket World Cup (2011 and 2015), the ICC

---

*Born in Rawalpindi, 1945, played for Government College Lahore, studied in Britain as a chartered accountant. From 1989, he was PCB representative on the ICC and, crucially, chaired the ICC Finance and Marketing Committee, 1996–2002. He became president of the ICC in 2003.

Under-19 World Cup (2008, 2010, 2012, 2014), the ICC World T20 (2007, 2009, 2010, 2012, 2014), the ICC Women's World Cup (2009 and 2013), the ICC Champions Trophy (2009 and 2013) and four minor events. The commercial rights were split between TV (broadcast) rights and sponsorship rights. The successful bids totalled $1.5 billion, with ESPN Star Sports (News Corp and partners) winning the broadcast rights for $1.1 billion, and individual bids by Pepsi, LG, Reliance Corp of India, Emirates Airlines and others acquiring the sponsorship rights for a further $400 million. A direct comparison between the 2000–07 and the 2007–15 periods is not possible because of the important inclusion from 2007 of the ICC World T20 commercial rights. However, the list of competitions and the sums achieved, plus the arrival of the annual ICC Awards and the ICC Hall of Fame, are testament to international cricket's arrival as a world entertainment phenomenon.

BILATERAL TOURNAMENTS AND THE POWER OF INDIA

These arrangements for international competitions generated huge windfall gains for both full and associate members based on the share-out established in the far-off days of 1993. They depended crucially on the enduring goodwill of India, which has far and away the biggest viewer market for cricket, in conventional television and in new media. India could undoubtedly have obtained a far higher revenue if it had sold its own rights separately, or if it simply demanded a higher share-out of the international tournament revenues. Given the success of the Indian Premier League, India would also profit handsomely if it had removed T20 competitions from the ICC bundle and negotiated rights sales for them on its own account.

India's power has been even more marked in bilateral tournaments, where the ICC settlement has been based on a simple rule: all television rights, from all countries, accrue to the host, even if the host, like Pakistan, plays its 'home matches' in another country. Since Indian viewing revenues are so much more important than any other country's, a tour by India makes a critical difference to any other country's cricket finances. An English tour comes second to India as an earner for a host, then at some distance

Australia, while other tourists trail far behind them. The ICC Future Tours Programme of the 1993 settlement essentially aims for each country to visit each other over a cycle of years, so that each shares the gain of an Indian tour and the relative pain of receiving a lesser financial power.

India's long refusal to be hosted by Pakistan (which last happened in 2005–06) has therefore imposed a major penalty on Pakistan cricket.

PAKISTAN AND CRICKET'S BIG BANG

In 2000, the year in which the ICC bundled its rights for the first time, the PCB broke even, with income and expenditure balanced at $4.6 million. Bangladesh, the weakest cricketing nation, were the tourists. With more attractive opposition (in terms of viewer rights) such as England or Australia, the figure would have been $8–10 million, generating, after adjustment of costs, a surplus of $4 million.

From 2002 to 2013, Pakistan's total receipts from ICC-organised tournaments alone was $74 million, of which $13.25 million were hosting fees for tournaments, and $3.5 million from participation fees (Champions Trophy 2008, and World Cup 2011). The remaining $57.5 million came from its share of ICC revenues under the formula for a full member.

The PCB's aggregate income over sixteen years 1998–2013 amounted to $365 million, and generated a cumulative surplus after tax of $131 million, a respectable net margin of 35%. Previous generations would be astonished to see the Board contributing to the national exchequer.

But a deeper look at the figures reveals an underlying volatility that reflects the reality of the finance of cricket in Pakistan.

Of the total surplus, approximately $43 million came from the surpluses arising from the two Indian tours of 2004 and 2008, of $18 million and $25 million respectively. The growth in these figures demonstrates clearly the effect of the ICC bilateral tours settlement and the rising value of host country rights, especially if the touring nation is India.

This volatility of income is clearly demonstrated by the immediate financial consequences of the events of the attacks on Mumbai in November 2008 and on the Sri Lankan touring team in Lahore in 2009. In October 2008, one month before the Mumbai incident, Ten Sports (by 2008, a subsidiary of Subhash Chandra's Zee Corp) bought the Pakistan broadcast rights for 2008–13 for $125 million, predicated on a full tour by India including Tests and one-day internationals. The cancellation of the Indian tour meant a reduction in PCB receipts to approximately $35 million. This represents a deficit over the life of the rights of $90 million.

India and Pakistan have yet to agree to a resumption of bilateral touring including neutral venue matches, or Pakistan 'home' matches played in India. Pakistan has received sympathy from the ICC members and has played 'home' matches against many of the full members, including Australia and England in England and the UAE. But the opportunity cost to Pakistan of the Indian impasse can be readily, if roughly calculated. Imagine three home bilateral series in Pakistan itself, against India, England and Australia, each with three Tests, five one-day internationals and five T20 matches. The India series would yield Pakistan approximately $70 million, the English and Australian series $35 million each – generating a total of $140 million. Now take away India, and imagine Pakistan playing the same series against England, Australia and South Africa in the United Arab Emirates. These might bring in $20 million each, for a total of $60 million. The opportunity cost to Pakistan cricket of the terrorist incidents is therefore at least $80 million.

THE EFFECT ON DEVELOPMENT

Confronted by such volatility, the PCB has managed to hold its operating expenses in the period 2009–13 at approximately $12 million. They had doubled from $6 million in 2006. After deficits in 2008–10, a degree of stability has returned, and after a strong income in 2011 from the World Cup, modest surpluses will be achievable in 2012 and 2013.

The revenues flowing into Pakistan cricket from the big bang in international cricket would be unimaginable to its pioneers. Both Najam Sethi, the acting PCB chairman, and his would-be successors have a huge task in ensuring that these revenues are not wasted. They need to address pressing issues of staffing and productivity with the PCB, the legitimacy and competence of representative local bodies, the share-out of revenues between competing claimants (including women's cricket and cricket for disabled

Hanif Mohammad introduces Khalid Ibadulla to the Queen at Lord's, 1967.

Early Pakistan women cricketers at the Gaddafi stadium wearing a *shalwar kameez*.

Two great players: Majid Khan and Asif Iqbal putting on their pads.

AH Kardar,
immaculately dressed
as ever but ill at ease
on the campaign trail
Lahore 1970.

Majid Khan caught Marsh bowled
Walker 158. Melbourne 1972. The not-
out batsman is Mushtaq Mohammad.

Sadiq Mohammad,
Wasim Bari, Aftab
Baloch, Zaheer Abbas,
Asif Masood and
Majid Khan on the
1974 tour of England.
Masood, wearing the
check trousers, had a
bowling run-up that
was compared by John
Arlott to 'Groucho
Marx chasing a pretty
waitress'.

Three Burki cousins: Majid Khan, Dr Farrakh Khan (team doctor) and Imran Khan. Pakistan tour of India 1979–80.

The Ladies stand at the Gaddafi stadium, Pakistan v India, second Test, Lahore, October 1978–79.

Women playing at the Lahore Gymkhana, 2013.

ZA Bhutto and Kardar discussing matters of state at the Gaddafi stadium.

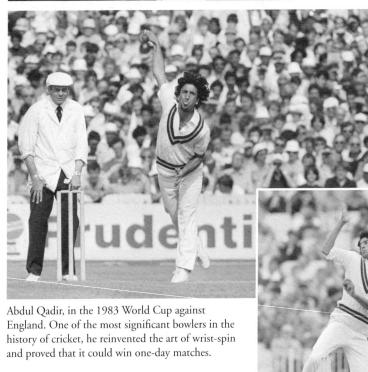

Abdul Qadir, in the 1983 World Cup against England. One of the most significant bowlers in the history of cricket, he reinvented the art of wrist-spin and proved that it could win one-day matches.

Wasim Akram plotting another reverse for England at Old Trafford in June 1987.

aved Miandad, Pakistan's highest scorer in Tests, on his way to 260 against England at The Oval in August 1987.

Pakistan's prime minister, Nawaz Sharif, shows off his square cut at a Commonwealth meeting in Zimbabwe in 1991. He is the latest Pakistani leader to have been a proficient cricketer.

Captain Imran Khan celebrates winning the 1992 'Cornered Tigers' World Cup final against England.

Lethal fast bowler Waqar Younis at the third Test match, at The Oval, in August 1996. Pakistan beat England by nine wickets.

Children playing in the street in Karachi.

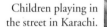

Inzamam-ul-Haq with popular Pakistan coach Bob Woolmer, who died suddenly in March 2007 during the World Cup in the West Indies.

Fans in Multan burn images of former captain Salman Butt and Mohammad Asif in November 2011. The pair had just been jailed for spot-fixing.

Shahid 'Boom Boom' Afridi is a hero to millions of Pakistan cricket followers.

Saeed Ahmed in retirement. He is now a fervent evangelist for Islam.

Inzamam-ul-Haq looking thoughtful.

Imran Khan makes a point at a party rally at the Quaid-e-Azam MA Jinnah mausoleum in Karachi during the 2013 election campaign.

Pakistan captain Misbah ul-Haq hits out against Sri Lanka at the Sheikh Zayed stadium in Abu Dhabi in January 2014. Sadly, there were few spectators to watch this 'home' Test.

Cricket at dusk in Rawalpindi, on the outskirts of Islamabad.

people), and the efficiency of current programmes. They need to tackle a host of problems whose causes are outside their control, including security, corruption and match-fixing, and the poor education of so many young cricketers. All of these issues have to be addressed against a financial background of volatile revenues, a substantial cost base, and repeated interference by the courts.

THE AGE OF INDIA

The tasks facing Pakistan's cricket administrators became all the more urgent in January 2014. During that month in Dubai, the ICC announced agreement in principle on proposals tabled by India, England and Australia to scrap the 1993 ICC settlement. As of March 2014 a process of negotiation, led by India, was under way which would replace the collective Future Tours Programme with a series of bilateral agreements. It would also re-cast the sharing of the proceeds of future ICC tournaments (essentially, broadcast and sponsorship rights which, had the old 'bundling' system been repeated for 2015–21, were expected to generate up to $3 billon). Instead of an equal distribution among all full members they would be allocated to members in proportion to their economic contribution. In this way, India, aided by England and Australia, would take effective control of the ICC and its revenue flows, reflecting the economic power of their domestic television markets.*

The importance of these negotiations for Pakistan cricket cannot be exaggerated. Although they risk relegating Pakistan (and six other Test-playing countries) to permanent second-class international status, they may make achievable the resumption of bilateral Test cricket series between Pakistan and India – a great prize for Pakistan.

Cricket's new settlement has been driven by the market power of India, which is greater than that of all the others combined. The Financial Revolution has given rise to the Age of India. She has a huge responsibility to use her power in the interests of the world game.

---

*In cricket terms, rather than economic power, the enduring importance of the other Test-playing nations was highlighted by the first ICC tournament after the January announcement. The final of the Under-19 World Cup in February 2014 was contested by Pakistan and South Africa, while the best innings of the tournament was played in the quarter-final by a West Indian.

LAST YEARS OF PEACE

'Be prepared to be bombed. Be prepared to go back to the stone age.'
– US WARNING TO PAKISTAN

When we last reported on the progress of the Pakistan cricket team, it had just crashed to a humiliating defeat at the hands of Australia at Lord's in the 1999 World Cup. The first casualty of this disaster was the PCB, replaced by yet another ad hoc committee.

In place of the experienced Khalid Mahmood, the new chairman was Mujeeb-ur-Rehman, head of the REDCO industrial concern. He had no cricketing background, but he was politically well connected and his company had been a major sponsor of domestic cricket. The other members of the ad hoc committee were Naushad Ali (a former Test cricketer and an army officer) and Javed Zaman, the much respected representative of the Burki clan.

The new regime opened Pakistan's long-awaited National Cricket Academy, at the Gaddafi stadium in Lahore, and appointed Wasim Raja as national coach – the third for the year, following the ousted Javed Miandad and Mushtaq Mohammad, who had departed by choice after the World Cup.[1]

Moin Khan was due to captain the national team, but Wasim Akram displaced him when he was cleared of corruption by the Ehtesab Bureau, the PCB's internal inquiry which had preceded the judicial Qayyum inquiry, whose report was still pending. Wasim's first major assignment could not have been more difficult: a Test series in Australia. Before the party set out, it had lost its coach. The independent-minded Wasim Raja resigned and was replaced by the South African Richard Pybus, who had been technical coach during the World Cup.

More seriously, it lost its government as well, when Nawaz Sharif was ousted in a coup d'état by Pervez Musharraf. Inevitably, Musharraf sacked Rehman, Nawaz Sharif's protégé, as chairman of the ad hoc committee. He was replaced, as a stopgap, by the veteran, Kardar-trained, Zafar Altaf.*

Pakistan lost all three Tests on that 1999–2000 Australia tour, the first and third by heavy margins, the second by four wickets after they felt aggrieved by an umpiring decision in Australia's second innings. It was given in favour of Justin Langer who went on to complete a century and take part in a match-winning stand with Australia's brilliant new wicketkeeper-batsman Adam Gilchrist.

There were some fine individual Pakistan performances. Inzamam-ul-Haq, Saeed Anwar and Ijaz Ahmed contributed centuries, and Saqlain Mushtaq baffled Australians with his doosra in the second Test. But there were too many batting collapses from strong positions, and the bowlers could not contain an Australian batting line-up in which Gilchrist, Langer and Michael Slater all averaged over 80.

Worst of all, Shoaib Akhtar was suspected of throwing. The PCB secretary, Shafqat Rana, denounced these suspicions as racist, without knowing that the match referee, John Reid of New Zealand, had requested Shoaib's action to be secretly filmed. When shown to the ICC, they concluded that he sometimes threw his bouncer. They handed out a ban from international cricket, but then surprisingly cleared him to play one-day internationals.[2]

The row cost Shafqat his job, and then Zafar Altaf was replaced as chairman of the PCB ad hoc committee by Musharraf's military colleague, General Tauqir Zia. He had some cricket pedigree, but was still a serving officer commanding the troops policing the Indian border. Initially, he tried to turn the job down, but Musharraf insisted.†

---

*The party had a selection surprise: Ghulam Ali replaced the experienced Aamer Sohail. A gesture to youth? Hardly, for Ghulam Ali was thirty-three, the same age as the ousted opener, and had been on no one's radar since playing three scattered one-day internationals in the early 1990s. Ghulam Ali played just one first-class innings in Australia, scoring 31. He performed well in domestic cricket for several years but never came close to another tour.

†Conversation with Tauqir Zia, 2011. Tauqir Zia says that as Director of Military Operations he would talk to his Indian opposite number every day, and their conversations would begin with banter about cricket.

The Australian whitewash ended Richard Pybus's role as Pakistan's first foreign national coach. After barely six weeks he was replaced by the great survivor, Intikhab Alam. Colonel Shuja-ud-Din, now one of the grand old men of Pakistan cricket, expostulated in his history that Pakistan's coaching turnover had got 'beyond a joke'. He had a point. In 1999 the Pakistan Cricket Board had three chairmen, who managed between them to give the team five different coaches, and three different captains.[3]

After a short break at home, Pakistan returned to Australia for the annual three-way World Series one-day tournament against Australia and India. There were four losses and four wins (one a last-ball thriller) in the preliminary rounds and the all-rounder Abdul Razzaq did enough to become man of the series, but Australia overwhelmed Pakistan in the best-of-three match final.[4]

Just nine days after their final defeat in Australia, Pakistan were back home to face Sri Lanka. Wasim Akram was officially 'relieved of the captaincy upon his own request.' In fact, he was sacked. Moin Khan refused to replace him and Saeed Anwar filled in. He was uninspiring, and Sri Lanka won the one-day series 3–0 and an ill-tempered Test series 2–1. Muttiah Muralitharan was too good for the Pakistan batsmen, although a young Pashtun, Younis Khan, became the seventh Pakistani to score a century on Test debut.

Pakistan's victory was a consolation after the series had been lost, and it was gained by Moin Khan, deputising for the injured Saeed Anwar. Waqar Younis returned to the team and took thirteen wickets. Before this Test, Javed Miandad ousted Intikhab Alam as national coach, provoking Intikhab into a rare outburst against the PCB.[5]

Moin Khan was now re-installed as captain, and led the team to victory in Sharjah in the Coca-Cola Cup against India and South Africa. He then took an injury-hit squad to West Indies for Pakistan's first visit since 1993. He won a one-day series against them and Zimbabwe, and then played three Tests. The first was drawn, with Pakistan in a strong position after rain. In the second, Moin and Javed were blamed for curiously defensive tactics after Imran Nazir, only eighteen, scored a rapid hundred. A delayed declaration gave West Indies a comfortable draw.

In the third Test in Antigua, a Yousuf Youhana century rescued Pakistan, after an early collapse and a great six-wicket burst by Wasim Akram limited

West Indies to a lead of only four runs. Inzamam-ul-Haq was infuriated by a dubious decision against him in the second innings from umpire Billy Doctrove. With West Indies pursuing 216 to win, Doctrove caused more fury by reprieving their captain, Jimmy Adams. However, it did not seem to matter when Wasim took another five wickets. West Indies still needed 19 to win when the last man came in. It was one of the world's worst batsmen, Courtney Walsh, but somehow he survived to accompany Adams. Then it was the turn of the other umpire, Doug Cowie of New Zealand, to infuriate Pakistan by denying a clear bat-pad chance offered by Walsh. Even so, Pakistan should have won, but a nervous Saqlain fumbled two easy run-outs; the second, with both batsmen at the same end, produced the winning leg-bye for West Indies.*

SURVIVING THE QAYYUM REPORT

At this stage of Pakistan's international programme, the buried Qayyum Report was finally made public. As already noted, it recommended life bans for Salim Malik and Ata-ur-Rehman, whose international careers were already effectively over. Key current players, including Wasim Akram, Waqar Younis, Mushtaq Ahmed, Saeed Anwar and Inzamam-ul-Haq were censured and fined for failure to co-operate.

Qayyum's judgement was especially important for Wasim. His censure had led him to withdraw from his post in England on Channel 4 television's commentary team, but the actual punishment allowed him to join the Pakistan team in Sri Lanka, in June 2000. He celebrated with a century and nine wickets in the series and became the first (and so far only) Pakistani to take 400 Test wickets.†

Younis Khan, Inzamam, and Saeed scored centuries in the same innings as Wasim; Waqar weighed in with eleven wickets; an off-spinner, Arshad Khan – described by Shuja-ud-Din as a 'lanky Pathan' – gave fine support and Abdul Razzaq claimed a hat-trick as Pakistan took the first two Tests.

---

* Wisden 2001, pp.1215–17, refers to 'glaring errors' by the two umpires against Pakistan. Curiously, both men were involved in another black day for Pakistan cricket, as supporting cast to Darrell Hair in the abandoned match at The Oval in 2006.

† It will take a long time for any Pakistani to equal him. As of September 2013, Pakistan's leading Test bowlers are Umar Gul (age twenty-nine) with 169 wickets and Saeed Ajmal (age thirty-five) with 147.

Perhaps exhausted, they yielded a record opening stand of 335 to the Sri Lankans Sanath Jayasuriya and Marvin Atapattu in the rain-affected third Test and lost all of their one-day matches in the subsequent Singer Cup against Sri Lanka and South Africa. Nonetheless, it looked as though Pakistan cricket had come through the long match-fixing trauma. *Wisden* commented on Moin's 'admirable' leadership and his successful partnership with Javed Miandad.[6]

Moin Khan's leadership credentials were, however, damaged irretrievably when England toured Pakistan in the winter of 2000–01, for three Tests preceded by three one-day internationals. In the first one-dayer, Pakistan failed to defend a total of 304, as a young Englishman, Andrew 'Freddie' Flintoff, carted an experienced attack including Wasim Akram and Waqar Younis for 84 off 60 balls. Shahid Afridi replied for Pakistan in the next game, with five for 40 and 61 off 69 balls. Shuja-ud-Din commented magisterially: 'Having got married the previous week, the hot-headed Pathan was determined to stamp his authority on the game.'[7] Saqlain Mushtaq mesmerised England in the third ODI and Pakistan took the series 2–1.

In the first Test at Lahore, Moin and Javed were criticised for timid, defensive tactics, as England took more than two days to reach 480 for 8 (all eight taken by Saqlain) before declaring. Graham Thorpe scored a century without a boundary. Pakistan were slow in reply, strangled by Ashley Giles and Craig White, but Saqlain played an important role with the bat, sharing a ninth-wicket partnership of 127 with the centurion Yousuf Youhana.

In the second Test at Faisalabad, Moin was attacked for a tardy declaration after Abdul Razzaq made his first Test century. The leg-spinner Danish Kaneria made his debut (the second Hindu to play for Pakistan after his cousin, the wicketkeeper Anil Dalpat), but he and his colleagues posed little threat as England showed no interest in their target.

After two draws, the series came down to the final Test in Karachi. Inzamam and Youhana scored centuries and shared a partnership of 259 but no one else did much in Pakistan's first innings of 405. England's reply of 388 was built on an innings of 125 in nine hours 36 minutes by Michael Atherton. He played 350 dot balls.[8]

The *Daily Telegraph*'s Michael Henderson commented: 'During this time one could hear the whole of *Gotterdammerung* twice and still nip out to the pub for last orders.'⁹ Pakistan were strangled again by Ashley Giles but at the end of the fourth day, the game seemed dead. However, on the fifth morning Moin and Razzaq were out cheaply and a panicked Pakistan lost six wickets for 30 against Giles and Darren Gough in tandem.

England were set 176 in 44 overs. Saqlain reduced them to 51 for 3 but there was a stabilising partnership of 91 between Thorpe and Graeme Hick, who exploited Moin's field settings to take a regular supply of singles and twos without risk. Moin delayed proceedings desperately with long conferences and field changes, but Thorpe (64 not out) and his captain Nasser Hussain were together as England completed victory in deepening darkness, amid muezzins chanting the calls for evening prayers. It was England's first win in Pakistan since Ted Dexter led the tour of 1961–62, and Pakistan's first loss to anyone at the National stadium, Karachi.¹⁰

Moin Khan survived this calamity and led a depleted Pakistan to New Zealand for their next engagement. This tour saw an astonishing parade of injuries and withdrawals, which meant that no fewer than twenty-four players played some part in it before it concluded.¹¹ Pakistan split the one-day series 2–2, but when New Zealand chased down 286 in the final match there were doubts about Moin's command over his team.

However, in the first Test at Auckland they won crushingly as New Zealand lost eight wickets for ten runs in their second innings. The destroyers were Saqlain and yet another fast-bowling prodigy, Mohammad Sami, the 'Karachi Kid'. Standing in for the (again) injured Shoaib Akhtar, he blasted out five New Zealanders for 36 on his debut.*

Another debutant had a quieter start but a longer career: Misbah-ul-Haq. This was Pakistan's first experience of a drop-in pitch. The bowlers did not enjoy the second, at Christchurch, which was so sedated that only nineteen wickets fell. Saqlain rewarded himself for his toil with a hundred, sharing a stand of 248 with Youhana, who made a double-century. New Zealand won the third Test by an innings, despite rain, as Pakistan subsided to 104 and 118 against the accurate but rarely world-beating seam of Daryl Tuffey and Chris Martin. Inzamam had an unhappy first taste of

---

*Mohammad Sami had an in-out career; his highs included hat-tricks in all three forms of international cricket but also the longest international over – 17 balls against Bangladesh in 2004 in the one-day Asia Cup. His 85 Test wickets cost nearly 53 runs apiece – no other bowler to take 50 wickets has paid so much for them.

captaincy, standing in for the injured Moin. His absence from this disaster earned Moin no reprieve; the selectors sacked him as both captain and wicketkeeper. Waqar Younis replaced him as captain for the short summer tour of England in 2001.

As wicketkeeper, the selectors dramatically restored Rashid Latif, after a four-year absence mainly spent attacking corruption and creating an independent cricket academy. Shoaib Akhtar was restored after convincing the ICC, on the basis of expert analysis from the University of Western Australia, that his joints had a natural hyper-extension. He arrived late and had to leave early because of a serious stomach complaint. His biggest impact on the Test series was to break Nasser Hussain's thumb. In great pain, the England captain complained about the vocal support for Pakistan from young Asian Britons. In fact, the series had been specifically promoted to Pakistan supporters.[12]

They did not have much to cheer at Lord's as England won by an innings: Darren Gough and Andy Caddick took eight wickets apiece. However, in the second, at Old Trafford, they enjoyed 114 and 85 from Inzamam, and fifties from Younis Khan and Latif, and in England's first innings a sharp run-out by Wasim, which induced a collapse from 282 for 2 to 357 all out. On the last day, England needed 285 to win off the now compulsory 90 overs. At lunch, they had made only 64 of them but lost only one wicket. Saqlain contained England by bowling into the rough, but England still had eight wickets left at tea time and a gettable target of 174 in 32 overs. With the second new ball, Waqar and Wasim bowled like men possessed, Saqlain returned to prey on English fears of the doosra – and the eight wickets melted away, four of them for one run in 13 balls. For once, Pakistan had cause to be grateful to the umpires (England's much-respected David Shepherd and the West Indian Eddie Nicholls); four English batsmen fell to clear no-balls which were not called.[13]

In the triangular one-day series which followed against England and Australia, Waqar achieved figures of seven for 36 against England, the best one-day performance by any Pakistan bowler. However, Pakistan were heavily beaten by Australia in the final, for which they mysteriously dropped Shahid Afridi.[14]

Pakistan then returned for an Asian Test Championship lacking India, who staged a late pull-out. Inzamam scored a century in his home town of Multan against Bangladesh. He was joined by Saeed Anwar, Yousuf Youhana, Abdul Razzaq and a new left-handed opening batsman, Taufeeq Umar, the eighth Pakistani to hit a Test century on debut. It was the first time five Pakistanis had scored centuries in the same Test innings.* Only Faisal Iqbal missed out (in front of his uncle Javed Miandad) as Pakistan declared on 546 for 3 (Inzamam retired with dehydration). Kaneria took twelve cheap wickets and Pakistan won by an innings and 264 runs.†

This easy victory over Bangladesh at Multan was the last moment of normality. A week later came the Al-Qaeda attack on New York's Twin Towers.

---

*Australia had done the same against West Indies in Kingston in 1954–55.
†The day after finishing this Test, Saeed Anwar lost his young daughter. The tragedy turned him into a devout Muslim and he followed former captain Saeed Ahmed as an evangelist for the Tablighi Jamaat movement. He never played another Test match but continued to play ODIs until the 2003 World Cup, when he was still only thirty-four.

PART FOUR

THE AGE OF ISOLATION

2001–PRESENT

INTRODUCTION

Pakistan now found herself at the heart of George W Bush's 'war on terror'. Within hours of Al-Qaeda's attack on the United States on the morning of 11 September 2001, the US president telephoned the Pakistan president, Musharraf, with an ultimatum: you're either with us or against us.

Musharraf chose cooperation. His decision produced lasting consequences. American support brought his regime a huge flow of aid and although this was concentrated overwhelmingly on the military rather than domestic priorities, it helped to sustain a long economic boom. During Musharraf's time in power, Pakistan's growth rate rose from 4% to 7% and per capita income doubled.[1]

All of these achievements were more than cancelled out by the costs of conflict. When the Taliban attempted a comeback in Afghanistan and attacked American forces there, the Americans ordered Musharraf to act against them.[2] In March 2004, he launched a major operation in Waziristan, on the Afghan border, against local allies of the Afghan Taliban. It ended in stalemate, with hundreds of army casualties. The operation killed far more local civilians than militants, who used their local knowledge and mobility to melt away before the Pakistan army. It began a cycle of violence which endures to this day, in which not only the Taliban but other Islamist militants have staged a wave of terrorist attacks all over Pakistan; some were in direct revenge for the casualties caused by the army but many more exploited resentment against the Americans and Musharraf as a pretext for sectarian violence or an extension of racketeering and organised crime.[3] Suicide bombings, previously unknown in Pakistan, became routine. The country is today ravaged by terrorism and civil war, which has claimed some 50,000 lives.

Musharraf was derided as a puppet of foreigners. After a failed attempt to impose martial law, he was compelled to accept the return of the exiled leaders, Nawaz Sharif and Benazir Bhutto; Bhutto was soon after assassinated at a public rally. Her family party, the PPP, fell into the hands of her husband Asif Ali Zardari. Ironically, the collapse of Musharraf's power was accelerated by his biggest single achievement, the liberalisation of media regulation. It encouraged massive growth of independent media in all sectors, and their coverage of events, including cricket, became far more dramatic and outspoken.[4] An important by-product was the ending of the state television service's monopoly of cricket coverage.

When Musharraf finally fell in August 2008, he left a raft of unsolved problems to his civilian successors – organised insurgencies, assassinations and routine daily violence, enduring corruption, underpaid and demoralised public servants, inequality – especially in the ownership of land and capital, a backward education system, environmental degradation and regular shortages of water and power.

Internationally, Pakistan's relations with India were wrecked in November 2009 by the terrorist attacks on Mumbai. Relations with the United States were worsened by drone strikes, from January 2006, which killed hundreds of civilians in the north-west and the tribal areas.

Since Musharraf, Pakistan has been ruled either by Zardari or Nawaz Sharif – politicians who represented a system which had brought Pakistan to the edge of bankruptcy in 1999, *before* the new costs created by the 'war on terror'. Their administrations did little to overcome Pakistan's deep problems but they did manage one historic achievement with the election of 2013 – Pakistan's first civilian transfer of power after a democratically elected government had completed a full five-year term.

This is the context for the descent of Pakistan cricket into the age of isolation.

CRICKET IN EXILE

'Twenty thousand Indian cricket fans visited Pakistan. You have sent back 20,000 Pakistan ambassadors to India.'
– INDIAN HIGH COMMISSIONER TO SHAHARYAR KHAN

The first consequence for cricket was the cancellation of New Zealand's projected tour of Pakistan, who could no longer play at home and were grateful for such international crumbs as the Khaleej Times Trophy in Sharjah against Sri Lanka and Zimbabwe.

Pakistan soon had their first experience of playing a 'home' Test series in the Gulf States. Their opponents were the West Indies, who had declined to visit Pakistan partly because of 9/11 and partly because of growing military tension with India. The two Tests, at Sharjah in January–February 2002, had only a few hundred live spectators and therefore no atmosphere or colour, but they preserved the vital revenue from television. Sri Lanka (from a nation ravaged by civil war and accustomed to terror) were the first team with the nerve to visit Pakistan post 9/11 when they arrived to compete in the Asia Test Championship in Lahore in March 2002. They easily beat a ragged Pakistan side, beset by rumours of divisions, from which Wasim Akram and Saqlain Mushtaq were controversially excluded.

New Zealand followed in May 2002, amid heavy security. They lost a one-day series 3–0. Shoaib Akhtar took six for 16 in the first match at

Karachi and broke the 100mph barrier in the third, which also saw a century from Shoaib Malik. In the first Test at Lahore, Inzamam became the second Pakistani after Hanif Mohammad to score a Test triple-century. He had to nurse the tail and battle cramp which made running singles and twos an agonising ordeal.* Forced to concentrate on boundaries, he hit 38 fours and nine sixes, and finally perished for 329, after nine hours and 39 minutes, trying to hit a tenth six.

Along the way, he overtook the disgraced Salim Malik to become Pakistan's second highest Test scorer, behind Javed Miandad. Shoaib then took over the match. To counter the dead pitch he ignored it, bowling a series of fast late-swinging yorkers which dismissed six batsmen for 11 runs, as New Zealand were all out for 73 in reply to Pakistan's 643.† He injured himself again, which allowed New Zealand to resist longer in the follow-on, but Pakistan still gained their biggest Test victory, by an innings and 324 runs.[1]

The second Test at Karachi never happened. A terrorist suicide bomber killed himself and thirteen other people in a blast near the Pearl Continental hotel where both teams were staying. The windows at the hotel were shattered and the New Zealand physiotherapist was injured by glass in the team bus. Only a few minutes later and it would have been full of players.

The New Zealand board called off the rest of the tour. Stephen Fleming, their captain, stepped out of the hotel driveway to take a look at the scene. In the words of his authorised biographer, 'He couldn't help noticing . . . the general acceptance from the locals. In most countries the area would be roped off as a crime scene and guarded around the clock to assist with a forensic examination. But Fleming saw shopkeepers out almost immediately afterwards, sweeping up the debris and evidence. Bodies were being carried away, the injured were being tended and traders were preparing to resume business.' New Zealand's captain might have been less shocked if he had been aware that Karachi had already endured more than a decade of ethnic, sectarian and politically driven violence. An overwrought Fleming broke down in tears at a press conference in Singapore on his team's way home.[2]

---

*The New Zealand captain, Stephen Fleming, denied him the use of a runner in the last two hours of his innings.
†This is the second highest Test match first-innings lead, beaten only by England's lead of 702 against Australia at The Oval in 1938, when Len Hutton scored his 364.

After the bomb blast, international cricket once again disappeared from Pakistan. The team wandered around the world playing one-day internationals in Australia, Canada, Colombo, Nairobi and even Tangier. The Morocco Cup, contested by Pakistan, South Africa and Sri Lanka, was another venture by Abdul Rahman Bukhatir, the creator of Sharjah cricket.

It was the first attempt to stage cricket in a place with almost no expatriate cricket lovers – but it was well suited to television. It must have been hard for Pakistan to concentrate in a fine, although slightly makeshift, stadium in front of a few bemused Moroccans. They might have enjoyed Shahid Afridi scoring 62 off 40 balls, with four sixes, against South Africa, but this was not enough to take Pakistan into the final, won by Sri Lanka, who remain holders of the only Morocco Cup ever contested.*

Pakistan resumed Test cricket with a 2–0 sweep in Zimbabwe in November 2002. If this gave Pakistan any heart for the forthcoming World Cup, it was destroyed in South Africa. 'Even to the naked eye,' commented Neil Manthorp and John Ward in *Wisden 2004*, 'the Pakistani team lacked cohesion and harmony, but in case anyone doubted it, the tour was awash with stories of infighting and argument.'

The 2003 World Cup confirmed this impression of disintegration. Pakistan disappeared at the group stage and their only victories came against the unrated Dutch and Namibians. In the wake of this catastrophe, the PCB chairman, General Tauqir Zia, tried to resign but was ordered to stay in his post by President Musharraf, and lingered until the end of the year.[3] Waqar did not survive that long. Pakistan were soon to come home from international exile, but under a new leader.

IMPROVEMENT UNDER SHAHARYAR KHAN

After the humiliating first-round exit from the 2003 World Cup, Pakistan cricket went through three years of revival, for which the credit belongs primarily to three men.

---

*The contest did inspire a vigorous local cricket scene. In 2004, a team representing the British Parliament played two matches in Tangier against a young all-Moroccan side, coached by the former Australian Test all-rounder Gary Cosier. The Moroccans won one and drew the other to claim their first international series victory in the approving presence of the Wali of Tangier (personal knowledge).

One was Shaharyar Khan, a former foreign secretary who was President Musharraf's surprise choice as chairman of the PCB in 2003. He had learnt his cricket under the Muslim legend of the 1930s Syed Wazir Ali. Shaharyar Khan brought a clear mind, personal integrity and political independence, and his diplomatic experience won Pakistan many friends internationally.

The second was Bob Woolmer, who replaced Javed Miandad as Pakistan's national coach in 2004. Woolmer won the trust of a disparate group of players, refused to allow dressing room coteries and privileges for senior players, and lifted the squad's physical, technical and mental performance. Woolmer himself absorbed and respected the culture of Pakistan and championed his players against prejudiced critics at home and abroad.[4]

The third was Inzamam-ul-Haq. In September 2003, he became Pakistan's tenth Test captain in a decade,* in circumstances which represented a familiar blend of heroism and scandal. The heroism came in the second Test against Bangladesh, Pakistan's first Test visitors since the New Zealanders had pulled out of their tour in February 2002. Out of form, and facing the axe, Inzamam produced a superb undefeated century to snatch a one-wicket victory for Pakistan.† The scandals involved a catch behind the wicket wrongly claimed against Bangladesh by his predecessor, Rashid Latif, and a selection row over Junaid Zia, the son of the then chairman of the PCB.[5]

Needless to say, all three faced regular criticism. Arif Abbasi thought Shaharyar Khan a poor decision-maker and Shoaib Akhtar called him weak.[6] Woolmer had to overcome resentment at being a foreign coach, particularly from the vocal partisans of Javed Miandad.‡ The most exposed of the trio was Inzamam. His critics attacked him for being tactically unaware (on some crucial occasions he was not even aware of the relevant laws or playing conditions). He was famously inarticulate, especially in English. He had favourite players and was on bad terms with his vice-captain, Younis Khan.[7] His religiosity grated on some key members of his team,

---

*Including one-day internationals, by my count the captaincy changed hands *eighteen* times during this period.
†Both of Pakistan's one-wicket Test victories have been gained with Inzamam at the crease.
‡Mushtaq Mohammad, who had had three spells as national coach all terminated abruptly, wrote in his autobiography, *Inside Out* (Pakistan, 2006), p.227, that Woolmer was appointed because, 'We still have an inferiority complex like from the days of the British Raj, where white man is God.'

notably Shoaib.[8] Against this, he offered experience and a link with the great victory of 1992, world-class batsmanship and dignity.

Inzamam was an injured onlooker when Yousuf Youhana became the first (and so far, only) Christian to captain Pakistan. Thanks to Shoaib and Danish Kaneria, who took thirteen wickets between them, he won a Test against the visiting South Africans. Asim Kamal became the third Test player to make 99 on debut. Inzamam was back in charge for the second Test to earn a draw and take the series 1–0. He then travelled to New Zealand for another two-Test series. After a drawn first Test in Hamilton, an eleven-wicket haul for Shoaib in the second Test gave Pakistan a series victory, despite the tourists conceding a big first-innings lead and Inzamam nearly throwing the game away by forgetting to claim the extra half-hour on the final day.[9]

Inzamam's first major series in charge could not have been more demanding – the first full visit of India for fourteen years. This sequence of games in 2003–04 turned out to be one of the most memorable series in the history of international cricket, between two great teams in extraordinary circumstances. Even the pre-Test ODIs were packed with drama.[10] The first which, under Pakistani pressure, was held in Karachi, produced 693 runs, then a record. Pakistan's pursuit of 349 was led by Inzamam's 122 off 102 balls. It was checked at the end by a sensational running catch by Mohammad Kaif, but even then, Moin Khan had the chance to win the match by hitting a six off the last ball. The second at Rawalpindi was almost a mirror image. Sachin Tendulkar hit a giant hundred for India, who just failed to overhaul Pakistan's 329, powered by a newcomer Yasir Hameed and Shahid Afridi, restored after a year. Hameed delighted his home fans in Peshawar with 98, as Pakistan successfully chased down 244 on a bowlers' pitch (a rarity in Pakistan).

In Lahore, packed with Indian supporters on cricket visas, Inzamam made another century in a lost cause. Pakistan had the game in the bag, until a superb match-winning partnership between Rahul Dravid and Mohammad Kaif led their bowlers and fielders to disintegrate. In the fifth match, also at Lahore, the Indian fans saw a typically cultured century from V V S Laxman, as India won easily to take the series.

The first Test took Inzamam to his home town of Multan. It was an unhappy return. Virender Sehwag hit India's first Test triple-century, off only

364 balls, and India's acting captain, Dravid, declared controversially on 675, before Tendulkar could complete a double-century. Dravid may have expected Pakistan to bat well on a flat track, but Inzamam got a poor decision from umpire Simon Taufel on 77, Yasir Hameed fell to a loose shot at 91 and Pakistan failed to avoid the follow-on. In the second innings, Inzamam was brilliantly run out. Yousuf Youhana hit a spectacular century, but neither he nor anyone else could prevent an innings defeat.

The second Test at Lahore produced a match-winning performance by Umar Gul, aged nineteen, and described in *Wisden* as 'a matchstick-thin seamer from Nawakheli, a village on the Afghan border and birthplace of two of history's greatest squash players, Jahangir and Jansher Khan.'[11] Moving and seaming the ball after the express bowlers Shoaib Akhtar and Mohammad Sami leaked runs, Gul took five for 31 and ended a record-breaking run of 497 Test runs for Tendulkar without dismissal. Centuries from Inzamam and Imran Farhat, and seventies from Youhana and newcomer, Asim Kamal, gave Pakistan a big lead and they won by nine wickets.

In the deciding Test at Rawalpindi, Pakistan were all out for 224, thanks mainly to India's popular workaday seamer, Lakshmipathy Balaji. Dravid then batted for over twelve hours for 270, supported by seventies from Laxman and Sourav Ganguly. This took India to exactly 600. The Pakistan attack looked threadbare. Umar Gul was injured; his replacement (also from the North-West) Fazl-e-Akbar offered little threat and Shoaib walked off injured after three cheap wickets. Only Asim Kamal defied Anil Kumble and Balaji as Pakistan lost by an innings. Omar Kureishi called this performance 'the blackest in Pakistan's cricket history'. Javed Miandad was sacked as national coach and Shaharyar Khan questioned Shoaib's commitment to the team and directed him to take a medical examination.[12]

These ructions were eclipsed by the genuine amity between both the teams and even more so between the fans. Rahul and Priyanka Gandhi (Indira's grandchildren) mingled with the fans in the public stand in the Karachi one-day international, and Indian VIPs joined President Musharraf in greeting MA Jinnah's daughter and grandson when they made a low-key visit to the first Lahore one-dayer.[13] Ordinary Pakistanis showered hospitality on Indian visitors, especially returnees who had fled at Partition. They were signalling their gratitude to the Indians for ending Pakistan's international isolation and their desire for peace.[14] At the end of the Test series, the Indian High Commissioner remarked to Shaharyar Khan: 'Twenty thousand Indian cricket fans visited Pakistan. You have sent back 20,000 Pakistan ambassadors to India.'[15]

Woolmer's Pakistan then split a home series 1–1 with Sri Lanka, but his first tour assignment was away to Australia and one of their greatest ever sides, featuring Matthew Hayden, Justin Langer, Ricky Ponting and Adam Gilchrist among the batsmen, and Glenn McGrath and Shane Warne in the bowling attack.

Pakistan duly lost the Test series 3–0, the first by a record margin of 491 runs. Inzamam contributed just one run in both innings and was then knocked out by a back injury, and Yousuf Youhana stood in again as captain. Abdul Razzaq was sidelined bizarrely by over-indulgence in spinach.[16]

But there were a few bright spots for Pakistan. Younis Khan averaged over 40, Shoaib Akhtar, despite injury and discipline problems, became a crowd favourite and was recognised as the fastest bowler in the world, and there was a fine century by a young man thought to have a big future – Salman Butt.

Woolmer's next assignment was Pakistan's tour of India, in return for India's visit the year before. The tour party was hit by the absence of Shoaib (with a hamstring injury which no one disputed). Mushtaq Mohammad thought that without him Pakistan were 'little better than a club side.'

In fact, they levelled the Test series with a massive win after a draw and a big defeat and took the one-day series 4–2. Yousuf Youhana averaged over 47 in the series, Inzamam over 80, and Younis Khan over 100. They were now recognised as three of the best batsmen in the world.

President Musharraf made a renewed attempt at cricket diplomacy when he went to watch the last one-day international in New Delhi. He was invited by the Indian prime minister, Manmohan Singh, following a sustained thaw initiated by his predecessor. Musharraf later wrote that his efforts at the match (easily won by Pakistan) were almost wrecked by Shahid Afridi, who kept hitting sixes towards the VIP enclosure. It was all he could do to avoid cheering. Musharraf's efforts did produce agreement to reduce tension on two Kashmiri flashpoints in Siachin and Sir Creek.

However, his offer to abandon Pakistan's claim to Kashmir, in exchange for demilitarisation and self-government in the province (the most dramatic diplomacy ever undertaken at a cricket match) made no headway before he fell from power in 2008.[17]

As in Pakistan the previous year, Indian supporters (and shops, hotels and restaurants) went out of their way to welcome travelling Pakistan supporters, although the Indian authorities were more restrictive and gave visas only for the so-called Reconciliation Test at Mohali.[18]

Pakistan then drew a short series in the West Indies. After losing the first Test at Bridgetown by 276 runs, Pakistan comfortably won the second, with centuries from Inzamam and Younis Khan.

England, fresh from winning the Ashes and a one-day series against Australia, were the next visitors to Pakistan in November 2005. Highlights of a 2–0 series win by the home side included Inzamam scoring a century in each innings in the second Test (his lowest score in the Test series was 53); Yousuf Youhana, converted to Islam and renamed Mohammad Yousuf, notching up a double-century in the same Test; Salman Butt continuing to impress, with a hundred in Lahore; and the bowling of Shoaib Akhtar. The Rawalpindi Express responded to thoughtful mentoring from Woolmer with his finest series: seventeen wickets, mostly with 95mph deliveries, occasionally with a beautifully disguised slower ball. It was a generally friendly series, although Shahid Afridi was fined and banned for an outrageous war dance in an attempt to scuff up the pitch during the second Test in Faisalabad. The England party made friends at the outset of the tour by helping young victims of an earthquake in northern Pakistan.

Pakistan followed this up with two draws and a thumping victory at home to India, the latter under Younis Khan, standing in once again as captain. He completed 553 runs in five innings in the series, and there were two hundreds for Kamran Akmal, who briefly established himself as a great wicketkeeper-batsman. Mohammad Yousuf and Shahid Afridi also excelled in this series, with two centuries apiece. There were some background dramas – Shoaib's 'suspect' action; a strange itinerary caused by a long row over allocating a Test to Rawalpindi, which produced the only result; and overprepared comatose wickets elsewhere. Inzamam had a brief spat with Rahul Dravid in the one-day series because he forgot the rule for 'obstructing the field'.[19] Otherwise the series confirmed Pakistan's progress under Woolmer and they ascended the Test rankings.

WEAK LEADERS AND A SEQUENCE OF CRISES

This process was soon checked and reversed. Pakistan cricket now entered a very dark period which mixed farce, tragedy and ultimately terror and national disgrace. During this era of continuous crisis, the issues went much deeper than cricket. They would have taxed the strongest leaders, and unfortunately there were none of these. Instead, in its time of trouble, Pakistan cricket was run by a series of people without the authority, character or constitutional legitimacy to cope.

The downhill trajectory started with the 2006 tour of England. The series was already lost when umpire Darrell Hair, acting without warning or explanation, suddenly docked Pakistan five runs for tampering with the ball.*

On return to Pakistan, Younis Khan was the replacement for Inzamam as captain in the forthcoming Champions Trophy one-day tournament. He asked for a couple of additions to the squad. When they were refused he stormed into a PCB press conference and announced his resignation as 'dummy captain'. He repented shortly after and agreed to go as an ordinary player under Mohammad Yousuf. At this point, Shaharayar Khan resigned. His successor was Dr Nasim Ashraf, a Musharraf minister.†

Ashraf's first act was to restore Younis Khan as captain. It was an inauspicious beginning to Ashraf's tenure, and worse was to follow. Pakistan crashed out of the first round of the Champions Trophy, and their two leading pace bowlers, Shoaib Akhtar and Mohammad Asif, were sent home after testing positive for a banned steroid. Ashraf's handling of the issue did not inspire confidence. The PCB handed a two-year ban to Shoaib, but only a one-year ban to Asif. Both appealed successfully, whereupon the World Anti-Doping Agency appealed against their clearance to the International

---

*The ructions caused by this incident are narrated minute by minute by Shaharyar Khan, op. cit. pp.235–62.

†Ashraf had been a doctor – specialising in the kidney – in the United States, before returning to Pakistan to become an adviser and minister for Musharraf. He had played three first-class matches as a batsman for Peshawar at the end of the 1960s, totalling just 50 runs.

Court of Arbitration for Sport in Switzerland, which decided that it had no jurisdiction, and the clearance stood.[20]

WORLD CUP FAILURE, RENEWED SUSPICIONS AND THE DEATH OF BOB WOOLMER

The two banned bowlers were not missed when Pakistan played West Indies in Pakistan for the first time in nine years (the 'home' series of 2001–02 was played in temporary exile in Sharjah). Their replacements Umar Gul and Shahid Nazir took twenty-seven wickets between them in the three Tests, backed by Danish Kaneria with fourteen. There was a colossal performance by Mohammad Yousuf; 665 runs with four centuries in five innings. Inzamam, who was still captain, had a moderate time of it but Pakistan seemed to have regained cohesion in winning the Test series 2–0 and the one-day series 3–1.[21]

The banned bowlers were back for Pakistan's tour of South Africa, although Inzamam made it clear that he did not want Shoaib. He appeared in the second Test just long enough to take four for 11 in his opening burst, came near to blows with Woolmer over his knee and hamstring injuries, and flew home again. Mohammad Asif took over the burden of the attack and bowled Pakistan to their lone victory in the Test series against two for South Africa.[22]

This unhappy tour was forgotten amid the disasters of the World Cup in the West Indies. Pakistan lost to the host country, and then, astonishingly, were defeated by the part-timers of Ireland, ensuring their exit at the group stage. That same night, a deeply depressed Bob Woolmer died, alone in his hotel room. The Pakistan team, and in particular Inzamam, were devastated with shock and grief, to which was added the agony of suspicion and rumour. This was largely instigated by Sarfraz Nawaz, who claimed that Woolmer was killed by the betting mafia, and that he had been about to expose wrongdoing in the Pakistan team.

As wilder and wilder rumours began to circulate (fed by a leaked pathologist's report), the Pakistan team were held in a separate hotel and questioned repeatedly by the Jamaican police.[23] Eventually, more reliable pathologists disputed the original assumption that Woolmer had been drugged and strangled, and concluded that he had died of natural causes. The head of the criminal investigation, Mark Shields, who had begun his work in a blaze of publicity, also came to this view.

This did not end the whispers against the Pakistan team, particularly when the Jamaican coroner's jury decided to return an open verdict.[24] During this ordeal, the PCB offered little support to the players, and was itself convulsed by a long dispute between the chairman, Nasim Ashraf, and one of its top administrators, the former Test opening bowler Saleem Altaf.*

Nasim Ashraf offered to resign after the World Cup debacle; Musharraf ordered him to stay in his post. Nothing improved for Pakistan in the subsequent Test series against South Africa at home and away to India both lost 0-1. In the hope of a fresh start for Pakistan cricket, Ashraf passed the captaincy to the young all-rounder Shoaib Malik.

Unfortunately, Malik did not have the personality or perhaps the cricketing credentials (Test batting and bowling averages both hovering in the low thirties) to impose unity in the Pakistan dressing room. His efforts at team-building were not made easier when the Board decided to give Inzamam an emotional farewell home Test at Lahore against the South Africans.

Inzamam had an embarrassing final dismissal, stumped off the unremarkable left-armer Paul Harris, and was stranded three runs short of Javed Miandad's record 8,832 Test runs for Pakistan.[25] In India, Shoaib Malik was condemned as 'indecisive and uninspiring'[26] before he damaged his ankle in a football kickabout. He was replaced by Younis Khan (who previously Ashraf had barred forever from the captaincy). There was yet another return for an injured Shoaib Akhtar – again despite Ashraf.

Pakistan's big success in India was Misbah-ul-Haq. He had played five scattered Tests since 2000, with a top score of 28. He then disappeared for three seasons into domestic cricket where he was a heavy scorer. Recalled against India, aged thirty, he averaged over 116 with two centuries.

The calendar year 2008 was the first since 1970 in which Pakistan played no Test cricket. This was not entirely due to Ashraf. The ICC's Future Tours Programme was set some years in advance, but the only scheduled series, against Australia, was abandoned on security grounds by the Australians

---

*The dispute came to a head the following year. Saleem Altaf was sacked for allegedly leaking an email from Nasim Ashraf over the team's performance, but then won a legal action against the PCB for tapping his telephone. Saleem Altaf: personal interview.

(without compensation) and the PCB made no apparent effort to attract
any other opponents, few believed their claims that they approached the
South Africans and the New Zealanders. To be brutal, no one really wanted
to play Pakistan, home or away.

HORROR IN LAHORE

'We owe our lives to the courageous Mohammad Khalil.'

– KUMAR SANGAKKARA

By the end of 2007, the Musharraf regime was tottering, as the political parties united in support of popular protests against his attempt to sack Pakistan's Chief Justice Iftikhar Chaudhry and then declare himself re-elected as president in a disputed election. Nawaz Sharif and Benazir Bhutto both returned from exile. A pro-Benazir rally was attacked by a suicide bomber, and dozens were killed. She herself was assassinated at a rally in Rawalpindi. As Musharraf staggered on into the New Year, the authority of Nasim Ashraf, his appointee as chairman of the PCB, diminished with that of his master.

Ashraf's weakness was demonstrated in his handling of the Pakistan players who tried to join the rival Indian Twenty20 leagues. The first into the field was the Indian Cricket League (ICL), founded by Subhash Chandra of Zee TV. Like Kerry Packer, he was a frustrated bidder for TV rights, meeting years of resistance from the Indian Board of Control. Chandra revived memories of Packer by signing Tony Greig as a director and public face, joining Kapil Dev (restored to iconic status after facing down charges of match-fixing). Unlike Packer, however, Chandra had no intention of staging Test matches or even one-day internationals to challenge the Board of

Control for Cricket in India (BCCI), and he knew he could never match the earnings of India's 'galactic' stars, which were linked to their Test status. He proposed an inter-city 20-over tournament, which did not have to clash with India's international programme or any other country's.[1]

Intriguingly, Chandra wanted to involve teams from Pakistan. He employed the former Pakistan captain, Moin Khan, as a recruiter, and attracted a number of international cricketers, of whom the best-known were Inzamam-ul-Haq and Mohammad Yousuf, both at or near the end of their careers.

ICL offered potential benefits to Pakistan cricket – strengthened ties with India and a share of the huge Indian television revenues for cricket. None of these were explored. Nasim Ashraf announced a blanket ban on all Pakistan players who signed for it, from both international and domestic cricket.[2]

It is interesting to compare this response to AH Kardar's hostility to the Packer players. Kardar, however misguidedly, was fighting for an ideal of Pakistan cricket, in which the players gave undisputed loyalty to their country and expected no greater reward than the honour of representing it.

Ashraf's PCB seemed to have no motives except to keep control of the players and to keep in with the BCCI, which was determined to crush the infant ICL. Predictably, and in another echo of Packer, Pakistan's ICL signings, led by the Test opener Imran Farhat, challenged the bans in the courts. With typical speed, the last cases were resolved only in April 2013, and freed all the players to play again in domestic cricket, with the exception of the now retired Inzamam and Saqlain Mushtaq.[3]

When the ICL's competitor, the Indian Premier League (IPL), was launched shortly after – under the aegis of the BCCI – some of Pakistan's greatest current talents were included in the initial auction. The highest-priced Pakistani was Shahid Afridi, who attracted a bid of $675,000 from the Deccan Chargers. Mohammad Asif went for $650,000 to Delhi Daredevils. Shoaib Malik attracted $500,000, Shoaib Akhtar $425,000, Younis Khan $225,000, Kamran Akmal and Umar Gul $150,000 apiece.[4]

With the exception of Shoaib Malik (in the midst of a personal dispute with Nasim Ashraf, who was suing him for libel,) none of these players were penalised by the PCB. In fact, Pakistan's oldest English-language newspaper *Dawn* noted on 18 March 2008: 'While adopting a liberal policy towards the IPL, which is bankrolled by the Indian cricket board, the PCB has banned the players who have signed up for the ICL.'[5]

Pakistan cricket had become a satellite of Indian cricket, and its policies were being shaped by the stronger party in a domestic Indian dispute. The impotence of the PCB was demonstrated in the IPL's second season. After the terrorist attack on Mumbai in December 2008, blamed widely in India on Pakistan, the IPL franchise holders decided that Pakistani players would be unpopular. They were excluded from the League for simple commercial reasons, and have never returned.

The ban once again turned Pakistan's leading cricketers into poor relations and deprived them of a legal means to obtain the wealth of their Indian counterparts. It thus provided an economic incentive for match-fixing.[6] However, this is to get ahead of the narrative.

ASHRAF DEPARTS, ENTER BUTT

In August 2008, Musharraf quit power, threatened with impeachment. On the very same day his appointee left the PCB, emphatically demonstrating that the control of Pakistan cricket was in the hands of the ruling regime.

Few mourned Nasim Ashraf. Critics had complained of his interference in team matters, and the appointment of a bloated administration. PCB staffing rose under his tenure from 300 to over 700 – but none of the extra staff had the wit to organise Pakistan's most popular domestic tournament, the Twenty20 championship. There were rumours of financial extravagance (eagerly confirmed by his eventual successor).

However, the Pakistan cricket public came to think more fondly of Ashraf after a year's experience of his successor, Ijaz Butt. I do not want to be unfair to Ijaz Butt. I asked to interview him, he declined. In dozens of other interviews for this history, with Pakistani and international cricketers or administrators, I could not find anyone who had a good word to say about him, with the exception of Yawar Saeed – whom he appointed as national team manager.

Ijaz Butt played eight Tests for Pakistan as a wicketkeeper-batsman from 1959 to 1962, averaging just below 20, although he was more successful in domestic cricket. After retirement from cricket, he had a career with Servis Industries, makers of footwear and tyres and intermittently sponsors of a team which competed in Pakistan's domestic tournaments.

He had managed Pakistan's tour of Australia in 1981–82 (they lost the Test series 2–1 and senior players revolted openly against the captain, Javed Miandad).[7] He also built a powerbase in Lahore cricket and politics, and was the brother-in-law of the powerful new defence minister, Chaudhry Ahmad Muktar. He was appointed PCB chairman by Musharraf's successor as president of Pakistan, Asif Ali Zardari, Benazir Bhutto's widower, after several weeks of politicking. He was already seventy years of age.[8]

Butt began his reign with a characteristic politician's manoeuvre, of denouncing the failings of the previous regime. He claimed that under Ashraf the PCB's reserves had fallen from US$42 million to US$19 million without good reason. Although promising an economy drive, he appointed a number of ex-players to high-profile positions within the PCB, notably Javed Miandad, who became its director-general.[9]

As already mentioned, in November 2008 the terrorist attack on Mumbai caused renewed tension between India and Pakistan. Pakistan's top cricketers lost their place in the new, lucrative Indian Premier League and India's planned Test and one-day international tour of Pakistan was cancelled. The Australians also pulled out of their scheduled tour.

Thanks to the goodwill of Sri Lanka, Pakistan were able to resume Test cricket at home in 2009. The first Test in Karachi, for which the Sri Lankans were promised 'presidential security',[10] was uneventful and produced enormous feats of scoring. The Sri Lankans opened with 644 for 7 declared, with double-centuries from Mahela Jayawardene and Thilan Samaraweera. Pakistan replied with 765 for 6, their highest Test total, before Younis Khan declared. The innings had occupied 1,493 balls,[11] during which Younis had become Pakistan's third triple-centurion, and Kamran Akmal recovered from recent failures with 158. Pakistan had brief hopes of a victory before the match expired as a draw.[12]

For the second Test, the teams travelled to Lahore. It was a questionable decision to play there; the Punjab was in turmoil, and Pakistan's new president had imposed federal rule on the province.* However, the PCB went ahead with the programme and the Sri Lankans took their word about security.

---

*The PCB received numerous warnings against playing the Test in Lahore, which were ignored. Security issues were left to the new Punjab administration. Qamar Ahmed: personal interview.

On the first two days, the Sri Lankans piled up another huge score, and Samaraweera posted another double-century. Pakistan had replied with a quick opening stand of over 100.

On the third day, the Sri Lankan team bus was driven to the Gaddafi stadium in company with a minibus containing the four match umpires and the match referee, England's Chris Broad.* The Sri Lankans' cricket coach, Trevor Bayliss, was already concerned that the bus had lost its armed escort, which had constantly accompanied it in Karachi, while Broad noted that the streets had not been cleared.[13]

However, the Sri Lankan players continued their normal routines of chatting, listening to music or trying to reach their families at home on their mobile telephones. Suddenly they heard an explosion and a shout of 'Get down!' from Tillekeratne Dilshan in the front seat.

The convoy was under attack from terrorists using machine guns, grenades and rockets. The opening burst killed five security men (and a traffic warden) in a leading vehicle and also immobilised the team bus, turning the Sri Lankans into sitting ducks.

Miraculously, none of them was killed. The assistant coach, Paul Farbrace, and seven players were injured by bullets or shrapnel, the most seriously wounded being the opener Tharanga Paranavitana, hit in the chest, and Samaraweera, struck in the thigh.

Two people contributed to the miraculous escape. One was Dilshan, in the front seat, who took the immense risk of lifting his head to size up the situation, and then ordered the driver to reverse and directed him as he resumed control of the vehicle. The other was the Pakistani driver, Mohammad Khalil, who drove the bus 500 metres and then crashed past iron barricades to get inside the Gaddafi stadium.

In the words of Kumar Sangakkara: 'We owe our lives to the courageous Mohammad Khalil ... The tyres of the bus had been shot out and he was in grave personal danger, exposed to gunfire at the front of the bus. But he was hell-bent on getting us to safety and somehow he got that bus moving again.'[14]

Sri Lanka's own experience of terrorist violence may have helped its players. Their great spinner Muttiah Muralitharan commented, 'The players

---

*The convoy did not include, as it normally did, the Pakistan team. Younis Khan had told the umpires that the Pakistan team were tired and would follow later: *Wisden 2010*, pp.28–9. Later this would be seized on by conspiracy theorists.

reacted instinctively and naturally, diving right down to the floor of the bus, rather than on the seats.'[15]

The umpire's minivan was in even greater danger as its driver, Zafar Khan, had been shot dead. Fortunately, he had managed first to pull up behind an ambulance, which gave the vehicle some cover, but it was hit by at least eighty-five bullets.

In an effort to protect the tall Broad, the fourth umpire Ahsan Raza stood up and was hit by bullets in the lung and liver. In unbearable pain, he began to recite the *Kalima*, an Islamic prayer, while Broad worked frantically to stop the flow of blood from Raza's body. After a delay of over ten minutes, the bus was finally boarded by Pakistan's armed elite force and Broad, still tending to Raza, had to prevail on one of them to drive the minivan into the stadium.* It was the first terrorist attack on a sports team since the massacre of Israeli athletes at the Munich Olympics of 1972.

Almost as shocking as the attack itself was the response of the PCB and Pakistan government officials.[16] Ijaz Butt said that there had been no security failures and condemned Broad for a 'big lie' in claiming that there were no police to protect the Sri Lankans and the officials.[17] Javed Miandad called for a life ban on Broad by the ICC[18] and the PCB registered a formal complaint against him.[19]

Meanwhile, the traumatised Sri Lankans had flown home, and the Lahore Test was abandoned. New Zealand and Bangladesh cancelled their projected tours later in the year. The ICC paid no attention to Butt's protest against Broad, still less to his claim that international cricket could resume in Pakistan within 'six to nine months'. It removed Pakistan as a co-host of the 2011 World Cup and effectively suspended tours of Pakistan for an indefinite period.

The PCB promptly tried to take the ICC to court, forfeiting more goodwill. Eventually it was allowed to keep around $18 million as a lost 'hosting' fee.[20] The ICC appointed a task force, headed by England's Giles Clarke, to help Pakistan back into the fold.

According to the Pakistan authorities, Lashkar-e-Jhangvi, a Punjabi terrorist group which has been blamed for numerous sectarian killings and

*See his account in 'No one came to our rescue', *Sunday Times,* 8 March 2009. Raza needed a transfusion of twenty pints of blood in hospital. Against medical advice he umpired in a senior game ten weeks later. *Wisden 2010,* p.34.

assassinations, was responsible.* Certainly the attack carried all the hallmarks of the LJ, which does not favour suicide bombings and tends to use machine guns and grenades, and has a long history of attacks on buses.

Eleven suspected terrorists were arrested in the wake of the attack, of whom three were still in custody at the time of writing and eight on bail (one of whom has reportedly been killed since in a drone attack). The trial of the accused has been rumbling on for four years now in Lahore's anti-terrorism court, and still less than half of the forty-eight witnesses have been cross-examined. Observers say that this is typical of terrorism cases, where convictions normally fail for lack of evidence.[21]

These terrorists managed through cricket to strike at the heart of Pakistan's nationhood. The loss of major international cricket has persisted ever since. It has hurt Pakistan cricket not only financially but psychologically. Every Pakistan team since then has been playing as foreigners, away from family and friends at home, supported only by expatriates or rich hangers-on.

AFTERMATH OF TERROR

Pakistan had one bright moment in 2009. Under Younis Khan, they won the ICC World Twenty20 trophy in England in June. Umar Gul was the best bowler in the tournament, backed up by Shahid Afridi and Saeed Ajmal.

Touchingly, Younis dedicated the trophy to Bob Woolmer, and pleaded for visiting teams to return to Pakistan. This did not happen but in a supportive (and commercially astute) gesture, the Pakistanis were given two Tests against Australia in England during their tour the following year.[22]

However, the aura of victory was soon dispelled and Pakistan cricket fell back into a familiar pattern after its exit from the Champions Trophy. Younis resigned the captaincy again, and Mohammad Yousuf took up the unwanted job. He had echoes of Inzamam, calm and religious, but was also unimaginative and defensive.

*See Mujahid Hussain, *Punjabi Taliban* (Pentagon Press, 2012), p.118: 'On 25 July 2009, the Ministry of Interior sent a report to National Assembly's Standing Committee on Sports and Culture stating that assailants of the Sri Lankan cricket team were activists of Lashkar-e-Jhangvi who wanted to hijack the bus in order to pressurise the government for the release of their leaders Malik Ishak and Akram Lahori.'

Pakistan shared a 'home' Test series with New Zealand which was played in New Zealand. Each side won one Test and then the bizarre timing of the final match, to suit Pakistan television viewers, in which play started at noon, helped Pakistan escape with a draw. One bright feature of this series was a seventeen-year-old bowler whose fast, late left-arm swing reminded watchers of Wasim Akram. More, much more, would be heard of Mohammad Amir.

Shahid Afridi was back as captain for his first Test in four years when Pakistan played Australia at Lord's in June 2010. He achieved little as player or captain and promptly resigned when Pakistan lost heavily.

Pakistan's lone batting success had experienced an intermittent Test career since 2003, with an average in the low thirties. He made 63 and 92 in this Test, he was educated, articulate and still young. The selectors decided that Salman Butt could give the team a new look. He had the best possible start – winning the next Test and ending a losing sequence of thirteen Tests against Australia. His pace trio of Umar Gul, Mohammad Amir and Mohammad Asif routed Australia in the first innings, he himself was top scorer in Pakistan's reply and the whole team kept cool under pressure when they chased a target of 178. The new captain made an excellent impression as he dedicated Pakistan's victory to the people at home who had not been able to see it on television.[23]

Pakistan's bowlers confirmed their quality in the Tests against England, although brittle batting condemned them to two heavy defeats. They bounced back to win the third Test, as Amir and another left-arm paceman Wahab Riaz each took five wickets in an innings.

In the final Test at Lord's, Amir produced one of the magic bowling spells of Pakistan cricket. It reduced England to 102 for 7. However, he also produced a no-ball with an overstep so outrageous, that Michael Holding in the commentary box came close to tears as he struggled to avoid a direct charge of wrongdoing.[24] (By contrast, the worldly Mohammad Asif managed to bowl no-balls without attracting any suspicion.)*

Amir continued to bowl good deliveries when not required to do otherwise, but he and the other Pakistan bowlers were frustrated by an

---

*Mohammad Amir overstepped by about a foot, Mohammad Asif by about two inches: *Wisden 2011*, p.34.

astonishing record eighth-wicket stand of 333, between Jonathan Trott and Stuart Broad. Pakistan crashed to an innings defeat, but by then the cricket had been overshadowed by the *News of the World* story, which emerged on the night of the third day.

Posing as a representative of an Indian bookmaking syndicate, the newspaper's investigative reporter, Mazher Mahmood, had handed £140,000 to Salman Butt's agent, Mazher Majeed, to secure the delivery of three no-balls within a set passage of play.[25] Mazher Majeed was arrested, and Salman Butt, Mohammad Amir and Mohammad Asif were questioned by police.

Ijaz Butt reacted to the story with a straight denial. 'These are just allegations. Anybody can stand up and say things about you – it doesn't make them true.' He refused to suspend them from the forthcoming one-day series, which was threatened with cancellation. Eventually, the tour manager, Yawar Saeed, announced they had 'voluntarily withdrawn', and it was left to the ICC to suspend them since the PCB continued to take no action against them.

Shahid Afridi returned as one-day captain, and, unlike Butt and the PCB, did something to win back friends for Pakistan by delivering an apology. 'On behalf of these boys, I want to say sorry to all cricket lovers and all cricket nations.'[26] Shoaib Akhtar was another prominent returnee. Pakistan levelled the one-day series after going 2–0 down, before losing the decider. This series might have done something to repair relationships – until the third match, at The Oval. After a tip-off from the *News of the World*'s sister paper, the *Sun*, the ICC announced that they were investigating a number of suspicious scoring patterns in the Pakistan innings.

The supposedly volatile Shahid Afridi reacted simply by rubbishing the allegation (which eventually was rejected by the ICC). His supposedly responsible chairman, Ijaz Butt, decided to accuse the *England* players of throwing The Oval one-day international match, without a shred of evidence. 'There is loud talk in the bookies' circle that some English players have taken enormous amounts of money to lose the match. No wonder there was such a collapse.'[27]

If Butt's comments had been meant for domestic audiences in Pakistan, they failed. The media and politicians turned on him as an incompetent who had failed to control wrongdoing and lost Pakistan friends when it most needed them. The Pakistan Assembly's sports committee pressed for his replacement and more significantly, Pakistan's High Commissioner in London, Wajid Shamsul Hasan, wrote a critical letter about him to President Zardari.[28]

Butt survived the domestic pressures, but at a two-day meeting of the ICC he was in effect put under supervision. He was given a month to introduce a strict anti-corruption code, and the existing ICC taskforce under Giles Clarke was strengthened and given a new remit – to conduct a comprehensive review of the governance of Pakistan cricket.[29]

The match-fixing story stayed alive as the three accused players faced long proceedings in the ICC and then criminal trials in England. It gained new life during Pakistan's next international series, at 'home' in Dubai against South Africa, when Zulqarnain Haider, the new young wicketkeeper-batsman, suddenly fled to London, claiming that he and his family were under threat because he had declined to get involved in match-fixing. Zulqarnain mentioned an approach by a mysterious figure speaking in Urdu, with an accent he could not identify. Over several days, he declined to be more specific about the threats and their origins and claimed that he could not trust the ICC's own Anti-Corruption and Security Unit. A few months later, Zulqarnain returned to Pakistan with assurances about his safety, and his family's, from the interior minister, and was allowed to resume a first-class career.[30] Pakistan cricket in the meantime moved into calmer waters with the appointment of a new Test captain.

MISBAH-UL-HAQ AND THE FUTURE

'The above mentioned structure arguably contributes to an environment of uncertainty (and instability) in which the Governing Board is accountable to the Patron rather than the game, and management are insufficiently empowered to manage day-to-day operations.'

– PAKISTAN TASK FORCE TEAM (PTT) REPORT

Misbah-ul-Haq was already thirty-six when he took over the Pakistan Test captaincy. The task he faced was far more difficult than any previous Test captain, including Kardar. He had to lead a cricket team in exile, deal with constant charges of corruption and match-fixing, and confront a chaotic administration.

It speaks volumes for Misbah that he rose to the challenge. He had been a consistent batsman in domestic cricket, but had enjoyed an in-and-out Test career, with one great series in India in 2007–08, and then nothing special. He had been discarded for the tour of England.

This did not affect his self-belief. He was a Pashtun, proud of being a Niazi from the same family as Imran Khan's father, and took Imran as his inspiration.[1] He had a fine cricket brain (which he also used to complete an MBA from Lahore University of Management Technology during his captaincy),[2] he was a fine motivator and mentor of younger players, and strengthened a fragile middle-order with his gift for scoring runs when they were most needed. He worked successfully with Mohsin Khan, the former Test batsman, who had become chief selector in March 2010 – the fourth within twelve months.*

Misbah led Pakistan to two draws at 'home' to South Africa in November 2010. The first was dominated by South Africa, who set Pakistan 419 to win. Misbah joined the restored Younis Khan at 157 for 3 and they shared an unbroken partnership of 186 in 58 overs to save the game. In the second Test, Misbah contributed 77 and 58 not out after AB de Villiers had smashed 278 not out (then a national record) in South Africa's first innings.

Misbah contributed another fifty to a ten-wicket victory away to New Zealand, in January 2011, and then 99 and 70 not out to draw the second Test and win the series. Shahid Afridi was captain for the World Cup in 2011, which Pakistan had been due to host until the attack on the Sri Lankan team. Pakistan cruised through their group matches, with five wins and one defeat by New Zealand.

Afridi took wickets for them at low cost and all the top-order batsmen, particularly Younis and Misbah, contributed runs when they were needed. However, in the semi-final Pakistan met India, who chose to bat first and made 260. Pakistan did their cause no good by dropping Sachin Tendulkar four times on the way to 85. A nervous Umar Gul bowled poorly and was blasted by Virender Sehwag, but Wahab Riaz bowled Pakistan back into contention with five for 46. Pakistan's reply began promisingly, but the Indian seamers, Ashish Nehra and Munaf Patel bowled many dot balls, the required run-rate began to creep up, and four batsmen were out to poor shots.

Misbah and Umar Akmal staged a rally, but when Umar was the fifth man out Pakistan needed 119 at more than seven an over. When Afridi skied a catch off a full toss, Misbah was the last hope. He accelerated but not enough and Pakistan lost by 29 runs.

Misbah and Younis were criticised for slow scoring, but Afridi made a gracious speech in defeat and in general Pakistan's performance was thought better than expected. Osman Samiuddin, one of Pakistan's leading cricket

*See 'Mohsin Khan becomes Pakistan team's chief selector', *BBC News Sport*, 2 March 2010. Mohsin had been married to the Indian film actress Reena Roy and enjoyed a brief career in Bollywood movies himself: www.myasia-bollywood.com/celebrity/mohsin-khan.

writers, summed up: 'A few incidents apart, Pakistan went through the tournament without any major scandal and a visible sense of unity and togetherness within the squad. That in itself was a minor triumph given what had gone before.'[3]

One Pakistan supporter was not prepared to accept this verdict. Azhar Siddiq claimed that the match had been fixed to promote good relations between India and Pakistan.* He petitioned the Lahore High Court to investigate and publish the contents of alleged telephone conversations between Shahid Afridi and two Pakistani ministers.[4] The court rejected his petition, the ICC chief Haroon Lorgat flatly rejected other calls for an investigation[5] and the suspicions subsided until November 2012, when the British author Ed Hawkins published his book, *Bookie, Gambler, Fixer, Spy: A Journey to the Corrupt Heart of Cricket's Underworld.* He narrated watching the semi-final and receiving a Twitter message from an Indian bookmaker predicting the precise pattern of runs and dismissals in Pakistan's innings.[6] The BCCI and the ICC maintained their positions that there was no call for an investigation and Hawkins provided no convincing evidence, but the story confirmed again that the miasma of match-fixing hangs over all international cricketers. Any poor decision or underperformance now excites automatic suspicion.

THE ICC'S PAKISTAN TASK FORCE TEAM REPORTS

Barely a month after the World Cup defeat, Misbah was back at the helm when Pakistan toured the West Indies. In the first Test, Saeed Ajmal, suddenly emerging from obscurity as the world's finest off-spinner in his mid-thirties, took eleven wickets in a low-scoring match, but Pakistan's batting let them down.

Misbah scored their only half-century as they lost by 40 runs in pursuit of a modest target of 219. Pakistan split the series with a crushing 196-run victory in the second Test, after second-innings centuries from Misbah and the opening batsman Taufeeq Umar (restored after a long gap).

---

*The match had been watched by both prime ministers, side by side. A few months later the two countries signed a series of Favoured Nations Status trade agreements and opened a new border terminal at Wagah-Attari. See 'Inside the Dark World of Match Fixing', *India Today*, 20 November 2012.

A month later, in June 2011, the ICC met in Hong Kong to receive the report from its Pakistan task force team (PTT). This formidable document struck at the core of the Pakistan cricket administration – its direct relationship with the state. This relationship had been deliberately created, for pragmatic reasons, by Justice Cornelius when Pakistan cricket came into being sixty years earlier.

The report commented strongly in its executive summary: 'It is highly unusual that the President of the country is entitled to appoint both the Chairman of the PCB and over half of the Governing Board. It is also inconsistent with the demands of modern sports administration that the Chairman also holds the powers of the CEO ... While recognising that changes may not happen overnight, the PTT believes that preserving the status quo will constrain the development of Pakistan cricket in the long term and is not in keeping with international best practice in sports administration.'[7]

The PCB's response was muted. Ijaz Butt noted, ominously, that action on the recommendations was entirely in the hands of the PCB.[8] However, the PCB's chief operating officer Subhan Ahmed took a more emollient line a few days later, and crucially indicated that the PCB would not challenge the ICC directive to remove political interference from cricket.*

FAREWELL IJAZ BUTT

While the PCB wrestled with the terms set by the ICC for Pakistan's continued status in international cricket, the players continued their gradual rehabilitation under Misbah.

A workaday seamer, Aizaz Cheema, backed by Saeed Ajmal and the subsidiary spin of Mohammad Hafeez, secured victory in a one-off Test in Zimbabwe after the hosts had scored 412 in their first innings. Pakistan then won a 'home' three-Test series against Sri Lanka in the United Arab Emirates.

*See 'Pakistan to abide by ICC directive on government interference', *Pakistan Express Tribune*, 5 July 2011, and 'ICC task team report: Pakistan soften stance', ibid. 20 July 2013. Subhan had the remarkable distinction of being the only member of the PCB to earn praise from Shoaib Akhtar. 'Actually, there is only one person who does any work within the board and that is Subhan. He works there in multiple capacities – as a typist, executive, tour organiser etc. He does all the work and no one else does anything of use.' S Akhtar, op. cit. p.214.

Amid this chain of victories, Ijaz Butt left the PCB in October 2011. There were few mourners. Writing in the UAE newspaper *The National,* Osman Samiuddin commented: 'A generous assessment of his time would have it as disastrous. On and off the field, the reputation of a once-proud cricket nation has been shredded. It has become a paranoid wreck and Butt has steered that transformation.'

After some weeks of hiatus and speculation, President Zardari appointed Zaka Ashraf (no relation of Nasim) as the new PCB chairman. He was a political associate with no cricket background, under fire for his performance as chief executive of the ZTBL Bank (formerly the Agricultural Development Bank, and under both names a long-term patron of Pakistan cricket).

Zaka Ashraf brought a quiet, subdued style to his chairmanship. Unlike his predecessors, he managed to keep hold of his senior staff, particularly the able Subhan Ahmed, who as at the time of writing retained his post as chief operating officer and lynchpin of Pakistan's cricket administration.

TEST WHITEWASH OF ENGLAND

Untroubled by embarrassments from their new chairman, Pakistan's cricketers continued to progress. They were far too good for Bangladesh in an away series which produced two easy wins. At the end of the year, the PCB named Misbah-ul-Haq the Pakistan Cricketer of the Year. A tribute noted that 'there is clear freshness and conviviality in the Pakistan dressing room, a welcome sign. The youngsters now have a firm and faithful hand on their shoulders. Internecine politics has been blown away along with petty quarrels in the Pakistan team to become a united team singing the song of unity waiting to dazzle in 2012.'*

Such a tribute would have jinxed most captains, but Misbah's greatest moments were to come. Pakistan's next engagement was a three-Test series against England at 'home' in the UAE. Pakistan achieved a clean sweep of three successive Test victories thanks to three bowlers: Umar Gul with eleven wickets at just over 22 apiece, Abdur Rehman's nineteen at 16.73 apiece and, above all, Saeed Ajmal's twenty-four at 14.7. Ajmal had mesmerised the

---

*See 'Misbah-ul-Haq is the Pakistan Cricketer of 2011', www.pcb.com.pk, 31 December 2011.

English batsmen with sharp but conventional off-spin and a mysterious doosra that spun the other way.

He was thirty-four – but still reached 100 Test wickets faster than any other Pakistani. It was a tribute to years of toil in domestic cricket. Ajmal was born in Faisalabad and made his debut for them in the Quaid-e-Azam Trophy as far back as 1996. His family background was modest. In interviews, he told the story of having an open-air sewage channel in front of the family home, and was proud of having it cleaned out and renamed a canal.[9] Like two other great spin bowlers, Bhagwat Chandrasekhar and Muttiah Muralitharan, he had overcome a handicapped right arm. He had survived a hostile umpires' report on his bowling action in 2009[10] and revived English suspicions (especially of the doosra) by an unguarded remark, in his scattergun English, about being allowed extra leeway in straightening his right arm.[11]

However, no one doubted Ajmal's personal integrity. During the match-fixing scandal of 2010, he had earned a backhanded tribute from the bookmaker Mazher Majeed, who said on a secret video that he was 'too religious' to get involved in spot-fixing.[12]

A SHORT HONEYMOON

In spite of the landmark series win, Misbah-ul-Haq and Mohsin Khan enjoyed only a short honeymoon with the Pakistan public. Mohsin was already on the way out, as the PCB were looking for another foreign coach. They eventually settled for the experienced Australian Dav Whatmore.*

Misbah was criticised as a one-day player and leader when England swept the 50-over series 4–0 and won the Twenty20 series 2–1. As a consequence, he stepped down as Twenty20 captain in favour of the opener and all-rounder Mohammad Hafeez, who was more than six years younger.

Before the series against England, Pakistan had made history by playing a one-day international against Afghanistan. It was their first return to Sharjah

---

*See 'Whatmore to take over as Pakistan coach next month,' Press Trust of India, 8 February 2012. This report suggests that Zaka Ashraf took against Mohsin and accused him of 'pressure tactics' against the PCB to secure his retention. If true, this would be a characteristic encounter between the latter-day PCB and a top official.

since it had been blacklisted under Indian pressure a decade earlier. Pakistan won by seven wickets, but it was the Afghans who delighted observers by competing for most of the match in their first encounter with a Test-playing country. When Saeed Ajmal, who had just destroyed England, came on to bowl, the well-upholstered Afghan opener, Mohammad Shahzad, reverse-swept his third ball for six without a care in the world.[13]

Meanwhile, Misbah led Pakistan to victory in the four-nation Asia Cup one-day tournament in Bangladesh, then lost series in Sri Lanka and South Africa in 2012–13.

Pakistan were blown away by Dale Steyn in the first Test against the South Africans in Johannesburg. He took six wickets for eight runs and Pakistan were all out for their lowest-ever score of 49. Misbah top scored with 64 in their second innings, but Pakistan lost by 211 runs. The second Test was more competitive. Younis and Asad Shafiq each scored 111 and Pakistan gained a narrow lead on first innings. Only Misbah and Azhar Ali showed much resistance in the second innings, and South Africa chased down a target of 182 without much alarm, despite four cheap wickets for Saeed Ajmal. Spectators enjoyed the Test debut of Pakistan's left-arm seamer Mohammad Irfan – over 7 ft and the tallest man known to have played first-class cricket.

Nonetheless, the first rumbles of criticism were heard against Misbah's leadership and on his return home he had to deny media stories of a rift between him and Mohammad Hafeez. Ijaz Butt, now in retirement, did not improve the situation by claiming that Hafeez had ganged up with the coach, Dav Whatmore, to isolate Misbah from the team.[14]

THE IMPACT OF EXILE

Pakistan have played 43 Test matches since their exile began in 2009, including the Sri Lankan series completed in January 2014 in the UAE. They have won 15, lost 18 and drawn 10. Fourteen of these Tests have been 'home' matches, two in England and the remainder in the UAE, with seven victories, three defeats and four draws. In that period, they have played 125 one-day internationals in bilateral series (that is, excluding the 2011 World Cup and other international tournaments), 36 of them at 'home' in the UAE.

Both of Pakistan's current international captains have spoken plainly about the impact of exile, during their Test and T20 series against Sri Lanka in 2013–14, in the UAE. Interviewed during the third Test, Misbah-ul-Haq made the simple point that, 'Most captains and cricketers improve their records at home, on grounds where they played their initial cricket and in front of home crowds. More than half of my side has never played for Pakistan in Pakistan. Apart from players like Younis [Khan], [Mohammad] Hafeez and I, most of the players in the side today have no idea what it means to play international cricket at home.'[15]

Misbah's comments are borne out by the record of his star bowler Saeed Ajmal. He had played 31 Test matches by the end of January 2014 – none of them in Pakistan. Of his 105 one-day international appearances, only his first two were made in Pakistan (both in Karachi in the 2008 Asia Cup).

In December 2013, Pakistan's T20 captain, Mohammad Hafeez, spoke about the pressures of exile when interviewed after the team's three-wicket victory over Sri Lanka in Dubai. 'We are playing away from Pakistan for the last four years and it is getting too much for us mentally. As players we are coping with too many things playing not at home. There is not support from Pakistan. Staying away from the family almost 11 months in a year is a big task and I think credit goes to the players the way they are . . . getting performances for Pakistan.'[16]

Again, it is instructive to study Saeed Ajmal, and his travels in the calendar year 2013. These began in India, with two one-day internationals. In February and March, he went to South Africa and played three Tests and five one-day internationals. In May, he had a jaunt to Scotland and Ireland for two one-day internationals, before playing three one-day matches for Pakistan in England, in the group stage of the ICC Champions Trophy. In July, he went to the West Indies for five one-day internationals. Next month, it was Zimbabwe, two Tests and three more one-day internationals. In October, he at last had a 'home' international Test and one-day series, against South Africa in the UAE. But only three days after completing the final one-day match in Sharjah, he appeared in the first match of the return one-day series in Cape Town. In December, he was back in the UAE for five more one-day matches against Sri Lanka. He closed the year by playing on the opening day of the first Test, also against Sri Lanka.

He played no first-class matches at all in Pakistan during 2013, compared to nine overseas (eight of them Tests). He did snatch four one-day matches at home, between 5 and 11 April, in the President's Cup, compared to 33 (all internationals) away from Pakistan.

It is sadly commonplace to see empty Test match grounds on the opening day, but I found it especially dispiriting to watch Pakistan take on South Africa in Dubai on 23 October 2013. The modern stadium sits in a sports complex in a place with no roots in cricket, or indeed in any sport except falconry. On the day, the spectators could be counted in dozens, barely enough to generate reaction shots for the television coverage. Although Dubai has many Pakistani expatriates, few could afford the price of a ticket or take the time off work. Those who did show up did try to create some noise and atmosphere for their team, although unfortunately they collapsed on the first morning against the South African attack (including, gallingly, the former Pakistani Imran Tahir).

Spending months at a time shuttling between foreign hotel rooms, hugely dependent on each other's company, cut off from all the supportive settings and networks which go with being at home – there is no early end in sight of this austere regime for Pakistan's international cricketers.

Their absence has an obvious impact on cricket within Pakistan. It reduces the quality of domestic teams and means that fans cannot see their best players in action, except through television. It makes it very much harder for younger players to learn from Pakistan's biggest stars unless and until they themselves break through into the international team, a point put to me frequently by administrators and former players. It also threatens one of the great romantic traditions of Pakistan cricket, which I have mentioned many times – the teenage prodigy or the forgotten journeyman who turns up at a practice session and dazzles the stars. If those stars are never at home, what hope is there for the next Wasim Akram or Tauseef Ahmed to become an overnight sensation?

PAKISTAN CRICKET'S FATE IN THE COURTS

In May 2013, Pakistan held nationwide parliamentary elections and provincial assembly elections. For the first time in the nation's history, a democratically elected government completed a five-year term and handed over power to a democratically elected successor. The national elections resulted in a hung parliament dominated by the Muslim League, led by Nawaz Sharif. After a few weeks of negotiation, he was able to recruit nineteen independent members to support a coalition government and became prime minister for the third time.

Meanwhile, by ICC decree, the PCB was expected to introduce democracy itself. This process did not fare as well as the national elections. In May President Zardari, still patron of the PCB, drew up a shortlist of candidates for election by the eleven governors of the PCB. It contained two names, the incumbent Zaka Ashraf (appointed by Zardari under the old system in October 2011) and Aftab Ahmad Khan, a man unknown in the cricket world, although he was a successful accountant and a former chairman of the Lahore Stock Exchange. The election was not publicly announced, and it is not apparent that Aftab Ahmad Khan fought a vigorous campaign. If so, it was fruitless; Ashraf was elected unanimously on 8 May, for a four-year term.[17]

Unfortunately for him, this 'election' was immediately challenged in the courts, in separate actions by Rashid Latif in Karachi and in Islamabad by Ahmad Nadeem, former coach of the Pakistan army. Nadeem's petition pointed out that Punjab, Pakistan's most populous province, had not been represented in the election. The Islamabad court suspended Ashraf and the judge commented that, 'The petitioner has a good arguable case in his favour, as the whole process of the election of the PCB chairman appears to be motivated and polluted.'[18]

A few weeks later, the Islamabad court ordered the government to replace Ashraf with an interim head of the PCB, who would represent Pakistan at the forthcoming meeting of the ICC. He or she was to be chosen by the inter-provincial committee looking after all sports in Pakistan. On its recommendation, Nawaz Sharif appointed Najam Sethi. To say the least, it was an interesting choice. Sethi, in his mid-sixties, had won international awards as an independent-minded journalist. He had founded a Lahore newspaper, edited several others, and was well-known as the presenter of a regular current affairs programme on Geo TV. In 1999, he had been arrested by the Inter-Services Intelligence (ISI) agency – Pakistan's notorious secret service – after an interview with the BBC about corruption in government; he was detained for a month without charges.[19] He had also campaigned against fundamentalism and received death threats from various Islamist groups.[20] In March 2013 he was chosen, by consensus between the Muslim League and the rival PPP, as the interim chief minister of Punjab in the run-up to the elections.*

Despite being an interim chairman, Najam Sethi took on the full responsibilities of the job. On 15 July, he appointed Moin Khan, the former Pakistan wicketkeeper and captain, as the new chairman of selectors, replacing the departing Iqbal Qasim, while retaining the remainder of the regionally balanced selection committee.[21] His first task was to pick a touring party for Zimbabwe.

However, a week later the Islamabad High Court judge, Shaukat Aziz Siddiqui, nullified his appointment. It ordered the PCB to draft a sports journalist, a cricket commentator and, separately, a 'keen follower of the game' from among the Pakistan cricket public to the selection panel. I have not been able to ascertain how many applicants submitted themselves for this dream job, and whether one was chosen. More importantly, the order stripped Najam Sethi of all power to make key decisions.[22] It directed the PCB to hold elections for a new chairman within ninety days through an election commission of representatives of all the regional and district cricket associations of Pakistan.†

A series of court actions since then succeeded only in adding further layers of confusion and uncertainty to the future of Pakistan cricket. Pakistan's prime minister, Nawaz Sharif, attempted to bolster Najam Sethi's position by a minor constitutional coup, in which he named himself as the patron of Pakistan cricket (replacing the role of the president or head of state established at the inception of Pakistan as a cricket nation). He then nominated Najam Sethi as chairman of an interim management committee, which also included Shaharyar Khan, Zaheer Abbas, Haroon Rashid and former team manager Naved Cheema.[23] This arrangement too was challenged in the

---

*See 'Najam Sethi takes oath as caretaker Punjab CM', *Dawn*, 27 March 2013. Sethi's admirers do not include Imran Khan, who has fiercely attacked Najam Sethi's role in Pakistan's national elections, his closeness to Nawaz Sharif and his possible conflict of interest with his role as a television journalist, particularly over the award of television rights in Pakistan cricket to the network which employs him. Imran Khan: personal interview. The PCB defended the award as representing the best offer to the PCB and that it was made by a fully transparent process. Source: 'PCB strikes up short-term TV rights deal', www.espncricinfo.com, 6 September 2013.

†The judge, Shaukat Aziz Siddiqui, was a high-profile right-winger with many critics. One pointed out that he was a former president of the Rawalpindi Bar Association, which in 2011 had supported the murderer of the Punjab governor Salman Taseer, who had condemned the misuse of Pakistan's blasphemy laws; see www.riazhaq.com/2013/04/pak-media-chyeers-as vindictive-right.html. He had stood as a candidate in the National Assembly elections of 2002 (under Musharraf), on a ticket from the MMA religious alliance: www.electionpakistani.com/ge2002/NA-54.html.

courts. Zaka Ashraf was restored by court order in January 2014 but was sacked a month later by Nawaz Sharif, who restored Najam Sethi and the ad hoc committee.[24]

Meanwhile Misbah-ul-Haq continued to lead the national team with great skill, determination and integrity. No one, not even the great Imran Khan, has had an easy ride captaining Pakistan down the years – but Misbah has had the toughest task of them all. Like most of his predecessors, he has had to cope with infighting, selectoral caprices and the chaotic administration of Pakistan cricket, aggravated by political and judicial interference. He also had to take over a team which had been tainted and demoralised by the match-fixing scandal of 2010. Finally, and most important, he has had to lead an international team in exile since the terrorist attack on the Sri Lankan cricketers in 2009. All of Misbah's 27 Test matches as captain (and 86 one-day internationals) have been played away from Pakistan. In January 2014 Misbah contributed vitally as captain and batsman when Pakistan secured a 'home' Test victory against Sri Lanka in Sharjah – setting a new fast-scoring record in scoring over 300 to win.

It is hard to imagine Pakistan without him, although he is nearly forty. He has spoken of the stresses of leading the team, pointing out how few of his players have played in front of their home supporters. Misbah's travels in 2013 make his point for him. They began in India, then took him to South Africa, Scotland, Ireland, England, West Indies, Zimbabwe, the UAE, South Africa again and back to the UAE. In that year, he played just one first-class match in Pakistan, compared to nine, all Test matches, overseas. He managed six one-day matches within a fortnight for his home team in Pakistan (Sui Northern Gas Pipelines Limited), compared to 34 overseas.

Such is life for Pakistan's international cricketers, a perpetual shuttle between foreign hotel rooms, playing 'home' matches in deserted stadiums in places with no roots in cricket, and cut off from extended family and community networks which are so important to Pakistanis. One wonders how much longer Misbah can continue to sustain the performance and mentality of his players.

At a time of intense difficulty and struggle, this brave and remarkable man held the national team together. He has proved himself a worthy successor to the great former captains, Kardar and Imran. There is no higher praise.

White on Green

> 'We are monotheists, our practice is to abjure customs, ritualism and
> Episcopal orders. For when factions and nationalities disappear they
> merge into faith.'
>
> – MIRZA GHALIB, THE POET

Abdul Hafeez Kardar died while asleep in the bedroom that he shared with his eleven-year-old grandson. Word quickly spread that 'Skipper' was gone, and crowds gathered in the Kardar house – family, politicians, intellectuals and of course cricketers. Fazal Mahmood and the team who attained such nation-defining success after Partition were all there. Imran Khan flew in from Islamabad.

Kardar had already withdrawn from the world by the time of his passing in April 1996, having been badly shaken by the death of his wife Shahzadi. In the final months, he would pray: 'I want to go, take me away. I am ready.'

I went to Kardar's grave in the Miani Sahib graveyard, just outside the city walls, to pay my own respects. His gravestone is simple, recording only his name and the dates of his birth and death. The gravedigger told me that Kardar had ordered the headstone to be prepared a year before he died, and had even supervised the digging of his grave, which was filled with sacks of wheat so that no other person could take that place for burial.

Thereafter, Kardar would go there almost every day. 'He used to come here and recite the Holy Quran over the grave of his wife,' the gravedigger told me. Kardar's first heart attack had struck him down during the 1987 tour of India, after he had reportedly climbed up several storeys to the commentary box during the Calcutta Test match. He returned for medical treatment in Lahore and thereafter turned away from the game in which he had played such a famous role. Indeed he was already disillusioned. According to his son Shahid, his father expressed foreboding about the future of cricket in Pakistan: 'A new element is coming. The greed that you see now, they will not be able to handle it.'[1] (Kardar's fastidiousness has been passed on to Shahid. When I went to see the only son of the great Pakistan cricket captain, he had just stepped down as Governor of the State Bank of Pakistan, reportedly in protest over President Zardari's policy of printing money.)

For a number of years, Abdul Hafeez Kardar was the leader of a small group of thinkers who tried to guide the future of Pakistan. They produced papers on energy policy, landholding reform, and energy policy, many of which were ahead of their time. Masood Hasan, a Lahore intellectual who edited this output, remembered how Kardar 'always came to see me in a three-piece suit. He had beautiful neckties. Towards the end he would shake a little as he entered the room, saying, "Digday, thainday, girday assi, aa, ee, gaey, aan." ["Stumbling, bumbling, falling, I have managed to arrive."] He maintained his superhuman standards of integrity.' Recalls Masood, 'It was a pain in the neck to run up a bill for him. Until he cleared every penny he wouldn't rest.'

Kardar became a writer. His books reflected on Pakistan's struggles after independence, brooded on the loss of Bangladesh, the drift to military rule, and Pakistan cricket. 'In my view,' wrote Kardar in a pamphlet calling for economic and social revolution, 'the only approach to the organisation of society which can guarantee a genuine emancipation of the people, is that of a centrally planned economy in which the means of production are not owned by individuals but are socialised.'

Mian Mohammad Saeed, the man Kardar displaced as Pakistan captain, also maintained his connection with cricket. He managed Pakistan Eaglets cricket tours to England, and in the summer of 1958 spent a season playing for Richmond Cricket Club, arranged by his close friend, the coach Alf Gover. 'At the age of 47, Saeed had now put on a little weight and the grey hairs were beginning to show. I heard afterwards that the young opposition fast bowlers, on his initial appearance, decided to bowl bouncers at the old gentleman,' recorded Gover in his autobiography. 'Much to Saeed's amusement and the bowlers' surprise and dismay, Saeed kept hooking them hard to the square-leg boundary.'

In 1974, Saeed suffered a stroke and the last few years of his life were spent in a wheelchair, in which friends would take him to watch the game he loved. The writer Sultan Mahmud was researching a study of Pakistan cricket after Partition. He went to Mian Saeed and implored him to allow him to write about the events surrounding Kardar and the captaincy. Saeed refused.

Like many Muslims, he grew a beard in old age. By chance, for a time, he lived, in the late 1970s, in the same apartment block – Mayfair Flats – as Kardar. The two men were polite when they met on the stairs, but too much had passed between them to allow them to become friends.

By the summer of 1979, Saeed was dying. As he lay in his bed, recalls his son Yawar, there was a knock. Kardar came in, and sat down beside Saeed for about half an hour. Neither man spoke but, as he left, there were tears in Kardar's eyes. The Pakistan cricket world attended the funeral, led by Jahangir Khan, who had played so much cricket alongside Saeed. When he met his son Yawar Saeed, Jahangir said, 'He used to go in before me every match. He would pad up and go in first. Now he's gone and done it again.'

After retirement from cricket, Fazal Mahmood, Saeed's son-in-law, stayed with the police force. When he was posted to different cities, it is said that his reputation for probity was so formidable that dishonest policemen would either arrange to be re-assigned, or leave the force in advance of his arrival. He was strict at home, forbidding his son Shahzad to be out after sunset. Shahzad remembers the fear he used to have of breaking this rule and incurring his father's wrath. (Shahid Kardar recalls the same treatment from AH Kardar.)

Fazal's final post was Deputy Inspector General of Traffic for the Punjab. Only those who have experienced Lahore's roads during rush-hour can understand what reserves of humour, understanding and steely patience that task must have required. While in this post, Fazal wrote the instruction manual *Speed with Safety: A Guide to Traffic in Lahore*. It stretches to approximately 200 pages, and is said to be definitive, although it has not yet been published.

I went to visit Fazal Mahmood's old home, wending my way past small phone shops, a bike-repair stall and fruit stalls. Local children had set up a game of cricket in the street outside. Did I spot one of them bowling a leg-cutter, Fazal's trademark delivery? In a row of detached two-storey houses, the Mahmood house is the largest, with a basement bomb shelter that was used in the 1965 and 1971 wars against India. But Fazal confined himself to the ground floor, rarely moving beyond his small bedroom, an equally modest living room and his wooden seat on the porch.

The two rooms remain exactly how Fazal left them at his death in 2005. A sofa stands by the window. Pakistan's national poet Muhammad Iqbal used to sit on it during visits to Fazal's father, Ghulam Hussain, while young Fazal served tea. Beside the sofa is a model of one of Pakistan's nuclear missiles and nearby a picture of the 1954 Oval team. On the opposite wall is a photograph of Mecca and beside that hangs Fazal's most prized and revered possession, a framed piece of the Ghilaf-e-Kaaba, the black cloth that covers the Holy Kaaba inside the Grand Mosque in Makkah, Saudi Arabia. There was no air conditioning; Fazal preferred to sleep outside in the hot weather, arguing that he would never have been able to hold up an end, bowling for hours a day, unless he was able to manage living through the heat.

Fazal became a student of the deep questions of life. This bore fruit in a remarkable book, *Urge to Faith*, a meditation on religion, philosophy and politics. The book demonstrates a profound faith and learning, containing many relevant quotations from the Holy Quran. Fazal doubted whether 'a democracy of western type' was capable of bringing about Islamic justice. He wrote: 'In democracy politics becomes personal. Persons are projected more than principles. Social values are thrown to the winds and the interest of a few persons (the mountebanks, the rich and the goondas [thugs]) are trumpeted as social ends.

'That is why in Pakistan, democracy will only run riot. It will be a "tamasha" [festivity] and useless luxury. There would be mud-slinging, abuse and corruption on a wide scale, a huge waste of energy and resources which the poverty-stricken masses can ill-afford to enjoy. The voters would be over-awed by feudal lords and hooligans, catch-words, slogans or lucre.

'Black money would buy votes in the black market to serve a black purpose. The mass of people in Pakistan are steeped in abject poverty and stark ignorance. Not more than ten or fifteen per cent are literate. They can be easily cajoled by slogans, trifling gifts or a show of force.'

Fazal wanted rule by wise men, acting according to the guidance of Allah. He considered entering politics and I was told that he contested a seat for the national assembly. However, his opponents raided the polling station, stealing the ballot boxes. Fazal chased them in his car but failed to recover the cast votes, losing the election and vowing never to contest another seat.

He also established a school for girls, originally called Sidra Model School. Following the 1954 Oval victory, the players had been gifted a plot of rural land to treat as they pleased. Fazal used his to support the education of women.

In his last years Fazal, once a partygoer, kept his distance from society. His mosque was two hundred metres from his house. In old age, Fazal acted as the muezzin, calling out worshippers for morning prayers. He would be waiting outside at 4am, even before the mullah arrived to unlock the gates. Fazal last performed this duty on the day that he died, 30 May 2005. From there he went to his office (he was then working for a textile concern), from where he spoke on the phone to his son, saying, 'God bless you.'

A few minutes later this splendid man, one of the most upright and courageous cricketers of all time, collapsed and died. To the end of his days, he regretted never having the chance to play against Don Bradman, as he would have done had he travelled to Australia with India in 1947.

Today, only four members of the team that clinched the famous victory at The Oval sixty years ago are still alive. I found Hanif Mohammad in the garden of his house in Karachi. To the sound of the call to prayer, Hanif told me his life story: how his family had lived a comfortable life in Junagadh before independence; how he used to go and watch his elder brothers Raees and Wazir play for the local Nawab's team; how one day there were tanks on the streets and his parents closed the windows and told the children to stay inside and not to move; how they escaped in a small steamer. 'We were afraid we might be caught going to Pakistan,' he said. 'I was too young to feel fear. My mother and father were so upset. But all they would say to us was, "Don't worry, everything will be all right."' It was an honour to talk to this delightful man, the symbol of early Pakistan fortitude. Hanif, who is 5ft 3in, explained it helps a batsman to be very small, citing Gavaskar, Hutton, Weekes, Hassett and Lara. He claimed that fast bowling is easier to face because bouncers passed harmlessly over their heads, while small men found short deliveries could easily be cut (CLR James noted the efficacy of Hanif's cut stroke at Worcester in 1954). He also argued that short men, being closer to the ground, could pick the length much more quickly, allowing them to decide which ball to hit a fraction earlier than others.

Hanif told me: 'I was not a great player like Viv Richards. I was just a mediocre batsman who wanted to play for his team and not take any chances.' This of course, is untrue. During his formative early years, Hanif was by far Pakistan's best batsman. He scored twelve centuries in Tests, including one against each contemporary Test-playing country (except South Africa), home and away. Hanif's 337 against the West Indies remains not just the highest score in a second innings, but the highest score ever made away from home, and the greatest defensive innings ever played.

Hanif, Kardar, Fazal and the others are part of the collective memory of Pakistan, a memory which has endured through many setbacks and much suffering. They remain a source of inspiration today. Hanif's fingers were like the twigs of an old tree, twisted, bent and broken from twenty years of cricket. In the days he played they didn't use X-rays and the broken fingers were just left to mend.

When I went to see him he was receiving a visit from his son Shoaib, who followed him with such success into the Pakistan Test team. Shoaib's own son Shehzar, who has already played first-class cricket in Karachi, also dropped by. His team shirt read: 'Let's Build a Better Pakistan', the campaign slogan of Imran Khan's political party. The cricket tradition remains powerful in the Mohammad family. But when I spoke to Majid Khan in Lahore, he told me that his Burki clan had dispersed and he did not believe another Burki would ever play first-class cricket. This was one of the saddest things I heard while researching this book.

As for Justice Cornelius, he died in 1991, aged 88, his integrity and scruple a byword. He is buried in Lahore's Christian cemetery. He and his wife lived alone in a pair of rooms in Faletti's Hotel, customarily used by visiting cricketing teams when they passed through Lahore. When his wife died following a marriage of fifty-eight years, he moved into a single room. Retiring to private practice after his public career, he dismayed the partners of his law firm by charging much lower fees than far less distinguished lawyers.* He

---

*In January 1980, after three years of persuasion by the firm and several polite but firm declinations by Cornelius, he became senior partner of the Lahore firm Lane, Mufti. The firm changed its name to Cornelius, Lane, Mufti.

eschewed social functions in order to maintain his judicial impartiality and aloofness. In yet another indication of his frugality, Cornelius drove the same green Wolseley car* he had acquired as a judge in the 1950s right up to his final days. 'For our people,' he used to remark 'affluence is poison.'

Towards the end of his life, he would present a distinctive figure in the early-morning queue outside Lahore's Gaddafi stadium on Test match days. Wearing a tweed jacket with grey trousers, suede shoes and a golf cap, he carried with him a lunch box and a shooting stick. An acquaintance once accosted him and asked him why he went to the cheapest seats, when a figure of his distinction would surely be an honoured guest in any of the official boxes. 'Nobody knows who I am any more,' he replied. 'And if they did know they wouldn't care.' Besides, he went on, he enjoyed himself far more perched on the shooting stick and listening to the banter from the crowd than he would in the corporate areas.†

I often made the journey by train between Hanif's Karachi and Cornelius and Majid's Lahore during the dozen or so trips I arranged to Pakistan to research this book. I would go to bed watching the sunset over Sindh and wake up to sunrise over the Punjab. Whenever I looked out of the window in daylight hours, I would see some kind of cricket match in progress – some organised on proper pitches, most of them improvised on any flat surface, all played intensely.

I made trips by train into the Punjabi towns of Bahawalpur (in order to inspect the Dring stadium) and by road to Multan, where the great Inzamam and Mushtaq Ahmed learnt their game. At Multan, I played street cricket with the local boys outside one of the famous shrines, only to be arrested by the police, who told me they were concerned for my safety. Thereafter, I was given an escort of half a dozen rangers, with machine guns, wherever I went.

In Peshawar two members of the ISI, the state intelligence service, followed me. They never talked to me personally but spoke at length with everyone I interviewed. By the end, so I was told, they had become great supporters of the project and eager to read the book.

---

*It will soon be donated to a special Courts Museum: *Dawn*, 29 October 2013.
†Najum Latif elicited this response from Cornelius.

I travelled up the Swat Valley, where every scrap of level ground seemed to be used up by young men playing tapeball cricket. I drove up through Malakand, where Winston Churchill made a brief sojourn in the country in 1897. He preferred polo, but when I passed Churchill's Point, I was glad to learn there were plenty of cricketers nowadays in Malakand.

I also journeyed across the Shandour Pass from Gilgit to Chitral, where I heard of an old shepherd who had died a few years earlier. He was totally blind, and had never even seen cricket played. He was, nevertheless, an inexhaustible source of information about cricket and cricketers, obtained over several decades of listening to Urdu commentary as he tended his sheep.

I was received with generosity and kindness. Ordinary fans, great players and harassed officials alike went out of their way to answer my questions. Like everyone who gets to know Pakistan at all well, I fell in love with the country, and always felt an intense excitement whenever I returned.

When this book was almost finished, I went to see Imran Khan, Pakistan's greatest cricketer. I left Imran until last because I felt he was too busy to be disturbed. When he retired from cricket he refused offers to stay in the game. In 1996, he founded his own political party, the Pakistan Tehreek-e-Insaf (PTI), which translates as Movement for Justice. He was elected as a member of the national assembly, representing his tribal home of Mianwali, in 2002, but he struggled to make national headway. For some time, he was written off as a joke.

But during the years this book was being written, Imran discovered his voice. He fought the national elections of 2013, in protest against the corruption of the main political parties and Pakistan's subordination to America. On the day his campaign was launched, I travelled by rickshaw from the Bagh-e-Jinnah, where I had been watching a cricket match, to witness the opening PTI rally in Lahore. The atmosphere was electric with anticipation, as I stood for hours at the back of a huge, worshipping crowd, many of whom had been waiting all day. The people around me – many of them young, and a large number, unusually for Pakistan, women – told me they saw Imran as a saviour. They believed that only he can bring to an end the cynicism and corruption that has brought their country to its knees over the past two decades.

They lapped up his message that their country has been betrayed by a greedy, western-backed political class, who have squandered Pakistan's natural resources and hidden their eye-watering profits in offshore bank accounts. Imran got a huge cheer when he said that, 'I will bowl out two opponents – Nawaz Sharif and President Zardari – with a single delivery.'

In the election itself, he did not quite manage that. But he made serious headway, winning thirty-five seats in the national assembly, and the PTI became the leading party in Khyber Pakhtunkhwa, the former North-West Frontier province. It dominates the coalition which rules the province, and has hurried to implement its promises, especially on corruption and education.

When the election was finished, I asked if I could talk cricket with Imran. When in Islamabad, he lives in a fine hilltop house an hour's drive out of town. A servant guided me through an internal courtyard, and an elegant drawing room, out onto a veranda beyond, which looked north towards the mountains and the tribal areas.

There I met Imran. He is still a superb figure of a man – fit, athletic and tanned, recovered from a serious accident at the end of the election campaign. We sat and drank tea in the thin winter sunshine, then went inside and talked in front of a log fire. 'You must know about my family to understand me,' he said. 'I came from, first of all, a Pashtun background. My father's family is from the Niazi tribe. My mother's family were from the Burki tribe. So I come from two Pashtun tribes.

'The Pashtuns have always been anti-slavery. The Pashtuns, you know, are anti-subservient to someone else. This is Pashtun history. So I was brought up completely in Pakistan. I was born in '52. I was born with a pride in a free country and how awful to be under colonial rule.'

He told me about growing up in the family home in Zaman Park, about a childhood dedicated to the outdoor activities of partridge-shooting, boar-hunting and playing cricket. His cousin Majid was his childhood hero. 'We would just be playing cricket, we would be together in the evenings and at his house. Majid's house was like a second home to me. I would call Majid's mother a second mother.' Jahangir Khan, Majid's father, was a powerful presence. 'He was a very upright man. Totally self-controlled. All I remember is listening to him talking about history. You know, he was a great historian.'

Imran recalled being taken to the hills on shooting trips by his maternal uncle, Ahmed Raza Khan: 'We would go into these colonial resting houses.

And it was how a shoot should be. It wasn't just a question of shooting partridge. In the evenings we would be sitting by the log fire and I would be listening to his stories about cricket and everything.'

When Imran was nine years old, his mother took him to watch a Test match between Pakistan and England led by Ted Dexter at Lahore stadium. His cousin Javed Burki scored a century: 'And that's when I decided I wanted to be a Test cricketer.'

Imran told me how national interest in cricket started to surge in the late seventies, with the India series against Pakistan. 'When television coverage became much better, that's when it took off. And then, 1992 – it went to a different level. We would go into these tribal areas and we would watch a match. And every now and then the match would stop, there would be a fight, and then they would start playing again. I read several times that someone's got killed during a cricket match.' He explained in detail his plans to develop serious cricket facilities in the tribal areas.

Most of all, I wanted to know what Abdul Hafeez Kardar had meant to Imran: 'I completely understood Kardar. Why he behaved that way. Because, you know, there was no cricket structure in Pakistan. It was very difficult. Kardar was somebody who understood cricket. He commanded respect because of his personality. He was a complete nationalist. He was anti-colonial and he chose the team completely on merit. If players were trying to bring the me and I into the team, he would be stern with them. And he made enemies. He would take on people. But the fact is that he made a tremendous contribution to Pakistan cricket.'

Imran is a much greater cricketer, and a far more formidable politician, than Kardar. But the two men brought an adamantine integrity and patriotism to their cricket and to their lives. After Pakistan achieved independence from Britain in 1947, cricket came to define what Pakistan stands for as a country. In the early days, that national team was an expression of the selflessness of the creators of Pakistan. More recently, the ossified arrogance of an entrenched political elite has brought the nation's politics to its knees. This was reflected in the match-fixing scandals. Salman Butt and his fellow cheats did not simply commit a criminal offence – they were guilty of an act of unspeakable treachery to tens of millions of Pakistani cricket fans who looked to them to bring hope and passion to their lives.

After Salman Butt was released from jail in England, he returned to

Pakistan, saying that he was innocent of wrong-doing and unfairly punished. He tried playing club cricket, but the Pakistan Cricket Board intervened to stop him. Then he tried making advertising films for TV, and turned up at the Lahore Gymkhana for a shoot. Word reached a furious Javed Zaman, the club secretary and Imran Khan's mentor and kinsman, who promptly ordered Butt to quit, declaring that he would not allow a criminal and a cheat to be presented as a role model to Pakistan youth. Butt and his film crew slunk away.

Everywhere I went in Pakistan, I was aware that people feel a huge sense of pride in their country. This pride expresses itself through the cricket team, whose white clothing against a green field neatly matches the colours of the national flag. Cricket is the game of the villages, it is the game of the towns. It is the game of the old, it is the game of the young, the rich and the poor. It is played in the plains of Sindh and in the mountains of the north. It is played by the army and the Taliban. It is enjoyed by all Pakistan's sects and religions. It is part of Pakistan's history and also its future. It is magical and marvellous. Nothing else expresses half so well the singularity, the genius, the occasional madness of the people of Pakistan, and their contribution to the world sporting community.

Appendix

Pakistani Names

Compiled by Murtaza Shibli, British Kashmiri writer and poet

The names of the Pakistani cricket players reflect a trend among Muslims across the world. They usually derive from those of the prophets who are mentioned in various *suras*, or chapters, of the Holy Quran. There are the ninety-nine names of Allah (most of them mentioned in the Quran), the ninety-nine names of the Prophet Muhammad given to him by Allah, and the names of the companions of the prophet such as Sadeeq, Umar, Uthman, Ali, Bilal, Salman, etc. Several biblical names, such as Moses (Musa), Jesus (Eesa), Gabriel (Jibreel), Aaron (Harun), Solomon (Sulaiman), Noah (Nooh), and Mary (Mariam) are also very common and considered Islamic.

It is important to note that the most important set of Islamic names start with the Arabic word *abd*, and is usually followed by one of the ninety-nine names of Allah, known as *asma'al husna* or the divine names. A very common name with the prefix 'abd' is Abdullah (Abd Allah), which means 'servant of Allah' or 'worshipper of Allah'.

Local variants of Islamic/Muslim names were common in pre-Partition India. The practice has largely died out now and is confined mostly to those living in far-off villages, with limited education. These include names such as Allah Rakha (the one who is sustained by Allah), Allah/ Muhammad Baksh (gifted by Allah/Muhammad), Alla/Muhammad Din (Allah's/ Muhammad's religion – not to be confused with Aladdin, of *The Arabian Nights*, which is Ala'-ad-din, meaning the nobility of the religion), Allah Wasaya, Allah Mangta (the one asked from Allah). Such common names were usually given by the local clergy to the village/towns folk that they catered for. These clergy (locally known as Pirs, Imams or Moulvis) would interpret religion for the common folk, give names to them and intercede on their behalf in all worldly and other worldly matters – birth, death, happiness and sadness. The names given to the common people were made in an attempt to distinguish them from the 'Islamic nobility'.

Another set of names prevalent in the Indian subcontinent has a Persian background. Names like Jahangir (the one who controls the world), Pervez, Jamshe(e)d, and Qaiser (Caeser) are widely used, though they are not exclusive to Muslim communities and are also commonly used among the Parsis in India.

A similar classification is followed in second names. The western idea of surnames, passed down from father to son, does not invariably apply in Pakistan. For example, two of the country's finest Test cricketers, Waqar Hasan and Pervez Sajjad, are brothers but have completely different names. Second names are broadly of three categories – of Arab naming convention, tribal names and ancestral names.

Muslim names in Pakistan and India can be a combination or amalgamation of Persian and Arabic (or Quranic) names. For example, Pervez Musharraf, the former military ruler of Pakistan, or Junaid Jamshed, the famous Pakistani pop singer turned born-again Muslim preacher. In the first example, Pervez is Persian, which means fortunate, or victorious. Musharraf, the second part of the name, is Arabic, and means honoured or exalted. In the next example, Junaid is Arabic and means soldier or warrior, whereas Jamshed is Persian and means rays of the sun. Jamshed is also the name of the famous Persian king whose goblet is famous and is used by several Persian and Urdu poets, while Junaid was a very famous Islamic Sufi.

Many of the Muslim names also start with the name Muhammad (or Mohammad/Mohammed/Muhammed), the most popular name of the Prophet Muhammad. This is considered lucky by Muslims, based on a *hadith* (a narration by the Prophet Muhammad): 'Whoever is named after me with the hope of being blessed, he will be blessed and will be in peace till the Day of Qiyaamah [Day of Judgement].' This is why many Muslims start their names with Muhammad. (Muhammad is now also the most popular first name in England.) For example, the full name of famous Pakistani cricketer Javed Miandad is Mohammad Javed Miandad Khan. However, as

is frequent practice, Mohammad does not form the part of the first name –
it has been shortened to Javed Miandad.

It is important to note that many Islamic/Muslim names are abbreviated
or shortened in a way that compromises the meaning of these names. The
shortened meaning can become 'blasphemous' in the Islamic creed, but such
practices are widespread. For example, Abdur Razzak, meaning servant of
the Razzak (the provider, one of the names of Allah) becomes Razzak as a
short form, which means the provider, thus diametrically changing the
meaning of the name. Similarly, Abdul Rehman, Abdul Wahab, Abdul A'ala
are shortened to Rehman, Wahab or A'ala, exclusive epithets of Allah and
therefore militating against the spirit of submitting to Allah.

Names of Pakistan Captains (Test, One-day and T20 Cricket)

Aamer Sohail: Aamer, Arabic, means civilised. Sohail, Arabic, means gentle.
It is also a name of a star. It can be written as Aamir, Amir. Sohail can be
written as Suhail, Suhaiyil, Sohale.

Abdul Hafeez Kardar: Abdul means servant or slave. It is also used with one
of the ninety-nine names of Allah, also known as *asma' al husna*, the divine
names. Hafeez, one of the names of Allah, means The Protector. Therefore,
Abdul Hafeez means slave or servant of The Protector.

Abdul Qadir: Qadir, Arabic, another name of Allah which means The
Omnipotent, The Able. Therefore, Abdul Qadir means the servant of The
Omnipotent/The Able.

Abdul Razzaq: The correct name (from its Arabic roots) would be Abdur
Razzaq. Razzaq is another name of Allah. It means The Sustainer. Therefore,
Abdur Razzaq means the servant/worshipper of The Sustainer.

Asif Iqbal: Asif, in Urdu, means a capable person. Iqbal, in Urdu, means
prosperity, good fortune, good luck, responsiveness, welfare. Iqbal is a very
famous name in Pakistan. The famous poet and philosopher Iqbal (full
name Muhammed Iqbal) provided the concept of Pakistan. He was
knighted by the British colonial powers and was a barrister at law.

Fazal Mahmood: Fazal, Arabic, means blessing. Mahmood, Arabic, means the commendable, praiseworthy. Mahmood is one of the ninety-nine names of the Prophet Muhammad.

Hanif Mohammad: Hanif (also written as Haneef), Arabic, means upright, true, true believer.

Imran Khan: Imran, Arabic, means population, civilisation, careful observance of rules of etiquette. According to the Islamic belief, Imran was the father of the Virgin Mary or Maryam, mother of Jesus. The Virgin Mary, according to Islam, is the most exalted woman in the history of mankind. On the Day of Judgement, she will be the mother of the faithful (all the faithful including Jews, Christians and Muslims).

Imtiaz Ahmed: Imtiaz (also written as Imtiyaz), Urdu, means distinction, privilege, mark of honour.

Intikhab Alam: This is a typical Persian/Urdu name. Intikhab means chosen or elected. Alam means the world. The full meaning of the name would be 'chosen by the world'. The plural of Intikhab is Intikhabat, which means elections.

Inzamam-ul-Haq: Inzamam, Arabic, means proximity or joining. Haq, Arabic, means the truth. Therefore, Inzamam-ul-Haq means close to the truth, or the one who has joined the truth. Inzamam was born in Multan, the spiritual capital of Pakistan which is dotted with Sufi shrines. Like Shahid Afridi, he belongs to a family of Sufi saints. His grandfather was Zia-ul-Haq, a famous local pir.

Javed Burki: Javed, Persian/Urdu, means eternal. Javed is frequently used as a prefix or suffix to the name Muhammed or Ahmed, both names of the Prophet Muhammad.

Javed Miandad: Javed, Persian and Urdu, means eternal, perpetual – it can also be written as Javaid or Javeid.

Majid Khan: Majid, Arabic, means the majestic. It is one of the names of Allah. The full correct version is Abdul Majid, servant/worshipper of the Majestic One.

Misbah-ul-Haq: Misbah, Arabic, means a lamp, a lamp light, lantern, a morning. Haq, means the truth. Misbah-ul-Haq means the lamp of the truth (which usually means Islam).

Mohammad Hafeez: Hafeez, Arabic, means guardian, protector, an attribute applied to Allah. Usually the name is Abdul Hafeez, servant/worshipper of the guardian/protector.

Mohammad Yousuf: This is a combination of two names of prophets – first, the Prophet Muhammad and second, the Prophet Yousuf (the biblical Joseph, son of prophet Yaqub, i.e. Jacob). Yousuf's Christian name was Yousuf Youhana which he changed to Mohammad Yousuf. Youhana means God's blessing.

Moin Khan: Moin (also written as Moeen, Moyeen), Arabic, means helper. Usually, Moeen is used as Moeen-ud-Din (helper of the din or religion, referring to Islam) or Moeen-ul-Haq (helper of the truth), which again refers to Islam. Moeen-ul-Islam is also used as a name.

Mushtaq Mohammad: Mushtaq, Persian/Urdu, means yearning. The name Mushtaq Mohammad means yearning for the (Prophet) Muhammad. However, it will never be written or said in that way.

Ramiz Hasan Raja: Ramiz/Rameez, Arabic, means a symbol. Hasan/Hassan was one of the two famous grandsons of the Prophet Muhammad, and means good-looking, handsome. His brother, Husain, was martyred in the battle of Karbala. Ramiz Hasan means symbol of Hassan.

Rashid Latif: Rashid (not to be confused with Rasheed which is sometimes also written as Rashid), Arabic, means rightly guided. Latif, Arabic, means subtle, gentle, friendly. Ironically, Rashid Latif is a notably undiplomatic man, frequently at odds with fellow players and officials and now an outspoken campaigner against corruption.

Saeed Ahmed: Saeed, Arabic, means auspicious, venerable, dignified, fortunate. It is also the name of a Sahabi, or the Prophet Muhammad's companion.

Saeed Anwar: Saeed, Arabic, means auspicious, venerable, dignified, fortunate. It is also the name of a Sahabi or the Prophet Muhammad's companion. Anwar, Arabic, means radiant. Nowadays, he is also referred to as Maulana

Saeed Anwar. Maulana (Arabic: literally 'our lord/master') is a title, mostly in the Indian subcontinent, preceding the name of respected Muslim religious leaders, in particular graduates of religious institutions, e.g. a madrassah or a *darululoom*, or scholars who have studied under other Islamic scholars. Although Saeed Anwar is not a graduate of any Islamic seminaries, he now delivers religious lectures and is associated with the Tablighi Jamaat, the famous Muslim organisation of South Asia.

Salim Malik: Salim, Persian/Urdu, means sound, affable, healthy, guarded, perfect, complete, safe, secure.

Salman Butt: Salman, Arabic, means safe, mild, affable, perfect. It is also the name of a famous Sahabi or a companion of the Prophet Muhammad. He was Persian and therefore is known as Salman Al-Farsi, Salman, the Persian. Butt is a Kashmiri surname, often written as Bhat in Indian-held Kashmir.

Sarfraz Nawaz: Another typical Persian/Urdu name. Sarfraz literally means holding ones' head up. It means esteemed, high. Nawaz in Persian/Urdu means kind, loving, generous. Nawaz has a Sufi background to it. Famous South Asian Sufi saint, Moeen-ud-Din Chisti is known as Gharib Nawaz, the one who loves the poor.

Shahid Afridi: Shahid, Arabic, means witness. It is one of the ninety-nine names of the Prophet Muhammad. Shahid Afridi belongs to a family of pirs (pir or peer means a Sufi teacher or a spiritual teacher). His father was known as Sahabzada Fazl-ur-Rehman of Bhutan Sharif. His grandfather, Maulana Muhammad Ilyas, was a well-known local spiritual figure. Bhutan Sharif is an area in Terah in Pakistan's Khyber Pakhtunkhwa province. Shahid Afridi was given the title 'The Prince of the Mountains' by the renowned Pakistani Urdu sports monthly *Akhbar-e-Watan*.

Shoaib Malik: Shoaib (also written as Shu'ayb), Arabic, means the one who knows the right path. Shoaib was a prophet who is believed to have lived after Abraham. In the Old Testament, he is referred to as Jethro who was an ancient Midianite prophet. Shoaib Malik is the husband of famous Indian tennis star, Sania Mirza. Another Shoaib played for Pakistan was Shoaib Mohammad, son of Hanif.

Waqar Younis: Waqar, Persian/Urdu, means majesty, veneration, dignity, gracefulness. Younis, Arabic, means a pillar and is the name of the Prophet Jonah.

Wasim Akram: Wasim, Arabic, means handsome, comely, of a fine countenance. Akram, Arabic, means generous. Akram is usually associated with Allah, but is not among his ninety-nine names.

Wasim Bari: Wasim, Arabic, means handsome, comely, of a fine countenance. Bari (al-Bari) is one of the names of Allah and it means 'The Evolver'.

Younis Khan: Younis, Arabic, means a pillar. It is the name of the Prophet Jonah.

Zaheer Abbas: Zaheer, Arabic, means radiant. Abbas, Arabic, means lion.

Names of Some Other Cricketers/Officials

Arif Abbasi: Arif, means acquainted, knowledgeable, devotee. Abbasi is a surname.

Ata-ur-Rehman: Ata/Atta, Arabic, means a gift. Rehman, one of the favourite names of Allah, means The Beneficent. Ata/Atta-ur-Rehman means a gift from The Beneficent.

Gul Mohammad: Gul has two meanings. It is a short form of Ghulam that means slave in Urdu. Gulam Muhammad, a common South Asian name which is not much in practice now, means slave of the Prophet Muhammad. Gul also means flower in Urdu, Persian and Turkish. The name of the current Turkish president is Abdullah Gul. Gul is pronounced differently in Turkish as 'Gi yul'. Gul Mohammad, who also played for India, was one of the earliest cricket players in Pakistan.

Haroon Rashid: (Actually it should be Rasheed, not to be confused with Rashid as in Rashid Latif or Lateef.) Haroon (also written as Haroun), Arabic, is the Arabic for Aaron. Haroon means chief, protector, guard, the wealth of the entire universe. Rasheed, Arabic, means 'the rightly guided' or 'the guide to the right path', one of the names of Allah. Haroon al-Rashid was a famous Abbasid Caliph, very well known because of his mentions in *The Arabian Nights (A Thousand and One Nights)*. Haroon Rashid was a well-known batsman in the 1980s. He started his career in 1976–77.

Ijaz Ahmed: Ijaz, Arabic, means miracle or astonishment. Ahmed is one of the names of the Prophet Muhammad. Ijaz Ahmed means a miracle of the Prophet Muhammad.

Ijaz Butt: Ijaz (Ajaz, Iajaz, Aijaz) means miracle, wondrous nature. Butt (or Bhat) is a Kashmiri surname.

Iqbal Qasim: Iqbal, Urdu, means prosperity, good fortune, good luck, responsiveness, welfare. Qasim, Arabic, is one of the names of the Prophet Muhammad. It means distributor.

Khalid Mahmood: Khalid, Arabic, means eternal, glorious. Mahmood, Arabic, means the commendable, praiseworthy. Mahmood is one of the ninety-nine names of the Prophet Muhammad. Khalid Mahmood was Pakistan team manager in their 1993 tour to the West Indies.

Mohsin Kamal: Mohsin, Arabic, means benevolent, benefactor, charitable, humanitarian. Kamal, Urdu/Arabic, means perfection, completion, integrity.

Mohsin Khan: (Full name Mohsin Hasan Khan). Mohsin, Arabic, means benevolent, benefactor, charitable, humanitarian. Mohsin Hasan means benefactor of Hasan, the grandson of the Prophet Muhammad. Mohsin Khan was a cricketer, film actor and later a Pakistan cricket coach. He retired from cricket in 1986 and joined Bollywood, the Indian film industry, with help from his then wife and Indian actress Reena Roy. He worked on about a dozen Indian and Pakistani films without any remarkable success.

Mudassar Nazar: Mudassar, Arabic, famous attribute of the Prophet Muhammad, given to him by Allah. It means wrapped in, enveloped, cloaked. There is a famous *sura* or chapter in the Quran called 'Mudassar'. Nazar, Urdu/Persian, means a vow, a promise made to God; a gift, charity, votive offering. Mudassar Nazar means a gift from Mudassar, the Prophet Muhammad or a gift to the Prophet Muhammad.

Nasim Hasan: (Nasim Hasan Shah, Justice). Nasim/Naseem, Urdu, means wind, fresh air, fragrant air, zephyr, a cool breeze. Nasim/Naseem Hassan means a breeze of Hassan, the grandson of the Prophet Muhammad. Justice Nasim Hasan Shah was chairman of the Pakistan Cricket Board.

Nazar Mohammad: Nazar Mohammad means the same as Mudassar Nazar – a gift from the Prophet Muhammad or a gift to the Prophet Muhammad.

Nur Khan: Nur means the (eternal) light, a common Muslim name. In the Middle East, it is a popular name for women, but in the subcontinent it is mainly used for men. Women usually have names like Noori.

Qasim Omar: Qasim, Arabic, one of the names of the Prophet Muhammad. It means a distributor. Omar, Arabic, means prosperous. Omar is also the name of the second Islamic Caliph, Omar ibn al-Khattab.

Sadiq Mohammad: Sadiq, Arabic, is one of the attributes/names of the Prophet Muhammad. It means sincere.

Saqlain Mushtaq: Saqlain (correct is Saqa-lain), Arabic, means the two worlds, the world and the hereafter.

Shaharyar Khan: Shaharyar means 'friend of a city', as transliterated into Urdu, but in Persian, Shaharyar means king.

Shakoor Rana: (Full name Abdul Shakoor Rana. The correct Arabic way to pronounce it is Abdush Shakoor.) Shakoor or Ash-Shakoor, Arabic, is one of the names of Allah. It means The Appreciative. Abdush Shakoor means the servant/slave of The Appreciative. Shakoor Rana was the famous Pakistani umpire involved in the flare-up with Mike Gatting.

Shoaib Akhtar: Shoaib (also written as Shu'ayb), Arabic, means the one who knows the right path. Shoaib was a prophet who is believed to have lived after Abraham. In the Old Testament, he is referred to as Jethro, who was an ancient Midianite prophet. Akhtar, Urdu, means a star, good luck.

Tauseef Ahmed: Tauseef, Urdu/Persian, means praise. Tauseef Ahmed means praise of Ahmed, the Prophet Muhammad.

Waqar Hasan: Waqar, Urdu/Persian, means dignity, grace. Waqar Hasan means dignity of Hasan, the grandson of the Prophet Muhammad. His brother, who played nineteen Test matches for Pakistan, has a completely different name: Pervez Sajjad. Pervez is Persian, meaning fortunate or victorious, while Sajjad means one who prostrates himself before Allah.

Wazir Mohammad: Wazir, Urdu/Persian, means vizier, an adviser or counsel.

Yawar Saeed: Yawar, Persian/Urdu, means aiding, friendly, friend. Yawar Saeed was a Pakistan team manager on several foreign tours.

Notes

1 I am grateful to Wasim Bari for bringing this quotation to my attention.

THE GREATEST GAME

1 Fazal Mahmood, *Fazal Mahmood aur Cricket* (*Fazal Mahmood and Cricket*), p.122. Translation by Murtaza Shibli.

CHAPTER 1

1 According to Fazal's own account. See Fazal Mahmood, *From Dusk to Dawn*, p.3. Like many students at the time, Ghulam Hussain would study under the street lampposts of Old Lahore as there was no electricity in their house.

2 Fazal Mahmood, *Urge to Faith*, p.viii.

3 Fazal Mahmood, *Fazal Mahmood aur Cricket*, p.23.

4 Fazal Mahmood, *From Dusk to Dawn*, p.5.

5 ibid. p.6.

6 Southern Punjab v Northern India, 4–6 March 1944, played at Patiala. Northern India 329 (Abdul Hafeez 94, Fazal Mahmood 38) and 127 (Abdul Hafeez 14, Fazal 2) Southern Punjab 326 (Fazal 1–22) and 104–8 (Fazal 2–29). Match drawn.

7 Fazal Mahmood, *Fazal Mahmood aur Cricket*, pp.32–34.

8 ibid. p.13.

9 Lawrence Ziring, *Pakistan in the Twentieth Century*, p.69.

10 *Wisden* 1947, p.154.

11 Fazal was playing in the Zonal Quadrangular Tournament for North Zone v South Zone. South Zone 227 (Fazal Mahmood 4–64) and 306 (Fazal Mahmood 2–42). North Zone 506–9 decl. (Kishenchand 218, Fazal Mahmood 100 not out) and 28–0. North Zone won by ten wickets. The match was played over 17, 18 and 19 February 1947. However, North Zone was heavily defeated by West Zone in the final. Source: Syed MH Maqsood, *Who's Who in Indian Cricket* 1947, p.38.

12 Denis Pitts (ed.) *Clem Attlee: The Granada Historical records interview*, London 1967, p.42. Quoted in Patrick French, *Liberty or Death*.

13 Maharajah of Patiala's XI v VM Merchant's XI, played at Feroz Shah Kotla Delhi on 15, 16, 17 and 18 March 1947. The Maharajah's team contained eight Hindus, two Muslims and one Sikh. VM Merchant's XI had four Muslims, six Hindus and one Parsi. VM Merchant's XI won by 29 runs. Source: MH Maqsood, op. cit. pp.41–42.

14 Fazal Mahmood, *From Dusk to Dawn*, p.14.

15 See Ziring, op. cit. p.57. 'Radcliffe was given responsibility for both committees even though he had never visited India, let alone served there, and did not possess even the most basic understanding of India demography or cultures.' Moreover Sir Cyril was given three weeks to complete the work of the two commissions.

16 I am indebted to Majid Khan for this information, although his father is not listed as a commissioner in two historical sources: Ian Talbot 'Radcliffe Award' in the *Oxford Companion to Pakistani History*, Justice Mohammad Munir, *From Jinnah To Zia*, p.12.

17 This account of Fazal's movements is based on Fazal Mahmood, op. cit. pp.14–15.

18 Mihir Bose, *A History of Indian Cricket*, pp.159–60.

19 Fazal Mahmood, op. cit. p.15.

20 ibid. pp.15–16.

21 ibid. p.16.

22 See for example, http://tribune.com.pk/story/88364/explosion–in–hangu–kills–5/

23 See Fazal Mahmood, *Fazal Mahmood aur Cricket*, p.61: 'Perhaps this was my biggest mistake in life, otherwise I would have achieved the position that I enjoy now at that time.'

24 ibid. p.65.

25 See AH Kardar, *Memoirs of an All-rounder*, pp.9–10: 'Referring specifically to the sports in my youth, there was always a distinction between the kinds of sports which were pursued in the towns and in the countryside. For instance, the country people excelled in wrestling and horse racing which were organised regularly in each village and at gatherings between villages . . . On the other hand, urbanisation led to increased interest in organised teams and individual sports, such as hockey, cricket, football, tennis, squash and volleyball.'

26 Its annual meetings, however, were confusingly held in other Indian cities.

27 Or Karachi, see Syed MH Maqsood, *Cricket in Pakistan, 1948–49 Edition*, p.47. The two turf wickets in Lahore were the Lahore Gymkhana and Aitchison College.

28 *The Times of India*, 11 August 1947.

29 ibid. 24 August 1947.

30 ibid. 9 July 1947.

31 ibid. 24 August 1947.

32 See SM Hussain, quoted in the *Pakistan vs Australia Official Souvenir Brochure*, Karachi 1959: 'As for England and the MCC, they were very well content that the membership previously by the subcontinent should after the Partition be appropriated to India. Worthy and well-intentioned Englishmen made the suggestion in all sincerity that Pakistan should get together with India to make a single cricketing country.'

33 In his essay on 'Growth of Pakistan Cricket', Abdul Hafeez Kardar referred to the 'characteristic national optimism' which accompanied the formation of the independent Board of Control for Cricket in Pakistan, 'under the stress and strain of multiple social, political and economic problems'. *Wisden 1954*, p.97.

34 KH Baloch and MS Parvez, *Encyclopaedia of Pakistan Cricket 1947–48 to 2004*, pp.629–30. After 1953 there was a new secretary, Syed Nazir Ali, who operated out of 29 Queen's Road, Karachi. See Syed MH Maqsood, op. cit. p.100.

35 Fazal Mahmood, *From Dusk to Dawn*, p.21.

36 For the Fazal quote see the-south-asian.com website article on the Lahore Gymkhana. I am grateful to Najum Latif for the anecdote about the young Fazal.

37 Interview with Yawar Saeed, Lahore 2012.

38 I am grateful to Sultan Mahmud for this anecdote.

39 'The West Indies accepted our invitation and agreed to play one Test in Lahore in November 1948.' Fazal Mahmood, *From Dusk to Dawn*, p.17.

40 Interview with Sultan Mahmud, Lahore 2012.

41 Shuja-ud-Din, *From Babes of Cricket*, p.4.

CHAPTER 2

1 CLR James, *Beyond A Boundary*, p.199.
2 Interview with Sultan Mahmud, Lahore 2012. Mahmud captained Government College and Punjab University, and toured England with the Pakistan Eaglets, before becoming a sports journalist. His book *Cricket After Midnight* is an indispensable source of understanding for the first quarter century of Pakistan Test cricket.
3 Interview with Sultan Mahmud, 2012.
4 Interview with Yawar Saeed, Lahore, 2012.
5 AH Kardar, *Memoirs of an All-rounder (MOAR)*, pp.120–125.
6 Ramachandra Guha, *A Corner of a Foreign Field*, pp.369–70, develops this theme more fully.
7 I am grateful to Kardar's son Shahid for this information.
8 JM Wikeley, *Punjabi Musalmans*, 1915, reprinted 1991, p.66. Members of the Arain caste are also renowned as agriculturalists.
9 AH Kardar, op. cit. p.15. Much of my information about Kardar's early life is drawn from this autobiographical memoir. I am also grateful to Shahid Kardar, Jalil Kardar (AH Kardar's nephew) and Najum Latif.
10 AH Kardar, op. cit. pp.19–20.
11 Kardar gives a moving account of his friendship with the Nawab of Pataudi in *MOAR*, pp.59–60.
12 AH Kardar, op. cit. pp.123–5.
13 In AH Kardar, op. cit. p134. Kardar declared that 'the above stands as a milestone in the history of Pakistan cricket. For, after this episode I decided to press and agitate for "specialists" of the administration and management of our cricket.'
14 *Wisden 1953*, pp.487–88.
15 I am grateful to Sultan Mahmud for this memory.
16 AH Kardar, op. cit. p.155.
17 Fazal Mahmood, *From Dusk to Dawn*, p.23.
18 Lawrence Ziring, *Pakistan in the Twentieth Century*, pp.116–32.
19 Fazal Mahmood, *From Dusk to Dawn*, p.23.

CHAPTER 3

1 Thanks to historians like Ramachandra Guha, Boria Majumdar and Mihir Bose, we now have a clear picture of the origins of cricket in south-east Asia. See particularly Ramachandra Guha, *A Corner of a Foreign Field*; Boria Majumdar, *Indian Cricket Through the Ages: A Reader*; and Mihir Bose, *A History of Indian Cricket*. This brief account of the early history of North West Indian cricket relies on their pioneering work.
2 R Guha, op. cit. p.14. Gladstone, upon becoming British prime minister in 1880, arranged the appointment of the Marquess of Ripon as Viceroy of India.
3 For more information see Vasant Raiji, *India's Hambledon Men*.
4 R Guha, op. cit. pp.33–36; *Wisden* notes that, although full records were not available, to judge from the names of the people who took wickets against the tourists, there were very few Indians playing, except in the Parsi side, Jonathan Rice (ed.), *Wisden on India: An Anthology*, p.9.
5 R Guha, op. cit. p.272.
6 Mihir Bose, op. cit. ch. 6 passim.
7 Mihir Bose, op. cit. pp.64–65.
8 Mihir Bose, *A Maidan View: The Magic of Indian Cricket*, pp.92–94.
9 John Keay, *The Honourable Company*, pp.13–14; VA Smith, *Oxford History of India (4th Ed.)*, p.607.
10 *The Bombay Times and Journal of Commerce*, 2 November 1842.
11 ibid. 23 August 1843.

12 ibid. 14 August 1844.

13 ibid. 31 January 1844, 11 November 1846.

14 Paddy Docherty, *The Khyber Pass: A History of Empire and Invasion*, p.209.

15 *The Bombay Times and Journal of Commerce*, 13 October 1849.

16 Rev. George Robert Gleig, *Sale's Brigade in Afghanistan, with an account of the seizure and defence of Jellalabad*, p.68. I am grateful to William Dalrymple for this reference.

17 Letters from Gordon Hugh Davidson, 15 November 1844, National Army Museum, Chelsea (Accession Number 2011–03–5).

18 ibid. 16 January 1845.

19 ibid. 10 November 1852.

20 All information on Abbottabad and Rawalpindi, unless otherwise stated, has been kindly prepared by Prof. Omer Tarin, historian of the North-West Frontier, to whom I am indebted. *Hazara District Gazetteer,* 1907, pp.11, 12 and 15.

21 See Jonathan Rice, 'Never a famous cricketer', *Wisden,* 138th edition, 2001, pp.38–42.

22 As with information on the other provincial towns of the Punjab, I am indebted to the work done by Prof. Omer Tarin on the history of Muree and it is his unpublished research which is reproduced here.

23 Photo 16, Collection of Major Keyes, 1st Punjab Infantry, National Army Museum, Chelsea (Accession Number 1966–11–30). Major Keyes was almost certainly the photographer. He was promoted to Major in 1861 for his part in putting down a Mehsud-Wazir uprising near Bannu in the same year; he was noted in this action for cutting down the leading Mehsud. He retired as General Sir CP Keyes, GCB, and was the father of Admiral Lord Keyes. His grandson, Lieutenant-Colonel Keyes, secured a posthumous Victoria Cross in a raid on General Rommel's HQ during World War Two. The large building on the right-hand side of the photograph is noted by the British Library as Major Keyes's house.

24 Compiled by various officers, *History of the Guides, 1846–1922*, p.278.

25 ibid. p.284.

26 ibid.

27 Col. GJ Younghusband, *A History of the Guides*, p.125

28 I am grateful to Dr Mubashar Hasan, finance minister of Pakistan 1971–75 for this anecdote, which concerns a cousin of his who played cricket against the British *c.*1910.

29 *Hazara District Gazetteer*, 1883–84, p.212. Sourced by Prof. Omer Tarin.

30 'Anglo-Vernacular Schools Report, Rawalpindi District', 1872–82, p.237. Sourced by Prof. Omer Tarin.

31 *Rawalpindi District Gazetteer*, 1893–94, p.187. Sourced by Prof. Omer Tarin.

32 TL Pennell, *Among the Wild Tribes of the Afghan Frontier: A record of sixteen years close intercourse with the natives of the Indian marches*, pp.140–41.

33 ibid. p.157.

34 ibid. p.150.

35 Some coverage was given in *Wisden 1891* with statistics recorded but little commentary. Even less space was given in *Wisden 1894* for Lord Hawke's tour in 1892–93 where only the two matches played against the Parsis were reported in any detail, most likely because of the Parsi success against Vernon's team two years previously.

36 Cecil Headlam, *Ten Thousand Miles Through India & Burma: An Account of the Oxford University Authentics' Cricket Tour with Mr KJ Key in the Year of the Coronation Durbar*, p.152.

37 ibid. p.162.

38 *Wisden 1903*, p.197.

39 AH Kardar, *Pakistan's Soldiers of Fortune*, p.3.

40 William Dalrymple's *The Last Mughal* is a sympathetic British account of the uprising and the subsequent destruction of Islamic culture.

41 Mushirul Hasan (ed.), *My Life, a Fragment: An Autobiographical Sketch of Maulana Mohamed Ali*, p.63.

42 David Lelyveld, *Aligarh's First Generation: Muslim Solidarity in British India*, p.102.

43 ibid. p.254.

44 Anonymous student, 'My College Life Twenty Years On', *The Aligarh Monthly*, (Vol 11:V), May 1904 (CC Mission Press, Cawnpore) p.41.
45 *Aligarh Institute Gazette*, 4 March 1882, quoted in Lelyveld, op. cit. p.255.
46 ibid.
47 For Jahangir Khan, see pp.6–7.
48 M Hasan (ed.), op. cit. p.41.
49 Morison, *History of the M.A.-O College*, p.14, quoted in Lelyveld, op. cit. pp.292–93.
50 Khadim Hussain Baloch and Mohammad Hussain Baluch, *Pakistan Cricket: A Compilation of the History, Volume 1 – 'A Century of Karachi Cricket'*, p.1.
51 ibid. p.iv.
52 ibid. p.2.
53 Syed MH Maqsood, *Who's Who in Indian Cricket*, p.72.
54 ibid.
55 BD Shankar, *40 Years of Active Cricket*, p.8.
56 Baloch and Baluch, op. cit. pp.2–4.
57 In the late 1920s Rubie and Shankar collaborated in the production of a *History of Sindh Cricket*. Unfortunately I have been unable to track down this volume.
58 Shankar, op. cit. p.16.
59 ibid. p.17.
60 ibid. p.61. The Quetta captain was AJ Holmes, who had played for Sussex.
61 ibid. p.116.
62 ibid. p.117.
63 ibid.
64 ibid. p.116.
65 ibid. p.118.
66 FS Aijazuddin, *Commanding Success: Aitchison College 1886–2011*, p.12.
67 HLO Garrett and Abdul Hamid, *A History of Government College, Lahore 1864–1964*, pp.4–5.
68 ibid. pp.20–25.
69 L Kashi Ram of Ferozepur remembers the club in these early days from his own experiences as a pupil in 1884–89: 'The College authorities did not evince the slightest interest, unless of course the payment of small subscriptions by the Professors each year, at the earnest request of some of the senior students to help them in their funds to carry on a cricket club, could be considered sufficient interest in that line . . . It had, as I have just mentioned, to depend upon its own enterprise and its own financial resources, helped as they were by subscriptions ranging between Rs.5 and Rs.16 each, received from the Professors and the Principal each year. The Director of Public Instruction used also to be approached for subscription and was more generous, paying Rs.20 whenever the Secretary of the club asked for help from him. For ordinary purposes the subscriptions received from the members were quite sufficient to keep the club going. The members appointed their own Secretary, who acted as ex-officio Captain of the team whenever a cricket match had to be played.' ibid. pp.49–57.
70 ibid.
71 ibid.
72 *Ravi* (January 1911) p.28.
73 *Ravi* (January 1909) p.28.
74 Interview with Professor AA Shakir, Lahore, 12 July 2012.
75 Mohammad Hanif Shahid, *The Role of Islamia College in the Pakistan Movement*, p.i.
76 Interview with Mohammad Hanif Shahid (author of *The Role of Islamia College in the Pakistan Movement*), 14 July 2012.
77 Fazal Mahmood *Fazal Mahmood aur Cricket*, pp.20–22.
78 Fazal Mahmood confided this information in later life to Najum Latif. Interview with Najum Latif, July 2012.
79 *Pakistan Times*, 4 February 1948, p.7.
80 *Ravi* (February 1947) p.28; *Ravi* (March–April 1947) p.43.
81 Fazal Mahmood, *From Dusk to Dawn*, p.6.

82 ibid. p.6. Fazal stresses that Hindu players represented the Islamia College team, saying that the 1945 Islamia team he captained contained two, Giyan Sagar and Naval Kishore. Both lived in Taxali Gate, Old Lahore. When the Pakistan team travelled to India in 1952, Sagar was there to welcome his old schoolfriends in Amritsar.

83 ibid. pp. 5–6.

84 AH Kardar, 'A Guide, Friend and a Philosopher,' in *100 Years of Islamia College Lahore, 1892–1992*, p.64.

85 ibid.; Interview with SF Rehman, 14 July 2012.

86 Fazal Mahmood, op. cit. p.7.

87 AH Kardar, op. cit. p.64.

88 Rajender Amarnath, *The Making of a Legend: Lala Amarnath Life & Times*, p.185.

89 ibid. p.4.

90 According to Fazal Mahmood, who told Najum Latif.

91 Crescent Cricket Club was formed by the cricket-loving residents of Mochi Gate Lahore. Bulaki Shah, a wealthy Hindu, was one of the main patrons of the Club. The Club held its nets at the Mochi Gate ground, moving later on in the early 1940s to the Minto Park ground. While Lala Amarnath was the most famous player, prominent Crescent cricketers included Haji Tawakkal Majeed, Mirza Mazaffar Baig, Wali Mohammad (famous for his 'accidental six' when he ducked into a rising ball from Learie Constantine, which hit the edge of the bat and flew over the slips and over the boundary), Gulzar Mohammad, Khadim Hussain, Qamaruddin, Ustad Gul, Ram Prakash, Surinder Khanna (who became President of the Board of Cricket Control in India), Shahab, Inayat Khan, Badaruddin, Raja Amir Elahi, Murawwat Hussain Shah, Agha Saadat Ali, Israr Ali, Maqsood Ahmed, Zulfiqar Ahmed, Duncan Sharpe, Ijaz Butt, Mohammad Ilyas, Younis Ahmed and Saleem Altaf. Kardar joined the Crescent Club after he had developed differences with the Mamdot Club.

92 Interview with Jamil (Jimmy) Rana, 2012.

93 Ayesha Jalal, *The Sole Spokesman: Jinnah, The Muslim League and the Demand for Pakistan*, pp.12fn, 53–55. The 'i' in the name was added later for ease of pronunciation. Rahmat Ali was swiftly disillusioned by his creation and ordered out of the country in 1948 (Khursheed Kamal Aziz, *Rahmat Ali: A Biography*, pp.303, 316).

94 Choudhary Rahmat Ali, 'Now or Never: Are We to Live or Perish Forever?' in G. Allana, *Pakistan Movement Historical Documents* (Karachi: Department of International Relations, University of Karachi, nd [1969]), pp. 03–110. Sourced through http://www.columbia.edu/itc/mealac/pritch-ett/00islamlinks/txt_rahmatali_1933.html (accessed 31 May 2013).

95 Ayesha Jalal, op. cit. pp.55–61.

96 R Guha, op. cit. In his recent book *Cricket Cauldron*, Shaharyar Khan, former PCB chairman does not mention Northern India at all in his account of the origins of Pakistan cricket.

97 R Guha, op. cit. pp.164–65.

98 ibid. pp.169–70.

99 S Khan, op. cit. p.7, R Guha, op. cit. pp.270, 280.

100 Guha, op. cit. pp.294–95, 309.

101 ibid. p.295.

102 AH Kardar, *Green Shadows*, pp.101–102.

CHAPTER 4

1 For which see Alex von Tunzelmann, *Indian Summer: The Secret History of the End of an Empire*, p.228.

2 *Tribune* (Ambala), 11 October 1952, p.6. Quoted in Stuart Jackson, 'Post-Partition nationalism in the Pakistan tour of India, 1952–3'; unpublished university dissertation submitted as part of the Tripos Examination in the Faculty of History, Cambridge University, April 2010.

3 *Dawn*, (Karachi), 9 October 1952 and 12 October 1952. This account of the political tensions around the tour is taken from Jackson, see above.

4 ibid. 9 October 1952. Quoted in Jackson, see above.

5 ibid. 10 October 1952. Quoted in Jackson, see above.

6 AH Kardar, *Inaugural Test Matches* (*ITM*), p.81.

7 Waqar Hasan, *An Autobiography*, p.15.

8 AH Kardar, op. cit. p.4.

9 *Dawn*, 13 October 1952. Quoted in Jackson, see above.

10 AH Kardar, op. cit. p.12.

11 Fazal Mahmood, *Fazal Mahmood aur Cricket*, pp.87–88.

12 ibid. pp.90–91.

13 ibid.

14 ibid. pp.96–98.

15 AH Kardar, op. cit. p.20.

16 Fazal Mahmood op. cit. p.100.

17 AH Kardar, op. cit. p.24.

18 ibid. p.69.

19 ibid. pp.72–73.

20 ibid. p.74.

21 Fazal Mahmood, op. cit. p.107.

22 Foreword by the Hon'ble Mr Justice Cornelius of the Federal Court of Pakistan, AH Kardar, op. cit. p.iii.

CHAPTER 5

1 Omar Noman, *Pride and Passion*, p.69. I have not found the original version of this Kureishi quotation.

2 Waqar Hasan, *An Autobiography*, p.46.

3 Personal interview with General Pervez Musharraf, former commander-in-chief.

4 I am grateful to General Tauqir Zia for this information.

5 Hanif Mohammad, *Playing for Pakistan, an Autobiography*, p.25.

6 Noman, op. cit. p.102; Syed MH Maqsood, *Twenty Years Of Pakistan Cricket 1947–67*, p.50.

7 Hanif Mohammad, op. cit. p.28.

8 ibid. See also the Pir's obituary in the *Daily Telegraph*, 19 January 2012.

9 Wallis Mathias, a gentle but courageous middle-order batsman who Hanif Mohammad called 'the best slip fielder I ever saw'. Son of the groundsman at the Karachi Gymkhana, he was often known as Wallis Mathias, even though Mathias was his Christian name. Became the first non-Muslim to play for Pakistan, this was against New Zealand at Dacca in 1955–56. He enjoyed a decent run in the side until a finger injury in nets ended his Test career. He was soon joined in the Test side by another Christian, Duncan Sharpe, an Anglo-Indian from Rawalpindi. He was a different person-ality. Contemporary photographs show someone who could have been a matinee idol on the English stage of the 1950s and his short Test career was terminated by theatrical disputes with Fazal Mahmood and the selectors over his claims to be the first-choice wicketkeeper. Sharpe even-tually migrated to South Australia, with the help of Barry Jarman and played for the state in the Sheffield Shield, although ironically Jarman, his patron, kept him out of the wicketkeeping role.

Apart from the British, the first Christians to contribute to cricket in what became Pakistan were entrepreneurial Goans who tired of Portuguese rule and migrated to Karachi in the mid-nineteenth century. They formed a cricket club in the Goa Portuguese Association and created one of Karachi's best grounds, which staged regular first-class fixtures to the 1950s. Wallis Mathias was the first representative of this Goan community to play for Pakistan. He was fol-lowed by Antao D'Souza, an unsuccessful opening bowler in Pakistan's disastrous tour of England in 1962.

Then there was a gap of thirty-five years until the appearance of Yousuf Youhana, who played just about half of his 90 Test matches before converting to Islam and changing his name to Mohammad Yousuf.

10 Wazir Mohammad interview, November 2012.

11 Syed MH Maqsood, op. cit. p.309.

12 Alfred Gover, *The Long Run: An Autobiography*, p.160. According to Hanif, Gover said 'he is a natural player and should play as he does and he will improve as time passes.' Hanif Mohammad, op. cit. p.8. In his account of the Pakistani Eaglets in his autobiography, Alf Gover seems to mix up the Eaglets teams of 1952 and 1953. I am grateful to Afzal Ahmed for pointing this out, and thus saving me from error.

13 Interview with Sultan Mahmud, fellow tourist for the Eaglets, Lahore, 2012.

14 ibid.

15 Gover, op. cit. p.159. Fazal Mahmood more or less confirms this account: 'after teaching me in-swing and out-swing, he clearly told me that he had no additional technical points to teach me which was not already present in my bowling.' Fazal Mahmood, *Fazal Mahmood aur Cricket*, p.118.

16 ibid. p.124 and Introduction by Sheikh Inam Ashraf.

17 ibid. p.124.

18 AH Kardar wrote a confusing and one-sided account of the political manoeuvring that preceded the tour in *Memoirs of an All-rounder (MOAR)*, pp.272–75.

19 See the invaluable account in *From Babes of Cricket* by Shuja-ud-Din, a member of the touring party who played in three of the Tests.

20 AH Kardar, *MOAR*, p.162.

21 See Shuja-ud-Din, op. cit. p.20. See also Noman, op. cit. p.82. Nazar's absence was a serious blow to Pakistan's fielding.

22 Shuja-ud-Din, op. cit. p.20.

23 AH Kardar, *Test Status on Trial (TSOT)*, p.105.

24 I am grateful to Shahid Kardar for this information.

25 Fazal Mahmood, op. cit. p.35.

26 ibid. p.36.

27 CLR James, *Cricket*, pp.76–77.

28 ibid. p.80.

29 'Owing to this day's cricket there were grave suggestions in certain quarters that Pakistan should not have been given Test status.' AH Kardar, *TSOT*, p.43.

30 Shuja-ud-Din, op.cit. p.23.

31 AH Kardar, *TSOT*, p.55.

32 Quoted in *Sportimes, the Magazine for Sportsmen*, October 1961. I have not traced the article from which the Cardus quote was taken.

33 AH Kardar, *TSOT*, p.69.

34 Fazal Mahmood, op. cit. p.234.

35 ibid. p.126.

36 Gover, op. cit. p.161.

37 Interview with Wazir Mohammad, November 2012.

38 Shuja-ud-Din, op. cit. p.25.

39 Fazal boasted that Hutton 'could not read my in-cutters or leg-cutters. He was repeatedly beaten and was not comfortable.' Fazal Mahmood, op. cit. p.44.

40 ibid. p.49.

41 ibid. pp.263–266.

42 ibid. p.49.

43 ibid. pp.266–67.

CHAPTER 6

1 WR Hammond, 'Cricket My World', quoted in *Cricket Without Challenge*, p.268.

2 *Tribune*, 18 February 1955.

3 *Sportsweek*, (Bombay) 22 July 1973. This is Sarbadhikary's account, and the bracketing and

emphasis are his own: 'Some British enthusiasts, say, at Lord's and the Oval, spot Kardar as a member of the 1946 Indian touring team. They tell him: "Christ – but you don't play negative cricket like the **Indians**, you don't run away from our fast bowlers to square-les [*sic*] like the **Indians** (mischievous, provocative and highly exaggerated reference to Umrigar's drawing away from Trueman on a really nasty wicket during the Manchester Test of the 1952 India-England series), you don't play for a draw like the **Indians**, you play attacking cricket, you play for a win." And Kardar, humbly, oh so humbly, clarifies: "But, then, we are no **Indians**, Sir, we are Pakistanis."'

4 Shuja-ud-Din, *The Chequered History of Pakistan Cricket*, p.27.

5 ibid. p.29.

6 I am relying heavily on Stuart Jackson's original research, see p.525, ch. 4, note 2 for the account of the atmosphere surrounding the Lahore Test.

7 *Tribune*, 4 February 1955.

8 O Kureishi, *Home To Pakistan*, p.67–68.

9 Shuja-ud-Din, op. cit. p.32.

10 Qamaruddin Butt, *Cricket without Challenge*, p.201.

11 For Imtiaz's defiance of orders, see Omar Noman, *Pride and Passion*, p.92.

12 Butt, op. cit. see Foreword by AH Kardar: 'It is rather amusing to relate that when our Board approached the Indians to play the final Test to a finish in view of the first four having been drawn, the Indians promptly declined to accede to our request.'

CHAPTER 7

1 Alan Ross, *Observer*, 11 March 1956. It is quite chilly – and certainly not 'stinking hot' – in Peshawar in February, when the Baig incident took place. A chota peg is a small container used for making individual servings of alcohol. '*Chota*' is the Urdu word for 'small measure'.

2 Throughout the records of the tour, consisting of internal MCC and BCCP communications, telegrams and newspaper reports, various spellings of Baig's name are adopted. I have followed the spelling adopted by AH Kardar in *Green Shadows*; however, it should be noted that the MCC uses the spelling 'Beg' consistently whilst others have used the spelling 'Baig', including the commentator and journalist Omar Kureishi. Where direct quotations are included, the source's spelling has been used.

3 Fazal Mahmood, *From Dusk to Dawn*, p.58. However, I have not been able to trace the source of this quotation, and wonder whether Carr really said it. The 1954 victory meant more for Pakistan than England, meaning that Carr's desire for revenge may have been less than Fazal thought.

4 Tony Lock, *For Surrey and England*, p.104. Lock claims that the phrase was misreported and was no more than 'a most regrettable error but one which could not be blamed on MCC.'

5 Stephen Chalke, *At the Heart of English Cricket: The Life and Memories of Geoffrey Howard*, p.169. Stephen Chalke's account of the incident, based on interviews with the English captain Donald Carr and the tour manager Geoffrey Howard, is invaluable.

6 ibid. pp.171–2.

7 ibid. p.182.

8 Brian Close, *I Don't Bruise Easily*, p.189.

9 Shuja-ud-Din Butt, *From Babes of Cricket to World Champions*, p.36.

10 Hanif Mohammad, *Playing for Pakistan, an Autobiography*, p.83.

11 I am grateful to Najum Latif, who was there, for this description of the crowd's reaction.

12 Chalke, op. cit. p.173.

13 The view of the England team was most clearly set out by Crawford White in the *News Chronicle*: 'Pakistani spectators, as well as MCC fans, seemed surprised at such prompt dismissals against men like Barrington, Tompkin and Swetman – who were at full stretch down the pitch when the ball hit them. If they were between wicket and wicket at that point, it would need a tremendous amount of spin, from a bowler bowling round the wicket as wide as Kardar, to bring the ball back to hit the wicket.'

14 Quoted in Chalke, op. cit. p.180.

15 I am grateful to Con Coughlin of the *Daily Telegraph* for this information.

16 Tony Lock, op. cit. p.119.

17 Chalke, op. cit. p.174.

18 Minutes of meeting held at Lord's, 17 March 1956 at 12.15pm. MCC Library Archive, MCC/CRI/5/1/62 (2 of 2).

19 ibid. The MCC were pressuring the Pakistan cricket authorities to stand Baig down for the fourth Test, so had reason to believe he would not be present. (G Howard to Group Captain Cheema, 13 February 1956, MCC Library Archive, MCC/CRI/5/1/63.)

20 Close, op. cit. p.190.

21 How many tongas were hired? Brian Close, op. cit. p.191, says four, but Lock, op. cit. p.119, says two.

22 AH Kardar, op. cit. p.125.

23 Close, op. cit. p.191.

24 Ken Barrington, *Playing It Straight*, p.42.

25 Chalke, op. cit. p.191.

26 Minutes of meeting held at Lord's, 17 March 1956 at 12.15pm. MCC Library Archive MCC/CRI/5/1/62 (2 of 2).

27 Chalke, op. cit. p.191.

28 See Shuja-ud-Din, op. cit. p.38, for an eyewitness account by a senior, though anonymous, member of the Pakistan team.

29 Minutes of meeting held at Lord's, 17 March 1956 at 12.15pm. MCC Library Archive MCC/CRI/5/1/62 (2 of 2).

30 Kardar, op. cit. p.125.

31 ibid. pp.126–7.

32 ibid.

33 ibid.

34 ibid. p.128.

35 Omar Kureishi, 'The Idrees Beg [*sic*] Incident – Inside Story Revealed', *Times of Karachi*, 3 January 1957.

36 ibid. Interestingly, this decision by the journalists is the opposite of that taken by the reporters present in Dacca during India's tour of Pakistan the year before, when Kardar's inflammatory speech was suppressed for the good of the tour.

37 'MCC Players and Manager Apologise to Umpire Idrees Baig' *Nawa-e-Waqt* (29 February 1956) p.1.

38 ibid.

39 Close, op. cit. p.192.

40 'Fuming Reaction of MCC's Action', *Nawa-e-Waqt*, 29 February 1956, back page.

41 Barrington, op. cit. p.40 and Shuja-ud-Din, op. cit. p.37.

42 Mirza Sajid Ali Baig to Viscount Alexander, 13 March 1956. MCC Library Archive, MCC/CRI/5/1/62.

43 G Howard to R Aird, 1 March 1956, MCC Library Archive MCC/CRI/1/5/63.

44 *Wisden 1957*, p.792. The telegram was sent on 2 March 1956, MCC Library Archive, MCC/CRI/5/1/62.

45 Lock, op. cit. p.122.

46 Trevor Bailey, *Wickets, Catches and the Odd Run*, p.64.

47 'Offer to cancel tour declined' *Pakistan Times*, 7 March 1956, MCC Library Archive, MCC/CRI/5/1/62.

48 Minutes of meeting held at Lord's on Saturday, 17 March 1956 at 12.15pm. MCC Library Archive MCC/CRI/5/1/62.

49 ibid.

50 *Wisden 1957*, p.793.

51 'The MCC, however, took a tolerant view of the whole sorry affair and no bonuses were lost.' Tony Lock, op. cit. p.129.

52 R Aird to President, Yorkshire CCC, 17 April 1956, MCC Library Archive, MCC/CRI/5/1/62.

53 R Aird to President, Surrey CCC, 17 April 1956, MCC Library Archive MCC/CRI/5/1/62.

54 Statement by the MCC Committee, 20 March 1956. Taken from *Wisden 1957*, p.793.

55 'A bottle of beer containing about two pints costs about 6/-d, which was more or less the price where we were there, and everything generally is expensive.' G Howard to R Aird, 22 June 1955, MCC Library Archive MCC/CRI/5/1/63.

56 G Howard to Group Captain Cheema, 28 February 1956, MCC Library Archive MCC/CRI/5/1/63.

57 D Carr to R Aird, 28 February 1956, MCC Library Archive MCC/CRI/5/1/63.

58 Geoffrey Howard Tour Report, 27 March 1956 (counter-signed by Donald Carr), MCC Library Archive MCC/CRI/5/1/63.

59 ibid.

60 ibid.

61 G Howard to S C Griffith, 24 February 1956, MCC Library Archive MCC/CRI/5/1/63.

62 ibid. Howard went on: 'One does not want to say too much and I will not do so but what I do want to say is that the lads took it very well indeed and did not show by as much as a glance that they were not happy – either when batting or later in the field.'

63 Chalke, op. cit. p.181.

64 ibid. p.182.

65 Qamar Ahmed, personal correspondence, 7 November 2012.

66 G Howard to R Aird, 22 June 1955, MCC Library Archive MCC/CRI/5/1/63.

67 Henry Cooper to R Aird, 21 November 1955. New Zealander John Reid endorsed this view in his book *Sword of Willow*. 'All I can say is that by comparison with his colleagues of the white coat in Pakistan and India, Idrees Baig was a Frank Chester.'

68 MH Maqsood, *Twenty Years of Pakistan Cricket*, pp.311–12.

69 Chalke, op. cit. p.192.

CHAPTER 8

1 Interview with Jamsheed Marker.

2 I am grateful to Shahid Kardar for this information.

3 AH Kardar, *Green Shadows*, p.4. Mymensingh and Rajshahi are two towns in East Pakistan (modern Bangladesh) approximately 100 miles apart.

4 I am grateful to SF Rehman for this information.

5 I am grateful to Najum Latif, who knew Fazal well, for this insight.

6 Interview with Hanif Mohammad, July 2012.

7 The BCCP had asked for two Tests, according to Fazal Mahmood. See Fazal Mahmood, *From Dusk to Dawn*, p.58.

8 ibid. p.59.

9 Jack Pollard, *The Complete Illustrated History of Australian Cricket*, p.825.

10 ibid.

11 Gul Mohammad became the third and last player to represent both India and Pakistan.

12 Shuja-ud-Din, *The Chequered History of Pakistan Cricket*, p.40.

13 Fazal Mahmood, op. cit. p.60.

14 Syed MH Maqsood, *Twenty Years of Pakistan Cricket*, pp.53–54.

15 Cited by Omar Noman, *Pride and Passion*, p.43.

16 Wazir Mohammad: interview with author.

17 Qamar Ahmed: personal interview.

18 C Valiotis, in, S Wagg (ed.), *Cricket and National Identity in the Postcolonial Age: Following On*, p.116.

19 Noman, op. cit. p.50.

20 Hanif Mohammad, *Playing for Pakistan, an Autobiography*, p.226.

21 Noman, op. cit. p.73.

22 Wazir Mohammad: interview with author.

23 The Lahore journalist and editor Hamid Sheikh commentated in Hindi, alongside John Arlott, for the BBC World Service on India's 1946 tour of England. I am indebted to Najum Latif for this information. Vernacular commentary then seems to have disappeared from domestic broadcasting in Pakistan.

24 Hussain is cited in Noman, op. cit. pp.173–74.

25 Hanif Mohammad, op. cit. p.226.

26 Anatol Lieven, *Pakistan: A Hard Country.*

27 Mubashir played for Lahore.

28 I am relying on Hanif Mohammad, op. cit. pp.6–16.

29 Hanif, op. cit. pp.7–8.

30 ibid.

31 Mushtaq Mohammad, *Inside Out: An Autobiography*, p.14.

32 ibid. p.21.

33 Hanif Mohammad, op. cit. p.18.

34 ibid. p.1. Ameer Bee died in 1994, aged eighty-four, living long enough to see her grandson Shoaib play Tests for Pakistan.

35 ibid. p.18.

36 ibid. p.20.

37 Mushtaq Mohammad, op. cit. p. 27.

38 Hanif Mohammad, op. cit. p.23.

39 Mushtaq Mohammad, op. cit. p.31.

40 AH Kardar, op. cit. p.4.

41 Interview with Nasim-ul-Ghani, March 2012.

42 AH Kardar, op. cit. p.5.

43 Interview with Nasim-ul-Ghani, March 2012.

44 AH Kardar, op. cit. p.16.

45 ibid. p.29.

46 ibid. p.30.

47 Interview with Hanif Mohammad.

48 Hanif Mohammad, *Playing for Pakistan, an Autobiography*, p.102.

49 Interview with Nasim-ul-Ghani, March 2012.

50 Hanif Mohammad, op. cit. p.102.

51 *Wisden* says it lasted 16 hours and 13 minutes, but Hanif in his autobiography insists that the true time was 16 hours and 39 minutes. See Hanif Mohammad, op. cit. pp.100–101.

52 Hanif Mohammad, op. cit. p.105.

CHAPTER 9

1 Shuja-ud-Din, *The Chequered History of Pakistani Cricket*, p.51.

2 Reference to this resignation is made in a draft letter from Flt Lt AH Kardar to the Commander in Chief of RPAF College, Risalpur, to be found in the Kardar papers, dated 15 October 1953. An anguished Kardar tells the commander-in-chief that he has retired from first-class cricket, adding that he has already issued a statement to that effect to Peter Jackson, the Reuters representative in Karachi. However, I have been unable to find any newspaper report or even reference to this resignation, and there is no way of telling whether the Kardar letter to the commander-in-chief was ever sent.

3 Hanif Mohammad, *Playing for Pakistan, an Autobiography*, and Wazir Mohammad, interview with the author.

4 Fazal Mahmood, *From Dusk to Dawn*, p.65. 'Kardar was made the chairman of the selection committee. However, I had clearly told the BCCP that I would not allow the selection committee to impose its team on me and that I should have a definite say in the selection.'

5 ibid. p.65.

6 Hanif Mohammad, op. cit. p.120. Fazal challenges this account in his autobiography, dismissing

Hanif's injury as 'mysterious'. But Hanif's version is more coherent and should be preferred. See Fazal Mahmood, op. cit. p.66.

7 Fazal Mahmood, op. cit. p.67.

8 Interview with Imran Khan.

9 Shuja-ud-Din, op. cit. p.57.

10 *Sunday Morning News Karachi*, dated 16 October 1960, p.7. Asked whether he would play even if not selected to captain, Kardar replied, 'My offer is unconditional.' He further said, 'Our batting is fairly strong but our fast bowling is rather weak.'

11 See *Dawn*, 2 October 1960, p.10.

12 ibid.

13 *Nawa-e-Waqt*, 23 October 1960, back page.

14 I am grateful to Najum Latif for his eye-witness account of Kardar's downfall. Mr Latif has also supplied many details concerning Kardar's hopeless comeback attempt. See also *Sportime*, November 1960.

15 Mushtaq Mohammad, *Inside Out*, pp.43–4.

16 See Omar Kureishi, *Ebb and Flow*. 'I learnt, unofficially, that Ayub Khan had been furious and called the players *goondas*. He had indicated too that henceforth the manager of the cricket team should be a senior army officer, a sort of martial law within a martial law.'

CHAPTER 10

1 See Omar Noman, *Pride and Passion*, p.107. 'One of the most intriguing counter-factuals of the decade is whether Pakistan should have prepared spinning wickets to take advantage of a trio of match-winning spinners – Mushtaq, Intikhab and Pervez Sajjad – instead of relying on a series of extremely mediocre medium pacers.'

2 Constituent Assembly (Legislature) of Pakistan Debates, Tuesday, 24 March 1953, Official Report, p.643.

3 Statement showing the grants-in-aid released to National Games and Sports Organisations from 1958–59 to 1967–68. National Assembly of Pakistan, 29 January 1969.

4 Shuja-ud-Din, *The Chequered History of Pakistan Cricket*, p.70.

5 *Pakistan Times*, 19 April 1962.

6 See Humayun Mirza, *From Plassey to Pakistan*, p.230.

7 See *Wisden 1963*, p.302: 'That the tour went through so pleasantly was due to the courtesy of the manager, Brigadier RG Hyder, and his assistant Major SA Rahman . . . '

8 Tom Graveney, *Tom Graveney on Cricket*, p.119.

9 Rafiushan Qureshi, 'The Irresponsibility of Pakistani Players', *Nawa-e-Waqt*, 5 July 1962.

10 Sultan Arif, 'Defeat in Third Test', *Nawa-e-Waqt*, 10 July 1962.

11 ibid.

12 Malik Fateh Khan, 'Cricket: A Problem,' *Nawa-e-Waqt*, 3 July 1962.

13 'Poor captaincy; reason for defeat', *Nawa-e-Waqt*, 17 July 1962.

14 Fazal Mahmood, *From Dusk to Dawn*, p.87.

15 See ibid. pp.85–90 for how Fazal believed that Cornelius had been pressurised into dropping him ahead of the tour. His account should be treated with caution.

16 ibid. p.88.

17 ibid.

18 Quoted in ibid. p.89.

19 ibid. p.88.

20 Javed Burki himself told me that he has never seen a copy. Personal interview.

21 Mushtaq Mohammad, *Inside Out*, p.80.

22 *Wisden 1966*, p.832.

23 Shuja-ud-Din, op. cit. p.89. Khalid Ibadulla was a great lost talent for Pakistan cricket. Bitterly disappointed at being excluded from the 1954 tour of England, he became the first Pakistani to qualify as a professional in English county cricket, for Warwickshire. He actually played more

matches against Pakistan than for them. Later he was decorated for his services as a cricket coach – in New Zealand, not Pakistan. (Khalid Ibadulla: personal interview.)

24 Zahid Zia Cheema, *Majestic Khan*, p.12. However, Pervez Sajjad has told me that there was no complaint from the Australians and suggested that this story was a cover for domestic intrigue.

25 Hanif thought he was not out. Hanif Mohammad, *Playing for Pakistan, an Autobiography*, pp.166–7. In the short tour Hanif made 402 runs in three completed innings, and he confounded the prediction of the recently retired Neil Harvey that he would be barracked by Australian crowds. (See N Harvey, *My World of Cricket 1963*, p.124.)

26 See above p.234 *et seq.*

27 *Wisden 1966*, p.832.

28 Imran Khan, *Pakistan: A Personal History*, p.38.

29 ibid.

CHAPTER 11

1 My narrative of political and military events is condensed heavily from two main sources: Sir Morrice James, *Pakistan Chronicle*, pp.166–91, and Owen Bennett Jones, *Pakistan: Eye of the Storm*, ch. 4.

2 Interview with Asif Iqbal.

3 ibid. Idris Baig was the umpire drenched by the MCC tourists in 1956. Perhaps Asif Iqbal was his delayed revenge.

4 Zahid Zia Cheema, *Majestic Khan*. Foreword by Wasim Bari.

5 ibid. p.8.

6 A description of the early nineteenth century Burkis can be found in Elphinstone's *An Account of the Kingdom of Caubol, Vol 1*, p.411: 'The next class of Taujaks are the Burrukees, inhabit Logur and part of the Boot Khauk. Though mixed with the Ghilijies, they differ from the other Taujkas, in as much as they form a tribe under chiefs of their own, furnish a good many troops to government, closely resemble the Afghans in their manners, and are more respected than any other Taujaks.'

7 K Hussan Zia, *The Pashtuns of Jullundur*, p.2.

8 Imran Khan claims in his autobiography that the Burkis came to India 'after a dispute within their tribe'. I have found no evidence of any dispute. *All Round View*, p.1.

9 K Hussan Zia, op. cit. p.3.

10 Interview with Majid Khan, March 2013.

11 Prof. Farrakh A Khan (ed.), *Reminiscences of an Officer, Aghajan's Service Diary*, pp.18–19.

12 The quotes which follow are all taken from K Hussan Zia, op. cit. pp 99–102.

13 ibid. p.101.

14 Prof. Farrakh A Khan (ed.), op. cit. pp.68–78.

15 K Hussan Zia, op. cit. p.104.

16 According to Aftab Gul.

17 Hanif Mohammad, *Playing for Pakistan, an Autobiography*, p.186.

18 ibid. p.187. One of the headlines in the following day's newspapers announced: 'Only the Police can remove Hanif.'

19 'This strange and (to the bowler) maddening shot, executed by hitting the ball backwards towards third man without changing the grip of the bat, Hanif played during his classic innings of 187 not out against England at Lord's in 1967. The bewildered bowler was Robin Hobbs, a leg-spinner, and Hanif played the shot three times during the innings. Hobbs had never seen it before and recalled years later how very surprised he was.' See Khalid Hasan, Khalid Hasan Online, The Little Master, http://www.khalidhasan.net/2002/08/16/the-little-master/.

20 Interview with Asif Iqbal, London 2012.

21 See Peter Oborne, *Basil D'Oliveira: Cricket and Conspiracy*.

22 See The MCC team's 'Tour Programme in Pakistan' in the 'Special Cricket Souvenir' published by *Sportimes*, January 1969.

23 K Fletcher, *Captain's Innings*, p.43: 'While we were still in Colombo, our manager Les Ames had the first of many meetings with High Commissioners, and emerged poker-faced with the news that both these places were so torn by rioting that the games would inevitably be moved.' See also John Snow, *Cricket Rebel*, p.67: 'When there had been a doubt about our arrival, Dacca had been removed from the schedule because it was considered too dangerous.' According to Shuja-ud-Din, however, Dacca was originally destined to be the second Test. Shuja-ud-Din is in agreement with Fletcher and Snow on the essential fact that Dacca was removed from the original touring schedule ahead of the MCC arrival in Karachi.

24 Snow, ibid.

25 Tom Graveney, *Tom Graveney on Cricket*, p.70.

26 I am grateful to Mustafa Khan, long-serving BCCP official, for this information.

27 Shuja-ud-Din, *The Chequered History of Pakistan Cricket*, p.110.

28 Fletcher, op. cit. p.45.

29 Graveney, op. cit. p.71. The paragraphs above are based on Graveney's admirable and clear account.

30 Snow, op. cit. p.69.

31 Oborne, op. cit. p.79. Gul, today a well-known Lahore lawyer, confirms D'Oliveira's version of events.

32 ibid.

33 Snow, op. cit. p.67.

34 ibid.

35 Graveney, op. cit. p.72.

36 Fletcher, op. cit. p.45.

37 ibid.

38 Oborne, op. cit. p.83.

39 R Sisson and LE Rose, *War and Secession*, p.23.

40 Bennett Jones, op. cit. p.141.

41 The evidence for this is contradictory. See *Wisden 1971* Report pp.968–69 by Ghulam Mustafa Khan: 'In all, 27 teams from both wings of the country were to participate but the teams from East Pakistan withdrew at the last moment, leaving 20 teams from West Pakistan to compete in the [Ayub Trophy] tournament.' And Nauman Niaz, *The Fluctuating Fortunes*, vol 1, p.731: 'Initially, 27 teams got themselves enrolled with the BCCP but later on seven withdrew citing objection against the title and name of the championship. They wanted it to be changed on political grounds and authoritatively, the cricket board refused to budge down, rightly so. Four teams from East Pakistan tendered their inability to play in the tournament.'

42 Nauman Niaz, vol 1, op. cit. pp.731–33; *Wisden 1971*, pp.968–70.

43 I am grateful to Najum Latif for information about the attack.

44 See *Sportimes*, November 1969, p.2.

45 This account is entirely based on the version in Hanif's biography, *Playing for Pakistan*, pp.200–1. It is, however, corroborated in broad outline by Shuja-ud-Din, who wrote that 'the circumstances in which Hanif Mohammad bade farewell to the international arena were most unfortunate to say the least.' Shuja-ud-Din, op. cit. p.115.

46 Hanif Mohammad, op. cit. pp.200–203.

47 ibid.

48 ibid. ch. 32.

49 Nauman Niaz, vol 1, op. cit. p.975.

50 ibid. p.48.

51 So the future Test captain recalled. See Imran Khan, *Imran*, p.54.

52 Personal interviews: Sarfraz Narwaz, Aftab Baloch.

53 Stephen Chalke, *Micky Stewart and the Changing Face of Cricket*, p.186.

54 Interview in www.espncricinfo.com/ci/content/story/88526.html and see also www.thedaily star.net/newDesign/news-details.php?nid=227712.

55 Zakir Hussain, *The Young Ones*, pp.1–2.

56 Sultan F Hussain, *The Fourth Trip*, p.12.

57 ITN transcript on jiscmediahub.ac.uk/mediaContent/open/Scripts/1971/19710619 _LT_01_ITN.

And see Zakir Hussain, ibid., which suggests that there was no prior consultation with the Pakistan players or management over the request to sign the bat.

58 Zakir Hussain, op. cit. pp.13–14.

59 Personal interview with Aftab Gul. Saeed had done this before, according to KH Baloch: 'A temperamental individual, Saeed made a point of defying the management by taking his wife on a tour of Australia and New Zealand in 1964–65. He did the same in England in 1967, contrary to the tour guidelines. On the tour of England in 1971, when not picked for the first two Test matches Saeed simply abandoned the tour party, without leaving any clue as to his whereabouts.' KH Baloch, *Encyclopaedia of Pakistan Cricket, vol II*, pp.268–72.

60 *Wisden 1972*, p.296.

61 Accounts of the Test matches from *Wisden 1972*, pp.295–96, 308–09, 311–12, 316–18 and Nauman Niaz, vol 2, op. cit. pp.1032–43.

62 Eventually the prisoners were repatriated after an agreement in August 1973 (see Sir Morrice James, op. cit. pp.190–91). For prisoners' cricket, see the obituary of Shuja-ud-Din in the *Pakistan Daily Times*, 12 February 2006, p.2. It is pleasant to record that DB Carr (captain of the 'Idris Baig' MCC tour) helped to secure cricket kit for him from the MCC.

63 Sarmila Bose's invaluable *Dead Reckoning*, esp. ch. 9. See also Gary J Bass, *The Blood Telegram*.

CHAPTER 12

1 AH Kardar, *Memoirs of an All-rounder (MOAR)*, p.283.

2 Owen Bennett Jones, *Pakistan: Eye of the Storm*, pp.266–67.

3 'Zulfikar [*sic*] Ali Bhutto: The People's President', a Pictorial Record by the Sindh government information office 1972.

4 Stanley Wolpert, *Zulfi Bhutto of Pakistan*, p.234.

5 Burki made this comment in 1988. It is cited in Chris Valiotis, 'Cricket in a nation imperfectly imagined: identity and tradition in postcolonial Pakistan', in Stephen Wagg (ed.), *Cricket and National Identity in the Postcolonial Age: Following On*, pp.123–24.

6 'Of all the politicians that I knew my longest association and the oldest was with Zulfiqar Ali Bhutto. I first met him in Bombay in 1942 when he came to see the members of the Punjab University Team at the Brabourne Stadium.' AH Kardar, *MOAR*, p.282.

7 I am grateful to Najum Latif, who was told this by Alimuddin. When he became president of Pakistan, Bhutto sought to bring S Mushtaq Ali to Pakistan, but without success.

8 AH Kardar, *MOAR*, pp.282–83.

9 http://timesofindia.indiatimes.com/sports/cricket/top-stories/When-Zulfikar-Ali-Bhutto-played-for-Sunder-Cricket-Club/articleshow/11984125.cms.

10 AH Kardar, *MOAR*, p.283.

11 ibid.

12 http://www.bhutto.org/article55.php.

13 Interview with Shahid Kardar.

14 AH Kardar, *MOAR*, p.142.

15 ibid. p.285.

16 Kardar's nephew Zubair stood for the PPP in Lahore in the national elections of May 2013 but was heavily defeated: www.votepk.com/natioinialassembly-na/na-120-lahore-iii/na-120-election-2013-results-final.

17 See AH Kardar, *Bangladesh: The Price of Political Failure*. Kardar's *Pakistan's Soldiers of Fortune* also contains a full account of his adventures in East Pakistan, where he visited in March, May and November 1970.

18 ibid.

19 ibid. p.158.

20 ibid. In Pakistan government terminology the 'health secretary' is the senior civil servant, equivalent to permanent secretary in Britain. Kardar was offered the post of health minister – equivalent to health secretary in Britain.

21 ibid.

22 AH Kardar, *MOAR*, pp.181–82.

23 Interview with Ghulam Mustafa Khan, November 2012.

24 Zafar Altaf: personal interview.

25 Omar Noman, *Pride and Passion*, pp.52–53.

26 AH Kardar, *MOAR*, pp.188–89.

27 For a fuller account see Shuja-ud-Din, *The Chequered History of Pakistan*, p.155.

28 Zafar Altaf: personal interview.

29 AH Kardar, *MOAR*, p.244.

30 ibid. p.227.

31 ibid. p.208.

32 ibid. pp.220–21. It is not explicitly clear from the context who these 'quislings' were, but on p.221 Kardar refers to Mr Rungta, president of the Indian Cricket Board in 1975, stating that he took him aside during the finals of the World Cup at Lord's 'and proposed that I should undertake a visit to South Africa as a representative of the ICC to assess and report on the progress of the gradual transition in the relations between white and non-white cricketers.

   'Although deeply shocked at the suggestion put to me, I politely asked Mr Rungta, "Are you familiar with the policies of the Indian government on this issue? I believe there is no room for any such visit until the racist government of South Africa changes."'

33 ibid. pp.221–22.

34 Zafar Altaf: personal interview.

35 AH Kardar, *MOAR*, pp.208–9.

36 Zafar Altaf; personal interview.

37 ibid.

38 Tim Caldwell, right-arm fast medium and right-handed batsman, played for New South Wales in the Sheffield Shield, 1935–37.

39 AH Kardar, *MOAR*, pp.233–34.

40 For example AR Cornelius, Jahangir Khan, Fazal Mahmood, Majid Khan, Hanif Mohammad, Saeed Ahmed, Imran Khan.

41 Nauman Niaz, *The Fluctuating Fortunes*, vol 2, p.1052.

42 Zafar Altaf: personal interview.

43 Shuja-ud-Din, op. cit. p.132. Shuja-ud-Din says that 'the tour committee was of the opinion that Saeed was simply afraid of facing Dennis Lillee and fellow fast bowlers on a green top and thus was guilty of lame excuses.

   'With the blessing of AH Kardar, the committee declined to hand his return ticket to Pakistan unless he provided a written apology. On his refusal to do so, he was left in Sydney, an extraordinary punishment, as the team proceeded on their New Zealand leg of the tour. At that stage the Pakistan Sports Board intervened and arranged for Saeed to return home.' Shuja-ud-Din judiciously concludes that 'whatever be the nature of intent of the misdemeanour or irresponsible behaviour of Saeed as a selected player in the national team on tour abroad, the punishment meted out to him by leaving him in the lurch in a foreign country can under no circumstances be considered a wise step.'

44 I am grateful to Najum Latif for passing on this remark. Najum himself remembers Saeed's cover drive as the most exciting stroke in world cricket during his heyday.

45 Noman, op. cit. p.143.

46 KH Baloch and MS Parvez, *Encyclopaedia of Pakistan Cricket*, p.270.

47 Saeed Ahmed: personal interview.

48 Ilyas was sacked shortly afterwards. Interview with the author during third England–Pakistan Test match in Dubai, February 2012.

49 Noman, op. cit. p.146.

50 *Wisden 1974*, p.912 *et seq.*

51 Christopher Martin-Jenkins, *The Complete Who's Who of Test Cricketers*, p.501.

52 Zahid Zia Cheema, *Majestic Khan*, p.40. Cheema provides an invaluable analysis of the sacking

of Intikhab, and the role played by Kardar. I am also grateful to Asif Iqbal for an account of this incident (interview with author, London 2012).

53 Niaz, vol 2, op. cit. p.1097.

54 *Wisden 1975*, p.343; Niaz, vol 2, op. cit. pp.1113–15.

55 For a critique of Zaheer, see Noman, op. cit. pp.149–50: 'And alas, he always seemed to fail under pressure. The double century at the Oval released some of the tension on Zaheer, but a 240 on a flat track was perhaps worth less than a fifty or so on a difficult wicket in trying circumstances,' sighs Noman.

56 Niaz, vol 2, op. cit. pp.1129–1130.

57 Sadiq Mohammad: personal interview.

58 *Wisden 1975*, p.994. Niaz, vol 2, op. cit. p.1133.

59 Niaz, vol 2, op. cit. p.1146.

60 Javed Miandad, *Cutting Edge: My Autobiography*, p.16.

61 Niaz, vol 2, op. cit. p.1138. However, there is no evidence that Majid ever sought to pass off the blame to Kardar. Majid himself told me 'I ignored his little notes' (personal interview).

62 Shuja-ud-Din, op. cit. p.150.

63 ibid. Asif Iqbal was out of action with a sinus operation and Majid Khan, Sadiq Mohammad and Mushtaq Mohammad – all potential captains – all failed to commit themselves to the tour.

64 ibid. p.151.

65 ibid.

66 Intikhab Alam gave this self-assessment in a personal interview, although he promised me that his imminent memoirs would be outspoken.

67 Noman quotes Saleem Altaf as follows: 'I have played under many captains – Hanif, Intikhab, Asif, Majid, Mushtaq. Mushtaq was the best of the lot. He was a courageous captain, and led from the front, somewhat similar in that sense to Imran.' Noman, op. cit. p.155.

68 Mushtaq learnt he would be captain only three days before, while captaining ZA Bhutto's XI against the tourists at Rawalpindi. See Mushtaq Mohammad, *Inside Out*, p.142.

69 ibid. p.143.

70 For example, see Kardar's account of meeting his team at Karachi station for the match against the MCC in 1951: 'I was furious to see the Englishmen alighting from first-class compartments and ours from second class . . . I made the board agree never to repeat this practice.' Kardar appears to have been annoyed not that his players were travelling second class but at the public disparity with their opponents. AH Kardar, *MOAR*, pp.186, 243.

71 Hanif and Mushtaq Mohammad: personal interviews.

72 Wasim Bari: personal interview.

73 Sadiq Mohammad, Mushtaq Mohammad: personal interviews.

74 Majid Khan: personal interview. *Wisden 1977*, p.1082.

75 Majid Khan: personal interview.

76 ibid.

77 Mushtaq Mohammad, op. cit. p.144. The Karachi Test concluded on 4 November 1976, and the first fixture of the Australia tour, against Western Australia, was played on 18 December. Mushtaq's claim that the team was due to fly to Australia three days after the Karachi Test is baffling.

78 See the illuminating account by Qamar Ahmed, 'Rebellions, Revolts not Uncommon to Pakistan cricket,' *Dawn*, 13 July 2009, http://archives.dawn.com/archives/177574.

79 AH Kardar, *The Cricket Conspiracy*, p.14.

80 Mushtaq, op. cit. p.145.

81 ibid. p.146.

82 Henry Blofeld, *The Packer Affair*, p.151.

83 See Press Release published after BCCP meeting in Lahore, 21 November 1976: 'In view of the above serious nature of the situation created by Mushtaq Mohammad the Council deemed it necessary to appoint as captain a person of impeccable integrity and proved [*sic*] service to the cause of Pakistan cricket and therefore decided to appoint Mr Intikhab Alam as captain of the Pakistan Team touring Australia and the West Indies. Mr Zaheer Abbas was appointed Vice-Captain of the team.' Reprinted in AH Kardar, *The Cricket Conspiracy*, p.59.

84 AH Kardar, op. cit. p.246. The account of the resignation is based on a conversation with Shahid Kardar.

85 Sadiq Mohammad: personal interview.

86 Telephone interview: May 2013.

PART TWO – INTRODUCTION

1 Omar Noman, *Pride and Passion*, pp.18–24.

CHAPTER 13

1 Omar Noman, *Pride and Passion*, p.160.

2 ibid. p.164.

3 *Wisden 1978*, p.921.

4 I have drawn heavily on the inspired discussion of the impact of Packer on world cricket in Noman, op. cit. p.164–66. For a well-sourced and superbly written contemporary account, see Henry Blofeld, *The Packer Affair*.

5 Personal interview.

6 See Shuja-ud-Din, *The Chequered History of Pakistan*, p.174. The move was almost certainly aimed at the rebels, all of whom (bar Majid and Wasim Bari) were playing county cricket.

7 ibid.

8 ibid.

9 See *Wisden 1979*, p.897.

10 ibid. *Wisden* records that the radio announcement was as much a mystery to Imtiaz Ahmed, chairman of selectors, as to anyone else.

11 *Wisden* recorded of McGlew that 'although as a feat of endurance and concentration it was remarkable, it is doubtful whether South Africa benefited by it.'

12 Blofeld, op. cit. p.195.

13 ibid. Probably the rioting began as a result of an attack on Bhutto supporters by a rival faction.

14 ibid.

15 According to Shuja-ud-Din, op. cit. pp.175–6. Shuja-ud-Din says that 'as a direct result of Sarfraz Nawaz's bizarre action, the match fee for Pakistan players was increased from Rs 5,000 to Rs 7,000, although the fast bowler had to make a public apology'. He also states, not implausibly, that it was only an intervention from General Zia that forced the cricket board to give in to Sarfraz's demands. Blofeld (op. cit. pp.154–5) also provides a colourful account of Sarfraz's peregrinations.

16 Personal interview: Henry Blofeld.

17 See Henry Blofeld, *The Packer Affair*, pp.155–70, a key source for the events which followed. Blofeld lists Imtiaz Ahmed (chairman of selectors), Fazal Mahmood, Colonel Zafar (board secretary), Mahmood Hussain, Kardar, Hanif Mohammad and Omar Kureishi as attending the meeting. He says that Hanif and Kureishi were the only two opponents of the Pakistan Board at the meeting.

18 Shuja-ud-Din, op. cit. p.182. Shuja-ud-Din says there was another meeting in the cantonment at Lahore.

19 According to Blofeld, 'After the meeting in Pindi, Kureishi contacted Packer, who told him that he was prepared to release his players only in return for a surety they would be selected.' Blofeld, op. cit. p.157.

20 According to Majid Khan, Packer players were thrown out of their jobs with PIA and banks and other state enterprises, even though they were not in breach of their contracts of employment. He believed this was due to government influence. Majid Khan: personal interview.

21 'The situation was complicated', records *Wisden*, 'by the inability of the touring party to discover whether the recall of the Packerites was by direct or indirect invitation of the Board or

was the result of an unofficial action by the pro-Packer faction, a try-on by the Packer organisation, or by command of one of the country's rulers.'

22 Blofeld, op. cit. p.166.
23 Noman, op. cit. p.168.
24 Javed Miandad, *Cutting Edge*, p.34.
25 *Wisden 1979*, pp.288–89.
26 Shuja-ud-Din, op. cit. p.181.
27 Arif Abbasi: personal interview.
28 Javed Miandad, op. cit. p.37.
29 *Wisden 1980*, pp.963–64.
30 Majid Khan: personal interview.
31 BS Bedi interview in the *Hindustan Times*, 2 January 2013.
32 Ramachandra Guha, *A Corner of a Foreign Field*, p.394.
33 Mushtaq Mohammad, *Inside Out*, pp.188–90.
34 Shashi Tharoor, *Shadows Across the Playing Field*, p.40. He added that India 'left the second Test convinced they were facing thirteen opponents, not eleven.' And see Mushtaq Mohammad, ibid.
35 ibid. p.41.
36 *Wisden 1980*, pp.963–64. Bedi had a history of demonstrative protest against what he considered unfair tactics and weak umpiring. On India's West Indies tour in 1975–76 he declared in the first innings at Kingston, Jamaica with just six wickets down, in protest against persistent bouncers. India's second innings ended with five wickets down, only 13 ahead, and Bedi announced that the remaining batsmen were all injured. Mihir Bose, *A History of Indian Cricket*, p.284.
37 Noman, op. cit. p172.
38 ibid.
39 According to Shuja-ud-Din, 'During the New Zealand tour, Pakistan's manager Omar Kureishi was suddenly recalled without even a replacement . . . Omar had allegedly indulged in excessive drinking and created ungainly scenes during official functions, which greatly embarrassed the touring squad.' Shuja-ud-Din, op. cit. p.188.
40 *Wisden 1980*, p.1006.
41 See p.354.
42 Miandad, op. cit. pp.247–48.
43 *Wisden 1980*, pp.1020–21.
44 Miandad, op. cit. pp.122–23.
45 Noman, op. cit. p.178.
46 *Wisden 1980*, pp.303–06 and 310–11.
47 Miandad, op. cit. pp.121–22.
48 Personal interview with Asif Iqbal.
49 ibid.
50 Miandad, op. cit. p.123.
51 *Wisden 1981*, p.994.
52 Majid Khan and Professor Dr Farrakh Khan: personal interviews.
53 There are repeated accounts of this alleged incident, including Part III of the Qayyum Report in 1998, which suggested that there had been heavy betting on the result of the toss. www.espncricinfo.com/db/NATIONAL /PAK/NEWS/qayyumreport.html.

CHAPTER 14

1 Sir Morrice James, *Pakistan Chronicle*, p.210.
2 See 'Economic policy under Zia 1977–88' faculty.lahoreschool,edu.pk/Academics/Lectures/ . . . /PH%204.pdf.
3 See p.423–24. However, in 1983 Zia did resist a bid in 1983 from Dr Asrar Ahmad, an Islamic

scholar, to ban televised cricket because 'it paralysed all constructive activity and . . . was likely to arouse an erotic sensation among feminine spectators.' Reported in *Dawn*, 20 July 1983.

4 James, op. cit. p.208.

5 Mushtaq Mohammad, *Inside Out*, p.219.

6 Omar Noman, *Pride and Passion*, p.186.

7 Javed Miandad, *Cutting Edge*, p.45.

8 Noman, op. cit. pp.192–94.

9 Miandad, op. cit. p.180.

10 By the owner of his local club, Sangam CC, whom Qamar Ahmed described to me as an expatriate Pakistani businessman, based in Bradford. See Noman, op. cit. p.187 and Shuja-ud-Din (with Mohammed Salim Pervez), *The Chequered History Of Pakistan Cricket 1947–2003*, p.198. Mushtaq himself claims credit for Tauseef's selection: Mushtaq Mohammad, op. cit. p.220.

11 Shuja-ud-Din, op. cit. p.201.

12 ibid. p.203.

13 ibid. p.202.

14 Noman, op. cit. p.189. Jack Bailey was watching this match as an ICC observer. Arif Abbasi told me that Bailey offered to ban Clarke if the BCCP protested. Abbasi refused, since Clarke had retaliated rather than provoked the attack. The issue was smoothed over by a visit and gifts from Clarke to his attacker. Arif Abbasi: personal interview.

15 Shuja-ud-Din, op. cit. p.203; Noman, op. cit. p.189.

16 Shuja-ud-Din, op. cit. p.202.

17 Miandad, op. cit. p.246.

18 Noman, op. cit, p.191.

19 Shuja-ud-Din, op. cit. pp.211–12.

20 Miandad, op. cit. p.58.

21 Imran was the key figure. Arif Abbasi said later that he was ready to return for the Test but was prevented by other senior players. 'They knew that if he returned the rest would have a very weak bargaining position.' Arif Abbasi told me that on the eve of the Lahore Test, Imran was willing to play but disappeared in the early hours to talk to Sarfraz Nawaz. Arif Abbasi: personal interview.

22 Miandad, op. cit. p.52.

23 Noman, op. cit. p.193.

24 ibid. p.194.

CHAPTER 15

1 Imran Khan, *All Round View* (*ARV*), p.4.

2 Personal interview.

3 There is an interesting short account of this tour in *History of Pakistan Junior Cricket*, compiled by Maqsood Ahmed Khan. Imran played in the side match at Sahiwal for Multan Zone Under-19s, which was drawn. Details of his performance are not recorded, but Maqsood Ahmed Khan wrote that he impressed with the bat in the trials. This tour coincided with MCC's much-troubled visit but appears to have passed off without disturbance.

4 Imran Khan, *ARV*, p.6.

5 ibid. p.7.

6 Personal interview: Javed Zaman.

7 Omar Noman, *Pride and Passion*, pp.196–7.

8 Imran Khan, *ARV*, p.53.

9 Majid Khan: personal interview; see also Javed Miandad, *Cutting Edge*, pp.142–43.

10 Cited in Noman, op. cit. p.198, and confirmed to me by Imran in a personal interview.

11 *Wisden 1983*, pp.341–42; Shuja-ud-Din, *The Chequered History of Pakistan Cricket*, p.217; Noman, op. cit. p.195.

12 *Wisden 1983*, pp.343–45; Shuja-ud-Din, op. cit. p.218.

13 Omar Noman brilliantly notes that 'while Pakistan were whitewashing Australia, the West Indies were doing the same to England. The world of cricket had undergone a revolution in just a few years. The two teams that had dominated cricket for much of its history were now being annihilated.' Noman, op. cit. p.198.

14 The analysis of the Test series is based on Noman, op. cit. p.199.

15 Javed Miandad, op. cit. ch. 7.

16 Christopher Sandford, *Imran Khan*, p.164.

17 Shuja-ud-Din, op. cit. p.228; Sandford, op. cit. p.166.

18 Shuja-ud-Din, op. cit. p.231.

19 Noman, op. cit. pp.199–200.

20 This account is based on Imran's own long, detailed description of his battle against injury in *ARV*, pp.57–67.

21 Imran Khan, *ARV*, p.59.

22 Shuja-ud-Din, op. cit. p.232.

23 *Wisden 1984*, pp.295–314; Shuja-ud-Din, op. cit. pp.232–34.

24 According to Shuja-ud-Din, op. cit. p.236.

25 Noman, op. cit. p.202; Shuja-ud-Din, op. cit. pp.234–36.

26 Imran Khan, *ARV*, p.62.

27 Shuja-ud-Din, op. cit. p.239.

28 See 'Pakistan's whistle-blower', news.bbc.co.uk/sport1/hi/cricket/1158386.

29 Imran Khan, *ARV*, p.65.

30 ibid.

31 *Wisden 1985*, pp.984–94. Mohsin Khan later changed his mind and played another fifteen Tests.

32 Javed Miandad, op. cit. pp.127–29.

33 In his long career, Botham played only one Test in Pakistan, on which evidence he rated the country 'the kind of place to send your mother-in-law for a month, all expenses paid.' This throwaway remark would come back to haunt him. It also earned Mrs Waller, the mother-in-law in question, a free holiday in Pakistan courtesy of the *Daily Mirror*, which she greatly enjoyed. See Ian Botham, *Botham: My Autobiography*, p.223 and the author's article 'Are we wrong about Pakistan?' *Daily Telegraph*, 28 February 2012.

34 *Wisden 1985*, pp 909–10; Noman, op. cit. pp.206–07.

35 Noman, op. cit. p208.

36 ibid. pp.209–10; *Wisden 1986*, p.926. Coney regularly supervised the pitch preparations in the series when the umpires did not appear to carry out their responsibilities: Shuja-ud-Din, op. cit. p.252.

37 Osman Samiuddin, 'Left Arm Explorer', www.espncricinfo.com/magazine/content/story/457209.html.

38 John Crace, *Wasim and Waqar*, p.25.

39 *Wisden 1986*, p.948.

40 Crace, op. cit. p.27.

41 Shuja-ud-Din, op. cit. p.254 (Abdul Qadir was already injured and the match was drifting to a draw).

CHAPTER 16

1 Imran Khan *All Round View (ARV)*, p.84.

2 ibid. p.67.

3 ibid. p.68.

4 ibid. p.69.

5 There is a vivid tribute in Javed Miandad, *Cutting Edge*, p.92.

6 Shuja-ud-Din, *The Chequered History of Pakistan Cricket*, p.259.

7 ibid. p.260.

8 ibid.

9 Miandad, op. cit. p.91.

10 Shuja-ud-Din, op. cit. p.262.

11 Imran Khan, *ARV*, p.74.

12 Shuja-ud-Din, op. cit. p.265.

13 Javed's own enthralling account is in Miandad, op. cit. pp.100–03.

14 Imran Khan, *ARV*, p.75.

15 *Wisden 1988*, pp.944–56; Omar Noman, *Pride and Passion*, pp.219–21. There was one on-field spat between Gavaskar and Younis Ahmed (brother of Saeed) who had been recalled to the side after a record interval of seventeen years: Noman, op. cit. p.222.

16 *Wisden 1988*, p.997.

17 ibid. p.990. Gavaskar might have been unhappy at his treatment by the Eden Gardens crowds.

18 Owen Bennett Jones, *Pakistan*, p.124 and see 'War Talk Evaporates on First Pitch: Zia's Cricket Diplomacy Gets High Score in India', *Los Angeles Times*, 23 February 1987.

19 Noman, op. cit. p.223.

20 Javed paid a handsome tribute in his autobiography, op. cit. p.136.

21 Imran Khan, *ARV*, p.84.

22 Shuja-ud-Din, op. cit. p.277.

23 Noman, op. cit. pp.225–26.

24 Imran Khan, *ARV*, p.85.

25 ibid. p.86.

26 Shuja-ud-Din, op. cit. pp.280–81; *Wisden 1988*, p.314.

27 Noman, op. cit. pp.227–28.

28 *Wisden 1988*, pp.328–30.

29 Javed Miandad, op. cit. p.146.

30 They overtook it with 765 in February 2009 against Sri Lanka.

31 *Wisden 1988*, pp.331–32.

32 Osman Samiuddin, 'Nur Khan: A Man who expanded the sport's boundaries', obituary tribute to Nur Khan, *The National*, 19 December 2011.

33 Pakistan's World Cup organiser, Arif Abbasi, had already lined up the Hinduja brothers as sponsors, but they were unacceptable to the Indian government. Arif Abbasi: personal interview. Strictly speaking, Reliance were not a sponsor; they acquired ticketing rights for their money.

34 Ayaz Memon, 'Start of the power shift' article in www.livemint.com, 4 April 2012.

35 *Wisden 1988*, p.263.

36 ibid. p.271.

37 ibid. pp.274–83.

38 Javed Miandad, op. cit. pp.156–58 and *Wisden 1988*, pp.283–84.

39 Imran Khan, *ARV*, p.93.

CHAPTER 17

1 Omar Noman, *Pride and Passion*, p.235.

2 Graham Gooch, *My Autobiography*, p.126.

3 Scyld Berry, *A Cricket Odyssey*, p.138. Berry is one of those cricket journalists who asks broader questions about the cultural and political context of the game. His *Cricket Odyssey* is a minor classic.

4 Gooch, op. cit. p.126.

5 Derek Birley, *A Social History of English Cricket*, p.332.

6 *Wisden 1989*, p.909. This quote is taken from Martin Johnson's long article, 'England in Pakistan, 1987–88', pp.909–13, an invaluable survey of the tour. Chris Broad later would face a much more desperate crisis in Pakistan cricket, when as a match referee in 2009 he became a victim of the attack on the Sri Lankan Test team. See p.481.

7 Shafqat Rana: personal interview.

8 ibid.

9   In Jeremy Coney's whimsical autobiography, *The Playing Mantis*, the chapter on this Pakistan tour strikes the only note of bitterness.

10 *Wisden*, p.911.

11 Imran Khan, *Pakistan*, p.93.

12 Shuja-ud-Din, *The Chequered History of Pakistan Cricket*, p.297.

13 Javed Miandad, *Cutting Edge*, p.171.

14 Shuja-ud-Din, op. cit. p.298.

15 Javed Miandad, op. cit. p.172.

16 Shuja-ud-Din, op. cit. p.300.

17 Noman, op. cit. p.241.

18 See the discussion in Owen Bennett Jones, *Pakistan*, pp.233–34.

19 Sir Morrice James, *Pakistan Chronicle*, pp.208–11; Bennett Jones, op. cit. pp.234–35; Anatol Lieven, *Pakistan: A Hard Country*, pp.79–80.

20 *Daily Telegraph* obituary, 27 October 2007.

21 Lieven, op. cit. p.79.

22 Bennett Jones, op. cit. p.238.

23 ibid. pp.235–36

24 See LM Surhone and others, *Zahid Ali Akbar Khan*.

25 Lieven, op. cit. p.319

26 *Wisden 1990*, p.935.

27 Noman, op. cit. p.241.

28 Mike Coward, *Cricket Beyond the Bazaar*. This book remains one of the finest accounts of an overseas tour ever written.

29 ibid. p.65.

30 Imran Khan, op. cit. pp.131–32. Such was Imran Khan's account. However the *Pakistan Times* of 5 October 1987 tells a slightly more flattering story: as self-imposed opener, Nawaz Sharif was caught at silly point off Winston Benjamin for a duck. It reports his bemused opening partner as Zaeem Qadri, who had a first-class career of two innings without scoring. Nawaz Sharif was more successful at a light-hearted match at the Commonwealth summit in Zimbabwe in 1991, striking five sixes in his two-over innings. Shaharyar Khan and Ali Khan, *Cricket Cauldron*, pp.117–18. Nawaz Sharif outshone John Major and Australia's best cricketing prime minister Bob Hawke, who played in a trial match at Oxford University in 1954, dismissed for 2 by a bowler called R Hadlee (no relation).

31 As attested in personal interviews with Imran himself, Javed Burki, Intikhab Alam and Arif Abbasi.

32 *Express Tribune of Pakistan* report, 23 May 2013.

33 See 'Wanted WAPDA chief jumps through legal loophole to escape capture', *Express News* (Pakistan), 8 July 2013.

CHAPTER 18

1   Javed Miandad, *Cutting Edge*, pp.189–90.

2   Quoted in Omar Noman, *Pride and Passion*, p.264.

3   Javed managed one more in 1996.

4   Noman, op. cit. p.266.

5   Javed Miandad, op. cit. p.201.

6   Inzamam-ul-Haq: personal interview.

7   Miandad, op. cit. p.209.

8   ibid.

9   Among many criticisms, see Noman, op. cit. p.271.

10 Javed Zaman: personal interview.

11 Miandad, op. cit. p.215. The repetition is deliberate, either by Javed himself or his skilled collaborator, Saad Shafqat.

12 Imran Khan, *All Round View (ARV)*, p.95.

13 Shahid Kardar: personal interview.

14 Amol Rajan, *Twirlymen*, p.274.

15 Javed Miandad, op. cit. p.2.

16 Javed also traces the influence of rooftop cricket matches, without pads, against his elder brother, which did wonders for his hand-eye co-ordination. Miandad, op. cit. pp.7–8.

17 ibid. p.51.

18 ibid. p.212. Javed Miandad's chapter on Imran (pp.212–222) is a classic of cricket writing, and without it no full understanding of Imran as a cricketer or a man is possible.

CHAPTER 19

1 Iain Wilton, *CB Fry King Of Sport*, p.25.

2 That remains the accepted story, but Jack Hobbs believed that it was invented by an unsung Oxford undergraduate called Herbert Page. Leo McKinstry, *Jack Hobbs: England's Greatest Cricketer*, p.100.

3 See www.espncricinfo/com/magazine/content/story/310734.html The exotic quality of the chinaman has fascinated cricket writers, as witness Shehan Karunatilaka's wonderful novel *Chinaman*. My friend and collaborator Richard Heller exploits it in his cricket novel *The Network*.

4 Ramadhin did generate a permanent change in the lbw law, as the result of his marathon spell at Edgbaston against England in 1957, when Peter May and Colin Cowdrey kept him out with their pads, for which see Michael Manley, *A History Of West Indies Cricket*, p.115.

5 For the origins of the doosra see http://www.dailytimes.com.pk/default.asp?page=story_30–5-2004_pg3_6. However, Mushtaq Mohammad credits its invention to Prince Aslam, heir to the Nawab of Manavadar, the crowdpleasing Royal spinner of the 1950s.

6 Wasim Akram, *Wasim*, pp.28–29.

7 B Woolmer, T Noakes (with H Moffett), *Bob Woolmer's Art And Science Of Cricket*, p.69 *et seq*, especially pp.283–84. Intriguingly, one of the scientists cited by Woolmer, Dr Rabi Mehta, opened the bowling with Imran Khan at the Royal Grammar School, Worcester, in 1972 (W Bown and R Mehta, 'The seamy side of swing bowling', *New Scientist 1993*, pp.21–24).

8 ibid. pp.261–62.

9 See Rahul Bhattacharya, *Pundits From Pakistan*, p.150 (which inaccurately dates Farrakh Khan's club career to the 1970s); and Sidharth Monga in http://www.espncricinfo.com/maazine/content/ story/604354.html.

10 As team doctor on Pakistan's India tour in 1979–80, Dr Farrakh was one of the first to recommend Imran as a future captain, see Imran Khan, *Imran*, p.107; in 1984 he instigated a medical conference which led to Imran's electrical treatment on his fractured leg, see Imran Khan, *All Round View*, p.65.

11 He scored 1,016 runs in 45 innings, according to MH Maqsood, *Twenty Years Of Pakistan Cricket 1947–67*, p.314. Interestingly, the leading scorer, with 1,608 runs in 38 innings, was the Anglo-Pakistani wicketkeeper-batsman Duncan Sharpe, who played three Tests before falling out with the authorities and emigrating to Australia.

12 Professor Dr Farrakh Khan: personal interview. Another possible mentor for Sarfraz was Saleem Altaf, who shared the new ball with him for Pakistan in several Tests. Saleem was noted for being able to achieve late swing in unfavourable conditions, see Harry Pearson, *The Trundlers*, p.233.

13 Wasim Bari: personal interview.

14 Sarfraz Nawaz: personal interview.

15 Christopher Sandford, *Imran Khan*, p.138.

16 www.geoffboycott.com/index.php/boycotts-world-view/pakistan.

17 See Sambit Bal, 'The birth of reverse swing', www.espncricinfo.com/ci/content/story/ 145722.html and Sidharth Monga, 'Reverse swing', www.espncricinfo.com/ci/content/story/ 145722.html

18 See Wasim Akram, op. cit. ch. 3, 'In At The Deep End'.

19 Wasim Akram, op. cit. and Osman Samiuddin, 'Left Arm Explorer', www. espncricinfo.com/ magazine/content/story457209.html.

20 However, Javed Burki also claims credit for Waqar's discovery: personal interview.

21 John Crace, Wasim and Waqar, ch. 4, 'The Burewala Bombshell'.

22 Lawrence Booth, Arm-Ball To Zooter, gives an entertaining explanation of the zooter.

23 Wasim Akram, op. cit. p.98.

24 Simon Rae, It's Not Cricket, pp.200–01.

25 ibid. pp.199–201 and Ken Piesse, Cricket's Greatest Scandals, pp.164–65.

26 Rae and Piesse op. cit.; Kishore Bhimani, Director's Special Book of Cricket Controversies.

27 Jack Bannister and Don Oslear, Tampering With Cricket, p.58.

28 Martin Crowe, Out On A Limb, pp.131–32.

29 Omar Noman, Pride and Passion, p.170. Faisalabad, third-largest city in Pakistan, formerly known as Lyallpur. Its name (which translates literally as 'city of Faisal') was changed in honour of Prince Faisal of Saudi Arabia.

30 Rae, op. cit. p.204; Crace, op. cit. pp.90–91.

31 Wasim Akram, op. cit. p.64.

32 I am indebted particularly to three sources for this section: Mike Marqusee, Anyone But England, ch. 5, 'The Level Playing Field'; Jack Williams, Cricket And Race, ch. 6; and Murray Hedgecock, 'The Cricket Press in 1992' in Wisden 1993, pp.1313–15.

33 Sun newspaper 10, 16, and 21 December 1987.

34 Adam Licudi and Wasim Raja, Cornered Tigers, p.40.

35 Wisden Cricket Monthly July 1987, p.3.

36 The Times, 21 April 1990. Tebbit's son William was a talented cricketer who is on the Honours Board of the Lord's Indoor Academy as a Young Cricketer of the Year.

37 Marqusee, op. cit. p.153 and Daily Mirror, 8 July 1992, my italics.

38 Sunday Telegraph, 12 July 1992. The article produced a lawsuit, settled out of court by payments to charities nominated by the PCB.

39 In 1987 Pakistan felt a sense of grievance over the appointment of his brother, Ken, to the Test match umpires panel. See Wisden 1988, p.304.

40 Marqusee, op. cit. p.134.

41 ibid. p.159 and Wisden 1993, p.301.

42 Marqusee, ibid. and Wisden 1993, p.1313.

43 Bannister and Oslear, op. cit. pp.16–18.

44 See Daily Mirror and the Sun, 24 and 25 August 1992.

45 Marqusee, op. cit. pp.161–2, and Wisden 1993, pp.264–5.

46 See Martin Williamson, 'An Establishment Fudge,' www.espncricinfo/magazine/content/story/ 478574.html.

47 See in particular Donald Saunders in the Daily Telegraph, 24 September 1992.

48 Wisden 1993, pp.206–07, and Marqusee, op. cit. p.166.

49 Rae, op. cit. p.212.

50 Wisden 1993, p.1315, and Marqusee, op. cit. p.160.

51 Wisden 1993, pp.16–18.

52 Wisden 1993, pp.39–41.

53 Scyld Berry, 'Reverse swing – a rough guide', www.espn.cricinfo.com/fanzone/content/story/ 14221.html.

54 Bhattacharya, op. cit. pp.150–151.

55 ibid. pp.154–55.

CHAPTER 20

1 Omar Noman, Pride and Passion, p.277; Wisden 1994, pp.1066–67.

2 Javed Miandad, Cutting Edge, p.224.

3 Justice Nasim was detested by the opposition Pakistan People's Party for his role in upholding the death sentence against ZA Bhutto. As recently as 2010, Bhutto's son-in-law, president Zardari, described him as a murderer. *Business Recorder* (Pakistan), 26 February 2010.

4 Shuja-ud-Din, *The Chequered History of Pakistan Cricket*, p.365.

5 Javed Miandad, op. cit. p.225.

6 Noman, op. cit. p.280.

7 Javed Miandad, op. cit. p.228. For a full account of the scandal see Qamar Ahmed, *Showdown: The Story of Pakistan's Tour of the West Indies.*

8 Shuja-ud-Din, op. cit. p.375.

9 Noman, op. cit. pp.282–83; *Wisden 1994*, pp.1087–91.

10 Noman, op. cit. pp.285–86; Shuja-ud-Din, op. cit. pp.376–77.

11 Javed Miandad, op. cit. p.234.

12 Shuja-ud-Din, op. cit. p.408.

13 See for example Ken Piesse, *Cricket's Greatest Scandals*, p.20.

14 See his profile as a Cricketer of the Year in *Wisden 1988.*

15 S & A Khan, *Cricket Cauldron*, p.208.

16 Shuja-ud-Din, op. cit. p.379.

17 ibid. p.380 and dailymailnews.com/0411/08/Sports/index.php?id=3. As in the Asif Iqbal coin-toss incident in India, Salim Malik had no business, as the visiting captain, in touching the coin.

18 Noman, op. cit. pp.287–88.

19 Javed Miandad, op. cit. pp.235–37.

20 Noman, op. cit. pp.290–91; Shuja-ud-Din, op. cit. pp.387–88.

21 Shuja-ud-Din, op. cit. pp.389–90.

22 Noman, op. cit. pp.291–92.

23 Shuja-ud-Din, op. cit. pp.392–95.

24 See p.367. Tapeball cricket is a fine training for swing bowlers, and batsmen who have to face them.

25 This account is partially based on Michael Atherton's comprehensive article in *The Times*, 20 March 2012.

26 Shuja-ud-Din, op. cit. p.197.

27 Qayyum Report, Part 1, p.3.

28 For an invaluable discussion of the incident with the toss, see Simon Wilde, *Caught*, pp.28–9.

29 'Return to Sharjah "where match-fixing started",' *Daily Telegraph*, 2 November 2011.

30 See especially 'Bukhatir surprised at ICC's "clearance",' *Gulf News*, 23 March 2000. Bukhatir is warmly defended by Javed Miandad. Source: Miandad, op. cit. pp.94–5, 159–61.

31 Simon Rae, *It's Not Cricket*, p.268.

32 Majid Khan: personal interview; Aamer Sohail: personal interview.

33 Piesse, op. cit. p.260.

34 Shuja-ud-Din, op. cit. p.398.

35 Piesse, op. cit. pp.22–23.

36 *Wisden 1996*, p.1086.

37 Piesse, op. cit. p.24.

38 ibid. pp.24–25; Shuja-ud-Din, op. cit. pp.400–1.

39 Shuja-ud-Din, op. cit. p.405.

40 ibid.

41 Shuja-ud-Din, op. cit. pp.418–19.

42 Noman, op. cit. p.300.

43 According to KH Baloch's normally reliable *Encyclopaedia of Pakistan Cricket 1947–48 to 2004*, Majid was sacked as national team manager in November 1995 then resigned from the World Cup Technical Committee: see Baloch and Parvez, op. cit. p.188.

44 *Wisden 1997*, p.1110.

45 Javed Miandad, op. cit. pp.238–40; Noman, op. cit. p.307.

46 Javed Miandad, op. cit. pp.239–40.

47 ibid. p.241; Shuja-ud-Din, op. cit. p.437.

48 Source: Wasim Akram's evidence to the Qayyum Commission (Part III, paragraph 22 and Findings, Reasons and Recommendations, paragraph 6).

49 It looks like a pointed comment on Intikhab: Yawar Saeed had far less experience of England and of management (he had last managed in 1985 when Pakistan toured New Zealand).

50 Imran was sued over articles which cited him in *India Today* and the *Sun*. Botham and Lamb claimed that he had accused them of being lower-class, ill-educated and racist. Botham also maintained that he had been accused of ball-tampering. After a long trial packed with cricket stars and other celebrities, the jury found for Imran. See 'Cricket and the Law' in *Wisden 1997*, pp.1378–9

51 ibid. p.394.

52 See http://www.cricketarchive.com/Archive/Records/Test/Overall/Players/Youngest_Players_on_Debut.html.

53 Geoffrey Dean, *Daily Telegraph*, 29 October 1996.

54 www.pcboard.com.pk/4/4168/4168.

55 www.unicef.org/pakistan/medi_7993.htm, UNICEF press release 19 November 2011.

56 Arif Abbasi: personal interview. Shaharyar Khan also clamped down on overage players when he became chairman of the PCB in 2004: S & A Khan op. cit. pp.165–66.

57 unesco.org.pk/education/teachereducation/files/sa4.pdf, p.7.

58 See pdffileebook.com/cricket-world-cup-schedue.html 'Age Determination Policy for ICC Under 19 World Cricket Cup'.

59 See for example http://www.app.com.pk/en_/index.php?option=com_content&task=view&id=85323&Itemid=62.

60 R Bhattacharya, *Pundits From Pakistan*, pp.140–43. Wasim Raja was a fine talent-spotter. One of his other finds was Inzamam-ul-Haq (personal interview).

61 http://www.espncricinfo.com/magazine/content/story/225512.html.

62 Mushtaq Mohammad, Sadiq Mohammad: personal interviews.

63 http://news.bbc.co.uk/sport1/hi/cricket/979530.stm and Mushtaq Mohammad: personal interview.

64 Noman, op. cit. pp.311–13. Tendulkar himself eventually eclipsed Saeed Anwar with a one-day double century against South Africa in 2010, and then they were both overtaken by Virender Sehwag's 219 against West Indies in 2011.

65 *Wisden 1999*, pp.1094–96.

66 ibid. pp.1135–38, 1143–44.

67 ibid. pp.1144–49.

68 Piesse, op. cit. p.263. Qayyum Report, paragraphs 8 and 9.

69 Piesse, op. cit. p.27.

70 Qayyum Report, *The Australian Evidence*.

71 Piesse, op. cit. p.27.

72 Qayyum Report, Part I, 1.

73 ibid. Part VI, 64.

74 ibid. Part V, 44.

75 ibid. Part V, 27 quotes Intikhab Alam's match report on the South Africa-Zimbabwe tour of 1994–95 as follows: 'Basit Ali is the only player in the Pakistan team who have [*sic*] made a confession that he has been involved in betting, his retirement from cricket is just to save himself.' Here is a summary of the fines recommended for players by Qayyum: Salim Malik: 10 lakh rupees; Wasim Akram: 3 lakh rupees; Mushtaq Ahmed: 3 lakh rupees; Ata-ur-Rehman: 1 lakh; Inzamam: 1 lakh; Akram Raza: 1 lakh; Saeed Anwar: 1 lakh. In addition, Wasim Akram was removed from the Pakistan team captaincy alongside a recommendation that he should 'be censured, kept under watch and his finances should be investigated'. The judge also recommended that Ata-ur-Rehman, surely a bit-part player, should be banned from international cricket. See ibid. Part VIII, 6.

76 ibid. Part VI, 64.

77 General Musharraf: personal interview.

78 *Wisden 1999*, p.413.

79 Javed Miandad, op. cit. p.274.

80 Mushtaq Mohammad, *Inside Out*, p.256.
81 ibid. pp.261–62.
82 Mushtaq Mohammad: personal interview.
83 See report in www.espncricinfo.com/ci/content/story/118001.html.

CHAPTER 21

1   Mushtaq Ahmed, *Twenty20 Vision*, p.7.
2   ibid. p.8.
3   ibid. p.9.
4   ibid. p.10.
5   ibid. p.12.
6   ibid. p.23.
7   ibid. p.18.
8   For some of the cultural difficulties faced by Mushtaq after leaving Sahiwal, see ibid. pp.25–36.
9   Shoaib Akhtar, *Controversially Yours*, pp.6–9.
10 ibid. pp.34–5.
11 ibid. p.40.
12 ibid. pp.45–51.
13 ibid. p.52.
14 ibid. p.55.
15 ibid. p.56.
16 ibid. p.81.
17 Most of the interviews were carried out by Abdur Rauf, Peshawar journalist.
18 Zulfiqar Ali, 'In Waziristan, craze for cricket knows no bounds', *Express Tribune*, 3 January 2013.
19 In 1970–71, captaining Peshawar, he forfeited a Quaid-e-Azam Trophy match against Rawalpindi in protest at being given out lbw.
20 Rahul Bhattacharya, *Pundits From Pakistan*, p.110.
21 *Wisden 2003*, p.1504 *et seq.*
22 *Wisden 2006*, p.1357.
23 I have adopted the spelling in *Wisden* and the PCB website, although I have seen reports that he prefers Younus.
24 S & A Khan, *Cricket Cauldron*, p.55; R Bhattacharya, op. cit. p.104. In 2009 both the Indian team hotel and the Kissa Khawani bazaar where they shopped were ravaged by terrorist attacks.
25 Source: Cricket Archive.
26 For an eye-witness account, see Rahul Pandita, 'That Day in 1986. How cricket died for me that day 25 years ago', www.openthemagazine.com, 9 April 2011.
27 Quoted in Gowhar Geelani's brilliant account, 'Can Bedi turn it in Kashmir?' *Gowhar Geelani, Kashmir Life, Volume 03, Issue 36,* Monday 14 November 2011.
28 Muzzafar Raina, 'Acquittal for 1983 pitch "diggers"', Muzzafar Raina, *Telegraph* (Calcutta, India), Wednesday 30 November 2011.
29 Acquittals over Kashmir 1983 cricket pitch sabotage', *Mid Day*, Mumbai, 30 November 2011.
30 'Acquittal for 1983 pitch "diggers"', Muzzafar Raina, *Telegraph* (Calcutta, India), Wednesday 30 November 2011.
31 See 'Wind in the willows: A cricket bat paradise', *Al Jazeera*, Azad Essa, 2 August 2011.
32 M Saleem Pandit, 'Cricket as tool to crystallise peace in Kashmir', *Times of India*, 5 July 2011.
33 http://in.news.yahoo.com/army–helping–youths–kashmir–hone–cricket–skills–102536004.html.
34 Kashmir cricketer Abid Nabi Friday joined the rebel Indian Cricket League (ICL). Faisul Yaseen, *www.Kashmirnews.com,* Srinagar, 29 September 2007.
35 http://www.mid-day.com/sports/2011/mar/290311-India-Pakistan-fans-pray-Srinagar.htm. There are also plausible reports that Indian victories are supported in parts of Baluchistan. On 30 March 2011 an Indian newspaper *The Examiner* claimed that 'jubilant crowds' in 'occupied Baluchistan' had celebrated Pakistan's defeat by India in the World Cup. However, in January 2013, a

Baluchistan provincial minister showed his loyalty to the Pakistan team, after their one-day series victories against India, by offering each player a camel worth over 400,000 rupees (around £2,700). See *Pakistan Today*, 7 January 2013.

36 Kashmir catches cricket fever. Section 144 In City, No Big Screens Allowed. *Wasim Khalid, Greater Kashmir*, Srinagar, Wednesday, 30 March 2011.

37 ibid.

38 See 'Kashmiri students briefly charged with sedition for rooting for wrong cricket team', *New York Times*, 7 March 2014.

39 'National cricket selector Asif Baloch injured in attack', 9 December 2012 in www.defence.pk.

CHAPTER 22

1 Nancy Joy, *Maiden Over*, p.20.

2 John Major, *More Than A Game*, p.59.

3 Joy, op. cit. p.23.

4 ibid. pp.26–27; Pete Davies, *Mad Dogs And English Women*, p.13.

5 Davies, op. cit. p.14.

6 Joy, op. cit. pp.45–56 gives a full account of the origins of women's cricket in Australia.

7 Davies, op. cit. pp.14–15.

8 ibid. p.16.

9 ibid.

10 Rachael Heyhoe Flint and Netta Rheinberg, *Fair Play*, p.113. Bombay won a two-innings match over Maharashtra in the final in only one day.

11 ibid. However, on the eve of the 2013 women's World Cup, Diana Edulji slammed the current BCCI for discriminating against India's women cricketers. www.espncricinfo.com/women/content/current/site/207455.html.

12 Javed Burki: personal interview.

13 Mrs Bushra Aitzaz: personal interview.

14 Ayesha Ashhar: personal interview.

15 www.espncricinfo.com/db/National/PAK/Associations/PWCA.

16 For the factional rivalries, see Report on Scrutiny of Women's Cricket Associations, January 2003.

17 Unless otherwise indicated, the narrative in this section is based on personal interviews with Shaiza and Sharmeen Khan and Pakistan's record-breaking Test batter, Kiran Baloch. Match results are derived from Cricket Archive.

18 This is taken from the 2003 Report to the PCB on the Scrutiny of Women's Cricket Associations in Pakistan.

19 Report on Scrutiny of Women's Cricket Associations, January 2003.

20 Kiran Baloch; personal interview.

21 C Shekhar Luthra, in *The Asian Age*, 9 December 1997.

22 Majid Khan: personal interview.

23 Report on Scrutiny of Women's Cricket Associations, January 2003.

24 Mrs Bushra Aitzaz: personal interview.

25 Ayesha Ashhar: personal interview.

26 Mrs Bushra Aitzaz: personal interview.

27 Shaiza and Sharmeen Khan, Kiran Baloch: personal interviews.

28 Report on Scrutiny of Women's Cricket Associations in Pakistan, January 2003.

29 Mrs Bushra Aitzaz: personal interview.

30 Arif Abbasi: personal interview.

31 S & A Khan, *Cricket Cauldron*, pp.109–10.

32 Mrs Bushra Aitzaz: personal interview

33 Certainly none had appeared internationally.

34 Najum Latif: personal information.

35 www.espncricinfo.com/ci/content/story/487927.html

36 beta.dawn.com/news/675691.
37 http://twocircles.net/2013jan29/heavysecuritypakistanwomenscricketteam.html.
38 www.dawn.com/2011/03/22/ex-colleagues-players-praise-shirin-javed.
39 According to Cricket Archive, the online resource which records every significant match played
    in the world (and many insignificant ones).

CHAPTER 23

1 Conversation with Imtiaz Ahmed at the PCB, 31 October 2011. Imtiaz, now 86, contributed
   to this famous 1954 victory with seven dismissals.
2 See above p.39.
3 Conversation with Shaharyar Khan.
4 Arif Abbasi: conversations with author.
5 See above p.320.
6 Arif Abbasi: conversations with author.
7 See Abid Ali Kazi, in *Wisden 1991*, pp.1179 et seq.
8 Ehsan Mani: conversations with author.

CHAPTER 24

1 Shuja-ud-Din, *The Chequered History of Pakistan Cricket*, pp.518–19.
2 *Wisden 2001*, p.1124; Shuja-ud-Din, op. cit. p.525.
3 Shuja-ud-Din, op. cit. p.526.
4 ibid. pp.527–28.
5 ibid. pp.529–30; *Wisden 2011*, pp.1168–69.
6 Shuja-ud-Din, op. cit. pp.546–48; *Wisden 2001*, p.1218.
7 Shuja-ud-Din, op. cit. p.555.
8 Len Hutton faced 636 dot balls in his then record innings of 364 against Australia at The Oval
   in 1938. See www.cricketweb.net/forum/cricket-chat/6217-can-you-beat-cricket-guru-title-
   232.html. I have not been able to ascertain the number of dot balls faced by Hanif Mohammad
   in his 970-minute innings of 337 at Bridgetown in 1958.
9 *Daily Telegraph,* 11 December 2000.
10 Shuja-ud-Din, op. cit. pp.557–58; *Wisden 2002*, pp.1051–53.
11 Shuja-ud-Din, op. cit. pp.58–560. Twenty-four tourists is a record for any cricket country.
12 *Wisden 2002*, p.399.
13 ibid. pp.399–400, 413–15.
14 Shuja-ud-Din, op. cit. pp.566–68.

PART FOUR – INTRODUCTION

1 See Owen Bennett Jones, *Pakistan*, pp.272 and 308–09. At the end of Musharraf's time, the
   armed forces absorbed 18% of Pakistan's national budget compared to 2% for education.
2 Anatol Lieven, *Pakistan: A Hard Country*, p.413.
3 For the spread of sectarian violence, see in particular Bennett Jones, op. cit. p.311.
4 Lieven, op. cit. pp.229–33.

CHAPTER 25

1 Shuja-ud-Din, *The Chequered History of Pakistan Cricket*, pp.580–82, and see 'Inzamam steals
   thunder with masterly 329', 3 May 2002, in www.espncricinfo.com.

2 Richard Boock, *Stephen Fleming*, pp.96–97.

3 S & A Khan, *Cricket Cauldron*, p.19.

4 For a fine tribute to Woolmer, see ibid. pp.68–79.

5 *Wisden 2004*, pp.1142–43.

6 Arif Abbasi: personal interview; Shoaib Akhtar, *Controversially Yours*, p.213.

7 S & A Khan, op. cit. p.77.

8 See S & A Khan, op. cit. pp.76–77; Shoaib Akhtar, op. cit. pp.231, 238–39.

9 *Wisden 2005*, p.1139.

10 ibid. pp.1192–98.

11 ibid. p.1208.

12 ibid. pp.1211–13.

13 Khan and Khan, op. cit. pp.58–59, 63.

14 *Wisden 2005*, p.1198.

15 Khan and Khan, op. cit. p.64.

16 *Wisden 2005*, p.1309. Razzaq later claimed that it was food poisoning rather than excess spinach, see interview in www.pakpassion.net, 15 July 2008.

17 Owen Bennett Jones, *Pakistan*, p.124, and see Soutik Biswas, 'The chequered history of cricket diplomacy', www.bbc.co.uk, 29 March 2011.

18 *Wisden 2006*, p.1021.

19 *Wisden 2007*, p.1090.

20 S Akhtar, op. cit. pp.151–52; *Wisden 2008*, pp.1140, 1389.

21 *Wisden 2007*, pp.1189–92.

22 S Akhtar, op. cit. pp.157–58; *Wisden 2008*, pp.1140–43.

23 S & A Khan, op. cit. pp.269–70.

24 *Wisden 2008*, p.46.

25 ibid. p.1179.

26 ibid. p.1188.

CHAPTER 26

1 For the origins of the ICL see the account in James Astill, *The Great Tamasha*, pp.82–86.

2 See 'PCB bans Pakistan's ICL players', in www.espncricinfo.com, 24 December 2007.

3 See 'Pakistan clears last six ICL players', *AFP Karachi*, 19 April 2013.

4 Figures cited in 'IPL Auction: Players' Worth' on Rediffusion Sports broadcast 20 February 2008.

5 See 'PCB to form policy for IPL players', *Dawn*, 19 March 2008.

6 James Astill makes this connection. See J Astill, op. cit. p.152.

7 See p.284 *et seq.*

8 'Ijaz Butt appointed new PCB chairman', www.espncricinfo.com/pakistan/content/story/372861.html, 7 October 2008.

9 *Wisden 2009*, p.1210.

10 *Wisden 2010*, p.1205.

11 Sri Lanka in 1997 had used 1,626 balls to score the Test record of 952 for 7 declared.

12 *Wisden 2010*, pp.1213–14.

13 ibid. pp.25 and 1205.

14 ibid. p.27. Mohammad Khalil was decorated at a ceremony in Sri Lanka in April 2009, and his family had a holiday there. The Sri Lankans honoured him before Pakistan and the PCB did so. See 'Sri Lanka honour the bus-driving hero of Lahore attacks', *Guardian*, 6 April 2009.

15 ibid. p.27.

16 ibid. p.1202.

17 'Pakistan accuses Chris Broad of "lying" about terror attack', *Daily Telegraph*, 5 March 2009.

18 'Miandad demands life ban for outspoken Broad', *Guardian*, 6 March 2009.

19 'Pakistan register Broad complaint', BBC report, 10 March 2009.

20 *Wisden 2010*, p.1202.
21 Source: conversation with journalists and court officials.
22 *Wisden 2010*, pp.527–33.
23 *Wisden 2011*, p.321.
24 Astill, op. cit. p.152.
25 'The Most Sensational Sporting Scandal Ever', *News of the World*, 29 August 2013.
26 *Wisden 2011*, p.34.
27 ibid. pp.350–51.
28 See 'Clouds gather ahead of Butt's return', www.espncricinfo.com, 5 October 2010.
29 See 'Clean Up Your Act, ICC tells PCB', www.espncricinfo.com, 13 October 2010.
30 *Wisden 2011*, p.1007 and 'Zulqarnain Haider: the man who bid adieu to his career after receiving threats from the bookies' in www.cricketcountry.com, 4 April 2013.

CHAPTER 27

1 See 'Like Imran, Misbah is a Niazi', *Telegraph* (Calcutta, India) 2 January 2013.
2 www.topnews.in/sports/Misbah-ul-Haq-lone-post-graduate-in-Pakistani-cricket-team-211307.
3 See 'Shahid Afridi proud of Pakistan's performance' in www.espncricinfo.com, 30 March 2011.
4 See www.ibtimes.com/cricket-world-cup-pakistan-accused-match-fixing-after-semi-final-loss-india-278201.
5 See 'India-Pakistan ICC World Cup semi-final: BCCI rubbishes match-fixing claims', Press Trust of India report, 11 November 2012.
6 See Ed Hawkins's article in the *Daily Mail*, 9 November 2012.
7 ibid. Executive Summary, paras 2.12–2.13. The PTT's comments could also have been directed at Zimbabwean and Sri Lankan cricket, whose administrations were also strongly influenced by their governments.
8 See 'PCB raises questions about task force report', www.espncricinfo.com, 13 July 2013.
9 See Osman Samiuddin's profile, 'Saeed Ajmal – Cricketer of the Year 2011' in *Wisden India 2012*.
10 See 'Ajmal Action gets ICC's green signal', www.espncricinfo.com, 24 May 2009.
11 See 'Saeed Ajmal claims clarified by Pakistan Cricket Board', on www.bbc.co.uk/sport/0/cricket/16929410, 7 February 2012.

GREEN ON WHITE

1 Shahid Kardar: personal interview.

Bibliography

BOOKS

Abid Ali Kazi, *First-Class Cricket in Pakistan, Vol 1* (Pakistan Association of Cricket Statisticians and Scorers, 1997), *Vol 2* (1998), *Vol 3* (1999), *Vol 4* (2000), *Vol 5* (2003)

Aijazuddin, FS, *Commanding Success: Aitchison College 1886–2011* (Lahore: Lé Topical, 2011)

Akbar, Mubashar Jawed (M J), *Tinderbox: The Past and Future of Pakistan* (Noida: Harper Collins Publishers India, 2011)

Amarnath, Rajender, *The Making of a Legend: Lala Amarnath Life & Times* (Cheltenham: Sportsbooks Ltd, 2007)

Ansari, Sarah, *Sufi Saints and State Power: The Pirs of Sind, 1843–1947* (Cambridge: Cambridge University Press, 1992)

Anwar Ahmed Khan, *ANWAR: The Autobiography of Anwar Ahmed Khan* (Karachi: Liliana International Publishers, 1990)

Astill, James, *The Great Tamasha* (Wisden Sports Writing, 2013)

Bahadur, Nawab Jiwan Yar Jung, *My Life Being The Autobiography Of Nawab Server-Ul-Mulk Bahadur* (Nabu Public Domain, 1923)

Bailey, Trevor, *Wickets, Catches and the Odd Run* (London: Willow Books, 1986)

Bala, Rajan, *The Covers Are Off: A Socio-historical Study of Indian Cricket, 1932–2003* (New Delhi: Rupa & Co., 2004)

Baloch, Khadim Hussain, *Summer of Swing* (Pakistan: Akhbar-e-Waten, September 1992)

Baloch, Khadim Hussain with Baluch, Mohammad Hussain, Statistics by M. Shoaib Ahmed, *Pakistan Cricket: A Compilation of the History. A Century of Karachi Cricket* (Karachi: Mujahid Book Stall, no publication date given)

Baloch, Khadim Hussain and Parvez, Mohammad Salim, *Encyclopaedia of Pakistan Cricket 1947–48 to 2004, Vols I and II* (published privately in Pakistan) (Karachi: Al-Asad Printers, 2005)

Bannister, Jack and Oslear, Don, *Tampering With Cricket* (London: Collins Willow, 1996)

Barrington, Ken, *Playing It Straight* (London: Stanley Paul, 1968)

Barrington, Ken as told to Pilley, Phil, *Running Into Hundreds* (London: Stanley Paul,1963)

Bashir Khan, *Over to Bashir Khan: Pakistan in India 1987. An eyewitness account of Pakistan 1987 cricket tour of India* (Karachi: Karachi Type Foundaries (Pvt) Ltd, 1989)

Bass, Gary J, *The Blood Telegram* (Knopf, 2013)

Bateman, Anthony and Hill, Jeffrey (eds), *The Cambridge Companion to Cricket* (Cambridge: Cambridge University Press, 2011)

Begg, WD, *Cricket and Cricketers in India* (Allahabad, India: Press Ltd, 1929)

Bellamy, Rex, *Squash: A History* (London: Heinemann Kingswood, 1988)

Bennett Jones, Owen, *Pakistan: Eye of the Storm* (Yale University Press, 2009)

Berry, Scyld, *A Cricket Odyssey: England on Tour 1987–88* (London: Pavilion Books Ltd, 1988)

Bhattacharya, Rahul, *Pundits From Pakistan* (Picador, 2005; Penguin India, 2012)

Bhatti, Mukhtar (compiled and edited), *Pakistan Sports: Golden Jubilee of Pakistan 1947–1997* (Lahore: Bhatti Publications, 1997)

—— (comp. & ed), *Golden Jubilee of Test Cricket,* (Lahore: Ababeel Publications, 2003)

—— (comp. & ed), *Silver Jubilee of One-Day Cricket* (Lahore: Ababeel Publications, 2006)

—— (comp. & ed), *Cricket World Cup Guide* (Lahore: Ababeel Publications, 2008)

—— (comp. & ed), *Pakistan Sports: An Almanac of Pakistan Sports with complete records 1947–1999* (no publisher given)

Bhimani, Kishore, *Director's Special Book Of Cricket Controversies* (Allied Publishers Bombay, 1992)

Bhutto, Benazir, *Daughter of the East: An Autobiography* (London: Pocket Books, 2008)

Birley, Derek, *A Social History of English Cricket* (Aurum, 2003)

Blackburne Hamilton, Col Henry, *Historical Record of the 14th (King's) Hussars from 1715 to 1900* (London: Greene & Co, 1901)

Blofeld, Henry, *The Packer Affair* (London: Collins, 1978)

Bolitho, Hector, *Jinnah: Creator of Pakistan* (Oxford: Oxford University Press, 2006)

Boock, Richard, *Stephen Fleming: Balance of Power* (Hodder Moa Beckett, New Zealand, 2004)

Booth, Lawrence, *Arm-ball To Zooter* (Penguin, 2007)

Bose, Mihir, *A History of Indian Cricket* (London: Andre Deutsch, 2002)

—— *A Maidan View: The Magic of Indian Cricket* (London: George Allen & Unwin, 1986)

—— *Game Changer* (London: Marshall Cavendish, 2012)

Bose, Sarmila, *Dead Reckoning: Memories of the 1971 Bangladesh War* (Pakistan: C Hurst & Co Publishers Ltd, 2011)

Botham, Ian, *Botham: My Autobiography – Don't Tell Kath* (London: Collins Willow, 1994)

—— *Head On: Ian Botham, The Autobiography* (London: Ebury Press, 2007)

Bowen, Rowland, *Cricket: A History of Its Growth and Development Throughout The World* (London: Eyre & Spottiswoode, 1970)

Braibanti, Ralph, *Chief Justice Cornelius of Pakistan: An Analysis with Letters and Speeches* (Oxford: Oxford University Press, 2000)

Chalke, Stephen, *At the Heart of English Cricket: The Life and Memories of Geoffrey Howard* (London: Fairfield Books, 2001)

—— *Micky Stewart and the Changing Face of Cricket* (Bath: Fairfield Books, 2011)

Cheema, Zahid Zia, *Majestic Khan* (Islamabad: DIA Publications, The Wall Street Printers, 1996)

Close, Brian, *I Don't Bruise Easily* (London: MacDonald and Jane's, 1978)

Cohen, Stephen Philip, *The Idea of Pakistan* (Washington, DC: Brookings Institution Press, 2004)

Coney, Jeremy, *The Playing Mantis* (Moa, New Zealand, 1985)

Copland, Ian, *The Princes of India in the Endgame of Empire, 1917–1947* (Cambridge: Cambridge University Press, 1997)

Coward, Mike, *Cricket Beyond the Bazaar* (London: Allen and Unwin, 1990)

Cox, Peter, *Sixty Summers: English Cricket Since World War 2* (Cambridge: Labatie Books, 2006)

Crace, John, *Wasim and Waqar: Imran's Inheritors* (London: Boxtree Ltd, 1992)

Crowe, Martin, *Out On A Limb* (Reed New Zealand, 1995)

Dalrymple, William, *The Last Mughal* (London: Bloomsbury, 2006)

Davies, Pete, *Mad Dogs And English Women* (Abacus, 1998)

De Mello, Anthony, *Portrait of Indian Sport* (London: Macmillan, 1959)

Docherty, Paddy, *The Khyber Pass: A History of Empire and Invasion* (London: Faber & Faber, 2007)

Ellis, Clive, *C.B.: The Life of Charles Burgess Fry* (London: JM Dent & Sons Ltd, 1984)

Elphinstone, Mountstuart, *An Account of the Kingdom of Caubol, Vol 1* (London: R Bentley, 1842)

Fazal Mahmood, *Urge to Faith* (Lahore: The Lion Art Press Limited, 1970)

Fazal Mahmood with Ashraf, Sheikh Inam, *Fazal Mahmood aur Cricket* (*Fazal Mahmood and Cricket*) (Lahore: Darul Balagh, 1955)

Fazal Mahmood with Asif Sohail, *From Dusk To Dawn: Autobiography of a Pakistan Cricket Legend* (Oxford: Oxford University Press, 2003)

Fletcher, Keith, *Captain's Innings: An Autobiography* (London: Hutchinson, 1983)

French, Patrick, *Liberty or Death* (London: HarperCollins, 1997)

Garrett, HLO and Hamid, Abdul, *A History of Government College, Lahore 1864–1964* (Lahore Government College, 1964)

Gavaskar, Sunil, *Runs and Ruins* (India: Rupa & Co, 1984)

Gleig, Rev. George Robert, *Sale's Brigade in Afghanistan, with an account of the seizure and defence of Jellalabad* (London: John Murray, 1846)

Gooch, Graham with Keating, Frank, *My Autobiography* (London: Collins Willow, 1995)

Gover, Alfred, *The Long Run: An Autobiography* (London: Pelham Books, 1991)

Graveney, Tom, *Tom Graveney on Cricket* (London: Frederick Muller, 1965)

Guha, Ramachandra, *A Corner of a Foreign Field: The Indian History of British Sport* (London: Picador, 2003)

Haigh, Gideon (ed.), *Peter the Lord's Cat and Other Unexpected Obituaries from Wisden* (London: Aurum Press, 2006)

—— *Sphere of Influence: Writings on cricket and its discontents* (London: Simon & Schuster, 2011)

Halliday, Tony (ed.), *Insight Guides: Pakistan* (Singapore: Apa Publications GmbH & Co. Verlag KG, 2008)

Hanif Mohammad, *Playing for Pakistan, An Autobiography* (Karachi: Hamdard Press, 1999)

Hanif Raza, M, *Pakistan Travellers' Companion* (Rawalpindi: no publication date given)

Harvey, Neil, *My World of Cricket* (Sportsman's Book Club, 1964)

Haskell, CW, *A Sinner in Sind* (Wellington: Wright & Carman Ltd, 1957)

Hawkins, Ed, *Bookie Gambler Fixer Spy* (Bloomsbury, 2013)

Hazare, Vijay, *Cricket Replayed* (Calcutta: Rupa & Co., 1976)

Headlam, Cecil, *Ten Thousand Miles Through India & Burma* (London: JM Dent & Co., 1903)

Heyhoe Flint, Rachael and Rheinberg, Netta, *Fair Play* (London: Angus and Robertson, 1976)

Hopkirk, Peter, *Quest for Kim: In Search of Kipling's Great Game* (London: John Murray (Publishers) Ltd, 1996)

Hussain, Mujahid, *Punjabi Taliban* (Pentagon Press, 2012)

Hussain, SM, *Pakistan vs Australia Official Souvenir Brochure* (Karachi: 1959)

Hussain, Dr Syed Sultan Mahmood, *56 Years of Islamia College Lahore, 1892–1947* (Lahore: Izharsons, 2011)

Imran Khan, *All Round View* (London: Chatto & Windus, 1988)

—— *Imran* (London: Pelham, 1983)

—— *Pakistan: A Personal History* (London: Bantam Press, 2011)

Jalal, Ayesha *The Sole Spokesman: Jinnah, The Muslim League and the Demand for Pakistan* (Cambridge: Cambridge University Press, 1994)

—— (ed.), *The Oxford Companion to Pakistani History* (Oxford: Oxford University Press, 2012)

James, CLR, *Beyond A Boundary* (London: Stanley Paul & Co., 1963)

—— *Cricket* (London: Allison & Busby, 1986)

James, Lawrence, *Rise and Fall of the British Empire* (London: Abacus, 1994)

James, Sir Morrice, *Pakistan Chronicle* (Hurst, 1993)

Javed Miandad, with Saad Shafqat, *Cutting Edge: My Autobiography* (Oxford: Oxford University Press, 2003)

Jawed Iqbal, *How Is That? Cricket in Cartoons* (Lahore: Azmat Ltd, 1980)

Joy, Nancy, *Maiden Over* (Unwin, 1950)

Kardar, Abdul Hafeez, *Our Trust* (Lahore: Kardar Publications, 1950)

—— *Test Status On Trial: The Story of Pakistan Cricket Team's Historic Tour to England* (Karachi: National Publications, 1954)

—— *Inaugural Test Matches: An Eye-witness Account of the Pakistan Cricket Team's Tour of India* (Karachi: Asad Ali of Asad Son & Co., 1954)

—— *Green Shadows* (Karachi: [self-published] 1959)

—— *The Cricket Conspiracy* (Lahore: Allied Press, 1977)

—— *Bangladesh: The price of political failure* (Lahore: Awami Press, 1985)

—— *Memoirs of an All-rounder* (Lahore: Progressive Publishers, 1987)

—— *Pakistan's Soldiers of Fortune* (Lahore: Ferozsons, 1988)

—— *The Diary of an Ambassador* (Lahore: SH Ghulam Ali & Sons, 1994)

—— *Failed Expectations* (Lahore: Book Traders, 1995)

Kazimi, Muhammad Reza, *A Concise History of Pakistan* (Oxford: Oxford University Press, 2009)

Keay, John, *The Honourable Company* (London: HarperCollins, 1993)

Khan, Prof. Farrakh A (ed), *Reminiscences of an Officer, Aghajan's Service Diary* (Privately printed, 2010)

Khan, Shaharyar and Khan, Ali, *Cricket Cauldron* (IB Tauris, 2013)

Kipling, Rudyard, edited & annotated by Trivedi, Harish, *Kim* (London: Penguin Books, 2011)

Kureishi, Omar, *Well Played Pakistan!* (International Communications, 1983)

—— *Once Upon a Time* (Lahore: Ferozsons (Pvt.) Ltd, 2000)

—— *Home To Pakistan* (Lahore: Ferozsons, 2003)

—— *Ebb and Flow* (Lahore: Ferozsons, 2006)

—— (ed.), *Cricket Fever* (no publisher given)

Lamb, Allan, *Allan Lamb: My Autobiography* (London: Collins Willow, 1996)

Lelyveld, David, *Aligarh's First Generation: Muslim Solidarity in British India* (New Delhi: OUP, 2010)

Licudi, Adam and Wasim Raja, *Cornered Tigers: A History of Pakistan's Test Cricket* (Antigua: Hansib Publishing (Caribbean), 1997)

Lieven, Anatol, *Pakistan: A Hard Country* (Penguin, 2012)

Lock, Tony, *For Surrey and England* (London, Hodder & Stoughton, 1957)

Major, Rt Hon Sir John, *More Than A Game* (Harper, 2007)

Majumdar, Boria, *Twenty-Two Yards to Freedom: A Social History of Indian Cricket* (India: Viking, Penguin Books, 2004)

—— (ed.), *Indian Cricket Through the Ages: A Reader* (New Delhi: Oxford University Press, 2005)

—— *Cricket in Colonial India,1780–1947* (Abingdon: Routledge, 2008)

—— *The Illustrated History of Indian Cricket* (New Delhi: Roli & Janssen/Roli Books, 2009)

Mangan, JA, *The Games Ethic and Imperialism: Aspects of the Diffusion of an Ideal* (London: Frank Cass, 1986)

Manley, Michael, *A History Of West Indies Cricket* (London: Pan, 1990)

Maqsood Ahmed Khan, *History of Pakistan Junior Cricket* (Lahore, 2012)

Maqsood, Syed, MH, *Who's Who in Indian Cricket* (Delhi: ZR Commercial Corporation, Model Press, 1947)

—— (ed.), *Cricket in Pakistan [1st Edition] 1948–49 Edition* (Karachi: ZR Commercial Corporation, 1949)

—— (ed.), *Cricket in Pakistan [2nd Edition]* (Karachi: Karachi Universal Cricket Club, 1951)

—— (ed.), *Cricket in Pakistan [3rd Edition]* (Karachi: Karachi Universal Cricket Club, 1954)

—— *Twenty Years of Pakistan Cricket 1947–67* (Karachi: Pakistan Printing Works, 1968)

Maqsood, Syed, MH and Merchant, MI, *Pakistan vs England* (Karachi: Pakistan Printing Works, 1954)

Marker, Jamsheed, *Quiet Diplomacy: Memoirs of an Ambassador of Pakistan* (Oxford: Oxford University Press, 2010)

Marqusee, Mike, *Anyone But England* (Verso, 1994)

—— *War Minus The Shooting: A journey through South Asia during Cricket's World Cup* (London: Heinemann, 1996)

Martin-Jenkins, Christopher, *The Complete Who's Who of Test Cricketers* (London: Guild Publishing, 1987)

Maulana Mohamed Ali, *My Life, a Fragment: An Autobiographical Sketch of Maulana Mohamed Ali,* edited & annotated by Hasan, Mushirul (New Delhi: Manohar Publishers and Distributors, 1999)

McKinstry, Leo, *Jack Hobbs: England's Greatest Cricketer* (London: Yellow Jersey Press, 2011)

Meher-Homji, Kersi, *Cricket's Great Families* (Australia: Kangaroo Press, 2000)

Merchant, MI, *100 Best Cricketers* (Karachi: 'Union' Press Ltd, no publication date given)

Miles, Keith with Khan, Rahmat, *Jahangir and the Khan Dynasty* (London: Pelham Books, 1988)

Mirza, Humayun, *From Plassey to Pakistan: The Family History of Iskander Mirza, The First President of Pakistan* (Pakistan: Ferozans (Pvt) Ltd, 1999)

Modi, Rusi, *Cricket Forever* (Bombay: Rusi Modi, 1964)

Morris, Jan, *Heaven's Command: An Imperial Progress* (London: Faber & Faber, 1998)

Munir, Justice Mohammad, *From Jinnah To Zia* (University of Virginia: Vanguard Books, 1980)

Mushtaq Ahmed, with Sibson, Andy, *Twenty20 Vision: My Life and Inspiration* (London: Methuen Publishing Ltd, 2006)

Mushtaq Mohammad, *Inside Out: An Autobiography* (Karachi: UniPrint, 2006)

Munir, Iqbal (ed.), *Red & White Book of Snooker: A Chronicle of the Game of Style* (Karachi: Laser Dot & Hamdard Press (Pvt.) Ltd, no publication date given)

Naipaul, VS, *India: A Wounded Civilization* (London: Picador, 2010)

Nandy, Ashis, *A Very Popular Exile* (New Delhi: Oxford University Press, 2007)

Natwar-Singh, Kunwar, *The Magnificent Maharaja: The Life and Times of Maharaja Bhupinder Singh of Patiala 1891–1938* (New Delhi: Rupa Publications India Pvt. Ltd, 2009)

Niaz, Dr Nauman, *Pakistan Cricket: The Story of Betrayal* (Rawalpindi: Printing Avenue House, 2009)

—— *The Fluctuating Fortunes: Official History of Pakistan Cricket.* Four volumes (Lahore: Pakistan Cricket Board, no publication date given)

Nicolson, Nigel, *Alex* (London: Weidenfeld, 1973)

Noman, Omar, *Pride and Passion: An Exhilarating Half Century of Cricket in Pakistan* (Karachi: Oxford University Press, 1998)

Oborne, Peter, *Basil D'Oliveira: Cricket and Conspiracy: The Untold Story* (Time Warner Books, London, 2005)

Pataudi, The Nawab of Pataudi, *Tiger's Tale: The story of one of India's greatest cricketers* (London: Stanley Paul & Co Ltd, 1969)

Pearson, Harry, *The Trundlers* (London: Hachette, 2013)

Pennell, TL, *Among the Wild Tribes of the Afghan Frontier: A record of sixteen years close intercourse with the natives of the Indian marches* (OUP, Orig. 1909; repr. Karachi, 1975)

Piesse, Ken, *Cricket's Greatest Scandals* (Australia: Viking Australia, 2000)

Pollard, Jack, *The Complete Illustrated History of Australian Cricket* (London: Pelham, 1992)

Pringle, Chris, *Save The Last Ball For Me* (Celebrity Books New Zealand, 1998)

Qamar Ahmed, *Testing Time* (Karachi: Liberty Books, 1983)

—— *Showdown: The story of Pakistan's tour of the West Indies 1993* (Karachi: Cricketprint Publication, no publication date given)

Qamaruddin Butt, *Cricket Without Challenge* (Sialkot and Lahore: Maliksons publishers, 1955)

—— *Playing for a Draw: Covering Pakistan's Tour of India* (Jahanaisons, 1962)

—— *Cricket Reborn Covering Commonwealth Cricket Team's Tour of Pakistan 1963* (Rawalpindi: Civil & Military Press, c.1964)

—— *Sporting Wickets Eye-witness Accounts of the Tours of M.C.C. and New Zealand to Pakistan 1969* (no publisher given, c.1970)

Rae, Simon, *It's Not Cricket* (London: Faber & Faber, 2001)

Raiji, Vasant, *India's Hambledon Men* (Bombay: Tyeby Press, 1986)

Rajan, Amol, *Twirlymen* (London: Yellow Jersey, 2011)

Rajaraman, G, *Match-Fixing: The Enemy Within* (New Delhi: Har-Anand Publications PVT Ltd, 2001)

Raz, Dr Tariq, *Commanders of Pakistan Cricket (Updated Edition)* (Karachi: Saad Publications, 2003)

Rehmatullah, A Aziz, *35 Years of Pakistan Test Cricket* (Karachi: Mohammed Moin Aziz. no publication date given)

Reid, John, *Sword of Willow* (Wellington, New Zealand: AH and AW Reed, 1962)

Rice, Jonathan (ed.), *Wisden on India: An Anthology* (London: John Wisden & Co., 2011)

Rice, Jonathan, and Renshaw, Andrew, *The Wisden Collector's Guide* (London: John Wisden & Co, 2011)

Ricquier, Bill, *The Pakistani Masters* (New Delhi: Lotus Collection, Roli Books Pvt Ltd, 2010)

Roy, SK, *Indian Cricketers* (Calcutta Illustrated News, 1946)

Rumford, Chris and Wagg, Stephen (eds), *Cricket and Globalization* (Newcastle Upon Tyne: Cambridge Scholars Publishing, 2010)

Salma Ahmed, *Cutting Free: The Extraordinary Memoir of a Pakistani Woman* (New Delhi: Lotus Collection, Roli Books, 2007)

Sandford, Christopher, *Imran Khan: The Cricketer, The Celebrity, The Politician, The Biography* (London: HarperCollins Publishers, 2009)

Sarbadhikary, Berry, *My World Of Cricket (A Century Of Tests) 1964* (Publisher unknown, 1964)

Schofield, Carey *Inside the Pakistan Army: A Woman's Experience on the Frontline of the War on Terror* (London: Biteback Publishing Ltd, 2011)

Searle, Chris, *Pitch of Life: Writings on Cricket* (Manchester: The Parrs Wood Press, 2001)

Shahid, Mohammad Hanif, *The Role of Islamia College in the Pakistan Movement* (Riyadh: International Islamic Research Institute, 1992

Shahzad, Syed Saleem, *Inside Al-Qaeda and the Taliban: Beyond Bin Laden and 9/11* (London: Pluto Press, 2011)

Shaikh, Mohammad Ali, *Sindh Madressah: The Institution and the Alumni* (Karachi: Sindh Madressatul Islam, 2005)

—— *Hassanally Effendi (1830–1895): The Founder of Sindh Madressatul* (Karachi: Sindh Madressatul Islam, 2010)

—— *Islam* (Karachi: Sindh Madressatul Islam (SMI) College in collaboration with Orient Books Publishing House, 2010*)*

Shankar, BD, *40 Years of Active Cricket* (Lucknow: Pioneer Press, 1955)

Shoaib Akhtar with Dogra, Anshu, *Controversially Yours* (India: HarperCollins, 2011)

Shuja-ud-Din Butt, Lt. Col (Retd) and Mohammed Salim Parvez, *From Babes of Cricket to World Champions* (Karachi: Bun, 1996)

Shuja-ud-Din Butt, Lt. Col (Retd) and Mohammed Salim Parvez, *The Chequered History of Pakistan Cricket. A Complete Account of Fifty-five Years (1947–48 to 2002–03)* (Pakistan: Milestone Communications, 2003)

Siddiqui, Islahuddin, *Dash Through my Life: An Autobiography* (Karachi: Islahuddin Siddiqui, 2009)

Sisson, R and Rose, LE, *War and Secession* (California: University of California Press, 1992)

Smith, VA, *Oxford History of India, Fourth Edition* (Delhi: Oxford University Press, 1981)

Snow, John, *Cricket Rebel: An Autobiography* (London: Hamlyn, 1976)

Sultan Mahmud, *Cricket After Midnight* (Book Traders Lahore, no publication date given)

Surhone, LM and others, *Zahid Ali Akbar Khan* (Betascript Publishing, 2010)

Talbot, Ian, *Pakistan: A Modern History* (New Delhi: Foundation Books, 2009)

Talyarkhan, AFS, *Official Souvenir of the Silver Jubilee of the Bombay Cricket Association 1930–1954* (Bombay, 1954)

Tennant, Ivo, *Imran Khan* (London: Gollancz/Witherby, 1995)

Tharoor, Shashi and Khan, Shaharyar, *Shadows Across the Playing Field: 60 Years of India-Pakistan Cricket* (New Delhi: Lotus Collection, Roli Books Pvt. Ltd, 2009)

von Tunzelmann, Alex, *Indian Summer: The Secret History of The End of an Empire* (London: Simon & Schuster, 2007)

Wagg, Stephen (ed.), *Cricket and National Identity in the Postcolonial Age: Following On* (Abingdon & New York: Routledge, 2005)

Waqar Hasan and Qamar Ahmed, *For Cricket and Country: An Autobiography* (Karachi: A Cricket Print Publication, 2002)

Warne, Shane, *My Autobiography* (London: Hodder & Stoughton, 2002)

Wasim Akram, *Wasim* (London: Piatkus, 1998)

Wikeley, JM, *Punjabi Musalmans* (1915, repr. 1991)

Wilde, Simon, *Caught: The Full Story of Cricket's Match-fixing Scandal* (London: Aurum Press Ltd, 2001)

—— *Ian Botham: The Power and the Glory* (London: Simon & Schuster, 2011)

Williams, Jack, *Cricket And Race* (Berg, 2001)

Wilson Hunter, Sir William, *The Indian Musalmans: Are They Bound In Conscience To Rebel Against The Queen?* (USA: Nabu Public Domain, 1923)

Wilton, Iain, *CB Fry: King Of Sport* (Metro, 2002)

Wolpert, Stanley, *Zulfi Bhutto of Pakistan: His Life and Times* (Oxford: Oxford University Press, 1993)

Woolmer, Bob and Noakes, Tim (with Moffett, Helen), *Bob Woolmer's Art And Science Of Cricket* (New Holland, 2008)

Younghusband, Col. GJ, *A History of the Guides* (London: Macmillan & Co Ltd, 1908)

Zaheer Abbas, with Foot, David, *Zed: Zaheer Abbas* (Surrey: The Windmill Press, World's Work Ltd, 1983)

Zakir Hussain, Syed, *The Young Ones: A Coverage of Pakistan Cricket Team's Tour of England 1971* (Lahore–Islamabad: West Pak Publishing Co. Ltd, 1972)

Zawwar Hasan, *Pakistan Sports: Story of Excellence* (Karachi: Export Promotion Bureau, 1996)

Zia, K Hussan, *The Pashtuns of Jullundur* (Lahore, 1994)

Zia, Mahmood, *Bridge My Way* (London: Faber & Faber Ltd, 1991)

Ziring, Lawrence, *Pakistan in the Twentieth Century: A Political History* (Oxford: Oxford University Press, 1999)

PAMPHLETS

Aziz, KK, *Are we living in a democratic society?* (Lahore: Group 2000 Series, January 1994)

Gauhar, Altaf, *Arab Petrodollars: Dashed Hope for a New Economic Order* (Lahore: Group 83 Series, 22 December 1987)

Hasan, Dr Mubashir and Rahman, IA, *National Unity: What is to be done?* (Lahore: Group 83 Series, March 1986)

Hussain, Dr Akmal, *The Land Reforms in Pakistan* (Lahore: Group 83 Series, 1983)

Hyder, Sajjad, *Aspects of Foreign Policy: How Should Pakistan Negotiate?* (Lahore: Group 83 Series, 1 August 1986)

Intikhab Alam, *Intikhab Alam Benefit Year 1978* (Pakistan and Surrey CCC, no publication date given)

Kardar, AH, *The Energy Crisis II: A Case For Public Takeover of Gas Fields* (Lahore: Group 83 Series, April 1983)

—— *Is The Economic Future of Our Youth Secure?* (Midlink, 1 June 1985)

—— *Provincial Autonomy: Concept and Framework* (Lahore: Group 83 Series, 29 November1987)

—— *Defence: Objectives, Strategy, and Cost* (Lahore: Group 83 Series, 1998)

Kardar, Shahid, *The Sixth Plan: Is It A Solution To Pakistan's Problems?* (Lahore: Group 83 Series, July 1983)

—— *The Gathering Economic Crisis and the Dwindling Options.* M.L Qureshi Memorial Lecture (Lahore: Group 83 Series, 27 June 1986)

Loan, AU, *The Energy Crisis III: Need for Accelerated Development of Hydrocarbon Reserves* (Lahore: Group 83 Series, October 1985)

—— *Pakistan Economy: Gas Power Generation* (Lahore: Group 2000 Series, February 1994)

Masud, M, *The Crisis In Education: The Medium of Instruction* (Lahore: Group 83 Series, May 1983)

Zulfiqar Ali Khan, Air Chief Marshal (Retd); Zafar Chaudhry, Air Marshal (Retd); Habib, and MR Hasan, *Mechanics of Transfer of Power & Its Retention by the People* (Lahore: Group 83 Series, May 1986)

Picture Credits

The author and publishers would like to thank the following SOURCES for images used in the plate sections:

A very rare photograph of Fazal Mahmood's father Ghulam Hussain (COURTESY OF MUEEN AFZAL)

British soldiers playing cricket at Kohat (NATIONAL ARCHIVES OF PAKISTAN)

The Burkis of Jullundur (MAJID KHAN)

Jahangir Khan shakes hands with King George V (MAJID KHAN)

Emperor and retainer (SHAHID KARDAR)

Imtiaz Ahmed and Maqsood Ahmed going out to bat (NAJUM LATIF)

Prime Minister Nazimuddin meets Pakistan cricket stars (MUEEN AFZAL)

Many great figures of Pakistan cricket (MAJID KHAN)

Mian Saeed, Pakistan's first captain (NAJUM LATIF)

Ameer Bee, cricket's greatest matriarch (MUSHTAQ MOHAMMAD)

A unique photograph. The mothers of three Pakistan cricket captains (MAJID KHAN)

Pakistan take their first ever Test wicket (KEYSTONE/GETTY IMAGES)

The Pakistan cricket team for the 1954 tour of England (POPPERFOTO/ GETTY IMAGES)

'At half-past three this well-built and powerful man . . .' (NAJUM LATIF)

Fazal Mahmood and his Pakistan side leave the field (CENTRAL PRESS/HULTON ARCHIVE/GETTY IMAGES)

Shuja-ud-Din, right, going out with Alimuddin (NAJUM LATIF/NASREEN ILAHI)

MCC tourists to Pakistan, 1955–56 (POPPERFOTO/GETTY IMAGES)

Two men in overcoats (SHAHID KARDAR)

Justice Cornelius, presenting a prize (NOSHEEN HANIF, KINNAIRD COLLEGE LAHORE)

President Iskander Mirza watching Pakistan (NAJUM LATIF)

President Eisenhower and President Ayub Khan (NAJUM LATIF)

Saeed Ahmed rehearses his legendary cover drive (NAJUM LATIF)

Height of fashion (MAJID KHAN)

Brigadier 'Gussy' Haider towering over the 1962 Pakistan touring team (NAJUM LATIF)

Hanif Mohammad introduces Khalid Ibadulla to the Queen (NAJUM LATIF)

Early Pakistan women cricketers (NOSHEEN HANIF, KINNAIRD COLLEGE LAHORE)

Two great players: Majid Khan and Asif Iqbal (MAJID KHAN)

AH Kardar, immaculately dressed as ever (SHAHID KARDAR)

Majid Khan caught Marsh bowled Walker 158 (MAJID KHAN)

Sadiq Masood et al. (MAJID KHAN)

Three Burki cousins (DR FARRAKH AHMED KHAN)

The Ladies stand at the Gaddafi stadium (PATRICK EAGAR VIA GETTY IMAGES)

Women playing at the Lahore Gymkhana (RICHARD HELLER)

ZA Bhutto and Kardar discussing matters of state (SHAHID KARDAR)

Abdul Qadir, in the 1983 World Cup (BOB THOMAS/GETTY IMAGES)

Wasim Akram plotting another reverse for England (POPPERFOTO/GETTY IMAGES)

Javed Miandad, Pakistan's highest scorer in Tests (BOB THOMAS/GETTY IMAGES)

Pakistan's prime minister, Nawaz Sharif, shows off his square cut (ALLSTAR PICTURE LIBRARY/ALAMY)

Captain Imran Khan celebrates winning the 1992 'Cornered Tigers' World Cup final (JOE MANN/ALLSPORT/GETTY IMAGES)

Lethal fast bowler Waqar Younis (BOB THOMAS/GETTY IMAGES)

Children playing in the street in Karachi (LAURENCE GRIFFITHS/ALLSPORT/GETTY IMAGES)

Inzamam-ul-Haq with popular Pakistan coach Bob Woolmer (PRAKASH SINGH/AFP/GETTY IMAGES)

Fans in Multan burn images of former captain Salman Butt and Mohammad Asif (SS MIRZA/AFP/GETTY IMAGES)

Shahid 'Boom Boom' Afridi (ASIF HASSAN/AFP/GETTY IMAGES)

Saeed Ahmed, in retirement (RICHARD HELLER)

Inzamam-ul-Haq looking thoughtful (RICHARD HELLER)

Imran Khan makes a point at a party rally (ASIF HASSAN/AFP/GETTY IMAGES)

Pakistan captain Misbah-ul-Haq hits out (ISHARA S KODIKARA/AFP/GETTY IMAGES)

Cricket at dusk in Rawalpindi (NICOLAS ASFOURI/AFP/GETTY IMAGES)

Index